4-4-60

UNDER THE EDITORSHIP OF

Lucius Garvin

University of Maryland

THE
EXAMINED LIFE

An Introduction to Philosophy

edited by

TROY WILSON ORGAN

Ohio University

HOUGHTON MIFFLIN COMPANY

Boston · The Riverside Press Cambridge

"Philosophic study
means the habit
of always seeing
an alternative."

William James

1114490

Preface

This volume is designed to meet the following four needs;

1. *The need for a course in philosophy which is both introductory and terminal.* The traditional introductory course in departments of philosophy acquaints the student with the principal concepts, problems, and methods of the subject. After the introduction the student is expected to register for another course in philosophy in which he will get to the "meat" of philosophy. In some departments the introductory course is frankly recognized as a "feeder course." But many students — perhaps most students — do not take another course in philosophy. It is my conviction that if students are to derive the maximum benefit from philosophy, each philosophy department must offer an introductory course which is valuable in itself rather than one which is valuable merely as a preparation for advanced work in philosophy.

2. *The need for a course in philosophy which helps young people develop democratic attitudes and values.* Knowledge is not sufficient in these disintegrative and disruptive times. A few men who possess knowledge and skill but are not motivated by humanitarian ideals can become a menace to all men. If our civilization is to survive and if individuals are to live effectively and happily, we must discover and create the order and the values which make human life significant. Knowledge without wisdom can plunge mankind into barbarism. This is no longer a theory. Recent and contemporary totalitarian states supply the most obvious evidence. We have had ample warning of the foolishness of increasing knowledge, production, transportation, and communication without regard to their possible contribution to the good life for man. Liberal education must meet this challenge. Educators have too often hidden behind the cloak of objective scholarship and have ignored their students' development with respect to attitudes and values. Although teachers in colleges of liberal arts have recognized that they must not indoctrinate their students, they must realize that they are obliged as liberal educators to help their students to understand the concepts and attitudes which have made liberalism possible. No teacher in our democracy can shirk this obligation. We who teach philosophy ought to be especially sensitive to this obligation. We must reinstate philosophy in the

Socratic and Pythagorean tradition as a way of life. We can profit by examining Eastern philosophy. Each school of philosophy originating in China and India (with the possible exception of Cārvāka) has as its primary purpose the betterment of human life: the elimination of suffering (Hinduism and Buddhism), the achievement of peace of mind (Taoism), the improvement of man in society (Confucianism). Philosophy in the West must return to its early concern for the good life for man. Philosophy must be philosophy of life.

3. *The need for presenting philosophy as controversy.* Many of the textbooks which introduce philosophy to college students give an utterly false impression of the nature of philosophy. Students come to the conclusion that in the past philosophers have wrangled over curious problems which by this time have been either discarded or solved. The students are given the dry bones of the conclusion of the argument, rather than the lifeblood of the controversy. They fail to understand that the controversy is eternal because the basic problems of philosophy arise out of man's finitude. Different ages may use different words and techniques in dealing with the issues of philosophy, but the problems of man's relation to his fellow men, to his physical environment, and to the ultimate mysteries remain as problems whose solution requires fresh insight in each generation. A philosophical argument is never won. Philosophy is never finished, for each man must be his own philosopher.

4. *The need for a textbook which does not usurp the rôle of the instructor.* The textbook should stimulate philosophical discussion, not stifle it. Philosophical arguments probably promote more student thought than do expositions about philosophical positions. If the textbook contains selections from the polemic writings of the philosophers, students will come to realize that each position in philosophy, no matter how peculiar it may seem, is held, or has been held, by a man who believed as he did with mind and heart. The lifeless description of problems and solutions which unfortunately characterizes many textbooks is largely to blame for the dryness which many undergraduates associate with philosophy. Furthermore, since the only philosophic work which many students read is a textbook in which one man describes what another man thought, they can scarcely be blamed for concluding that philosophy is neither exciting nor practical. The ideal textbook should whet the students' appetite for classroom discussion.

This volume, which I have prepared to meet these four needs, consists of readings on topics which seem to me to be fundamental in a philosophy of life. I have selected for each topic two readings which present conflicting solutions of the same problem. (Occasionally it may prove interesting and profitable for the students and instructor to determine whether the paired readings actually concern the same problem.) The pairing of opposing selections has two values: (1) If the issue seems important to students they must either join with one author against the other or propose and defend an alternative view — in either case they are forced to philosophize; and (2) students are introduced to intellectual tolerance, one of the most essential requirements for the success of a democracy — i.e., the idea that men of good will can differ on very significant issues, that conflicting points of view can be supported by cogent arguments, that when two men differ in intellectual matters it does not follow that one of them is a fool.

I am fully aware that many topics which would belong in a traditional "Introduction to Philosophy" are not included in this volume — e.g., the problem of universals, the mind–body problem, the problem of causality. My defense, to repeat what has been said above, is that this textbook was not prepared for a course which is a prerequisite for advanced courses in philosophy. The topics are those which I have found to be fruitful in helping undergraduates to find their own life philosophy. I have tried to be fair to the various philosophical schools, but it would be very strange indeed if my own position had not been reflected in the selection of the topics or the readings.

I have found that students are better prepared to discuss the topics in class if as they read a selection they try to answer the following questions:

1. What is the problem the author is attempting to solve?
2. What are his methods of solution?
3. What is his solution?
4. Does his proposed solution actually solve the problem?
5. What would his solution mean in practice?
6. What is your evaluation of
    (a) his statement of the problem?
    (b) his methods of solution?
    (c) his solution?

Students who can make an intelligent exposition of a selection from a great philosopher are a cause for rejoicing in any department of philosophy. This volume has been prepared, however, with the conviction that students who have thought out a tentative, workable, and personal solution to a live philosophical problem have engaged in an enterprise that is far more significant than mere exposition. The study of philosophy should lead to philosophizing. It is the author's hope that this volume will help young men and women to formulate a personal philosophy of life adequate to the times and places in which they live. May they find that the examined life is worth living.

I wish to acknowledge my gratitude to the following: To The Fund for the Advancement of Education for a fellowship in 1952–53 which gave me the opportunity to study some of the problems in teaching philosophy. To Dr. Paul R. Anderson, President of Chatham College, who encouraged me to try new ideas during the eight years I taught under his leadership. To the editors and publishers who have kindly given permission to use material on which they hold copyrights. To my students whose impatience with sophistical ideas constantly reminds me that life is the ultimate testing ground of philosophy.

Contents

PART THREE · THE CREATIVE WORLD

PART FOUR · THE SOCIAL WORLD

INTRODUCTION

PHILOSOPHY AND LIFE

Philosophy begins with questions. Some of the earliest questions of children are the same questions which puzzle the wisest philosophers: "Who am I? Where did I come from? What happens to me when I die? How did the world come to be? What is God like?" Well-meaning but weary parents and teachers often stifle this native inquisitiveness and channel these early questions into less puzzling areas of thought. Somewhere between kindergarten and college most young people have lost the habit of asking questions. Formal education has done its work: the imagination has been deadened. One of the big jobs in philosophy is to revive the uninhibited curiosity of early childhood. Within this context a philosopher might be described as one who can return to childhood at will! For the philosopher, the lover of wisdom, is one who continues to ask questions even though some others may think his questions are unnecessary or even silly. Probably the chief difference between philosophers and laymen is that the former are more persistent, more systematic, more imaginative, and less restrained in question-raising. — Or, as William James has said, philosophers are "men curious beyond practical needs."

Sometimes the philosopher seems to be partial to those questions which cannot be answered! The layman may ask: "But why raise questions which cannot be answered? Why seriously consider a question which merely leads to other questions? Why not limit inquiries to those for which definite and conclusive answers can be found?" To which the philosopher replies: "Your questions are most interesting. In raising these very questions you have confirmed my belief that man is never more philosophical than when he questions his own questioning. My dear fellow, you are not rejecting philosophy, *you are philosophizing!*"

1

Many a tired intellectual has at times agreed with Whitman that he "could turn and live with animals."

> They do not sweat and whine about their condition,
> They do not lie awake in the dark and weep for their sins,
> They do not make me sick discussing their duty to God.

But only a few like Nebuchadnezzar have actually tried the life of the lower animals. Rousseau wrote about the joys of primitive and animal existence, but he never lived the life of a primitive. Voltaire told him that although his exposition was very persuasive it was some time since he himself had last gone about on all fours and he had no intention of relearning that mode of travel. Life might be simpler if we stooped to the level of the beasts, and perhaps we would be happier if we did not ask philosophical questions. However, before glorifying the unexamined life we ought to consider what has motivated man in the philosophic quest.

Plato contended that man is by nature a philosophical animal — that he is born to intellectual disquietude. Plato thought that man would never be satisfied with a society in which only the basic needs of food, clothing, and shelter were met. He wants other goods: recreation, beauty, work, peace, love, knowledge, something to worship. He wants these even before he has fully satisfied his primary physical needs. Man seeks shelter from the sun and the rain; he also seeks to know what causes the sun to shine and the rain to fall. Like the ant, he stores the fruits of the summer for the bleak winter months, but unlike the ant he seeks to explain the forces which bring summer and winter. He adjusts himself to his environment; he also tries to understand his environment. Man, in other words, is driven to philosophize by the same elemental and instinctive drives by which he is driven to seek nourishment and self-preservation. Such is Plato's answer to the question "Why is man philosophical?"

Others believe that man philosophizes because he enjoys it — even the sweating and whining about his condition and the weeping for his sins! He enjoys speculating about the world and his place in it. The search for that which is hidden is fun whether it be a baby playing peek-a-boo, a schoolboy playing hide-and-go-seek, a reader following a detective thriller, a paleontologist digging for fossils, an astronomer speculating about the interior of a star, or a theologian theorizing upon the nature of God. What if the seeker does not find what he sought? Well, the game itself was fun; the pursuit justified itself. The quest for the unknown has satisfactions which remain even when the quest is fruitless. A dog chases a cat for the fun of the chase; he doesn't want the cat! Lessing once said: "Did the Almighty, holding in His right hand truth and in His left search for truth, deign to proffer me the one I might prefer, in all humility, but without hesitation, I should request search after truth." And Malebranche remarked in the same vein: "If I held truth captive in my hand, I should open my hand and let it fly, in order that I might again pursue and capture it." Philosophizing is fun; it is also a serious activity, and many philosophers have been so impressed by the urgency of their task that they missed the enjoyment of the activity. Samuel Johnson said he had a friend who had always wanted to be a philosopher but was unable to be one because of his native cheerfulness. Voltaire warned: "Woe to philosophers who cannot laugh away their learned wrinkles." Pascal thought that to make light of philosophy was to be a true philosopher. A long face does not make a philosopher.

But neither will a happy countenance make a philosopher, add those who support a third motive for philosophizing. Is philosophy just a pleasant recreation for idle hours? The intellectual dilettante fails to achieve the real purpose of philosophy, which is to attain wisdom about man and his universe. Philosophy is not a game; it is an attempt to solve living problems. Man continues to philosophize because he needs intelligence in the conduct of life. Voltaire and Pascal were probably right about the seriousness of philosophers; most of them have been in dead earnest. Through philosophizing man gains insight into his world, solves problems of how life ought to be lived, and perfects his own being by acquiring new breadth of mind and depth of perspective. The confusion of modern living and the multitude of conflicting theories on how life ought to be spent force all of us back upon our intellectual resources. Although man may be said to be philosophical by nature, and although philosophizing is an enjoyable enterprise, it is the usefulness of philosophizing which sanctifies the activity. There is always the possibility that the philosopher may enjoy raising questions and forget that questions were originally asked for the purpose of getting answers. When questions are raised without concern for answers, philosophy has become a disease rather than a cure. — So contend those who stress philosophy as a problem-solving activity.

Why do *you* raise questions? What are your motives for philosophizing? Are you sometimes like Alice when she got into "that state of mind that she wants to deny something — only she doesn't know what to deny"? What do you expect to receive from a course in philosophy? Many young people come to the study of formal philosophy desiring to find a substitute for religious beliefs and practices which no longer have significance for them. Some seek information about the relation of science and art, the difference between good and evil, the conflict of freedoms and obligations. Others want to know more about themselves: Is man an immortal being? Does he have free will? What do I really want? Perhaps these are some of the problems that bother you; perhaps you feel a need to find moorings in our fast-moving world. One assumption that underlay the preparation of this book is that these are the sort of problems which bother a good many young people and the sort of problems upon which philosophy should give some illumination. We assume that you as an average young person living in the modern world are interested in forming what we shall call a philosophy of life. This book will not give you the answers to all your problems; rather it will suggest some of the answers that have been given to a few of the problems of men.

When one is perplexed and confused there are two courses of action open to him: one is to *flee* from the confusion and the other is to *reason* to a workable conclusion. One is the way of retreat; the other is the way of attack. One is the way of illusion; the other, the way of reality. One is the way of pessimism; the other, the way of optimism. It is true that some philosophers have been pessimistic about man and his place in the universe; and others have claimed to be pessimistic about man's ability to philosophize. However, the actions of philosophers speak louder than their words. Philosophizing is evidence of the basic optimism of philosophers. They raise questions because they believe that answers can be attained. They refuse to allow fear or failure to drive them to irrationalities. The philosophers are not Messiahs; they are but voices crying in behalf of the rational powers of man. Their message can be heard above the confusions of our day: "Don't give up hope. We'll think a way out of this yet. Trust your head, not a good-luck charm. There are better days to come. Prepare yourself for those days; for, in the words of Thoreau, 'Only that day dawns to which we are awake. There is more day to dawn. The sun is but a morning star'."

In a philosophy of life two questions are raised: "What is its nature?" and "What is its worth?" We assume that these questions are raised about a specific thing or idea or activity: a flower, an automobile, a human being, a nation, the enjoyment of painting, an act of worship, the concept of God. The words which answer the first question may be said to be the expression of the *facts;* the words which answer the second question are the expression of *values.* In a philosophy of life, as in a science, we seek knowledge about the world, but in a philosophy of life we also want to know the human worth of things, ideas, and activities. It is the emphasis on values which is unique in a philosophy of life. Questions about reality are raised only in order that the problems of value may be solved. For example, before deciding on the worth of leprechauns a wise person would want to decide whether or not there are such things in the real world. We are frequently tempted to decide which objects are desirable before we decide whether they exist; our wants quickly outdistance our resources. This is the incentive for the creation of folk tales and myths. Aladdin's lamp, fairy godmothers, and magic wands are the creation of minds that wish to believe that the real world does not limit the possibilities of values. Although it might be pleasant to believe that one had $1000 in his checking account, before one acted on that pleasant belief the course of wisdom would consist of finding out exactly how much one did have in the bank. The banker might not be convinced that "wishing will make it so." We do not live in Gondore, nor in Shangri-La, nor even in a Brave New World. A philosophy of life is a consideration of what is significant for human beings in the real world. Or, to assert the same idea in another way, it is an examination of the world of reality under the aspect of values.

A philosophy of life cannot be avoided. If a disgruntled person were to claim: "I have no philosophy of life. I see no meaning in life," we could reply: "On the contrary, you do have a philosophy of life. And you have expressed it — or at least you have suggested what it is. Can you refine your statement? Do you contend that there *is* no meaning in life? Or that there is no meaning in life *for you?* Or that you are skeptical of man's ability to find a meaning in life?" The question we need to ask ourselves is not "Shall I have a philosophy of life?" Rather it is "What sort of philosophy of life do I have already, and how can I make it more harmonious with reality, more internally consistent, more complete?" All people — except very young children and the insane — may be said to have a philosophy of life, but few people have consciously and critically developed these philosophies. Everyman philosophy is unconscious, unsystematic, sketchy, and often inconsistent; the philosopher's philosophy is conscious, systematic, and usually consistent.

No one comes to a study of philosophical problems without some preconceptions of what is real and what is valuable. Experience precedes reflection. By the time a young person reaches college years his prejudices and his convictions — they are hard to differentiate! — may be so deeply ingrained that he lacks the open-mindedness essential to all learning experiences. If we are unwilling to examine critically our most cherished beliefs, we shall derive little from a study such as the one upon which we are now launched. We are examining our beliefs in order to understand, to appreciate, and, only when necessary, to alter or destroy.

There have been periods in human history when an acceptable philosophy of life was easy to acquire. These were times of limited knowledge when people were offered only one philosophy. The common people simply accepted that which was given to them and let the proper authorities worry about the sort of problems we are considering in this study. We are not now living in an age of faith. No longer can we simply "believe . . . and be saved." The orderly world view which gave meaning and purpose to men in the thirteenth century — the last "ready-to-wear" philosophy of life — cannot be lifted over the centuries and applied to our day; for in spite of the "unchanging human spirit" and the "eternal verities" the matrix which shapes modern man is vastly different from, and more complex than, that of the Middle Ages. Today if one has an adequate philosophy of life it is a personal achievement rather than an acceptance of an authoritative pattern of thought and action.

Religion was an effective integrating agent in previous centuries, but today the voices of churches and synagogues must compete with political, cultural, intellectual, economic, and recreational agencies demanding our support and determined to mold our lives. Religious institutions have lost their sovereignty. However, religion is not the only authority which has weakened: many of us refuse to accept a philosophy of life on the basis of any authority, whether that authority be church, state, Holy Writ, king, priest, or parent. Furthermore, churches, because of their understandable conservatism, often find themselves wedded to views of the universe which have been superseded by the results of scientific research. Religions have clung so tenaciously to old conceptions and outmoded values, and have resisted with such tenacity the new, that many educated and progressive people of our day give financial support to churches and synagogues yet reject the philosophy of life set forth by these institutions. Others sever themselves completely from religious organizations. They call themselves "the emancipated." Churchmen call them "the lost generation."

We might place blame for the present difficulty of forming an adequate philosophy of life on the extremely vigorous and successful advances of the sciences in the last one hundred years — during which we have been presented with more knowledge than we have been able to assimilate into our value systems. Our knowledge surpasses our controls. Human knowledge is now so vast that if any one of us is to know anything thoroughly he must limit himself to a small segment of knowledge. In the twentieth century an Aristotle — a man erudite in all areas of learning — is an impossibility. Consequently, we are a generation of specialists; each of us must know more and more about less and less. We are left with the uneasy feeling that some of the most relevant information — relevant, that is, both to the understanding of our own specialty and to our own richest living — escapes us because we have narrowed our learning. The medical profession is an excellent example. A generation ago a great majority of physicians were general practitioners; they examined the patients who came to their offices, located the source of the physical disorder, and prescribed the treatment. Today knowledge about the human body and its ills and the means of therapy is so vast that a majority of physicians, particularly in urban areas, become specialists. In many parts of the country the patient now goes directly to a clinic for diagnosis. There he passes from specialist to specialist and is examined part by part until he is almost convinced that he is not a single person but a collection of lungs, kidneys, stomach, heart, gall bladder, and other organs rather loosely related to each other. The patient, the man, is lost somewhere among the specialists. Thus there has arisen the need for other specialists — psychologists, psychiatrists, psychoanalysts — to examine the patient as a person. Specialization is now so advanced that men of different professions can carry on a conversation only if one talks about his specialty while the others politely listen, or if the conversation centers on one of the few remaining topics of common knowledge and interest: practical politics, the weather, and the opposite sex! At a recent philosophical meeting the chairman asked those of the two hundred philosophers present who thought they understood the philosophical paper they had just heard to raise their hands. Not a hand was raised! Still another example of the specialization and consequent fragmentation of present-day living is the common experience of house owners who are compelled to seek the services of plumber, carpenter, mason, electrician, painter, paperhanger, and locksmith. Modern frustrated landlords recall with nostalgia that their fathers simply hired a general repair man.

Again, the complexity of our daily lives makes for disintegration. We agree with Robert Louis Stevenson that the "world is . . . full of a number of things"; but we cannot agree with him that this is a cause for rejoicing. It is difficult to feel significant if we have jobs that are frustrating, tedious, and boring, or if our days are filled with contacts with many people but with few whom we know well enough to understand as unique individuals. The people we see on the streetcar are strangers to us; they are merely bodies occupying space. "Neighbor" is a word seldom used in large cities except during the annual Community Chest drive. Life is more varied and physically less arduous in the city than in rural communities, but the price we pay is loneliness and the loss of individuality. In the city we know each other only in fragments: as a member of the club, as a golf partner, as a fellow guest at a party, as a man in the next pew, as a cruncher of popcorn in the movies, as a pedestrian, as a body that beat us to the seat in the streetcar.

Today's rapid social, political, and economic changes further confuse us. The periodic alternation of inflation and deflation, of depression and prosperity, of war and peace, of cooperation and competition leaves us in an exhausted and confused state of mind. We become unable to identify friend or foe. We do not know where to find security. The toll is indicated by the fact that one half of the hospital beds in the United States are occupied by the mentally ill. Jules Masserman once taught cats to respond to light as a signal for food. Later when the cats saw the light and anticipated food a blast of air was turned on them. They sprang away and cowered in the corner of the cage. When the cats discovered that the light was not a dependable sign, they showed great fear and excitement when the light appeared and stayed as far as possible from the food. Masserman reported that the cats developed the characteristics of a "nervous breakdown," just as people do who need work and cannot find it, or who seek secure investments in a fluctuating economy, or who desire peace and find frustration. Even the good old sign of the American dollar is not as dependable as we once thought it was!

To summarize: A philosophy of life that is adequate to the problems of our day is difficult to form because: (1) we have few, if any, dependable integrating agents; (2) our common store of information is too vast for any one person to grasp; (3) our daily lives are too complex to permit us to catch the relative significance of the activities of our days; and (4) the changes in social living outrun the tempo of human psychological adjustments.

A little more than one hundred years ago, when life became complex (!) in Concord, Massachusetts, a young man of twenty-eight years named Henry David Thoreau retired to Walden Pond, a few miles outside the city limits, to work out his philosophy of life. In his report of that experiment he wrote: "I went to the woods because I wished to live deliberately, to front only the essential facts of life, and see if I could not learn what it had to teach, and not, when I came to die, discover that I had not lived. I did not wish to live what was not life, living is so dear; nor did I wish to practice resignation, unless it was quite necessary, I wanted to live deep and suck out all the marrow of life, to live so sturdily and Spartan-like as to put to rout all that was not life, to cut a broad swath and shave close, to drive life into a corner, and reduce it to its lowest terms, and, if it be proved to be mean, why then to get the whole and genuine meanness of it, and publish its meanness to the world; or if it were sublime, to know it by experience, and be able to give a true account of it in my next excursion. For most men, it appears to me, are in a strange uncertainty about it, whether it is of the devil or of God, and have somewhat hastily concluded that it is the chief end of man to 'glorify God and enjoy Him forever'." Few of us are able to retire to a Walden Pond to learn what life has to teach, but each of us needs to find the good, the beautiful, and the true, and to fit facts and values like parts of a jigsaw puzzle into a total pattern of life.

There are at least three different methods of forming a philosophy of life. The first is the daydreamer's method. This consists of the idle, carefree spinning of values which could be found only in a "never-never land." Thomas More, Francis Bacon, and Samuel Butler followed this method when they wrote their conceptions of the ideal commonwealth. If we ask *when* these plans will become a reality, they may be said to reply in the well-known words of Plato: when "philosophers are kings, or the kings and princes of this world have the spirit and power of philosophy." If we ask *where* these states are to be found they reply with Thomas More, "Utopia" (that is, "nowhere").

This was the method of philosophizing that Thomas White, a rich merchant of London, had in mind when he remarked to David Hume: "I am surprised, Mr. Hume, that a man of your good sense should think of being a philosopher. Why, I now took it into my head to be a philosopher for some time, but tired of it most confoundedly, and very soon gave it up."

"Pray, sir," asked Mr. Hume, "in what branch of philosophy did you employ your researches? What books did you read?"

"Books?" said Mr. White. "Nay, sir, I read no books, but I used to sit for whole forenoons a-yawning and poking the fire." [1]

Armchair philosophizing is not the best method. Philosophers are not to

> ". . . sit apart on a hill retired,
> In thoughts more elevate . . ."

Earl Balfour described the daydreaming philosophers as men who "to the world at large seem to sit (as it were) far apart from their fellowmen, seeking wisdom by methods hard of comprehension, and gently quarrelling with each other in an unknown tongue."

The second method is the defense of prejudices. This is the method of philosophizing commonly thought to have been used by the philosophers in medieval times. It is a method not entirely absent from the work of contemporary philosophers. The Scholastics used philosophy as the handmaiden of theology, the "queen of the sciences." Philosophy was the way of supporting and defending religious beliefs. Some contemporary schools of philosophy are diametrically opposed to Scholasticism in all ways except one: philosophy for them is still a handmaiden, only this time her mistress is science. It is a limited and dangerous use of philosophy to use her only to defend ideas, regardless of whether those ideas be the teachings of the church, the conclusions of the sciences, or the doctrines of the state.

---

[1] Ernest Campbell Mossner, *The Forgotten Hume,* Columbia University Press, 1943, p. xii. Reprinted by permission of the publisher.

Philosophy, when so used, may be defined as the activity of seeking good reasons for believing what one would believe without good reasons. There is a better method of forming a philosophy of life than merely justifying the values one already has.

In using this better method we first analyze the knowing process and the facts gathered through this process; then we select values which are in harmony with these facts. This method is a contribution of western philosophers since 1600. When traditional authorities fell during the Renaissance, philosophers were obliged to examine the ways of knowing. Descartes sought by the method of doubt to find one idea so certain that it could not be doubted; Spinoza built a magnificent structure upon a foundation of truths taken to be self-evident; Locke, recognizing the errors into which human reason falls when it acts before it considers its abilities and limitations, outlined the origin, certainty, and extent of human knowledge; Kant warned against the dangers of translating into the external world that which is merely an aspect of knowing minds.

This method has three steps. The first is to analyze the modes of knowing. How often a discussion comes to a stalemate because the participants have not decided what are the means, tests, and limits of knowledge. It was such an experience that prompted Locke to make his famous study, *An Essay Concerning Human Understanding.* In the "Epistle to the Reader" he wrote: "Were it fit to trouble thee with the history of this Essay, I should tell thee, that five or six friends, meeting at my chamber, and discoursing on a subject very remote from this, found themselves quickly at a stand by the difficulties that arose on every side. After we had awhile puzzled ourselves, without coming any nearer a resolution of those doubts which perplexed us, it came into my thoughts, that we took a wrong course; and that, before we set ourselves upon inquiries of that nature, it was necessary to examine our own abilities, and see what objects our understandings were and were not fitted to deal with." Once the ways of knowing most appropriate to the subject matter to be studied have been selected, the next step is to use these tools to produce dependable knowledge. And the third step is to consider the human worth of the information thus gained. This is the order of philosophizing at its best.

In the philosophical journey which lies before us we shall begin with ourselves. We first consider the problem of self-knowledge, and then move to questions about the significant values of the self. The self does not live in a vacuum; it lives in — some philosophers would prefer to say that it is compounded from — three worlds: the natural world, the social world, and the creative world. The natural world is the world of matter and life; the social world is the world of the self in its relationships to other selves; and the creative world is the world of aesthetic achievements and religious aspirations through which man strives to enrich his life by the liberal use of the imagination. In the examination of each world we ask how knowledge is established, what are the important realities, and what this world contributes to human values. As you proceed through the selections you will undoubtedly become aware of many problems in creating a philosophy of life which are not included in the topics listed in this volume. Life contains riches and meanings which defy containment within the pages of any book. There are more things both in heaven and in earth than are dreamed of in philosophy.

SUGGESTIONS FOR THOUGHT

1. At what age should one expect to have formed an adequate philosophy of life? Harold Dunkel says that it is beyond the ability of college students (although he adds that college students should begin the study of the problems involved in a philosophy of life). Havelock Ellis says age sixty is early enough. T. V. Smith says perhaps no person has an altogether satisfactory one.

2. "Mankind can flourish in the lower stages of life with merely barbaric flashes of thought. But when civilization culminates, the absence of a coordinating philosophy of life, spread throughout the community, spells decadence, boredom, and the slackening of effort." (A. N. Whitehead) What is a coordinating philosophy of life? How can a philosophy of life be spread throughout the community?

3. What advice might have been given Theodore Dreiser when he grumbled: "Life is to me too much of a welter and play of inscrutable forces to permit any significant comment. . . . I catch no meaning for all I have seen, and pass quite as I came, confused and dismayed"?

4. Which goals in life seem to receive most attention from the average modern person? Is it true that "the average person is more concerned with the state of his bowels than with the state of his conscience"? Compare the life goals of a typical man of this century with those of a typical man of the thirteenth century.

5.

"Ah, but a man's reach should exceed his grasp,
Or what's a heaven for?"
                    (Browning, "Andrea del Sarto")

What are the relative merits of attainable and unattainable goals in life? How might a visionary person justify his existence?

6. What arguments would you raise to one who argued as follows: "Morality is the self-conscious living of life. One is moral when one knows what one is doing — it is living one's life knowingly. Therefore, to live by habit is to live non-morally — if not immorally"?

7. How great is your love for truth? Would you exchange a comforting delusion for an uncomfortable truth? E.g., suppose there is no God; would you prefer to know with certainty of the non-existence of God, or would you rather retain a mistaken but comforting belief in God's existence? Do men have any beliefs which are too sacred to be examined?

8. Does it require any courage to be philosophical today? What are some of the possible dangers of critical thinking in religion, in ethics, in politics, and in economics? Can you name any public figures who have suffered because they tried to be philosophical?

9. G. B. Shaw once said, "You cannot be a philosopher and a good man, although you may be a philosopher and a great man." What do you think Shaw meant?

10. What groups in our society are opposed to the stimulation of thinking? How can their point of view be defended?

11. Pascal has written, "To make light of philosophy is to be a true philosopher." Why is it dangerous to take philosophy too seriously? Can one take philosophy too lightly?

12. It has been said that the average person takes about eighty years to wake up and see the meaning of what he has been doing all his life.

Philosophy is the attempt to awake a few years earlier. What is the value of waking up?

13. Philosophers have been criticized as people who know where they want to go but have no facilities for getting there; practical people are those who get there but usually find they have gotten to the wrong place. How would you evaluate this distinction between philosophers and practical people?

14. Here are three statements about the meaning of life. Criticize them. "The three most serious losses which a man can suffer are those affecting money, health, and reputation. Loss of money is far the worst, then comes ill-health, and then loss of reputation." (Samuel Butler) "For many men . . . to live up to one's ideals is not so difficult as it is to find an ideal that is worth living up to." (C. Delisle Burns) "The good life is one motivated by love and guided by knowledge." (Bertrand Russell)

SUGGESTIONS FOR FURTHER READING

BODE, B. H., "Why Do Philosophical Problems Persist?" *The Journal of Philosophy, Psychology, and Scientific Methods,* Vol. 15, 1918, pp. 169–177.

BRADLEY, F. H., *The Principles of Logic,* Second Edition, London, Oxford University Press, 1922, Essay 12.

BROWN, WILLIAM ADAMS, "The Future of Philosophy as a University Study," *The Journal of Philosophy,* Vol. 18, 1921, pp. 673–682.

BROWNELL, BAKER, *The Philosopher in Chaos,* New York, D. Van Nostrand Co., 1941, ch. 1.

DEWEY, JOHN, *The Quest for Certainty,* New York, Minton, Balch, and Co., 1929, ch. 3.

HÖFFDING, HARALD, "Philosophy and Life," *The International Journal of Ethics,* Vol. 12, 1902, pp. 137–151.

JAEGER, WERNER, "The Moral Value of the Contemplative Life," in *Moral Principles of Action,* edited by Ruth Nanda Anshen, New York, Harper and Brothers, 1952, pp. 77–93.

JOAD, C. E. M., "Appeal to Philosophers," *Philosophy,* Vol. 15, 1940, pp. 400–416.

LADD, GEORGE TRUMBULL, "The Mission of Philosophy," *The Philosophical Review,* Vol. 14, 1905, pp. 113–137.

LARRABEE, HAROLD A., *What Philosophy Is,* New York, The Vanguard Press, 1928, ch. 5.

MONTAGUE, WILLIAM PEPPERELL, "The Modern Distemper of Philosophy," *The Journal of Philosophy,* Vol. 48, 1951, pp. 429–435.

OTTO, MAX, "Meditation on a Hill," *The Philosophical Review,* Vol. 39, 1930, pp. 329–350.

PERRY, RALPH BARTON, "The Practical Man and the Philosopher," *The International Journal of Ethics,* Vol. 13, 1903, pp. 482–493.

ROYCE, JOSIAH, *William James and Other Essays on the Philosophy of Life,* New York, The Macmillan Company, 1911, Essay I.

SEARS, LAURENCE, "Responsibilities of Philosophy Today," *The Journal of Philosophy,* Vol. 41, 1944, pp. 147–155.

PART ONE THE SELF

1

THE SELF
AND SELF-KNOWLEDGE

KNOW THYSELF was Socrates' favorite advice to the young men of ancient Athens. However, the Scottish empiricist Hume has difficulty in even finding a self. James, on the other hand, finds not one self but four! David Hume (1711–1776) wrote widely in the fields of philosophy, history, and political economy. Not the least of Hume's contributions to philosophy was the arousing of Kant from his "dogmatic slumbers." William James (1842–1910) is commonly regarded as the most creative philosopher America has produced. He began teaching physiology at Harvard University in 1872, but within a few years he transferred his interest to the new science of psychology. After the publication of his *Principles of Psychology* (1891) he turned from psychology, which he now called "a nasty little subject," to philosophy and religion. He and Charles Saunders Peirce are credited with the foundation of the pragmatic school of philosophy.

A

There are some philosophers who imagine we are every moment intimately conscious of what we call our *self;* that we feel its existence and its continuance in existence; and are certain, beyond the evidence of a demonstration, both of its perfect identity and simplicity. The strongest sensation, the most violent passion, say they, instead of distracting us from this view, only fix it the more intensely, and make us consider their influence on *self* either by their pain or pleasure. To attempt a further proof of this were to weaken its evidence; since no proof can be derived from any fact of which we are so intimately conscious; nor is there anything of which we can be certain if we doubt of this.

David Hume, *A Treatise of Human Nature,* 1738, Book I, Part IV, Section VI.

Unluckily all these positive assertions are contrary to that very experience which is pleaded for them; nor have we any idea of *self,* after the manner it is here explained. For, from what impression could this idea be derived? This question it is impossible to answer without a manifest contradiction and absurdity; and yet it is a question which must necessarily be answered, if we would have the idea of self pass for clear and intelligible. It must be some one impression that gives rise to every real idea. But self or person is not any one impression, but that to which our several impressions and ideas are supposed to have a reference. If any impression gives rise to the idea of self, that impression must continue invariably the same, through the whole course of our lives; since self is supposed to exist after that manner. But there is no impression constant and invariable. Pain and pleasures, grief and joy, passions and sensations succeed each other, and never all exist at the same time. It cannot therefore be from any of these impressions, or from any other, that the idea of self is derived; and consequently there is no such idea.

But further, what must become of all our particular perceptions upon this hypothesis? All these are different, and distinguishable, and separable from each other, and may be separately considered, and may exist separately, and have no need of anything to support their existence. After what manner therefore do they belong to self, and how are they connected with it? For my part, when I enter most intimately into what I call *myself,* I always stumble on some particular perception or other, of heat or cold, light or shade, love or hatred, pain or pleasure. I never can catch *myself* at any time without a perception, and never can observe anything but the perception. When my perceptions are removed for any time, as by sound sleep, so long am I insensible of *myself,* and may truly be said not to exist. And were all my perceptions removed by death, and could I neither think, nor feel, nor see, nor love, nor hate, after the dissolution of my body, I should be entirely annihilated, nor do I conceive what is further requisite to make me a perfect nonentity. If any one, upon serious and unprejudiced reflection, thinks he has a different notion of *himself,* I must confess I can reason no longer with him. All I can allow him is, that he may be in the right as well as I, and that we are essentially different in this particular. He may, perhaps, perceive something simple and continued, which he calls *himself;* though I am certain there is no such principle in me.

But setting aside some metaphysicians of this kind, I may venture to affirm of the rest of mankind, that they are nothing but a bundle or collection of different perceptions, which succeed each other with an inconceivable rapidity, and are in a perpetual flux and movement. Our eyes cannot turn in their sockets without varying our perceptions. Our thought is still more variable than our sight; and all our other senses and faculties contribute to this change; nor is there any single power of the soul, which remains unalterably the same, perhaps for one moment. The mind is a kind of theatre, where several perceptions successively make their appearance; pass, repass, glide away, and mingle in an infinite variety of postures and situations. There is properly no *simplicity* in it at one time, nor *identity* in different, whatever natural propension we may have to imagine that simplicity and identity. The comparison of the theatre must not mislead us. They are the successive perceptions only, that constitute the mind; nor have we the most distant notion of the place where these scenes are represented, or of the materials of which it is composed.

What then gives us so great a propension to ascribe an identity to these successive perceptions, and to suppose ourselves possessed of an invariable and uninterrupted existence through the whole course of our lives? In order to answer this question we must distinguish betwixt personal identity, as it regards our thought or imagination, and as it regards our passions or the concern we take in ourselves. The first is our present subject; and to explain it perfectly we must take the matter pretty deep, and account for that identity, which we attribute to plants and animals; there being a great analogy betwixt it and the identity of a self or person.

We have a distinct idea of an object that remains invariable and uninterrupted through a supposed variation of time; and this idea we call that of *identity* or *sameness*. We have also a distinct idea of several different objects existing in succession, and connected together by a close relation; and this to an accurate view affords as perfect a notion of *diversity* as if there was no manner of relation among the objects. But though these two ideas of identity, and a succession of related objects, be in themselves perfectly distinct, and even contrary, yet it is certain that, in our common way of thinking, they are generally confounded with each other. That action of the imagination, by which we consider the uninterrupted and invariable object, and that by which we reflect on the succession of related objects, are almost the same to the feeling; nor is there much more effort of thought required in the latter case than in the former. The relation facilitates the transition of the mind from one object to another, and renders its passage as smooth as if it contemplated one continued object. This resemblance is the cause of the confusion and mistake, and makes us substitute the notion of identity, instead of that of related objects. However at one instant we may consider the related succession as variable or interrupted, we are sure the next to ascribe to it a perfect identity, and regard it as invariable and uninterrupted. Our propensity to this mistake is so great from the resemblance above mentioned, that we fall into it before we are aware; and though we incessantly correct ourselves by reflection, and return to a more accurate method of thinking, yet we cannot long sustain our philosophy, or take off this bias from the imagination. Our last resource is to yield to it, and boldly assert that these different related objects are in effect the same, however interrupted and variable. In order to justify to ourselves this absurdity, we often feign some new and unintelligible principle, that connects the objects together, and prevents their interruption or variation. Thus we feign the continued existence of the perceptions of our senses, to remove the interruption; and run into the notion of a *soul*, and *self*, and *substance*, to disguise the variation. But, we may further observe, that where we do not give rise to such a fiction, our propension to confound identity with relation is so great, that we are apt to imagine something unknown and mysterious, connecting the parts, beside their relation; and this I take to be the case with regard to the identity we ascribe to plants and vegetables. And even when this does not take place, we still feel a propensity to confound these ideas, though we are not able fully to satisfy ourselves in that particular, nor find anything invariable and uninterrupted to justify our notion of identity.

Thus the controversy concerning identity is not merely a dispute of words. For when we attribute identity, in an improper sense, to variable or interrupted objects, our mistake is not confined to the expression, but is commonly attended with a fiction, either of something invariable and uninterrupted, or of something mysterious and inexplicable, or at least with a propensity to such fictions. What will suffice to prove this hypothesis to the satisfaction of every fair inquirer, is to show, from daily experience and observation, that the objects which are variable or interrupted, and yet are supposed to continue the same, are such only as consist of a succession of parts, connected together by resemblance, contiguity, or causation. For as such a succession answers evidently to our notion of diversity, it can only be by mistake we ascribe to it an identity; and as the relation of parts, which leads us into this mistake, is really nothing but a quality, which produces an association of ideas, and an easy transition of the imagination from one to another, it can only be from the resemblance, which this act of the mind bears to that by which we contemplate one continued object, that the error arises. Our chief business, then, must be to prove, that all objects, to which we ascribe identity, without observing their invariableness and uninterruptedness, are such as consist of a succession of related objects.

In order to this, suppose any mass of matter, of which the parts are contiguous and connected, to be placed before us; it is plain we must attribute a perfect identity to this mass, provided all the parts continue uninterruptedly and invariably the same, whatever motion or change of place we may observe either in the whole or in any of the parts. But supposing some very *small* or *inconsiderable* part to be added to the mass, or subtracted from it; though this absolutely destroys the identity of the whole, strictly speaking, yet as we seldom think so accurately, we scruple not to pronounce a mass of matter the same, where we find so trivial an alteration. The passage of the thought from the object before the change to the object after it, is so smooth and easy, that we scarce per-

ceive the transition, and are apt to imagine, that it is nothing but a continued survey of the same object.

There is a very remarkable circumstance that attends this experiment; which is, that though the change of any considerable part in a mass of matter destroys the identity of the whole, yet we must measure the greatness of the part, not absolutely, but by its *proportion* to the whole. The addition or diminution of a mountain would not be sufficient to produce a diversity in a planet; though the change of a very few inches would be able to destroy the identity of some bodies. It will be impossible to account for this, but by reflecting that objects operate upon the mind, and break or interrupt the continuity of its actions, not according to their real greatness, but according to their proportion to each other; and therefore, since this interruption makes an object cease to appear the same, it must be the uninterrupted progress of the thought which constitutes the imperfect identity.

This may be confirmed by another phenomenon. A change in any considerable part of a body destroys its identity; but it is remarkable, that where the change is produced *gradually* and *insensibly,* we are less apt to ascribe to it the same effect. The reason can plainly be no other, than that the mind, in following the successive changes of the body, feels an easy passage from the surveying its condition in one moment, to the viewing of it in another, and in no particular time perceives any interruption in its actions. From which continued perception, it ascribes a continued existence and identity to the object.

But whatever precaution we may use in introducing the changes gradually, and making them proportionable to the whole, it is certain, that where the changes are at last observed to become considerable, we make a scruple of ascribing identity to such different objects. There is, however, another artifice, by which we may induce the imagination to advance a step further; and that is, by producing a reference of the parts to each other, and a combination to some *common end* or purpose. A ship, of which a considerable part has been changed by frequent reparations, is still considered as the same; nor does the difference of the materials hinder us from ascribing an identity to it. The common end, in which the parts conspire, is the same under all their variations, and affords an easy transition of the imagination from one situation of the body to another.

But this is still more remarkable, when we add a *sympathy* of parts to their *common end,* and suppose that they bear to each other the reciprocal relation of cause and effect in all their actions and operations. This is the case with all animals and vegetables; where not only the several parts have a reference to some general purpose, but also a mutual dependence on, and connection with, each other. The effect of so strong a relation is, that though every one must allow, that in a very few years both vegetables and animals endure a *total* change, yet we still attribute identity to them, while their form, size, and substance, are entirely altered. An oak that grows from a small plant to a large tree is still the same oak, though there be not one particle of matter or figure of its parts the same. An infant becomes a man, and is sometimes fat, sometimes lean, without any change in his identity. . . .

★ ★ ★

We now proceed to explain the nature of *personal identity,* which has become so great a question in philosophy, especially of late years, in England, where all the abstruser sciences are studied with a peculiar ardour and application. And here it is evident the same method of reasoning must be continued which has so successfully explained the identity of plants, and animals, and ships, and houses, and of all compounded and changeable productions either of art or nature. The identity which we ascribe to the mind of man is only a fictitious one, and of a like kind with that which we ascribe to vegetable and animal bodies. It cannot therefore have a different origin, but must proceed from a like operation of the imagination upon like objects.

But lest this argument should not convince the reader, though in my opinion perfectly decisive, let him weigh the following reasoning, which is still closer and more immediate. It is evident that the identity which we attribute to the human mind, however perfect we may imagine it to be, is not able to run the several different perceptions into one, and make them lose their characters of distinction and difference, which are essential to them. It is still true that every distinct perception which enters into the composition of the mind, is a distinct existence, and is different, and distinguishable, and separable from every other perception, either contemporary or successive. But as, notwithstanding this distinction and separability, we suppose the whole train of perceptions to be united by identity, a question naturally arises concerning this relation of identity, whether it be something that really binds our several perceptions together, or only associates their ideas in the imagination; that is, in other words, whether, in pronouncing concerning the identity of a person, we observe some real bond among his perceptions, or only feel one among the ideas we form of them. This question we might easily decide, if we would recollect what has been already proved at large, that the understanding never observes any real connection among objects, and that even the union of cause and effect, when strictly examined, resolves itself into a customary association of ideas. For from thence it evidently follows, that identity is nothing really belonging to these different perceptions, and uniting them together, but is merely a quality which we attribute to them, because of the union of their ideas in the imagination when we reflect upon them. Now, the only qualities which can give ideas a union in the imagination, are these three relations above mentioned. These are the uniting principles in the ideal world, and without them every distinct object is separable by the mind, and may be separately considered, and appears not to have any more connection with any other object than if disjoined by the greatest difference and remoteness. It is therefore on some of these three relations of resemblance, contiguity, and causation, that identity depends; and as the very essence of these relations consists in their producing an easy transition of ideas, it follows that our notions of personal identity proceed entirely from the smooth and uninterrupted progress of the thought along a train of connected ideas, according to the principles above explained.

The only question, therefore, which remains is, by what relations this uninterrupted progress of our thought is produced, when we consider the successive existence of a mind or thinking person. And here it is evident we must confine ourselves to resemblance and causation, and must drop contiguity, which has little or no influence in the present case.

To begin with *resemblance;* suppose we could see clearly into the breast of another, and observe that succession of perceptions which constitutes his mind or thinking principle, and suppose that he always preserves the memory of a considerable part of past perceptions, it is evident that nothing could more

contribute to the bestowing a relation on this succession amidst all its variations. For what is the memory but a faculty, by which we raise up the images of past perceptions? And as an image necessarily resembles its object, must not the frequent placing of these resembling perceptions in the chain of thought, convey the imagination more easily from one link to another, and make the whole seem like the continuance of one object? In this particular, then, the memory not only discovers the identity, but also contributes to its production, by producing the relation of resemblance among the perceptions. The case is the same, whether we consider ourselves or others.

As to *causation;* we may observe that the true idea of the human mind, is to consider it as a system of different perceptions or different existences, which are linked together by the relation of cause and effect, and mutually produce, destroy, influence, and modify each other. Our impressions give rise to their correspondent ideas; and these ideas, in their turn, produce other impressions. One thought chases another, and draws after it a third, by which it is expelled in its turn. In this respect, I cannot compare the soul more properly to anything than to a republic or commonwealth, in which the several members are united by the reciprocal ties of government and subordination, and give rise to other persons who propagate the same republic in the incessant changes of its parts. And as the same individual republic may not only change its members, but also its laws and constitutions; in like manner the same person may vary his character and disposition, as well as his impressions and ideas, without losing his identity. Whatever changes he endures, his several parts are still connected by the relation of causation. And in this view our identity with regard to the passions serves to corroborate that with regard to the imagination, by the making our distant perceptions influence each other, and by giving us a present concern for our past or future pains or pleasures.

As memory alone acquaints us with the continuance and extent of this succession of perceptions, it is to be considered, upon that account chiefly, as the source of personal identity. Had we no memory, we never should have any notion of causation, nor consequently of that chain of causes and effects, which constitute our self or person. But having once acquired this notion of causation from the memory, we can extend the same chain of causes, and consequently the identity of our persons beyond our memory, and can comprehend times, and circumstances, and actions, which we have entirely forgot, but suppose in general to have existed. For how few of our past actions are there, of which we have any memory? Who can tell me, for instance, what were his thoughts and actions on the first of January 1715, the eleventh of March 1719, and the third of August 1733? Or will he affirm, because he has entirely forgot the incidents of these days, that the present self is not the same person with the self of that time; and by that means overturn all the most established notions of personal identity? In this view, therefore, memory does not so much *produce* as *discover* personal identity, by showing us the relation of cause and effect among our different perceptions. It will be incumbent on those who affirm that memory produces entirely our personal identity, to give a reason why we can thus extend our identity beyond our memory.

The whole of this doctrine leads us to a conclusion, which is of great importance in the present affair, viz. that all the nice and subtile questions concerning personal identity can never possibly be decided, and are to be regarded rather as grammatical than as philosophical difficulties. Identity depends on the relations of ideas; and these relations produce identity, by means of that easy transition they occasion. But as the relations, and the easiness of the transition may diminish by insensible degrees, we have no just standard by which we can decide any dispute concerning the time when they acquire or lose a title to the name of identity. All the disputes concerning the identity of connected objects are merely verbal, except so far as the relation of parts gives rise to some fiction or imaginary principle of union, as we have already observed.

B

In its widest possible sense . . . a man's self is the sum total of all that he can call his, not only his body and his psychic powers, but his clothes and his house, his wife and children, his ancestors and friends, his reputation and works, his lands and horses, and yacht and bank-account. All these things give him the same emotions. If they wax and prosper, he feels triumphant; if they dwindle and die away, he feels cast down, — not necessarily in the same degree for each thing, but in much the same way for all. . . .

William James, *The Principles of Psychology,* Vol. 1, New York, Henry Holt and Company, 1893, ch. 10 (in part).

The constituents of the self may be divided

into two classes, those which make up respectively —

    (a) The material self;
    (b) The social self;
    (c) The spiritual self; and
    (d) The pure ego.

The body is the innermost part of the *material self* in each of us; and certain parts of the body seem more intimately ours than the rest. The clothes come next. The old saying that the human person is composed of three parts — soul, body and clothes — is more than a joke. We so appropriate our clothes and identify ourselves with them that there are few of us who, if asked to choose between having a beautiful body clad in raiment perpetually shabby and unclean, and having an ugly and blemished form always spotlessly attired, would not hesitate a moment before making a decisive reply. Next, our immediate family is a part of ourselves. Our father and mother, our wife and babes, are bone of our bone and flesh of our flesh. When they die, a part of our very selves is gone. If they do anything wrong, it is our shame. If they are insulted, our anger flashes forth as readily as if we stood in their place. Our home comes next. Its scenes are part of our life; its aspects awaken the tenderest feelings of affection; and we do not easily forgive the stranger who, in visiting it, finds fault with its arrangements or treats it with contempt. All these different things are the objects of instinctive preferences coupled with the most important practical interests of life. We all have a blind impulse to watch over our body, to deck it with clothing of an ornamental sort, to cherish parents, wife and babes, and to find for ourselves a home of our own which we may live in and 'improve.'

An equally instinctive impulse drives us to collect property; and the collections thus made become, with different degrees of intimacy, parts of our empirical selves. The parts of our wealth most intimately ours are those which are saturated with our labor. There are few men who would not feel personally annihilated if a life-long construction of their hands or brains — say an entomological collection or an extensive work in manuscript — were suddenly swept away. The miser feels similarly towards his gold, and although it is true that a part of our depression at the loss of possessions is due to our feeling that we must now go without certain goods that we expected the possessions to bring in their train, yet in every case there remains, over and above this, a sense of the shrinkage of our personality, a partial conversion of ourselves to nothingness, which is a psychological phenomenon by itself. We are all at once assimilated to the tramps and poor devils whom we so despise, and at the same time removed farther than ever away from the happy sons of earth who lord it over land and sea and men in the full-blown lustihood that wealth and power can give, and before whom, stiffen ourselves as we will by appealing to anti-snobbish first principles, we cannot escape an emotion, open or sneaking, of respect and dread.

A man's *social self* is the recognition which he gets from his mates. We are not only gregarious animals, liking to be in sight of our fellows, but we have an innate propensity to get ourselves noticed, and noticed favorably, by our kind. No more fiendish punishment could be devised, were such a thing physically possible, than that one should be turned loose in society and remain absolutely unnoticed by all the members thereof. If no one turned round when we entered, answered when we spoke, or minded what we did, but if every person we met 'cut us dead,' and acted as if we were non-existing things, a kind of rage and impotent despair would ere long well up in us, from which the cruellest bodily tortures would be a relief; for these would make us feel that, however bad might be our plight, we had not sunk to such a depth as to be unworthy of attention at all.

Properly speaking, a man has as many social selves as there are individuals who recognize him and carry an image of him in their minds. To wound any one of these his images is to wound him. But as the individuals who carry the images fall naturally into classes, we may practically say that he has as many different social selves as there are distinct groups of persons about whose opinion he cares. He generally shows a different side of himself to each of these different groups. Many a youth who is demure enough before his parents and teachers, swears and swaggers like a pirate among his 'tough' young friends. We do not show ourselves to our children as to our club-companions, to our customers as to the laborers we employ, to our own masters and employers as to our intimate friends. From this there results what practically is a division of the man into several selves; and this may be a discordant splitting, as where one is afraid to let one set of his acquaintants know him as he is elsewhere; or it may be a perfectly harmonious division of labor, as where one tender to his children is stern to the soldiers or prisoners under his command.

The most peculiar social self which one is apt to have is in the mind of the person one is in love with. The good or bad fortunes of this self cause the most intense elation and dejection — unreasonable enough as measured by every other standard than that of the organic feeling of the individual. To his own consciousness he *is* not, so long as this particular social self fails to get recognition, and when it is recognized his contentment passes all bounds. . . .

*   *   *

By the *spiritual self,* so far as it belongs to the empirical me, I mean a man's inner or subjective being, his psychic faculties or dispositions, taken concretely; not the bare principle of personal unity, or 'pure' ego, which remains still to be discussed. These psychic dispositions are the most enduring and intimate part of the self, that which we most verily seem to be. We take a purer self-satisfaction when we think of our ability to argue and discriminate, of our moral sensibility and conscience, of our indomitable will, than when we survey any of our other possessions. Only when these are altered is a man said to be *alienatus a se.* . . .

*   *   *

Now, let us try to settle for ourselves as definitely as we can, just how this central nucleus of the self may feel, no matter whether it be a spiritual substance or only a delusive word. . . .

*   *   *

First of all, I am aware of a constant play of furtherances and hindrances in my thinking, of checks and releases, tendencies which run with desire, and tendencies which run the other way. Among the matters I think of, some range themselves on the side of the thought's interests, whilst others play an unfriendly part thereto. The mutual inconsistencies and agreements, reinforcements and obstructions, which obtain amongst these objective matters reverberate backwards and produce what seem to be incessant reactions of my spontaneity upon them, welcoming or opposing, appropriating or disowning, striving with or against, saying yes or no. This palpitating inward life is, in me, that central nucleus which I just tried to describe in terms that all men might use.

But when I forsake such general descriptions and grapple with particulars, coming to the closest possible quarters with the facts, it is difficult for me to detect in the activity any purely spiritual element at all. Whenever my introspective glance succeeds in turning round quickly enough to catch one of these manifestations of spontaneity in the act, all it can ever feel distinctly is some bodily process, for the most part taking place within the head. Omitting for a moment what is obscure in these introspective results, let me try to state those particulars which to my own consciousness seem indubitable and distinct.

In the first place, the acts of attending, assenting, negating, making an effort, are felt as movements of something in the head. In many cases it is possible to describe these movements quite exactly. In attending to either an idea or a sensation belonging to a particular sense-sphere, the movement is the adjustment of the sense-organ, felt as it occurs. I cannot think in visual terms, for example, without feeling a fluctuating play of pressures, convergences, divergences, and accommodations in my eyeballs. The direction in which the object is conceived to lie determines the character of these movements, the feeling of which becomes, for my consciousness, identified with the manner in which I make myself ready to receive the visible thing. My brain appears to me as if all shot across with lines of direction, of which I have become conscious as my attention has shifted from one sense-organ to another, in passing to successive outer things, or in following trains of varying sense-ideas.

When I try to remember or reflect, the movements in question, instead of being directed towards the periphery, seem to come from the periphery inwards and feel like a sort of withdrawal from the outer world. As far as I can detect, these feelings are due to an actual rolling outwards and upwards of the eyeballs, such as I believe occurs in me in sleep, and is the exact opposite of their action in fixating a physical thing. In reasoning, I find that I am apt to have a kind of vaguely localized diagram in my mind, with the various fractional objects of the thought disposed at particular points thereof; and the oscillations of my attention from one of them to another are most distinctly felt as alternations of directions in movements occurring inside the head.

In consenting and negating, and in making a mental effort, the movements seem more complex, and I find them harder to describe. The opening and closing of the glottis play a great part in these operations, and, less distinctly, the movements of the soft palate, etc., shutting off the posterior nares from the mouth. My glottis is like a sensitive valve, intercepting my breath instantaneously at every mental hesitation or felt aversion to the objects of my thought, and as quickly opening, to let the air pass through my throat and nose, the moment the repugnance is overcome. The feeling of the movement of this air is, in me, one strong ingredient of the feeling of assent. The movements of the muscles of the brow and eyelids also respond very sensitively to every fluctuation in the agreeableness or disagreeableness of what comes before my mind.

In effort of any sort, contractions of the jaw-muscles and of those of respiration are added to those of the brow and glottis, and thus the feeling passes out of the head properly so called. It passes out of the head whenever the welcoming or rejecting of the object is strongly felt. Then a set of feelings pour in from many bodily parts, all 'expressive' of my emotion, and the head-feelings proper are swallowed up in this larger mass.

In a sense, then, it may be truly said that, in one person at least, the 'self of selves,' when carefully examined, is found to consist mainly of the collection of these peculiar motions in the head or between the head and throat. I do not for a moment say that this is all it consists of, for I fully realize how desperately hard is introspection in this field. But I feel quite sure that these cephalic motions are the portions of my innermost activity of which I am most distinctly aware. If the dim portions which I cannot yet define should prove to be like unto these distinct portions in me, and I like other men, it would follow that our entire feeling of spiritual activity, or what commonly passes by that name, is really a feeling of bodily activities whose exact nature is by most men overlooked. . . .

★   ★   ★

I have said all that need be said of the constituents of the phenomenal self . . . Our decks are consequently cleared for the struggle with that pure principle of personal identity which has met us all along our preliminary exposition, but which we have always shied from and treated as a difficulty to be postponed. Ever since Hume's time, it has been justly regarded as the most puzzling puzzle with which psychology has to deal; and whatever view one may espouse, one has to hold this position against heavy odds. If, with the Spiritualists, one contend for a substantial soul, or transcendental principle of unity, one can give no positive account of what that may be. And if, with the Humians, one deny such a principle and say that the stream of passing thoughts is all, one runs

against the entire common-sense of mankind, of which the belief in a distinct principle of selfhood seems an integral part. Whatever solution be adopted in the pages to come, we may as well make up our minds in advance that it will fail to satisfy the majority of those to whom it is addressed. The best way of approaching the matter will be to take up first the sense of personal identity.

In the last chapter it was stated in as radical a way as possible that the thoughts which we actually know to exist do not fly about loose, but seem each to belong to some one thinker and not to another. Each thought, out of a multitude of other thoughts of which it may think, is able to distinguish those which belong to its own ego and those which do not. The former have a warmth and intimacy about them of which the latter are completely devoid, being merely conceived, in a cold and foreign fashion, and not appearing as blood-relatives, bringing their greetings to us from out of the past.

Now this consciousness of personal sameness may be treated either as a subjective phenomenon or as an objective deliverance, as a feeling, or as a truth. We may explain how one bit of thought can come to judge other bits to belong to the same ego with itself; or we may criticize its judgment and decide how far it may tally with the nature of things.

As a mere subjective phenomenon the judgment presents no difficulty or mystery peculiar to itself. It belongs to the great class of judgments of sameness; and there is nothing more remarkable in making a judgment of sameness in the first person than in the second or the third. The intellectual operations seem essentially alike, whether I say 'I am the same,' or whether I say 'the pen is the same, as yesterday.' It is as easy to think this as to think the opposite and say 'neither I nor the pen is the same.'

This sort of *bringing of things together into*

the object of a single judgment is of course essential to all thinking. The things are conjoined *in* the thought, whatever may be the relation in which they appear to the thought. The thinking them is *thinking* them together, even if only with the result of judging that they do not *belong* together. This sort of *subjective synthesis,* essential to knowledge as such (whenever it has a complex object), must not be confounded with *objective synthesis* or union instead of difference or disconnection, known among the things. The subjective synthesis is involved in thought's mere existence. Even a really disconnected world could only be *known* to be such by having its parts temporarily united in the object of some pulse of consciousness.

The sense of personal identity is not, then, this mere synthetic form essential to all thought. It is the sense of a sameness perceived *by* thought and predicated of things *thought-about*. These things are a present self and a self of yesterday. The thought not only thinks them both, but thinks that they are identical. The psychologist, looking on and playing the critic, might prove the thought wrong, and show there was no real identity, — there might have been no yesterday, or, at any rate, no self of yesterday; or, if there were, the sameness predicated might not obtain, or might be predicated on insufficient grounds. In either case the personal identity would not exist as a *fact;* but it would exist as a *feeling* all the same; the consciousness of it by the thought would be there, and the psychologist would still have to analyze that, and show where its illusoriness lay.

SUGGESTIONS FOR THOUGHT

1. An author quoting from another book which he had written wrote in the footnote, "I hereby give myself permission to quote myself when I feel like it." How many selves are denoted?

2. What are the selves referred to in the following directives: Be yourself. Forget yourself. Deny yourself. Develop yourself. Find yourself. Blame yourself. Behave yourself. Be true to yourself.

3. Has an amputee lost part of his self? Did Carlyle lose part of himself when his manuscript was accidentally burned in the fireplace? Has a man who lost his wealth on Wall Street lost part of himself? Has a divorcee lost part of herself? Has a mother whose baby has died lost part of herself? What do your answers to these questions suggest about the physical limits of the self?

4. What differences are there in subject and object in knowing (1) that a pencil is on the table, (2) that two plus two equals four, (3) another person, (4) one's self?

5. A little child refers to itself in the third person, but later recognizes itself as a person and uses the first person. At what age have you noticed this change? What brings about this self-recognition?

6. "Once upon a time, I, Chuang Tze, dreamt I was a butterfly, fluttering hither and thither, to all intents and purposes a butterfly. I was conscious only of following my fancies as a butterfly, and was unconscious of my individuality as a man. Suddenly, I awakened, and there I lay, myself again. Now I do not know whether I was then a man dreaming I was a butterfly, or whether I am now a butterfly dreaming I am a man." How can Chuang Tze find his real self?

7. What do you think Albert Schweitzer meant when he said that it is becoming more and more difficult to be a personality?

8. A modern philosopher distinguishes between mind and body by claiming that wholes determine parts for mind, whereas parts determine wholes for body. Does this seem to be true? Why is the relationship between mind and body a problem?

9. When one is asleep, what is the "I" that is asleep and the "I" that is not asleep? What is the "I" that dreams?

10. Why is the argument for solipsism, i.e., that only the self and its sensations and thoughts exist, also an argument against solipsism?

11. "Of no action can we say simply that it is selfish or unselfish, for in everything that we say or do some one aspect or direction of our character, some one self, is affirmed, and another or others are denied." (R. A. Tsanoff) Show how a miser, a spendthrift, an ascetic, and a libertine are both selfish and unselfish.

In the Preface a few questions were presented as an outline for the study of the selections. You will find it profitable occasionally to write out answers to these questions. One of our students at Ohio University, André Sauvageot, wrote the following after he had read the selection from Hume:

1. What is the problem Hume is attempting to solve?

Hume is trying to find out if there is any real basis for our belief in an underlying unity which unites our various sensations and thoughts. The problem is both ontological and epistemological, for on the answer depends both something of the nature of reality and a clue to what the human mind is capable of knowing or discovering about the nature of reality.

2. What are Hume's methods of solution?

Hume tries to show that we have no separate, independently existing self, or that there is no impression (i.e., sensation) of an independent self, but that it is a name given a group of independent percepts among which the mind feigns data to fill in the gaps, thus unifying that which is not unified in reality. Hume stays rigidly with the empirical method throughout his investigation.

3. What is Hume's solution?

His solution is that there is no independently existing entity called the self. We are not justified in supposing the existence of a self which underlies our percepts, for it is in the nature of our minds to feign data which disguise the gaps among our percepts in such a way as to give them a unity or identity. Identity depends on the memory, which discovers and produces identity, by relating percepts causally. All that exists and all that we can know are individual impressions and ideas.

4. Does Hume's proposed solution actually solve the problem?

I do not think that his solution solved the problem, but rather it is just a statement that the problem cannot be solved. Hume does not give us anything to replace our old idea of self.

5. What would Hume's solution mean in practice?

Since reality consists of separate, independent phenomena only with no underlying metaphysical unity, it would follow that knowledge is very limited. Hume's conclusions about the self would undermine all the knowledge on which identity depends and this would either directly or indirectly include most of our knowledge.

6. What is your evaluation of (a) Hume's statement of the problem, (b) Hume's methods of solution, and (c) Hume's solution?

a. I think that his statement of the problem is very good. He was thorough in stating it so that from his starting point his conclusion follows logically. However, he started with the assumption that ideas are always derived from impressions.

b. I think that his methods of solution are clear to follow and are consistent within Hume's system. I do feel that he sidesteps some strong objections to his solution.

c. His solution is really a conclusion that we cannot solve the problem. It leaves much to be desired in that it is an unfruitful theory in a practical sense. No physical or social science can be built on Hume's conclusions. It would seem that there must be some degree of unity of the self, or how can we even contemplate the problem of the self?

SUGGESTIONS FOR FURTHER READING

ALEXANDER, S., "Self as Subject and as Person," *Proceedings of the Aristotelian Society,* Vol. 11, 1911, pp. 1–28.

BOYCE GIBSON, W. R., "Self-Introspection," *Proceedings of the Aristotelian Society,* Vol. 5, 1905, pp. 38–52.

BRADLEY, F. H., *Essays on Truth and Reality,* London, Oxford University Press, 1914, pp. 409–427.

COPLESTON, F. C., "Know Thyself: But How?" *The Hibbert Journal,* Vol. 41, 1942–43, pp. 12–17.

EWING, A. C., *The Fundamental Questions of Philosophy,* New York, The Macmillan Company, 1951, ch. 5.

GARNETT, A. CAMPBELL, *Reality and Value,* New Haven, Yale University Press, 1937, ch. 3.

HOCKING, WILLIAM ERNEST, *The Self: Its Body and Freedom,* New Haven, Yale University Press, 1928, ch. 1.

LAIRD, JOHN, *Problems of the Self,* New York, The Macmillan Company, 1917.

LEWIS, C. I., *Mind and the World-Order,* New York, Charles Scribner's Sons, 1929, pp. 412–427.

MAY, ROLLO, *Man's Search for Himself,* New York, W. W. Norton and Co., 1953.

MEAD, GEORGE H., "The Social Self," *The Journal of Philosophy, Psychology, and Scientific Methods,* Vol. 10, 1913, pp. 374–380.

MELLONE, S. H., "The Nature of Self-Knowledge," *Mind,* Vol. 10, 1901, pp. 318–355.

MOORE, JARED S., "The Problem of the Self," *The Philosophical Review,* Vol. 42, 1933, pp. 487–499.

PARKER, DEWITT H., *The Self and Nature,* Cambridge, Mass., Harvard University Press, 1917, chs. 1, 2.

SPAULDING, E. G., *What Am I?,* New York, Charles Scribner's Sons, 1928, ch. 1.

WEISS, PAUL, *Nature and Man,* New York, Henry Holt and Company, 1947, ch. 12.

2

HAPPINESS

F. H. Bradley, in one of his essays, writes: "Yes, happiness is the end which indeed we all reach after. . . . Alas! the one question which no one can answer is, What is happiness?" Aristotle attempts to give an answer to that question. Hartmann confines himself to the common observation that happiness is an accompaniment which defies the one who would seek it directly. Aristotle (384–322 B.C.) and Plato were the two greatest philosophers of the ancient Greek world — if not the greatest philosophers of all time. Dante described Plato as the master of those who dream, Aristotle as the master of those who know. Aristotle's studies in biology, psychology, logic, ethics, politics, metaphysics, and aesthetics support Dante's encomium. Nicolai Hartmann (1882–) is a German moral philosopher who has taught at the Universities of Marburg, Cologne, and Berlin. He is best known for his three-volume work *Ethik* (1926).

A

Now that we have spoken of the virtues, the forms of friendship, and the varieties of pleasure, what remains is to discuss in outline the nature of happiness, since this is what we state the end of human nature to be. Our discussion will be the more concise if we first sum up what we have said already. We said,

Aristotle, *Nicomachean Ethics,* Book X, Sections 6–8, translated by W. D. Ross, in *The Works of Aristotle Translated into English,* Vol. 9, edited by W. D. Ross, Oxford, The Clarendon Press, 1925. Reprinted by permission of the publishers.

then, that it is not a disposition; for if it were it might belong to some one who was asleep throughout his life, living the life of a plant, or, again, to some one who was suffering the greatest misfortunes. If these implications are unacceptable, and we must rather class happiness as an activity, as we have said before, and if some activities are necessary, and desirable for the sake of something else, while others are so in themselves, evidently happiness must be placed among those desirable in themselves, not among those desirable for the sake of something else; for happiness does not lack anything, but is self-sufficient. Now those activities are desirable in themselves from which nothing is sought beyond the activity. And of this nature virtuous actions are thought to be; for to do noble and good deeds is a thing desirable for its own sake.

Pleasant amusements also are thought to be of this nature; we choose them not for the sake of other things; for we are injured rather than benefited by them, since we are led to neglect our bodies and our property. But most of the people who are deemed happy take refuge in such pastimes, which is the reason why those who are ready-witted at them are highly esteemed at the courts of tyrants; they make themselves pleasant companions in the tyrants' favourite pursuits, and that is the sort of man they want. Now these things are thought to be of the nature of happiness because people in despotic positions spend their leisure in them, but perhaps such people prove nothing; for virtue and reason, from which good activities flow, do not depend on despotic position; nor, if these people, who have never tasted pure and generous pleasure, take refuge in the bodily pleasures, should these for that reason be thought more desirable; for boys, too, think the things that are valued among themselves are the best. It is to be expected, then, that, as different things seem valuable to boys and to men, so they should to bad men and to good. Now, as we have often maintained, those things are both valuable and pleasant which are such to the good man; and to each man the activity in accordance with his own disposition is most desirable, and, therefore, to the good man that which is in accordance with virtue. Happiness, therefore, does not lie in amusement; it would, indeed, be strange if the end were amusement, and one were to take trouble and suffer hard-

ship all one's life in order to amuse oneself. For, in a word, everything that we choose we choose for the sake of something else — except happiness, which is an end. Now to exert oneself and work for the sake of amusement seems silly and utterly childish. But to amuse oneself in order that one may exert oneself, as Anacharsis puts it, seems right; for amusement is a sort of relaxation, and we need relaxation because we cannot work continuously. Relaxation, then, is not an end; for it is taken for the sake of activity.

The happy life is thought to be virtuous; now a virtuous life requires exertion, and does not consist in amusement. And we say that serious things are better than laughable things and those connected with amusement, and that the activity of the better of any two things — whether it be two elements of our being or two men — is the more serious; but the activity of the better is *ipso facto* superior and more of the nature of happiness. And any chance person — even a slave — can enjoy the bodily pleasures no less than the best man; but no one assigns to a slave a share in happiness — unless he assigns to him also a share in human life. For happiness does not lie in such occupations, but, as we have said before, in virtuous activities.

If happiness is activity in accordance with virtue, it is reasonable that it should be in accordance with the highest virtue; and this will be that of the best thing in us. Whether it be reason or something else that is this element which is thought to be our natural ruler and guide and to take thought of things noble and divine, whether it be itself also divine or only the most divine element in us, the activity of this in accordance with its proper virtue will be perfect happiness. That this activity is contemplative we have already said.

Now this would seem to be in agreement both with what we said before and with the truth. For, firstly, this activity is the best (since not only is reason the best thing in us, but the objects of reason are the best of knowable objects); and, secondly, it is the most continuous, since we can contemplate truth more continuously than we can *do* anything. And we think happiness has pleasure mingled with it, but the activity of philosophic wisdom is admittedly the pleasantest of virtuous activities; at all events the pursuit of it is thought to offer pleasures marvellous for their purity and their enduringness, and it is to be expected that those who know will pass their time more pleasantly than those who inquire. And the self-sufficiency that is spoken of must belong most to the contemplative activity. For while a philosopher, as well as a just man or one possessing any other virtue, needs the necessaries of life, when they are sufficiently equipped with things of that sort the just man needs people towards whom and with whom he shall act justly, and the temperate man, the brave man, and each of the others is in the same case, but the philosopher, even when by himself, can contemplate truth, and the better the wiser he is; he can perhaps do so better if he has fellow-workers, but still he is the most self-sufficient. And this activity alone would seem to be loved for its own sake; for nothing arises from it apart from the contemplating, while from practical activities we gain more or less apart from the action. And happiness is thought to depend on leisure; for we are busy that we may have leisure, and make war that we may live in peace. Now the activity of the practical virtues is exhibited in political or military affairs, but the actions concerned with these seem to be unleisurely. Warlike actions are completely so (for no one chooses to be at war, or provokes war, for the sake of being at war; any one would seem absolutely murderous if he were to make enemies of his friends in order to bring about battle and slaughter); but the action of the statesman is also unleisurely, and — apart from the political action itself — aims at despotic power and honours, or at all events happiness, for him and his fellow citizens — a happiness different from political action, and evidently sought as being different. So if among virtuous actions political and military actions are distinguished by nobility and greatness, and these are unleisurely and aim at an end and are not desirable for their own sake, but the activity of reason, which is contemplative, seems both to be superior in serious worth and to aim at no end beyond itself, and to have its pleasure proper to itself (and this augments the activity), and the self-sufficiency, leisureliness, unweariedness (so far as this is possible for man), and all the other attributes ascribed to the supremely happy man are evidently those connected with this activity, it follows that this will be the complete happiness of man, if it be allowed a complete term of life (for none of the attributes of happiness is *in*complete).

But such a life would be too high for man; for it is not in so far as he is man that he will live so, but in so far as something divine is present in him; and by so much as this is superior to our composite nature is its activity superior to that which is the exercise of the other kind of virtue. If reason is divine, then, in comparison with man, the life according to it is divine in comparison with human life. But we must not follow those who advise us, being men, to think of human things, and, being mortal, of mortal things, but must, so far as we can, make ourselves immortal, and strain every nerve to live in accordance with the best thing in us; for even if it be small in bulk, much more does it in power and worth surpass everything. This would seem, too, to be each man himself, since it is the authoritative and better part of him. It would be strange, then, if he were to choose not the life of his self but that of something else. And what we said before will apply now; that which is proper to each thing is by nature best and most pleasant for each thing; for man, therefore, the life according to reason is best and pleasantest, since reason more than anything else *is* man. This life therefore is also the happiest.

But in a secondary degree the life in accordance with the other kind of virtue is happy; for the activities in accordance with this befit our human estate. Just and brave acts, and other virtuous acts, we do in relation to each other, observing our respective duties with regard to contracts and services and all manner of actions and with regard to passions; and all of these seem to be typically human. Some of them seem even to arise from the body, and virtue of character to be in many ways bound up with the passions. Practical wisdom, too, is linked to virtue of character, and this to practical wisdom, since the principles of practical wisdom are in accordance with the moral virtues and rightness in morals is in accordance with practical wisdom. Being connected with the passions also, the moral virtues must belong to our composite nature; and the virtues of our composite nature are human; so, therefore, are the life and the happiness which correspond to these. The excellence of the reason is a thing apart; we must be content to say this much about it, for to describe it precisely is a task greater than our purpose requires. It would seem, however, also to need external equipment but little, or less than moral virtue does. Grant that both need the necessaries, and do so equally, even if the statesman's work is the more concerned with the body and things of that sort; for there will be little difference there; but in what they need for the exercise of their activities there will be much difference. The liberal man will need money for the doing of his liberal deeds, and the just man too will need it for the returning of services (for wishes are hard to discern, and even people who are not just pretend to wish to act justly); and the brave man will need power if he is to accomplish any of the acts that correspond to his virtue, and the temperate man will need opportunity; for how else is either he or any of the others to be recognized? It is debated, too, whether the will or the deed is more essential to virtue, which is assumed to involve both; it is surely clear that its perfection involves both; but for deeds many things are needed, and more, the greater and nobler the deeds are. But the man who is contemplating the truth needs no such thing, at least with a view to the exercise of his activity; indeed they are, one may say, even hindrances, at all events to his contemplation; but in so far as he is a man and lives with a number of people, he chooses to do virtuous acts; he will therefore need such aids to living a human life.

But that perfect happiness is a contemplative activity will appear from the following consideration as well. We assume the gods to be above all other beings blessed and happy; but what sort of actions must we assign to them? Acts of justice? Will not the gods seem absurd if they make contracts and return deposits, and so on? Acts of a brave man, then, confronting dangers and running risks because it is noble to do so? Or liberal acts? To whom will they give? It will be strange if they are really to have money or anything of the kind. And what would their temperate acts be? Is not such praise tasteless, since they have no bad appetites? If we were to run through them all, the circumstances of action would be found trivial and unworthy of gods. Still, every one supposes that they *live* and therefore that they are active; we cannot suppose them to sleep like Endymion. Now if you take away from a living being action, and still more production, what is left but contemplation? Therefore the activity of God, which surpasses all others in blessedness, must be contemplative; and of human activities, therefore, that which is most akin to this must be most of the nature of happiness.

This is indicated, too, by the fact that the other animals have no share in happiness, being completely deprived of such activity. For while the whole life of the gods is blessed, and that of men too in so far as some likeness of such activity belongs to them, none of the other animals is happy, since they in no way share in contemplation. Happiness extends, then, just so far as contemplation does, and those to whom contemplation more fully belongs are more truly happy, not as a mere concomitant but in virtue of the contemplation; for this is in itself precious. Happiness, therefore, must be some form of contemplation.

But, being a man, one will also need external prosperity; for our nature is not self-sufficient for the purpose of contemplation, but our body also must be healthy and must have food and other attention. Still, we must not think that the man who is to be happy will need many things or great things, merely because he cannot be supremely happy without external goods; for self-sufficiency and action do not involve excess, and we can do noble acts without ruling earth and sea; for even with moderate advantages one can act virtuously (this is manifest enough; for private persons are thought to do worthy acts no less than despots — indeed even more); and it is enough that we should have so much as that; for the life of the man who is active in

accordance with virtue will be happy. Solon, too, was perhaps sketching well the happy man when he described him as moderately furnished with externals but as having done (as Solon thought) the noblest acts, and lived temperately; for one can with but moderate possessions do what one ought. Anaxagoras also seems to have supposed the happy man not to be rich nor a despot, when he said that he would not be surprised if the happy man were to seem to most people a strange person; for they judge by externals, since these are all they perceive. The opinions of the wise seem, then, to harmonize with our arguments. But while even such things carry some conviction, the truth in practical matters is discerned from the facts of life; for these are the decisive factor. We must therefore survey what we have already said, bringing it to the test of the facts of life, and if it harmonizes with the facts we must accept it, but if it clashes with them we must suppose it to be mere theory. Now he who exercises his reason and cultivates it seems to be both in the best state of mind and most dear to the gods. For if the gods have any care for human affairs, as they are thought to have, it would be reasonable both that they should delight in that which was best and most akin to them (i.e. reason) and that they should reward those who love and honour this most, as caring for the things that are dear to them and acting both right and nobly. And that all these attributes belong most of all to the philosopher is manifest. He, therefore, is the dearest to the gods. And he who is that will presumably be also the happiest; so that in this way too the philosopher will more than any other be happy.

B

Eudaemonism is too old and honourable a form of the moral consciousness to allow us, in criticizing it, to forget the really valuable element in it. This is not exhausted by saying that for centuries it has been a trusted vehicle of the genuine, though misunderstood, valuational consciousness. It could never have been this, if the value, selected by it as a guiding star, were not fundamentally a genuine, indisputable value.

To prove this is superfluous. Everyone feels directly the value of happiness as such and the opposite character of unhappiness. That not every form of happiness is of equal worth does not matter. Indeed one may further concede that even pleasure is a value. These values exist; and to turn man away from this self-evident fact by fictitious theory, would be a futile undertaking. A genuine valuational consciousness cannot be argued away. But from this fact it does not follow either that all striving is towards happiness or that it ought to be so. In other words, happiness and pleasure are indeed values, but not the only ones and not the highest. The eudaemonistic point of view rightly plays a part in man's moral consciousness, but it has no right to play the leading rôle. The indisputable value of happiness does not justify "eudaemonism," no matter what form it takes, just as little as the indisputable value of pleasure justifies hedonism.

Happiness evidently holds a unique place among the other values. We cannot reckon it as one of the moral values in the stricter

Nicolai Hartmann, *Ethics,* Vol. 1, translated by Stanton Coit, New York, The Macmillan Company, and London, George Allen & Unwin Ltd., 1932 (German original, 1926), pp. 146–151. Reprinted by permission of The Macmillan Company and George Allen & Unwin Ltd.

sense. It is not a moral quality of a person; and it is neutral as regards good and evil, is anterior to both. We cannot make anyone directly responsible for our happiness and unhappiness. But it is also difficult to reckon happiness among goods — as the word is commonly understood; it is of too general a character and, besides, never inheres in a real carrier of values; it always remains an emotional value. Nevertheless it is essentially related to everything which has the character of a "good," or, more correctly, to the reality and existence, to the possession, of a good.

Perhaps one comes nearest to its essence in defining it as the emotional value accompanying every real conscious possession; it is therefore a necessary emotional reaction to every valuational reality and relation — or, one might say, to every participation in values — and has its own secondary scale of values. Formulas of this kind can fit only approximately the relation which here confronts us. But we may venture upon two suggestions:

First, there is a universal connection of happiness with the whole series of values, from the highest and the most spiritual of the moral virtues to the last and most commonplace of external goods — wherein is to be found the inner reason for the extraordinary diversity in the valuational shades of happiness.

And, secondly, the eudaemonistic principle has a peculiar capacity to be a vehicle of genuine moral values, because of the remarkable scope which it gives to the most varied and most contradictory values of human conduct.

Thus we can understand that happiness, although in fact only an accompanying phenomenon, has still in all ages of immature consciousness played the rôle of a universal form of the valuational sense — that is, the rôle of an ethical category. That this rôle does not by right belong to it does not detract from the force of the historical fact. We have examples enough of a similar extension of single categories beyond bounds in the domain of theory. There have been times when the teleological category has dominated the whole concept of nature; to-day science has reduced the sphere of its validity to very narrow limits. But just as there has been a theoretical consciousness which could not see a mere event except as the execution of a purpose, so has there been for perhaps a still longer time a moral consciousness which could not imagine a "good" in any other form than that of a "happiness." And here also a stringent limitation of the category within justifiable boundaries is the correction required. The correction, however, does not mean a rejection of the category, but a bringing forward of the really determining principles which are hidden behind it.

Happiness is not the highest value; it is always relatively subordinate, an accompaniment, as we have seen. But notwithstanding all this it is nevertheless a value proper which, in those higher and lower masses of value which it accompanies as an emotion, never disappears. It is something different from them all. And to its difference is attached a moral claim of a peculiar kind. The happiest man is certainly not the best — no one would contradict that statement; but it is justifiable to add: The best man ought to be the happiest. It is of the essence of moral goodness to be worthy of happiness.

This claim is only a desideratum. But it reveals the distinctive value of happiness. Whether this desideratum may expect fulfilment is not an ethical question. It falls under the religious inquiry: What may we hope? But the claim as such is independent of its fulfilment.

Only in so far as the consciousness of being worthy of happiness is itself already a happiness does the fulfilment attach to the essence of the matter. But here we are anticipating our investigation. For exactly this essence of the matter, the being worthy of happiness, does not inhere in the relation of man to the eudaemonistic value but to the higher, the properly ethical, values.

Apart from the ultimate question as to what kind of value may be peculiar to happiness and how it is to be graded, there is a series of further ethical questions which are suggested by eudaemonism and make it an extremely ambiguous phenomenon. Here we can only consider the one question, whether striving after happiness is rational.

That it is so is not self-evident nor does it depend alone upon the valuational character of happiness, but also essentially upon the material involved. To strive for external goods is possible only within very narrow limits; but to strive for qualities of character, if one does not possess a predisposition towards them, is altogether impossible. Still more doubtful would be a striving for love. The striving for happiness is closely related to this latter. **1114490**

Everyone knows what is involved in the search for happiness. The mythological figure of the whimsical Fortuna hits the nail on the head. It is more than a mere figure of speech. It is in the very nature of "happiness" to tease man and to mock him as long as he lives, to lure him on, to mislead him and leave him standing with empty hands. It pursues him jealously so long as he, diverted from it, is pursuing other values. But it escapes from him the moment he snatches at it. It flees beyond his reach if he passionately pursues it. But if he modestly turns away, it flatters him again. If in despair he gives up the struggle, it mocks him behind his back.

If one omits from this characterization the popular poetic hyperbole, there still remains in it a kind of essential law, an inner necessity.

Happiness does not depend solely upon the attainable goods of life to which it seems to be attached. It depends at the same time, or rather primarily, upon an inner predisposition, a sensitiveness of the individual himself, his capacity for happiness. But this capacity suffers under the effort to attain happiness. It is greatest where the good involved was least sought for, where it falls unexpectedly into one's lap. And it is smallest, where it is passionately yearned for and striven after.

To what this decline in the capacity for happiness is properly due is a difficult psychological question. It is conceivable that the anticipation of happiness, the mere Epicurean dwelling upon it before it is there, diminishes it. It never quite equals what was expected. The anticipation has already falsified it, by prejudicing the sense of value against the reality, in favour of some fantastic image. Or is it that the capacity of enjoyment has simply exhausted itself beforehand? However this may be, the striving itself nullifies the eudaemonistic value of the thing striven for, before it has been attained. The attainment becomes illusory through the striving itself, because thereby the thing attained is no longer the same happiness which was striven for.

In other words, happiness allows itself to be yearned for and striven after, but not to be attained by striving. The pursuit of happiness reacts unfavourably upon the capacity for it. At the same time it always vitiates the thing pursued. When the pursuit dominates a man, it sweeps all happiness out of his life, makes him restless and unsteady, and precipitates him into unhappiness. This is the meaning of that alluring and fleeing, that flattery and mockery.

Real happiness always approaches from another side than one expects. It always lies where one is not seeking it. It always comes as a gift and never permits itself to be wrung from life or extorted by threats. It exists in the richness of life which is always there. It opens itself to him who sets his gaze upon this abundance — that is, upon the primary values. It flees from him who is looking out only for pleasant sensations, charmed only by the emotions which accompany all values. Thus his vision for the values themselves is blurred. But he who yearns for them, without coquetting with his sensations, wins the reality.

Is it a curse upon man, an eternal infatuation, that all striving assumes so easily the form of a search for happiness and that every gain in value takes on the guise of happiness? Or is it a part of eternal wisdom and justice which is fulfilled in the fact that all genuine striving after genuine ethical values of itself brings happiness as its own reward, and this the more, the higher in the scale the value is to which the striving is directed? May we believe that in this sense the man who is most worthy of happiness is also in reality the happiest — because he is the one who is the most capable of happiness? Does it not look as though, in its higher meaning, the proposition that the best man is the happiest is still true? And is not eudaemonism, then, in the end rehabilitated?

These are no longer ethical questions. Moreover, man cannot answer them. But an affirmative answer to them — in case it were justified — certainly would not be a justification of eudaemonism. Happiness, as a moral postulate, is an eternal requirement of the human heart; but "eudaemonism," as the morality of striving for it, is a tendency which destroys itself, in that it systematically leads to an incapacity for happiness.

SUGGESTIONS FOR THOUGHT

1. Older people frequently look back on their youth as the happiest period of their lives, whereas young people look forward to happiness. Which period of life might be regarded as the happiest period? Would the memory of an event give more happiness than the event itself?

2. John Stuart Mill advised that "the conscious ability to do without happiness gives the best prospect of realizing such happiness as is attainable." Is this because happiness depends on self-control, even the control of our own desire for happiness? How would you defend Mill's position?

3. Why do you think the pursuit of happiness is listed as an "inalienable right" in our Declaration of Independence?

4. How successful are most people in the pursuit of happiness? Are people unsuccessful because happiness is difficult to achieve, or because they do not recognize happiness when they possess it?

5. Timothy Dwight, a former president of Yale University, once said that the happiest person is the person who thinks the most interesting thoughts. Does happiness seem to you to be a matter of thinking? What are some of the factors which foster deep and lasting happiness?

6. Does the increase of learning foster a decrease of happiness? Kant observed: "We do indeed find that the more a cultivated reason concerns itself with the meaning of happiness and the enjoyment of life, the farther away man gets from true satisfaction." Do college-trained men and women seem to enjoy life more than those who did not go to college? If Kant is right, can you suggest some ways by which a person might acquire a college education and still not lose his happiness?

7. "The root of joy as of duty is to put all one's powers toward some great end." (Justice O. W. Holmes) Will any "great end" serve this function? What does this quotation suggest about the relation of duty and happiness?

8. The first sentence in Tolstoy's *Anna Karenina* is puzzling and tantalizing: "Happy families are all alike; every unhappy family is unhappy in its own way." What do you make of it?

9. W. T. Stace thinks that one of the reasons for the unhappiness that bedevils mankind is that man generally mistakes pleasure for happiness. What are the differences between pleasure and happiness?

10. A number of years ago the following advertisement appeared in the *London Times:* "Wanted: Two domestic servants. Christian. Cheerful if possible." In what ways has religion prevented men from being fully happy? In what ways has religion enhanced the happiness of men? How do the other-worldly aspects of religion affect human happiness?

SUGGESTIONS FOR FURTHER READING

AUGUSTINE, *De beata vita* (The Happy Life), translated by Ludwig Schopp, *The Fathers of the Church*, Vol. 2, edited by Ludwig Schopp, New York, Cima Publishing Company, 1948, pp. 29–84.

BROCHMANN, GEORG, *Humanity and Happiness*, New York, Viking Press, 1950.

JOAD, C. E. M., *The Pleasure of Being Oneself*, New York, The Philosophical Library, 1951.

LAMPRECHT, STERLING, *Nature and History*, New York, Columbia University Press, 1950, pp. 123–155.

LANGDON-DAVIES, JOHN, *Man Comes of Age*, New York, Harper and Brothers, 1932, ch. 11.

MERCIER, CHARLES A., "Are we happier than our forefathers?" *The Hibbert Journal,* Vol. 15, 1916–17, pp. 75–89.

MOFFITT, JOHN, JR., "The Pursuit of Human Happiness," *The International Journal of Ethics,* Vol. 49, 1938, p. 1–17.

POTTER, CHARLES FRANCIS, *Technique of Happiness,* London, Macaulay Press, 1935.

POWYS, JOHN COWPER, *The Art of Happiness,* New York, Simon and Schuster, 1935.

RUSSELL, BERTRAND, *New Hopes for a Changing World,* New York, Simon and Schuster, 1951, chs. 20, 21.

RUSSELL, MRS. BERTRAND, *The Right to Be Happy,* New York, Harper and Brothers, 1927.

SOKOLOFF, BORIS, *The Achievement of Happiness,* New York, Simon and Schuster, 1935.

WATTS, ALAN W., *The Meaning of Happiness,* New York, Harper and Brothers, 1940.

WOLFE, W. BERAN, *How To Be Happy though Human,* New York, Farrar and Rinehart, 1931.

WOODBRIDGE, FREDERICK J. E., *An Essay on Nature,* New York, Columbia University Press, 1940, ch. 5.

3

WORK AND PLAY

TOM SAWYER believed that work and play were quite distinct: "Work consists of whatever a body is obliged to do . . . Play consists of whatever a body is not obliged to do." Most other philosophers doubt that these two forms of human activity can be, or should be, so completely separated. In the following selections Bradley seems to be closer to Tom than is Perry, but both agree that one's attitude toward work and play is an important part of one's philosophy of life. Francis Herbert Bradley (1846–1924) was forced by ill health to retire to his apartment at Oxford shortly after his appointment as a Fellow of Merton College. Yet the books and essays written in the seclusion of his apartment made him the acknowledged leader of idealism in the later part of the nineteenth century and the first quarter of the twentieth century. Ralph Barton Perry (1876–   ) taught philosophy at Harvard University from 1902 until his retirement in 1946. He is a leader of the American philosophical school known as New Realism. He is probably best known for his volume *General Theory of Value* (1926), although in more recent years he has become known beyond philosophical circles as an interpreter and defender of democracy.

A

What is play? It is activity, we may say,

F. H. Bradley, "On Floating Ideas and the Imaginary," *Mind,* New Series, Vol. 15, 1906, pp. 462–472. This essay also appears in: F. H. Bradley, *Essays on Truth and Reality,* Oxford, The Clarendon Press, 1914, pp. 50–63. Reprinted by permission of the Editor of *Mind* and The Clarendon Press.

so far as that is felt to be unconstrained. And hence the activity must in the first place be pleasant. It must be enjoyed and exercised for its own sake, and, so far as it is mere play, it must not be felt as subject to any sort of control. In play I have nothing, which I do or seek because I am forced from the outside, because I am driven by desire, or because there is a valuable end which I pursue and which thus is able to dictate. Play is therefore mere amusement, and, so far as it remains mere play, it owns no master but caprice. In playing I realize myself not only apart from the compulsion of force or appetite, but as free from anything that could define and so limit and constrain me. Play is thus incompatible with foreign control, and again it is further opposed to earnest. Where you have something that is valuable and that matters, you have so far no play, or rather you have no play here except within restraint and limits. For, wherever I am in earnest, my activity is defined by an end. And, even if there is no end outside the activity, the control is still present. For where my activity is valuable, its detail is relative to the whole, and its detail is therefore more or less subordinate and subject to restraint. And, so far as I feel this, I lose the sense of mere play and caprice. Play is thus activity spontaneous and agreeable and qualified by the absence of compulsion or earnest.

It may be asked if this contrast is really inherent in the sense of play. The opposition to earnest, it may be objected, need exist nowhere except in the spectator's mind. There is natural activity which bursts forth apart from any sense of limit and restraint. Such activity we can find everywhere in the young, and we may even imagine it, if we please, as existing in a perfect mind. And here, it will be said, there is a sense of freedom and of self-assertion and of play, uncoloured by any feeling of contrast or restraint. But the above objection turns, I think, upon a question of words. I fully agree that there is such a sense of spontaneous activity, but, apart from a felt contrast, I could not myself call it an experience of play. And at any rate I propose here

to use the word otherwise. Where there is play, felt as play, I shall suppose the more or less remote contrast with a more or less withdrawn earnest. I shall assume the presence of a more or less specified sense of something, more or less prominent or in the background, which is felt as control or limit. Restraint, whether as what is forced on me or as what matters, I shall take therefore as a necessary element implied in play. But in what follows I shall confine myself to the consideration of play as limited not by force but by earnest.

If you ask what is earnest and what matters, then in the end it is life as a whole which matters. Every pleasant activity therefore is so far good, and all matters because and so far as it realizes the main end. But on the other hand within the contents of this whole there are degrees of necessity and of importance. In general or in particular, against something that either is indispensable or that matters more, some aspect of life may be unimportant. And any aspect which thus relatively does not matter, can be felt here and now not to matter at all. Here is the province of play in its contrast with earnest. Where there is activity which as a whole or in its detail is thus relatively of no moment, we have a limited sphere of caprice and amusement and, in a word, of play.

But there is no hard division in life between play and earnest, and there is in short no genuine human end which in principle excludes play. The absolute separation in life of optional and necessary, of play and work, leads essentially to error. And the error is palpable where everything except maintenance of life is identified with play. Certainly my bare subsistence is an end which may be said to come first, because everything in life is lost if there is no more living. But on the other hand a mere living which is not good itself or for the sake of something good, is neither necessary nor desirable. Work for the sake of work and practice for practice' sake are, in fact, ends which no one apart from illusion could accept.

And generally the sundering of life into spheres of work and spheres of play is indefensible. It is true that in life there are things which are everywhere necessary. There is a certain amount of physical well-being and a certain degree of mental and moral development which are fundamental. Human life is impossible except on this basis of individual and social virtue. But beyond this common basis are those special stations in social life the occupation of which is more or less a matter of choice. And further there are non-social modes of human self-realization which in a sense are higher and in a sense are still more optional. They are optional in the sense that deprived of them life could be lived, and that with regard to them the individual has a right and a duty to choose. But on the other hand to treat these higher functions as mere play would be obviously absurd. We have in the next place what may be called the minor graces of life, things the detail of which is more or less variable at our pleasure. And finally we end in what are called amusements. Here, where the amusement is *mere* amusement, the detail is optional. It has no value in itself, but is desirable solely for the sake of its effect on human welfare.

Play may be called necessary in the sense that without play human life is not fully realized, and hence we may speak of a general duty and obligation to play. But on the other hand the obligation stops short of prescribing the details, which in the main are left to our pleasure. Hence we may find here the merely optional, which we may oppose to the merely necessary, and may forget that neither of these in abstraction and by itself is a human end. In short to identify the barely necessary with that which matters and is to be taken in earnest, is in principle indefensible. You cannot in life make a hard division into separate spheres of work and play, for play in a word exists everywhere so far as I am able to play there.

I will point out briefly first how in principle every human activity admits of play, and in the next place how more or less all plays in a sense are serious pursuits.

It is possible first to take a serious pursuit and to amuse myself with it. I may, that is, occupy myself with this activity just so far as it amuses me, and I may treat it as something which, for me, falls outside of what really matters. In comparison with other things the pursuit has no serious claim on me. I am not in earnest with it, I may do with it as I please, and in a word I may play with it. But to distinguish here between mere trifling on one side, and on the other side interests which are serious though limited, is often impossible. There are again interests with which, in the case of this or that man or of every man, no trifling is permissible. But, without attempting further explanation, it is safe to conclude that within limits it is possible and right to play at a serious pursuit. What, however, I here desire to insist on is this, that in principle every human activity, however grave and even sacred, admits of some play. Play is here the expression of certain conquest and of absolute mastery over detail. And this joyous aspect is wholly absent from work only where, as too often happens, the conditions are inhuman. The most serious aspects of human life admit of play in this sense. In religions, not one-sided, there is an element of merry-making and sport, such as comes naturally with a sense of full security and triumph. And the morality which ignores the charm of sportive well-doing, has lost sight of the full ideal of human goodness. To trifle with a principle, to make it the sport of mere self-will, is forbidden. It is another thing to be filled with an implicit sense of relative value, and in the service of a higher principle to enjoy its triumph over the fixed detail and limits of human duties. This is a gracious element seldom absent from the highest wisdom and love.

There is no serious pursuit, we have seen, which in principle excludes play. And on the other hand play hardly can maintain complete severance from earnest. Mere amusements, it appeared, as general amusement are necessary for our welfare, and in most cases perhaps they are more than mere amusements. Plays may advance some social end, or may develop some individual faculty which in its effects or in itself is really valuable. They tend in other words, so far, to pass into useful performances, or into accomplishments worth having because adding to the sum of human perfection. And again from another side plays are something more than mere playing. They are subject in each case to special restraint by the rule of the game. They are limited not only by a more or less specified world of earnest, but they become in various degrees defined in themselves. And so far as in playing you must not trifle with the rule of the game, your playing has taken on a feature of earnest.

Plays contain usually a large element of chance and caprice, but apart from that, as plays, they keep essentially the following character. They have no individual worth, their detail in itself does not matter, and one of them has, in itself as against the others, no value at all. You are therefore, so far, free to choose amongst them at your caprice. If one of them is your best way of playing, that one has special value for you. But, on the other

side, its value is generic merely, and it has worth only as a means to an end. In this point plays differ from accomplishments, which have value so far as they each contribute individually to human perfection. Plays on the other hand, so far as mere plays, have no end but a general end which falls outside of all taken individually. And where this principle is ignored, and where the rule of the game perhaps gains more than a conventional value, we are too familiar with the result. Plays are perverted into the serious pursuits of life, the moral perspective is distorted or destroyed, and the effect on life is, according to circumstances, more or less injurious or even ruinous. The above distinction, however, between mere plays and accomplishments, though clear in principle, is often in practice not easy to maintain.

Play is any activity in life so far as that is agreeable, is unconstrained, and is felt here and now not to matter. Play is not in principle excluded, we have seen, from any aspect of life. And when we come to mere amusements which exist for the sake of playing, they tend, as we have seen, to develop a character, too often perverted, of work and earnest. There is in short no natural separation of life into spheres of necessary work and of mere play. And, when we consider these extremes, we find that, differing otherwise, they share the same essential feature. Neither has its end in itself, neither contributes, individually and in itself, a special element to human value. Each on the contrary is desirable solely for the sake of an effect, particular or general, which it produces.

The division of human existence into spheres of necessary work and of optional play leads therefore, when developed, to confusion and absurdity. The world of play turns out to be the only world which a man could seriously desire, and the world of earnest, when you examine it, proves to be that which by itself has no importance or value. Everything which possesses human interest becomes mere play, while the residue could be an end only for irrational caprice. Any such view breaks down at once when confronted with the facts of actual life. Thus a stage-play, to take that instance, is even to the spectator not mere playing, while to the actor it is the serious business of life. It is not merely the work by which he lives, but it is the main end of his being, the special function by which he at once contributes to humanity and realizes himself. On the other side the necessity of living is no real necessity, unless the life, which in oneself or others it subserves, is really desirable. A mere inhuman subsistence and an empty practice are (I would repeat) things which, except through an illusion, no one could take in earnest.

Play, we have thus seen, is one aspect of life. It is, or in principle it may be, everywhere present. The division of life into spheres of work and play may be most important and even necessary, but any such division after all is not absolute but relative. If you take it otherwise it becomes an error which even practically may have bad results, and which theoretically cannot fail to be more or less injurious. It is parallel to the separation of the world into real and imaginary, matter of fact and mere ideas. And it proves, when we consider it, to be another offshoot of the same fundamental error. It will, I think, tend further to illustrate the same theme if I add some words on the supposed connexion of make-believe with play.

Play has been held to contain essentially the presence of make-believe and illusion. It has been alleged in short to depend upon a sense of the imaginary in its contrast with the real. This doctrine to my mind is in such obvious collision with plain fact, that I think it

better to begin by asking how it can come to be adopted. And there is (i) the undoubted presence of make-believe in *some* playing. This feature, having been wrongly generalized and taken as essential, is then postulated in spite of appearance as existing everywhere. We have again (ii) the so-called imitative actions in young animals. These, or many of these, it is natural to call playing. And our minds are thus insensibly led to regard such actions as performed in imitation and with a consciousness of unreality. And (iii) there is finally the more or less specified sense of limitation and restraint, which, we have seen, is essentially involved in playing. Hence, where the erroneous division of the world into imaginary and real is accepted, the former of these tends to be taken as that which in playing is limited by the latter. Thus we conclude that in play we essentially have a sense of the imaginary as opposed to matter of fact. We shall realize both the character and the extent of this mistake when we ask as to the nature of that restraint which, we agree, is present in play.

But it is better first to illustrate briefly the collision of the above doctrine with fact. When two young dogs are chasing one another or biting, when boys let out of school behave in much the same manner, when a man aimlessly strikes at this or that with his stick, or falls into some other trifling activity where, as we say, he has nothing to do — it seems obvious that make-believe here has no concern in the matter. And when we take part in the athletic pastimes of boyhood or manhood, and play at hockey, football or cricket, or again at such games as cards or chess — how can it be seriously maintained that illusion is present always and essentially? The opposite conclusion, to my mind at least, seems too clear for argument. When for example I play at cricket, what am I pretending to do other than the thing which I do? An outsider doubtless can insist that everywhere we have a mimic battle of this or that kind, but the mimicry surely exists only in the mind of the outsider, and for my mind, as I play, has no existence at all. And if it is objected that in play we have a sense of limit, and that the restraint must come from a sense of the real as against the imaginary, that brings me to the point which I wish to discuss. On the one hand I agree that in play we have some sense of limit, but on the other hand I urge the absence in many cases of anything like make-believe. And I will proceed to show the real nature of that restraint which seems everywhere present in play.

In many cases of play the restraint, we may say in a word, is not theoretical but moral. Consider the natural sporting of a young dog or a child. There are certain natural activities which in themeslves are pleasant. To bite, for instance, or to struggle or run is delightful. But — and here is the point — with my play-fellow I must not bite beyond a limit. If I go too far and hurt my playfellow the result is unpleasant, unless indeed I am angry and want to fight and am not afraid to do so. Hence I exercise my delightful activities so as to stop short of that result. I need not be thinking of this all the time, but any approach to excess brings on what is discordant with my pleasant condition, both in my own mind and perhaps palpably outside my mind also. Such a result is felt to be incongruous, and, as soon as it is suggested, it suppresses the excess of the activity. If the reader will observe a young dog gnawing the flesh of his hand and watching him to observe if the line is at any time crossed, he will, I think realize my meaning. There is absolutely no illusion here, but there is restraint, a restraint which later may be formulated as the rule of the game. On the other hand when a dog exercises his ac-

tivity on a stick, the rule of the game, we may say, is simply that he is not to hurt himself.

It may be objected that so far we have not the distinction between play and earnest. But so far, I reply, I am endeavouring merely to establish the presence of restraint without illusion. I am pointing out that the limit to pleasant activity may be, in a word, not theoretical but moral. And this result still holds, I now go on to urge, where the specific sense of play is clearly present. In cricket, for example, or in cards I am obviously under restraint, while as obviously, at least to my mind, there is no trace of make-believe. Unless I am a professional or a devotee, I am aware that these activities are optional. They do not matter in themselves, and their scope is limited by that in life which really does matter. And, in the second place, to secure a better exercise of the activity it is carried on subject to conventional restraints. I am, in other words, limited by the rules of the game, which exclude at once mere trifling and violence, as well as by the consciousness that, as against what is more serious, my activity does not matter. This is the nature of the restraint which, to my mind, is both effective and obvious. Illusion and make-believe on the other hand I am unable to discern.

'But,' I shall be told, 'you are ignoring the play in which make-believe is obvious. A girl with her doll, a boy with a wooden sword, are plain instances which confute you. And the actor in stage-plays, you seem to forget, is called a player. And to deny here the presence of every kind of make-believe and illusion is surely irrational.' To this I reply that such a denial is no part of my case. All that I have been urging so far is that illusion does not belong essentially or everywhere to play. Playing, on the contrary, we may now go on to see, is of various kinds. And playing of one kind undoubtedly involves make-believe. It implies within limits the treatment of the imaginary as if it were real. If you take make-believe as the playing at practical belief, as our acting within limits as if the facts here and now were qualified, as we know that in fact they are not qualified — then make-believe, it is obvious, belongs to some play. But to argue from this that, where I do *not* play at believing, I must pretend in order to play, seems clearly illogical. Whether in short, and how far, in any play there is illusion, depends in each case — that is all I urge — upon the nature of the play.

We have seen that in some play there is no pretence or illusion. The exercise of the activity involves no excursion into the imaginary world. But, as can easily be seen with children, this imaginary element soon appears, and in playing it occupies a great space, how great I need not discuss. The perceived facts here do not suffice for the required activity. They are therefore extended by imaginary qualifications, and the activity becomes possible. And at this point a new kind of restraint and limit can be observed.

All playing involves a limit, but in some plays this limit, we saw, was simply what we called moral. Beyond a certain point, that is, I must not. But where make-believe comes in, we find a new sort of control. The child that pretends in play knows that morally it must not cross a certain line. But it knows now also that it has an imaginary world, which is limited by real fact, and again in some cases by conventional suppositions. A schoolboy playing at soldiers knows first that he must hurt no one too much, but he knows also that he is a schoolboy as well as a soldier. And he knows that, so long as certain conventions are observed, no consistency is required even in his imaginary character.

The control, in a word, has become theoretical as well as moral. The playing dog knows, we may say, that beyond a certain point *he must not*. The playing boy knows this in all his playing, and in some cases he knows no more. But in other cases he knows also that beyond a certain point *the thing is not*. He has here a world of imagination, qualifying the real world but always subject to and restrained by that world.

These two controls, the moral and theoretical, are in much play so joined and blended that to separate their several effects would be hard or impossible. In 'playing a part,' on the stage or again in real life, this intimate mingling may be observed. We have first of all the letting-go of certain activities subject to a certain moral restraint. But we have in addition the entrance, for ourselves or for others or for both, into the sphere of pretence, make-believe and illusion. This entrance is limited by our consciousness of the real fact, and again by conventional rules, wherever and so far as these exist. And to what extent the control is before the mind, and how far illusion actually is present, depends in every case upon the conditions and the individual.

Thus pretence and make-believe do not belong to the general essence of play. They are obviously present often where there is no playing and where they are used consciously as means to a serious end. On the other side there are many plays (we have seen) from which illusion certainly is absent. In other plays again the activity is exercised within an area more or less qualified as imaginary. Lastly there are cases where illusion and pretense are not essential, but where more or less they tend to come in. And the extent here will be determined by the individual conditions.

B

In all cases of playful interest, from the play of animals to the play of the human imagination, there appears to be one common principle. An action-system having a certain normal result, is only partially executed; not because it is externally thwarted, but because it is only partially consistent with some predominant action-system. The most evident characteristic of playful activity is self-imposed restraint. The cat that plays with the mouse *almost* kills its prey, but stops just short of the consummation of the performance. The dog at play bites, but bites gently; runs away, but does not run far away. The spectator at the melodrama feels moved to rescue the heroine, and may even warn her of her danger, but he remains in his seat. The man who playfully imagines that he is a millionaire does some of the things that a millionaire would do, but not all. In these cases restraint is evidently a very different thing from failure, the interest being checked not by external circumstances but by some internal and interested control. In no case is the agent carrying the activity as far as he *could*. The dog could bite harder, but he does not want to; the imaginary millionaire could be more extravagant, but he is deterred by his own recognition of the facts. Playful activity is also commonly characterized by make-believe or pretence. But except in so far as it is confused with imitation, this turns out to be also a form of restraint. The child who pretends to be a soldier or a mother is executing some

but not all of the characteristic combative or parental activities. Indeed the examples cited above to illustrate restraint could equally well be cited as illustrations of pretence. The playful dog is pretending to fight or to run away, and the imaginary millionaire is pretending to possess wealth.

How shall we interpret this limitation of interested activity that is characteristic of play? The limitation does not relate to the type of performance, for one may play at anything. Play is not limited out of regard for other interests, for it is not the same thing as prudence, moderation or self-sacrifice. The boy who plays at being a soldier or pirate, is not controlling his warlike or piratical propensities out of regard for his own or another's well-being. There is some sense in which he is not a soldier or pirate at all, — some sort of flat difference between reality and pretence.

In order to understand this difference, it is necessary first to conceive of an interested activity as taking effect in certain changes which have both conditions and consequences beyond the activity itself. It unites with a given situation so as to produce a subsequent situation which, in turn, will inaugurate an ulterior train of effects. Such activity is characterized by a recognition of the existing situation, a search for means, and a regard for the future; and is commonly named for that normal ulterior consequence whose expectation is its governing motive. Now the phenomenon of play seems to consist, first, in the fact that part of such an interested performance occurs without the expectation for which it is named. Some care is needed in the statement of this principle, if make-believe is not to be confused with error. An expectation may occur and may inaugurate action, in the absence of the external conditions which render its fulfilment possible. In this case the interest is 'real' or 'earnest,' but is founded on error and "doomed to defeat." The case of make-believe, on the other hand, is the case in which the requisite external conditions are not only absent, but known to be absent; so that the action is checked from within, short of that point at which their absence is fatal.

Let us consider, for example, the case of the dog romping with his master. The dog is said to be playing in so far as certain of its activities are organized parts of other activities, dissociated from the normal expectations for which they are named. Thus, for example, the dog springs upon its master, seizes his hand, bites at it, and growls. These activities are primarily associated with a train of other consequences, such as injury, retaliation on the part of the object attacked, death or devouring of prey. These ulterior consequences do not, however, occur, nor are they expected or sought. The dog is not mistaking his master for his enemy or prey, or deceived into misapplied effort, as he might be by a dummy cunningly contrived to simulate the proper object of ferocity. He recognizes his master throughout, and deals with him as such. But though differently motivated the dog's performance coincides in part with that which he would execute in the presence of a rival, an intruder, or his natural prey. The performance is called playful in so far as there is this partial coincidence, and is the playful form of that activity which in its entirety is called the real, earnest or serious activity.

In the second place, however, the dog who is playfully fighting, or pretending to be ferocious, is 'really' romping with his master. In other words, although the normal expectation for which the fictitious activity is named is lacking, there is an expectation which *is* governing the performance. Although divorced from the circumstances with which it is nominally associated, the activity is related to the circumstances which actually exist. It is transposed to unnatural circumstances, and so abridged or modified as to be consistent with these circumstances. There is a change of control which sets limits to it. In the case of the playful dog this control or actually dominating motive is an interest of the recurrent type, which is substituted for the progressive interest of attacking and slaying. There is, in other words, a tendency to prolong the existing situation, and the development of the activity is arrested at a point which will guarantee its repetition. This is commonly described as interest in the activity itself rather than in its result.

Such an analysis serves to correct two standard theories of play which are ordinarily thought to be inconsistent. Thus Professor William McDougall, following Schiller and Spencer, holds that play is "a purposeless activity, striving toward no goal," and explicable as an overflow of surplus energy. He bases this opinion on the evident fact that playful activity is not the same either in its effects or in its accompanying emotion, as the real activity for which it is named; and on the association of play with the abundant vitality which characterizes youth, health and freshness. Such a view, while emphasizing the absence of the motivation commonly governing the activity, does not sufficiently emphasize that resemblance between earnest and playful activity owing to which the one is named for the other. The opposing view, maintained by Groos, Schneider and James, takes this resemblance as its point of departure, and interprets play as the partial exercise of instinctive activities. But this view tends to neglect the fact that these instinctive activities do not really occur. Both views neglect the actual motivation of play, the former by viewing play as aimless, and the latter by identifying its motivation with that of the instincts which it resembles.

All writers on the subject are influenced by the unnecessary supposition that if play is to be governed by any motive at all, it must be either the same as that of the several instincts, or a new and unique motive invented *ad hoc*, — an "instinct to play." The former alternative is excluded because of the absolute difference between doing a thing in fun and in earnest, and the latter by the fact that play reproduces all of the performances of real life without having any specific form of its own. To avoid this *impasse* it is only necessary to suppose that all partial activities are capable, whether by inheritance, or by experience, of possessing a motive power of their own. According to James, "all simple active games are attempts to gain the excitement yielded by certain primitive instincts, through feigning that the occasions for their exercise are there." But this statement fails to explain what is meant by "feigning," and implies that the excitement is the same in the playful and real exercise of the instinct. We may now understand the feigning to consist in the fact that an instinctive activity, suitable to a certain situation, is executed only so far as it is consistent with the recognition of a contrary situation. The playful dog is treating his master like an enemy so far as this is compatible with treating him as a friend. The accompanying excitement will not be that of ferocity but that of love, tinged with ferocity. The component of fighting which is embodied in romping will carry with it some portion of the fighting impulse.

We are now in a position to understand something of the place of play in life. The playful form of any activity is an abridgement of the activity under the control of inopportune or inauspicious circumstance. It is such transformation of an activity as may enable it to fit into an action-system which is based on the recognized absence of the conditions suitable to the activity's full performance.

Play, so constructed, provides, in the first place a means of circumventing the rule that "you cannot both eat your cake and have it." It is a means of reconciling consumption and possession. It is the cat-and-mouse manner of life. It expresses the fact that you can both eat your cake and have it, *if you do not carry the eating too far.* There is a crucial point at which the rule takes effect, but by stopping short of that point one can escape its application. One cannot swallow one's cake and have it, but one can handle it, look at it, gloat over it or even mouth it, — and still have it. The dog can bite his master's hand and still have it to bite again, provided he bites gently; or he can run away from his master and still have his master to run away from, provided he remains within range and tempts pursuit. In play, activity is changed from a rectilinear to an asymptotic or elliptical form, stopping just short of consummation for the sake of prolongation or recurrence. Play thus provides a means by which an activity may be saved from its own natural dénouement.

This aspect of play may be generalized as immunity from consequences. One can dance without paying the piper. In "real life" consequences are taken account of; as events in the environment, and having their own train of effects, they require a general readjustment to the future, or a systematic correction of expectations. The playful activity is somehow dissociated and insulated from this causal field. In the case of the child, eventualities are looked out for by others. The child, like the lilies of the field, is delivered by parental care from the necessity of toiling and spinning. The adult who takes a holiday or an hour of recreation, has made provision for it by "arranging his affairs," that is by securing his future. The holiday activities themselves are characterized by their discontinuity with that series of means and ends that constitutes his main current of endeavor. A man's sports and recreation are so organized as to have the minimum of consequences, being conducted on a plane that does not intersect with that of his imperative needs or his vocational purpose. They are artificially contrived so that they may be performed spontaneously, that is, without calculation of consequences. This mood of spontaneity is further induced by a change of scene in which the habitual tomorrow may for a time be forgotten. The adult at play is thus said to be relieved from his "cares," or from that watchfulness and persistent effort with which his ordinary occupations are attended. Like the horse at pasture he may be healed from the fatigue and friction of harness. Recreation may therefore be playful in a double sense, as being divorced from the context of work, and as consisting in activities which simulate those of real performance.

Activity is deemed frivolous or excessively playful when, like Nero's fiddling, it disregards facts or consequences that press for consideration. From the standpoint of the devout all worldly living is frivolous, because it ignores reality, both present and future. A serious life, on the other hand, is a life wholly permeated by the conviction of reality, and closely applied to the main purpose. If "life is real! life is earnest!" this means "to act that each tomorrow find us farther than today." The grim spirit of Puritanism expresses itself in the resolve: "Never to lose one moment of time, but to improve it in the most profitable way I can. Never to allow any pleasure or grief, joy or sorrow, nor any affection at all, nor any degree of affection, nor any circumstance relating to it, but what helps religion." (From the *Resolutions* of Jonathan Edwards, 1722–1723.)

If play denotes an activity delivered from consequences, it also denotes an activity delivered from circumstances. It is not only a means of eating one's cake without ceasing to have it, but also a means of eating one's cake without having it at all. It provides a way of making bricks without straw. Here lies the great compensatory value of play, or the so-called "pleasures of the imagination." The principle is the same, consisting in the fact that a complete performance which requires the support of external conditions may be partially executed in the absence of these conditions. One cannot wholly be a millionaire without the effective possession of wealth, but there is no man so poor that he cannot assume some of the postures of the millionaire. 'Wishing' in the limited sense, as something less than earnest desire, is interest attended by the recognized absence of auspicious conditions. That which distinguishes the 'idle' wish from the genuine interest is the absence of endeavor. The object of mere wishing does not operate as a governing expectation. One *does nothing about it:* that is to say, one does not react to the given situation with a view to fulfilling the wish, because there is nothing in the given situation that *promises* this fulfilment. A wish is a governing propensity without trial or effort; or a longing without hope, though not without satisfaction. The modern who wishes he had been born an ancient Greek, or the self-confessed failure who wishes for power and leadership, does not fit the object of his dreams into his living environment, present or future. Nevertheless he indulges in some of the activities appropriate to that other environment; and conducts himself implicitly, if not overtly, as one whose "game is empires," or as one who dwells "where burning Sappho loved and sung."

SUGGESTIONS FOR THOUGHT

1. "Man only plays," says Schiller, "when in the full meaning of the word he is a man, and he is only completely a man when he plays." How does adult play differ from child play? What values does play have in the life of a mature person?

2. Can a full life be achieved without work, or must even those with independent income find some work to do in order to live a satisfactory life? Plato doubted that a person who worked for a living could be a responsible citizen. Voltaire, on the other hand, said of work: "It becomes in the long run the greatest of pleasures, and takes the place of the illusions of life."

3. How is it possible to escape the tediousness of some of the jobs which have to be done in modern life? Has power machinery promoted the greater happiness of mankind? What are the human values of automation?

4. Can you argue on non-economic grounds that it is an obligation of the state to provide work for its citizens?

5. How does a woman's choice of a vocation differ from a man's? Women are often embarrassed when they must list their vocation as "housewife." Why this embarrassment, and what can be done about it?

6. Diderot once remarked, "Only the evil man seeks solitude." This remark broke the friendship between Rousseau and Diderot. Do you agree with Diderot? What might have prompted this observation?

7. "There is no happiness without idleness, and only the useless is pleasurable." (Tchekhov) Many Americans seem to believe that only activity and a feeling of being useful bring happiness. Which view do you support?

8. Augustine has warned: "No man has a right to lead such a life of contemplation as to forget in his own ease the service due to his neighbor; nor has any man a right to be so immersed in active life as to neglect the contemplation of God." This advice from Augustine may sound good, but what does it mean in action?

9. An inspector for certain schools in England reported in 1901: "I know cases in which parents have deplored the final ruin of their child's education at its higher school and for its future life, from its having drunk in as gospel, at a so-called Kindergarten institution, this deadly error, viz., that in a truly human education a child should not be able clearly to distinguish whether it is at work or at play." Wherein is the danger in disguising work as play?

10. Much has been said about how a person's vocation shapes his character, e.g., "The truth seems to be, indeed, that all people should be very careful in selecting their callings and vocations. . . . Gardeners are almost always pleasant, affable people to converse with; but beware of quarter-gunners, keepers of arsenals, and lonely light-house men." (Herman Melville in *White Jacket*) And Demosthenes long ago said, "Whatever be the pursuits of men, their character must be similar." We do commonly associate certain personality traits with certain vocations, e.g., taxi drivers, cowboys, preachers, miners, YMCA workers, etc. To what extent are we justified in these generalizations? How might one argue against them?

11. What are some of the most satisfying vocations? What makes them satisfying?

SUGGESTIONS FOR FURTHER READING

BOSANQUET, BERNARD, "The Place of Leisure in Life," *The International Journal of Ethics,* Vol. 21, 1911, pp. 153–165.

DE MAN, HENRI, *Joy in Work,* translated by Eden and Cedar Paul, New York, Henry Holt and Company, 1929.

DEWEY, JOHN, *How We Think,* Boston, D. C. Heath and Company, 1910, ch. 12.

GREENBIE, SIDNEY, *Leisure for Living,* Edinburgh, George Stewart and Company, 1940.

JACKS, L. P., "The Ethics of Leisure," *The Hibbert Journal,* Vol. 27, 1928–29, pp. 270–281.

JAMES, WILLIAM, *Talks to Teachers on Psychology and to Students on Some of Life's Ideals,* New York, Henry Holt and Company, 1904, pp. 199–228.

JOAD, C. E. M., *Diogenes: or, The Future of Leisure,* New York, E. P. Dutton and Company, 1928.

LIN YUTANG, *The Importance of Living,* New York, Reynal and Hitchcock, 1937, ch. 7.

OVERSTREET, H. A., *A Guide to Civilized Leisure,* New York, W. W. Norton and Company, 1934.

RIESMAN, DAVID, *The Lonely Crowd,* New Haven, Yale University Press, 1950, chs. 15–17.

RIEZLER, KURT, "Play and Seriousness," *The Journal of Philosophy,* Vol. 38, 1941, pp. 505–517.

SCUDDER, VIDA D., "Work," *The Hibbert Journal,* Vol. 33, 1933–34, pp. 498–510.

SMITH, T. V., "Work as an Ethical Concept," *The Journal of Philosophy,* Vol. 21, 1924, pp. 543–554.

STEVENSON, ROBERT LOUIS, *Virginibus Puerisque and Other Papers,* New York, Charles Scribner's Sons, 1900, pp. 107–127.

STEWARD, GEORGE, "Play as Art," *The Journal of Philosophy,* Vol. 41, 1944, pp. 178–184.

VITELES, MORRIS S., *The Science of Work,* New York, W. W. Norton and Company, 1934, chs. 1, 11.

4

LOVE AND FRIENDSHIP

PLATO (c.428–c.348 B.C.) gives us a treatise on friendship in the *Lysis,* one of the earlier of his dialogues. Here Socrates, in a manner which we believe to be true of the historical Socrates, enthusiastically examines a number of definitions of friendship which are suggested to him by young men who have an immediate experience of friendship. But he discovers that although the young men are friends they do not know what friendship is, and Socrates, who "knows nothing," goes away empty-handed. Aristotle (384–322 B.C.), on the other hand, performs his usual careful, objective classification of the subject at hand.

A

All people have their fancies; some desire horses, and others dogs; and some are fond of gold, and others of honour. Now, I have no violent desire of any of these things; but I have a passion for friends; and I would rather have a good friend than the best cock or quail in the world: I would even go further, and say the best horse or dog. Yea, by the dog of Egypt, I should greatly prefer a real friend to all the gold of Darius, or even to Darius himself: I am such a lover of friends

Plato, *Lysis* (in part), *The Dialogues of Plato,* Vol. 1, translated by Benjamin Jowett, Oxford, The Clarendon Press, Third Edition, 1892, pp. 59–75.

as that. And when I see you and Lysis, at your early age, so easily possessed of this treasure, and so soon, he of you, and you of him, I am amazed and delighted, seeing that I myself, although I am now advanced in years, am so far from having made a similar acquisition, that I do not even know in what way a friend is acquired. But I want to ask you a question about this, for you have experience: tell me then, when one loves another, is the lover or the beloved the friend; or may either be the friend?

Either may, I should think, be the friend of either.

Do you mean, I said, that if only one of them loves the other, they are mutual friends?

Yes, he said; that is my meaning.

But what if the lover is not loved in return? which is a very possible case.

Yes.

Or is, perhaps, even hated? which is a fancy which sometimes is entertained by lovers respecting their beloved. Nothing can exceed their love; and yet they imagine either that they are not loved in return, or that they are hated. Is not that true?

Yes, he said, quite true.

In that case, the one loves, and the other is loved?

Yes.

Then which is the friend of which? Is the lover the friend of the beloved, whether he be loved in return, or hated; or is the beloved the friend; or is there no friendship at all on either side, unless they both love one another?

There would seem to be none at all.

Then this notion is not in accordance with our previous one. We were saying that both were friends, if one only loved; but now, unless they both love, neither is a friend.

That appears to be true.

Then nothing which does not love in return is beloved by a lover?

I think not.

Then they are not lovers of horses, whom the horses do not love in return; nor lovers of quails, nor of dogs, nor of wine, nor of gymnastic exercises, who have no return of love; no, nor of wisdom, unless wisdom loves them in return. Or shall we say that they do love them, although they are not beloved by them; and that the poet was wrong who sings —

'Happy the man to whom his children are dear, and steeds having single hoofs, and dogs of chase, and the stranger of another land'?

I do not think that he was wrong.

You think that he is right?

Yes.

Then, Menexenus, the conclusion is, that what is beloved, whether loving or hating, may be dear to the lover of it: for example, very young children, too young to love, or even hating their father or mother when they are punished by them, are never dearer to them than at the time when they are being hated by them.

I think that what you say is true.

And, if so, not the lover, but the beloved, is the friend or dear one?

Yes.

And the hated one, and not the hater, is the enemy?

Clearly.

Then many men are loved by their enemies, and hated by their friends, and are the friends of their enemies, and the enemies of their friends. Yet how absurd, my dear friend, or indeed impossible is this paradox of a man being an enemy to his friend or a friend to his enemy.

I quite agree, Socrates, in what you say.

But if this cannot be, the lover will be the friend of that which is loved?

True.

And the hater will be the enemy of that which is hated?

Certainly.

Yet we must acknowledge in this, as in the preceding instance, that a man may be the friend of one who is not his friend, or who may be his enemy, when he loves that which does not love him or which even hates him. And he may be the enemy of one who is not his enemy, and is even his friend: for example, when he hates that which does not hate him, or which even loves him.

That appears to be true.

But if the lover is not a friend, nor the beloved a friend, nor both together, what are we to say? Whom are we to call friends to one another? Do any remain?

Indeed, Socrates, I cannot find any.

But, O Menexenus! I said, may we not have been altogether wrong in our conclusions?

I am sure that we have been wrong, Socrates, said Lysis. And he blushed as he spoke, the words seeming to come from his lips involuntarily, because his whole mind was taken up with the argument; there was no mistaking his attentive look while he was listening.

I was pleased at the interest which was shown by Lysis, and I wanted to give Menexenus a rest, so I turned to him and said, I think, Lysis, that what you say is true, and that, if we had been right, we should never have gone so far wrong; let us proceed no further in this direction (for the road seems to be getting troublesome), but take the other path into which we turned, and see what the poets have to say; for they are to us in a manner the fathers and authors of wisdom, and they speak of friends in no light or trivial manner, but God himself, as they say, makes them and draws them to one another; and this they express, if I am not mistaken, in the following words: —

'God is ever drawing like towards like, and making them acquainted.'

I dare say that you have heard those words.

Yes, he said; I have.

And have you not also met with the treatises of philosophers who say that like must love like? they are the people who argue and write about nature and the universe.

Very true, he replied.

And are they right in saying this?

They may be.

Perhaps, I said, about half, or possibly, altogether, right, if their meaning were rightly apprehended by us. For the more a bad man

has to do with a bad man, and the more nearly he is brought into contact with him, the more he will be likely to hate him, for he injures him; and injurer and injured cannot be friends. Is not that true?

Yes, he said.

Then one half of the saying is untrue, if the wicked are like one another?

That is true.

But the real meaning of the saying, as I imagine, is, that the good are like one another, and friends to one another; and that the bad, as is often said of them, are never at unity with one another or with themselves; for they are passionate and restless, and anything which is at variance and enmity with itself is not likely to be in union or harmony with any other thing. Do you not agree?

Yes, I do.

Then, my friend, those who say that the like is friendly to the like mean to intimate, if I rightly apprehend them, that the good only is the friend of the good, and of him only; but that the evil never attains to any real friendship, either with good or evil. Do you agree?

He nodded assent.

Then now we know how to answer the question 'Who are friends?' for the argument declares 'That the good are friends.'

Yes, he said, that is true.

Yes, I replied; and yet I am not quite satisfied with this answer. By heaven, and shall I tell you what I suspect? I will. Assuming that like, inasmuch as he is like, is the friend of like, and useful to him — or rather let me try another way of putting the matter: Can like do any good or harm to like which he could not do to himself, or suffer anything from his like which he would not suffer from himself? And if neither can be of any use to the other, how can they be loved by one another? Can they now?

They cannot.

And can he who is not loved be a friend?

Certainly not.

But say that the like is not the friend of the like in so far as he is like; still the good may be the friend of the good in so far as he is good?

True.

But then again, will not the good, in so far as he is good, be sufficient for himself? Certainly he will. And he who is sufficient wants nothing — that is implied in the word sufficient.

Of course not.

And he who wants nothing will desire nothing?

He will not.

Neither can he love that which he does not desire?

He cannot.

And he who loves not is not a lover or friend?

Clearly not.

What place then is there for friendship, if, when absent, good men have no need of one another (for even when alone they are sufficient for themselves), and when present have no use of one another? How can such persons ever be induced to value one another?

They cannot.

And friends they cannot be, unless they value one another?

Very true.

But see now, Lysis, whether we are not being deceived in all this — are we not indeed entirely wrong?

How so? he replied.

Have I not heard some one say, as I just now recollect, that the like is the greatest enemy of the like, the good of the good? — Yes, and he quoted the authority of Hesiod, who says:

'Potter quarrels with potter, bard with bard, Beggar with beggar;'

and of all other things he affirmed, in like manner, 'That of necessity the most like are most full of envy, strife, and hatred of one another, and the most unlike, of friendship. For the poor man is compelled to be the friend of the rich, and the weak requires the aid of the strong, and the sick man of the physician; and every one who is ignorant, has to love and court him who knows.' And indeed he went on to say in grandiloquent language, that the idea of friendship existing between similars is not the truth, but the very reverse of the truth, and that the most opposed are the most friendly; for that everything desires not like but that which is most unlike: for example, the dry desires the moist, the cold the hot, the bitter the sweet, the sharp the blunt, the void the full, the full the void, and so of all other things; for the opposite is the food of the opposite, whereas like receives nothing from like. And I thought that he who said this was a charming man, and that he spoke well. What do the rest of you say?

I should say, at first hearing, that he is right, said Menexenus.

Then are we to say that the greatest friendship is of opposites?

Exactly.

Yes, Menexenus; but will not that be a monstrous answer? and will not the all-wise eristics be down upon us in triumph, and ask, fairly enough, whether love is not the very opposite of hate; and what answer shall we make to them — must we not admit that they speak the truth?

We must.

They will then proceed to ask whether the enemy is the friend of the friend, or the friend the friend of the enemy?

Neither, he replied.

Well, but is a just man the friend of the unjust, or the temperate of the intemperate, or the good of the bad?

I do not see how that is possible.

And yet, I said, if friendship goes by contraries, the contraries must be friends.

They must.

Then neither like and like nor unlike and unlike are friends.

I suppose not.

And yet there is a further consideration: may not all these notions of friendship be erroneous? but may not that which is neither good nor evil still in some cases be the friend of the good?

How do you mean? he said.

Why really, I said, the truth is that I do not know; but my head is dizzy with thinking of the argument, and therefore I hazard the conjecture, that 'the beautiful is the friend,' as the old proverb says. Beauty is certainly a soft, smooth, slippery thing, and therefore of a nature which easily slips in and permeates our souls. For I affirm that the good is the beautiful. You will agree to that?

Yes.

This I say from a sort of notion that what is neither good nor evil is the friend of the beautiful and the good, and I will tell you why I am inclined to think so: I assume that there are three principles — the good, the bad, and that which is neither good nor bad. You would agree — would you not?

I agree.

And neither is the good the friend of the good, nor the evil of the evil, nor the good of the evil; — these alternatives are excluded by the previous argument; and therefore, if there be such a thing as friendship or love at all, we must infer that what is neither good nor evil must be the friend, either of the good, or of that which is neither good nor evil, for nothing can be the friend of the bad.

True.

But neither can like be the friend of like, as we were just now saying.

True.

And if so, that which is neither good nor evil can have no friend which is neither good nor evil.

Clearly not.

Then the good alone is the friend of that only which is neither good nor evil.

That may be assumed to be certain.

And does not this seem to put us in the right way? Just remark, that the body which is in health requires neither medical nor any other aid, but is well enough; and the healthy man has no love of the physician, because he is in health.

He has none.

But the sick loves him, because he is sick?

Certainly.

And sickness is an evil, and the art of medicine a good and useful thing?

Yes.

But the human body, regarded as a body, is neither good nor evil?

True.

And the body is compelled by reason of disease to court and make friends of the art of medicine?

Yes.

Then that which is neither good nor evil becomes the friend of good, by reason of the presence of evil?

So we may infer.

And clearly this must have happened before that which was neither good nor evil had become altogether corrupted with the element of evil — if itself had become evil it would not still desire and love the good; for, as we were saying, the evil cannot be the friend of the good.

Impossible.

Further, I must observe that some substances are assimilated when others are present with them; and there are some which are not assimilated: take, for example, the case of an ointment or colour which is put on another substance.

Very good.

In such a case, is the substance which is anointed the same as the colour or ointment?

What do you mean? he said.

This is what I mean: Suppose that I were to cover your auburn locks with white lead, would they be really white, or would they only appear to be white?

They would only appear to be white, he replied.

And yet whiteness would be present in them?

True.

But that would not make them at all the more white, notwithstanding the presence of white in them — they would not be white any more than black?

No.

But when old age infuses whiteness into them, then they become assimilated, and are white by the presence of white.

Certainly.

Now I want to know whether in all cases a substance is assimilated by the presence of another substance; or must the presence be after a peculiar sort?

The latter, he said.

Then that which is neither good nor evil may be in the presence of evil, but not as yet evil, and that has happened before now?

Yes.

And when anything is in the presence of evil, not being as yet evil, the presence of good arouses the desire of good in that thing; but the presence of evil, which makes a thing evil, takes away the desire and friendship of the good; for that which was once both good and evil has now become evil only, and the good was supposed to have no friendship with the evil?

None.

And therefore we say that those who are already wise, whether Gods or men, are no longer lovers of wisdom; nor can they be lovers of wisdom who are ignorant to the extent of being evil, for no evil or ignorant person is a lover of wisdom. There remain those who have the misfortune to be ignorant, but are not yet hardened in their ignorance, or void of understanding, and do not as yet fancy that they know what they do not know: and therefore those who are the lovers of wisdom are as yet neither good nor bad. But the bad do not love wisdom any more than the good; for, as we have already seen, neither is unlike the friend of unlike, nor like of like. You remember that?

Yes, they both said.

And so, Lysis and Menexenus, we have discovered the nature of friendship — there can be no doubt of it: Friendship is the love which by reason of the presence of evil the neither good nor evil has of the good, either in the soul, or in the body, or anywhere.

They both agreed and entirely assented, and for a moment I rejoiced and was satisfied like a huntsman just holding fast his prey. But then a most unaccountable suspicion came across me, and I felt that the conclusion was untrue. I was pained, and said, Alas! Lysis and Menexenus, I am afraid that we have been grasping at a shadow only.

Why do you say so? said Menexenus.

I am afraid, I said, that the argument about friendship is false: arguments, like men, are often pretenders.

How do you mean? he asked.

Well, I said; look at the matter in this way: a friend is the friend of some one; is he not?

Certainly he is.

And has he a motive and object in being a friend, or has he no motive and object?

He has a motive and object.

And is the object which makes him a

friend, dear to him, or neither dear nor hateful to him?

I do not quite follow you, he said.

I do not wonder at that, I said. But perhaps, if I put the matter in another way, you will be able to follow me, and my own meaning will be clearer to myself. The sick man, as I was just now saying, is the friend of the physician — is he not?

Yes.

And he is the friend of the physician because of disease, and for the sake of health?

Yes.

And disease is an evil?

Certainly.

And what of health? I said. Is that good or evil, or neither?

Good, he replied.

And we were saying, I believe, that the body being neither good nor evil, because of disease, that is to say because of evil, is the friend of medicine, and medicine is a good: and medicine has entered into this friendship for the sake of health, and health is a good.

True.

And is health a friend, or not a friend?

A friend.

And disease is an enemy?

Yes.

Then that which is neither good nor evil is the friend of the good because of the evil and hateful, and for the sake of the good and the friend?

Clearly.

Then the friend is a friend for the sake of the friend, and because of the enemy?

That is to be inferred.

Then at this point, my boys, let us take heed, and be on our guard against deceptions. I will not again repeat that the friend is the friend of the friend, and the like of the like, which has been declared by us to be an impossibility; but, in order that this new statement may not delude us, let us attentively examine another point, which I will proceed to explain: Medicine, as we were saying, is a friend, or dear to us for the sake of health?

Yes.

And health is also dear?

Certainly.

And if dear, then dear for the sake of something?

Yes.

And surely this object must also be dear, as is implied in our previous admissions?

Yes.

And that something dear involves something else dear?

Yes.

But then, proceeding in this way, shall we not arrive at some first principle of friendship or dearness which is not capable of being referred to any other, for the sake of which, as we maintain, all other things are dear, and, having there arrived, we shall stop?

True.

My fear is that all those other things, which, as we say, are dear for the sake of another, are illusions and deceptions only, but where that first principle is, there is the true ideal of friendship. Let me put the matter thus: Suppose the case of a great treasure (this may be a son, who is more precious to his father than all his other treasures); would not the father, who values his son above all things, value other things also for the sake of his son? I mean, for instance, if he knew that his son had drunk hemlock, and the father thought that wine would save him, he would value the wine?

He would.

And also the vessel which contains the wine?

Certainly.

But does he therefore value the three measures of wine, or the earthen vessel which contains them, equally with his son? Is not this rather the true state of the case? All his anxiety has regard not to the means which are provided for the sake of an object, but to the object for the sake of which they are provided. And although we may often say that gold and silver are highly valued by us, that is not the truth; for there is a further object, whatever it may be, which we value most of all, and for the sake of which gold and all our other possessions are acquired by us. Am I not right?

Yes, certainly.

And may not the same be said of the friend? That which is only dear to us for the sake of something else is improperly said to be dear, but the truly dear is that in which all these so-called dear friendships terminate.

That, he said, appears to be true.

And the truly dear or ultimate principle of friendship is not for the sake of any other or further dear.

True.

Then we have done with the notion that friendship has any further object. May we then infer that the good is the friend?

I think so.

And the good is loved for the sake of the evil? Let me put the case in this way: Suppose that of the three principles, good, evil, and that which is neither good nor evil, there remained only the good and the neutral, and that evil went far away, and in no way affected soul or body, nor ever at all that class of things which, as we say, are neither good nor evil in themselves; — would the good be of any use, or other than useless to us? For if there were nothing to hurt us any longer, we should have no need of anything that would do us good. Then would be clearly seen that we did but love and desire the good because of the evil, and as the remedy of the evil, which was the disease; but if there had

been no disease, there would have been no need of a remedy. Is not this the nature of the good — to be loved by us who are placed between the two, because of the evil? but there is no use in the good for its own sake.

I suppose not.

Then the final principle of friendship, in which all other friendships terminated, those, I mean, which are relatively dear and for the sake of something else, is of another and a different nature from them. For they are called dear because of another dear or friend. But with the true friend or dear, the case is quite the reverse; for that is proved to be dear because of the hated, and if the hated were away it would no longer be dear.

Very true, he replied: at any rate not if our present view holds good.

But, oh! will you tell me, I said, whether if evil were to perish, we should hunger any more, or thirst any more, or have any similar desire? Or may we suppose that hunger will remain while men and animals remain, but not so as to be hurtful? And the same of thirst and the other desires, — that they will remain, but will not be evil because evil has perished? Or rather shall I say, that to ask what either will be then or will not be is ridiculous, for who knows? This we do know, that in our present condition hunger may injure us, and may also benefit us: — Is not that true?

Yes.

And in like manner thirst or any similar desire may sometimes be good and sometimes an evil to us, and sometimes neither one nor the other?

To be sure.

But is there any reason why, because evil perishes, that which is not evil should perish with it?

None.

Then, even if evil perishes, the desires

which are neither good nor evil will remain?

Clearly they will.

And must not a man love that which he desires and affects?

He must.

Then, even if evil perishes, there may still remain some elements of love or friendship?

Yes.

But not if evil is the cause of friendship: for in that case nothing will be the friend of any other thing after the destruction of evil; for the effect cannot remain when the cause is destroyed.

True.

And have we not admitted already that the friend loves something for a reason? and at the time of making the admission we were of opinion that the neither good nor evil loves the good because of the evil?

Very true.

But now our view is changed, and we conceive that there must be some other cause of friendship?

I suppose so.

May not the truth be rather, as we were saying just now, that desire is the cause of friendship; for that which desires is dear to that which is desired at the time of desiring it? and may not the other theory have been only a long story about nothing?

Likely enough.

But surely, I said, he who desires, desires that of which he is in want?

Yes.

And that of which he is in want is dear to him?

True.

And he is in want of that of which he is deprived?

Certainly.

Then love, and desire, and friendship would appear to be of the natural or con-genial. Such, Lysis and Menexenus, is the inference.

They assented.

Then if you are friends, you must have natures which are congenial to one another?

Certainly, they both said.

And I say, my boys, that no one who loves or desires another would ever have loved or desired or affected him, if he had not been in some way congenial to him, either in his soul, or in his character, or in his manners, or in his form.

Yes, yes, said Menexenus. But Lysis was silent.

Then, I said, the conclusion is, that what is of a congenial nature must be loved.

It follows, he said.

Then the lover, who is true and no coun-terfeit, must of necessity be loved by his love.

Lysis and Menexenus gave a faint assent to this; and Hippothales changed into all manner of colours with delight.

Here, intending to revise the argument, I said: Can we point out any difference between the congenial and the like? For if that is possible, then I think, Lysis and Menexenus, there may be some sense in our argument about friendship. But if the congenial is only the like, how will you get rid of the other argument, of the uselessness of like to like in as far as they are like; for to say that what is useless is dear, would be absurd? Suppose, then, that we agree to distinguish between the congenial and the like — in the intoxication of argument, that may perhaps be allowed.

Very true.

And shall we further say that the good is congenial, and the evil uncongenial to every one? Or again that the evil is congenial to the evil, and the good to the good; and that which is neither good nor evil to that which is neither good nor evil?

They agreed to the latter alternative.

Then, my boys, we have again fallen into the old discarded error; for the unjust will be the friend of the unjust, and the bad of the bad, as well as the good of the good.

That appears to be the result.

But again, if we say that the congenial is the same as the good, in that case the good and he only will be the friend of the good.

True.

But that too was a position of ours which, as you will remember, has been already refuted by ourselves.

We remember.

Then what is to be done? Or rather is there anything to be done? I can only, like the wise men who argue in courts, sum up the arguments: — If neither the beloved, nor the lover, nor the like, nor the unlike, nor the good, nor the congenial, nor any other of whom we spoke — for there were such a number of them that I cannot remember all — if none of these are friends, I know not what remains to be said.

Here I was going to invite the opinion of some older person, when suddenly we were interrupted by the tutors of Lysis and Menexenus, who came upon us like an evil apparition with their brothers, and bade them go home, as it was getting late. At first, we and the by-standers drove them off; but afterwards, as they would not mind, and only went on shouting in their barbarous dialect, and got angry, and kept calling the boys — they appeared to us to have been drinking rather too much at the Hermaea, which made them difficult to manage — we fairly gave way and broke up the company.

I said, however, a few words to the boys at parting: O Menexenus and Lysis, how ridiculous that you two boys, and I, an old boy, who would fain be one of you, should imagine ourselves to be friends — this is what the by-standers will go away and say — and as yet we have not been able to discover what is a friend!

B

After what we have said, a discussion of friendship would naturally follow, since it is a virtue or implies virtue, and is besides most necessary with a view to living. For without friends no one would choose to live, though he had all other goods; even rich men and those in possession of office and of dominating power are thought to need friends most of all; for what is the use of such prosperity without the opportunity of beneficence, which is exercised chiefly and in its most laudable form towards friends? Or how can prosperity be

Aristotle, *Nicomachean Ethics,* Book VIII, Sections 1–6, translated by W. D. Ross, *The Works of Aristotle Translated into English,* Vol. 9, edited by W. D. Ross, Oxford, The Clarendon Press, 1925. Reprinted by permission of the publishers.

guarded and preserved without friends? The greater it is, the more exposed is it to risk. And in poverty and in other misfortunes men think friends are the only refuge. It helps the young, too, to keep from error; it aids older people by ministering to their needs and supplementing the activities that are failing from weakness; those in the prime of life it stimulates to noble actions — 'two going together' — for with friends men are more able both to think and to act. Again, parent seems by nature to feel it for offspring and offspring for parent, not only among men but among birds and among most animals; it is felt mutually by members of the same race, and especially by men, whence we praise lovers of their fellowmen. We may see even in our travels how near and dear every man is to every other. Friendship seems too to hold states together, and lawgivers to care more for it than for justice; for unanimity seems to be something like friendship, and this they aim at most of all, and expel faction as their worst enemy, and when men are friends they have no need of justice, while when they are just they need friendship as well, and the truest form of justice is thought to be a friendly quality.

But it is not only necessary but also noble; for we praise those who love their friends, and it is thought to be a fine thing to have many friends; and again we think it is the same people that are good men and are friends.

Not a few things about friendship are matters of debate. Some define it as a kind of likeness and say like people are friends, whence come the sayings 'like to like', 'birds of a feather flock together', and so on; others on the contrary say 'two of a trade never agree'. On this very question they inquire for deeper and more physical causes, Euripides saying that 'parched earth loves the rain, and stately heaven when filled with rain loves to fall to earth', and Heraclitus that 'it is what opposes that helps' and 'from different tones comes the fairest tune' and 'all things are produced through strife'; while Empedocles, as well as others, expresses the opposite view that like aims at like. The physical problems we may leave alone (for they do not belong to the present inquiry); let us examine those which are human and involve character and feeling, e.g. whether friendship can rise between any two people or people cannot be friends if they are wicked, and whether there is one species of friendship or more than one. Those who think there is only one because it admits of degrees have relied on an inadequate indication; for even things different in

species admit of degree. We have discussed this matter previously.

The kinds of friendship may perhaps be cleared up if we first come to know the object of love. For not everything seems to be loved but only the lovable, and this is good, pleasant, or useful; but it would seem to be that by which some good or pleasure is produced that is useful, so that it is the good and the useful that are lovable as ends. Do men love, then, *the* good, or what is good for *them?* These sometimes clash. So too with regard to the pleasant. Now it is thought that each loves what is good for himself, and that the good is without qualification lovable, and what is good for each man is lovable for him; but each man loves not what is good for him but what seems good. This however will make no difference; we shall just have to say that this is 'that which seems lovable'. Now there are three grounds on which people love; of the love of lifeless objects we do not use the word 'friendship'; for it is not mutual love, nor is there a wishing of good to the other (for it would surely be ridiculous to wish wine well; if one wishes anything for it, it is that it may keep, so that one may have it oneself); but to a friend we say we ought to wish what is good for his sake. But to those who thus wish good we ascribe only goodwill, if the wish is not reciprocated; goodwill when it *is* reciprocal being friendship. Or must we add 'when it is recognized'? For many people have goodwill to those whom they have not seen but judge to be good or useful; and one of these might return this feeling. These people seem to bear goodwill to each other; but how could one call them friends when they do not know their mutual feeling? To be friends, then, they must be mutually recognized as bearing goodwill and wishing well to each other for one of the aforesaid reasons.

Now these reasons differ from each other

in kind; so, therefore, do the corresponding forms of love and friendship. There are therefore three kinds of friendship, equal in number to the things that are lovable; for with respect to each there is a mutual and recognized love, and those who love each other wish well to each other in that respect in which they love one another. Now those who love each other for their utility do not love each other for themselves but in virtue of some good which they get from each other. So too with those who love for the sake of pleasure, it is not for their character that men love ready-witted people, but because they find them pleasant. Therefore those who love for the sake of utility love for the sake of what is good for *themselves,* and those who love for the sake of pleasure do so for the sake of what is pleasant to *themselves,* and not in so far as the other is the person loved but in so far as he is useful or pleasant. And thus these friendships are only incidental; for it is not as being the man he is that the loved person is loved, but as providing some good or pleasure. Such friendships, then, are easily dissolved, if the parties do not remain like themselves; for if the one party is no longer pleasant or useful the other ceases to love him.

Now the useful is not permanent but is always changing. Thus when the motive of the friendship is done away, the friendship is dissolved, inasmuch as it existed only for the ends in question. This kind of friendship seems to exist chiefly between old people (for at that age people pursue not the pleasant but the useful) and, of those who are in their prime or young, between those who pursue utility. And such people do not live much with each other either; for sometimes they do not even find each other pleasant; therefore they do not need such companionship unless they are useful to each other; for they are pleasant to each other only in so far as they

rouse in each other hopes of something good to come. Among such friendships people also class the friendship of host and guest. On the other hand the friendship of young people seems to aim at pleasure; for they live under the guidance of emotion, and pursue above all what is pleasant to themselves and what is immediately before them; but with increasing age their pleasures become different. This is why they quickly become friends and quickly cease to be so; their friendship changes with the object that is found pleasant, and such pleasure alters quickly. Young people are amorous too; for the greater part of the friendship of love depends on emotion and aims at pleasure; this is why they fall in love and quickly fall out of love, changing often within a single day. But these people do wish to spend their days and lives together; for it is thus that they attain the purpose of their friendship.

Perfect friendship is the friendship of men who are good, and alike in virtue; for these wish well alike to each other qua good, and they are good in themselves. Now those who wish well to their friends for their sake are most truly friends; for they do this by reason of their own nature and not incidentally; therefore their friendship lasts as long as they are good — and goodness is an enduring thing. And each is good without qualification and to his friend, for the good are both good without qualification and useful to each other. So too they are pleasant; for the good are pleasant both without qualification and to each other, since to each his own activities and others like them are pleasurable, and the actions of the good *are* the same or like. And such a friendship is as might be expected permanent, since there meet in it all the qualities that friends should have. For all friendship is for the sake of good or of pleasure — good or pleasure either in the abstract or such as will be enjoyed by him who has the friendly feeling — and is based on a certain resemblance; and to a friendship of good men all the qualities we have named belong in virtue of the nature of the friends themselves; for in the case of this kind of friendship the other qualities also are alike in both friends, and that which is good without qualification is also without qualification pleasant, and these are the most lovable qualities. Love and friendship therefore are found most and in their best form between such men.

But it is natural that such friendships should be infrequent; for such men are rare. Further, such friendship requires time and familiarity; as the proverb says, men cannot know each other till they have 'eaten salt together'; nor can they admit each other to friendship or be friends till each has been found lovable and been trusted by each. Those who quickly show the marks of friendship to each other wish to be friends, but are not friends unless they both are lovable and know the fact; for a wish for friendship may arise quickly, but friendship does not.

This kind of friendship, then, is perfect both in respect of duration and in all other respects, and in it each gets from each in all respects the same as, or something like what, he gives; which is what ought to happen between friends. Friendship for the sake of pleasure bears a resemblance to this kind; for good people too *are* pleasant to each other. So too does friendship for the sake of utility; for the good are also useful to each other. Among men of these inferior sorts too, friendships are most permanent when the friends get the same thing from each other (e.g. pleasure), and not only that but also from the same source, as happens between ready-witted people, not as happens between lover and beloved. For these do not take pleasure in the same things, but the one in seeing the beloved and the other in receiving attentions from his lover; and when the bloom of youth is passing the friendship sometimes passes too (for the one finds no pleasure in the sight of the other, and the other gets no attentions from the first); but many lovers on the other hand are constant, if familiarity has led them to love each other's characters, these being alike. But those who exchange not pleasure but utility in their amour are both less truly friends and less constant. Those who are friends for the sake of utility part when the advantage is at an end; for they were lovers not of each other but of profit.

For the sake of pleasure or utility, then, even bad men may be friends of each other, or good men of bad, or one who is neither good nor bad may be a friend to any sort of person, but for their own sake clearly only good men can be friends; for bad men do not delight in each other unless some advantage come of the relation.

The friendship of the good too and this alone is proof against slander; for it is not easy to trust any one's talk about a man who has long been tested by oneself; and it is among good men that trust and the feeling that 'he would never wrong me' and all the other things that are demanded in true friendship are found. In the other kinds of friendship, however, there is nothing to prevent these evils arising.

For men apply the name of friends even to those whose motive is utility, in which sense states are said to be friendly (for the alliances of states seem to aim at advantage), and to those who love each other for the sake of pleasure, in which sense children are called friends. Therefore we too ought perhaps to call such people friends, and say that there are several kinds of friendship — firstly and in the proper sense that of good men *qua* good, and by analogy the other kinds; for it is in virtue of something good and something akin to what is found in true friendship that they are friends, since even the pleasant is good for the lovers of pleasure. But these two kinds of friendship are not often united, nor do the same people become friends for the sake of utility and of pleasure; for things that are only incidentally connected are not often coupled together.

Friendship being divided into these kinds, bad men will be friends for the sake of pleasure or of utility, being in this respect like each other, but good men will be friends for their own sake, i.e. in virtue of their goodness. These, then, are friends without qualification; the others are friends incidentally and through a resemblance to these.

As in regard to the virtues some men are called good in respect of a state of character, others in respect of an activity, so too in the case of friendship; for those who live together delight in each other and confer benefits on each other, but those who are asleep or locally separated are not performing, but are disposed to perform, the activities of friendship; distance does not break off the friendship absolutely, but only the activity of it. But if the absence is lasting, it seems actually to make men forget their friendship; hence the saying 'out of sight, out of mind'. Neither old people nor sour people seem to make friends easily; for there is little that is pleasant in them, and no one can spend his days with one whose company is painful, or not pleasant, since nature seems above all to avoid the painful and to aim at the pleasant. Those, however, who approve of each other but do not live together seem to be well-disposed rather than actual friends. For there is nothing so characteristic of friends as living together (since while it is people who are in need that desire benefits, even those who are supremely happy desire to spend their days together; for solitude suits

such people least of all); but people cannot live together if they are not pleasant and do not enjoy the same things, as friends who are companions seem to do.

The truest friendship, then, is that of the good, as we have frequently said; for that which is without qualification good or pleasant seems to be lovable and desirable, and for each person that which is good or pleasant to him; and the good man is lovable and desirable to the good man for both these reasons. Now it looks as if love were a feeling, friendship a state of character; for love may be felt just as much towards lifeless things, but mutual love involves choice and choice springs from a state of character; and men wish well to those whom they love, for their sake, not as a result of feeling but as a result of a state of character. And in loving a friend men love what is good for themselves; for the good man in becoming a friend becomes a good to his friend. Each, then, both loves what is good for himself, and makes an equal return in goodwill and in pleasantness; for friendship is said to be equality, and both of these are found most in the friendship of the good.

Between sour and elderly people friendship arises less readily, inasmuch as they are less good-tempered and enjoy companionship less; for these are thought to be the greatest marks of friendship and most productive of it. This is why, while young men become friends quickly, old men do not; it is because men do not become friends with those in whom they do not delight; and similarly sour people do not quickly make friends either. But such men may bear goodwill to each other; for they wish one another well and aid one another in need; but they are hardly *friends* because they do not spend their days together nor delight in each other, and these are thought the greatest marks of friendship.

One cannot be a friend to many people in

the sense of having friendship of the perfect type with them, just as one cannot be in love with many people at once (for love is a sort of excess of feeling, and it is the nature of such only to be felt towards one person); and it is not easy for many people at the same time to please the same person very greatly, or perhaps even to be good in his eyes. One must, too, acquire some experience of the other person and become familiar with him, and that is very hard. But with a view to utility or pleasure it is possible that many people should please one; for many people are useful or pleasant, and these services take little time.

Of these two kinds that which is for the sake of pleasure is the more like friendship, when both parties get the same things from each other and delight in each other or in the same things, as in the friendships of the young; for generosity is more found in such friendships. Friendship based on utility is for the commercially minded. People who are supremely happy, too, have no need of useful friends, but do need pleasant friends; for they wish to live with *some one* and, though they can endure for a short time what is painful, no one could put up with it continuously, nor even with the Good itself if it were painful to him; this is why they look out for friends who are pleasant. Perhaps they should look out for friends who, being pleasant, are also good, and good for them too; for so they will have all the characteristics that friends should have.

People in positions of authority seem to have friends who fall into distinct classes; some people are useful to them and others are pleasant, but the same people are rarely both; for they seek neither those whose pleasantness is accompanied by virtue nor those whose utility is with a view to noble objects, but in their desire for pleasure they seek for ready-witted people, and their other friends they choose as being clever at doing what they are told, and these characteristics are rarely combined. Now we have said that the *good* man *is* at the same time pleasant and useful; but such a man does not become the friend of one who surpasses him in station, unless he is surpassed also in virtue; if this is not so, he does not establish equality by being proportionally exceeded in both respects. But people who surpass him in both respects are not so easy to find.

However that may be, the aforesaid friendships involve equality; for the friends get the same things from one another and wish the same things for one another, or exchange one thing for another, e.g. pleasure for utility; we have said, however, that they are both less truly friendships and less permanent. But it is from their likeness and their unlikeness to the same thing that they are thought both to be and not to be friendships. It is by their likeness to the friendship of virtue that they seem to be friendships (for one of them involves pleasure and the other utility, and these characteristics belong to the friendship of virtue as well); while it is because the friendship of virtue is proof against slander and permanent, while these quickly change (besides differing from the former in many other respects), that they appear *not* to be friendships; i.e. it is because of their unlikeness to the friendship of virtue.

SUGGESTIONS FOR THOUGHT

1. How do you account for the popularity of books like Dale Carnegie's *How to Win Friends and Influence People?* Are we to assume that we have lost the art of making friends?

2. Villars, a Marshal of France in the 18th century, once said, "Defend me from my friends; I can defend myself from my enemies." What might be some of the dangers of friendship? E.g., "Even your best friend won't tell you!"

3. Have modern means of communication and transportation fostered richer and more lasting friendships? Are friendships possible in modern impersonal industrial and business relationships? E.g., compare relationships that exist between the country grocer and his customers and between a big chain grocery and its customers.

4. Is the "battle of the sexes" a healthy state of affairs, or should we try to ignore sex differentiation and emphasize our common humanity? To what extent can we ignore sex distinctions? What is the argument for separate education for men and women? For coeducation?

5. Jason says to Medea in Euripides' *Medea,* "You women have such strange ideas, that you think all is well so long as your married life runs smooth." Is this observation generally true for women? Is it less true for men? How do women and men differ in their attitudes toward marriage?

6. What are some of the chief problems of marriage? What can be done to insure the formation of satisfying and lasting marriages in modern society? What are the most satisfactory substitutes for marriage?

7. "The man who prefers his dearest friend to the call of duty, will soon show that he prefers himself to his dearest friend." (Frederick Robertson) What are some of the occasions in which there is a conflict between duty and friendship? Can friendship itself be a duty?

8. In August, 1952, the National Vigilance Association of London disbanded its patrols designed to protect young women from strangers in railroad stations with the announcement: "Today it's the young men who need protecting and looking after." What has brought about this change?

9. "Intimacy has its risks. It is easier and in most cases better to be acquaintances than friends." (James Baillie) What are the risks of friendship? Is friendship worth the risks?

SUGGESTIONS FOR FURTHER READING

BACON, FRANCIS, "Of Friendship."

CABOT, RICHARD C., *What Men Live By,* Boston, Houghton Mifflin Company, 1914, Part III.

CADMAN, S. PARKES, *Adventure for Happiness,* New York, The Macmillan Company, 1936, ch. 9.

COE, GEORGE A., "On Having Friends: A Study of Social Values," *The Journal of Philosophy, Psychology, and Scientific Methods,* Vol. 12, 1915, pp. 155–161.

D'ARCY, M. C., *The Mind and Heart of Love,* New York, Henry Holt and Company, 1947.

EMERSON, RALPH WALDO, "Friendship."

FROMM, ERICH, "Selfishness and Self-Love," *Psychiatry,* November 1939.

HAMBRIDGE, GOVE, *Time to Live,* New York, Whittlesey House, 1933, ch. 6.

JORDAN, E., *The Good Life,* Chicago, University of Chicago Press, 1949, ch. 13.

KAGAWA, TOYOHIKO, *Love, The Law of Life,* Philadelphia, John C. Winston Company, 1929.

MARTIN, HERBERT, *The Philosophy of Friendship,* New York, Dial Press, 1935.

MAUROIS, ANDRE, *The Art of Living,* translated by James Whittal, New York, Harper and Brothers, 1940, ch. 4.

RIGGS, AUSTEN FOX, *Intelligent Living,* New York, Doubleday, Doran and Company, 1929, ch. 3.

SOROKIN, PITIRIM, *Altruistic Love,* Boston, The Beacon Press, 1950.

WEISS, PAUL, *Man's Freedom,* New Haven, Yale University Press, 1950, ch. 20.

5

FREEDOM OF THE SELF

ALL THEORY is against the freedom of the will, all experience is for it," observed Samuel Johnson. Man feels free, yet when he speculates about human freedom in its relation to either an omniscient God or a deterministic science, he finds difficulty in defending his freedom. Much of the intellectual confusion about freedom is due to the fact that it may be conceived of either as indeterminism or as self-determinism. Thilly regards freedom as the former, Ritchie as the latter. Frank Thilly (1865–1934) was a teacher of philosophy at the University of Missouri, Princeton University, and Cornell University; he was also Dean of Liberal Arts at Cornell. For a time he was editor of the *International Journal of Ethics*. David George Ritchie (1853–1903) was a tutor at Oxford University. In 1894 he became professor of logic and metaphysics at the University of St. Andrews.

A

If we look, then, at a single individual, we find, in the first place, that his will is subject to intellectual laws, that his thoughts and actions are dependent upon the time in which he lives as well as upon the character of the nation to which he belongs, upon the character of his ancestors, upon the conditions of life into which he has been born, upon the reli-

Frank Thilly, "The Freedom of the Will," *The Philosophical Review*, Vol. 3, 1894, pp. 393–411 (in part).

gious, political, intellectual, and physical education which he has enjoyed, upon his personal experiences, and upon the state of his body. "It is generally admitted," says Tyndall, "that the man of to-day is the child and product of incalculable antecedent times. His physical and intellectual textures have been woven for him during his passage through phases of history and forms of existence which lead the mind back to an abysmal past." All the factors mentioned above are determining influences on his mode of action. A German philosopher will act differently from a South Sea cannibal; that he does so is altogether due to conditions. The latter can no more will to search for the causes of things than the former can to eat human flesh, unless, of course, certain influences conducive to a change are excited.

It is noticed, too, that society everywhere presupposes the possibility of determining the actions of its members. Its laws, its rewards and punishments, its educational efforts, all are meant to be determinants of the will. The individual, in his dealings with men, acts on the same principle.

That the conduct of man is determined by certain causes is a fact. There can be question only as to how this causation takes place. Actions are, as was seen, the external manifestation of inner will-activity. Instinctive actions are the results of an inner feeling of uneasiness produced either by physiological conditions or by sense impressions, which occasion psychical actions. This psychical side of the instinct depends on the general condition of the apperceptive process, which is a product of many past conditions, and the stimulus, while the bodily expression depends on the nature of the body. The impulse is aroused by the presence in consciousness of an idea and its relation to apperception. The higher will-acts result from the presence in consciousness of many ideas, and the preference given to one of them.

The attention is directed first to one, then to another, until it finally chooses one to the exclusion of all others. That it chooses or remains fixed upon this one and not that, is due to the peculiar nature of the individual apperception or will, which nature is, of course, the product of countless influences. It is a texture woven *for* us, not *by* us. I quote as an example a case given by Dr. Ward: "But now take the instance of a military officer — possessing real piety and steadfastly purposing to grow therein — who receives at the hand of a brother officer some stinging and (as the world would say) 'intolerable' insult. His nature flames forth; his spontaneous impulse, his real present desire, is to inflict some retaliation, which shall at least deliver him from the 'reproach' of cowardice. Nevertheless, it is his firm resolve, by God's grace, to comport himself Christianly. His resolve contends vigorously against his desire, until the latter is brought into harmony with his principles." In this case the apperception or will at first rivets itself on the idea of some destructive effect; it is involuntary in the sense of having been aroused by some external cause. If the attention were for a longer space of time fixed upon this idea to the exclusion of others, that is, if the mind were unable to turn to other ideas, the injurious movement would follow. The state of mind resulting in the blow would be the effect of certain feelings, these feelings would be due to the nature of the apperception, which in turn is the product of race and individual education, etc. Whether a remark made by any one is insulting or not, depends altogether on the apperceptive attitude of the party against whom it is directed. A military man would be more likely to flame forth upon hearing a slur than the shrewd and careful business-man. The former has been, as it were, saturated with certain ideas of honor. The German lieutenant would cut you to pieces for saying what would in no way affect the American lawyer. Now in the case cited, the attention does not remain fixed; distinct religious teachings arise in the mind of the offended person and ultimately determine his will. That such ideas can arise and inhibit the first impulse, is due to the character of the agent, who has received a religious training. A savage would not have comported himself so "Christianly." We have here not a case of free-will, as Ward maintains, but an excellent instance of determined conduct.

What often makes deterministic theories objectionable, is their failure to recognize the significance of the character or will or apperception on motives. On the one hand they place these forces impelling the will now in this direction, now in that; on the other, a thing moved, a will utterly helpless, the mere shuttlecock of forces. In its craving for logical simplification and classification the human mind often sets up such schemes as these. The philosopher makes his analysis, the roles are given out, and the play begins. It must be remembered, however, that motives are nothing apart from the person himself; they are phases or tendencies of the being, the individual tending now hither, now thither. Whether an idea or feeling is to have motive power or not, depends altogether on the character of the individual, which has been formed by a multitude of influences and conditions, and is continually acted upon, while it itself acts upon the contents offered it. Just as an object can mean nothing unless it be the object of some subject, so also a motive is meaningless except in its relation to some person or agent. As was said before, whether an idea or sensation or feeling is to have influence on my conduct, depends on my character. The prospect of obtaining an honorable and lucrative position may not have the slightest effect on my behavior, while the desire to pass my time in undisturbed reflection may serve as a powerful incentive to me, and determine me to act in a way utterly inexplicable to me, and determine me to act in a way utterly inexplicable to my friends. What to me is a motive, may be to another a deterrent. The desire for fame which forms so mighty an impulse in the case of some men, in no way affected Spinoza. It is true, I, as I now exist, am not

the creature but the creator of motives. Many libertarians have been so overjoyed at the discovery of this fact that they straightway laid down their work and cheered for free-will, forgetting, for the moment, that the active personality, as it now exists, is to be and can be accounted for. It is not a *causa sui,* standing outside of the chain of events, but an activity determined in its manner of manifestation by the sum of manifold causes. As Wundt asserts: "Character determines the will before all motives. The character implicitly contains a sum of psychological causes whose total effects we always measure in predicting a person's conduct." This character has been formed, and the actions resulting from it will depend altogether on the nature of its formation. It is not a causeless cause, but a caused cause. Wherever several ideas are presented to consciousness the choice of the one or the other will be wholly determined by the nature of this apperception. And every decision of the will reacts upon it, in some manner influencing all future action. I have the power to concentrate my thoughts, and ward off all disturbances. This power has been acquired; it is the result of education. The child is unable to fix its attention, and it is the whole business of the teacher to apply such motives as may appeal to the pupil, and assist him in acquiring this faculty of attention.

To sum up briefly: Every action is the product of a chain of causes. Man acts in accordance with his character, which is determined in its nature by inherited tendencies, education, and life-conditions.

I have attempted to give in the above a statement of the facts, avoiding as carefully as possible the use of a terminology which is apt to arouse prejudice and to obscure intellectual vision. Nor do I intend to offer any metaphysical hypothesis concerning this psychical activity. These seem to me to be the facts as far as I can discover them in my own consciousness, and with these facts I am willing to content myself. I shall now turn to the examination of some of the deterministic and libertarian theories.

There are mechanical theories which, basing all their arguments on the existence of matter and motion, examine and try to explain the external aspect of volition only, namely movements. Every movement is the product of physical causes. However purposive an action may appear to be, it is of the same nature as the simplest reflex act. Certain useful movements of the organism survive. In the course of time these movements become more and more complicated. By phylogenetic generation and natural adaptation a nerve-apparatus arises which is so arranged as to be able, in spite of the infinite variety of external conditions, to liberate upon external stimulation movements that are adapted to the conditions of the outer world. The complexity of this apparatus presents no difficulty to the explanation. It is not an immediate factor, but a gradual development from the lowest stages of movement. As Münsterberg recapitulates: "All muscular contractions ensue in consequence of the excitation of the sensorimotor apparatus by external stimuli, which conditions movement and in a given apparatus necessarily conditions a definite movement. This apparatus had to arise through selection. The external material process of every movement, be it reflex, or impulse, or voluntary action, is explicable according to the principles of physio-chemical science as a necessary occurrence, without the help of an immaterial factor."

According to this physical view, every movement is physically determined. No account is taken of consciousness at all, and where it is recognized it is regarded as a mere spectator. These movements would go right on in the same way, whether consciousness were present or not. At any rate, consciousness can neither occasion nor even direct a single change in the external world. Every change of this kind would signify a violation of the law of the conservation of energy and make the world altogether irrational. In order to save this law, consciousness can be nothing more than an 'epiphenomenon.' It is clear that such a scheme presents the most thorough-going physical determinism possible. However simple and seductive it may be, it nevertheless disregards certain facts that must be taken account of. The chief fault of the theory lies in its assuming the unwarrantable metaphysical hypothesis that matter is the world-principle and that mind is its function. Or it assumes a dualistic standpoint, but regards matter as active, consciousness as passive. Now let us not forget, in the first place, that consciousness is a fact. Secondly, it is not a mere epiphenomenon. Thirdly, if it is something more than a function of matter, and yet affected by motion, the law of the conservation of energy is as much violated in this case as when mind acts on matter. In the fourth place, if it is but a function of matter, it is miraculous how a function can philosophize about itself and that of which it is the function.

Now we have as little right to say that consciousness is the product of external motion as that it produces motion in the external world. All that we know and all that we can say is, (1) that consciousness is active, and (2) that external movements correspond to psychical impulses. That the one phenomenon should in any way be the cause of the other seems inconceivable to us, simply because we implicitly base our reasoning on the hypothesis that mind and matter are two entirely distinct substances, or at any rate, that they are two distinct phenomena. This, of course, is altogether gratuitous metaphysical hypothesis, which makes an explanation of the facts an impossibility. I can offer no satisfactory hypothesis, but it seems to me that until such an hypothesis is forthcoming, all we can do is to content ourselves with the facts. We have no right to deny certain facts because they do not fit into an assumed scheme of the world. We cannot say that psychical phenomena cause physical changes, and *vice versa*, if we have already separated these two realms. Still it remains a fact that what we call a psychical phenomenon precedes what we call a physical phenomenon, and the reverse. A psychical impulse is followed by a movement; how the thing is done, I do not know. If the thing is utterly inconceivable on dualistic principles, so much the worse for these principles.

Together with physical determinism we rule out as insufficient all such indeterministic theories as base themselves on the dualistic hypothesis, and then endeavor to show how a psychical impulse or will can exert an influence on matter. According to some, the will does not cause motion but simply directs it, and hence does not violate the law of the conservation of energy, because directing requires no putting forth of new energy; others say the effort put forth is so small, that really you ought not to count it as new energy at all.

I therefore leave the question as to how movement is caused by will-action unanswered; in fact I repudiate the manner of putting the question. — Let me return now to the subject of psychical activity, and examine these theories which hold that the will is free. What is meant by saying that this psychical activity, the will, is free? Evidently this: The will is not subject to the law of causality; it is cause without being effect. Freedom means, as Schopenhauer and Kant put it, the faculty of beginning a causal series. A man is free when he has the power of beginning a causal series without being in any way determined thereto. This psychical activity is free when it acts without cause; when the manner of its action depends on no antecedent event. I will to perform a certain act; nothing has determined me to will as I did; under the same conditions I could have willed otherwise. However the view may be modified, freedom essentially means a causeless will.

1. Now it has been seen, first, that this psychical function cannot act unless there be some cause or occasion for its action, and that the manner in which it acts depends wholly upon conditions. Therefore to assert that the will is free belies the facts.

2. In the second place, such a thing as free will is inconceivable. We have psychical activity; we cannot conceive of this acting without cause. We cannot think otherwise than in terms of causality. If, therefore, we would understand this mental activity or will at all, we must inquire into its causes. A free will means a will that has no cause, the power to act without a sufficient cause; to postulate this of the will is equivalent to waiving all explanation of it. Even those who approach the subject from the Kantian standpoint must think in causal terms or else forego every attempt at a scientific explanation, for knowledge is possible only under certain conditions, the forms of the mind. When you repudiate these forms, you simply yield up your only possibility of knowing.

Wherever in the world we have a phenomenon we seek for its cause in some antecedent phenomenon or sum of phenomena. If we acknowledge the application of the law to the events of physical nature, and deny its validity in the mental sphere, we present an exception to the uniformity of nature. And as Bain says: "Where there is no uniformity, there is clearly no rational guidance, no prudential foresight." Every act, be it ever so insignificant, has its antecedent cause. I can sit down or get up as I please, but whether I please or not depends on conditions which may be apparent or concealed. James holds in his article on "The Dilemma of Determinism" that the world would be no less rational if actions like the bending into one street rather than into another were left to absolute volition. However, such a slight deviation from the law would be, as far as the principle is concerned, as great a miracle as though the planet Jupiter should sway from its path. It would make the entire universe irrational. In the words of Riehl: "However infinitely small the difference between such a world and the real one might appear to the fancy, for the understanding an infinitely small deviation from the law of determination of occurrences, from the general law of causality, would still remain an infinitely great miracle. There would arise out of the ability to perform apparently insignificant acts with absolute freedom, the ability to pervert the entire order of nature in continually increasing extents. The consequences of a single element of irrationality, an exception to the law of causation, could not but make the whole of nature irrational, just as a very little amount of ferment is able to produce fermentation in an entire organic mass. Nature could not exist alongside of an undetermined power of freedom."

In order to escape these difficulties many devices are resorted to. We must think in terms of causality; true. But, nevertheless, the will is free. In order to make these two contradictions agree, causality is simply interpreted to mean freedom or noncausality. In other words, a special theory of causality is manufactured to meet the requirements of the libertarian doctrine. Dr. Ward is guilty of such a fabricated scheme of harmonizing opposites. He will not grant that 'free' and 'uncaused' are synonyms. There are two kinds of causation: in the one case it means a law of uniform phenomenal sequence. By this kind of causation the physical world is ruled, *the important exception being miracles.* But there is also such a thing as *originative* causation. An intelligent substance, for example, acts as an originative cause. Such a substance is the human soul. Dr. Ward bases his interpretation of the causal law on the hypothesis of freedom, which is the very thing to be proved. You say, he exclaims, there is no such a thing as an originative cause? Look at the human will. You have anti-impulsive will-acts due to the soul's power of absolute choice. You say, he continues, that free-will violates the causal principle? Not at all, for what does causation signify but originative cause? — It is evident we have here an excellent example of the *circulus vitiosus.*

Martineau may be accused of the same vicious reasoning. The will, he says, is a cause, i.e., "it is something which terminates the balance of possibilities in favor of this phenomenon rather than that." This notion he applies to the universe, then back again to the will. He wants to show that the idea of causality applied does not make for determinism but for freedom; he begins by assuming that causality equals freedom. His false reasoning is very apparent. Determinists say, according to him, every action must have a cause, the will must be controlled by motives, for nothing can be without a cause. The will cannot be free because of this causal principle. Yes, answers Martineau, if causality means that different effects must have different causes, then the will is not free. But it is not true that different effects must have different causes. The will is not determined, because different effects need not have different causes. They need not have different causes, because in the will we have an example of a cause which has the power to determine an alternative, i.e., a free cause. This amounts to saying, the will is free because it is free. Martineau also asserts that the counterpart of this idea is found in the cosmos in a like *preferring* power. We see nothing of the kind in the cosmos unless we read it into the cosmos ourselves.

3. We observe, then, that a free will is wholly inconceivable; it violates the law of causality. The psychological investigation has already shown that it contradicts the facts. We must now also insist that, if the will *is* free, it is utterly useless to attempt to determine it. And yet everybody acts on the conviction that this may be done. If nothing can determine it, what is the use of education, of laws, of arguments, of entreaties, of moral suasion, of punishment, and all those means employed to determine conduct? How can an utterly groundless willing be in any way held responsible? The voluntary activity has been initiated without being caused. Hence nothing can be done to affect it. Like a *deus ex machina*, the free will enters upon the scene of action, and in the same mysterious manner disappears. How can it be approached, this guilty party? Why offer it motives if these have no influence? Besides, if the will does not come under the causal law, why speak of its development during the various periods of race and individual life? If it cannot be determined, how explain the influences of disease and stimulants on it? Why should it ever degenerate? What becomes of it in sleep? Where is it in the hypnotized state? What would morality be to a person absolutely free? "Indeterminism," says Riehl, "would subject our moral life to contingency." The free will cannot be impelled by reason to act; it can in no way be determined to adopt the more reasonable course, but. acts groundlessly. Nor can conscience be of avail, nor remorse, nor any other ethical feeling. A person acting without cause would be utterly unreliable; in fact, the ideal

free man's actions would resemble those of the lunatic. To desire such freedom would, indeed, as Leibniz exclaims, be to desire to be a fool. Or, in Schelling's words: "To be able to decide for A and non-A without any motives whatsoever, would, in truth, simply be a prerogative to act in an altogether irrational manner."

I also fail to see in what respect the cause of libertarianism is helped by granting that the will cannot act without motives, but that it is, in some cases, able to choose one motive to the exclusion of the other, and that, too, without cause. The same fallacy obtains in the reasoning, whether you extend or limit this faculty of the will to begin a new causal series. When Martineau asserts the will to be a cause "which terminates the balance of possibilities in favor of this phenomenon rather than that," he maintains absolute freedom of volition, and lays himself open to all the objections urged above.

4. To say that the will is free, in the sense of being uncaused, is to make it altogether inconceivable. If the causal law cannot be applied to this psychical activity, nothing can be said of it at all, perhaps not even that it exists, for we are not, I believe, directly conscious of it; and even if we were, we should have to be conscious of it in terms of consciousness. We can speak and think only in intellectual terms. Many attempts have been made to bring some meaning into this notion of freedom, but without success. Every undertaking of this kind ends, and must end, in contradictions, which ought to convince philosophers of the futility of their efforts to think otherwise than in terms of thought. Right here is the point, they will reply, you are applying forms of thought to the phenomena of mind, but you forget that they are but forms. When you theorize concerning the will, when you look at will-acts, it must nec-

essarily seem to you that the will is determined, because you are applying mental forms.
But strip your mind of all these categories,
and you have the *Ding an sich,* the real thing
in itself, *"wie es leibt und lebt,"* as the Ger-
mans say. You must think of it without applying mental functions at all, and then you
have the intelligible self. This intelligible
self is uncaused, free. In the same breath Kant
holds the intelligible to be *"unerkennbar,"*
and proceeds to describe it in detail. According to Kant's own statements and principles,
the thing in itself is unknowable. Besides, it
is a violation of his own principles even to
hypostasize any such being as the thing in
itself. It is an abstraction — a something supposed to be the bearer of the mental functions.
These we abstract, and then set up this logical
creation of ours as a reality. According to
Kantian philosophy such a product of the
functions of the intellect is a phenomenon
merely, no reality. . . .

There are, it is said, certain facts which
make for free will. "I hold, therefore," says
Sidgwick, "that against the formidable array
of cumulative evidence offered for Determinism, there is but one argument of real force;
the immediate affirmation of consciousness in
the moment of deliberate action."

1. Now, if it were really true that we have
a consciousness of being free in the sense in
which this term has been used, this feeling
would have as little weight as a scientific proof
as the feeling that the sun moves around the
earth has for astronomy. Where a man accepts this "immediate intuition of the soul's
freedom" as a proof of its actuality, he is
simply asserting that his soul is free because
he feels it to be free.

2. And even granting that such a feeling
can prove anything, must we not show (1)
that it exists, (2) what it tells us? Libertarians
claim that men are conscious of being free,
and see herein a proof of their thesis. But the
all-important question is, whether men really
say and believe themselves to be free in the
sense in which these philosophers claim that
they are. The libertarian throws into this consciousness his entire doctrine, thereby garbling
the facts to suit his theory.

It is necessary, therefore, to analyze this
consciousness of freedom. Before the volition
takes place there may be present in consciousness a feeling that I can do either this or that.
In the moment of willing no such feeling exists, while after the act has been willed and
executed I say to myself, I might have done
otherwise. Now all the possibilities of *action*
occur to me, my mind is in a different state,
certain painful feelings that formerly exerted
an irresistible influence are no longer present,
or only dimly remembered. All the conditions
being changed, I feel as though I could have
acted differently. And so I could have done,
if only I had willed differently, and so I could
have willed differently, if only the conditions
of willing had been different. I can do what I
will to do; I am free to get up or sit down,
free to go home or stay here, to give up all
my prospects of life, if only I will to do so.
Never does my consciousness tell me that a
volition is uncaused, that there was no reason
for my willing as I did will, that the will is
the absolute beginning of an occurrence, that
at any moment any volition may arise regardless of all antecedent processes. Least of all
does it tell me that I am the manifestation of
an intelligible self which I feel to be free.

If, then, this feeling has any value as evidence, it proves no more than the logical possibility of acting otherwise. Besides, I cannot
grant that this so-called sense of freedom is

an immediate consciousness. The subject simply *reasons* concerning his acts, weighs the different possibilities against each other. If any feeling accompanies this process, it is due to a misconception.

But do I *feel* that I could have *willed* otherwise? I think not. I may reason about my willing, and finally *conclude* that I could have willed otherwise. I may feel that there was a *possibility* of willing otherwise than as I did will. But I am reasoning when I say that under the same conditions I could have willed otherwise. And this conclusion, for it is a conclusion, is due to the agent's ignorance of causes. To this ignorance Spinoza attributes the entire subjective illusion of freedom. At any rate our *immediate* consciousness gives us no account whatever of the real question, *viz.*, whether we will without cause. As we have seen, the action is the expression of the person's character. With this character the agent identifies himself, and, being unconscious of the influences that have moulded this personality of his, he regards his will as an originative faculty.

Against those who so strongly emphasize the sense of freedom, we may urge the deterministic standpoint generally accepted in all the affairs of life. We regard the actions of men as necessary functions of their character. In all historical sciences, we invariably seek for the causes of events, we analyze the characters of the actors, and show the influences of the times and surroundings. Our entire social life is based on the conviction that under certain conditions men will act in a certain way. That this is so, let the methods of education and government attest.

The feeling of responsibility is also urged against determinism, and accepted as a proof of liberty. This, however, may be explained. The person regards every voluntary action of his as the expression of his personality, with which he identifies himself, even though it is the product of manifold causes. It is held that if a man could be taught to recognize his conduct as a necessary outcome of certain conditions, he would cease to blame himself for it. This might be the case if he regarded his personality as something over and against certain moving forces, pushing the will now hither now thither. He feels himself as an agent, the acts as *his* acts, and sees no reason why this self from which the acts emanated, should not be held responsible.

But if action is the necessary expression of character, and character the necessary product of conditions, why *hold* any one responsible, even though he feel himself responsible? If man's acts are the effects of causes, why punish him for what he cannot help? Because punishment is a powerful determining cause. Why should I be held responsible for my deeds? "The reply is," in Tyndall's words, "the right of society to protect itself against aggressive injurious forces, whether they be bound or free, forces of nature or forces of man." Punishment can have a meaning only in a deterministic scheme of things. We can by education make a moral being out of man, that is, determine him to act for the social good. As Riehl expresses it epigrammatically: "Man is not held responsible because he is by birth a moral being; he becomes a moral being because he is held responsible."

There are many men who, while acknowledging the arguments of the deterministic theory to be unanswerable, yet reject it on practical grounds. However, even if it were so that man cannot live by it, this would by no means impair its truth. The fact that the knowledge of certain things might produce injurious consequences can have no weight with the philosopher. Truth is one thing, expediency another. The history of the world has shown us thus far that we need have no fear of the truth. The proclamation of new truths has invariably been met with denunciations. Morality was believed to be in danger, but gradually the hated theory became an axiom, and the world is living right on.

The deterministic theory is not, as has been claimed, a discouraging and paralyzing doctrine. On the contrary, the knowledge that we are determined must determine us to avoid certain conditions and seek others more favorable. Determinism does not destroy the energy of action. Fatalistic nations like the Mohammedans were far more energetic than Christian ascetics, who believed in the will's absolute freedom. Determinism is the strongest motive to action. If I am exceedingly desirous of fame how can the knowledge that this desire has been caused by conditions affect me? Why should it make me less ambitious? If I have been morally educated, I shall continue to strive after certain things in spite of my belief in determinism. I shall go right on deliberating and choosing as heretofore, and

make an effort to live an honorable, useful life. "Now when it is said by a fatalist," Butler writes, "that the whole constitution of nature, and the actions of men, that every thing and every mode and circumstance of every thing, is necessary, and could not possibly have been otherwise, it is to be observed, that this necessity does not exclude deliberation, choice, preference, and acting from certain principles and to certain ends; because all this is a matter of undoubted experience, acknowledged by all, and what every man may, every moment, be conscious of. . . . The author of nature then being certainly of some character or other, notwithstanding necessity, it is evident this necessity is as reconcilable with the particular character of benevolence, veracity, and justice, in him, which attributes are the foundation of religion, as with any other character; since we find their necessity no more hinders *men* from being benevolent than cruel; true than faithless; just than unjust, or, if the fatalist pleases, what we call unjust."

B

"Free will" (in some undefined form or other) is usually supposed to be an essential doctrine that the champions of religion and morality are bound to maintain against the doctrine of necessity which is asserted by the champions of scientific thought. The "antinomy," or contradiction in thought, which troubles the modern mind, is not expressed in the form of an opposition between the eternal decrees of the Almighty on the one side and on the other the freedom of the human will, which is supposed to be implied in man's re-

David G. Ritchie, "Free-will and Responsibility," *The International Journal of Ethics*, Vol. 5, 1895, pp. 409–431 (in part).

sponsibility to God; but in the form of an opposition between the necessity of the causal nexus, which is presupposed by all the sciences of nature and of human nature on the one side, and on the other the freedom of the human will which is supposed to be implied in man's responsibility even to his fellow-men. From a metaphysical point of view the necessity of nature may seem to be only an element in the eternal decrees of God: but it is the requirements of science and not the requirements of systematic theology which seem to trouble the present-day defenders of free-will. There is an appearance of conflict between what is scientifically true and what is supposed to be good moral doctrine. Now an opposition between science and morality, if it is a real opposition, is a very serious matter; and it is an opposition which people cannot escape, as they think they escape the older form of the difficulty by simply disregarding theology and metaphysics as a futile waste of thought. It is worth while attempting to discuss it in order to see whether the opposition is a real one or not, and whether it may not be due to some misunderstanding of the term "necessity" on the one hand and of the term "moral responsibility" on the other. We are always too apt to discuss whether a thing is true or not, without asking first what it means and whether it means anything at all.

First of all, then, let us see what "necessity" means as postulated by science. It means nothing except the necessity of logical sequence: A is the cause of B; if A happens B must happen, — i.e., from A I can infer B. If you throw a ball up in the air, it *must* come down again. The "must" here is not the "must" of command, as if there were some despot outside the whole universe who arbitrarily interfered with what, apart from his interference, would be the course of events we might reasonably expect. The "if — must" is simply an expression for the course of events which we may and do reasonably expect. The "if — must" is simply an expression for the course of events which we may and do reasonably expect. The necessity of natural causation is presupposed by all scientific investigation; but this presupposition is identical with our presupposition that nature is an intelligible whole, a universe, and not simply a chaos of isolated and disconnected events. Our presupposition in interpreting nature is simply that nature is capable of being interpreted. There can be no science of nature unless we do assume that nature is intelligible and coherent. We understand very little of nature

as yet; a great deal we human beings may never be able to understand. But all science proceeds on the assumption that phenomena are connected together in such a way that if, and when, we are sufficiently acquainted with the conditions under which an event happens, we can predict the happening of that event, whenever the conditions are fulfilled. The statement of scientific "cause," the statement of a law of nature, is never strictly accurate unless we put in the "if," or perhaps several "ifs." If you throw a ball up in the air, it must come down again, if nothing interferes with gravitation. If the ball should alight on the roof of a house, or be caught in the branches of a tree, or by the hands of a human being, it may not come down to the earth so long as these obstacles are in the way. If you swallow a sufficient quantity of poison you will die, unless you can have a sufficient antidote administered soon enough; and so on.

Now, if there is to be a science of psychology dealing with the phenomena of the human mind, if there is to be a science of sociology dealing with the phenomena of human society, the principle of "necessity" must apply to the phenomena of human life in the same sense in which it applies to the phenomena of nature, but in the same sense only. When it is said that a frequent experience of two phenomena in immediate combination — say a double knock and the postman delivering letters — will lead to a mental association being formed such that the thought of the one phenomenon tends to recall the thought of the other phenomenon, it is not meant that at any given time you will necessarily think of the postman, but only that if you hear a double knock you will most probably think of the postman, unless you happen to have a playful friend who imitates the postman's knock, or unless there be some other

counteracting cause to interfere with the association. So, if it is said that centuries of oppression and misgovernment tend to incapaci-
tate a people from managing their affairs well
when they obtain their liberty, it is not meant
that any given people must necessarily mis-
manage their affairs, but that under such conditions, unless their leaders show conspicuous
energy and ability, a people are most likely to
do so.

The opponents of "necessity" generally
confuse it with fatalism. The difference between the necessity which I have been trying
to explain and fatalism is just the difference
between a statement of what under certain
conditions may be foreseen and a statement
of what must happen whatever the conditions
may be. The necessitarian says, as every reasonable person might say, if you have sufficient ability, and if you have a sufficiently
good training, and if you keep your health, you
will succeed in your business, unless some particularly unfavorable combination of circumstances are against you. The fatalist or the
fortune-teller predicts success irrespective of
all conditions — in spite of all conditions. You
are born under a lucky planet; you have certain lines on your hand, *therefore* you must
succeed. Necessity means an orderly, intelligible world in which like causes produce like
events. Fatalism or fortune-telling implies a
chaotic world in which events may happen
anyhow, or, at least, in which there are arbitrary interferences with the orderly sequence
of events. Fate is thus the very opposite of
necessity.

J. S. Mill sought to avoid the misleading
associations apt to be connected with the word
"necessity" by calling his theory not "necessitarianism" but "determinism." I do not think
anything was really gained by the substitution
of the latter term. It is quite as capable of
gathering misleading associations round it as

the other. To say that the will is "determined"
by motives, and that these are "determined"
by the character and circumstances of the individual, and so on, may be misunderstood to
mean that some outside force intrudes and
overrules the intelligible connection between
cause and effect. For these misunderstandings,
it must be admitted that necessitarians or determinists are a good deal to blame. They
have often spoken as if the laws of nature
were some despotic external authority against
which man struggled in vain; they have ignored the fact that in so speaking they were
opposing man to nature at the very moment
when they were professedly reducing him to
a part of nature, and ignoring the fact that
nature, including human volitions, is not the
same as nature exclusive of human volitions.

I pass now to the other side of the antinomy. What is meant by free-will? If we
define free acts as those acts (of course,
thoughts, volitions, etc., are "acts") of which
the cause is in the agent himself, — a definition of "the voluntary" which satisfied Aristotle and St. Thomas Aquinas, — there is no
conflict between necessitarianism, as just explained, and free-will. But such a definition
is very wide and general; "the cause being in
the agent" is a phrase that needs further analysis: (1) Where the cause of some movement
of a person's body is external to the person
— i.e., where the person is not properly an
agent, but is only a passive object or instrument, — there, clearly, there is not "freedom,"
nor is there responsibility. If you are knocked
down by the fall of some scaffolding, or if
you are seized by a couple of policemen and
carried off to the police-station, you are not a
free agent in falling down or in being carried
off, and you are not held directly responsible
for falling down or for being carried off,
though you may be responsible by going near
the scaffolding or for arousing the suspicions

that have led to your being arrested. (2) Where the compulsion exercised is not directly a physical compulsion, the case is more complicated. If a brigand holds a pistol at your head and demands "Your money or your life!" your handing over your purse to him is obviously a voluntary act in a sense in which we could not apply the term to your having the purse torn from you by force. In the one case *you* do not act, in the other *you* do, though under terror of physical compulsion. Responsibility enters more largely into this second case than into the first. Still, the responsibility does not seem complete. The person who does even wrong or base acts under fear of death or great pain or suffering to himself or to others may be excused in a way in which he could not be excused if these threats of violence were absent. Yet there is no absolute gap between the handing over a purse to the brigand who holds at your head a pistol, which you know to be loaded and which you know he is likely to use, and assenting to a disagreeable arrangement through a remote fear of possible unpleasant consequences to yourself or to other persons; both are voluntary acts, "free" acts, in the sense of being acts springing from your own volition to move your muscles. But both may be called "involuntary" acts in the sense of being acts that you do with reluctance and with a feeling of pain and aversion. (3) We are only said to act quite freely, quite voluntarily, when the act is one that we do "with our whole heart," one that we choose not only in the sense that it is our act, for which we are in some degree responsible, but in the sense that we put ourselves into it, so to speak. For such acts, acts which are the outcome of our inclinations, we are obviously responsible in the fullest sense.

Now, so far as this goes, there is nothing yet to conflict with the statement that our volitions are due to causes in the same sense — and in the same sense only — as any other events are. Fear of pain, inclination towards an object are causes of our volition in the same sense in which rain and sunshine are causes of the growth of plants. "Yes," it may be said, "but the more important cause is left out in these statements. The plant's own nature is among the causes of its growth (a rose will not grow into a thistle), and so the individual in each case is the most important and the real cause. The external circumstances are only the occasion of his acting." But the plant's own nature, the person's own nature are not theoretically incapable of further analysis, — however difficult or impossible at present it may seem to understand them. Just as in the Indian mythology the world is supposed to rest on an elephant and the elephant on a tortoise, but there the search for causes comes to an end, so in practical matters we are often contented with a very short exploration of causes. The self-choosing how to act, choosing sometimes against inclination and sometimes with inclination, is the point beyond which we do not go in the ordinary analysis of conduct which is sufficient, e.g., for the procedure of the law courts. When conduct is brought home to a person as the result of his own choice, he is held responsible for it. But where the lawyer may be content to stop, the psychologist and the moralist must go farther; and so must any person conscientiously examining his own conduct. Why did we choose this course rather than the other? We may wonder, perhaps, how we could have been so foolish; but if we are quite candid with ourselves, and have sufficiently good memories and sufficiently clear insight into our own habits of thinking and feeling, we shall discover what it was that made us choose the course we did. There is fallacy of retrospection, if I may call it, which is very apt to vitiate our examination of our own conduct in the past. We suppose ourselves back at the moment of choice with the same knowledge and experience that we have acquired since, in part as the result of that choice and of its consequences; and, besides, we suppose ourselves back at the moment of choice with the possible alternatives spread out before us in the same calm, clear light as that in which we are now looking on them. We forget that emotion remembered in tranquillity is a very different thing from emotion as actually felt. Now this familiar fallacy of retrospection seems to me to have a good deal to do with the belief that our choice is something undetermined and arbitrary; we picture ourselves in a calm and indifferent mood, surveying the possible logical alternatives, and we are loath to recognize that *in the frame of mind in which we were at the moment of choice* our choice was the inevitable outcome of that frame of mind, in the same sense in which an explosion is the inevitable outcome of a match applied to a cask of powder. If the match had gone out before it touched the powder, or if the powder had had its quality affected by damp, the result would have been different; and so it would have been with our conduct if our frame of mind had been altered. It may be seen here how, not determinism, but indeterminism is allied to fatalism. Indeterminism, like fatalism, supposes a want of continuity between different parts of psychical experience. To say that I must inevitably choose in a particular way, whatever frame of mind I am in, is to assert that the effect is independent of its cause. To say that I am equally able and equally likely to choose in one way or in its opposite, although my frame of mind is of a certain sort, is to assert, also, that the effect is independent of its cause. The necessitarian or determinist theory asserts that, if my frame of mind is of a certain

sort, certain consequences will follow; it implies a connection between cause and effect. In other words, the motives of action are asserted to be causes of the same kind, so far as inevitableness of sequence and possibility of prediction are concerned, as the causes of physical events; and it is implied that if we could analyze with sufficient care we should always be able to see how volitions were the outcome of motives, and how motives were the outcome of our character and circumstances, and how our character was the outcome of previous acts and abstentions from acting, and so on. . . .

★   ★   ★

When we find ourselves without a sufficient motive to decide our choice, we may ask some one else to decide for us, or we may "toss up." But our decision to "toss up" is not itself unmotived. It is due probably to the discomfort of indecision, the feeling that we are wasting time, or something of that sort. Suppose I am going out for a walk, and cannot make up my mind whether to turn to the right or the left. I may purposely let my decision depend on some mere "chance" in order to start myself definitely in one direction.

In arguing for the truth of determinism as against indeterminism, there is no need to deny the obvious psychological fact of indecision. But it seems rather a strange thing to think that indecision is a necessary characteristic of moral and responsible action. The plain man, who is an honest man, would rather resent being told that when he found a purse belonging to somebody else, nobody could really tell whether he would keep it or restore it to its owner. If the honest man is a quick-tempered person, you had better get out of his way after telling him that. There are, of course, "doubtful characters;" but those are just the people on whom the police have to keep an eye — in order that fear of the policeman may form a stronger motive than the temptation to pick conveniently accessible pockets. The people who are constantly wavering between right and wrong are, surely, not the only class of persons who can act morally and be held responsible for their actions. As Mr. Bradley has very ingeniously put it, it is a strange way of proving man to be accountable to make him out to be an altogether unaccountable creature. What we call the "reliable" person is just the person whose actions you can forecast. Would it not be absurd, if the most satisfactory person morally were just the person who through want of indecision was not properly responsible?

Of course, I do not mean that the mere facility of predicting a person's conduct proves that he is responsible. A person subject to some habitual delusion may be quite certain to act in a particular way under a particular set of circumstances. A dipsomaniac may be certain to get drunk when liquor is placed in his way. A suicidal maniac may be certain to cut his throat if knives are left about when the fit is on him. In these cases particular actions follow a particular external stimuli, just as a plant turns to the sunlight or a cat springs at a mouse. The rational will of the man is temporarily or permanently, in certain respects at least, in abeyance. Mere facility of prediction does not necessarily imply responsibility; but the power of predicting conduct is not inconsistent with responsibility. On the contrary, as I have just been urging the thoroughly upright and responsible person is the person whose conduct can be predicted with more certainty than the conduct of the person of weak and unsettled character.

If we appeal to the plain man, — i.e., to the ordinary experience and practice of people who are not interested in attacking or defining a philosophical dogma, — it is obvious enough that we are constantly in the habit of making fairly successful predictions about human conduct. When we make engagements with some people, we know that they will be on the spot punctually to the minute; other people we know are almost equally certain to be so many minutes late. If you arrange a picnic, you can generally be more certain that the people who have promised to come will turn up than that the day will be fine — in Great Britain. That is to say, we can predict human conduct in some matters with greater certainty than we can predict the weather. When it comes to forecasting the conduct of human beings on a large scale, the risk of failure is diminished. A shopkeeper who lays in a stock of goods for the season is predicting that a certain number of persons, more or less, will desire to purchase a certain quality and quantity of goods. He knows that a certain way of displaying his foods in the shop-windows, or certain forms of advertisement will increase his sales. The whole huge advertising business, which relieves the ugliness of some of our streets and railway stations and disfigures the beauty of much of our scenery, is a proof of the possibility of predicting human conduct and of the fact that volitions are the outcome of motives.

Some people would, indeed, admit that we can predict the conduct of human beings in the mass or on the average, but would urge that the impossibility of precisely predicting how any particular person will act on any particular occasion allows a loophole for free-will in the sense of arbitrary, undetermined choice. Now, it is quite true that the most experienced shopkeeper cannot certainly predict that A or B will buy particular commodities; he may be more certain about what A will do than about what B will do, because he knows A's usual tastes better, or because B is by nature a more capricious customer than A. But on the average he may forecast a sale of a certain quantity of foods. In this uncertainty of particular prediction, however, there is nothing that is peculiar to human conduct. Of a given packet of seeds you may predict that fifty per cent will come up, of another packet that seventy per cent will come up, etc., but you cannot predict certainly that any particular seed will come up, though an experienced eye may see that *this* particular seed is more likely to come up than that. The principle of averages applies to voluntary human actions just as it does to any other natural phenomena, and it is vain to look for "free-will" lurking in the holes and corners of incomplete and inaccurate calculations. An argument from the fact that predictions have only a rough accuracy would prove too much; for it would prove that turnip-seed had free-will as much as men and women. As I have already had occasion to say, chance, if we are thinking carefully, is only a name for our ignorance. That we cannot in any given case make a certain prediction does not prove that events happen without a cause, "spontaneously," but only that we do not know the facts sufficiently. More perfect knowledge, which we, of course, may in this particular case never be able to obtain, would make prediction possible. As I said at the outset, the necessity of causal connection means "IF *a, then b,*" and if we are mistaken in thinking *a* is present, we should of course be mistaken in expecting *b,* unless some other cause were present from which *b* could arise. . . .

★ ★ ★

The determinist theory has suffered greatly from the crude and injudicious way in which it has too often been presented. Thus, when it is argued that human volitions are the out-come of "character" and "circumstances," both the advocates of the theory and its opponents are apt to think of these as if they were two determinate quantities which simply needed to be joined together in order to give the result. Now, in the first place, "circumstances" which we may speak of as being "the same" are not the same, as antecedents of volition, to persons of different characters. A purse lying on the road is one circumstance to an honest character and a quite different circumstance to a dishonest or "doubtful" character. Secondly, the character is not something fixed and constant, but is being continually modified, however slightly, by circumstances, or rather by its own reaction upon circumstances; for the character is the real "self," and to say that actions are self-determined is the same thing as to say that they are determined by the character. In speaking of the causal nexus, or the causal chain, we are too apt to be led away by the easy image or picture of a continuous series, as if the movement of causation were all in one direction, and as if causes and effects could always be clearly separated off as antecedents and consequents in time. And to this fallacious simplification of the problem we are apt to add another, by thinking of a combination of causes as if it simply meant the adding of two quantities, each of which remained unaffected in quality by the other. Now, this is a false way of thinking about any organic life — even the lowest (I need not here discuss whether it is correct even as applied to inorganic existences). A plant's growth, its "behavior," is not a mathematical resultant of so much soil and air and sunshine added on to a given quantity — the plant's nature; the plant's behavior is the outcome of its own nature as reacting on external stimuli. The environment in which a plant finds itself may determine whether it will have luxuriant or scanty foliage, and, within limits, whether its blossoms are single or double, nay, even whether they are darker or lighter in color; but the environment will not turn a hyacinth into a tulip nor a blue hyacinth into a red one. That is the result of the plant's own nature. The power of variation which some plants inherit is very considerable, but there is a very definite limit. In the case of human beings the power of variation is very much greater, although even here there are limits. . . .

People sometimes speak as if "free-will" were not true, or, at least, were incapable of being proved true, and yet were, in this same sense, a doctrine necessary for morality, a useful lie. Now this is a somewhat dangerous attitude of mind, which accepts a fundamental contradiction between science and morality. But is it so certain that the free-will doctrine is more favorable to the interests of morality than the necessitarian? Robert Owen urged the doctrine of necessitarianism in the interests of his endeavors after social reform. The free-will doctrine, — the notion that at any moment any human being is "free" to choose between right and wrong, and that all moral evil and a great part of the physical evil in the world are due entirely to the wrong choice of individuals who might equally well have chosen rightly, — this notion has undoubtedly helped to blind people to the necessity of putting individuals in good surroundings, of giving them strong motives to choose rightly. The free-will doctrine applied in this way has been bad for society. It is also bad for the individual. The idea that at any moment we are free to choose aright leads to a neglect of the fact that habits are gradually, though silently, growing up which may make it al-

most impossible for us to choose a year hence in the way in which we may still be able to choose now. We do not expect a plant to grow vigorous and strong under unfavorable conditions. We are too apt to expect human beings to do so. "Lead us not into temptation." What is the meaning of that prayer, if not that surroundings do act upon the will? And those who seek a good life must not only avoid temptations, but must get into healthy surroundings as much as they can. A negative morality is a one-sided ideal, and it is a very inadequate discipline for the soul. The great defect of ascetic morality has been, not its rigid system of discipline (we all need discipline in our lives), but its negative character. The good life is made to seem simply a series of denials, of abstinences. For the average human being this is a somewhat dangerous training, — apt to produce terrible reactions. It is not enough to cast out an unclean spirit and leave the house empty, however swept and garnished. Such a spirit is very apt to return with seven other spirits more evil than himself. Many very devout and serious persons, absorbed in their own religious life, have been slow to recognize this; and that is probably one explanation why such persons have so often failed more conspicuously in bringing up their children than more worldly persons who have had a considerable number of varied and healthy interests. "Satan finds some mischief still for idle hands to do" is an excellent warning even for those who have cast out Satan from their creed. It is a moral duty not merely to avoid evil, but to cultivate varied and healthy interests. And this is also the best way of avoiding evil. A morbid concentration of thought on the things that ought not to be done is apt even to lead to the doing of them. There is a good deal of sound moral doctrine to be got out of a full recognition of the truth which there is in psychological determinism.

At the same time there is an element of truth in the belief that free-will is a morally useful idea, an element of truth which is neglected by most exponents of determinism: I mean the importance of getting people to think that they *can* do a thing. The idea of oneself as acting in a certain way becomes a new factor in the mind; it may attract desires and feelings round it, and so become a new motive determining conduct. A man may be turned from idle and evil courses by the image of himself as a good man and a useful citizen, provided, of course, this image of himself as acting rightly is not merely a piece of day-dreaming, but an ideal that stimulates effort. Herein lies the good of examples in morality. That "men of like passions with ourselves" should overcome difficulties and sloth and temptation restores faith in the possibilities of the human nature we share with them. But in all this there is no contradiction of scientific determinism. There is nothing in any carefully understood scientific truth to contradict the enormous modifiability and adaptability of the normal human being — within limits, certainly, but limits which we have no right to fix too narrowly till every effort has been made. It is this modifiability of human nature which gives so much power to external influences whether good or evil.

Ideas which seem entirely to contradict freedom may have the same beneficial effect as the idea of freedom. The theological doctrine of prevenient and irresistible grace has helped those who have accepted it, and who have felt themselves "saved" by such grace, to change almost the whole course of their lives, believing that it was no longer frail, corrupt human nature that was acting, but God's omnipotence working in them to will and to do that which is good. Probably more persons have been helped to reform their conduct by a sincere belief in some such high Augustinian or Calvinistic doctrine than have been helped by a belief in the arbitrary power of choice at any moment. The latter seems to me only a safe doctrine in the minds of persons of good character who are likely therefore to choose aright, and whose confidence in their freedom is really a confidence in their strength. The theological doctrine of grace in its extreme form has also undoubtedly considerable dangers. It may lead to spiritual pride and contempt for ordinary "carnal" morality on the one side and to despair and helpless misery on the other. But it contains in a mystical and somewhat irrational form the important philosophical and ethical truths that man as a moral being is raised above the merely natural; it accentuates just that element which the necessitarian theory, as ordinarily stated, leaves out, — the gap between man and mere unconscious, unreflecting nature. The protest of the advocates of free-will against necessitarianism seems to me a protest, in a mistaken form, in favor of this neglected truth. Man thinks, and therefore his thoughts, his aspirations, his ideals, become a factor in his conduct and raise him above the mere passive instrument of natural (i.e., animal) appetites and impulses. The necessitarian too often represents men as merely passive, as merely a series of events; man is an agent, and is more than a mere series of events. He can act, to use a famous phrase, not merely according to law but with a consciousness of law.

To conclude, I must call attention to the ambiguity in the term "freedom" as applied to the will. Man is "free" in the sense that the actions for which he can be held responsible are the outcome of his own conscious self, and not determined by external causes. But this is only the negative sense of freedom. He is free in a higher sense only when he acts according to the dictates of his reason, when his reason determines the content of his volitions, when motives are not merely motives as distinct from mere impulses, but are such motives as his reason approves. In this sense of freedom there is no appearance even of an opposition between freedom and necessity. Freedom in this sense is opposed to slavery, and is identical with rationality. Freedom in this sense may be described as the end or aim of morality. In the other sense it is only its presupposition. Freedom in this higher sense is the very opposite of arbitrary caprice. It is the freedom, not of lawlessness, but of self-government ("autonomy of the will," in Kant's phrase). We are not self-governing to start with, nor do we become so by being left to "the freedom of our own will," — i.e., to the blind guidance of instinct and impulse. Self-government, so far as we ever attain it, is the result of training and discipline which must at first be given us by others, and can only afterwards be directed by ourselves.

Benjamin Franklin tells us in his Autobiography how at one time he tried to form a band of young men united by no elaborate theological doctrines but chiefly by the common desire of helping each other to lead good and useful lives — an "ethical society," in fact, in one at least of its aspects. To this society he proposed to give what seems to us the rather curious name of "The Society of the Free and Easy." "Free," he explains, "as being, by the general practice and habits of the virtues, free from the dominion of vice, and particularly by the practice of industry and frugality, free from debt, which exposes a man to constraint and a species of slavery to his creditors." Franklin had a somewhat prosaic way of preaching great and good causes, but he brings out in his odd title this important aspect of freedom, — that same aspect which Spinoza was thinking of when he identified "the slavery of man" with the strength of the passions and the freedom of man with the power of the reason. Free-will in the sense of incalculable, unmotived caprice would not be worth having, even if it were an intelligible idea; free-will, in this higher sense, is the will that can only exist by obedience to the dictates of reason. "Where there is no law there is no freedom" is a sound maxim in ethics as well as in politics.

SUGGESTIONS FOR THOUGHT

1. Why is the doctrine of freedom of the self important in ethical theory? In legal practices? In interpretation of history?

2. Julian S. Huxley has said: "I protest that if some great Power would agree to make me always think what is true and do what is right, on condition of being turned into a sort of clock. . . . I should instantly close with the offer." Would you? Give a defense of your answer.

3. Some have said that people interpret the beliefs and actions of other people in terms of heredity and environment but refuse so to interpret their own beliefs and actions. Why?

4. What are the differences between the Calvinistic doctrine of predestination and the Greek conception of fate?

5. Has modern physics in its principle of indeterminacy established human freedom? Defend the position that an act may be caused and still be a free act.

6. How can one escape the paradox involved in an argument that one is not free? For example, "If you argue that you have no freedom, you imply that you are *compelled* to argue in this way, and that thus your opinion is not a free and rational decision but a compulsive

mechanism of no more significance than a nervous tic." (Alan W. Watts)

7. Lyman Beecher, a liberal New England preacher of the last century, had arranged to exchange pulpits with a neighboring preacher. On Sunday morning, when the two clergymen met going to each other's churches, the neighboring minister said: "Dr. Beecher, did you realize that before the creation of the world God arranged that you were to preach in my pulpit and I in yours on this Sabbath?" Beecher replied, "Is that so? Then I won't do it." And he turned his horse around and returned to his own church. Did Beecher's action refute the doctrine of predestination? How might one argue that Beecher's action did not refute predestination? How can the doctrine of predestination be refuted?

SUGGESTIONS FOR FURTHER READING

ADAMS, G. P., and others, *Knowledge and Society,* New York, D. Appleton-Century Company, 1938, ch. 6.

ALEXANDER, S., "Freedom," *Proceedings of the Aristotelian Society,* Vol. 14, 1914, pp. 322–354.

AYER, ALFRED J., *The Foundations of Empirical Knowledge,* New York, The Macmillan Company, 1947, pp. 207–220.

BROAD, C. D., *Determinism, Indeterminism, and Libertarianism,* New York, The Macmillan Company, 1934.

HARTMANN, NICOLAI, *Ethics,* Vol. III, translated by Stanton Coit, New York, The Macmillan Company, 1932.

HOBART, R. E., "Free Will as Involving Determinism and Inconceivable Without It," *Mind,* Vol. 43, 1934, pp. 1–27.

HOOPER, SIDNEY E., "Freedom," *The Journal of Philosophical Studies,* Vol. 2, 1937, pp. 212–219.

JAMES, WILLIAM, "The Dilemma of Determinism," in *The Will to Believe and Other Essays in Popular Philosophy,* New York, Longmans, Green and Company, 1931, pp. 145–183.

LAIRD, JOHN, *On Human Freedom,* London, George Allen and Unwin, 1947.

MILL, JOHN STUART, *An Examination of Sir William Hamilton's Philosophy,* New York, Henry Holt and Company, 1884, ch. 26.

PALMER, GEORGE HERBERT, *The Problem of Freedom,* Boston, Houghton Mifflin Company, 1911.

RUSSELL, BERTRAND, *Our Knowledge of the External World,* London, Open Court Company, 1914, ch. 8.

STACE, W. T., *Religion and the Modern Mind,* Philadelphia, J. B. Lippincott Company, 1952, pp. 248–258.

SWABEY, WILLIAM CURTIS, *Being and Being Known,* New York, Dial Press, 1937, ch. 20.

WILLIAMS, GARDNER, "Free-will and Determinism," *The Journal of Philosophy,* Vol. 38, 1941, pp. 701–712.

6

IMMORTALITY

"IF A MAN DIE, will he live again?" must be one of the very oldest philosophical questions. Most cultures appear to have tried to answer the question in the affirmative. Socrates, in Plato's dialogue the *Phaedo*, concludes not only that the soul of man is immortal but also that death is the goal which he as a philosopher has been seeking all during his life in the flesh. F. H. Bradley suspects that the belief in immortality is a "degrading superstition" and that the educated world can soon, if not now, dispense with it.

A

And now, O my judges, I desire to prove to you that the real philosopher has reason to be of good cheer when he is about to die, and that after death he may hope to obtain the greatest good in the other world. And how this may be, Simmias and Cebes, I will endeavour to explain. For I deem that the true votary of philosophy is likely to be misunderstood by other men; they do not perceive that he is always pursuing death and dying; and if this be so, and he has had the desire of death all his life long, why when his time comes should he repine at that which he has been always pursuing and desiring?

Plato, *Phaedo* (in part), *The Dialogues of Plato*, Vol. 2, translated by Benjamin Jowett, Oxford, The Clarendon Press, Third Edition, 1892, pp. 202–207, 236–240, 245–255.

Simmias said laughingly: Though not in a laughing humour, you have made me laugh, Socrates; for I cannot help thinking that the many when they hear your words will say how truly you have described philosophers, and our people at home will likewise say that the life which philosophers desire is in reality death, and that they have found them out to be deserving of the death which they desire.

And they are right, Simmias, in thinking so, with the exception of the words 'they have found them out;' for they have not found out either what is the nature of that death which the true philosopher deserves, or how he deserves or desires death. But enough of them: — let us discuss the matter among ourselves. Do we believe that there is such a thing as death?

To be sure, replied Simmias.

Is it not the separation of soul and body? And to be dead is the completion of this; when the soul exists in herself, and is released from the body and the body is released from the soul, what is this but death?

Just so, he replied.

There is another question, which will probably throw light on our present enquiry if you and I can agree about it: — Ought the philosopher to care about the pleasures — if they are to be called pleasures — of eating and drinking?

Certainly not, answered Simmias.

And what about the pleasures of love — should he care for them?

By no means.

And will he think much of the other ways of indulging the body, for example, the acquisition of costly raiment, or sandals, or other adornments of the body? Instead of caring about them, does he not rather despise anything more than nature needs? What do you say?

I should say that the true philosopher would despise them.

Would you not say that he is entirely concerned with the soul and not with the body? He would like, as far as he can, to get away from the body and to turn to the soul.

Quite true.

In matters of this sort philosophers, above all other men, may be observed in every sort of way to dissever the soul from the communion of the body.

Very true.

Whereas, Simmias, the rest of the world are of opinion that to him who has no sense of pleasure and no part in bodily pleasure, life is not worth having; and that he who is indifferent about them is as good as dead.

That is also true.

What again shall we say of the actual acquirement of knowledge? — is the body, if invited to share in the enquiry, a hinderer or a helper? I mean to say, have sight and hearing any truth in them? Are they not, as the poets are always telling us, inaccurate witnesses? and yet, if even they are inaccurate and indistinct, what is to be said of the other senses? — for you will allow that they are the best of them?

Certainly, he replied.

Then when does the soul attain truth? — for in attempting to consider anything in company with the body she is obviously deceived.

True.

Then must not true existence be revealed to her in thought, if at all?

Yes.

And thought is best when the mind is gathered into herself and none of these things trouble her — neither sounds nor sights nor pain nor any pleasure, — when she takes leave of the body, and has as little as possible to do with it, when she has no bodily sense or desire, but is aspiring after true being?

Certainly.

And in this the philosopher dishonours the body; his soul runs away from his body and desires to be alone and by herself?

That is true.

Well, but there is another thing, Simmias: Is there or is there not an absolute justice?

Assuredly there is.

And an absolute beauty and absolute good?

Of course.

But did you ever behold any of them with your eyes?

Certainly not.

Or did you ever reach them with any other bodily sense? — and I speak not of these alone, but of absolute greatness, and health, and strength, and of the essence or true nature of everything. Has the reality of them ever been perceived by you through the bodily organs? or rather, is not the nearest approach to the knowledge of their several natures made by him who so orders his intellectual vision as to have the most exact conception of the essence of each thing which he considers?

Certainly.

And he attains to the purest knowledge of them who goes to each with the mind alone, not introducing or intruding in the act of thought sight or any other sense together with reason, but with the very light of the mind in her own clearness searches into the very truth of each; he who has got rid, as far as he can, of eyes and ears and, so to speak, of the whole body, these being in his opinion distracting elements which when they infect the soul hinder her from acquiring truth and knowledge — who, if not he, is likely to attain to the knowledge of true being?

What you say has a wonderful truth in it, Socrates, replied Simmias.

And when real philosophers consider all these things, will they not be led to make a reflection which they will express in words something like the following? 'Have we not found,' they will say, 'a path of thought which seems to bring us and our argument to the conclusion, that while we are in the body, and while the soul is infected with the evils of the body, our desire will not be satisfied? and our desire is of the truth. For the body is a source of endless trouble to us by reason of the mere requirement of food; and is liable also to diseases which overtake and impede us in the search after true being: it fills us full of loves, and lusts, and fears, and fancies of all kinds, and endless foolery, and in fact, as men say, takes away from us the power of thinking at all. Whence come wars, and fightings, and factions? whence but from the body and the lusts of the body? Wars are occasioned by the love of money, and money has to be acquired for the sake and in the service of the body; and by reason of all these impediments we have no time to give to philosophy; and, last and worst of all, even if we are at leisure and betake ourselves to some speculation, the body is always breaking in upon us, causing turmoil and confusion in our enquiries, and so amazing us that we are prevented from seeing the truth. It has been proved to us by experience that if we would have pure knowledge of anything we must be quit of the body — the soul in herself must behold things in themselves: and then we shall attain the wisdom which we desire, and of which we say that we are lovers; not while we live, but after death; for if while in company with the body, the soul cannot have pure knowledge, one of two things follows — either knowledge is not to be attained at all, or, if at all, after death. For then, and not till then, the soul will be parted from the body and exist in herself alone. In this present life, I reckon that we make the nearest approach to knowledge when we have the least possible intercourse or communion with the body, and are not surfeited with the bodily nature, but keep ourselves pure until the hour when God himself is pleased to release us. And thus having got rid of the foolishness of the body we shall be pure and hold converse with the pure, and know of ourselves the clear light everywhere, which is no other than the light of truth.' For the impure are not permitted to approach the pure. These are the sort of words, Simmias, which the true lovers of knowledge cannot help saying to one another, and thinking. You would agree; would you not?

Undoubtedly, Socrates.

But, O my friend, if this be true, there is a great reason to hope that, going whither I go, when I have come to the end of my journey, I shall attain that which has been the pursuit of my life. And therefore I go on my way rejoicing, and not I only, but every other man who believes that his mind has been made ready and that he is in a manner purified.

Certainly, replied Simmias.

And what is purification but the separation of the soul from the body, as I was saying before; the habit of the soul gathering and collecting herself into herself from all sides out of the body; the dwelling in her own place alone, as in another life, so also in this, as far as she can; — the release of the soul from the chains of the body?

Very true, he said.

And this separation and release of the soul from the body is termed death?

To be sure, he said.

And the true philosophers, and they only, are ever seeking to release the soul. Is not the separation and release of the soul from the body their special study?

That is true.

And, as I was saying at first, there would be a ridiculous contradiction in men studying to live as nearly as they can in a state of death, and yet repining when it comes upon them.

Clearly.

And the true philosophers, Simmias, are always occupied in the practice of dying, wherefore also to them least of all men is death terrible. Look at the matter thus: — if they have been in every way the enemies of the body, and are wanting to be alone with the soul, when this desire of theirs is granted, how inconsistent would they be if they trembled and repined, instead of rejoicing at their departure to that place where, when they arrive, they hope to gain that which in life they desired — and this was wisdom — and at the same time to be rid of the company of their enemy. Many a man has been willing to go to the world below animated by the hope of seeing there an earthly love, or wife, or son, and conversing with them. And will he who is a true lover of wisdom, and is strongly persuaded in like manner that only in the world below he can worthily enjoy her, still repine at death? Will he not depart with joy? Surely he will, O my friend, if he be a true philosopher. For he will have a firm conviction that there, and there only, he can find wisdom in her purity. And if this be true, he would be very absurd, as I was saying, if he were afraid of death.

He would indeed, replied Simmias.

And when you see a man who is repining at the approach of death, is not his reluctance a sufficient proof that he is not a lover of wisdom, but a lover of the body, and probably at the same time a lover of either money or power, or both?

Quite so, he replied. . . .

And now let us proceed, he said. And first of all let me be sure that I have in my mind what you were saying. Simmias, if I remember rightly, has fears and misgivings whether the soul, although a fairer and diviner thing than the body, being as she is in the form of harmony, may not perish first. On the other hand, Cebes appeared to grant that the soul was more lasting than the body, but he said that no one could know whether the soul, after having worn out many bodies, might not perish herself and leave her last body behind her; and that this is death, which is the destruction not of the body but of the soul, for in the body the work of destruction is ever going on. Are not these, Simmias and Cebes, the points which we have to consider?

They both agreed to this statement of them.

He proceeded: And did you deny the force of the whole preceding argument, or of a part only?

Of a part only, they replied.

And what did you think, he said, of that part of the argument in which we said that knowledge was recollection, and hence inferred that the soul must have previously existed somewhere else before she was enclosed in the body?

Cebes said that he had been wonderfully impressed by that part of the argument, and that his conviction remained absolutely unshaken. Simmias agreed, and added that he himself could hardly imagine the possibility of his ever thinking differently.

But, rejoined Socrates, you will have to think differently, my Theban friend, if you still maintain that harmony is a compound, and that the soul is a harmony which is made out of strings set in the frame of the body; for you will surely never allow yourself to say that a harmony is prior to the elements which compose it.

Never, Socrates.

But do you not see that this is what you imply when you say that the soul existed before she took the form and body of man, and was made up of elements which as yet had no existence? For harmony is not like the soul, as you suppose; but first the lyre, and the strings, and the sounds exist in a state of discord, and then harmony is made last of all, and perishes first. And how can such a notion of the soul as this agree with the other?

Not at all, replied Simmias.

And yet, he said, there surely ought to be harmony in a discourse of which harmony is the theme?

There ought, replied Simmias.

But there is no harmony, he said, in the two propositions that knowledge is recollection, and that the soul is a harmony. Which of them will you retain?

I think, he replied, that I have a much stronger faith, Socrates, in the first of the two, which has been fully demonstrated to me, than in the latter, which has not been demonstrated at all, but rests only on probable and plausible grounds; and is therefore believed by the many. I know too well that these arguments from probabilities are impostors, and unless great caution is observed in the use of them, they are apt to be deceptive — in geometry, and in other things too. But the doctrine of knowledge and recollection has been proven to me on trustworthy grounds; and the proof was that the soul must have existed before she came into the body, because to her belongs the essence of which the very name implies existence. Having, as I am convinced, rightly accepted this conclusion, and on sufficient grounds, I must, as I suppose, cease to argue or allow others to argue that the soul is a harmony.

Let me put the matter, Simmias, he said, in another point of view: Do you imagine that a harmony or any other composition can be in a state other than that of the elements, out of which it is compounded?

Certainly not.

Or do or suffer anything other than they do or suffer?

He agreed.

Then a harmony does not, properly speaking, lead the parts or elements which make up the harmony, but only follows them.

He assented.

For harmony cannot possibly have any motion, or sound, or other quality which is opposed to its parts.

That would be impossible, he replied.

And does not the nature of every harmony depend upon the manner in which the elements are harmonized?

I do not understand you, he said.

I mean to say that a harmony admits of degrees, and is more of a harmony, and more completely a harmony, when more truly and fully harmonized, to any extent which is possible; and less of a harmony, and less completely a harmony, when less truly and fully harmonized.

True.

But does the soul admit of degrees? or is one soul in the very least degree more or less, or more or less completely, a soul than another?

Not in the least.

Yet surely of two souls, one is said to have intelligence and virtue, and to be good, and the other to have folly and vice, and to be an evil soul: and this is said truly?

Yes, truly.

But what will those who maintain the soul to be a harmony say of this presence of virtue and vice in the soul? — will they say that here is another harmony, and another discord, and that the virtuous soul is harmonized, and herself being a harmony has another harmony within her, and that the vicious soul is inharmonical and has no harmony within her?

I cannot tell, replied Simmias; but I suppose that something of the sort would be asserted by those who say that the soul is a harmony.

And we have already admitted that no soul is more a soul than another; which is equivalent to admitting that harmony is not more or less harmony, or more or less completely a harmony?

Quite true.

And that which is not more or less a harmony is not more or less harmonized?

True.

And that which is not more or less harmonized cannot have more or less of harmony, but only an equal harmony?

Yes, an equal harmony.

Then one soul not being more or less absolutely a soul than another, is not more or less harmonized?

Exactly.

And therefore has neither more nor less of discord, nor yet of harmony?

She has not.

And having neither more nor less of harmony or of discord, one soul has no more vice or virtue than another, if vice be discord and virtue harmony?

Not at all more.

Or speaking more correctly, Simmias, the soul, if she is a harmony, will never have any vice; because a harmony, being absolutely a harmony, has no part in the inharmonical.

No.

And therefore a soul which is absolutely a soul has no vice?

How can she have, if the previous argument holds?

Then, if all souls are equally by their nature souls, all souls of all living creatures will be equally good?

I agree with you, Socrates, he said.

And can all this be true, think you? he said; for these are the consequences which seem to follow from the assumption that the soul is a harmony?

It cannot be true.

Once more, he said, what ruler is there of the elements of human nature other than the soul, and especially the wise soul? Do you know of any?

Indeed, I do not.

And is the soul in agreement with the affections of the body? or is she at variance with them? For example, when the body is hot and thirsty, does not the soul incline us against drinking? and when the body is hungry, against eating? And this is only one instance out of ten thousand of the opposition of the soul to the things of the body.

Very true.

But we have already acknowledged that the soul, being a harmony, can never utter a note at variance with the tensions and relaxations and vibrations and other affections of the strings out of which she is composed; she can only follow, she cannot lead them?

It must be so, he replied.

And yet do we not now discover the soul to be doing the exact opposite — leading the elements of which she is believed to be composed; almost always opposing and coercing them in all sorts of ways throughout life, sometimes more violently with the pains of medicine and gymnastic; then again more gently; now threatening, now admonishing the desires, passions, fears, as if talking to a thing which is not herself, as Homer in the Odyssee represents Odysseus doing in the words —

'He beat his breast, and thus reproached
    his heart:
Endure, my heart; far worse hast thou
    endured!'

Do you think that Homer wrote this under the idea that the soul is a harmony capable of being led by the affections of the body, and not rather of a nature which should lead and master them — herself a far diviner thing than any harmony?

Yes, Socrates, I quite think so.

Then, my friend, we can never be right in saying that the soul is a harmony, for we should contradict the divine Homer, and contradict ourselves.

True, he said. . . .

★   ★   ★

There is nothing new, he said, in what I am about to tell you; but only what I have been always and everywhere repeating in the previous discussion and on other occasions: I want to show you the nature of that cause which has occupied my thoughts. I shall have to go back to those familiar words which are in the mouth of every one, and first of all assume that there is an absolute beauty and goodness and greatness, and the like; grant me this, and I hope to be able to show you the nature of the cause, and to prove the immortality of the soul.

Cebes said: You may proceed at once with the proof, for I grant you this.

Well, he said, then I should like to know whether you agree with me in the next step; for I cannot help thinking, if there be anything beautiful other than absolute beauty should there be such, that it can be beautiful only in so far as it partakes of absolute beauty — and I should say the same of everything. Do you agree in this notion of the cause?

Yes, he said, I agree.

He proceeded: I know nothing and can understand nothing of any other of those wise causes which are alleged; and if a person says to me that the bloom of colour, or form, or any such thing is a source of beauty, I leave all that, which is only confusing to me, and simply and singly, and perhaps foolishly, hold and am assured in my own mind that nothing makes a thing beautiful but the presence and participation of beauty in whatever way or manner obtained; for as to the manner I am uncertain, but I stoutly contend that by beauty all beautiful things become beautiful. This appears to me to be the safest answer which I can give, either to myself or to another, and to this I cling, in the persuasion that this principle will never be overthrown, and that to myself or to any one who asks the question, I may safely reply, That by beauty beautiful things become beautiful. Do you not agree with me?

I do.

And that by greatness only great things

become great and greater greater, and by smallness the less become less?

True.

Then if a person were to remark that A is taller by a head than B, and B less by a head than A, you would refuse to admit his statement, and would stoutly contend that what you mean is only that the greater is greater by, and by reason of, greatness, and the less is less only by, and by reason of, smallness; and thus you would avoid the danger of saying that the greater is greater and the less less by the measure of the head, which is the same in both, and would also avoid the monstrous absurdity of supposing that the greater man is greater by reason of the head, which is small. You would be afraid to draw such an inference, would you not?

Indeed, I should, said Cebes, laughing.

In like manner you would be afraid to say that ten exceeded eight by, and by reason of, two; but would say by, and by reason of, number; or you would say that two cubits exceed one cubit not by a half, but by magnitude? — for there is the same liability to error in all these cases.

Very true, he said.

Again, would you not be cautious of affirming that the addition of one to one, or the division of one, is the cause of two? And you would loudly asseverate that you know of no way in which anything comes into existence except by participation in its own proper essence, and consequently, as far as you know, the only cause of two is the participation in duality — this is the way to make two, and the participation in one is the way to make one. You would say: I will let alone puzzles of division and addition — wiser heads than mine may answer them; inexperienced as I am, and ready to start, as the proverb says, at my own shadow, I cannot afford to give up the sure ground of a principle. And if any one

assails you there, you would not mind him, or answer him, until you had seen whether the consequences which follow agree with one another or not, and when you are further required to give an explanation of this principle, you would go on to assume a higher principle, and a higher, until you found a resting place in the best of the higher; but you would not confuse the principle and the consequences in your reasoning, like the Eristics — at least if you wanted to discover real existence. Not that this confusion signifies to them, who never care or think about the matter at all, for they have the wit to be well pleased with themselves however great may be the turmoil of their ideas. But you, if you are a philosopher, will certainly do as I say.

What you say is most true, said Simmias and Cebes, both speaking at once.

Ech. Yes, Phaedo; and I do not wonder at their assenting. Any one who has the least sense will acknowledge the wonderful clearness of Socrates' reasoning.

Phaed. Certainly, Echecrates; and such was the feeling of the whole company at the time.

Ech. Yes, and equally of ourselves, who were not of the company, and are now listening to your recital. But what followed?

Phaed. After all this had been admitted, and they had agreed that ideas exist, and that other things participate in them and derive their names from them, Socrates, if I remember rightly, said: —

This is your way of speaking; and yet when you say that Simmias is greater than Socrates and less than Phaedo, do you not predicate of Simmias both greatness and smallness?

Yes, I do.

But still you allow that Simmias does not really exceed Socrates, as the words may seem to imply, because he is Simmias, but by reason of the size which he has; just as Simmias does not exceed Socrates because he is Simmias, any more than because Socrates is Socrates, but because he has smallness when compared with the greatness of Simmias?

True.

And if Phaedo exceeds him in size, this is not because Phaedo is Phaedo, but because Phaedo has greatness relatively to Simmias, who is comparatively smaller?

That is true.

And therefore Simmias is said to be great, and is also said to be small, because he is in a mean between them, exceeding the smallness of the one by his greatness, and allowing the greatness of the other to exceed his smallness. He added, laughing, I am speaking like a book, but I believe that what I am saying is true.

Simmias assented.

I speak as I do because I want you to agree with me in thinking, not only that absolute greatness will never be great and also small, but that greatness in us or in the concrete will never admit the small or admit of being exceeded: instead of this, one of two things will happen, either the greater will fly or retire before the opposite, which is the less, or at the approach of the less has already ceased to exist; but will not, if allowing or admitting of smallness, be changed by that; even as I, having received and admitted smallness when compared with Simmias, remain just as I was, and am the same small person. And as the idea of greatness cannot condescend ever to be or become small, in like manner the smallness in us cannot be or become great; nor can any other opposite which remains the same ever be or become its own opposite, but either passes away or perishes in the change.

That, replied Cebes, is quite my notion.

Hereupon one of the company, though I do not exactly remember which of them, said: In heaven's name, is not this the direct contrary of what was admitted before — that out of the greater came the less and out of the less the greater, and that opposites were simply generated from opposites; but now this principle seems to be utterly denied.

Socrates inclined his head to the speaker and listened. I like your courage, he said, in reminding us of this. But you do not observe that there is a difference in the two cases. For then we were speaking of opposites in the concrete, and now of the essential opposite which, as is affirmed, neither in us nor in nature can ever be at variance with itself: then, my friend, we were speaking of things in which opposites are inherent and which are called after them, but now about the opposites which are inherent in them and which give their name to them; and these essential opposites will never, as we maintain, admit of generation into or out of one another. At the same time, turning to Cebes, he said: Are you at all disconcerted, Cebes, at our friend's objection?

No, I do not feel so, said Cebes; and yet I cannot deny that I am often disturbed by objections.

Then we are agreed after all, said Socrates, that the opposite will never in any case be opposed to itself?

To that we are quite agreed, he replied.

Yet once more let me ask you to consider the question from another point of view, and see whether you agree with me: — There is a thing which you term heat, and another thing which you term cold?

Certainly.

But are they the same as fire and snow?

Most assuredly not.

Heat is a thing different from fire, and cold is not the same with snow?

And yet you will surely admit, that when snow, as was before said, is under the influence of heat, they will not remain snow and heat; but at the advance of the heat, the snow will either retire or perish?

Very true, he replied.

And the fire too at the advance of the cold will either retire or perish; and when the fire is under the influence of the cold, they will not remain as before, fire and cold.

That is true, he said.

And in some cases the name of the idea is not only attached to the idea in an eternal connection, but anything else which, not being the idea, exists only in the form of the idea, may also lay claim to it. I will try to make this clearer by an example: — The odd number is always called by the name of odd?

Very true.

But is this the only thing which is called odd? Are there not other things which have their own name, and yet are called odd, because, although not the same as oddness, they are never without oddness? — that is what I mean to ask — whether numbers such as the number three are not of the class of odd. And there are many other examples: would you not say, for example, that three may be called by its proper name, and also be called odd, which is not the same with three? and this may be said not only of three but also of five, and of every alternate number — each of them without being oddness is odd; and in the same way two and four, and the other series of alternate numbers, has every number even, without being evenness. Do you agree?

Of course.

Then now mark the point at which I am aiming: — not only do essential opposites exclude one another, but also concrete things, which, although not in themselves opposed, contain opposites; these, I say, likewise reject the idea which is opposed to that which is contained in them, and when it approaches them they either perish or withdraw. For example; Will not the number three endure annihilation or anything sooner than be converted into an even number, while remaining three?

Very true, said Cebes.

And yet, he said, the number two is certainly not opposed to the number three?

It is not.

Then not only do opposite ideas repel the advance of one another, but also there are other natures which repel the approach of opposites.

Very true, he said.

Suppose, he said, that we endeavour, if possible, to determine what these are.

By all means.

Are they not, Cebes, such as compel the things of which they have possession, not only to take their own form, but also the form of some opposite?

What do you mean?

I mean, as I was just now saying, and as I am sure that you know, that those things which are possessed by the number three must not only be three in number, but must also be odd.

Quite true.

And on this oddness, of which the number three has the impress, the opposite idea will never intrude?

No.

And this impress was given by the odd principle?

Yes.

And to the odd is opposed the even?

True.

Then the idea of the even number will never arrive at three?

No.

Then three has no part in the even?

None.

Then the triad or number three is uneven?

Very true.

To return then to my distinction of natures

which are not opposed, and yet do not admit opposites — as, in the instance given, three, although not opposed to the even, does not any the more admit of the even, but always brings the opposite into play on the other side; or as two does not receive the odd, or fire the cold — from these examples (and there are many more of them) perhaps you may be able to arrive at the general conclusion, that not only opposites will not receive opposites, but also that nothing which brings the opposite will admit the opposite of that which it brings, in that to which it is brought. And here let me recapitulate — for there is no harm in repetition. The number five will not admit the nature of the even, any more than ten, which is the double of five, will admit the nature of the odd.

The double has another opposite, and is not strictly opposed to the odd, but nevertheless rejects the odd altogether. Nor again will parts in the ratio 3 : 2, nor any fraction in which there is a half, nor again in which there is a third, admit the notion of the whole, although they are not opposed to the whole: You will agree?

Yes, he said, I entirely agree and go along with you in that.

And now, he said, let us begin again; and do not you answer my question in the words in which I ask it: let me have not the old safe answer of which I spoke at first, but another equally safe, of which the truth will be inferred by you from what has been just said. I mean that if any one asks you 'what that is, of which the inherence makes the body hot,' you will reply not heat (this is what I call the safe and stupid answer), but fire, a far superior answer, which we are now in a condition to give. Or if any one asks you 'why a body is diseased,' you will not say from disease, but from fever; and instead of saying that oddness is the cause of odd numbers, you will say that

the monad is the cause of them: and so of things in general, as I dare say that you will understand sufficiently without my adducing any further examples.

Yes, he said, I quite understand you.

Tell me, then, what is that of which the inherence will render the body alive?

The soul, he replied.

And is this always the case?

Yes, he said, of course.

Then whatever the soul possesses, to that she comes bearing life?

Yes, certainly.

And is there any opposite to life?

There is, he said.

And what is that?

Death.

Then the soul, as has been acknowledged, will never receive the opposite of what she brings.

Impossible, replied Cebes.

And now, he said, what did we just now call that principle which repels the even?

The odd.

And that principle which repels the musical or the just?

The unmusical, he said, and the unjust.

And what do we call that principle which does not admit of death?

The immortal, he said.

And does the soul admit of death?

No.

Then the soul is immortal?

Yes, he said.

And may we say that this has been proven?

Yes, abundantly proven, Socrates, he replied.

Supposing that the odd were imperishable, must not three be imperishable?

Of course.

And if that which is cold were imperishable, when the warm principle came attacking the snow, must not the snow have retired whole and unmelted — for it could never have perished, nor could it have remained and admitted the heat?

True, he said.

Again, if the uncooling or warm principle were imperishable, the fire when assailed by cold would not have perished or have been extinguished, but would have gone away unaffected?

Certainly, he said.

And the same may be said of the immortal: if the immortal is also imperishable, the soul when attacked by death cannot perish; for the preceding argument shows that the soul will not admit of death, or ever be dead, any more than three or the odd number will admit of the even, or fire, or the heat in the fire, of the cold. Yet a person may say: 'But although the odd will not become even at the approach of the even, why may not the odd perish and the even take the place of the odd?' Now to him who makes this objection, we cannot answer that the odd principle is imperishable; for this has not been acknowledged, but if this had been acknowledged, there would have been no difficulty in contending that at the approach of the even the odd principle and the number three took their departure; and the same argument would have held good of fire and heat and any other thing.

Very true.

And the same may be said of the immortal: if the immortal is also imperishable, then the soul will be imperishable as well as immortal; but if not, some other proof of her imperishableness will have to be given.

No other proof is needed, he said; for if the immortal, being eternal, is liable to perish, then nothing is imperishable.

Yes, replied Socrates, and yet all men will agree that God, and the essential form of life, and the immortal in general, will never perish.

Yes, all men, he said — that is true; and what is more, gods, if I am not mistaken, as well as men.

Seeing then that the immortal is indestructible, must not the soul, if she is immortal, be also imperishable?

Most certainly.

Then when death attacks a man, the mortal portion of him may be supposed to die, but the immortal retires at the approach of death and is preserved safe and sound?

True.

Then, Cebes, beyond question, the soul is immortal and imperishable, and our souls will truly exist in another world!

I am convinced, Socrates, said Cebes, and have nothing more to object; but if my friend Simmias, or any one else, has any further objection to make, he had better speak out, and not keep silence, since I do not know to what other season he can defer the discussion, if there is anything which he wants to say or to have said.

But I have nothing more to say, replied Simmias; nor can I see any reason for doubt after what has been said. But I still feel and cannot help feeling uncertain in my own mind, when I think of the greatness of the subject and the feebleness of man.

Yes, Simmias, replied Socrates, that is well said: and I may add that first principles, even if they appear certain, should be carefully considered; and when they are satisfactorily ascertained, then, with a sort of hesitating confidence in human reason, you may, I think, follow the course of the argument; and if that be plain and clear, there will be no need for any further enquiry.

Very true.

But then, O my friends, he said, if the soul is really immortal, what care should be taken of her, not only in respect of the portion of time which is called life, but of eternity! And the danger of neglecting her from this point of view does indeed appear to be awful. If death had only been the end of all, the wicked would have had a good bargain in dying, for they would have been happily quit not only of their body, but of their own evil together with their souls. But now, inasmuch as the soul is manifestly immortal, there is no release or salvation from evil except the attainment of the highest virtue and wisdom. For the soul when on her progress to the world below takes nothing with her but nurture and education; and these are said greatly to benefit or greatly to injure the departed, at the very beginning of his journey thither.

B

Immortality of the Soul . . . is a topic on which for several reasons I would rather keep silence, but I think that silence here might fairly be misunderstood. It is not easy, in the first place, to say exactly what a future life means. The period of personal continuance obviously need not be taken as endless. And again precisely in what sense, and how far, the survival must be personal is not easy to lay down. I shall assume here that what is meant is an existence after death which is conscious of its identity with our life here and now. And the duration of this must be taken as sufficient to remove any idea of unwilling extinction or of premature decease. Now we seem to desire continuance (if we do desire it) for a variety of reasons, and it might be interesting elsewhere to set these out and to clear away confusions. I must however pass at once to the question of possibility.

There is one sense in which the immortality of souls seems impossible. We must remember that the universe is incapable of increase. And to suppose a constant supply of new souls, none of which ever perished, would clearly land us in the end in an insoluble difficulty. But it is quite unnecessary, I presume, to hold the doctrine in this sense. And, if we take the question generally, then to deny the possibility of a life after death would be quite ridiculous. There is no way of proving, first, that a body is required for a soul. And though a soul, when bodiless, might (for all we know) be even more subject to mortality, yet obviously here we have passed into a region of ignorance. And to say that in this region a personal continuance could not be, appears simply irrational. And the same result holds, even if we take a body as essential to every soul, and, even if we insist also (as we cannot) that this body must be made of our everyday substance. A future life is possible even on the ground of common crude Materialism. After an interval, no matter how long, another nervous system sufficiently like our own might be developed; and in this case memory and a personal identity must arise. The event may be as improbable as you please, but I at least can find no reason for calling it impossible. And we may even go a step further still. It is conceivable that an indefinite number of such bodies should exist, not in succession merely, but all together and all at once. But, if so, we might gain a personal continuance not single but multiform, and

F. H. Bradley, *Appearance and Reality,* New York, The Macmillan Company, 1893, pp. 501–510. Reprinted by permission of George Allen & Unwin Ltd.

might secure a destiny on which it would be idle to enlarge. In ways like the above it is clear that a future life is possible, but, on the other hand, such possibilities are not worth much.

A thing is impossible absolutely when it contradicts the known nature of Reality. It is impossible relatively when it collides with some idea which we have found good cause to take as real. A thing is possible, first, as long as it is not quite meaningless. It must contain some positive quality belonging to the universe; and it must not at the same time remove this and itself by some destructive addition. A thing is possible further, according as its meaning contains without discrepancy more and more of what is held to be real. We, in other words, consider anything more possible as it grows in probability. And "Probability," we are rightly told, "is the guide of life." We want to know, in short, not whether a thing is merely and barely possible, but how much ground we have for expecting it and not something else.

In a case like the present, we cannot, of course, hope to set out the chances, for we have to do with elements the value of which is not known. And for probability the unknown is of different kinds. There is first the unknown utterly, which is not possible at all; and this is discounted and treated as nothing. There is next something possible, the full nature of which is hidden, but the extent and value of which, as against some other "events," is clear. And so far all is straightforward. But we have still to deal with the unknown in two more troublesome senses. It may stand for a mere possibility about which we know nothing further, and for entertaining which we can find no further ground. Or again, the unknown may cover a region, where we can specify no details, but which still we can judge to contain a great diversity of possible events.

We shall soon find the importance of these dry distinctions. A bodiless soul is possible because it is not meaningless, or in any way known to be impossible. But I fail to find any further and additional reason in its favour. And, next, would a bodiless soul be immortal? And, again, why after death should *we*, in particular, have any bodiless continuance? The original slight probability of a future life seems not much increased by these considerations. Again, if we take body to be essential — a body, that is, consisting of matter either familiar or strange — what, on this ground, is our chance of personal continuance after death? You may here appeal to the unknown, and, where our knowledge seems nothing, you may perhaps urge, "Why not this event, just as much as its contrary and opposite?" But the question would rest on a fallacy, and I must insist on the distinction which above we laid down. In this unknown field we certainly cannot particularize and set out the chances, but in another sense the field is not quite unknown.

We cannot say that, of the combinations possible there, one half is, for all we know, favourable to a life after death. For, to judge by actual experience, the combinations seem mostly unfavourable. And, though the character of what falls outside our experience *may* be very different, yet our judgment as to this must be affected by what we do know. But, if so, while the whole variety of combinations must be taken as very large, the portion judged favourable to continued life, whether multiform or simple, must be set down as small. Such will have to be our conclusion if we deal with this unknown field. But, if we may not deal with it, the possibility of a future life is, on this ground, quite unknown;

and, if so, we have no right to consider it at all. And the general result to my mind is briefly this. When you add together the chances of a life after death — a life taken as bodiless, and again as diversely embodied — the amount is not great. The balance of hostile probability seems so large that the fraction on the other side to my mind is not considerable. And we may repeat, and may sum up our conclusion thus. If we appeal to blank ignorance, then a future life may even have no meaning, and may fail wholly to be possible. Or if we avoid this worst extreme, a future life may be but barely possible. But a possibility, in this sense, stands unsupported face to face with an indefinite universe. And its value, so far, can hardly be called worth counting. If, on the other hand, we allow ourselves to use what knowledge we possess, and if we judge fairly of future life by all the grounds we have for judging, the result is not much modified. Among those grounds we certainly find a part which favours continuance; but, taken at its highest, that part appears to be small. Hence a future life must be taken as decidedly improbable.

But in this way, it will be objected, the question is not properly dealt with. "On the grounds you have stated," it will be urged, "future life may be improbable; but then those grounds really lie outside the main point. The positive evidence for a future life is what weighs with our minds; and this is independent of discussions as to what, in the abstract, is probable." The objection is fair, and my reply to it is plain and simple. I have ignored the positive evidence because for me it has really no value. Direct arguments to show that a future life is, not merely possible, but real, seem to me unavailing. The addition to general probability, which they make, is to my mind trifling; and, without examining these arguments in detail, I will add a few remarks.

Philosophy, I repeat, has to justify all sides of our nature; and this means, I agree, that our main cravings must find satisfaction. But that every desire of every kind must, as such, be gratified — this is quite a different demand, and it is surely irrational. At all events it is opposed to the results of our preceding discussions. The destiny of the finite, we saw everywhere, is to reach consummation, but never wholly as such, never quite in its own way. And as to this desire for a future life, what is there in it so sacred? How can its attainment be implied in the very principles of our nature? Nay, is there in it, taken by itself, anything moral in the least or religious at all? I desire to have no pain, but always pleasure, and to continue so indefinitely. But the literal fulfilment of my wish is incompatible with my place in the universe. It is irreconcileable with my own nature, and I have to be content therefore with that measure of satisfaction which my nature permits. And am I, on this account, to proclaim philosophy insolvent, because it will not listen to demands really based on nothing?

But the demand for future life, I shall be told, is a genuine postulate, and its satisfaction is implicated in the very essence of our nature. Now, if this means that our religion and our morality will not work without it — so much the worse, I reply, for our morality and our religion. The remedy lies in the correction of our mistaken and immoral notions about goodness. "But then," it will be exclaimed, "this is too horrible. There really after all will be self-sacrifice; and virtue and selfishness after all will not be identical." . . . "But then strict justice is not paramount." No, I am sure that it is not so. There is a great deal in the universe, I am sure, beyond mere morality; and I have yet to learn that, even in the moral world, the highest law is justice. "But, if we die, think of the loss of all our hard-won gains." But is a thing lost, in the first place, because *I* fail to get it or retain it? And, in the second place, what seems to us sheer waste is, to a very large extent, the way of the universe. We need not take on ourselves to be anxious about that. "But without endless progress, how reach perfection?" And *with* endless progress (if that means anything) I answer, how reach it? Surely perfection and finitude are in principle not compatible. If you are to be perfect, then you, as such, must be resolved and cease; and endless progress sounds merely like an attempt indefinitely to put off perfection. And as a function of the perfect universe, on the other hand, you are perfect already. "But after all we must wish that pain and sorrow should be somewhere made good." On the whole, and in the whole, if our view is right, this is fully the case. With the individual often I agree it is not the case. And I wish it otherwise, meaning by this that my inclination and duty as a fellow-creature impels me that way, and that wishes and actions of this sort among finite beings fulfil the plan of the Whole. But I cannot argue, therefore, that all is wrong if individuals suffer. There is in life always, I admit, a note of sadness; but it ought not to prevail, nor can we truly assert that it does so. And the universe in its attitude towards finite beings must be judged of not piecemeal but as a system. "But, if hopes and fears are taken away, we shall be less happy and less moral." Perhaps, and perhaps again both more moral and more happy. The question is a large one, and I do not intend to discuss it, but I will say so much as this. Whoever argues that belief in a future life has, on the whole, brought evil to humanity, has at least a strong case. But, the question here seems irrelevant. If it could indeed be urged that the essence of a finite being is such, that it can only regulate its conduct by keeping sight of another world and of another life — the matter, I agree, would be altered. But if it comes merely to this, that human beings now are in such a condition that, if they do not believe what is probably untrue, they must deteriorate — that to the universe, if it were the case, would be a mere detail. It is the rule that a race of beings so out of agreement with their environment should deteriorate, and it is well for them to make way for another race constituted more rationally and happily. And I must leave the matter so.

All the above arguments, and there are others, rest on assumptions negatived by the general results of this volume. It is about the truth of these assumptions, I would add, that discussion is desirable. It is idle to repeat, "I want something," unless you can show that the nature of things demands it also. And to debate this special question, apart from an enquiry into the ultimate nature of the world, is surely unprofitable.

Future life is a subject on which I had no desire to speak. I have kept silence until the subject seemed forced before me, and until in a manner I had dealt with the main problems involved in it. The conclusion arrived at seems the result to which the educated world, on the whole, is making its way. A personal continuance is possible, and it is but little more. Still, if any one can believe in it, and finds himself sustained by that belief, — after all it is possible. On the other hand it is better to be quit of both hope and fear, than to lapse back into any form of degrading superstition. And surely there are few greater responsibilities which a man can take on himself, than to have proclaimed, or even hinted, that without immortality all religion is a cheat and all morality a self-deception.

SUGGESTIONS FOR THOUGHT

1. Does death have any positive values or is it the cessation of all values? Is death ever a blessing? Are there times when death is to be chosen in preference to life? What values are more precious than life?

2. What is it that people fear when they say they are afraid of death?

3. How much consideration should one give to the fact of one's own immortality? Socrates says in the *Apology*, " . . . a man who is good for anything ought not to calculate the chance of living or dying; he ought only to consider whether in doing anything he is doing right or wrong," but in the *Phaedo* Socrates says that the philosopher is always pursuing death. How can these be reconciled?

4. Compare the attitudes of young people and of the aged toward death. Of the happy and the unhappy. Of the rich and the poor.

5. How does religious faith assist men in facing death? Bergson has suggested that religion may be a self-preservative effort to keep man from suicide when he becomes fully aware of the fact of death. Do you agree?

6. What is the argument for and against euthanasia? Why have most societies disapproved of suicide?

7. In what various ways may the self be said to be immortal? Why has an immortality of absorption in the impersonal universe been accepted in the Orient whereas the Occident has usually thought of immortality in terms of persistence of the person after the death of the body?

8. What are the values of belief in personal immortality? What are the dangers of such belief?

9. Is the hope of personal immortality an effective sanction of human behavior?

10. Are people who believe in and long for life beyond the grave less concerned with the improvement of life on earth than those who do not believe in life beyond the grave?

11. Rousseau wrote in one of his letters: "All the subtleties of metaphysics would not lead me to doubt for a moment the immortality of my soul." How can we account for this refusal to disbelieve? If it were possible to establish scientifically the complete mortality of man, would people even then give up the belief in immortality?

12. The *Bhagavad-Gita* says that the greatest marvel in the world is that even though each man sees death come to other people he somehow feels that he will not die. How can we account for this refusal to face the facts?

SUGGESTIONS FOR FURTHER READING

BROAD, C. D., *The Mind and Its Place in Nature,* New York, Harcourt, Brace and Company, 1929, chs. 11, 12.

COE, GEORGE ALBERT, "A Realistic View of Death" in *Religious Realism,* edited by D. C. MacIntosh, New York, The Macmillan Company, 1931, ch. 7.

GRANT, FREDERICK C., *Can We Still Believe in Immortality?,* Louisville, The Cloister Press, 1944.

HOCKING, WILLIAM ERNEST, *Thoughts on Death and Life,* New York, Harper and Brothers, 1937, ch. 1.

KEYSER, CASSIUS J., "The Significance of Death," *The Hibbert Journal,* Vol. 12, 1913–14, pp. 886–892.

KNIGHT, RAY, "Contempt for Death among the Uncivilized," *The Hibbert Journal,* Vol. 39, 1940–41, pp. 277–286.

LAMONT, CORLISS, *The Illusion of Immortality*, New York, G. P. Putnam's Sons, 1935.

MOORE, VIRGINIA, *Ho For Heaven!*, New York, E. P. Dutton and Company, 1946.

PERRY, RALPH BARTON, *The Hope of Immortality*, New York, The Vanguard Press, 1945.

PRINGLE-PATTISON, A. SETH, *The Idea of Immortality*, London, Oxford University Press, 1922.

RITCHIE, A. D., "Theories of Immortality," *Philosophy*, Vol. 17, 1942, pp. 117–127.

STEERE, DOUGLAS, *On Beginning From Within*, New York, Harper and Brothers, 1943, ch. 5.

STREETER, B. H., and others, *Immortality*, New York, The Macmillan Company, 1917.

TSANOFF, RADOSLAV A., *The Problem of Immortality*, New York, The Macmillan Company, 1917.

WEISS, PAUL, "Immortality," *The Review of Metaphysics*, Vol. 1, 1948, pp. 87–103.

WHITEHEAD, A. N., "Immortality," in *Essays in Science and Philosophy*, New York, The Philosophical Library, 1947, pp. 77–96.

PART TWO   THE NATURAL WORLD

7

KNOWLEDGE OF THE NATURAL WORLD

THE PROBLEMS in establishing reliable knowledge about the natural world may be classified into three groups: (1) those concerned with the *methods* of knowing; (2) those concerned with the *objects* of knowledge; and (3) those concerned with the *limits* of knowledge. The readings from Berkeley and Pearson are chiefly concerned with the latter two groups of problems. Berkeley thinks that the real and the known are equivalent (except in the case of mind) because a thing cannot exist unless it is known, whereas Pearson believes that the known is only a small portion of the real. George Berkeley (1685–1753) was an Irish bishop and philosopher who devoted himself with religious zeal to the refutation of the view that matter is an independent reality. His *Treatise Concerning the Principles of Human Knowledge* was published in 1710. Karl Pearson (1857–1936) was a professor of eugenics at the University of London.

A

It is evident to any one who takes a survey of the objects of human knowledge, that they are either ideas actually imprinted on the senses, or else such as are perceived by attending to the passions and operations of the mind; or lastly, ideas formed by help of memory and imagination, either compounding, divid-

George Berkeley, *A Treatise Concerning the Principles of Human Knowledge,* 1710, Part I (in part).

ing, or barely representing those originally perceived in the aforesaid ways. By sight, I have the ideas of light and colours, with their several degrees and variations. By touch, I perceive, for example, hard and soft, heat and cold, motion and resistance; and of all these more and less either as to quantity or degree. Smelling furnishes me with odours; the palate with tastes; and hearing conveys sounds to the mind in all their variety of tone and composition. And as several of these are observed to accompany each other, they come to be marked by one name, and so to be reputed as one thing. Thus, for example, a certain colour, taste, smell, figure, and consistence, having been observed to go together, are accounted one distinct thing, signified by the name *apple.* Other collections of ideas constitute a stone, a tree, a book, and the like sensible things; which, as they are pleasing or disagreeable, excite the passions of love, hatred, joy, grief, and so forth.

But besides all that endless variety of ideas or objects of knowledge, there is likewise something which knows or perceives them, and exercises divers operations, as willing, imagining, remembering about them. This perceiving, active being is what I call *Mind, Spirit, Soul,* or *Myself.* By which words I do not denote any one of my ideas, but a thing entirely distinct from them, *wherein they exist,* or, which is the same thing, whereby they are perceived; for the existence of an idea consists in being perceived.

That neither our thoughts, nor passions, nor ideas formed by the imagination, exist *without* the mind, is what *everybody will allow.* And (to me) it seems no less evident that the various sensations or ideas imprinted on the sense, however blended or combined together (that is, whatever objects they compose), cannot exist otherwise than *in* a mind perceiving them. I think an intuitive knowledge may be obtained of this, by any one that shall attend to *what is meant by the term exist,* when applied to sensible things. The table I write on, I say, exists, that is, I see and feel it; and if I were out of my study I should say it existed, meaning thereby that if I was in my study I might perceive it, or that some other spirit actually does perceive it. There was an odour, that is, it was smelled; there was a sound, that is to say, it was heard; a colour or figure, and

it was perceived by sight or touch. This is all that I can understand by these and the like expressions. For as to what is said of the absolute existence of unthinking things without any relation to their being perceived, that seems perfectly unintelligible. Their *esse* is *percipi,* nor is it possible they should have any existence, out of the minds or thinking things which perceive them.

It is indeed an opinion *strangely* prevailing amongst men, that houses, mountains, rivers, and in a word all sensible objects, have an existence natural or real, distinct from their being perceived by the understanding. But with how great an assurance and acquiescence soever this principle may be entertained in the world; yet whoever shall find in his heart to call it in question, may, if I mistake not, perceive it to involve a manifest contradiction. For what are the forementioned objects but the things we *perceive* by sense, and what do we perceive *besides our own ideas or sensations;* and is it not plainly repugnant that any one of these or any combination of them should exist unperceived?

If we thoroughly examine this tenet, it will, perhaps, be found at bottom to depend on the doctrine of *abstract ideas.* For can there be a nicer strain of abstraction than to distinguish the existence of sensible objects from their being perceived, so as to conceive them existing unperceived? Light and colours, heat and cold, extension and figures, in a word the things we see and feel, what are they but so many sensations, notions, ideas, or impressions on the sense; and is it possible to separate, even in thought, any of these from perception? For my part I might as easily divide a thing from itself. I may indeed divide in my thoughts or conceive apart from each other those things which, perhaps, I never perceived by sense so divided. Thus I imagine the trunk of a human body without the limbs, or conceive the smell of a rose without thinking on the rose itself. So far I will not deny I can abstract, if that may properly be called *abstraction,* which extends only to the conceiving separately such objects as it is possible may really exist or be actually perceived asunder. But my conceiving or imagining power does not extend beyond the possibility of real existence or perception. Hence as it is impossible for me to see or feel any thing without an actual sensation of that thing, so is it impossible for me to conceive in my thoughts any sensible thing or object distinct from the sensation or perception of it.

Some truths there are so near and obvious to the mind, that a man need only open his eyes to see them. Such I take this important one to be, to wit, that all the choir of heaven and furniture of the earth, in a word all those bodies which compose the mighty frame of the world, have not any substance without a mind, that their *being (esse)* is to be perceived or known; that consequently so long as they are not actually perceived by me, or do not exist in my mind or that of any other *created spirit,* they must either have no existence at all, *or else subsist in the mind of some eternal spirit:* it being perfectly unintelligible and involving all the absurdity of abstraction, to attribute to any single part of them an existence independent of a spirit. To be convinced of which, the reader need only reflect and try to separate in his own thoughts the being of a sensible thing from its being perceived.

From what has been said, it follows, there is *not any other substance than spirit,* or that which perceives. But for the fuller proof of this point, let it be considered, the sensible qualities are colour, figure, motion, smell, taste, and such like, that is, the ideas perceived by sense. Now for an idea to exist in an unperceiving thing is a manifest contradiction; for *to have an idea is all one as to perceive:* that therefore wherein colour, figure, and the like qualities exist, must perceive them; hence it is clear there can be no *unthinking* substance or *substratum* of those ideas.

But, say you, though the ideas themselves do not exist without the mind, yet there may be things *like* them whereof they are copies or resemblances, which things exist without the mind, in an unthinking substance. I *answer,* an idea can be like nothing but an idea; a colour or figure can be like nothing but another colour or figure. If we look but ever so little into our thoughts, we shall find it impossible for us to conceive a likeness except only between our ideas. Again, I ask whether those supposed originals or external things, of which our ideas are the pictures or representations, be themselves perceivable or no? if they are, *then they are ideas,* and we have gained our point; but if you say they are not, I appeal to any one whether it be sense, to assert a colour is like something which is invisible; hard or soft, like something which is intangible; and so of the rest.

Some there are who make a *distinction* betwixt *primary* and *secondary* qualities: by the former, they mean extension, figure, motion, rest, solidity or impenetrability, and number: by the latter they denote all other sensible qualities, as colours, sounds, tastes, and so forth. The ideas we have of these they acknowledge not to be the resemblances of anything existing without the mind or unperceived; but they will have our ideas of the primary qualities to be patterns or images of things which exist without the mind, in an unthinking substance which they call *matter.* By *matter* therefore we are to understand an inert, senseless substance, in which extension, figure, and motion, *do actually subsist.* But it is evident from what we have already shown, that extension, figure, and motion, are *only ideas existing in the mind,* and that an idea can be like nothing but another idea, and that consequently neither they nor their archetypes can exist in an *unperceiving* substance. Hence it is plain, that the very notion of what is called *matter, or corporeal substance,* involves a contradiction in it.

They who assert that figure, motion, and the rest of the primary or original qualities, do exist without the mind, in unthinking substances, do at the same time acknowledge that colours, sounds, heat, cold, and such like secondary qualities, do not, which they tell us are sensations existing *in the mind alone,* that depend on and are occasioned by the different size, texture, and motion of the minute particles of matter. This they take for an undoubted truth, which they can demonstrate beyond all exception. Now if it be certain, that those original qualities are *inseparably united with the other sensible qualities,* and not, even in thought, capable of being abstracted from them, it plainly follows that they exist only in the mind. But I desire any one to reflect and try, whether he can, by any abstraction of thought, conceive the extension and motion of a body, without all other sensible qualities. For my own part, I see evidently that it is not in my power to frame an idea of a body extended and moved, but I must withal give it some colour or other sensible quality which is *acknowledged* to exist only in the mind. In short, extension, figure, and motion, abstracted from all other qualities, are inconceivable. Where therefore the other sensible qualities are, there must these be also, to wit, in the mind and nowhere else. . . .

★   ★   ★

I am afraid I have given cause to think me needlessly prolix in handling this subject. For to what purpose is it to dilate on that which may be demonstrated with the utmost evidence in a line or two, to any one that is capable of the least reflection? It is but looking into your own thoughts, and so trying whether you can conceive it possible for a sound, or figure, or motion, or colour, to exist without the mind, or unperceived. This easy trial may make you see, that what you contend for is a downright contradiction. Insomuch that I am content to put the whole upon this issue; if you can but conceive it possible for one extended moveable substance, or in general, for any one idea, or any thing like an idea, to exist otherwise than in a mind perceiving it, I shall readily give up the cause: and as for all that *compages* of external bodies which you contend for, I shall grant you its existence, though *you cannot either give me any reason why you believe it exists, or assign any use to it when it is supposed to exist.* I say, the bare possibility of your opinion's being true, shall pass for an argument that it is so.

But, say you, surely there is nothing easier than to imagine trees, for instance, in a park, or books existing in a closet, and nobody to perceive them. I answer, you may say so, there is no difficulty in it: but what is all this, I beseech you, more than framing in your mind certain ideas which you call *books* and *trees,* and at the same time omitting to frame the idea of any one that may perceive them? *but do not you yourself perceive or think of them all the while?* this therefore is nothing to the purpose; it only shows you have the power of imagining or forming ideas in your mind; but it doth not show that you can conceive it possible the objects of your thought may exist without the mind: to make out this, *it is necessary that you conceive them existing unconceived or unthought-of, which is a manifest repugnancy.* When we do our utmost to conceive the existence of external bodies, we are all the while only contemplating our own ideas. But the mind, taking no notice of itself, is deluded to think it can and doth conceive bodies existing unthought-of or without the mind; though at the same time they are apprehended by or exist in itself. A little attention will discover to any one the truth and evidence of what is here said, and make it unnecessary to insist on any other proofs against the existence of material substance.

It is very obvious, upon the least inquiry into our own thoughts, to know whether it be possible for us to understand what is meant by the *absolute existence of sensible objects in themselves or without the mind.* To me it is evident those words mark out either a direct contradiction, or else nothing at all. And to convince others of this, I know no readier or fairer way, than to entreat they would calmly attend to their own thoughts: and if by this attention the emptiness or repugnancy of those expressions does appear, surely nothing more is requisite for their conviction. It is on this therefore that I insist, to wit, that the *absolute* existence of unthinking things are words without a meaning, or which include a contradiction. This is what I repeat and inculcate, and earnestly recommend to the attentive thoughts of the reader.

B

Now this is the peculiarity of scientific method, that when once it has become a habit of mind, that mind converts *all* facts whatsoever into science. The field of science is unlimited; its material is endless, every group of natural phenomena, every phase of social life, every stage of past or present development is material for science. *The unity of all science consists alone in its method, not in its material.* The man who classifies facts of any kind whatever, who sees their mutual relation and describes their sequences, is applying the scientific method and is a man of science. The facts may belong to the past history of mankind, to the social statistics of our great cities, to the atmosphere of the most distant stars, to the digestive organs of a worm, or to the life of a scarcely visible bacillus. It is not the facts themselves which form science, but the method in which they are dealt with. The material of science is coextensive with the whole physical universe, not only that universe as it now exists, but with its past history and the past history of all life therein. When every fact, every present or past phenomenon of that universe, every phase of present or past life therein, has been examined, classified, and coordinated with the rest, then the mission of science will be completed. What is this but saying that the task of science can never end till man ceases to be, till history is no longer made, and development itself ceases?

It might be supposed that science has made such strides in the last two centuries, and notably in the last fifty years, that we might look forward to a day when its work would be practically accomplished. At the beginning of this century it was possible for an Alexander von Humboldt to take a survey of the entire domain of then extant science. Such a survey would be impossible for any scientist now, even if gifted with more than Humboldt's powers. Scarcely any specialist of today is really master of all the work which has been done in his own comparatively small

Karl Pearson, *The Grammar of Science,* London, Walter Scott, Ltd., 1892; J. M. Dent & Sons, Ltd., London, and E. P. Dutton & Co., Inc., New York (Everyman's Library) 1937, chs. 1, 10 (in part).

field. Facts and their classification have been accumulating at such a rate, that nobody seems to have leisure to recognize the relations of sub-groups to the whole. It is as if individual workers in both Europe and America were bringing their stones to one great building and piling them on and cementing them together without regard to any general plan or to their individual neighbour's work; only where someone has placed a great cornerstone, is it regarded, and the building then rises on this firmer foundation more rapidly than at other points, till it reaches a height at which it is stopped for want of side support. Yet this great structure, the proportions of which are beyond the ken of any individual man, possesses a symmetry and unity of its own, notwithstanding its haphazard mode of construction. This symmetry and unity lie in scientific method. The smallest group of facts, if properly classified and logically dealt with, will form a stone which has its proper place in the great building of knowledge, wholly independent of the individual workman who has shaped it. Even when two men work unwittingly at the same stone they will but modify and correct each other's angles. In the face of all this enormous progress of modern science, when in all civilized lands men are applying the scientific method to natural, historical, and mental facts, we have yet to admit that the goal of science is and must be infinitely distant.

For we must note that when from a sufficient if partial classification of facts a simple principle has been discovered which describes the relationship and sequences of any group, then this principle or law itself generally leads to the discovery of a still wider range of hitherto unregarded phenomena in the same or associated fields. Every great advance of science opens our eyes to facts which we had failed before to observe, and makes new de-

mands on our powers of interpretation. This extension of the material of science into regions where our great-grandfathers could see nothing at all, or where they would have declared human knowledge impossible, is one of the most remarkable features of modern progress. Where they interpreted the motion of the planets of our own system, we discuss the chemical constitution of stars, many of which did not exist for them, for their telescopes could not reach them. Where they discovered the circulation of the blood, we see the physical conflict of living poisons within the blood, whose battles would have been absurdities for them. Where they found void and probably demonstrated to their own satisfaction that there was void, we conceive great systems in rapid motion capable of carrying energy through brick walls as light passes through glass. Great as the advance of scientific knowledge has been, it has not been greater than the growth of the material to be dealt with. The goal of science is clear — it is nothing short of the complete interpretation of the universe. But the goal is an ideal one — it marks the *direction* in which we move and strive, but never a stage we shall actually reach. The universe grows ever larger as we learn to understand more of our own corner of it.

Now I want to draw the reader's attention to two results which flow from the above considerations, namely: that the material of science is coextensive with the whole life, physical and mental, of the universe, and furthermore that the limits to our perception of the universe are only apparent, not real. It is no exaggeration to say that the universe was not the same for our great-grandfathers as it is for us, and that in all probability it will be utterly different for our great-grandchildren. The universe is a variable quantity, which depends upon the keenness and structure of our organs of sense, and upon the fineness of our powers and instruments of observation. We shall see more clearly the important bearing of this latter remark when we come to discuss more closely in another chapter how the universe is largely the construction of each individual mind. For the present we must briefly consider the former remark, which defines the unlimited scope of science. To say that there are certain fields — for example, *metaphysics* — from which science is excluded, wherein its methods have no application, is merely to say that the rules of methodical observation and the laws of logical thought do not apply to the facts, if any, which lie within such fields. These fields, if indeed such exist, must lie outside any intelligible definition which can be given of the word *knowledge*. If there are facts, and sequences to be observed among those facts, then we have all the requisites of scientific classification and knowledge. If there are no facts, or no sequences to be observed among them, then the possibility of *all* knowledge disappears. The greatest assumption of everyday life — the inference which the metaphysicians tell us is wholly beyond science — namely, that other beings have consciousness as well as ourselves, seems to have just as much or as little *scientific* validity as the statement that an earth-grown apple would fall to the ground if carried to the planet of another star. Both are beyond the range of experimental demonstration, but to assume uniformity in the characteristics of brain 'matter' under certain conditions seems as scientific as to assume uniformity in the characteristics of stellar 'matter.' Both are only working hypotheses and valuable in so far as they simplify our description of the universe. Yet the distinction between science and metaphysics is often insisted upon, and not unadvisedly, by the devotees of both. If we take any group of physical or biological facts —

say, for example, electrical phenomena or the development of the ovum — we shall find that, though physicists or biologists may differ to some extent in their measurements or in their hypotheses, yet in the fundamental principles and sequences the professors of each individual science are in practical agreement among themselves. A similar if not yet so complete agreement is rapidly springing up in both mental and social science, where the facts are more difficult to classify and the bias of individual opinion is much stronger. Our more thorough classification, however, of the facts of human development, our more accurate knowledge of the early history of human societies, of primitive customs, laws, and religions, our application of the principle of natural selection to man and his communities, are converting anthropology, folk-lore, sociology, and psychology into true sciences. We begin to see indisputable sequence in groups of both mental and social facts. The causes which favour the growth or decay of human societies become more obvious and more the subject of scientific investigation. Mental and social facts are thus not beyond the range of scientific treatment, but their classification has not been so complete, nor for obvious reasons so unprejudiced, as those of physical or biological phenomena.

The case is quite different with metaphysics and those other supposed branches of human knowledge which claim exemption from scientific control. Either they are based on an accurate classification of facts, or they are not. But if their classification of facts were accurate, the application of the scientific method ought to lead their professors to a practically identical system. Now one of the idiosyncrasies of metaphysicians lies in this: that each metaphysician has his own system, which to a large extent excludes that of his predecessors and colleagues. Hence we must conclude that metaphysics are built either on air or on quicksands — either they start from no foundation in facts at all, or the super-structure has been raised before a basis has been found in the accurate classification of facts. I want to lay special stress on this point. There is no short cut to truth, no way to gain a knowledge of the universe except through the gateway of scientific method. The hard and stony path of classifying facts and reasoning upon them is the only way to ascertain truth. It is the reason and not the imagination which must ultimately be appealed to. The poet may give us in sublime language an account of the origin and purport of the universe, but in the end it will not satisfy our aesthetic judgment, our idea of harmony and beauty, like the few facts which the scientist may venture to tell us in the same field. The one will agree with all our experiences past and present, the other is sure, sooner or later, to contradict our observation because it propounds a dogma, where we are yet far from knowing the whole truth. Our aesthetic judgment demands harmony between the representation and the represented, and in this sense science is often more artistic than modern art.

The poet is a valued member of the community, for he is known to be a poet; his value will increase as he grows to recognize the deeper insight into nature with which modern science provides him. The metaphysician is a poet, often a very great one, but unfortunately he is not known to be a poet, because he strives to clothe his poetry in the language of reason, and hence it follows that he is liable to be a dangerous member of the community. The danger at the present time that metaphysical dogmas may check scientific research is, perhaps, not very great. The day has gone by when the Hegelian philosophy threatened to strangle infant science in Germany; — that it begins to languish at Oxford is a proof that it is practically dead in the country of its birth. The day has gone by when philosophical or theological dogmas of any kind can throw back for generations the progress of scientific investigation. There is no restriction now on research in any field, or on the publication of the truth when it has been reached. But there is nevertheless a danger which we cannot afford to disregard, a danger which retards the spread of scientific knowledge among the unenlightened, and which flatters obscurantism by discrediting the scientific method. There is a certain school of thought which finds the laborious process by which science reaches truth too irksome; the temperament of this school is such that it demands a short and easy cut to knowledge, where knowledge can only be gained, if at all, by the long and patient toiling of many groups of workers, perhaps through several centuries. There are various fields at the present day wherein mankind is ignorant, and the honest course for us is simply to confess our ignorance. This ignorance may arise from the want of any proper classification of facts, or because supposed facts are themselves inconsistent, unreal creations of untrained minds. But because this ignorance is frankly admitted by science, an attempt is made to fence off these fields as ground which science cannot profitably till, to shut them up as a preserve whereon science has no business to trespass. Wherever science has succeeded in ascertaining the truth, there, according to the school we have referred to, are the 'legitimate problems of science.' Wherever science is yet ignorant, there, we are told, its method is inapplicable; there some other relation than cause and effect (than the same sequence recurring with the like grouping of phenomena), some new but undefined relationship rules. In these fields, we are told, problems become philosophical and can only be treated by the method of philosophy. The philosophical method is opposed to the scientific method; and here, I think, the danger I have referred to arises. We have defined the scientific method to consist in the orderly classification of facts followed by the recognition of their relationship and recurring sequences. The scientific judgment is the judgment based upon this recognition and free from personal bias. If this were the philosophical method there would be no need of further discussion, but as we are told the subject-matter of philosophy is not the 'legitimate problem of science,' the two methods are presumably not identical. Indeed the philosophical method seems based upon an analysis which does not start with the classification of facts, but reaches its judgments by some obscure process of internal cogitation. It is therefore dangerously liable to the influence of individual bias; it results, as experience shows us, in an endless number of competing and contradictory systems. It is because the so-called philosophical method does not, when different individuals approach the same range of facts, lead, like the scientific, to practical unanimity of judgment, that science, rather than philosophy, offers the better training for modern citizenship.

It must not be supposed that science for a moment denies the existence of some of the problems which have hitherto been classed as philosophical or metaphysical. On the contrary, it recognizes that a great variety of physical and biological phenomena lead directly to these problems. But it asserts that the methods hitherto applied to these problems have been futile, because they have been unscientific. The classifications of facts hitherto made by the system-mongers have been hopelessly inadequate or hopelessly prejudiced. Until the scientific study of psychology, both by observation and experiment, has advanced immensely beyond its present limits

— and this may take generations of work — science can only answer to the great majority of 'metaphysical' problems, 'I am ignorant.' Meanwhile it is idle to be impatient or to indulge in system-making. The cautious and laborious classification of facts must have proceeded much further than at present before the time will be ripe for drawing conclusions.

Science stands now with regard to the problems of life and mind in much the same position as it stood with regard to cosmical problems in the seventeenth century. Then the system-mongers were the theologians, who declared that cosmical problems were not the 'legitimate problems of science.' It was vain for Galilei to assert that the theologians' classification of facts was hopelessly inadequate. In solemn congregation assembled they settled that:

'The doctrine that the earth is neither the centre of the universe nor immovable, but moves even with a daily rotation, is absurd, and both philosophically and theologically false, and at the least an error of faith.'

It took nearly two hundred years to convince the whole theological world that cosmical problems were the legitimate problems of science and science alone, for in 1819 the books of Galilei, Copernicus, and Kepler were still upon the index of forbidden books, and not until 1822 was a decree issued allowing books teaching the motion of the earth about the sun to be printed and published in Rome!

I have cited this memorable example of the absurdity which arises from trying to pen science into a limited field of thought, because it seems to me exceedingly suggestive of what must follow again, if any attempt, philosophical or theological, be made to define the 'legitimate problems of science.' Wherever there is the slightest possibility for the human mind to *know,* there is a legitimate problem of science. Outside the field of actual knowledge can only lie a region of the vaguest opinion and imagination, to which unfortunately men too often, but still with decreasing prevalence, pay higher respect than to knowledge.

We must here investigate a little more closely what the man of science means when he says: 'Here I am ignorant.' In the first place, he does not mean that the method of science is necessarily inapplicable, and accordingly that some other method is to be sought for. In the next place, if the ignorance really arises from the inadequacy of the scientific method, then we may be quite sure that no other method whatsoever will reach the truth. The ignorance of science means the enforced ignorance of mankind. I should be sorry myself to assert that there is any field of either mental or physical perceptions which science may not in the long course of centuries enlighten. Who can give us the assurance that the fields already occupied by science are alone those in which knowledge is possible? Who, in the words of Galilei, is willing to set limits to the human intellect? It is true that this view is not held by several leading scientists, both in this country and Germany. They are not content with saying: 'We *are* ignorant,' but they add, with regard to certain classes of facts: 'Mankind must *always* be ignorant.' Thus in England Professor Huxley has invented the term *Agnostic,* not so much for those who are ignorant as for those who limit the possibility of knowledge in certain fields. In Germany Professor E. du Bois-Reymond has raised the cry: '*Ignorabimus*' ('We shall be ignorant'), and both his brother and he have undertaken the difficult task of demonstrating that with regard to certain problems human knowledge is impossible. We must, however, note that in these cases we are not concerned with the limitation of the scientific method, but with the denial of the

possibility that any method whatever can lead to knowledge. Now I venture to think that there is great danger in this cry: 'We *shall* be ignorant.' To cry 'We are ignorant' is safe and healthy, but the attempt to demonstrate an endless futurity of ignorance appears a modesty which approaches despair. Conscious of the past great achievements and the present restless activity of science, may we not do better to accept as our watchword that sentence of Galilei: 'Who is willing to set limits to the human intellect?' — interpreting it by what evolution has taught us of the continual growth of man's intellectual powers.

Scientific ignorance may, as I have remarked, either arise from an insufficient classification of facts, or be due to the unreality of the facts with which science has been called upon to deal. Let us take, for example, fields of thought which were very prominent in medieval times, such as alchemy, astrology, witchcraft. In the fifteenth century nobody doubted the 'facts' of astrology and witchcraft. Men were ignorant as to how the stars exerted their influence for good or ill; they did not know the exact mechanical process by which all the milk in the village was turned blue by a witch. But for them it was nevertheless a fact that the stars did influence human lives, and a fact that the witch had the power of turning the milk blue. Have we solved the problems of astrology and witchcraft to-day?

Do we now know how the stars influence human lives, or how witches turn milk blue? Not in the least. We have learnt to look upon the facts themselves as unreal, as vain imaginings of the untrained human mind; we have learnt that they could not be described scientifically because they involved notions which were in themselves contradictory and absurd. With alchemy the case was somewhat different. Here a false classification of real facts was combined with inconsistent sequences — that is, sequences not deduced by a rational method. So soon as science entered the field of alchemy with a true classification and a true method, alchemy was converted into chemistry and became an important branch of human knowledge. Now it will, I think, be found that the fields of inquiry, where science has not yet penetrated and where the scientist still confesses ignorance, are very like the alchemy, astrology, and witchcraft of the Middle Ages. Either they involve facts which are in themselves unreal — conceptions which are self-contradictory and absurd, and therefore incapable of analysis by the scientific or any other method — or, on the other hand, our ignorance arises from an inadequate classification and a neglect of scientific method.

This is the actual state of the case with those mental and spiritual phenomena which are said to lie outside the proper scope of science, or which appear to be disregarded by scientific men. No better example can be taken than the range of phenomena which are entitled Spiritualism. Here science is asked to analyse a series of facts which are to a great extent unreal, which arise from the vain imaginings of untrained minds and from atavistic tendencies to superstition. So far as the facts are of this character, no account can be given of them, because, like the witch's supernatural capacity, their unreality will be found at bottom to make them self-contradictory. Combined, however, with the unreal series of facts are probably others, connected with hypnotic and other conditions, which are real and only incomprehensible because there is as yet scarcely any intelligent classification or true application of scientific method. The former class of facts will, like astrology, never be reduced to law, but will one day be recognized as absurd; the other, like alchemy, may grow step by step into an important branch of science. Whenever, therefore, we are tempted to desert the scientific method of seeking truth, whenever the silence of science suggests that some other gateway must be sought to knowledge, let us inquire first whether the elements of the problem, of whose solution we are ignorant, may not after all, like the facts of witchcraft, arise from a superstition, and be self-contradictory and incomprehensible because they are unreal.

If on inquiry we ascertain that the facts cannot possibly be of this class, we must then remember that it may require long ages of increasing toil and investigation before the classification of the facts can be so complete that science can express a definite judgment on their relationship. Let us suppose that the Emperor Karl V had said to the learned of his day: 'I want a method by which I can send a message in a few seconds to that new world, which my mariners take weeks in reaching. Put your heads together and solve the problem.' Would they not undoubtedly have replied that the problem was impossible? To propose it would have seemed as ridiculous to them as the suggestion that science should straightway solve many problems of life and mind seems to the learned of to-day. It required centuries spent in the discovery and classification of new facts before the Atlantic cable became a possibility. It may require the like or even a longer time to unriddle those psychical and biological enigmas to which I have referred; but he who declares that they can never be solved by the scientific method is to my mind as rash as the man of the early sixteenth century would have been had he declared it utterly impossible that the problem of talking across the Atlantic Ocean should ever be solved.

If I have put the case of science at all correctly, the reader will have recognized that modern science does much more than demand that it shall be left in undisturbed possession of what the theologian and metaphysician please to term its 'legitimate field.' It claims that the whole range of phenomena, mental as well as physical — the entire universe — is its field. It asserts that the scientific method is the sole gateway to the whole region of knowledge. The word science is here used in no narrow sense, but applies to all reasoning about facts which proceeds, from their accurate classification, to the appreciation of their relationship and sequence. The touchstone of science is the universal validity of its results for all normally constituted and duly instructed minds. Because the glitter of the great metaphysical systems becomes dross when tried by this touchstone, we are compelled to classify them as interesting works of the imagination, and not as solid contributions to human knowledge.

Although science claims the whole universe as its field, it must not be supposed that it has reached, or ever can reach, complete knowledge in every department. Far from this, it confesses that its ignorance is more widely extended than its knowledge. In this very confession of ignorance, however, it finds a safeguard for future progress. Science cannot give its consent to man's development being some day again checked by the barriers which dogma and myth are ever erecting round territory that science has not yet effectually occupied. It cannot allow theologian or metaphysician, those Portuguese of the intellect, to establish a right to the foreshore of our present ignorance, and so hinder the settlement in due time of vast and yet unknown continents of thought. In the like barriers erected in the past science finds some of the greatest difficulties in the way of intellectual progress and social advance at the present. It is the want of impersonal judg-

ment, of scientific method, and of accurate insight into facts, a want largely due to a non-scientific training, which renders clear thinking so rare, and random and irresponsible judgments so common, in the mass of our citizens to-day. Yet these citizens, owing to the growth of democracy, have graver problems to settle than probably any which have confronted their forefathers since the days of the Revolution. . . .

Our grandfathers stood puzzled before problems like the physical evolution of the earth, the origin of species, and the descent of man; they were, perforce, content to cloak their ignorance with time-honoured superstition and myth. To our fathers belongs not only the honour of solving these problems, but the credit of having borne the brunt of that long and weary battle by which science freed itself from the tyranny of tradition. Their task was the difficult one of daring to know. We, entering upon their heritage, no longer fear tradition, no longer find that to know requires courage. We, too, however, stand as our fathers did before problems which seem to us insoluble — problems, for example, like the genesis of living from lifeless forms, where science has as yet no certain descriptive formula, and perhaps no hope in the immediate future of finding one. Here we have a duty before us, which, if we have faith in the scientific method, is simple and obvious. We must turn a deaf ear to all those who would suggest that we can enter the stronghold of truth by the burrow of superstition, or scale its walls by the ladder of metaphysics. We must accomplish a task more difficult to many minds than daring to know. We must dare to be ignorant. *Ignoramus, laborandum est.*

SUGGESTIONS FOR THOUGHT

1. When looking down a railroad track, does one see the rails as they are or does he see them as they appear to him? Do we ever see reality as it is? Which is the real table, the one we see or the one described by nuclear physics? What is the world that science examines — the world of sense-data or an independently existing world?

2. Julian Huxley has described science as systematic common-sense. Nicholas Murray Butler says: "Science is a wholly different kind of knowledge from common-sense, and it contradicts common-sense at almost every point." What is common-sense anyway?

3. What do we mean when we say that something is scientifically true?

4. Why has science been so well accepted in the twentieth century? What is gained if psychology, history, economics, art criticism, etc., are established as sciences? What is the difference between a science and an art?

5. Is the distinction between pure science and practical science a valid one?

6. What motivates the scientist — the desire to know, to control, to serve, to win esteem, to make money, or what? What, for example, motivated Francis Bacon, Galileo, Darwin, Willard Gibbs, Thomas Edison, and George Washington Carver?

7. What would you say to a person who observes that science is precise because scientists will not bother themselves with anything that does not lend itself to exact measurement?

8. James H. Leuba once made a study of American scientists' belief in God and personal immortality. Among the answers to his very simple questions were these two: (1) "I cannot answer these questions. I do not know what they mean. I have no interest in them, and can hardly conceive of any one wishing to know." and (2) "How is it possible for a sane student to answer these questions? They do not deal with phenomena or material which we can investigate. I believe in everything that is." How might the scientific attitude of these two men be described?

9. Is it a serious limitation of science to point out that it cannot deal with ultimate reality but only with nature as known by the human mind?

10. What dangers are there in developing a method in advance of problems? Does it tend to make the student aware of only those phases of a problem for which he has a method of study? In what ways has modern scientific methodology become a metaphysic?

11. Why are some of our modern scientists so insistent on the limitations of science? Is this a reaction against the overconfidence of scientists of the latter part of the nineteenth century? E.g., C. S. Peirce said in 1878 that the time would come when all questions would be answered.

12. Why do philosophers generally have more difficulty than scientists in being objective toward their subject matter? Why is the history of philosophy more important than the history of science? Does philosophy make no progress? Are there any dangers in neglecting the historical aspects of science?

13. Exactly what do we mean when we accuse some one of being unscientific? What would a human society be like that was thoroughly scientific?

14. How does a philosopher compare with an artist and a scientist? N. Lossky says: "Philosophers stand midway between art and science in their view of the world; like artists, they are generally capable of seeing the wholeness of things, but like scientists they are concerned to express their discoveries in exact terms."

15. Albert Einstein is reported to have said: "No amount of experimentation can ever prove me right; a single experiment may at any time prove me wrong." What does this reveal to us

about the nature of the knowledge Einstein has formulated?

16. What evidence is there that man's sense organs do not give the whole of reality? When we say that we are seeing a star, what is it that we actually see?

17. A college education reminds us constantly of how little we know and of the tentative nature of the knowledge we have. What value is there in forcing us to recognize our intellectual poverty? Are there dangers in emphasizing our intellectual poverty?

SUGGESTIONS FOR FURTHER READING

BENJAMIN, A. CORNELIUS, "The Problem of Knowledge," *The Journal of Philosophy,* Vol. 27, 1930, pp. 381–390.

BROAD, C. D., *Scientific Thought,* New York, Harcourt, Brace and Company, 1927, Introduction.

CONANT, JAMES B., *On Understanding Science,* New Haven, Yale University Press, 1947, ch. 1.

EDDINGTON, A. S., *New Pathways of Science,* New York, The Macmillan Company, 1935, ch. 1.

GEORGE, WILLIAM H., *The Scientist in Action,* London, Williams and Norgate, 1936.

JEFFREYS, HAROLD, "Scientific Method, Causality, and Reality," *Proceedings of the Aristotelian Society,* Vol. 37, 1937, pp. 61–70.

LARRABEE, HAROLD A., *Reliable Knowledge,* Boston, Houghton Mifflin Company, 1945, ch. 13.

MURPHY, ARTHUR E., *The Uses of Reason,* New York, The Macmillan Company, 1943, Part IV, ch. 2.

RAMSPERGER, ALBERT G., *Philosophies of Science,* New York, F. S. Crofts and Company, 1942, ch. 10.

RUSSELL, BERTRAND, *Our Knowledge of the External World,* New York, W. W. Norton and Company, 1929, ch. 3.

RUSSELL, L. J., "Science and Philosophy," *Proceedings of the Aristotelian Society,* Vol. 24, 1924, pp. 61–76.

THOMSON, J. ARTHUR, *Introduction to Science,* New York, Henry Holt and Company, 1911, chs. 1–5.

WILL, FREDERICK L., "Is There a Problem of Induction?" *The Journal of Philosophy,* Vol. 39, 1942, pp. 505–513.

WOODBRIDGE, FREDERICK J. E., *An Essay on Nature,* New York, Columbia University Press, 1940, ch. 1.

8

THE ORIGIN OF
THE COSMOS

THE DAWN OF CREATION may be a theme more suitable for poets and artists than for scientists, but it is doubtful that any answer, poetic or scientific, will ever have universal human acceptance. St. Augustine and Herbert Spencer represent the two most divergent positions concerning the origin of the cosmos: creationism and agnosticism. St. Augustine (354–430), Bishop of Hippo in proconsular Africa, wrote his most famous book, *The City of God* (426), to reassure Christians that the fall of the Roman Empire would not end the Christian Church. Herbert Spencer (1820–1903) was a self-taught English philosopher. Before devoting himself to the writing of his many books, in which he developed his evolutionary principles, he was an engineer on the London and Birmingham Railway (1837–1846) and a sub-editor of the *Economist* (1848–1853).

A

Of all the visible things, the world is the greatest; of all invisible, the greatest is God. But, that the world is, we see; that God is, we believe. That God made the world, we can believe from no one more safely than from God Himself. But where have we heard

Augustine, *The City of God*, Book XI, chs. 4–6, translated by Marcus Dods, *A Select Library of the Nicene and Post-Nicene Fathers of the Christian Church*, Vol. 2, edited by Philip Schaff, Buffalo, The Christian Literature Society, 1887, pp. 206–208.

Him? Nowhere more distinctly than in the Holy Scriptures, where His prophet said, "In the beginning God created the heavens and the earth." Was the prophet present when God made the heavens and the earth? No; but the wisdom of God, by whom all things were made, was there, and wisdom insinuates itself into holy souls, and makes them the friends of God and His prophets, and noiselessly informs them of His works. They are taught also by the angels of God, who always behold the face of the Father, and announce His will to whom it befits. Of these prophets was he who said and wrote, "In the beginning God created the heavens and the earth." And so fit a witness was he of God, that the same Spirit of God, who revealed these things to him, enabled him also so long before to predict that our faith also would be forthcoming.

But why did God choose then to create the heavens and earth which up to that time He had not made? If they who put this question wish to make out that the world is eternal and without beginning, and that consequently it has not been made by God, they are strangely deceived, and rave in the incurable madness of impiety. For, though the voices of the prophets are silent, the world itself, by its well-ordered changes and movements, and by the fair appearance of all visible things, bears a testimony of its own, both that it has been created, and also that it could not have been created save by God, whose greatness and beauty are unutterable and invisible. As for those who own, indeed, that it was made by God, and yet ascribe to it not a temporal but only a creational beginning, so that in some scarcely intelligible way the world should always have existed a created world they make an assertion which seems to them to defend God from the charge of arbitrary hastiness, or of suddenly conceiving the idea of creating the world as a quite new idea, or of casually changing His will, though He be unchangeable. But I do not see how this supposition of theirs can stand in other respects, and chiefly in respect of the soul; for if they contend that it is co-eternal with God, they will be quite at a loss to explain whence there has accrued to it new misery, which through a previous eternity had not existed. For if they said that its happiness and misery ceaselessly alternate, they

must say, further, that this alternation will continue for ever; whence will result this absurdity, that, though the soul is called blessed, it is not so in this, that it foresees its own misery and disgrace. And yet, if it does not foresee it, and supposes that it will be neither disgraced nor wretched, but always blessed, then it is blessed because it is deceived; and a more foolish statement one cannot make. But if their idea is that the soul's misery has alternated with its bliss during the ages of the past eternity, but that now, when once the soul has been set free, it will return henceforth no more to misery, they are nevertheless of opinion that it has never been truly blessed before, but begins at last to enjoy a new and uncertain happiness; that is to say, they must acknowledge that some new thing, and that an important and signal thing, happens to the soul which never in a whole past eternity happened it before. And if they deny that God's eternal purpose included this new experience of the soul, they deny that He is the Author of its blessedness, which is unspeakable impiety. If, on the other hand, they say that the future blessedness of the soul is the result of a new decree of God, how will they show that God is not changeable with that mutability which displeases them? Further, if they acknowledge that it was created in time, but will never perish in time, — that it has, like number, a beginning but no end, — and that, therefore, having once made trial of misery, and been delivered from it, it will never again return thereto, they will certainly admit that this takes place without any violation of the immutable counsel of God. Let them, then, in like manner believe regarding the world that it too could be made in time, and yet that God, in making it, did not alter His eternal design.

Next, we must see what reply can be made

to those who agree that God is the Creator of the world, but have difficulties about the time of its creation, and what reply, also, they can make to difficulties we might raise about the place of its creation. For, as they demand why the world was created then and no sooner, we may ask why it was created just here where it is, and not elsewhere. For if they imagine infinite spaces of time before the world, during which God could not have been idle, in like manner they may conceive outside the world infinite realms of space, in which, if any one says that the Omnipotent cannot hold His hand from working, will it not follow that they must adopt Epicurus' dream of innumerable worlds? with this difference only, that he asserts that they are formed and destroyed by the fortuitous movements of atoms, while they will hold that they are made of God's hand, if they maintain that, throughout the boundless immensity of space, stretching interminably in every direction round the world, God cannot rest, and that the worlds which they suppose Him to make cannot be destroyed. For here the question is with those who, with ourselves, believe that God is spiritual, and the Creator of all existences but Himself. As for others, it is a condescension to dispute with them on a religious question, for they have acquired a reputation only among men who pay divine honors to a number of gods, and have been conspicuous among the other philosophers for no other reason than that, though they are still far from the truth, they are near it in comparison with the rest. While these, then, neither confine in any place, nor limit, nor distribute the divine substance, but, as is worthy of God, own it to be wholly though spiritually present everywhere, will they perchance say that this substance is absent from such immense spaces outside the world, and is occupied in one only, (and that a very little

one compared with the infinity beyond), the one, namely, in which is the world? I think they will not proceed to this absurdity. Since they maintain that there is but one world, of vast material bulk, indeed, yet finite, and in its own determinate position, and that this was made by the working of God, let them give the same account of God's resting in the infinite times before the world as they give of His resting in the infinite spaces outside of it. And as it does not follow that God set the world in the very spot it occupies and no other by accident rather than by divine reason, although no human reason can comprehend why it was so set, and though there was no merit in the spot chosen to give it the precedence of infinite others, so neither does it follow that we should suppose that God was guided by chance when He created the world in that and no earlier time, although previous times had been running by during an infinite past, and though there was no difference by which one time could be chosen in preference to another. But if they say that the thoughts of men are idle when they conceive infinite places, since there is no place beside the world, we reply that, by the same showing, it is vain to conceive of the past times of God's rest, since there is no time before the world.

For if eternity and time are rightly distinguished by this, that time does not exist without some movement and transition, while in eternity there is no change, who does not see that there could have been no time had not some creature been made, which by some motion could give birth to change, — the various parts of which motion and change, as they cannot be simultaneous, succeed one another, — and thus, in these shorter or longer intervals of duration, time would begin? Since then, God, in whose eternity is no change at all, is the Creator and Ordainer of time, I do not see how He can be said to have created the world after spaces of time had elapsed, unless it be said that prior to the world there was some creature by whose movement time could pass. And if the sacred and infallible Scriptures say that in the beginning God created the heavens and the earth, in order that it may be understood that He had made nothing previously, — for if He had made anything before the rest, this thing would rather be said to have been made "in the beginning," — then assuredly the world was made, not in time, but simultaneously with time. For that which is made in time is made both after and before some time, — after that which is past, before that which is future. But none could then be past, for there was no creature by whose movements its duration could be measured. But simultaneously with time the world was made, if in the world's creation change and motion were created, as seems evident from the order of the first six or seven days. For in these days the morning and evening are counted, until, on the sixth day, all things which God then made were finished, and on the seventh the rest of God was mysteriously and sublimely signalized. What kind of days these were it is extremely difficult, or perhaps impossible for us to conceive, and how much more to say!

B

Respecting the origin of the Universe three verbally intelligible suppositions may be made. We may assert that it is self-existent; or that it is self-created; or that it is created by an external agency. Which of these suppositions is most credible it is not needful here to inquire. The deeper question, into which this finally merges, is, whether any one of them is even conceivable in the true sense of the word. Let us successively test them.

When we speak of a man as self-supporting, of an apparatus as self-acting, or of a tree as self-developed, our expressions, however inexact, stand for things that can be realized in thought with tolerable completeness. Our conception of the self-development of a tree is doubtless symbolic. But though we cannot really represent in consciousness the entire series of complex changes through which the tree passes, yet we can thus represent the leading features of the series; and general experience teaches us that by long continued observation we could gain the power to realize in thought a series of changes more fully representing the actual series: that is, we know that our symbolic conception of self-development can be expanded into something like a real conception; and that it expresses, however inaccurately, an actual process in nature. But when we speak of self-existence, and, helped by the above analogies, form some vague symbolic conception of it, we delude ourselves in supposing that this symbolic conception is of the same order as the others. On joining the word *self* to the word *existence,* the force of association makes us believe we have a thought like that suggested by the compound word self-acting. An endeavour to expand this symbolic conception, however, will undeceive us. In the

Herbert Spencer, *First Principles of a New System of Philosophy,* New York and London, D. Appleton and Company, 1896, Part I, Section 11.

first place, it is clear that by self-existence we especially mean, an existence independent of any other — not produced by any other: the assertion of self-existence is simply an indirect denial of creation. In thus excluding the idea of any antecedent cause, we necessarily exclude the idea of a beginning; for to admit the idea of a beginning — to admit that there was a time when the existence had not commenced — is to admit that its commencement was determined by something, or was caused; which is contradiction. Self-existence, therefore, necessarily means existence without a beginning; and to form a conception of self-existence is to form a conception of existence without a beginning. Now by no mental effort can we do this. To conceive existence through infinite past-time, implies the conception of infinite past-time, which is an impossibility. To this let us add, that even were self-existence conceivable, it would not in any sense be an explanation of the Universe. No one will say that the existence of an object at the present moment is made easier to understand by the discovery that it existed an hour ago, or a day ago, or a year ago; and if its existence now is not made in the least degree more comprehensible by its existence during some previous finite period of time, then no accumulation of such finite periods, even could we extend them to an infinite period, would make it more comprehensible. Thus the Atheistic theory is not only absolutely unthinkable, but, even if it were thinkable, would not be a solution. The assertion that the Universe is self-existent does not really carry us a step beyond the cognition of its present existence; and so leaves us with a mere re-statement of the mystery.

The hypothesis of self-creation, which practically amounts to what is called Pantheism, is similarly incapable of being represented in thought. Certain phenomena, such as the precipitation of invisible vapour into cloud, aid us in forming a symbolic conception of a self-evolved Universe; and there are not wanting indications in the heavens, and on the earth, which help us to render this conception tolerably definite. But while the succession of phases through which the Universe has passed in reaching its present form, may perhaps be comprehended as in a sense self-determined; yet the impossibility of expanding our symbolic conception of self-creation into a real conception, remains as complete as ever. Really to conceive self-creation, is to conceive potential existence passing into actual existence by some inherent necessity; which we cannot do. We cannot form any idea of a potential existence of the universe, as distinguished from its actual existence. If represented in thought at all, potential existence must be represented as something, that is as an actual existence; to suppose that it can be represented as nothing, involves two absurdities — that nothing is more than a negation, and can be positively represented in thought; and that one nothing is distinguished from all other nothings by its power to develope into something. Nor is this all. We have no state of consciousness answering to the words — an inherent necessity by which potential existence became actual existence. To render them into thought, existence, having for an indefinite period remained in one form, must be conceived as passing without any external or additional impulse, into another form; and this involves the idea of a change without a cause — a thing of which no idea is possible. Thus the terms of this hypothesis do not stand for real thoughts; but merely suggest the vaguest symbols incapable of any interpretation. Moreover, even were it true that potential existence is conceivable as a different thing from actual existence; and that the transition from the one to the other can be mentally realized as a self-determined change; we should still be no forwarder: the problem would simply be removed a step back. For whence the potential existence? This would just as much require accounting for as actual existence; and just the same difficulties would meet us. Respecting the origin of such a latent power, no other suppositions could be made than those above named — self-existence, self-creation, creation by external agency. The self-existence of a potential universe is no more conceivable than we have found the self-existence of the actual universe to be. The self-creation of such a potential universe would involve over again the difficulties here stated — would imply behind this potential universe a more remote potentiality; and so on in an infinite series, leaving us at last no forwarder than at first. While to assign as the source of this potential universe an external agency, would be to introduce the notion of a potential universe for no purpose whatever.

There remains to be examined the commonly-received or theistic hypothesis — creation by external agency. Alike in the rudest creeds and in the cosmogony long current among ourselves, it is assumed that the genesis of the Heavens and the Earth is affected somewhat after the manner in which a workman shapes a piece of furniture. And this assumption is made not by theologians only, but by the immense majority of philosophers, past and present. Equally in the writings of Plato, and in those of not a few living men of science, we find it taken for granted that there is an analogy between the process of creation and the process of manufacture. Now in the first place, not only is this conception one that cannot by any cumulative process of thought, or the fulfilment of predictions based on it, be shown to answer to anything

actual; and not only is it that in the absence of all evidence respecting the process of creation, we have no proof of correspondence even between this limited conception and some limited portion of the fact; but it is that the conception is not even consistent with itself — cannot be realized in thought, when all its assumptions are granted. Though it is true that the proceedings of a human artificer may vaguely symbolize to us a method after which the Universe might be shaped, yet they do not help us to comprehend the real mystery; namely, the origin of the material of which the Universe consists. The artizan does not make the iron, wood, or stone he uses; but merely fashions and combines them. If we suppose suns, and planets, and satellites, and all they contain to have been similarly formed by a "Great Artificer," we suppose merely that certain pre-existing elements were thus put into their present arrangement. But whence the pre-existing elements? The comparison helps us not in the least to understand that; and unless it helps us to understand that, it is worthless. The production of matter out of nothing is the real mystery, which neither this simile nor any other enables us to conceive; and a simile which does not enable us to conceive this, may just as well be dispensed with. Still more manifest does the insufficiency of this theory of creation become, when we turn from material objects to that which contains them — when instead of matter we contemplate space. Did there exist nothing but an immeasurable void, explanation would be needed as much as now. There would still arise the question — how came it so? If the theory of creation by external agency were an adequate one, it would supply an answer; and its answer would be — space was made in the same manner that matter was made. But the impossibility of conceiving this is so manifest, that no one dares to assert it. For if space was created, it must have been previously non-existent. The non-existence of space cannot, however, by any mental effort be imagined. It is one of the most familiar truths that the idea of space as surrounding us on all sides, is not for a moment to be got rid of — not only are we compelled to think of space as now everywhere present, but we are unable to conceive its absence either in the past or the future. And if the non-existence of space is absolutely inconceivable, then, necessarily, its creation is absolutely inconceivable. Lastly, even supposing that the genesis of the Universe could really be represented in thought as the result of an external agency, the mystery would be as great as ever; for there would still arise the question — how came there to be an external agency? To account for this only the same three hypotheses are possible — self-existence, self-creation, and creation by external agency. Of these the last is useless: it commits us to an infinite series of such agencies, and even then leaves us where we were. By the second we are practically involved in the same predicament; since, as already shown, self-creation implies an infinite series of potential existences. We are obliged therefore to fall back upon the first, which is the one commonly accepted and commonly supposed to be satisfactory. Those who cannot conceive a self-existent universe; and who therefore assume a creator as the source of the universe; take for granted that they can conceive a self-existent creator. The mystery which they recognize in this great fact surrounding them on every side, they transfer to an alleged source of this great fact; and then suppose that they have solved the mystery. But they delude themselves. As was proved at the outset of the argument, self-existence is rigorously inconceivable; and this holds true whatever be the nature of the object of which it is predicated. Whoever agrees that the atheistic hypothesis is untenable be-

cause it involves the impossible idea of self-existence, must perforce admit that the theistic hypothesis is untenable if it contains the same impossible idea.

Thus these three different suppositions respecting the origin of things, verbally intelligible though they are, and severally seeming to their respective adherents quite rational, turn out, when critically examined, to be literally unthinkable. It is not a question of probability, or credibility, but of conceivability. Experiment proves that the elements of these hypotheses cannot even be put together in consciousness; and we can entertain them only as we entertain such pseud-ideas as a square fluid and a moral substance — only by abstaining from the endeavour to render them into actual thoughts. Or, reverting to our original mode of statement, we may say that they severally involve symbolic conceptions of the illegitimate and illusive kind. Differing so widely as they seem to do, the atheistic, the pantheistic, and the theistic hypothesis contain the same ultimate element. It is impossible to avoid making the assumption of self-existence somewhere; and whether that assumption be made nakedly, or under complicated disguises, it is equally vicious, equally unthinkable. Be it a fragment of matter, or some fancied potential form of matter, or some more remote and still less imaginable cause, our conception of its self-existence can be formed only by joining with it the notion of unlimited duration through past time. And as unlimited duration is inconceivable, all those formal ideas into which it enters are inconceivable; and indeed, if such an expression is allowable, are the more inconceivable in proportion as the other elements of the ideas are indefinite. So that in fact, impossible as it is to think of the actual universe as self-existing, we do but multiply impossibilities of thought by every attempt we make to explain its existence.

SUGGESTIONS FOR THOUGHT

1. What does it mean to create something? Does creation mean to fashion something out of nothing, i.e., *creatio ex nihilo?*

2. What are the possible meanings of a first cause? How has the theory of evolution modified our conception of first cause?

3. How have you been able to reconcile the Hebrew story of creation and the hypotheses of science about the origin of the world? How does the Hebrew story of creation compare with similar stories developed in other cultures?

4. Why are scientists not greatly concerned about origins, and particularly about the origin of the universe? Is it the inability of the scientific method to deal with origins that causes them to say that they are not interested in them?

5. If man is not able to arrive at a first cause of the universe, why does he not give up the search for first causes?

6. Stories of the creation of the world are said to be the effort of man to explain the world to himself. Just how does such a story explain the world? Do the sciences now satisfactorily explain the world to man?

SUGGESTIONS FOR FURTHER READING

ALLEN, JOHN STUART, and others, *Atoms, Rocks and Galaxies,* New York, Harper and Brothers, 1938, ch. 2.

AQUINAS, THOMAS, *Summa Theologica,* Questions 44–49, 65–74.

BOODIN, J. E., "Cosmic Evolution," *Proceedings of the Aristotelian Society,* Vol. 21, 1921, pp. 91–121.

CHAMBERLIN, THOMAS CHROWDER, *The Origin of the Earth,* Chicago, University of Chicago Press, 1916.

FARRELL, B. A., "In the Beginning . . . ," *Philosophy,* Vol. 15, 1940, pp. 285–300.

GAMOW, GEORGE, *Biography of the Earth,* New York, Viking Press, 1948, ch. 2.

HOYLE, FRED, *The Nature of the Universe,* New York, Harper and Brothers, 1951.

JEANS, JAMES, *The Universe Around Us,* New York, The Macmillan Company, 1929, chs. 4, 6.

LEMAITRE, GEORGES, *The Primeval Atom,* translated by Betty H. Korff and Serge A. Korff, New York, D. Van Nostrand Company, 1950.

MOULTON, FOREST RAY, *Astronomy,* New York, The Macmillan Company, 1938, ch. 14.

RUSSELL, HENRY NORRIS, *The Solar System and Its Origin,* New York, The Macmillan Company, 1935, ch. 3.

SHAPLEY, HARLOW, *Flights From Chaos,* New York, McGraw-Hill Book Company, 1930, chs. 12, 13.

WATTS, ALAN W., *Behold the Spirit,* New York, Pantheon Books, 1947, pp. 127–149.

WHIPPLE, FRED L., *Earth, Moon and Planets,* New York, Blakiston Company, 1941, ch. 14.

WHITTAKER, F. R. S., *The Beginning and End of the World,* London, Oxford University Press, 1942.

9

THE NATURE OF LIFE

THERE IS a story of a man in a railway compartment who claimed to be able to identify his fellow-passengers' vocations if they would answer but a single question. The question was: "What is life?" Two types of answers are possible: the mechanistic and the vitalistic. According to mechanism life is an activity of matter — Hobbes said that life is a movement of limbs. According to vitalism life is a substance independent of matter. Plato gives a simple statement of the vitalistic position in *The Laws* in these words: "The soul is prior to the body . . . the body is second and comes afterwards, and is born to obey the soul, which is the ruler." Herbert Wildon Carr (1857–1931) was for many years a professor of philosophy at King's College, the University of London. James Johnstone was Professor of Oceanography at the University of Liverpool when he wrote the article reprinted here. He is best known as the author of the volume *A Study of the Oceans*, which was published in 1926. Carr defends the vitalistic position; Johnstone defends mechanism.

A

It seems to me of fundamental importance that as a preliminary to any discussion of the nature of life we should conceive clearly the actual fact or phenomenon of life. It is wholly inadequate to classify natural objects into the inert and the living, into objects which are not responsive and objects which are responsive to external impressions, and

then seek to specify the property or character which differentiates the one class from the other. Life is a perfectly definite and distinctive phenomenon. It is not a thing nor is it the character of a thing. It is a purposive activity exercised within clearly ascertainable limits and having a definite range. I use the term purposive without any implication of awareness. Living activity is purposive in the meaning that it can only be understood by correlating the initiation of the activity with

Herbert Wildon Carr, "The Nature of Life," *The Personalist,* Vol. 11, 1930, pp. 5–12. Reprinted by permission of the editor of *The Personalist.*

the end. The nature of the activity is plainly recognizable however difficult it may be to conceive the agent, agents or agency which the activity implies.

The first important point is that life is a phenomenon of solar radiation. A certain amount of radiating energy of which the sun is the source is intercepted by this planet on its surface, and here and there on the surface minute portions of this energy are entrapped, captured, magazined, controlled, redirected and made to subserve the purpose of the agent or agency intercepting it, whatever that agent or agency be. Life does not create energy and it does not use the energy imprisoned in the atomic or molecular systems which enter into the composition of living organisms. For example, the atoms of oxygen and molecules of water at present in my blood stream are no different from the atoms of oxygen and molecules of water in the atmosphere outside me. There are, I am told, cases of bacterial activity where the energy transformed or redirected is not derived (at least not directly derived) from the solar radiation, but it will be agreed, I think, that this exceptional fact does not affect the main contention that life as we know it is a purposive activity depending for its means on solar radiation.

A second important point to make clear is that life is not a phenomenon of cosmic evolution. We believe the earth to have had its origin in the sun and to be like the sun in its constitution. Science schematizes its history as a thermodynamic system running down. Its present condition is a stage in a cooling process. There is no evidence and no ground for believing that at any stage of this cooling, or as a direct consequence of it, life must arise or supervene or emerge. The life on this planet and life on the planet Mars, if we are right in interpreting the appearance of that planet, and the life on Venus, if, as some con-

jecture, there is life on its cloud-screened surface, is an active, purposive utilization of radiant solar energy.

A third important consideration is that while we have no direct knowledge of life in itself, we know quite definitely the means by which it utilizes the solar energy. Life avails itself of the instability of carbon compounds under the prevailing temperature conditions of the earth's surface. Its activity is not sporadic. We cannot by producing the conditions of life generate living activity, or by assembling the constituents of an organism make life supervene. Only a living cell can generate a living cell. All the evidence confirms the view that life is single in origin and continuous in evolution.

If we are agreed that these are the facts which we have to interpret then it is quite clear that to suppose we explain life by saying it emerges is childish; and to arrange or classify life in a hierarchy, placing matter below it and mind above it, is unmeaning and futile.

Let us now consider the mode in which living activity is exercised.

Life is individual; it exists only in living beings and each living being is indivisible, a whole not constituted of parts. In so far as a living being has a nature of its own, its whole nature exists individually in it. Buds, germs, seeds, fertilized ova, possess, each individually, the complete nature to which its life can give expression. This existence may be potential, but, whether actualized or not, it is altogether present.

Though life exists only in the individual, the purpose of living activity transcends individuality, for one of the clearest facts of living activity is transformism, the evolution of organic forms towards greater complexity of organization and higher functions. This upward evolution appears to be effected, without any reversal of the second law of thermodynamics, simply by intercepting and controlling and redirecting the degrading energy.

The problem of the nature of life is to interpret these facts.

During the modern period two alternative and mutually contradictory theories have been proposed. They are named mechanism and vitalism. Mechanism is the original theory put forward by Descartes. It rested on the idea that there is a complete difference of kind between two substances, mind and matter. Life in Descartes' view was a phenomenon of material organization, and material organization had no necessary connection with conscious feeling and thinking. The variety of the material world was due, he held, to the movement which had been originally imparted to the extended or material world, and this movement, which he conceived as indestructible, must, he thought, once introduced, lead, by the simple mechanical working of its laws, to ever increasing complexity. In this way the most complicated organisms had been formed and they were in effect self-regulating machines. In man there is a soul, conscious and cognitive, so situated in the body that it is able to control and direct the machine, but he saw no reason to suppose a soul in animals or that animals were anything else than unconscious automata. The organization of the living body and all its functions, nutrition, growth, reproduction, could, he thought, be fully explained by the mechanics of movement, and this mechanistic principle was abundantly illustrated and confirmed in the study of anatomy and physiology.

Vitalism, the opposing principle, found its fullest expression in the philosophy of Leibniz. It rested on a new metaphysical conception of the constitution of the world. It denied the reality of the material world, and held that the real units or atoms which constitute the world are essentially living and active, each a subject of experience. A living thing possesses *vis viva* and is individual. Mechanical movement is only the outward expression of internal force. Force is like the bent bow, its reality is not its actuality but its potentiality. A living thing is not a complex machine of assembled interlocking parts, but an individual, acting integrally. It is what Aristotle had described by the word entelechy, a self-ruled force actively expressing itself. The universe consists of entelechies. The inert world of matter is a mass effect, a result of confused perception.

Thus in the seventeenth century, and before the great scientific development, there were definitely formulated two contrary principles of scientific interpretation. Their history is instructive. The mechanistic principle proved very attractive and tended to become identified with scientific method. The reason is not difficult to understand. Mechanism lent itself to precise mathematical formulation and it was conspicuously successful in astronomy and physics. It seemed almost axiomatic that if the living world was to be amenable to scientific treatment it could only be on the same principle and it seemed, therefore, hardly open to doubt that the most complex phenomena of living action might be traced to their origin in the simplest laws of mechanics. Vitalism, on the other hand, appeared eminently unscientific. It sinned against the scientific ideal, for it seemed to multiply entities without necessity. It seemed to be occult and therefore incomprehensible or else to be a mere device of creating *ad hoc* a suppositious entity and naming it entelechy. The old Aristotelian term "entelechy" has been revived in the recent philosophy of the organism, particularly in the work of Dr. Hans Driesch, and it has been criticized by mechanistic writers on these grounds.

In my view mechanism is not only insufficient and inadequate, it not merely falls short or fails, it is the wrong way to approach the problem and it cannot interpret life. We have not to supplement it but to reverse it. In declaring myself a vitalist I wish to defend the term "entelechy" from the reproach which has been cast upon it, due entirely in my view to a complete misunderstanding of its meaning and use. Rightly understood, entelechy is not something we claim to find in the organism or something which for theoretical reasons we affirm to be present, it is the principle of organization itself.

The vitalistic theory is generally represented as the view that a living organism is primarily a cunningly devised machine such as, say, an automobile, and then, as such a machine is useless without the mechanic at the driving wheel to direct and control it, to suppose that the organism has a director in control, and this director is then named "entelechy." Such at any rate is the usual way in which Driesch's theory is presented; whether he accepts it or not I do not know, but certainly this is not what Leibniz meant by "entelechy" nor is it possible to read such a meaning into Aristotle.

Leibniz says that every monad is entelechy. This is very different from saying that all or some monads have entelechies. Entelechy is not something one can have. What one can have, and what every living individual has, is the "perfection" which constitutes a whole, when the whole is individual and indivisible. A whole which is made up of the aggregate of the parts is not entelechy just because it can be separated into the parts of which it is composed. I think General Smuts in choosing the word Holism for his theory has chosen the wrong word. The right word is entelechy.

It is the principle of entelechy which alone can interpret the facts of the organism. The organism is not a machine, or if it is, then, as Leibniz says, it is unlike man-made machines inasmuch as all its parts are machines to infinity. The principle of entelechy is the principle by which a whole is an individual whole, and acts always as a whole, even when its constituent parts are themselves wholes acting as individual wholes. To suppose entelechy as existing distinct from the parts, controlling them and directing them as the mechanic the machine, is not only to contradict the principle, it is to lose all contact with the facts. Consider a personality, self-controlled, self-directed, self-identical — myself, for example. I can only act while my body functions, but I am my whole bodily organism functioning. Yet that organism which is myself is constituted of living cells, each with its own self-centered, individual interest in its action, each acting according to its own nature. I have no power to interfere with the activities of the constituent cells of my body, I give them no orders, exercise no influence on them, direct or indirect, yet apart from them I am nothing and apart from me they are nothing.

I have yet to show why vitalism reverses and does not supplement mechanism. The mechanistic principle is clearly defined by Descartes in the third of his maxims in the *Discourse on Method*. "To bring order to my thoughts, beginning with the simplest objects and those easiest to know, to rise gradually to the knowledge of the more composite, not assuming any order which is not that of natural precedence." Why, I shall be asked (perhaps with indignation), is this excellent maxim, expressing the very essence of scientific method, to be disregarded and disobeyed, when the nature of life is the subject of inquiry? The answer is not because this method fails, but because it falsifies the facts. It implies that the complexity of the whole is a disposition of the parts. Metaphysically it is unsound; logically it leads to the absurdity that there is no more in the more than there is in the less. Is not the emergent theory of evolution an attempt to rationalize such an irrationality?

What is the alternative? The alternative is the principle of entelechy. It is scientific, for it is the principle the biologist actually uses in his own special science and only discards when he seeks to relate his science to other sciences. No biologist is content to analyze a grain of wheat or a living cell as a chemist analyzes a sample of water. Wherever we are dealing with life we know there is more in the reality than exists in its actualization at any moment of observation. The reality of a living thing consists in potentiality and this potentiality is not less real because it is not, and may never be, actualized. This is the concept of entelechy and the biologist cannot dispense with it in his own domain. He abandons it only when he seeks the origin of living activity itself in a matter which by definition has no potentiality. Hence the impasse.

Many scientists and philosophers today are dissatisfied with mechanism and even convinced of its complete failure to interpret the nature of life and yet are unwilling to accept vitalism. What is their alternative? For the most part they take refuge in the new theory of "emergence." It seems to them that there must have been a natural precedence of matter to life and of life to mind. Unable to give any meaning to the idea of a creation of life out of matter or of mind out of life, they regard them as "emergents." Pressed to give some definite meaning to their descriptive term they postulate a principle in the cosmos which for some inexplicable reason is making for wholeness, a wholeness not already there.

My way is to adopt an entirely different concept of the substance of the world. For me its reality is activity and activity is distinguished from mechanical movement by its individuality. Anything is what it does and what does nothing is nothing. The concept of matter is of a reality which does nothing. Activity is essentially individual and purposive and in its higher form personal. Life and mind are therefore the essence of reality. They are not late-comers; they are there from the first. The principle of entelechy does not require that the real shall be actual. In its potentiality it is always perfect, a whole, whatever be its state of actualization at any moment. What then is matter and materiality? (I am not, of course, dealing with the physical and mathematical problems, but with perceptual matter.) I reply that it is phenomenon. It is not real on its own account or self-subsistent; it is a mass-effect, an aspect of the real forces which constitute the world, and the work of science is to extrapolate the scheme of those forces. Why do I call this vitalism? Because it rests on a concept which makes life and living activity original, which includes matter and mind in the concept of life instead of generating life out of matter and mind out of life.

B

Consider two fairly simple, natural occurrences: a storm at sea and an earthquake. Many descriptions of these things have been

James Johnstone, "The Mechanism of Life," *Journal of Philosophical Studies,* Vol. 1, 1926, pp. 183–191. Reprinted by permission of the Editor of *Philosophy,* the journal of The Royal Institute of Philosophy.

made, but what interests us here are their scientific descriptions. In the first case, then, we have to deal with changes in the pressure and temperature of the atmosphere, with violent motions of the air and with waves in the sea. In the second case we deal with stratified rocks that are in a state of severe strain. When this strain exceeds a certain limit the rocks are fractured and waves are set up in the elastic materials of the earth's crust. In most cases storms and earthquakes happen when we do not expect them, and so there is usually little time to investigate them in an adequate manner. But there is no doubt whatever that if we could make all the researches that are practicable we could "explain" individual storms and earthquakes. "Explanation" means re-describing the phenomena in the simplest manner possible, that is, in terms of space, time, gravitation, energy-transformations, chemical constitution of the materials concerned, etc. Such explanations can be (and indeed have been) made of the occurrences mentioned above, and the physical ideas we have noted are all that are included in the explanations.

Now an organism, as we see it in nature, is "something happening," that is, it is a series of occurrences that we tend to investigate in just the same way as we do storms at sea and earthquakes upon the land. Not only does such an attitude apply to the development, functioning, and behaviour of other animals, but it is also extended to the functioning and behaviour of the investigator himself, in so far as these things are studied by scientific methods and by introspection. Science regards living organisms as "bodies moving in nature" in very complex ways, and it sees nothing in them other than physical configurations undergoing changes, that is, systems of electrons, atoms, and molecules arranged in definite ways, and energy-transformations occurring also in definite ways. The configurations and transformations are to be described in formal language, which employs very definite physical concepts and makes use of mathematical symbols. This method of description applies to the cyclonic storm or the earthquake, or the

living organism just in the same way. It is true that most astronomical, physical, or geological occurrences are fairly simple ones (astronomical occurrences being the simplest of all, for they can be completely described mathematically). On the other hand, biological things and occurrences are very complex, and mathematical methods of investigation have, so far, hardly been applied (except in relation to the theory of probability, when they serve mainly to investigate the error of observational data). It is also true that all the methods necessary for the complete physico-mathematical descriptions of such phenomena as earthquakes, eclipses, and storms exist at the present time, and can be applied with success whenever an adequate basis of observation is made; on the other hand, all the resources, say of a Government about to engage in a protracted war, are inadequate to most cases of simple organic behaviour (to say nothing of development or evolution), because the methods of investigation have not yet been invented. But science does not doubt that such methods will in time be found, and that explanations of organic development, functioning, and behaviour that are essentially similar in their nature to the explanations, say, of planetary and tidal motions will ultimately be made. It believes that the explanations, or irreducibly simple descriptions of both kinds of natural occurrences, organic and inorganic, will contain the same concepts.

This, then, is the mechanistic conception of life.

It applies to the study of the living organism just those methods of investigation that have successfully been applied to the study of inorganic things, so that biology (or, at any rate, physiology) has always been simply the mechanics, physics, and chemistry of the period (always just a little behind the times, so to speak) applied to the investigation of functioning and behaviour. And so it is interesting to note that the mechanistic biology of any period reflects the state of physical science of a decade or two earlier. The Cartesian mechanism of life — quite the most thorough-going treatment yet made — was mechanical, presenting the results, applied to life, of the physics of Galileo and his school. It showed us an animal automaton — a thing of hydrostatic pressure, flow of liquids through tubes of varying calibre, stretched nerve-threads actuating valves, filters and sieves, liquids that were thin and mobile, or thick and viscous, liquids expansible by heat, liquids that distended hollow organs, etc., that is, the physical ideas current at the time. It was a visible, animal mechanism that was studied, for the microscope (if it had been invented) had not been applied to the investigation of the bodily parts, and it was believed that anatomical structure, as displayed by dissection, could explain organic functioning. There were no chemical ideas of life in the Cartesian mechanism, though a rude chemistry (that of the alchemists) had long been studied. Then came the invention and use of the microscope, and the coarse, anatomical description of the animal body became supplemented by the minute examination of the tissues: that was in the eighteenth century. The latter results were very striking, and it must have been expected that the more one could see of the structure of the body the more clearly would this structure explain functioning. About this time, also, the earlier chemistry (of Basil Valentine and Paracelsus) was again applied to the study of life (notably by Van Helmont), and organic functioning seemed to be largely an affair of fermentations. Physiology has not yet receded from this chemical conception of life, though the early conception of fermentation processes as the physical basis of life was not a remarkably

helpful one. About the end of the eighteenth and the beginning of the nineteenth centuries the true theory of combustion was worked out, and immediately the processes of animal respiration were seen to be those of oxidation and the output of carbonic acid gas. The inference was irresistible, so that the analogy of the body of the warm-blooded animal with the inorganic heat-engine followed as a matter of course (to be modified by investigations that belong to our own period). That brings us up to the early years of the nineteenth century.

Then came the great period of classic physiology — about 1820 to 1860, and most of our present notions of animal mechanism come from those years. The experimental investigation of the body of the mammal was carried on by methods that were largely physical ones: the modern compound microscope, the induction coil, the use of clockwork drums to obtain graphic records of motions of parts of the body under stimulation, injection of bloodvessels, stimulation of nerves, degeneration methods of studying nerve tracts, the use of galvanometers, etc., — all came from this time (when physics, especially electrical science, was making great strides forward). This kind of physical physiology is still that of the medical schools — the "horological laboratory method," as a well-known zoologist of the last generation described it. But chemical methods also advanced rapidly during the early part of the nineteenth century, and there are, in particular, three great landmarks: (1) the first synthesis of an organic compound, that is, of urea, by Köhler; (2) the conception of colloid structure (due to Graham); and (3) the notion of catalysis (worked out by Berzelius). The synthesis of urea by Köhler was "sensational" in a high degree, for it had been believed that organic compounds could only be produced in the living tissues. Colloids and their significance dominate physiology of to-day. Catalysis gave a new cue to physiology, so that, ever since 1878, when Kuhne introduced the term "enzyme," as meaning much the same thing as the old ferment, life has become an affair of enzymes, pro-enzymes (or zymogens) that precede enzymes, kinases that activate enzymes, anti-enzymes that inhibit enzymes, hormones, vitamins, etc. The multiplicity of these "substances," no one of which has yet been chemically isolated, much less synthesized, suggests that the fertility of the conception in physiology is beginning to fail. But, at all events, we see how intimately the mechanistic conception of life depends upon the advances made by the chemists and physicists.

The last three decades of the nineteenth century, along with our own generation, have seen the development of a biology with its own individuality and methods. All that we have surveyed above represents, not biology, but rather the application of physics and chemistry to the study of the modes of activity of the living organism; it remains, with us, as the classic physiology of the medical schools and what is called bio-chemistry. A new impetus to biology was given when, in the 'seventies and 'eighties of last century, Roux, the pupil of Pasteur, initiated what has been called "development-mechanics" and experimental embryology. Along with this came the modern study of cell-anatomy, the investigation of the "germ-plasm," or hypothetical substance of heredity, experimental breeding, and "genetics." The significance of all this for a new conception of life cannot be overestimated. No less profound in its influence has been the rigorous study of the nervous system — the micro-structural investigations and, above all, the experimental work of Sherrington and his pupils on nervous activity and its integrative function in animal life.

Here we have the indispensable data for the study of animal behaviour. The investigation of the behaviour of the intact, living organism, carried out by ordinary observation and supplemented by the experimental methods so brilliantly employed by Sherrington; the study of cell-anatomy (with its enormously difficult technique); the investigation of tissue-growth; the methods of experimental embryology; the application of radiational physics to biology — these are the fertile fields of biological investigation of the near future. For the present bio-chemistry is only a subsidiary method, occupying a limited field of research.

Now do the methods and results that we have just barely indicated — with those that are about to emerge from contemporary work — enable us to "explain" life? "Explanation," we repeat, is, for the scientific man, the re-description of phenomena in terms of the irreducibly simple concepts of mathematical physics: thus we explain (and predict) the complicated motions of the tides from our knowledge of the motions of the earth, sun, and moon; or we explain chemical valency by assuming that the atoms are built up of nuclear and satellite electrons. Nothing simpler than gravitation and electrons can, for the present, at all events, be conceived, so that our re-descriptions of tidal motions and chemical valencies are the simplest possible. But we cannot find any such explanation of organic activity. Enzymes provide the mechanism of, say, processes of digestion, but we are still ignorant of the chemical and physical nature of any one of these agents. The coagulation of the blood has been described in terms of chemical "interactions of colloids under the influence of electrolytes, especially calcium." Thus fibrinogen, prothrombin, prothrombokinase, anti-thrombokinase, etc., pass into fibrin, thrombin, thrombokinase, etc.; but no one of these substances is known in the way that we know, say, water and hydrogen peroxide. Behaviour, in general, is regarded as chains of reflex acts; reflex acts are the activities of systems of neurones in connection with muscular and sensory structures, and they depend on nervous impulses taking established paths through the labyrinth of the spinal cord and brain. These paths are determined by the varying resistances of the synapses, but we do not know what determines the varying permeability of the synaptic membranes to the passage of the nervous impulse, whatever *that* may be. Individual development, that is the establishment of the bodily organs, is due in some way to groups of developmental "factors" in the chromatoplasm of the nuclei of the germ-cells, but we do not know what is the physical and chemical constitution of these "factors." And so on, we "explain" any one organic mechanism by another mechanism which is generally just as complex. We see in the organism a "vista of exquisite mechanisms," but the final physical simplicity which must be the characteristic of our explanations eludes us. It is quite true that, in comparison with the mechanism of the solar system, that of the living organism is incredibly complex, so that we have still ever so much to find out before our explanations can be made. But, that being so, is not our life-mechanism a matter of faith rather than of physical demonstration?

It is also true that our mechanistic conception of life has been of extraordinary value in the practical sense. After all, it is now possible to set up city-communities of several millions of people living together in a huddled-up kind of way, but still remaining fairly healthy. Medical and biological research have lengthened life and have enabled normal men and women to last out their threescore and ten years (or more) with little disease or suffering. They have enabled us to meet and endure the inevitable accidents of life without the pain and suffering of even a century ago. We can breed and rear useful domestic animals, fruits, vegetables, etc., and we may be sure that our successes in these ways will become much greater in the future. Obviously our lives, in their variety and content, have become fuller than those of the men and women of the pre-scientific civilizations. It would be just as stupid to under-estimate the practical consequences of our mechanistic conception as it would be vain to argue that it has provided us with a physical explanation of life. And the history of physiological science shows clearly that our knowledge of the ways in which the animal body functions has always increased during those periods when materialistic or mechanistic conceptions were generally accepted, while those other phases of biology when animistic or vitalistic views were current have been characterized by relative sterility.

Now it is quite proper to inquire why it is that biology remains inveterately mechanistic in spite of the failure of the science to produce its physical explanations. For one thing it deliberately excludes a rather large field of human experience from its investigations. Returning to our analogy of the storm at sea, we find that, along with those intellectual processes that are active in our observations of the motions of sea, and wind and ship, and in our measurements of those phenomena, there are other states of mentality. Even the scientific mind may experience a certain discomposure: there are quite irrational fears; apprehensions of disaster; visceral reflexes with very prominent emotional concomitants, and a disturbance of intellectual calm which tends to inhibit exact observation. These aspects of a storm at sea have not been well described by meteorologists and oceanographers, and they have never been "explained" in the physical sense. In fact, scientists tend to regard them with a kind of disdain (afterwards!). Again, think about our plain, uncritical, common-sense knowledge of other animals — such knowledge as is possessed by a good gamekeeper, or dog-fancier, or a "man of the world." Certain quite remarkable feelings are aroused in us by intimate knowledge of animals: we may fear, or dislike them; we may have very strong affections for them; we may abuse, or praise, or punish, or reward them. We do not think in this way about inorganic things: the latter have interest and utility, and we may even admire them, or avoid them, or merely exhibit indifference, but obviously they do not excite in us the same kinds of feelings that accompany or express our intimate knowledge of domestic animals, to say nothing of other men and women. It is curious, also, how very well we can *recognize* life in spite of our difficulty in describing it: no biologist has trouble in deciding whether or not a thing is alive (and this applies not only to ordinary animals, but even to those exceedingly primitive organisms that we call bacteria and to the obscure living things that require the aid of the ultramicroscope even to be *seen*). And yet the difficulty of describing these organisms in physical terms, so as clearly to differentiate them from inorganic bodies, is very great.

Or think about our own activities, as exhibited in our behaviour and displayed to us by introspection. Just those same activities can be seen in other men and women, and we do not doubt for a moment that they are accompanied by those states of consciousness that we recognize in ourselves. Yet other men and women are only "bodies moving in nature" for a strictly mechanistic biology. "This animal machine that I call my wife," said a zoologist, "exhibits certain facial contortions and emits certain articulate sounds similar to those emitted by myself when I have a headache, but I have no right to say that she has a headache." This is the real mechanism, yet no sensible man would talk in that way to his wife! It is a plain and very obvious fact that we have built up our societies and social relationships on the basis of such quite irrational recognitions of life in other things than ourselves, and it is very curious that we should refuse to consider this experience as part of that which has to be explained in physical terms.

Yet it is quite certain that biology will never abandon its mechanistic attitude. The latter is something more than merely an hypothesis: it is a "demand" or an "ideal of explanation" that we *insist upon* in our investigation of life activity. We can "interrogate nature" in various ways. Merely to ask a question, or to sit down and think, or pray, or contemplate, are futilities: we must intervene in nature, and this we can do because we are parts of nature that have the powers of deliberation and choice. All our observations and experiments are interventions in the sense that we cause natural processes to take slightly different directions than they would have done but for our activities. When we find, by observation, that the Dog Star, Sirius, has a companion with a certain orbit, we obtain that knowledge by diverting the light of the star into our spectroscopes, thus interfering with its natural dissipation. When we make an hypothesis we say to nature, "Suppose, for the moment, you are such-and-such: then if I do *this,* you will do *that*." As a rule Nature does something different from that which we assume she will do, and then we simply abandon our hypothesis and make another one. By and by, however, we make the "right" hypothesis, and so we build up our formal explanations or laws of Nature. But, again, we may say to Nature: "You are such-and-such, and you may as well admit it": that is our demand, and we make it in much the same way as we demand cash from a bank, knowing that we have a credit balance, though we may not know how much it is. Our physical law of conservation is such a demand, and it is clear (from the history of physics) that no scientific result of any kind whatever can compel us to abandon the law. Thus it has been transferred from matter to energy, then to mass, then to electromagnetic mass, then to the "action" of the modern quantum physics (or so it appears, for an outsider may well be excused from error because of the perplexities and apparent contradictions of this hypothesis). We cannot, or rather we plainly refuse to think otherwise than according to our law of conservation, for it is our demand on Nature. And it is very clear that science has been justified by its insistence, in spite of all the apparent difficulties, that the law of conservation is "true," for every new hypothesis that has been made in order to preserve the validity of the law has led to new discoveries and new powers of control over Nature.

Our mechanistic conception of life is such a demand upon nature: it is an "ideal of explanation" which leads us insistently to look for facts that are relevant to it. It does not seem to be probable that we shall ever find an explanation of life that will realize our ideal, yet, none the less, we seem to be compelled to seek for it. Something in us, the impulse to act so as more and more to acquire power over the things that happen in our environment, impels us to look for the explanation of life in those processes of nature that we can in some measure control. In those other conceptions of life that are not physical we can have little interest — as scientists — for in their very nature they represent agencies which we cannot control. Mediaeval animism, with archei and souls and spirits and

vital forces or energies; the "neovitalism" with its entelechies and psychoids; the analogy of life with the "splash made by the entry of mental existences into the sea of inert matter" — such conceptions have been compared by a veteran cytologist with the Vestals of Classic Rome: they are dedicated to God and barren. (The original illustration is Bacon's, of course.) Science must continue to seek for its physical explanations of life. Even while it recognizes that the search has been unsuccessful, it does not evade its difficulties by transferring the explanation to the domain of non-physical existences because there it cannot investigate.

Is the search always to be an unsuccessful one? The huge output of contemporary physiology has a curiously limited range — enzymes, hormones, vitamines, colloids, hydrogen-ion-concentration, etc., — minutiae, and even trivialities, of research that do not ever appear to touch upon the problems of life, or bring us nearer to the desired physical explanations. But physics itself promises bigger things. The older science has had its crowning achievement, it is said, in the general theory of relativity, but the new physics which transforms itself almost every year — *that* interests us as biologists. Even the very incomprehensibilities of the modern science stimulate us. The universe that is assuredly "running down" and tending always towards its condition of greatest probability of occurrence — or utter inertia — and which must yet, somewhere, and at some time or other, "wind *itself* up"; here we have what is, for the moment, one of the recurring paradoxes of science, awaiting its resolution in some new physical conception. The more one thinks about life — as it is manifested in the chemical and physical events that make up organic metabolism — the more strongly will the notion force itself upon us that the living organism is resisting the process of physical "running-down." In life we get some idea of that other process which must, in moments of duration of the universe, lead towards the condition of least probability — when the universe "winds *itself* up." So we seem to be seeking our explanation of life in a transcendental physics, and, fortunately, the perplexities and even impossibilities of the new hypotheses do not deter investigators. It is a curious conclusion to which we come — that it is not in the conventional biology of the present time that we seem to look for an explanation of life, but rather in the study of mathematical physics.

SUGGESTIONS FOR THOUGHT

1. Liebig is reported to have replied to the question whether he believed that a leaf or a flower could be formed by chemical forces; "I would more readily believe that a book on chemistry or on botany could grow out of dead matter." Why do biologists today doubt their ability to find a scientific explanation of the origin of life?

2. Is Bergson's *élan vital* an explanation of life or a confession of ignorance? What is the status of vitalism in modern biology?

3. How would you define life? Julian Huxley has defined it as the capacity for continued cyclical self-reproduction. What are the essential characteristics of life?

4. What is dead matter, or must we revise our thinking and assume that all matter is alive? What are some of the values and difficulties of the theory of panpsychism?

5. Why has man been interested in the origin of his species? Has part of the resistance to the evolutionary theory of man's origin been due to our tendency to commit the genetic fallacy?

6. In the introduction to the first edition of *The Origin of Species* Darwin wrote: "I am con-vinced that natural selection has been the main but not the exclusive means of modification." What other means might he have recognized?

7. Are we justified in taking the theory of organic evolution and applying it to studies of the cosmos, human societies, religious concepts, etc.? Distinguish between "develop" and "evolve."

8. Why was Christianity for many years violently opposed to the theory of evolution? The following law was passed by the legislature of Tennessee on March 21, 1925: "Be it enacted by the General Assembly of the State of Tennessee that it shall be unlawful for any teacher in any of the universities, normals, or other public schools in the State, which are supported in whole or in part by the public school funds of the State, to teach the theory that denies the divine creation of man as taught in the Bible, and to teach instead that man has descended from a lower order of animal." Did the legislators correctly understand the Bible, the theory of evolution, and the function of higher education? How can the supposed conflict of the Bible and evolution be resolved?

SUGGESTIONS FOR FURTHER READING

BERGSON, HENRI, *Creative Evolution,* translated by Arthur Mitchell, New York, Henry Holt and Company, 1911, ch. 1.

BRADLEY, JOHN HODGDON, *Patterns of Survival,* New York, The Macmillan Company, 1938, ch. 1.

BURCH, GEORGE BOSWORTH, "The Nature of Life," *The Review of Metaphysics,* Vol. 5, 1951, pp. 1–10.

CHASE, CARL TRUEBLOOD, *Frontiers of Science,* New York, D. Van Nostrand Company, 1936, ch. 20.

EISELEY, LOREN C., "The Secret of Life," *Harpers Magazine,* Vol. 207, October 1953, pp. 64–68.

HALDANE, J. B. S., *What is Life?,* New York, Boni and Gaer, 1947.

JENKINSON, J. W., "Vitalism," *The Hibbert Journal,* Vol. 9, 1910–11, pp. 545–549.

LILLIE, RALPH S., "The Scientific View of Life," *The Journal of Philosophy,* Vol. 25, 1928, pp. 589–606.

MORGAN, C. LLOYD, *Life, Mind, and Spirit,* New York, Henry Holt and Company, 1925, Lecture 3.

OSBORN, HENRY FAIRFIELD, *The Origin and Evolution of Life,* New York, Charles Scribner's Sons, 1917, ch. 7.

SCHRÖDINGER, ERWIN, *What is Life?,* New York, The Macmillan Company, 1945.

SEARS, PAUL B., *This is Our World,* Norman, University of Oklahoma Press, 1937, ch. 7.

SELLARS, ROY WOOD, *Evolutionary Naturalism,* Chicago, Open Court Publishing Company, 1922, ch. 15.

WELLS, H. G., *The Science of Life,* London, Literary Guild, 1934, Book V, ch. 1.

10

THE COSMOS AND PURPOSE

AGAIN AND AGAIN teleology has been ridiculed and declared to be dead. Francis Bacon compared final causes to vestal virgins: "Like them they are dedicated to God, and are barren." William James asserted, "Darwinism has once and for all displaced design from the minds of the scientific." And Nicolai Hartmann rejoiced in "the greatest achievement of modern thought — deliverance from the nightmare of teleology." Yet men persist in finding design and purpose in nature. Is this a commentary on man's anthropomorphism, or is teleology a fact? Aristotle interpreted the natural world teleologically, but Benedictus de Spinoza (1632–1677), the great Jewish rationalist, rejected all final causes.

A

Now that we have established these distinctions, we must proceed to consider causes, their character and number. Knowledge is the object of our inquiry, and men do not think they know a thing till they have grasped the 'why' of it (which is to grasp its primary cause). So clearly we too must do this as regards both coming to be and passing away and every kind of physical change, in order that, knowing their principles, we may try to refer to these principles each of our problems.

In one sense, then, (1) that out of which a thing comes to be and which persists, is called 'cause', e.g. the bronze of the statue, the silver of the bowl, and the genera of which the bronze and the silver are species.

In another sense (2) the form of the archetype, i.e. the statement of the essence, and its

Aristotle, *Physics,* Book II, Sections 3, 7, 8, translated by R. P. Hardie and R. K. Gaye, *The Works of Aristotle Translated into English,* Vol. 2, edited by W. D. Ross, Oxford, The Clarendon Press, 1930. Reprinted by permission of the publishers.

genera, are called 'causes' (e.g. of the octave the relation of 2:1, and generally number), and the parts in the definition.

Again (3) the primary source of the change or coming to rest; e.g. the man who gave advice is a cause, the father is cause of the child, and generally what makes of what is made and what causes change of what is changed.

Again (4) in the sense of end or 'that for the sake of which' a thing is done, e.g. health is the cause of walking about. ('Why is he walking about?' we say. 'To be healthy', and, having said that, we think we have assigned the cause.) The same is true also of all the intermediate steps which are brought about through the action of something else as means toward the end, e.g. reduction of flesh, purging, drugs, or surgical instruments are means toward health. All these things are 'for the sake of' the end, though they differ from one another in that some are activities, others instruments.

This then perhaps exhausts the number of ways in which the term 'cause' is used.

As the word has several senses, it follows that there are several causes of the same thing (not merely in virtue of a concomitant attribute), e.g. both the art of the sculptor and the bronze are causes of the statue. These are causes of the statue *qua* statue, not in virtue of anything else that it may be — only not in the same way, the one being the material cause, the other the cause whence the motion comes. Some things cause each other reciprocally, e.g. hard work causes fitness and vice versa, but again not in the same way, but the one as end, the other as the origin of change. Further the same thing is the cause of contrary results. For that which by its presence brings about one result is sometimes blamed for bringing about the contrary by its absence.

Thus we ascribe the wreck of a ship to the absence of the pilot whose presence was the cause of its safety.

All the causes now mentioned fall into four familiar divisions. The letters are the causes of syllables, the material of artificial products, fire, &c., of bodies, the parts of the whole, and the premises of the conclusion, in the sense of 'that from which'. Of these pairs the one set are causes in the sense of substratum, e.g. the parts, the other set in the sense of essence — the whole and the combination and the form. But the seed and the doctor and the adviser, and generally the maker, are all sources whence the change or stationariness originates, while the others are causes in the sense of the end or the good of the rest; for 'that for the sake of which' means what is best and the end of the things that lead up to it. (Whether we say the 'good itself' or the 'apparent good' makes no difference.)

Such then is the number and nature of the kinds of cause.

Now the modes of causation are many, though when brought under heads they too can be reduced in number. For 'cause' is used in many senses and even within the same kind one may be prior to another (e.g. the doctor and the expert are causes of health, the relation 2:1 and number of the octave), and always what is inclusive to what is particular. Another mode of causation is the incidental and its genera, e.g. in one way 'Polyclitus', in another 'sculptor' is the cause of a statue, because 'being Polyclitus' and 'sculptor' are incidentally conjoined. Also the classes in which the incidental attribute is included; thus 'a man' could be said to be the cause of a statue or, generally, 'a living creature'. An incidental attribute too may be more or less remote, e.g. suppose that 'a pale man' or 'a musical man' were said to be the cause of the statue.

All causes, both proper and incidental, may be spoken of either as potential or as actual; e.g. the cause of a house being built is either 'house-builder' or 'house-builder building'.

Similar distinctions can be made in the things of which the causes are causes, e.g. of 'this statue' or of 'statue' or of 'image' generally, of 'this bronze' or of 'bronze' or of 'material' generally. So too with the incidental attributes. Again we may use a complex expression for either and say, e.g., neither 'Polyclitus' nor 'sculptor' but 'Polyclitus, sculptor'.

All these various uses, however, come to six in number, under each of which again the usage is twofold. Cause means either what is particular or a genus, or an incidental attribute or a genus of that, and these either as a complex or each by itself; and all six either as actual or as potential. The difference is this much, that causes which are actually at work and particular exist and cease to exist simultaneously with their effect, e.g. this healing person with this being-healed person and that house-building man with that being-built house; but this is not always true of potential causes — the house and the house-builder do not pass away simultaneously.

In investigating the cause of each thing it is always necessary to seek what is most precise (as also in other things): thus man builds because he is a builder, and a builder builds in virtue of his art of building. This last cause then is prior: and so generally.

Further, generic effects should be assigned to generic causes, particular effects to particular causes, e.g. statue to sculptor, this statue to this sculptor; and powers are relative to possible effects, actually operating causes to things which are actually being effected.

This must suffice for our account of the number of causes and the modes of causation. . . .

* * *

It is clear then that there are causes, and that the number of them is what we have stated. The number is the same as that of the things comprehended under the question 'why'. The 'why' is referred ultimately either (1), in things which do not involve motion, e.g. in mathematics, to the 'what' (to the definition of 'straight line' or 'commensurable', &c), or (2) to what initiated a motion, e.g. 'why did they go to war? — because there had been a raid'; or (3) we are inquiring 'for the sake of what?' — 'that they may rule'; or (4), in the case of things that come into being, we are looking for the matter. The causes, therefore, are these and so many in number.

Now, the causes being four, it is the business of the physicist to know about them all, and if he refers his problems back to all of them, he will assign the 'why' in the way proper to his science — the matter, the form, the mover, 'that for the sake of which'. The last three often coincide; for the 'what' and 'that for the sake of which' are one, while the primary source of motion is the same in species as these (for man generates man), and so too, in general, are all things which cause movement by being themselves moved; and such as are not of this kind are no longer inside the province of physics, for they cause motion not by possessing motion or a source of motion in themselves, but being themselves incapable of motion. Hence there are three branches of study, one of things which are incapable of motion, the second of things in motion, but indestructible, the third of destructible things.

The question 'why', then, is answered by reference to the matter, to the form, and to the primary moving cause. For in respect of coming to be it is mostly in this last way that causes are investigated — 'what comes to be after what? what was the primary agent or patient?' and so at each step of the series.

Now the principles which cause motion in a physical way are two, of which one is not physical, as it has no principle of motion in itself. Of this kind is whatever causes movement, not being itself moved, such as (1) that which is completely unchangeable, the primary reality, and (2) the essence of that which is coming to be, i.e. the form; for this is the end or 'that for the sake of which'. Hence since nature is for the sake of something, we must know this cause also. We must explain the 'why' in all the senses of the term, namely, (1) that from this that will necessarily result ('from this' either without qualification or in most cases); (2) that 'this must be so if that is to be so' (as the conclusion presupposes the premisses); (3) that this was the essence of the thing; and (4) because it is better thus (not without qualification, but with reference to the essential nature in each case).

We must explain then (1) that Nature belongs to the class of causes which act for the sake of something; (2) about the necessary and its place in physical problems, for all writers ascribe things to this cause, arguing that since the hot and the cold, &c., are of such and such kind, therefore certain things *necessarily* are and come to be — and if they mention any other cause (one his 'friendship and strife,' another his 'mind'), it is only to touch on it, and then good-bye to it.

A difficulty presents itself: why should not nature work, not for the sake of something, nor because it is better so, but just as the sky rains, not in order to make the corn grow, but of necessity? What is drawn up must cool, and what has been cooled must become water and descend, the result of this being that the corn grows. Similarly if a man's crop is spoiled on the threshing-floor, the rain did not fall for the sake of this — in order that the crop might be spoiled — but that result just followed. Why then should it not be the same with the parts in nature, e.g. that our teeth should come up *of necessity* — the front teeth sharp, fitted for tearing, the molars broad and useful for grinding down the food — since they did not arise for this end, but it was merely a coincident result; and so with all other parts in which we suppose that there is purpose? Wherever then all the parts came about just what they would have been if they had come to be for an end, such things survived, being organized spontaneously in a fitting way; whereas those which grew otherwise perished and continue to perish, as Empedocles says his 'man-faced ox-progeny' did.

Such are the arguments (and others of the kind) which may cause difficulty on this point. Yet it is impossible that this should be the true view. For teeth and all other natural things either invariably or normally come about in a given way; but of not one of the results of chance or spontaneity is this true. We do not ascribe to chance or mere coincidence the frequency of rain in winter, but frequent rain in summer we do; nor heat in the dog-days, but only if we have it in winter. If then, it is agreed that things are either the result of coincidence or for an end, and these cannot be the result of coincidence or spontaneity, it follows that they must be for an end; and that such things are all due to nature even the champions of the theory which is before us would agree. Therefore action for an end is present in things which come to be and are by nature.

Further, where a series has a completion, all the preceding steps are for the sake of that. Now surely as in intelligent action, so in nature; and as in nature, so it is in each action, if nothing interferes. Now intelligent action is for the sake of an end; therefore the nature of things also is so. Thus if a house, e.g., had been a thing made by nature, it would have been made in the same way as it is now by art; and if things made by nature were made also by art, they would come to be in the same way as by nature. Each step then in the series is for the sake of the next; and generally art partly completes what nature cannot bring to a finish, and partly imitates her. If, therefore, artificial products are for the sake of an end, so clearly also are natural products. The relation of the later to the earlier terms of the series is the same in both.

This is most obvious in the animals other than man: they make things neither by art nor after inquiry or deliberation. Wherefore people discuss whether it is by intelligence or by some other faculty that these creatures work, — spiders, ants, and the like. By gradual advance in this direction we come to see clearly that in plants too that is produced which is conducive to the end — leaves, e.g. grow to provide shade for the fruit. If then it is both by nature and for an end that the swallow makes its nest and the spider its web, and plants grow leaves for the sake of the fruit and send roots down (not up) for the sake of nourishment, it is plain that this kind of cause is operative in things which come to be and are by nature. And since 'nature' means two things, the matter and the form, of which the latter is the end, and since all the rest is for the sake of the end, the form must be the cause in the sense of 'that for the sake of which'.

Now mistakes come to pass even in the operations of art: the grammarian makes a mistake in writing and the doctor pours out the wrong dose. Hence clearly mistakes are possible in the operations of nature also. If

then in art there are cases in which what is rightly produced serves a purpose, and if where mistakes occur there was a purpose in what was attempted, only it was not attained, so must it be also in natural products, and monstrosities will be failures in the purposive effort. Thus in the original combinations the 'ox-progeny' if they failed to reach a determinate end must have arisen through the corruption of some principle corresponding to what is now the seed.

Further, seed must have come into being first, and not straightway the animals: the words 'whole-natured first . . .' must have meant seed.

Again, in plants too we find the relation of means to end, though the degree of organization is less. Were there then in plants also 'olive-headed vine-progeny', like the 'man-headed ox-progeny', or not? An absurd suggestion; yet there must have been, if there were such things among animals.

Moreover, among the seeds anything must have come to be at random. But the person who asserts this entirely does away with 'nature' and what exists 'by nature'. For those things are natural which, by a continuous movement originated from an internal principle, arrive at some completion: the same completion is not reached from every principle; nor any chance completion, but always the tendency in each is towards the same end, if there is no impediment.

The end and the means towards it may come about by chance. We say, for instance, that a stranger has come by chance, paid the ransom, and gone away, when he does so as if he had come for that purpose, though it was not for that that he came. This is incidental, for chance is an incidental cause, as I remarked before. But when an event takes place always or for the most part, it is not incidental or by chance. In natural products the sequence is invariable, if there is no impediment.

It is absurd to suppose that purpose is not present because we do not observe the agent deliberating. Art does not deliberate. If the ship-building art were in the wood, it would produce the same results *by nature*. If, therefore, purpose is present in art, it is present also in nature. The best illustration is a doctor doctoring himself: nature is like that.

It is plain then that nature is a cause, a cause that operates for a purpose.

B

In the foregoing I have explained the nature and properties of God. I have shown that he necessarily exists, that he is one: that he is, and acts solely by the necessity of his own nature; that he is the free cause of all things, and how he is so; that all things are in God, and so depend on him, that without him they could neither exist nor be conceived; lastly, that all things are predetermined by God, not through his free will or absolute fiat, but from the very nature of God or infinite power. I have further, where occasion offered, taken care to remove the prejudices, which might impede the comprehension of my demonstrations. Yet there still remain misconceptions not a few, which might and may prove very grave hindrances to the understanding of the concatenation of things, as I have explained it above. I have therefore thought it worth while to bring these misconceptions before the bar of reason.

All such opinions spring from the notion commonly entertained, that all things in nature act as men themselves act, namely, with an end in view. It is accepted as certain, that God himself directs all things to a definite goal (for it is said that God made all things for man, and man that he might worship

Spinoza, *Ethics,* Part I, Appendix, translated by R. H. M. Elwes, *The Chief Works of Benedick de Spinoza translated from the Latin,* London, George Bell and Sons, 1883.

him). I will, therefore, consider this opinion, asking first, why it obtains general credence, and why all men are naturally so prone to adopt it? Secondly, I will point out its falsity; and, lastly, I will show how it has given rise to prejudices about good and bad, right and wrong, praise and blame, order and confusion, beauty and ugliness, and the like. However, this is not the place to deduce these misconceptions from the nature of the human mind: it will be sufficient here, if I assume as a starting point, what ought to be universally admitted, namely, that all men are born ignorant of the causes of things, that all have the desire to seek for what is useful to them, and that they are conscious of such desire. Herefrom it follows, first, that men think themselves free inasmuch as they are conscious of their volitions and desires, and never even dream, in their ignorance, of the causes which have disposed them so to wish and desire. Secondly, that men do all things for an end, namely, for that which is useful to them, and which they seek. Thus it comes to pass that they only look for a knowledge of the final causes of events, and when these are learned, they are content, as having no cause for further doubt. If they cannot learn such causes from external sources, they are compelled to turn to considering themselves, and reflecting what end would have induced them personally to bring about the given event, and thus they necessarily judge other natures by their own. Further, as they find in themselves and outside themselves many means which assist them not a little in their search for what is useful, for instance, eyes for seeing, teeth for chewing, herbs and animals for yielding food, the sun for giving light, the sea for breeding fish, &c., they come to look on the whole of nature as a means for obtaining such conveniences. Now as they are aware, that they found these conveniences and did not make them, they think they have cause for believing, that some other being has made them for their use. As they look upon things as means, they cannot believe them to be self-created; but, judging from the means which they are accustomed to prepare for themselves, they are bound to believe in some ruler or rulers of the universe endowed with human freedom, who have arranged and adapted everything for human use. They are bound to estimate the nature of such rulers (having no information on the subject) in accordance with their own nature, and therefore they assert that the gods ordained everything for the use of man, in order to bind man to themselves and obtain from him the highest honour. Hence also it follows, that everyone thought out for himself, according to his abilities, a different way of worshipping God, so that God might love him more than his fellows, and direct the whole course of nature for the satisfaction of his blind cupidity and insatiable avarice. Thus the prejudice developed into superstition, and took deep root in the human mind; and for this reason everyone strove most zealously to understand and explain the final causes of things; but in their endeavour to show that nature does nothing in vain, i.e., nothing which is useless to man, they only seem to have demonstrated that nature, the gods, and men are all mad together. Consider, I pray you, the result: among the

many helps of nature they were bound to find some hindrances, such as storms, earthquakes, diseases, &c.: so they declared that such things happen, because the gods are angry at some wrong done them by men, or at some fault committed in their worship. Experience day by day protested and showed by infinite examples, that good and evil fortunes fall to the lot of pious and impious alike; still they would not abandon their inveterate prejudice, for it was more easy for them to class such contradictions among other unknown things of whose use they were ignorant, and thus to retain their actual and innate condition of ignorance, than to destroy the whole fabric of their reasoning and start afresh. They therefore laid down as an axiom, that God's judgments far transcend human understanding. Such a doctrine might well have sufficed to conceal the truth from the human race for all eternity, if mathematics had not furnished another standard of verity in considering solely the essence and properties of figures without regard to their final causes. There are other reasons (which I need not mention here) besides mathematics, which might have caused men's minds to be directed to these general prejudices, and have led them to the knowledge of the truth.

I have now sufficiently explained my first point. There is no need to show at length, that nature has no particular goal in view, and that final causes are mere human figments. This, I think, is already evident enough, both from the causes and foundations on which I have shown such prejudice to be based, and also from Prop. xvi., and the Corollary of Prop. xxxii., and, in fact, all those propositions in which I have shown, that everything in nature proceeds from a sort of necessity, and with the utmost perfection. However, I will add a few remarks, in order to overthrow this doctrine of a final cause utterly. That which is really a cause it considers as an effect, and *vice versa:* it makes that which is by nature first to be last, and that which is highest and most perfect to be most imperfect. Passing over the questions of cause and priority as self-evident, it is plain from Props. xxi., xxii., xxiii. that that effect is most perfect which is produced immediately by God; the effect which requires for its production several intermediate causes is, in that respect, more imperfect. But if those things which were made immediately by God were made to enable him to attain his end, then the things which come after, for the sake of which the first were made, are necessarily the most excellent of all.

Further, this doctrine does away with the perfection of God: for, if God acts for an object, he necessarily desires something which he lacks. Certainly, theologians and metaphysicians draw a distinction between the object of want and the object of assimilation; still they confess that God made all things for the sake of himself, not for the sake of creation. They are unable to point to anything prior to creation, except God himself, as an object for which God should act, and are therefore driven to admit (as they clearly must), that God lacked those things for whose attainment he created means, and further that he desired them.

We must not omit to notice that the followers of this doctrine, anxious to display their talent in assigning final causes, have imported a new method of argument in proof of their theory — namely, a reduction, not to the impossible, but to ignorance; thus showing that they have no other method of exhibiting their doctrine. For example, if a stone falls from a roof on to someone's head, and kills him, they will demonstrate by their new method, that the stone fell in order to kill the man; for, if it had not by God's will fallen with that object, how could so many circumstances (and there are often many concurrent circumstances) have all happened together by chance? Perhaps you will answer that the event is due to the facts that the wind was blowing, and the man was walking that way. "But why," they will insist, "was the wind blowing, and why was the man at that very time walking that way?" If you again answer, that the wind had then sprung up because the sea had begun to be agitated the day before, the weather being previously calm, and that the man had been invited by a friend, they will again insist: "But why was the sea agitated, and why was the man invited at that time?" So they will pursue their questions from cause to cause, till at last you take refuge in the will of God — in other words, the sanctuary of ignorance. So, again, when they survey the frame of the human body, they are amazed; and being ignorant of the causes of so great a work of art, conclude that it has been fashioned, not mechanically, but by divine and supernatural skill, and has been so put together that one part shall not hurt another.

Hence anyone who seeks for the true causes of miracles, and strives to understand phenomena as an intelligent being, and not to gaze at them like a fool, is set down and denounced as an impious heretic by those, whom the masses adore as the interpreters of nature and the gods. Such persons know that, with the removal of ignorance, the wonder which forms their only available means for proving and preserving their authority would vanish also. But I now quit this subject, and pass on to my third point.

After men persuaded themselves, that everything which is created is created for their sake, they were bound to consider as the chief quality in everything that which is most useful to themselves, and to account those things the best of all which have the most beneficial effect on mankind. Further, they were bound to form abstract notions for the explanation of the nature of things, such as *goodness, badness, order, confusion, warmth, cold, beauty, deformity,* and so on; and from the belief that they are free agents arose the further notions *praise* and *blame, sin* and *merit.*

I will speak of these latter hereafter, when I treat of human nature; the former I will briefly explain here.

Everything which conduces to health and the worship of God they have called *good,* everything which hinders these objects they have styled *bad;* and inasmuch as those who do not understand the nature of things do not verify phenomena in any way, but merely imagine them after a fashion, and mistake their imagination for understanding, such persons firmly believe that there is an *order* in things, being really ignorant both of things and their own nature. When phenomena are of such a kind, that the impression they make on our senses requires little effort of imagination, and can consequently be easily remembered, we say that they are *well-ordered;* if the contrary, that they are *ill-ordered* or *confused.* Further, as things which are easily imagined are more pleasing to us, men prefer order to confusion — as though there were any order in nature, except in relation to our imagination — and say that God has created all things in order; thus, without knowing it, attributing imagination to God, unless, indeed, they would have it that God foresaw human imagination, and arranged everything, so that it should be most easily imagined. If this be their theory, they would not, perhaps, be daunted by the fact that we find an infinite number of phenomena, far surpassing our imagination, and very many others which confound its weakness. But enough has been said on this subject. The other abstract notions are nothing but modes of imagining, in which the imagination is differently affected, though they are considered by the ignorant as the chief attributes of things, inasmuch as they believe that everything was created for the sake of themselves; and, according as they are affected by it, style is good or bad, healthy or rotten and corrupt. For instance, if the motion which objects we see communicate to our nerves be conducive to health, the objects causing it are styled *beautiful;* if a contrary motion be excited, they are styled *ugly.*

Things which are perceived through our sense of smell are styled fragrant or fetid; if through our taste, sweet or bitter, full-flavoured or insipid; if through our touch, hard or soft, rough or smooth, &c.

Whatsoever affects our ears is said to give rise to noise, sound, or harmony. In this last case, there are men lunatic enough to believe, that even God himself takes pleasure in harmony; and philosophers are not lacking who have persuaded themselves, that the motion of the heavenly bodies gives rise to harmony — all of which instances sufficiently show that everyone judges of things according to the state of his brain, or rather mistakes for things the forms of his imagination. We need no longer wonder that there have arisen all the controversies we have witnessed, and finally scepticism: for, although human bodies in many respects agree, yet in very many others they differ; so that what seems good to one seems bad to another; what seems well ordered to one seems confused to another; what is pleasing to one displeases another, and so on. I need not further enumerate, because this is not the place to treat the subject at length, and also because the fact is sufficiently well known. It is commonly said: "So many men, so many minds; everyone is wise in his own way; brains differ as completely as palates." All of which proverbs show, that men judge of things according to their mental disposition, and rather imagine than understand: for, if they understood phenomena, they would, as mathematics attest, be convinced, if not attracted, by what I have urged.

We have now perceived, that all the explanations commonly given of nature are mere modes of imagining, and do not indicate the true nature of anything, but only the constitution of the imagination; and, although they have names, as though they were entities, existing externally to the imagination, I call them entities imaginary rather than real; and, therefore, all arguments against us drawn from such abstractions are easily rebutted.

Many argue in this way. If all things follow from a necessity of the absolutely perfect nature of God, why are there so many imperfections in nature? such, for instance, as things corrupt to the point of putridity, loathsome deformity, confusion, evil, sin, &c. But these reasoners are, as I have said, easily confuted, for the perfection of things is to be reckoned only from their own nature and power; things are not more or less perfect, according as they delight or offend human senses, or according as they are serviceable or repugnant to mankind. To those who ask why God did not so create all men, that they should be governed only by reason, I give no answer but this: because matter was not lacking to him for the creation of every degree of perfection from highest to lowest; or, more strictly, because the laws of his nature are so vast, as to suffice for the production of everything conceivable by an infinite intelligence, as I have shown in Prop. xvi.

Such are the misconceptions I have undertaken to note; if there are any more of the same sort, everyone may easily dissipate them for himself with the aid of a little reflection.

SUGGESTIONS FOR THOUGHT

1. What adaptations of the natural world appear to you to be the expression of purpose? What maladjustments are you aware of?

2. Frederick W. H. Myers was once asked what question he would ask of the Sphinx if he could ask but one. Myers replied: "If I could ask the Sphinx one question and one only, and hope for an answer, I think it would be this: 'Is the Universe friendly?'" Why is this a good question?

3. Would it be possible to hold to a teleological view of the universe and believe that it is not man and his development which is the purpose of the universe? For example, could the purpose of the universe be the formation of better rocks?

4. Is it possible to base an adequate philosophy of life on a neutral view of the universe — that is, that the universe is neither hostile nor friendly to man? Can the theory of the hostility of nature to man be overthrown by claiming that nature is not hostile or we would not be here?

5. What effect does the study of astronomy have on your ego? Do you feel belittled by the immensity of astronomical space, or do you constantly remind yourself that it is man who is able to study this universe?

6. Bertrand Russell has warned, "We must learn that the world was not made for us." What evidence can you cite that the world was not made for man? Is there evidence that it was made for man?

7. Reinhold Niebuhr has said that modern culture "is to be credited with the greatest advances in the understanding of nature and with the greatest confusion in the understanding of man. Perhaps this credit and debit are logically related to each other." How can they be related? Why would advance in the understanding of na-

ture fail to promote advance in the understanding of the nature of man?

8. Does man's ability to know the universe, and the supposed inability of the universe to know man, suggest that man is superior or transcendent to the universe?

9. What effect have your studies of natural science had on your sense of the uniqueness and value of human beings?

10. "To me, and I cannot speak for any other, creation, growth, and, as the highest that I can conceive, growth of beauty, and especially of that beauty which inheres in persons, is the most restful, most satisfying aspect I can grasp of what may be Nature's purpose." (Maynard Metcalf) Can you suggest some alternative hypotheses concerning Nature's purpose?

11. "It is perhaps significant that in terms of simple magnitude man is the mean between macrocosm and microcosm. Stated crudely this means that a supergiant red star (the largest material body in the universe) is just as much bigger than man as an electron (tiniest of physical entities) is smaller." (Lincoln Barnett) What is the significance of this fact?

12. A critic of Galileo said that the satellites of Jupiter were invisible to the naked eye, that they exerted no influence on the earth, that they were useless, and that since they were useless they did not exist! What other things in the universe might be eliminated on this basis?

13. "Why do birds colour their eggs so beautifully for so short a time, and when it is not intended that they shall be seen by any but the parents? The sentimental turtle and the prosaic hen are alike satisfied to sit on a plain egg, without going to the trouble and expense of colouring it. Why can a hedge sparrow find no peace in anything short of turquoise?" (Samuel Butler) How would you answer Butler's questions?

SUGGESTIONS FOR FURTHER READING

BAHM, ARCHIE J., "Emergence of Purpose," *The Journal of Philosophy,* Vol. 44, 1947, pp. 633–636.

BOODIN, JOHN ELOF, *A Realistic Universe,* New York, The Macmillan Company, 1931, ch. 18.

BOUWSMA, O. K., "Variations on a Theme by Mr. Costello," *The Journal of Philosophy,* Vol. 43, 1946, pp. 157–161.

GOTSHALK, D. W., "A Suggestion for Naturalists," *The Journal of Philosophy,* Vol. 45, 1948, pp. 5–12.

HENDERSON, L. J., *The Order of Nature,* Cambridge, Harvard University Press, 1917.

HOBHOUSE, L. T., *Development and Purpose,* New York, The Macmillan Company, 1927, Part II, chs. 6, 7.

KNOX, HENRY HOBART, "Concerning Purpose in Nature," *The Personalist,* Vol. 19, 1938, pp. 32–40.

KRIKORIAN, Y. H., "Teleology and Causality," *The Review of Metaphysics,* Vol. 2, 1949, pp. 35–46.

LECOMTE DU NOÜY, PIERRE, *Human Destiny,* New York, Longmans, Green and Company, 1947.

SEARS, PAUL B., *This Is Our World,* Norman, University of Oklahoma Press, 1937, chs. 3–6.

STACE, W. T., *Religion and the Modern Mind,* Philadelphia, J. B. Lippincott Company, 1952, pp. 19–31.

URBAN, W. M., *The Intelligible World,* New York, The Macmillan Company, 1929, ch. 10.

VAN NUYS, KELVIN, *Science and Cosmic Purpose,* New York, Harper and Brothers, 1949.

WHITEHEAD, A. N., *The Function of Reason,* Princeton, Princeton University Press, 1929, ch. 1.

11

REALITY AND VALUES

Is THE WORLD mind-like or matter-like in its fundamental nature? This is the basic problem of metaphysics. In the past philosophers have spent much of their energy in trying to make their opponents look ridiculous. Thus the idealists, who contend that the world is mind-like, have tried to show that the naturalists, who contend that the world is matter-like, are nothing but crude materialists; and the naturalists have attempted to make idealists appear as romantic solipsists. Royce and Woodbridge, however, devote themselves in these selections to positive presentations of their own views rather than to the destruction of each other's metaphysics. Josiah Royce (1855–1916) was an outstanding American idealist. He taught at Harvard University from 1882 to the time of his death. Frederick James Eugene Woodbridge (1867–1940), a naturalist and neo-realist, taught at the University of Minnesota and at Columbia University. At the latter institution he was dean of the faculties of political science, philosophy, pure science, and fine arts from 1912 to 1920.

A

I must remind you that idealism has two aspects. It is, for the first, a kind of analysis of the world, an analysis which so far has no absolute character about it, but which undertakes, in a fashion that might be acceptable to any skeptic, to examine what you mean by all the things, whatever they are, that you believe in or experience. This idealistic analysis consists merely in a pointing out, by various devices, that the world of your knowledge, whatever it contains, is through and through such stuff as ideas are made of, that you never in your life believed in anything definable *but* ideas, that, as Berkeley put it, "this whole choir of heaven and furniture of earth" is nothing for any of us but a system of ideas which govern our belief and our conduct. Such idealism has numerous statements, interpretations, embodiments: forms part of the most

Josiah Royce, *The Spirit of Modern Philosophy,* Boston, Houghton Mifflin and Company, 1892, ch. 11 (in part).

various systems and experiences, is consistent with Berkeley's theism, with Fichte's ethical absolutism, with Professor Huxley's agnostic empiricism, with Clifford's mind-stuff theory, with countless other theories that have used such idealism as part of their scheme. In this aspect idealism is already a little puzzling to our natural consciousness, but it becomes quickly familiar, in fact almost commonplace, and seems after all to alter our practical faith or to solve our deeper problems very little.

The other aspect of idealism is the one which gives us our notion of the absolute Self. To it the first is only preparatory. This second aspect is the one which from Kant, until the present time, has formed the deeper problem of thought. Whenever the world has become more conscious of its significance, the work of human philosophy will be, not nearly ended (Heaven forbid an end!), but for the first time fairly begun. For then, in critically estimating our passions, we shall have some truer sense of whose passions they are.

I begin with the first and the less significant aspect of idealism. Our world, I say, whatever it may contain, is such stuff as ideas are made of. This preparatory sort of idealism is the one that, as I just suggested, Berkeley made prominent, and, after a fashion familiar. I must state it in my own way, although one in vain seeks to attain novelty in illustrating so frequently described a view.

Here, then, is our so real world of the senses, full of light and warmth and sound. If anything could be solid and external, surely, one at first will say, it is this world. Hard facts, not mere ideas, meet us on every hand. Ideas any one can mould as he wishes. Not so facts. In idea socialists can dream out Utopias, disappointed lovers can imagine themselves successful, beggars can ride horses, wanderers can enjoy the fireside at home. In the realm of facts, society organizes itself as

it must, rejected lovers stand for the time defeated, beggars are alone with their wishes, oceans roll drearily between home and the wanderer. Yet this world of fact is, after all, not entirely stubborn, not merely hard. The strenuous will can mould facts. We can form our world, in part, according to our ideas. Statesmen influence the social order, lovers woo afresh, wanderers find the way home. But thus to alter the world we must work, and just because the laborer is worthy of his hire, it is well that the real world should thus have such fixity of things as enables us to anticipate what facts will prove lasting, and to see of the travail of our souls when it is once done. This, then, is the presupposition of life, that we work in a real world, where house-walls do not melt away as in dreams, but stand firm against the winds of many winters, and can be felt as real. We do not wish to find facts wholly plastic; we want them to be stubborn, if only the stubbornness be not altogether unmerciful. Our will makes constantly a sort of agreement with the world, whereby, if the world will continually show some respect to the will, the will shall consent to be strenuous in its industry. Interfere with the reality of my world, and you therefore take the very life and heart out of my will.

The reality of the world, however, when thus defined in terms of its stubbornness, its firmness as against the will that has not conformed to its laws, its kindly rigidity in preserving for us the fruits of our labors, — such reality, I say, is still something wholly unanalyzed. In what does such stubbornness consist? Surely, many different sorts of reality, as it would seem, may be stubborn. Matter is stubborn when it stands in hard walls against us, or rises in vast mountain ranges before the path-finding explorer. But minds can be stubborn also. The lonely wanderer, who watches by the seashore the waves that roll between him and his home, talks of cruel facts, material barriers that, just because they *are* material, and not ideal, shall be the irresistible foes of his longing heart. "In wish," he says, "I am with my dear ones, but alas, wishes cannot cross oceans! Oceans are material facts, in the cold outer world. Would that the world of the heart were all!" But alas! to the rejected lover the world of the heart *is* all, and that is just his woe. Were the barrier between him and his beloved only made of those stubborn material facts, only of walls or of oceans, how lightly might his will erelong transcend them all! Matter stubborn! Outer nature cruelly the foe of ideas! Nay, it is just an idea that now opposes him, — just an idea, and that, too, in the mind of the maiden he loves. But in vain does he call this stubborn bit of disdain a merely ideal fact. No flint was ever more definite in preserving its identity and its edge than this disdain may be. Place me for a moment, then, in an external world that shall consist wholly of ideas, — the ideas, namely, of other people about me, a world of maidens who shall scorn me, of old friends who shall have learned to hate me, of angels who shall condemn me, of God who shall judge me. In what piercing north winds, amidst what fields of ice, in the labyrinths of what tangled forests, in the depths of what thick-walled dungeons, on the edges of what tremendous precipices, should I be more genuinely in the presence of stubborn and unyielding facts than in that conceived world of ideas! So, as one sees, I by no means deprive my world of stubborn reality, if I merely call it a world of ideas. On the contrary, as every teacher knows, the ideas of the people are often the most difficult of facts to influence. We were wrong, then, when we said that whilst matter was stubborn, ideas could be moulded at pleasure. Ideas are often the most implacable of facts. Even my own ideas, the facts of my own inner life, may

cruelly decline to be plastic to my wish. The wicked will that refuses to be destroyed, — what rock has often more consistency for our senses than this will has for our inner consciousness! The king, in his soliloquy in "Hamlet," — in what an unyielding world of hard facts does he not move! and yet they are now only inner facts. The fault is past; he is alone with his conscience.

> "What rests?
> Try what repentance can. What can it not?
> Yet what can it, when one cannot repent?
> O wretched state! O bosom black as death!
> O lìmëd soul, that, struggling to be free,
> Art more engaged!"

No, here are barriers worse than any material chains. The world of ideas has its own horrible dungeons and chasms. Let those who have refuted Bishop Berkeley's idealism by the wonder why he did not walk over every precipice or into every fire if these existed only in his idea, let such, I say, first try some of the fires and the precipices of the inner life, ere they decide that dangers cease to be dangers as soon as they are called ideal, or even subjectively ideal in me.

Many sorts of reality, then, may be existent at the heart of any world of facts. But this bright and beautiful sense-world of ours, — what, amongst these many possible sorts of reality, does that embody? Are the stars and the oceans, the walls and the pictures, real as the maiden's heart is real, — embodying the ideas of somebody, but none the less stubbornly real for that? Or can we make something else of their reality? For, of course, that the stars and the oceans, the walls and the pictures have *some* sort of stubborn reality, just as the minds of our fellows have, our analysis so far does not for an instant think of denying. Our present question is, what sort of reality? Consider, then, in detail, certain aspects of the reality that seems to be exemplified in our sense-world. The sublimity of the sky, the life and majesty of the ocean, the interest of a picture, — to what sort of real facts do these belong? Evidently here we shall have no question. So far as the sense-world is beautiful, is majestic, is sublime, this beauty and dignity exist only for the appreciative observer. If they exist beyond him, they exist only for some other mind, or as the thought and embodied purpose of some universal soul of nature. A man who sees the same world, but who has no eye for the fairness of it, will find all the visible facts, but will catch nothing of their value. At once, then, the sublimity and beauty of the world are thus truths that one who pretends to insight ought to see, and they are truths which have no meaning except for such a beholder's mind, or except as embodying the thought of the mind of the world. So here, at least, is so much of the outer world that is ideal, just as the coin or the jewel or the bank-note or the bond has its value not alone in its physical presence, but in the idea that it symbolizes to a beholder's mind, or to the relatively universal thought of the commercial world. But let us look a little deeper. Surely, if the objects yonder are un-ideal and outer, odors and tastes and temperatures do not exist in these objects in just the way in which they exist in us. Part of the being of these properties, at least, if not all of it, is ideal and exists for us, or at best is once more the embodiment of the thought or purpose of some world-mind. About tastes you cannot dispute, because they are not only ideal but personal. For the benumbed tongue and palate of diseased bodily conditions, all things are tasteless. As for temperatures, a well known experiment will show how the same water may seem cold to one hand and warm to the other. But even so, colors and sounds are at least in part ideal. Their causes

may have some other sort of reality; but colors themselves are not in the things, since they change with the light that falls on the things, vanish in the dark (whilst the things remained unchanged), and differ for different eyes. And as for sounds, both the pitch and the quality of tones depend for us upon certain interesting peculiarities of our hearing organs, and exist in nature only as voiceless sound-waves trembling through the air. All such sense qualities, then, are ideal. The world yonder may — yes, must — have attributes that give reasons why these qualities are thus felt by us; for so we assume. The world yonder may even be a mind that thus expresses its will to us. But these qualities need not, nay, cannot resemble the ideas that are produced in us, unless, indeed, that is because these qualities have place as ideas in some world-mind. Sound-waves in the air are not like our musical sensations; nor is the symphony as we hear it and feel it any physical property of the strings and the wind instruments; nor are the ether-vibrations that the sun sends us like our ideas when we see the sun; nor yet is the flashing of moonlight on the water as we watch the waves a direct expression of the actual truths of fluid motion as the water embodies them.

Unless, then, the real physical world yonder is itself the embodiment of some world-spirit's ideas, which he conveys to us, unless it is real only as the maiden's heart is real, namely, as itself a conscious thought, then we have so far but one result: that real world (to repeat one of the commonplaces of modern popular science) is in itself, apart from somebody's eyes and tongue and ears and touch, neither colored nor tasteful, neither cool nor warm, neither light nor dark, neither musical nor silent. All these qualities belong to our ideas, being indeed none the less genuine facts for that, but being in so far ideal facts. We must see colors when we look, we must hear music when there is playing in our presence; but this *must* is a must that consists in a certain irresistible presence of an idea in us under certain conditions. *That* this idea must come is, indeed, a truth as unalterable, once more, as the king's settled remorse in Hamlet. But like this remorse, again, it exists as an ideal truth, objective, but through and through objective *for* somebody, and not *apart from* anybody. What this truth implies we have yet to see. So far it is only an ideal truth for the beholder, with just the bare possibility that behind it all there is the thought of a world-spirit. And, in fact, *so* far we must all go together if we reflect.

But now, at this point, the Berkeleyan idealist goes one step further. The real outside world that is still left unexplained and unanalyzed after its beauty, its warmth, its odors, its tastes, its colors, and its tones, have been relegated to the realm of ideal truths, what do you now *mean* by calling it real? No doubt it *is* known as somehow real, but *what* is this reality *known as* being? If you know that this world is still there and outer, as by hypothesis you know, you are bound to say *what* this outer character implies for your thought. And here you have trouble. Is the outer world, as it exists outside of your ideas, or of anybody's ideas, something having shape, filling space, possessing solidity, full of moving things? That would in the first place seem evident. The sound isn't outside of me, but the sound-waves, you say, are. The colors are ideal facts; but the ether-waves don't need a mind to know them. Warmth is ideal, but the physical fact called heat, this playing to and fro of molecules, is real, and is there apart from any mind. But once more, *is* this so evident? What do I *mean* by the shape of anything, or by the size of anything? Don't I mean just the idea of shape or of size that I

am obliged to get under certain circumstances? What is the meaning of any property that I give to the real outer world? How can I express that property except in case I think it in terms of my ideas? As for the sound-waves and the ether-waves, what are they but things ideally conceived to explain the facts of nature? The conceptions have doubtless their truth, but it is an ideal truth. What I mean by saying that the things yonder have shape and size and trembling molecules, and that there is air with sound-waves, and ether with light-waves in it, — what I *mean* by all this is that experience forces upon me, directly or indirectly, a vast system of ideas, which may indeed be founded in truth beyond me, which in fact *must* be founded in such truth if my experience has any sense, but which, like my ideas of color and of warmth, are simply expressions of how the world's order must appear to me, and to anybody constituted like me. Above all, is this plain about space. The real things, I say, outside of me, fill space, and move about in it. But what do I mean by space? Only a vast sysem of ideas which experience and my own mind force upon me. Doubtless these ideas have a validity. They have *this* validity, that I, at all events, when I look upon the world, am bound to see it in space, as much bound as the king in Hamlet was, when he looked within, to see himself as guilty and unrepentant. But just as his guilt was an idea, — a crushing, an irresistible, an overwhelming idea, — but still just an idea, so, too, the space in which I place my world is one great formal idea of mine. That is just why I can describe it to other people. "It has three dimensions," I say, "length, breadth, depth." I describe them. I form, I convey, I construct, an idea of it through them. I know space, as an idea, very well. I can compute all sorts of unseen truths about the relations of its parts. I am sure that you, too, share this idea. But, then, for all of us alike it is just an idea; and when we put our world into space, and call it real there, we simply think one idea into another idea, not voluntarily, to be sure, but inevitably, and yet without leaving the realm of ideas. . . .

★   ★   ★

What I have desired thus far is merely to give each of you, as it were, the sensation of being an idealist in this first and purely analytical sense of the word idealism. The sum and substance of it all is, you see, this: you know your world in fact as a system of ideas about things, such that from moment to moment you find this system forced upon you by experience. Even matter you know just as a mass of coherent ideas that you cannot help having. Space and time, as you think them, are surely ideas of yours. Now, what more natural than to say that *if* this be so, the real world beyond you must in itself be a system of somebody's ideas? If it is, then you can comprehend what its existence means. If it isn't, then since all you can know of it is ideal, the real world must be utterly unknowable, a bare *x*. Minds I can understand, because I myself am a mind. An existence that has no mental attribute is wholly opaque to me. So far, however, from such a world of ideas, existent beyond me in another mind, seeming to coherent thought essentially *un*real, ideas and minds and their ways, are, on the contrary, the hardest and stubbornest facts that we can name. *If* the external world is in itself mental, then, be this reality a standard and universal thought, or a mass of little atomic minds constituting the various particles of matter, in any case one can comprehend what it *is*, and will have at the same time to submit to its stubborn authority as the lover accepts the reality of the maiden's moods. If the world *isn't* such

an ideal thing, then indeed all our science, which is through and through concerned with our mental interpretations of things, can neither have objective validity, nor make satisfactory progress towards truth. For as science is concerned with ideas, the world beyond all ideas is a bare *x*. . . .

★   ★   ★

There lies now just ahead of us the goal of a synthetic idealistic conception, which will not be content with this mere analysis of the colors and forms of things, and with the mere discovery that all these are for us nothing but ideas. In this second aspect, idealism grows bolder, and fears not the profoundest doubt that may have entered your mind as to whether there is any world at all, or as to whether it is in any fashion knowable. State in full the deepest problem, the hardest question about the world that your thought ever conceived. In this new form idealism offers you a suggestion that indeed will not wholly answer nor do away with every such problem, but that certainly will set the meaning of it in a new light. What this new light is, I must in conclusion seek to illustrate.

Note the point we have reached. *Either,* as you see, your real world yonder is through and through a world of ideas, an outer mind that you are more or less comprehending through your experience, *or else,* in so far as it is real and outer it is unknowable, an inscrutable *x,* an absolute mystery. The dilemma is perfect. There is no third alternative. Either a mind yonder, or else the unknowable; that is your choice. Philosophy loves such dilemmas, wherein all the mightiest interests of the spirit, all the deepest longings of human passion, are at stake, waiting as for the fall of a die. Philosophy loves such situations, I say, and loves, too, to keep its scrutiny as cool in the midst of them as if it were watching a game of chess, instead of the great world-game. Well, try the darker choice that the dilemma gives you. The world yonder shall be an *x,* an unknowable something, outer, problematic, foreign, opaque. And you, — you shall look upon it and believe in it. Yes, you shall for argument's sake first put on an air of resigned confidence, and say, "I do not only fancy it to be an extra-mental and unknowable something there, an impenetrable *x,* but I know it to be such. I can't help it. I didn't make it unknowable. I regret the fact. But there it is. I have to admit its existence. But I know that I shall never solve the problem of its nature." Ah, its nature is a *problem,* then. But what do you mean by this "problem"? Problems are, after a fashion, rather familiar things, — that is, in the world of ideas. There are problems soluble and problems insoluble in that world of ideas. It is a soluble problem if one asks what whole number is the square root of 64. The answer is 8. It is an insoluble problem if one asks me to find what whole number is the square root of 65. There is, namely, no such whole number. If one asks me to name the length of a straight line that shall be equal to the circumference of a circle of a known radius, that again, in the world of ideas, is an insoluble problem, because, as can be proved, the circumference of a circle is a length that cannot possibly be exactly expressed in terms of any statable number when the radius is of a stated length. So in the world of ideas, problems are definite questions which can be asked in knowable terms. Fair questions of this sort either may be fairly answered in our present state of knowledge, or else they could be answered if we knew a little or a good deal more, or finally they could not possibly be answered. But in the latter case, if they could not possibly be answered, they always must resemble the problem how to square the circle. They then always turn

out, namely, to be absurdly stated questions, and it is their absurdity that makes these problems absolutely insoluble. Any fair question could be answered by one who knew enough. No fair question has an unknowable answer. But now, *if* your unknowable world out there is a thing of wholly, of absolutely problematic and inscrutable nature, is it so because you don't *yet* know enough about it, or because in its very nature and essence it is an absurd thing, an *x* that *would* answer a question, which actually it is nonsense to ask? Surely one must choose the former alternative. The real world may be unknown; it can't be essentially unknowable.

This subtlety is wearisome enough, I know, just here, but I shall not dwell long upon it. Plainly *if* the unknowable world out there is through and through in its nature a really inscrutable problem, this must mean that in nature it resembles such problems as, What is the whole number that is the square root of 65? Or, What two adjacent hills are there that have no valley between them? For in the world of thought such are the *only* insoluble problems. All others either may now be solved, or would be solved if we knew more than we now do. But once more, *if* this unknowable is only just the real world as now unknown to us, but capable some time of becoming known, then remember that, as we have just seen, only a mind can ever become an object known to a mind. If I know you as external to me, it is only because you are minds. If I can come to know *any* truth, it is only in so far as this truth is essentially mental, is an idea, is a thought, that I can ever come to know it. Hence, if that so-called unknowable, that unknown outer world there, ever could, by any device, come within our ken, then it is already an ideal world. For just that is what our whole idealistic analysis has been proving. Only ideas are knowable. And nothing absolutely unknowable can exist.

For the absolutely unknowable, the *x* pure and simple, the Kantian thing in itself, simply cannot be admitted. The notion of it is nonsense. The assertion of it is a contradiction. Round-squares, and sugar salt-lumps, and Snarks, and Boojums, and Jabberwocks, and Abracadabras; such, I insist, are the only unknowables there are. The unknown, that which our human and finite selfhood hasn't grasped, exists spread out before us in a boundless world of truth; but the unknowable is essentially, confessedly, *ipso facto* a fiction. . . .

Either idealism, we said, *or* the unknowable. What we have now said is that the absolutely unknowable is essentially an absurdity, a nonexistent. For any fair and statable problem admits of an answer. If the world exists yonder, its essence is then already capable of being known by some mind. If capable of being known by a mind, this essence is then already essentially ideal and mental. A mind that knew the real world would, for instance, find it a something possessing qualities. But qualities are ideal existences, just as much as are the particular qualities called odors or tones or colors. A mind knowing the real world would again find in it relations, such as equality and inequality, attraction and repulsion, likeness and unlikeness. But such relations have no meaning except as objects of a mind. In brief, then, the world as known would be found to be a world that had all the while been ideal and mental, even before it became known to the particular mind that we are to conceive as coming into connection with it. Thus, then, we are driven to the second alternative. The real world must be a mind, or else a group of minds.

But with this result we come in presence of a final problem. All this, you say, depends upon my assurance that there is after all a real and therefore an essentially knowable and rational world yonder. Such a world would have to be in essence a mind, or a world of minds. But after all, how does one ever escape from the prison of the inner life? Am I not in all this merely wandering amidst the realm of my own ideas? *My* world, of course, isn't and can't be a mere *x*, an essentially unknowable thing, just because it *is my* world, and I have an idea of it. But then does not this mean that *my* world is, after all, forever just *my* world, so that I never get to any truth beyond myself? Isn't this result very disheartening? My world is thus a world of ideas, but alas! how do I then ever reach those ideas of the minds beyond me?

The answer is a simple, but in one sense a very problematic one. You, in one sense, namely, never *do* or can get beyond your own ideas, nor ought you to wish to do so, because in truth all those other minds that constitute your outer and real world are in essence one with your own self. This whole world of ideas is essentially *one* world, and so it is essentially the world of one self and *That art Thou.* . . .

You, for instance, are part of one larger self with me, or else I can't even be meaning to address you as outer beings. You are part of one larger self along with the most mysterious or most remote fact of nature, along with the moon, and all the hosts of heaven, along with all truth and all beauty. Else could you not even intend to speak of such objects beyond you. For whatever you speak of you will find that your world is meant by you as just your world. Talk of the unknowable, and it forthwith becomes your unknowable, your problem, whose solution, unless the problem be a mere nonsense question, your larger self must own and be aware of. The deepest problem of life is, "What is this deeper self?" And the only answer is, *It is the self that knows in unity all truth.* This, I insist, is no hypothesis. It is actually the presupposition of your deepest doubt. And that is why I say: Everything finite is more or less obscure, dark, doubtful. Only the Infinite Self, the problem-solver, the complete thinker, the one who knows what we mean even when we are most confused and ignorant, the one who includes us, who has the world present to himself in unity, before whom all past and future truth, all distant and dark truth is clear in one eternal moment, to whom far and forgot is near, who thinks the whole of nature, and in whom are all things, the Logos, the world-possessor, — only his existence, I say, is perfectly sure. . . .

★ ★ ★

The world, then, is such stuff as ideas are made of. Thought possesses all things. But the world isn't unreal. It extends infinitely beyond our private consciousness, because it is the world of an universal mind. What facts it is to contain only experience can inform us. There is no magic that can anticipate the work of science. Absolutely the *only* thing sure from the first about this world, however, is that it is intelligent, rational, orderly, essentially comprehensible, so that all its problems are somewhere solved, all its darkest mysteries are known to the supreme Self. This Self infinitely and reflectively transcends our consciousness, and therefore, since it includes us, it is at the very least a person, and more definitely conscious than we are; for what it possesses is self-reflecting knowledge, and what is knowledge aware of itself, but consciousness? Beyond the seeming wreck and chaos of our finite problems, its eternal insight dwells, therefore, in absolute and supreme majesty. Yet it is not far from every one of us. There is no least or most transient thought that flits through a child's mind, or that troubles with the faintest line of care a maiden's face, and that still does not contain and embody something of this divine Logos.

B

Two factors, mainly, have shaped our conception of nature — the theories of modern physical science, and the part that machinery has played in our industrial and social development. These two factors, one of which is theoretical and the other practical, have led us to think of nature as a sort of vast machine controlled only by mechanical methods. The history of the science of mechanics is suggestive reading for the student of civili-

F. J. E. Woodbridge, "Naturalism and Humanism," *The Hibbert Journal*, Vol. 6, 1907, pp. 7–17. Reprinted by permission of the editor of *The Hibbert Journal*.

sation, for it shows how a study of appliances has been turned into a theory of the universe. Men like Archimedes were interested in mechanics that they might make pumps and useful structures. But men like Galileo, Copernicus, Newton, and Laplace were interested that they might understand the processes of nature. Had Galileo used his knowledge as an architect might, or as an engineer, there had been no trial of his as a man hateful to God and dangerous to his fellows. Instead of being content to make machines, he essayed to make a world after a machinist's manner, and that was blasphemous. The tower of Pisa, illustrating in its wonderful structure many a mechanical law, was something to delight in and was assuredly no offence to Church or State. But Galileo, mounting its steps to drop his weights from its highest gallery, was a revolutionist. His offence, however, lay not in his ideas; they might have been pardoned, as were those of many another, had he not been measurably successful in his practice. Nature was responsible for his overthrow, for she answered readily to mechanical treatment.

From Galileo's time to our own day stretch several centuries. They mark in our intellectual history the steady and successful advance of the mechanical view of things, until today we can speak of the mechanism of thought and use no metaphor. To be sure, physical science is but a fraction of human knowledge; and the facts of life and mind do not readily yield to purely mechanical expression, yet mechanism has become the ideal of science. Indeed, our time does not lack historians who would make it the ideal of history also. In philosophy, idealism has made a valiant fight, but it has been a fight of defence. Its logic and dialectic produce a sense of bewilderment, while mechanism produces profitable industry.

Furthermore, the mechanical conception of nature has ceased long ago to be a speculation of scientists. It has become a popular conviction. The encyclopedia, the lecture, the magazine have brought the view within reach of everyone who can read. Your morning paper announces the latest scientific discovery as well as the latest divorce. The average man in the street knows as much about radium as the average college student. Galileo, in his day, was the exception. Today he is the exception whose view of nature is not essentially that which Galileo ventured to affirm. And this view has become a settled habit of thought. Who to-day thinks of the San Francisco earthquake as an act of God and not a mechanical occurrence?

In our industrial and social development mechanism has ruled fully as much as in our intellectual development, for we have become dependent on machinery and organisation. In such things we have put our faith, and that not without good reason. It is machinery that has made modern civilisation with all its variety and effectiveness possible. That is a common enough remark which one could reinforce with a wealth of illustration. But what is not so commonly remarked is the intellectual habit which our civilization has engendered, namely, the habit of demanding the appropriate machinery to make a cause effective before the cause itself may have an attentive hearing. We are no longer spontaneously visionary or romantic, but regard the man of visions and romances as mildly insane or as a man cultivating a pose. We may stand for ideas, as the saying is, but we are apt to do it from a sense of duty or from the desire to create an impression. We are not apt to do it instinctively as the free and natural expression of our settled habits; for our settled habits have been formed while we have conquered nature not through ideas, but by machinery. Attempts in that direction have been so abundantly justified both by theory and by practice that we no longer think readily of nature as a source of spontaneity and inspiration. We think of her rather as a vast machine.

Our background contains, thus, an altered view of man and an altered view of nature. Not only has man been dethroned from his exalted position as the lord of creation and made a part of nature, but he has been made a part of a machine. Wherever he turns, it is mechanism which confronts him and mechanical methods which commend themselves. He has by no means thought the matter out to a liberal acceptance of it and its consequences. It has been forced upon him without his free consenting, as a thing inevitable, aggressive, and dominating. Did we consult our inclinations and preferences we might choose a more personal world, people with divinities responsive to our moods and their expression; but such inclinations on our part are rudely inhibited by our intellectual habits. To personify the world with success, it must be done instinctively and spontaneously, with no meddling intellect to stop the free impulse; but how can one personify the world if he is convinced that it is essentially mechanical?

I have likened the background to the geography which is often neglected in a campaign because knowledge of the land is taken for granted. So I would not suggest that it is my opinion that we are living our lives, meeting our problems and our promises with the philosophical proposition currently on our lips, "Nature is a mechanism, and man is a part of that machine." I mean, rather, that what that proposition signifies has become a settled intellectual habit about which we do not think because it is a habit, but which, for the same reason, controls our actions and attitudes, colouring all that we instinctively and spontaneously do. I have tried to indicate how this habit has been formed and what its justification has been. I have suggested that what is often condemned as our materialism, utilitarianism, and loss of ideals, is not a negative matter signifying a sinful deterioration of human nature, but a positive matter, the natural expression of an altered background forced upon us by the progress of events. All this I have done professedly in the interest of philosophy and education, convinced that what we need in these days of so much agitation and reform is a clear knowledge of the controlling forces of our civilisation.

In spite of its significance and its justification, naturalism has not been, however, emotionally satisfactory. Our greatest poets have been blindly optimistic, like Browning, or despairingly reflective, like Arnold. The social influence of the two men is interesting. Browning's poetry produced clubs to make of him a cult and to preserve his philosophy through sectarian discipleship. Arnold's poetry produced strong individuals tenderly yet critically appreciative of human interests, but incapable of arousing great enthusiasm. He was by far the sounder thinker of the two; but he drew his inspiration from a past he could not justify, seeing in the future the intensity of human need more than an assured promise of good. Emotions, however, are not kept young and vigorous by clubs designedly constituted for raptures, or by beautiful expressions of despair; they must well up spontaneously from the background, and be so natural that they will need no cult and so instinctive that they will need no justification. It is just here that naturalism has failed. A mechanical world is emotionally bankrupt. In such a world one star does not differ from another star in glory; the difference is to be expressed directly in terms of mass, and inversely in terms of the square of the distance. To speak of glory in such a world is to speak theatrically.

Had not naturalism been marked by such emotional poverty, it would doubtless never have found humanism arrayed as its enemy. In that event humanism might have been enlarged or its best elements incorporated in a new inspiration. It was destined, however, to suffer a shrinkage and a diminution of its powers, so that it could fight only on the defensive and yield fortress after fortress. Yet it has been strong enough, in spite of successive defeats, still to preserve the front of a compact foe. At the outset, humanism had a distinct advantage, for it possessed culture as a lawful inheritance. That human treasure was not acquired by it through violence, but came as the natural legacy of an age grown sensitive to the accomplishments of man. Remember that in the inception of humanism man had achieved little as a student of nature, while he had achieved much as a student of his own impressions and ideas. Indeed, such a study is the characteristic note and definition of humanism. Such a study had produced a wonderful literature giving expression to noble sentiments. It had embodied itself in institutions which it maintained as the treasuries of its wealth, giving to them a sanctity which history seemed to confirm. Humanism became, consequently, conservative and traditional, a tendency which naturalism forced into a habit. Remember, too, that for several centuries humanism was educationally effective. The classics presented models of statesmanship and social excellence which could serve admirably in a civilisation still owning kinship with the impressions and ideas of older times. Humanism could, therefore, claim the warrant of experience when naturalism assailed its system of education. But its strongest claim has been in its emotional richness. Under the spell of literature and art, of moral aspiration and religion, the spirit of man has been quickened and ennobled. The claim is true that naturalism tends to produce efficiency merely, while humanism tends to produce character, refinement, sensitiveness, and sympathy. Even to-day we admire the naturalist, but we love the humanist. To the latter we still assign a kind of superior excellence as we do to gentlemen of the old school. There, indeed, is a man.

It must be set down as a misfortune that humanism has found so little to support it in the background of the modern spirit and to make it effective. But misfortunes have their causes, and we can assign as a chief cause of the steady decline of humanism its foolish educational programme. I have said that it has been educationally effective, and can point to experience in proof. But its educational programme has a serious defect which naturalism has not failed to make apparent. That defect resides in the fact that the materials of its education are limited and can be exhausted by a progressive age. The source of Greek intelligence and its products was not antiquity, but nature. Those ancients drew from an inexhaustible source, one not located in the past or traditionally guarded, but one surrounding them and enfolding them with wonders daily new. The moment they forgot that source, they might still teach the wisdom of the fathers to the Romans; but they ceased to be productive. They could hold up examples to imitate, but they could produce no new models. Now, humanism in its educational programme has interested itself in the past of man, in what he has accomplished rather than in the immediate sources of his inspiration. It has sedulously cultivated the classic tendency. By that I mean that it has placed the foundations of human excellence in the past achievements of certain men, and not in the experience of living persons. It has shut human life up in books, making these books authoritative and forgetting that the men who wrote them, wrote, not out of contemplation of the past, but out of the richness of their own experience. That is why humanism was bound to exhaust itself.

I would not be understood as not valuing history, for it is man's great teacher. Our plight would be sad indeed if we had to relearn everything. We could enjoy such a condition only if the records of the past were periodically destroyed. That might prove an interesting experiment, but it would be folly to accomplish such destruction by our volition, for we have grown too dependent for that. But history should be studied not as a record of the past, but as the story of the present, as the backward look of current experience. Then it is illuminating and instructive. America to-day is what lends significance to the performance of Columbus. We are guilty of a foolish anachronism when we credit him with its discovery. Similarly, our own achievements can have significance only as the future owns them as its past.

But humanism tended to seal up the past and refuse to let it have its rightful vindication. We were bidden to write commentaries on it and introductions to it, as if a man could grow strong through the perennial contemplation of his youth. Thus it was that humanism in its educational programme provided mainly for reminiscence and little for the immediate sources of the imagination. It divided time into epochs, the least important of which was the present. It lived constantly in another world than its own. It thus became a producer of evil. Grant all its rich contributions to what we call the humanities, what has it done to lighten pain or poverty or disease? Why has it nearly always been impotent in the crises of history? The answer lies in its method and its educational programme, for its sources were secondary, and not the primary and immediate fountains of life.

My object, however, has not been to disparage humanism any more than it has been to exalt naturalism. I have rather aimed at exhibiting their emergence from the background of the modern spirit as rival claimants for our acceptance. I have suggested that they might not have contended with each other had naturalism been able to supply that emotional uplift which is so characteristic of humanism at its best. In that case, each had doubtless ministered to the other's health. But naturalism, with its altered conception of man and nature could see in humanism only a beautiful illusion, and, having nature to draw upon with ever-increasing justification of its draft, it has rapidly and signally altered our opinions and our practices. Without performing the interesting experiment of destroying the records of the past, we face, it seems to me, the present as men who must learn for themselves. We have returned to nature and learned the lesson of mechanism, with the result that both naturalism and humanism have become unsatisfactory philosophies of life. The times and the manners appear to be the natural expression of that result.

Philosophy, exercising that historical function of which I spoke in the beginning, might rest content with this diagnosis. But it has a critical function as well. It is never content until it has made an estimate, for in seeking knowledge it would aim at teaching wisdom. What estimates, we may therefore ask, does our study suggest? Surely it must be, after all, a high estimate we put upon the lessons of mechanism when we are mindful both of its achievements and its promises. A mechanical nature may not warm the heart or fire the imagination, but it is certainly a powerful and tractable instrument capable of being put to countless uses. It is too valuable to be neglected. Still, to deepen the consciousness that every end we may desire, every hope we may wish to see fulfilled, has, could we but discover it, the machinery appropriate to its realisation, is decidedly worth while. This deepening consciousness begets a sturdy confidence. A mechanical nature is not whimsical, but a thing to be relied on, striking the proper hour at the proper time. It shelters no subtle malevolence which might elude our greatest care. It allows one no longer to have his hopes depressed and his will enfeebled by the belief that any evils are incurable. Our moral responsibility is thus put in a clear light, reinforced by a demonstration of the old saying that ignorance is the greatest of evils. For when once the appropriate mechanism for the achievement of any good is made known, no one can excuse the failure of its realisation, for the condemnation is that of folly; indeed, it is a great thing for man to be able to blame his stupidity rather than Providence for the greater share of his ills. We are entering to-day on the full significance of this truth and its many applications. We insist, for instance, as never before, and our insistence will grow to a relentless importunity, that we be allowed to live in sanitary conditions and that our food and water shall be pure. This we do not out of humanitarian benevolence simply, but because mechanism has taught us that there is no good reason why unsanitary conditions should exist. Such insistence is a prophecy of a new social order when we shall universally demand that knowledge shall minister to the public good, conscious that none can gainsay the justice of that demand. Consider Japan. Immobile for centuries, she has suddenly acquired our science of nature and given such an exhibition of civilisation that the world looks on amazed. That illustration seems to me to be typical of the future, for we have learned that the knowledge which counts is not primarily that of man's impressions and ideas, but knowledge of the mechanism of nature, which, when applied, yields its inevitable result. Yes, our estimate of mechanism must be high, convinced as we have become of its essential truth.

To deepen this conviction is the great business of education, and such education will be profoundly moral. There seems, therefore, to be no good reason to conclude that what has been called naturalism is the only philosophy of life which our altered background can afford. It appears rather to be the superficial exhibition of a profounder view of life, something bound to pass in its crudity, to be replaced by a quickened and eminently rational view of human goods and the means of their attainment. That newer philosophy might still be called naturalism, for it would own nature as its source; but it might equally well be called humanism, for it would realise that nature affords the proper mechanism to minister to the ambitions and hopes of humanity.

If the narrow and straitened humanism which we have discussed erred in its educational programme, the narrow and straitened naturalism has erred in its estimate of nature. Having learned that nature works by machinery, it neglected the obvious fact that the machinery exists to support and maintain its product. The future historian will note the neglect and characterise our age as one strikingly lacking in intelligence. He will note our vast industry, and comment on the fact that while we made great machines to support and sustain the products of that industry, we could none the less regard nature as purely mechanical, with no product to exalt and sustain. We have been so afraid of the doctrine of final causes and of assigning deliberate intentions to nature, that we have forgotten that she has produced, supported, and sustained human civilisation. For man is a part of nature, carried on by her forces to work the works of intelligence. In him she bursts forth into sustained consciousness of her own evolution, producing in him knowledge of her procesess, estimation of her goods, and suspicions of her ultimate significance. This is a truth of nature and not a product of human fancy; and it is a truth fraught with the profoundest emotional import. Without such creatures as man, nature might well exist, but she would exist unvalued and unobserved. Her natural beauties would fire no imagination, her wonders would rouse no curiosity, the fact that her vast machinery supported and sustained a varied world would excite no comment and kindle no aspiration. Add man — ah! but you cannot add him as some extraneous figure tacked on as a negligible quantity to a sum already total, for he has grown out of nature's own stuff and been wrought in her workshop. He is, then, no mere commentator on the world or spectator of it; he is one of its integrations, so to speak, a supreme instance where nature has measurably evaluated herself. His comments are nature's self-estimate.

Led by an enlightened naturalism, therefore, we cannot regard the mechanism of nature as a factory where the machines run on, but where there is supreme indifference to the product. Rather must we regard it as that which supports and maintains what we choose to call ideal products, and finds in them its significance and justification, as the germ finds its reason for existence in the life it engenders. We have been half-hearted evolutionists, seeking the causes of variation and neglecting the fact that nature is always achieving results which may justify her labours. Yes, something must be achieved. It need not be something long ago devised or originally intended, but we know it must be something with a value suited to give the struggle significance. It is impossible, therefore, for philosophy to regard the emergence of reason as but the opportunity to condemn the cosmic process as the begetter of illusions, and to convince us that the ideal aspirations of man are the one great error in the universe. Nay, rather, an enlightened naturalism will call upon reason constantly to illumine our path with ever fresh glimpses of the light of nature, so that human life may be at once natural, rational, and joyous. Such a philosophy would be also an enlightened humanism, calculated to sustain culture and give birth to impressions and ideas suffused with spontaneous emotion. And such a philosophy, I am bound to believe, is a solid foundation for enlightened educational progress.

SUGGESTIONS FOR THOUGHT

1. Edwin A. Burtt has said: "Our view of man and his destiny depends in the main on our answer to this problem about the essential structure of the universe." Why is this the case?

2. What are the differences between mind and matter? How could mind have developed out of matter? How could matter be considered as an expression of mind?

3. What is the appeal of metaphysical monism? Do you believe that there is a basic unity of the universe? Is dualism a satisfactory theory, or is it the theory of one who can't make up his mind?

4. When do you feel that you are getting closest to reality — when you deal with ideas or when you are working with material things?

5. It has been said that the difference between an idealist and a materialist is primarily a difference in temperament. How would you defend this view? How refute it?

6. Do you change your view of the ultimate nature of the world in church on Sunday mornings? If so, in what way?

7. W. E. Hocking has written: "Our occupations always define for us some aspect of reality; whatever we are daily occupied with and can

deal with successfully, making it respond to our wills, — that we regard as real." What occupations might encourage one to become a naturalist? Which might stimulate idealism?

8. How can man know when he has finally reached the real nature of things? A. A. Michelson, America's first winner of a Nobel Prize, predicted in the early 1890's that the future of physics would be in the refinement of measurement rather than in new discovery.

9. Sir William Bragg has said that physics uses the classical theory on Mondays, Wednesdays, and Fridays, and the quantum theory on Tuesdays, Thursdays, and Saturdays. Could it be that reality is such that it requires conflicting, even contradictory, theories to explain it? What reason do we have for assuming that reality must conform to our laws of thought?

10. Many modern philosophers are convinced that values cannot be derived from the real world. If this is the case, what characteristics would values have?

SUGGESTIONS FOR FURTHER READING

ALEXANDER, S., "Naturalism and Value," *The Personalist,* Vol. 9, 1938, pp. 243–250.

AUBREY, EDWIN E., "Naturalism and Religious Thought," *The Journal of Philosophy,* Vol. 48, 1951, pp. 57–66.

BALFOUR, ARTHUR JAMES, *The Foundations of Belief,* New York, Longmans Green and Company, 1895, Part I, chs. 1–4.

BOODIN, JOHN ELOF, *Three Interpretations of the Universe,* New York, The Macmillan Company, 1934.

EDDINGTON, ARTHUR, *The Nature of the Physical World,* New York, The Macmillan Company, 1929, chs. 8, 15.

EWING, A. C., *Idealism: A Critical Survey,* London, Methuen and Company, 1934, ch. 8.

GOTSHALK, D. W., *Metaphysics in Modern Times,* Chicago, University of Chicago Press, 1940, ch. 2.

HOCKING, W. E., *Types of Philosophy,* New York, Charles Scribner's Sons, 1929, chs. 3–7, 19–26.

LADD, GEORGE T., "Is the Universe Friendly?" *The Hibbert Journal,* Vol. 10, 1911–12, pp. 328–343.

OAKELEY, H. D., "Reality and Value," *Proceedings of the Aristotelian Society,* Vol. 11, 1911, pp. 80–107.

PARKER, DEWITT H., "Value and Existence," *The International Journal of Ethics,* Vol. 48, 1938, pp. 475–486.

PRATT, J. B., *Personal Realism,* New York, The Macmillan Company, 1937, ch. 23.

ROYCE, JOSIAH, *Lectures on Modern Idealism,* New Haven, Yale University Press, 1919.

SCHNEIDER, HERBERT W., "Natural Thought and the World of Religion," *The Journal of Philosophy,* Vol. 48, 1951, pp. 66–74.

STACE, W. T., *Time and Existence,* Princeton, Princeton University Press, 1952, pp. 127–131.

12

SCIENCE AND VALUES

THE RELEASE of the fearful energy of the atom has pointed up this problem in the minds of millions of people. It is far more than an academic issue. Dewey and Russell, writing in 1931, express attitudes which are quite typical of these men: Dewey — optimistic, hopeful, progressive; Russell — pessimistic, fearful, skeptical. John Dewey (1859–1952) was one of the most influential philosophers America has produced. He early broke from the Hegelian tradition which first appealed to him and turned to the pragmatism of William James. Dewey, however, avoided the word "pragmatism" and preferred to call his own philosophy "instrumentalism." Although he made many contributions to theoretical philosophy, he is best known as the father of progressive education. Dewey's professional career included professorships at the universities of Minnesota, Michigan, and Chicago and at Columbia University. Bertrand Russell (1872–   ), like Dewey, has contributed to both the theory and the practice of philosophy. Lord Russell has often championed unpopular social issues, e. g., pacificism, companionate marriage, socialism. His *Principia Mathematica* (written with A. N. Whitehead) is one of the most learned books of this century. For many years he has been a fellow and lecturer at Trinity College, Cambridge University. His philosophical position has changed through the years, but it can be most accurately described as realistic.

A

The significant outward forms of the civilization of the western world are the product of the machine and its technology. Indirectly, they are the product of the scientific revolution which took place in the seventeenth century. In its effect upon men's external habits, dominant interests, the conditions under which

John Dewey, *Philosophy and Civilization,* New York, G. P. Putnam's Sons, 1931, pp. 318–330. Reprinted by permission of the publishers.

they work and associate, whether in the family, the factory, the state, or internationally, science is by far the most potent social factor in the modern world. It operates, however, through its undesigned effects rather than as a transforming influence of men's thoughts and purposes. This contrast between outer and inner operation is the great contradiction in our lives. Habits of thought and desire remain in substance what they were before the rise of science, while the conditions under which they take effect have been radically altered by science.

When we look at the external social consequences of science, we find it impossible to apprehend the extent or gauge the rapidity of their occurrence. Alfred North Whitehead has recently called attention to the progressive shortening of the time-span of social change. That due to basic conditions seems to be of the order of half a million years; that due to lesser physical conditions, like alterations in climate, to be of the order of five thousand years. Until almost our own day the time-span of sporadic technological changes was of the order of five hundred years; according to him, no great technological changes took place between, say, 100 A.D. and 1400 A.D. With the introduction of steam-power, the fifty years from 1780 to 1830 were marked by more changes than are found in any previous thousand years. The advance of chemical techniques and in use of electricity and radio-energy in the last forty years makes even this last change seem slow and awkward.

Domestic life, political institutions, international relations and personal contacts are shifting with kaleidoscopic rapidity before our eyes. We cannot appreciate and weigh the changes; they occur too swiftly. We do not have time to take them in. No sooner do we begin to understand the meaning of one such

change than another comes and displaces the former. Our minds are dulled by the sudden and repeated impacts. Externally, science through its applications is manufacturing the conditions of our institutions at such a speed that we are too bewildered to know what sort of civilization is in process of making.

Because of this confusion, we cannot even draw up a ledger account of social gains and losses due to the operation of science. But at least we know that the earlier optimism which thought that the advance of natural science was to dispel superstition, ignorance, and oppression, by placing reason on the throne, was unjustified. Some superstitions have given way, but the mechanical devices due to science have made it possible to spread new kinds of error and delusion among a larger multitude. The fact is that it is foolish to try to draw up a debit and credit account for science. To do so is to mythologize; it is to personify science and impute to it a will and an energy on its own account. In truth science is strictly impersonal; a method and a body of knowledge. It owes its operation and its consequences to the human beings who use it. It adapts itself passively to the purposes and desires which animate these human beings. It lends itself with equal impartiality to the kindly offices of medicine and hygiene and the destructive deeds of war. It elevates some through opening new horizons; it depresses others by making them slaves of machines operated for the pecuniary gain of owners.

The neutrality of science to the uses made of it renders it silly to talk about its bankruptcy, or to worship it as the usherer in of a new age. In the degree in which we realize this fact, we shall devote our attention to the human purposes and motives which control its application. Science is an instrument, a method, a body of technique. While it is an end for those inquirers who are engaged in its pursuit, in the large human sense it is a means, a tool. For what ends shall it be used? Shall it be used deliberately, systematically, for the promotion of social well-being, or shall it be employed primarily for private aggrandizement, leaving its larger social results to chance? Shall the scientific attitude be used to create new mental and moral attitudes, or shall it continue to be subordinated to service of desires, purposes and institutions which were formed before science came into existence? Can the attitudes which control the use of science be themselves so influenced by scientific technique that they will harmonize with its spirit?

The beginning of wisdom is, I repeat, the realization that science itself is an instrument which is indifferent to the external uses to which it is put. Steam and electricity remain natural forces when they operate through mechanisms; the only problem is the purposes for which men set the mechanisms to work. The essential technique of gunpowder is the same whether it be used to blast rocks from the quarry to build better human habitations, or to hurl death upon men at war with one another. The airplane binds men at a distance in closer bonds of intercourse and understanding, or it rains missiles of death upon hapless populations. We are forced to consider the relation of human ideas and ideals to the social consequences which are produced by science as an instrument.

The problem involved is the greatest which civilization has ever had to face. It is, without exaggeration, the most serious issue of contemporary life. Here is the instrumentality, the most powerful, for good and evil, the world has ever known. What are we going to do with it? Shall we leave our underlying aims unaffected by it, treating it merely as a means by which unco-operative individuals may advance their own fortunes? Shall we try to improve the hearts of men without regard to the new methods which science puts at our disposal? There are those, men in high position in church and state, who urge this course. They trust to a transforming influence of a morals and religion which have not been affected by science to change human desire and purpose, so that they will employ science and machine technology for beneficent social ends. The recent Encyclical of the Pope is a classic document in expression of a point of view which would rely wholly upon inner regeneration to protect society from the injurious uses to which science may be put. Quite apart from any ecclesiastical connection, there are many "intellectuals" who appeal to inner "spiritual" concepts, totally divorced from scientific intelligence, to effect the needed work. But there is another alternative: to take the method of science home into our own controlling attitudes and dispositions, to employ the new techniques as means of directing our thoughts and efforts to a planned control of social forces.

Science and machine technology are young from the standpoint of human history. Though vast in stature, they are infants in age. Three hundred years are but a moment in comparison with thousands of centuries man has lived on the earth. In view of the inertia of institutions and of the mental habits they breed, it is not surprising that the new technique of apparatus and calculation, which is the essence of science, has made so little impression on underlying human attitudes. The momentum of traditions and purposes that preceded its rise took possession of the new instrument and turned it to their ends. Moreover, science had to struggle for existence. It had powerful enemies in church and state. It needed friends and it welcomed alliance with the rising capitalism which it so effectively promoted. If it tended to foster secularism and to create predominantly material interests, it could still be argued that it was in essential harmony with traditional morals and religion. But there were lacking the conditions which are indispensable to the serious application of scientific method in reconstruction of fundamental beliefs and attitudes. In addition, the development of the new science was attended with so many internal difficulties that energy had to go to perfecting the instrument just as an instrument. Because of all these circumstances the fact that science was used in behalf of old interests is nothing to be wondered at.

The conditions have now changed, radically so. The claims of natural science in the physical field are undisputed. Indeed, its prestige is so great that an almost superstitious aura gathers about its name and work. Its progress is no longer dependent upon the adventurous inquiry of a few untrammeled souls. Not only are universities organized to promote scientific research and learning, but one may almost imagine the university laboratories abolished and still feel confident of the continued advance of science. The development of industry has compelled the inclusion of scientific inquiry within the processes of production and distribution. We find in the public prints as many demonstrations of the benefits of science from a business point of view as there are proofs of its harmony with religion.

It is not possible that, under such conditions, the subordination of scientific techniques to purposes and institutions that flourished before its rise can indefinitely continue. In all affairs there comes a time when a cycle of growth reaches maturity. When this stage is reached, the period of protective nursing comes to an end. The problem of securing proper use succeeds to that of securing conditions of growth. Now that science has established itself and has created a new social en-

vironment, it has (if I may for the moment personify it) to face the issue of its social responsibilities. Speaking without personification, we who have a powerful and perfected instrument in our hands, one which is determining the quality of social changes, must ask what changes we want to see achieved and what we want to see averted. We must, in short, plan its social effects with the same care with which in the past we have planned its physical operation and consequences. Till now we have employed science absent-mindedly as far as its effects upon human beings are concerned. The present situation with its extraordinary control of natural energies and its totally unplanned and haphazard social economy is a dire demonstration of the folly of continuing this course.

The social effects of the application of science have been accidental, even though they are intrinsic to the private and unorganized motives which we have permitted to control that application. It would be hard to find a better proof that such is the fact than the vogue of the theory that such unregulated use of science is in accord with "natural law," and that all effort at planned control of its social effects is an interference with nature. The use which has been made of a peculiar idea of personal liberty to justify the dominion of accident in social affairs is another convincing proof. The doctrine that the most potent instrument of widespread, enduring, and objective social changes must be left at the mercy of purely private desires for purely personal gain is a doctrine of anarchy. Our present insecurity of life is the fruit of the adoption in practice of this anarchic doctrine.

The technologies of industry have flowed from the intrinsic nature of science. For that is itself essentially a technology of apparatus, materials and numbers. But the pecuniary aims which have decided the social results of the use of these technologies have not flowed from the inherent nature of science. They have been derived from institutions and attendant mental and moral habits which were entrenched before there was any such thing as science and the machine. In consequence, science has operated as a means for extending the influence of the institution of private property and connected legal relations far beyond their former limits. It has operated as a device to carry an enormous load of stocks and bonds and to make the reward of investment in the way of profit and power one out of all proportion to that accruing from actual work and service.

Here lies the heart of our present social problem. Science has hardly been used to modify men's fundamental acts and attitudes in social matters. It has been used to extend enormously the scope and power of interests and values which anteceded its rise. Here is the contradiction in our civilization. The potentiality of science as the most powerful instrument of control which has ever existed puts to mankind its one outstanding present challenge.

There is one field in which science has been somewhat systematically employed as an agent of social control. Condorcet, writing during the French Revolution in the prison from which he went to the guillotine, hailed the invention of the calculus of probabilities as the opening of a new era. He saw in this new mathematical technique the promise of methods of insurance which should distribute evenly and widely the impact of the disasters to which humanity is subject. Insurance against death, fire, hurricanes and so on have in a measure confirmed his prediction. Nevertheless, in large and important social areas, we have only made the merest beginning of the method of insurance against the hazards of life and death. Insurance against the risks

of maternity, of sickness, old age, unemployment, is still rudimentary; its idea is fought by all reactionary forces. Witness the obstacles against which social insurance with respect to accidents incurred in industrial employment had to contend. The anarchy called natural law and personal liberty still operates with success against a planned social use of the resources of scientific knowledge.

Yet insurance against perils and hazards is the place where the application of science has gone the furthest, not the least, distance in present society. The fact that motor cars kill and maim more persons yearly than all factories, shops, and farms is a fair symbol of how backward we are in that province where we have done most. Here, however, is one field in which at least the idea of planned use of scientific knowledge for social welfare has received recognition. We no longer regard plagues, famine and disease as visitations of necessary "natural law" or of a power beyond nature. By preventive means of medicine and public hygiene as well as by various remedial measures we have in idea, if not in fact, placed technique in the stead of magic and chance and uncontrollable necessity in this one area of life. And yet, as I have said, here is where the socially planned use of science has made the most, not least, progress. Were it not for the youth of science and the historically demonstrated slowness of all basic mental and moral change, we could hardly find language to express astonishment at the situation in which we have an extensive and precise control of physical energies and conditions, and in which we leave the social consequences of their operation to chance, *laissez-faire,* privileged pecuniary status, and the inertia of tradition and old institutions.

Condorcet thought and worked in the Baconian strain. But the Baconian ideal of the systematic organization of all knowledge, the planned control of discovery and invention, for the relief and advancement of the human estate, remains almost as purely an ideal as when Francis Bacon put it forward centuries ago. And this is true in spite of the fact that the physical and mathematical technique upon which a planned control of social results depends has made in the meantime incalculable progress. The conclusion is inevitable. The outer arena of life has been transformed by science. The effectively working mind and character of man have hardly been touched.

Consider that phase of social action where science might theoretically be supposed to have taken effect most rapidly, namely, education. In dealing with the young, it would seem as if scientific methods might at once take effect in transformation of mental attitudes, without meeting the obstacles which have to be overcome in dealing with adults. In higher education, in universities and technical schools, a great amount of research is done and much scientific knowledge is imparted. But it is a principle of modern psychology that the basic attitudes of mind are formed in the earlier years. And I venture the assertion that for the most part the formation of intellectual habits in elementary education, in the home and school, is hardly affected by scientific method. Even in our so-called progressive schools, science is usually treated as a side line, an ornamental extra, not as the chief means of developing the right attitudes. It is treated generally as one more body of ready-made information to be acquired by traditional methods, or else as an occasional diversion. That it is the method of all effective mental approach and attack in all subjects has not gained even a foothold. Yet if scientific method is not something esoteric but is a realization of the most effective operation of intelligence, it should be axiomatic that the development of scientific attitudes of thought, observation, and inquiry is the chief business of study and learning.

Two phases of the contradiction inhering in our civilization may be especially mentioned. We have long been committed in theory and words to the principle of democracy. But criticism of democracy, assertions that it is failing to work and even to exist are everywhere rife. In the last few months we have become accustomed to similar assertions regarding our economic and industrial system. Mr. Ivy Lee, for example, in a recent commencement address, entitled *This Hour of Bewilderment,* quoted from a representative clergyman, a railway president, and a publicist, to the effect that our capitalistic system is on trial. And yet the statements had to do with only one feature of that system: the prevalence of unemployment and attendant insecurity. It is not necessary for me to invade the territory of economics and politics. The essential fact is that if both democracy and capitalism are on trial, it is in reality our collective intelligence which is on trial. We have displayed enough intelligence in the physical field to create the new and powerful instrument of science and technology. We have not as yet had enough intelligence to use this instrument deliberately and systematically to control its social operations and consequences.

The first lesson which the use of scientific method teaches is that control is co-ordinate with knowledge and understanding. Where there is technique there is the possibility of administering forces and conditions in the region where the technique applies. Our lack of control in the sphere of human relations, national, domestic, international, requires no emphasis of notice. It is proof that we have not begun to operate scientifically in such matters. The public press is full of discussion of the five-year plan and the ten-year plan in Russia. But the fact that the plan is being tried by a country which has a dictatorship foreign to all our beliefs tends to divert attention from the fundamental consideration. The point for us is not this political setting nor its communistic context. It is that by the use of all available resources of knowledge and experts an attempt is being made at organized social planning and control. Were we to forget for the moment the special Russian political setting, we should see here an effort to use co-ordinated knowledge and technical skill to direct economic resources toward social order and stability.

To hold that such organized planning is possible only in a communistic society is to surrender the case to communism. Upon any other basis, the effort of Russia is a challenge and a warning to those who live under another political and economic regime. It is a call to use our more advanced knowledge and technology in scientific thinking about our own needs, problems, evils, and possibilities so as to achieve some degree of control of the social consequences which the application of science is, willy-nilly, bringing about. What stands in the way is a lot of outworn traditions, moth-eaten slogans and catchwords, that do substitute duty for thought, as well as our entrenched predatory self-interest. We shall only make a real beginning in intelligent thought when we cease mouthing platitudes; stop confining our idea to antitheses of individualism and socialism, capitalism and communism, and realize that the issue is between chaos and order, chance and control: the haphazard use and the planned use of scientific techniques.

Thus the statement with which we began, namely, that we are living in a world of change extraordinary in range and speed, is only half true. It holds of the outward applications of science. It does not hold of our intellectual and moral attitudes. About physical conditions and energies we think scientifically; at least, some men do, and the results of their thinking enter into the experiences of all of us. But the entrenched and stubborn institutions of the past stand in the way of our thinking scientifically about human relations and social issues. Our mental habits in these respects are dominated by institutions of family, state, church, and business that were formed long before men had an effective technique of inquiry and validation. It is this contradiction from which we suffer to-day.

Disaster follows in its wake. It is impossible to overstate the mental confusion and the practical disorder which are bound to result when external and physical effects are planned and regulated, while the attitudes of mind upon which the direction of external results depends are left to the medley of chance, tradition, and dogma. It is a common saying that our physical science has far outrun our social knowledge; that our physical skill has become exact and comprehensive while our humane arts are vague, opinionated, and narrow. The fundamental trouble, however, is not lack of sufficient information about social facts, but unwillingness to adopt the scientific attitude in what we do know. Men floundered in a morass of opinion about physical matters for thousands of years. It was when they began to use their ideas experimentally and to create a technique or direction of experimentation that physical science advanced with system and surety. No amount of mere fact-finding develops science nor the scientific attitude in either physics or social affairs. Facts merely amassed and piled up are dead; a burden which only adds to confusion. When ideas, hypotheses, begin to play upon facts, when they are methods for experimental use in action, then light dawns; then it becomes possible to discriminate significant from trivial facts, and relations take the place of isolated scraps. Just as soon as we begin to use the knowledge and skills we have to control social consequences in the interest of shared abundant and secured life, we shall cease to complain of the backwardness of our social knowledge. We shall take the road which leads to the assured building up of social science just as men built up physical science when they actively used the techniques of tools and numbers in physical experimentation.

In spite, then, of all the record of the past, the great scientific revolution is still to come. It will ensue when men collectively and cooperatively organize their knowledge for application to achieve and make secure social values; when they systematically use scientific procedures for the control of human relationships and the direction of the social effects of our vast technological machinery. Great as have been the social changes of the last century, they are not to be compared with those which will emerge when our faith in scientific method is made manifest in social works. We are living in a period of depression. The intellectual function of trouble is to lead men to think. The depression is a small price to pay if it induces us to think about the cause of the disorder, confusion, and insecurity which are the outstanding traits of our social life. If we do not go back to their cause, namely our half-way and accidental use of science, mankind will pass through depressions, for they are the graphic record of our unplanned social life. The story of the achievement of science in physical control is evidence of the possibility of control in social affairs. It is our human intelligence and human courage which are on trial; it is incredible that men who have brought the technique of physical discovery, invention, and use to such a pitch of perfection will abdicate in the face of the infinitely more important human problem.

B

The impulse towards scientific construction is admirable when it does not thwart any of the major impulses that give value to human life, but when it is allowed to forbid all outlet to everything but itself it becomes a form of cruel tyranny. There is, I think, a real danger lest the world should become subject to a tyranny of this sort, and it is on this account that I have not shrunk from depicting the darker features of the world that scientific manipulation unchecked might wish to create.

Science in the course of the few centuries of its history has undergone an internal development which appears to be not yet completed. One may sum up this development as the passage from contemplation to manipulation. The love of knowledge to which the growth of science is due is itself the product of a twofold impulse. We may seek knowledge of an object because we love the object or because we wish to have power over it. The former impulse leads to the kind of knowledge that is contemplative, the latter to the kind that is practical. In the development of science the power impulse has increasingly prevailed over the love impulse. The power impulse is embodied in industrialism and in governmental technique. It is embodied also in the philosophies known as pragmatism and

Reprinted from *The Scientific Outlook* by Bertrand Russell. By permission of W. W. Norton & Company, Inc., and of George Allen & Unwin Ltd. Copyright 1931 by Bertrand Russell. Pp. 260–269.

instrumentalism. Each of these philosophies holds, broadly speaking, that our beliefs about any object are true in so far as they enable us to manipulate it with advantage to ourselves. This is what may be called a governmental view of truth. Of truth so conceived science offers us a great deal; indeed there seems no limit to its possible triumphs. To the man who wishes to change his environment science offers astonishingly powerful tools, and if knowledge consists in the power to produce intended changes, then science gives knowledge in abundance.

But the desire for knowledge has another form, belonging to an entirely different set of emotions. The mystic, the lover, and the poet are also seekers after knowledge — not perhaps very successful seekers, but none the less worthy of respect on that account. In all forms of love we wish to have knowledge of what is loved, not for purposes of power, but for the ecstacy of contemplation. "In knowledge of God standeth our eternal life," but not because knowledge of God gives us power over Him. Wherever there is ecstacy or joy or delight derived from an object there is the desire to know that object — to know it not in the manipulative fashion that consists of turning it into something else, but to know it in the fashion of the beatific vision, because in itself and for itself it sheds happiness upon the lover. In sex love as in other forms of love the impulse to this kind of knowledge exists, unless the love is purely physical or practical. This may indeed be made the touchstone of any love that is valuable. Love which has value contains an impulse towards that kind of knowledge out of which the mystic union springs.

Science in its beginnings was due to men who were in love with the world. They perceived the beauty of the stars and the sea, of the winds and the mountains. Because they loved them their thoughts dwelt upon them, and they wished to understand them more intimately than a mere outward contemplation made possible. "The World," said Heraclitus, "is an ever-living fire, with measures kindling and measures going out." Heraclitus and the other Ionian philosophers, from whom came the first impulse to scientific knowledge, felt the strange beauty of the world almost like a madness in the blood. They were men of Titanic passionate intellect, and from the intensity of their intellectual passion the whole movement of the modern world has sprung. But step by step, as science has developed, the impulse of love which gave it birth has been increasingly thwarted, while the impulse of power, which was at first a mere camp-follower, has gradually usurped command in virtue of its unforeseen success. The lover of nature has been baffled, the tyrant over nature has been rewarded. As physics has developed, it has deprived us step by step of what we thought we knew concerning the intimate nature of the physical world. Colour and sound, light and shade, form and texture, belong no longer to that external nature that the Ionians sought as the bride of their devotion. All these things have been transferred from the beloved to the lover, and the beloved has become a skeleton of rattling bones, cold and dreadful, but perhaps a mere phantasm. The poor physicists, appalled at the desert that their formulae have revealed, call upon God to give them comfort, but God must share the ghostliness of His creation, and the answer that the physicists think they hear to their cry is only the frightened beating of their own hearts. Disappointed as the lover of nature, the man of science is becoming its tyrant. What matters it, says the practical man, whether the outer world exists or is a dream, provided I can make it behave as I wish? Thus science has more and more substituted power-knowledge for love-knowledge, and as this substitution becomes completed science tends more and more to become sadistic. The scientific society of the future as we have been imagining it is one in which the power impulse has completely overwhelmed the impulse of love, and this is the psychological source of the cruelties which it is in danger of exhibiting.

Science, which began as the pursuit of truth, is becoming incompatible with veracity, since complete veracity tends more and more to complete scientific scepticism. When science is considered contemplatively, not practically, we find that what we believe we believe owing to animal faith, and it is only our disbeliefs that are due to science. When, on the other hand, science is considered as a technique for the transformation of ourselves and our environment, it is found to give us a power quite independent of its metaphysical validity. But we can only wield this power by ceasing to ask ourselves metaphysical questions as to the nature of reality. Yet these questions are the evidence of a lover's attitude towards the world. Thus it is only in so far as we renounce the world as its lovers that we can conquer it as its technicians. But this division in the soul is fatal to what is best in man. As soon as the failure of science considered as metaphysics is realized, the power conferred by science as a technique is only obtainable by something analogous to the worship of Satan, that is to say, by the renunciation of love.

This is the fundamental reason why the prospect of a scientific society must be viewed with apprehension. The scientific society in its pure form, which is what we have been trying to depict, is incompatible with the pursuit of truth, with love, with art, with spontaneous delight, with every ideal that men have hitherto cherished, with the sole exception of ascetic renunciation. It is not knowledge that is the source of these dangers. Knowledge is good and ignorance is evil: to this principle the lover of the world can admit no exception. Nor is it power in and for itself that is the source of danger. What is dangerous is power wielded for the sake of power, not power wielded for the sake of genuine good. The leaders of the modern world are drunk with power: the fact that they can do something that no one previously thought it possible to do is to them a sufficient reason for doing it. Power is not one of the ends of life, but merely a means to other ends, and until men remember the ends that power should subserve, science will not do what it might to minister to the good life. But what then are the ends of life, the reader will say. I do not think that one man has a right to legislate for another on this matter. For each individual the ends of life are those things which he deeply desires, and which if they existed would give him peace. Or, if it be thought that peace is too much to ask this side of the grave, let us say that the ends of life should give delight or joy or ecstacy. In the conscious desires of the man who seeks power for its own sake there is something dusty: when he has it he wants only more power, and does not find rest in contemplation of what he has. The lover, the poet and the mystic find a fuller satisfaction than the seeker after power can ever know, since they can rest in the object of their love, whereas the seeker after power must be perpetually engaged in some fresh manipulation if he is not to suffer from a sense of emptiness. I think therefore that the satisfactions of the lover, using that word in its broadest sense, exceed the satisfactions of the tyrant, and deserve a higher place among the ends of life. When I come to die I shall not feel that I have lived in vain. I have seen the earth turn red at evening, the dew sparkling in the morning, and the snow shining under a frosty sun; I have smelt rain after drought, and have heard the stormy Atlantic beat upon the granite shores of Cornwall. Science may bestow these and other joys upon more people than could otherwise enjoy them. If so, its power will be wisely used. But when it takes out of life the moments to which life owes its value, science will not deserve admiration, however cleverly and however elaborately it may lead men along the road to despair. The sphere of values lies outside science, except in so far as science consists in the pursuit of knowledge. Science as the pursuit of power must not obtrude upon the sphere of values, and scientific technique, if it is to enrich human life, must not outweigh the ends which it should serve.

The number of men who determine the character of an age is small. Columbus, Luther and Charles V dominated the sixteenth century; Galileo and Descartes governed the seventeenth. The important men in the age that is just ended are Edison, Rockefeller, Lenin, and Sun Yat-sen. With the exception of Sun Yat-sen these were men devoid of culture, contemptuous of the past, self-confident, and ruthless. Traditional wisdom had no place in their thoughts and feelings; mechanism and organization were what interested them. A different education might have made all these men quite different. Edison might in his youth have acquired a knowledge of history and poetry and art; Rockefeller might have been taught how he had been anticipated by Crœsus and Crassus; Lenin, instead of having hatred implanted in him by the execution of his brother during his student days, might have made himself acquainted with the rise of Islam and the development of Puritanism from piety to plutocracy. By means of such an education some little leaven of doubt might have entered the souls of these great men. Given a little doubt their achievement

would perhaps have been less in volume, but much greater in value.

Our world has a heritage of culture and beauty, but unfortunately we have been handing on this heritage only to the less active and important members of each generation. The government of the world, by which I do not mean its ministerial posts but its key-positions of power, has been allowed to fall into the hands of men ignorant of the past, without tenderness towards what is traditional, without understanding of what they are destroying. There is no essential reason why this should be the case. To prevent it is an educational problem, and not a very difficult one. Men in the past were often parochial in space, but the dominant men of our age are parochial in time. They feel for the past a contempt that it does not deserve, and for the present a respect that it deserves still less. The copy-book maxims of a former age have become outworn, but a new set of copy-book maxims is required. First among these I should put: "It is better to do a little good than much harm." To give content to this maxim it would of course be necessary to instil some sense of what is good. Few men in the present day, for example, can be induced to believe that there is no inherent excellence in rapid locomotion. To climb from Hell to Heaven is good, though it be a slow and laborious process; to fall from Heaven to Hell is bad, even though it be done with the speed of Milton's Satan. Nor can it be said that a mere increase in the production of material commodities is in itself a thing of great value. To prevent extreme poverty is important, but to add to the possessions of those who already have too much is a worthless waste of effort. To prevent crime may be necessary, but to invent new crimes in order that the police may show skill in preventing them is less admirable. The new powers that science has given to man can only be wielded safely by those who, whether through the study of history or through their own experience of life, have acquired some reverence for human feelings and some tenderness towards the emotions that give colour to the daily existence of men and women. I do not mean to deny that scientific technique may in time build an artificial world in every way preferable to that in which men have hitherto lived, but I do say that if this is to be done it must be done tentatively and with a realization that the purpose of government is not merely to afford pleasure to those who govern, but to make life tolerable for those who are governed. Scientific technique must no longer be allowed to form the whole culture of the holders of power, and it must become an essential part of men's ethical outlook to realize that the will alone cannot make a good life. Knowing and feeling are equally essential ingredients both in the life of the individual and in that of the community. Knowledge, if it is wide and intimate, brings with it a realization of distant times and places, an awareness that the individual is not omnipotent or all-important, and a perspective in which values are seen more clearly than by those to whom a distant view is impossible. Even more important than knowledge is the life of the emotions. A world without delight and without affection is a world destitute of value. These things the scientific manipulator must remember, and if he does his manipulation may be wholly beneficial. All that is needed is that men should not be so intoxicated by new power as to forget the truths that were familiar to every previous generation. Not all wisdom is new, nor is all folly out of date.

Man has been disciplined hitherto by his subjection to nature. Having emancipated himself from this subjection, he is showing something of the defects of slave-turned-master. A new moral outlook is called for in which submission to the powers of nature is replaced by respect for what is best in man. It is where this respect is lacking that scientific technique is dangerous. So long as it is present, science, having delivered man from bondage to nature, can proceed to deliver him from bondage to the slavish part of himself. The dangers exist, but they are not inevitable, and hope for the future is at least as rational as fear.

SUGGESTIONS FOR THOUGHT

1. Compare a scientific and a poetic description of a rainbow. Can either description be said to give us the rainbow "as it is"?

2. If you were not living in the twentieth century, in what century would you want to live? Would a modern printing press and a telephone have made the Age of Pericles more cultural? Would a typewriter have helped Shakespeare write better plays? In what ways have the radio and the airplane made our lives happier? In what ways have they decreased our happiness?

3. A mathematician is said to have thanked God that his new theory was not of the slightest practical use to anyone. Why was he grateful? Why do scientists seek a value-free science? Can scientists rightfully be held accountable for the uses to which their discoveries are put? In what ways are scientists concerned about the practicality of their discoveries?

4. Can facts and values be separated? W. R. Inge once said: "I am prepared to maintain that a fact which has no value is not a fact, and that a value which has no existence is not a value."

5. How soon should new theories and discoveries in science be made popular informa-

tion? Should scientists withhold information that might be of benefit to humanity until they have worked out all the details? Is a nation justified in trying to keep scientific information secret? Should scientists be unrestrained in their research, or is society right in setting certain limits to scientific research? E.g., vivisectionism.

6. "Hence when the physical sciences describe objects and the world as being such and such, it is thought that the description is of reality as it exists in itself. Since all value-traits are lacking in objects as science presents them to us, it is assumed that reality has no such characteristics." (John Dewey) Is this a justified assumption? Defend your answer.

7. "The development of science is not merely a means toward the realization of certain values, but actually influences the course of values themselves, the things that men prize." (Charles W. Morris) Name some of the values that have been influenced by science.

8. May Kendall wrote the following parody addressed to T. H. Huxley:

> Primroses by the river's brim
> Dicotyledons were to him,
> And they were nothing more.

What more could they be?

9. Bernard Shaw once raised an interesting question: "How much better would the world be if it were all knowledge and no mercy?" Why do you suppose Shaw placed knowledge and mercy in opposition? What does St. Paul say about knowledge and charity? (I Corinthians 13)

10. "Nothing . . . can do more harm to democracy than the thesis, so popular with many contemporary moral and religious leaders, that science is neutral, if not positively evil, with respect to human values. The truth of the matter is that the scientific attitude of mind is one of the highest values, and a primary value in democracy." (F. S. C. Northrop) Why? What are other ways in which science is involved in human values?

11. Compare the quotation from Northrop with this one from John Dewey: "The great mistake of historic philosophy has been to admit values in any shape within the sacred enclosure of perfect science."

12. W. M. Urban says that "Science tries to forget men's wishes." What wishes of men are the ones science tries to forget? "True philosophy," Urban adds, "not only remembers them but tries to understand them."

SUGGESTIONS FOR FURTHER READING

BROWNELL, BAKER, *The College and the Community,* New York, Harper and Brothers, 1952, ch. 5.

COMPTON, ARTHUR H., *The Human Meaning of Science,* Chapel Hill, University of North Carolina Press, 1940.

DINGLE, HERBERT, *The Scientific Adventure,* New York, Pitman Publishing Corporation, 1952, ch. 18, 19.

GEIGER, GEORGE R., *Philosophy and the Social Order,* Boston, Houghton Mifflin Company, 1947, ch. 6.

HOCKING, W. E., *What Man Can Make of Man,* New York, Harper and Brothers, 1942, ch. 4.

LUNDBERG, GEORGE A., *Can Science Save Us?,* New York, Longmans Green and Company, 1947.

LYND, ROBERT S., *Knowledge for What?,* Princeton, Princeton University Press, 1939, ch. 5.

MATHER, KIRTLEY F., *Science in Search of God,* New York, Henry Holt and Company, 1928.

MCCRACKEN, D. J., *Thinking and Valuing,* New York, The Macmillan Company, 1950, pp. 1–23.

MEES, C. E. KENNETH, *The Path of Science,* New York, John Wiley and Sons, 1946, ch. 10.

MUMFORD, LEWIS, *Values for Survival,* New York, Harcourt, Brace and Company, 1946, pp. 78–130.

NORTHROP, F. S. C., *The Logic of the Sciences*

and the Humanities, New York, The Macmillan Company, 1947, ch. 23.

RUSSELL, L. J., "Science and Value," *The Journal of Philosophical Studies,* Vol. 5, 1930, pp. 257–265.

WHITE, ANDREW DICKSON, *A History of the Warfare of Science with Theology in Christendom,* New York, D. Appleton and Company, 1897.

WHITEHEAD, A. N., *Science and the Modern World,* New York, The Macmillan Company, 1925, ch. 12.

PART THREE

THE CREATIVE WORLD

13

THE NATURE OF RELIGION

FRIEDRICH ERNST DANIEL SCHLEIERMACHER (1768–1834) is best known for his definition of religion as a feeling of absolute dependence. Schleiermacher was reared as a Moravian. Although he later left the Moravians, their intense religious spirit stayed with him throughout his life. He held preaching and teaching positions at Halle and Berlin. Sarvepalli Radhakrishnan (1888–) is a Hindu who has devoted his life to the improvement of East–West relationships through the interpretation of religious and philosophical points of view. After many years of teaching in Indian universities, he became the leader of the Indian delegation to the United Nations Educational, Scientific and Cultural Organization. In 1952 he was elected Vice-President of the Republic of India. Radhakrishnan, unlike Schleiermacher, emphasizes the intellectual facets of religion.

A

Religion is for you at one time a way of thinking, a faith, a peculiar way of contemplating the world, and of combining what meets us in the world: at another, it is a way of acting, a peculiar desire and love, a special kind of conduct and character. Without this

distinction of a theoretical and practical you could hardly think at all, and though both sides belong to religion, you are usually accustomed to give heed chiefly to only one at a time. Wherefore, we shall look closely at religion from both sides.

We commence with religion as a kind of activity. Activity is twofold, having to do with life and with art. You would ascribe with the poet earnestness to life and cheerfulness to

Friedrich Schleiermacher, *On Religion: Speeches to Its Cultured Despisers,* translated by John Oman, London, Kegan Paul, Trench, Trübner & Company, 1893, Lecture 2 (in part). Reprinted by permission of Routledge & Kegan Paul Ltd.

art; or, in some other way, you would contrast them. Separate them you certainly will. For life, duty is the watchword. The moral law shall order it, and virtue shall show itself the ruling power in it, that the individual may be in harmony with the universal order of the world, and may nowhere encroach in a manner to disturb and confuse. This life, you consider, may appear without any discernible trace of art. Rather is it to be attained by rigid rules that have nothing to do with the free and variable precepts of art. Nay, you look upon it almost as a rule that art should be somewhat in the background, and nonessential for those who are strictest in the ordering of life. On the other hand, imagination shall inspire the artist, and genius shall completely sway him. Now imagination and genius are for you quite different from virtue and morality, being capable of existing in the largest measure along with a much more meagre moral endowment. Nay you are inclined, because the prudent power often comes into danger by reason of the fiery power, to relax for the artist somewhat of the strict demands of life.

How now does it stand with piety, in so far as you regard it as a peculiar kind of activity? Has it to do with right living? Is it something good and praiseworthy, yet different from morality, for you will not hold them to be identical? But in that case morality does not exhaust the sphere which it should govern. Another power works alongside of it, and has both right and might to continue working. Or will you perhaps betake yourselves to the position that piety is a virtue, and religion a duty or section of duties? Is religion incorporated into morality and subordinated to it, as a part to the whole? Is it, as some suppose, special duties towards God, and therefore a part of all morality which is the performance of all duties? But, if I have rightly appreci-

ated or accurately reproduced what you say, you do not think so. You rather seem to say that the pious person has something entirely peculiar, both in his doing and leaving undone, and that morality can be quite moral without therefore being pious.

And how are religion and art related? They can hardly be quite alien, because, from of old, what is greatest in art has had a religious character. When, therefore, you speak of an artist as pious, do you still grant him that relaxation of the strict demands of virtue? Rather he is then subjected, like every other person. But then to make the cases parallel, you must secure that those who devote themselves to life do not remain quite without art. Perhaps this combination gives its peculiar form to religion. With your view, there seems no other possible issue.

Religion then, as a kind of activity, is a mixture of elements that oppose and neutralize each other. Pray is not this rather the utterance of your dislike than your conviction? Such an accidental shaking together, leaving both elements unaltered, does not, even though the most accurate equality be attained, make something specific. But suppose it is otherwise, suppose piety is something which truly fuses both, then it cannot be formed simply by bringing the two together, but must be an original unity. Take care, however, I warn you, that you do not make such an admission. Were it the case, morality and genius apart would be only fragments of the ruins of religion, or its corpse when it is dead. Religion were then higher than both, the true divine life itself. But, in return for this warning, if you accept it, and discover no other solution, be so good as tell me how your opinion about religion is to be distinguished from nothing? Till then nothing remains for me but to assume that you have not yet, by examination, satisfied yourselves about this side of religion. Perhaps we shall have better fortune with the other side — what is known as the way of thinking, or faith.

You will, I believe, grant that your knowledge, however many-sided it may appear, falls, as a whole, into two contrasted sciences. How you shall subdivide and name belongs to the controversies of your schools, with which at present I am not concerned. Do not, therefore, be too critical about my terminology, even though it come from various quarters. Let us call the one division physics or metaphysics, applying both names indifferently, or indicating sections of the same thing. Let the other be ethics or the doctrine of duties or practical philosophy. At least we are agreed about the distinction meant. The former describes the nature of things, or if that seems too much, how man conceives and must conceive of things and of the world as the sum of things. The latter science, on the contrary, teaches what man should be for the world, and what he should do in it. Now, in so far as religion is a way of thinking of something and a knowledge about something, has it not the same object as these sciences? What does faith know about except the relation of man to God and to the world — God's purpose in making him, and the world's power to help or hinder him? Again it distinguishes in its own fashion a good action from a bad. Is then religion identical with natural science and ethics? You would not agree, you would never grant that our faith is as surely founded, or stands on the same level of certainty as your scientific knowledge! Your accusation against it is just that it does not know how to distinguish between the demonstrable and the probable. Similarly, you do not forget to remark diligently that very marvelous injunctions both to do and leave undone have issued from religion. You may be quite right; only do not forget that it has been the same with that

which you call science. In both spheres you believe you have made improvements and are better than your fathers.

What then, are we to say that religion is? As before, that it is a mixture — mingled theoretical and practical knowledge? But this is even less permissible, particularly if, as appears, each of these two branches of knowledge has its own characteristic mode of procedure. Such a mixture of elements that would either counteract or separate, could only be made most arbitrarily. The utmost gain to be looked for would be to furnish us with another method for putting known results into shape for beginners, and for stimulating them to a further study. But if that be so, why do you strive against religion? You might, so long as beginners are to be found, leave it in peace and security. If we presumed to subject you, you might smile at our folly, but, knowing for certain that you have left it far behind, and that it is only prepared for us by you wiser people, you would be wrong in losing a serious word on the matter. But it is not so, I think. Unless I am quite mistaken, you have long been labouring to provide the mass of the people with just such an epitome of your knowledge. The name is of no consequence, whether it be "religion" or "enlightenment" or aught else. But there is something different which must first be expelled, or, at least, excluded. This something it is that you call belief, and it is the object of your hostility, not an article you would desire to extend.

Wherefore, my friends, belief must be something different from a mixture of opinions about God and the world, and of precepts for one life or for two. Piety cannot be an instinct craving for a mess of metaphysical and ethical crumbs. If it were, you would scarcely oppose it. It would not occur to you to speak of religion as different from your knowledge, however much it might be distant. The strife of the cultured and learned with the pious would simply be the strife of depth and thoroughness with superficiality; it would be the strife of the master with pupils who are to emancipate themselves in due time. . . .

★ ★ ★

In order to make quite clear to you what is the original and characteristic possession of religion, it resigns, at once, all claims on anything that belongs either to science or morality. Whether it has been borrowed or bestowed it is now returned. What then does your science of being, your natural science, all your theoretical philosophy, in so far as it has to do with the actual world, have for its aim? To know things, I suppose, as they really are; to show the peculiar relations by which each is what it is; to determine for each its place in the Whole, and to distinguish it rightly from all else; to present the whole real world in its mutually conditioned necessity; and to exhibit the oneness of all phenomena with their eternal laws. This is truly beautiful and excellent, and I am not disposed to depreciate. Rather, if this description of mine, so slightly sketched, does not suffice, I will grant the highest and most exhaustive you are able to give.

And yet, however high you go; though you pass from the laws to the Universal Lawgiver, in whom is the unity of all things; though you allege that nature cannot be comprehended without God, I would still maintain that religion has nothing to do with this knowledge, and that, quite apart from it, its nature can be known. Quantity of knowledge is not quantity of piety. Piety can gloriously display itself, both with originality and individuality, in those to whom this kind of knowledge is not original. They may only know it as every-

body does, as isolated results known in connection with other things. The pious man must, in a sense, be a wise man, but he will readily admit, even though you somewhat proudly look down upon him, that, in so far as he is pious, he does not hold his knowledge in the same way as you.

Let me interpret in clear words what most pious persons only guess at and never know how to express. Were you to set God as the apex of your science as the foundation of all knowing as well as of all knowledge, they would accord praise and honour, but it would not be their way of having and knowing God. From their way, as they would readily grant, and as is easy enough to see, knowledge and science do not proceed.

It is true that religion is essentially contemplative. You would never call anyone pious who went about in impervious stupidity, whose sense is not open for the life of the world. But this contemplation is not turned, as your knowledge of nature is, to the existence of a finite thing, combined with and opposed to another finite thing. It has not even, like your knowledge of God — if for once I might use an old expression — to do with the nature of the first cause, in itself and in its relation to every other cause and operation. The contemplation of the pious is the immediate consciousness of the universal existence of all finite things, in and through the Infinite, and of all temporal things in and through the Eternal. Religion is to seek this and find it in all that lives and moves, in all growth and change, in all doing and suffering. It is to have life and to know life in immediate feeling, only as such an existence in the Infinite and Eternal. Where this is found religion is satisfied, where it hides itself there is for her unrest and anguish, extremity and death. Wherefore it is a life in the infinite nature of the Whole, in the One and in the All, in God, having and possessing all things in God, and God in all. Yet religion is not knowledge and science, either of the world or of God. Without being knowledge, it recognizes knowledge and science. In itself it is an affection, a revelation of the Infinite in the finite, God being seen in it and it in God.

Similarly, what is the object of your ethics, of your science of action? Does it not seek to distinguish precisely each part of human doing and producing, and at the same time to combine them into a whole, according to actual relations? But the pious man confesses that, as pious, he knows nothing about it. He does, indeed, contemplate human action, but it is not the kind of contemplation from which an ethical system takes its rise. Only one thing he seeks out and detects, action from God, God's activity among men. If your ethics are right, and his piety as well, he will not, it is true, acknowledge any action as excellent which is not embraced in your system. But to know and to construct this system is your business, ye learned, not his. If you will not believe, regard the case of women. You ascribe to them religion, not only as an adornment, but you demand of them the finest feeling for distinguishing the things that excel: do you equally expect them to know your ethics as a science?

It is the same, let me say at once, with action itself. The artist fashions what is given him to fashion, by virtue of his special talent. These talents are so different that the one he possesses another lacks; unless someone, against heaven's will, would possess all. But when anyone is praised to you as pious, you are not accustomed to ask which of these gifts dwell in him by virtue of his piety. The citizen — taking the word in the sense of the ancients, not in its present meagre significance — regulates, leads, and influences in virtue of his morality. But this is something different

from piety. Piety has also a passive side. While morality always shows itself as manipulating, as self-controlling, piety appears as a surrender, a submission to be moved by the Whole that stands over against man. Morality depends, therefore, entirely on the consciousness of freedom, within the sphere of which all that it produces falls. Piety, on the contrary, is not at all bound to this side of life. In the opposite sphere of necessity, where there is no properly individual action, it is quite as active. Wherefore the two are different. Piety does, indeed, linger with satisfaction on every action that is from God, and every activity that reveals the Infinite in the finite, and yet it is not itself this activity. Only by keeping quite outside the range both of science and of practice can it maintain its proper sphere and character. Only when piety takes its place alongside of science and practice, as a necessary, an indispensable third, as their natural counterpart, not less in worth and splendour than either, will the common field be altogether occupied and human nature on this side complete.

But pray understand me fairly. I do not mean that one could exist without the other, that, for example, a man might have religion and be pious, and at the same time be immoral. That is impossible. But, in my opinion, it is just as impossible to be moral or scientific without being religious. But have I not said that religion can be had without science? Wherefore, I have myself begun the separation. But remember, I only said piety is not the measure of science. Just as one cannot be truly scientific without being pious, the pious man may not know at all, but he cannot know falsely. His proper nature is not of that subordinate kind, which, according to the old adage that like is only known to like, knows nothing except semblance of reality.

His nature is reality which knows reality,

and where it encounters nothing it does not suppose it sees something. And what a precious jewel of science, in my view, is ignorance for those who are captive to semblance. If you have not learned it from my Speeches or discovered it for yourselves, go and learn it from your Socrates. Grant me consistency at least. With ignorance your knowledge will ever be mixed, but the true and proper opposite of knowledge is presumption of knowledge. By piety this presumption is most certainly removed, for with it piety cannot exist.

Such a separation of knowledge and piety, and of action and piety, do not accuse me of making. You are only ascribing to me, without my deserving it, your own view and the very confusion, as common as it is unavoidable, which it has been my chief endeavour to show you in the mirror of my Speech. Just because you do not acknowledge religion as the third, knowledge and action are so much apart that you can discover no unity, but believe that right knowing can be had without right acting, and *vice versa*. I hold that it is only in contemplation that there is division. There, where it is necessary, you despise it, and instead transfer it to life, as if in life itself objects could be found independent one of the other. Consequently you have no living insight into any of these activities. Each is for you a part, a fragment. Because you do not deal with life in a living way, your conception bears the stamp of perishableness, and is altogether meagre. True science is complete vision; true practice is culture and art self-produced; true religion is sense and taste for the Infinite. To wish to have true science or true practice without religion, or to imagine it is possessed, is obstinate, arrogant delusion, and culpable error. It issues from the unholy sense that would rather have a show of possession by cowardly purloining than have secure possession by demanding and waiting.

What can man accomplish that is worth speaking of, either in life or in art, that does not arise in his own self from the influence of this sense for the Infinite? Without it, how can anyone wish to comprehend the world scientifically, or if, in some distant talent, the knowledge is thrust upon him, how should he wish to exercise it? What is all science, if not the existence of things in you, in your reason? what is all art and culture if not your existence in the things to which you give measure, form and order? And how can both come to life in you except in so far as there lives immediately in you the external unity of Reason and Nature, the universal existence of all finite things in the Infinite?

Wherefore, you will find every truly learned man devout and pious. Where you see science without religion, be sure it is transferred, learned up from another. It is sickly, if indeed it is not empty appearance which serves necessity and is no knowledge at all. And what else do you take this deduction and weaving together of ideas to be, which neither live nor correspond to any living thing? Or in ethics, what else is this wretched uniformity that thinks it can grasp the highest human life in a single dead formula? The former arises because there is no fundamental feeling of that living nature which everywhere presents variety and individuality, and the latter because the sense fails to give infinity to the finite by determining its nature and boundaries only from the Infinite. Hence the dominion of the mere notion; hence the mechanical erections of your systems instead of an organic structure; hence the vain juggling with analytical formulas, in which, whether categorical or hypothetical, life will not be fettered. Science is not your calling, if you despise religion and fear to surrender yourself to reverence and aspiration for the primordial. Either science must become as low as your life, or it must be separated and stand alone, a division that precludes success. If man is not one with the Eternal in the unity of intuition and feeling which is immediate, he remains, in the unity of consciousness which is derived, for ever apart.

What, then, shall become of the highest utterance of the speculation of our days, complete rounded idealism, if it do not again sink itself in this unity, if the humility of religion do not suggest to its pride another realism than that which it so boldly and with such perfect right, subordinates to itself? It annihilates the Universe, while it seems to aim at constructing it. It would degrade it to a mere allegory, to a mere phantom of the one-sided limitation of its own empty consciousness. Offer with me reverently a tribute to the manes of the holy, rejected Spinoza. The high World-Spirit pervaded him; the Infinite was his beginning and his end; the Universe was his only and his everlasting love. In holy innocence and in deep humility he beheld himself mirrored in the eternal world, and perceived how he also was its most worthy mirror. He was full of religion, full of the Holy Spirit. Wherefore, he stands there alone and unequalled; master in his art, yet without disciples and without citizenship, sublime above the profane tribe. . . .

There then you have the three things about which my Speech has so far turned, — perception, feeling and activity, and you now understand what I mean when I say they are not identical and yet are inseparable. Take what belongs to each class and consider it by itself. You will find that those moments in which you exercise power over things and impress yourselves upon them, form what you call your practical, or, in the narrower sense, your

moral life; again the contemplative moments, be they few or many, in which things produce themselves in you as intuition, you will doubtless call your scientific life. Now can either series alone form a human life? Would it not be death? If each activity were not stimulated and renewed by the other, would it not be self-consumed? Yet they are not identical. If you would understand your life and speak comprehensively of it, they must be distinguished. As it stands with these two in respect of one another, it must stand with the third in respect of both. How then are you to name this third, which is the series of feeling? What life will it form? The religious as I think, and as you will not be able to deny, when you have considered it more closely.

The chief point in my Speech is now uttered. This is the peculiar sphere which I would assign to religion — the whole of it, and nothing more. Unless you grant it, you must either prefer the old confusion to clear analysis, or produce something else, I know not what, new and quite wonderful. Your feeling is piety, in so far as it expresses, in the manner described, the being and life common to you and to the All. Your feeling is piety in so far as it is the result of the operation of God in you by means of the operation of the world upon you. This series is not made up either of perceptions or of objects of perception, either of works or operations or of different spheres of operation, but purely of sensations and the influence of all that lives and moves around, which accompanies them and conditions them. These feelings are exclusively the elements of religion, and none are excluded. There is no sensation that is not pious, except it indicate some diseased and impaired state of the life, the influence of which will not be confined to religion. Wherefore, it follows that ideas and principles are all foreign to religion. This truth we here come upon

194

for the second time. If ideas and principles are to be anything, they must belong to knowledge which is a different department of life from religion.

Now that we have some ground beneath us, we are in a better position to inquire about the source of this confusion. May there not be some reason for this constant connection of principles and ideas with religion? In the same way is there not a cause for the connection of action with religion? Without such an inquiry it would be vain to proceed farther. The misunderstanding would be confirmed, for you would change what I say into ideas and begin seeking for principles in them. Whether you will follow my exposition, who can tell? What now is to hinder that each of the functions of life just indicated should not be an object for the others? Or does it not rather manifestly belong to their inner unity and equality that they should in this manner strive to pass over into one another? So at least it seems to me. Thus, as a feeling person, you can become an object to yourself and you can contemplate your own feeling. Nay, you can, as a feeling person, become an object for yourself to operate upon and more and more to impress your deepest nature upon. Would you now call the general description of the nature of your feelings that is the product of this contemplation a principle, and the description of each feeling, an idea, you are certainly free to do so. And if you call them religious principles and ideas, you are not in error. But do not forget that this is scientific treatment of religion, knowledge about it, and not religion itself.

Nor can the description be equal to the thing described. The feeling may dwell in many sound and strong, as for example in almost all women, without ever having been specially a matter of contemplation. Nor may you say religion is lacking, but only knowl-

edge about religion. Furthermore, do not forget what we have already established, that this contemplation presupposes the original activity. It depends entirely upon it. If the ideas and principles are not from reflection on a man's own feeling, they must be learned by rote and utterly void. Make sure of this, that no man is pious, however perfectly he understands these principles and conceptions, however much he believes he possesses them in clearest consciousness, who cannot show that they have originated in himself and, being the outcome of his own feeling, are peculiar to himself. Do not present him to me as pious, for he is not. His soul is barren in religious matters, and his ideas are merely supposititious children which he has adopted, in the secret feeling of his own weakness. As for those who parade religion and make a boast of it, I always characterize them as unholy and removed from all divine life. One has conceptions of the ordering of the world and formulas to express them, the other has prescriptions whereby to order himself and inner experiences to authenticate them. The one weaves his formulas into a system of faith, and the other spins out of his prescriptions a scheme of salvation. It being observed that neither has any proper standing ground without feeling, strife ensues as to how many conceptions and declarations, how many precepts and exercises, how many emotions and sensations must be accepted in order to conglomerate a sound religion that shall be neither specially cold nor enthusiastic, dry nor shallow. O fools, and slow of heart! They do not know that all this is mere analysis of the religious sense, which they must have made for themselves, if it is to have any meaning.

But if they are not conscious of having anything to analyze, whence have they those ideas and rules? They have memory and imitation, but that they have religion do not believe.

They have no ideas of their own from which formulas might be known, so they must learn them by rote, and the feelings which they would have accompanying them are copies, and like all copies, are apt to become caricatures. And out of this dead, corrupt, second-hand stuff, a religion is to be concocted! The members and juices of an organized body can be dissected; but take these elements now and mix them and treat them in every possible way; and will you be able to make heart's blood of them? Once dead, can it ever again move in a living body? Such restoration of the products of living nature out of its component parts, once divided, passes all human skill, and, just as little, would you succeed with religion, however completely the various kindred elements be given from without. From within, in their original, characteristic form, the emotions of piety must issue. They must be indubitably your own feelings, and not mere stale descriptions of the feelings of others, which could at best issue in a wretched imitation.

Now the religious ideas which form those systems can and ought to be nothing else than such a description, for religion cannot and will not originate in the pure impulse to know. What we feel and are conscious of in religious emotions is not the nature of things, but their operation upon us. What you may know or believe about the nature of things is far beneath the sphere of religion. The Universe is ceaselessly active and at every moment is revealing itself to us. Every form it has produced, everything to which, from the fulness of its life, it has given a separate existence, every occurrence scattered from its fertile bosom is an operation of the Universe upon us. Now religion is to take up into our lives and to submit to be swayed by them, each of these influences and their consequent emotions, not by themselves but as a part of the Whole, not as limited and in opposition

to other things, but as an exhibition of the Infinite in our life. Anything beyond this, any effort to penetrate into this nature and substance of things is no longer religion, but seeks to be a science of some sort.

On the other hand, to take what are meant as descriptions of our feelings for a science of the object, in some way the revealed product of religion, or to regard it as science and religion at the same time, necessarily leads to mysticism and vain mythology. For example, it was religion when the Ancients, abolishing the limitations of time and space, regarded every special form of life throughout the whole world as the work and as the kingdom of a being who in this sphere was omnipresent and omnipotent, because one peculiar way in which the Universe operates was present as a definite feeling, and they described it after this fashion. It was religion when they assigned a peculiar name and built a temple to the god to whom they ascribed any helpful occurrence whereby in an obvious, if accidental, way, the laws of the world were revealed, because they had comprehended something as a deed of the Universe, and after their own fashion set forth its connection and peculiar character. It was religion when they rose above the rude iron cage, full of flaws and inequalities, and sought again the golden age on Olympus in the joyous life of the gods, because beyond all change and all apparent evil that results only from the strife of finite forms, they felt the ever-stirring, living and serene activity of the World and the World-Spirit. But when they drew up marvellous and complex genealogies of the gods, or when a later faith produced a long series of emanations and procreations, it was not religion. Even though these things may have their source in a religious presentation of the relation of the human and the divine, of the imperfect and the perfect, they were, in themselves, vain mythology, and, in respect of science, ruinous mysticism. The sum total of religion is to feel that, in its highest unity, all that moves us in feeling is one; to feel that aught single and particular is only possible by means of this unity; to feel, that is to say, that our being and living is a being and living in and through God. But it is not necessary that the Deity should be presented as also one distinct object. To many this view is necessary, and to all it is welcome, yet it is always hazardous and fruitful in difficulties. It is not easy to avoid the appearance of making Him susceptible of suffering like other objects. It

is only one way of characterizing God, and, from the difficulties of it, common speech will probably never rid itself. But to treat this objective conception of God just as if it were a perception, as if apart from His operation upon us through the world the existence of God before the world, and outside of the world, though for the world, were either by or in religion exhibited as science is, so far as religion is concerned, vain mythology. What is only a help for presentation is treated as a reality. It is a misunderstanding very easily made, but it is quite outside the peculiar territory of religion.

B

Religion as an integral experience is a genuine form of spiritual life. It is what is deepest and most distinctive in man, belonging to the very essence of his life. As the child is afraid to be alone in the dark, so is man in awful fear in this world until he finds some consoling support in it. Religious experience starts from this need. Man tries to place himself in harmony with the secret of the universe. The religious impulse craves for unity with God or oneness with the whole of being. The characteristic note of all true religious experience is the feeling of an intuitive or perceptual or immediate certitude of God. Religion does not consist in the celebration of ceremonies or acceptance of academic abstractions, but is an experience of reality, an immediate awareness of God. It is the inevitable flowering of man's life, not estranged from tradition and practice, emotion and reason. The inner experience which each man can have for him-

self is the only religious revelation possible. It is nothing mysterious or miraculous. It is not something given to man once and for all, in some remote past or distant land. It comes to each man in his own life and with great authority. Each individual is immediately aware of an infinitely greater mind and soul than his own. When overlaid by the traditional element, the object of this awareness seems to vary, and the experience itself seems to take a thousand shapes, from the superstitions of the savage to the universal love of Buddha, the mystic joy of the Upanishadic seers, or the philosophical faith of Plato, in the essential unity and ultimate supremacy of beauty, goodness, and truth. The fashions of approach towards the establishing of a harmonious relation between the finite man and the power greater than himself, also vary from the barbarous sacrifices of the primitive peoples up to the faith and love of the most advanced. From this, it is clear that the religious idea dominates the whole life of man, though its essence consists in the immediate aware-

S. Radhakrishnan, "Religion and Philosophy," *The Hibbert Journal,* Vol. 20, 1921, pp. 36–45. Reprinted by permission of the Editor of *The Hibbert Journal.*

ness or felt certainty of God. The revelation of reality in the religious experience has a compelling power over the mind of man. In spite of the overwhelmingly emotional character of this experience, the rational element is not absent from it. The sense of objectivity is intense. Before proceeding further, I may observe how philosophy has here an important function to fulfil. Philosophy, or theology as it is called while it functions in the department of religion, has to reconcile this experimental datum with the rest of experience and the rest of experience with it. This is mainly a philosophical problem directly relevant only to those who share the spiritual experience, though it has also its use for others who, though they do not share the experience, still believe in its existence and validity. Thus, even if religion bases itself on an experienced fact, though it does not care to submit to any other authority, there remains for philosophy the essential task of harmonising the different experiences and thereby rendering religion itself self-conscious. Without such a philosophical rethinking into a whole of knowledge, religion would remain a mere superstition.

Religion, as we have described it, though *sui generis,* is a complex experience, a many-sided fact. As an attitude of the whole mind, it involves elements of knowing, feeling, and willing. These aspects cannot be separated from each other, though they can all be distinguished with the complex fact of religion. Separation in thought is not separation in existence. We may now briefly pass in review the various characters manifested in religious experience, and notice the part played by tradition or dogma, mystic fact or feeling, ethical value, and rational judgment.

Tradition or dogma. — In living religion there is no subjection to any authority except to the compelling one of immediate spiritual perception. To him who feels the presence of God no further logical proof is necessary. God is *felt* by him, and the feeling seems to silence all doubt. But the compulsion of feeling is subjective and imperfectly communicable. For others who do not share the feeling, the reality of God is uncertain. They have not personally realised the experience. The experimental basis is wanting for them. They have to depend on other people's experiences as embodied in their reflections. They have to work by faith till it becomes sight. They have not yet seen, they can only believe. Living in a fog, they must worship the sun that they have not seen. Through the acceptance of faith they have to gain the experience. The traditional or dogmatic religion becomes the pathway to reality. It provides the clue to the attainment of the truth. Without it, it may not be possible to gain the religious experience. So St. Paul wished his Roman correspondents to be filled with "the joy and peace in believing." The venture of faith will be progressively justified in life. The tradition does not become vital truth until it is made one's own, a part of one's life and seen with one's spirit. Only then does religion cease to be external to the mind of man and become the all-pervading principle of life. Tradition is the stepping-stone to truth.

Tradition determines the problems, raises the difficulties, and suggests modes of approach to the attainment of the true. We cannot wholly break away from it. The spiritual truth happens to be formulated in different ways simply because the seers are bred in different traditions. A first view of the history of religion tells us that there are no dependable realities at all in it, while a second view inclines us to think that the experience of the spiritual reality is one, though its logical elaborations are many. There is agreement in the foundational fact that the soul of man is included in something greater and more permanent than itself.

The difficulties of attaining the religious insight scare away many who are tempted to lean on other people's experiences, and thus acquire a religion which is only second-hand. The weaker brethren are content to enjoy the consolation of religion without themselves being religious. Tradition helps them to live in conformity with the religious requirements, though not out of the religious motive. Religion, popularly understood, is of this kind, dogmatic, traditional, and authoritarian. The distinguishing marks of conventional religion are belief in dogma and dependence on authority. Such a religion is that of the spinal cord and not of the brain. As animals exercise vital functions by the mere force of habit, even when the brain is removed, so do men live believing in the shadow of a shade, doing good to please God, whose reality they have faith in, though not perception of. If the tradition depresses, it is always open to us to say what the good curate said to his parishioners whom he threw all into tears when preaching to them on the Passion: "My children, do not weep so much as that; it happened long ago, and even, perhaps, it is not quite true."

All the same, respect for tradition is not altogether illogical. Tradition tends to convey the intense spiritual experience to other people and, if possible, rouse it in them. It serves as the basis of reflection. It interprets the spiritual experience of man in accordance with the intellectual and moral needs of the age in which it is formulated. The Bible, the Talmud, the Quran, and the Hindu scriptures embody different traditions which speak in different voices. Traditional beliefs deserve considerate treatment, since they have the experience of the ages behind them. Only, we have to remember that the experience is one thing and its expression another. The conception of truth or reality is different from its realisation. The feeling is private and ineffable, while the formula employs words and symbols which are common counters with settled connotations. If we forget the tentative and instrumental character of traditions, we shall be disloyal to the spirit of religion and begin to fight about false issues. The experience is profounder than any theory or tradition. At the time of its formulation, perhaps, the tradition may have represented in an adequate manner what is felt then to be overwhelmingly vital in the experience. We have no need to doubt its value so long as it is stimulating and satisfying. It is supreme till it is surpassed, as being only a partial or one-sided expression of truth. Advance in knowledge makes the formula lose its value, and attempts are made to recover the spirit underlying it and express it in more adequate terms. Beliefs which once had religious value are now discarded, since they are not appropriate to the new intellectual environment. The idea of eternal punishment possessed for Christendom enormous value for centuries. To-day we feel it to be outraging to our ethical sense of justice, and we are wondering how good people ever came to believe it. The founders of religion have been distinguished by their indifference, if not opposition, to tradition. Taking their stand on immediate perception or direct personal experience, they sometimes flout and fight tradition. They know that every tradition has an idea incorporated in it, and so long as the idea is vital the tradition is valued. But if the idea is extinct the tradition becomes an anachronism. It becomes the task of religious leaders to reinforce tradition and create forms of faith and utterance which would more adequately express the religious experience. By discarding traditional religion, or recasting it, they push religion along. Traditions can live only through an incessant process of testing and reshaping. The history of religion is little else than a repeated reinterpretation and re-shaping of old beliefs in view of advancing knowledge and thought. Philosophy insists that religious beliefs should agree with the dictates of a true nationality. Only through the work of reflection can we make traditions and faiths, feelings and emotions, symbols of truth and vehicles of ideals. Only then does traditional faith become the substance of things unseen.

We must, now and again, ask whether the traditional religion has any genuine experience behind it, and whether it expresses it in terms of the time spirit. If we avoid such an inquiry, the tradition tends to become a dead one, intolerant of truth and destructive of the spiritual sense. Traditional faith which survives the decay of dogma is ineffective and artificial and opposed to all true religion.

At the present day, we are forced to reconsider inherited beliefs, and bring about a harmony between them and the rest of our experience. Crises in life put ideas to the test and the recent international war has been very unsettling in its character. The rapid progress of scientific knowledge and the deeper interest in religion have led to a widespread tendency to reform or reconstruct traditional religion, if not replace it by something more rational and less superstitious. Here again is an excellent chance for philosophy.

Mystic Feeling. — Religious experience starts from a fact or a datum. It is a consciousness of God, emotionally coloured. A sense of certitude accompanies it. Philosophy is called upon to scrutinise the subjective feeling and find out to what extent it possesses truth and objectivity. A feeling is valuable only by its results for reflection. A caustic critic, speaking of James's *Varieties of Religious Experience,* remarks that James arrives at no distinction between religion and delirium tremens. The savage finds comfort in his superstition, and the savant strength in his religion. Totems and fetishes are not without psychological efficiency, though they cannot hope to thrive to-day in the world of thought. Through the help of philosophy, we have to find out whether there is anything objective about the religious feeling which is obviously private and personal to each individual. Were religious experience devoid of any objective element, then we should be landed in difficulties. The living God of truth and spirit will be displaced by our ideas of God, the cheap substitutes for which our new prophets are the advertising agents. What has cast ridicule on religion and led some well-intentioned men to discredit all mystic experience as pathological, being only an illusory illumination, mystical ecstasy, or emotional rapture, is traceable to a neglect of rational reflection in religious matters. What is not rational cannot be real. If philosophy does not establish the reality of the object of the mystic consciousness, the mystic experience loses its integrity and value. The attempt of Mr. B. Russell to substitute art for religion, and lead us to aesthetic contemplation with its temporary freedom from the Sisyphean struggle with desire, is not satisfactory either as philosophy or as religion. He tells us that the power which exists is evil, and the God whom we can worship is a creation of our own conscience and has no existence outside it. If we do not refuse to recognise facts we have to worship either the wicked reality that exists or a God that does not exist. But we cannot love an unreality or pursue a phantom. It is a vain stretching forth of arms towards something that can never fill them. Religious consciousness firmly believes in the existence of its object, in an ontological sense. There *is* an ultimate and independently existing reality. The consciousness of immediate contact with reality is no illusion. The truest religion has for its object the highest reality. "That which is filled with the more real is more really filled" (Plato).

Not only should philosophy test the value of the subjective assurances, but it should also take them into account and, so far as they are valid, fit them into its explanatory theory. The implications of the mystic experience which is capable of being roused at any time on compliance with ascertained conditions, require to be explained by any satisfactory philosophy. Mysticism believes in the ultimate oneness of subject and object, the observer and the observed. Mystic knowledge is the immediate witness of reality to itself. Logical proof comes later and is secondary in its character. The mystic education assumes the position that at the bottom of his soul every individual is in contact with the real. We must rend the veil of appearances to see the eternal life in things. Mystic training consists in a "hindrance of hindrances," or the removal of the clogging obstructions to the manifestation of the real. To break down these separating veils, different religions insist on different disciplines. Worship, which is an essential feature of all religions, in addition to the discovery of truth and the pursuit of the good, has this end in view. It is possible to attain the revelation of the supreme reality in each mind and heart through its own special path. We need not prescribe any one way for all. Through logical insight, through emotional intensity, through the constant practice of some form of the highest, the end may be gained; and when it is gained, the experience seems to have a self-certifying character. And a true philosophy must account for it.

Ethical Implications. — The spiritual intuition gives strength and support, peace and consolation, to man, and sanctifies all phases of his life. Religion is not a mere belief which floats on the surface of man's life, but a dynamic force which stirs the very depths of his soul. Religious views have their implications for life in this world. Religion is also practice of the presence of God. Love of God passes into an intense longing for union with Him, inspiring the individual to an effort to become as perfect as "the Father in Heaven." The ethical aspect of religion has attracted in a special degree the attention of European writers, particularly those of Great Britain. God is more goodness than truth or beauty. From the time the ancient Greeks taught the European world, the good has been put at the centre of the universe. Plato makes Socrates say in the *Phaedo* that it is the good which holds the universe together, and the final justification of all things in the world is that they represent the *best* possible arrangement. Kant bases religious truth on ethical consciousness. Religion to him is a postulate of morality. To Butler the secret of the universe is revealed through morals. To him God is the "great moral governor." Carlyle and Newman, Martineau and Matthew Arnold, are preoccupied with the sense of moral responsibility. To Matthew Arnold religion is nothing more than morality touched with emotion, and God the everlasting power, not ourselves, that makes for righteousness. According to Dr. Galloway, religious consciousness is "man's faith in a power beyond himself, whereby he seeks to satisfy emotional needs and gain stability of life, and which he expresses in acts of worship and service." Mr. B. Russell in his latest book on Bolshevism defines religion as "a set of beliefs held as dogmas dominating the conduct of life, going beyond or contrary to evidence, and inculcated by methods which are emotional or authoritarian, not intellectual." According to Croce, we have the full and consistent vindication of the moral life in the religious.

It is true that a good life is the service of God, and that ethical considerations establish the reality of God. Yet religion cannot be identified with moral life. The essence of religion consists in the spiritual intuition. However self-evident this intuition may be, it is not philosophically sound till it is known to be adequate in all respects, theoretical and practical alike.

Rational Factor. — The "reason" aspect of religion is emphasised by the thinkers of India as well as Germany, who seek in religion for an ultimate solution of the doubts, disputes, and distractions which beset the thinking mind in this enigmatical world. This enthusiasm for reason has inspired the many mighty efforts of system-building in Germany. Hegel sums up the spirit of German speculative adventure in the statement that "thinking too is divine service." It is the form of worship which the intellectually-minded offer to the divine reality. Simply because religion is a vital issue concerning the deepest needs of humanity, we need not ask philosophy to hold its tongue. The destructive effect of rational criticism on the orthodox beliefs has led some to free religion from the criticism of reason. But reason, which had dealt a deathblow to religious mythology, has in it healing virtues as well. If reflection has inflicted wounds on religious faith, further reflection will heal up the wounds. It is useless to ask us to suppress all thought. We cannot be saved from the exercise of reason. Philosophy is a natural bent of the human mind. Ultimately there cannot be any discord between religious certainty and philosophical truth. God is Eternal Reason. He inspires the deep, religious yearning, and has granted us the gift of reason. It is the function of philosophy to show that the hope in us is not an unreasonable one, and it is possible to reconcile the strenuous life of reason with the reality of religious experience. It is wrong to think, as did some mediaeval theologians, and Alfred Ritschl in modern times, that philosophical truth is one thing and religious truth another. However useful such a position may be as a temporary expedient to keep the two, religion and philosophy, safe from mutual interference, on the day of trial they will be found to regret this artificial separation. It is no use considering a theory to be true religiously simply because it has religious value. It cannot have religious value if it has not philosophical justification. A religion which cuts itself off from philosophy cannot meet the deeper needs of our consciousness. Truth is "what man recognises as value when his life is fullest and his soul at its highest stretch." Ultimately, nothing can be religiously valuable unless it is logically true. False ideas supposed to possess religious value are tolerated only so long as we refuse to think them or state them clearly to ourselves. In unreflective consciousness, contradictory ideas may sleep together in unbroken harmony without coming into any active collision. But this naïveté and apparently healthy indifference to ultimate problems cannot last long. Even commonsense believes in the unity of thought; and when it becomes aware of contradictions in it, it is forced to reconcile them or give them up. The moment we notice the discord, the effort after inward harmony starts. Not only philosophy but even religion emphasises this unity of thought. The religious experience lifts man above the divided and fragmentary existence in which he usually lives, and reveals to him a unity which only philosophy can bring home to his thought. Mind cannot give up its faith in itself, and philosophy cannot help asserting its rights. Truth is a harmony, and there cannot be a gulf between religion and philosophy.

There are some who ask us to give up all philosophy since it cramps, stifles and kills life. It is much better to live, love and believe than think, argue and debate. Blessed are they that feel but do not think. This is a false view of philosophy which shuts it off from life. Philosophy, rightly understood, is the inspiring and controlling energy of life. Quoting Chesterton, we might say that the most important thing about a man is his view of the universe; and the question is not whether our philosophy affects our life, but whether in the long run anything else does.

Religious consciousness is practical and personal, being a blend of faith, reason, emotion and will. According as the one or the other element predominates, we have the one or the other kind of religion. Where faith dominates, we have the traditional religion; where reason determines, we have the philosophical religion; where emotion is uppermost, we have mystic religions; and with most men of the modern times religion is essentially a promoting of morality and goodness. In all genuine religion these four elements are found together, and it is dangerous to the vitality

of religion if any one of them is exaggerated out of all proportion or completely sacrificed. Mere tradition, unsupported by reason and lacking the warmth of feeling or the zeal of heroism, is little better than mummery. Purely intellectual religion lands us in empty forms. Mysticism, if it is not to lapse into emotionalism, stands in need of self-criticism. Mechanical goodness, uninspired by spiritual assurance, is boring and ineffective. True religion has in it the four elements of a historic tradition, a mystic fact, an ethical life, and a philosophic judgment. Of them all, the last is the most important, since it has to decide how far the tradition is sustainable, or meaningful; whether the mystic fact is a true revelation of reality; whether the certitude it conveys is merely suggestive or also objective; and whether the ethical value it has is at the expense of truth or otherwise. When such vital questions are to be decided by philosophy, it is not right for the philosopher to start with any prejudice in favour of or against any of the elements. It is philosophy that has to determine the worth of religion, and not religion the philosophic outlook.

SUGGESTIONS FOR THOUGHT

1. When did you first have an experience that might be called religious? What prompted the experience? What has been most influential in the development of your religion? What influence has college had upon your religion?

2. Why are creeds emphasized in so many religions? Isn't ethical behavior more important than creedal uniformity? What is the relation between religious belief and moral behavior?

3. "The world has been too serious about religion, and through seriousness is near losing it." (Baker Brownell) Why has man found difficulty in taking his religion lightly? Why should he take it lightly?

4. Do you accept the reality of all entities mentioned in the Bible including angels, demons, devils, etc.? On what basis do you accept or reject the reality of such beings?

5. Augustine said, in the fifth century, "I should not be a Christian, but for the miracles." John Wesley said, in the eighteenth century, "The giving up of witchcraft is, in effect, giving up the Bible." Are miracles and witches essential to Christianity?

6. "When I pray for something, I do not pray. When I pray for nothing, I really pray." (Eckhart) What does Eckhart mean?

7. Is prayer a means of escaping effort? Who prays — the laborer or the loafer? Santayana says: "Prayer is not a substitute for work; it is a desperate effort to work further and to be efficient beyond the range of one's powers. It is not the lazy who are most inclined to prayer; those pray most who care most, and who, having worked hard, find it intolerable to be defeated."

8. What psychological changes may take place in a person who prays? Are the subjective values of prayer the only values? Could an atheist pray? Must prayer be directed to a deity? Couldn't one's words of encouragement delivered to one's self be called a form of prayer?

9. Why do people worship in groups? What is supposed to happen in a worship experience?

10. What is the function of the church? Does it guide people's moral and intellectual life? How can it be improved? What possibility is there of bringing together the two extreme views of organized religion, viz., an autocratic institution and a fellowship of believers? What is meant when churches claim that they are divine?

11. Do people join churches because they are religious or because they want to become religious? Schleiermacher once said that the church becomes of less consequence the more people increase in religion and that "the most pious sever themselves coldly and proudly." "The organized religions of the world have been religion's greatest foe." (Baker Brownell) "When organization comes in at the door, religion flies out at the window." (Warner Fite) In what respects have organized religions been a foe of religion?

12. How necessary are churches? Could there be religion without the churches? W. R. Inge has said: "Institutional churches are really secular corporations moulded to attract average humanity."

SUGGESTIONS FOR FURTHER READING

AVEY, ALBERT E., *Re-thinking Religion,* New York, Henry Holt and Company, 1936, chs. 1, 10.

DEWEY, JOHN, *A Common Faith,* New Haven, Yale University Press, 1934, ch. 1.

FERM, VERGILIUS, *First Adventures in Philosophy,* New York, Charles Scribner's Sons, 1936, ch. 3.

HOBBES, THOMAS, *Leviathan,* Part I, ch. 12.

HOWERTH, IRA W., "What Is Religion?" *The International Journal of Ethics,* Vol. 13, 1903, pp. 185–206.

KANT, IMMANUEL, *Religion Within the Limits of Reason Alone,* Book IV, Part I.

LEWIS, C. S., *The Case for Christianity,* New York, Charles Scribner's Sons, 1933, ch. 3.

LYMAN, EUGENE WILLIAM, *The Meaning and Truth of Religion,* New York, Charles Scribner's Sons, 1933, ch. 3.

MONTAGUE, W. P., *Belief Unbound,* New Haven, Yale University Press, 1930, ch. 1.

SPERRY, WILLARD L., *What We Mean by Religion,* New York, Harper and Brothers, 1940, ch. 1.

TRUEBLOOD, D. ELTON, *The Essence of Spiritual Religion,* New York, Harper and Brothers, 1936, ch. 1.

WARD, LESTER F., "The Essential Nature of Religion," *The International Journal of Ethics,* Vol. 8, 1898, pp. 169–192.

WICKENDEN, A. C., *Youth Looks at Religion,* New York, Harper and Brothers, 1939.

WRIGHT, WILLIAM KELLEY, *A Student's Philosophy of Religion,* New York, The Macmillan Company, 1931, chs. 1, 2.

14

GOD

St. Thomas Aquinas (1225–1274) created one of the most comprehensive intellectual syntheses that the world has ever had. In 1323 he was canonized by Pope John XXII, and in 1879 Pope Leo XIII directed that the teachings of St. Thomas should be the basis of theology in the Roman Catholic Church. The *Summa Theologica* is the greatest of his many works. George Edward Moore (1873–   ) is a leader of the English analytical movement. He lectured at Cambridge University from 1911 to 1939, and was editor of the philosophical journal *Mind* from 1921 to 1947. Perhaps it would not be unfair to say that Professor Moore is at his best when he is refuting ideas. He has turned his analytical powers with great effectiveness upon idealism, upon utilitarianism, and, in the essay which follows, upon the belief in God.

A

Because the chief aim of sacred doctrine is to teach the knowledge of God, not only as He is in Himself, but also as He is the beginning of things and their last end, and especially of rational creatures, as is clear from what has been already said, therefore, in our endeavour to expound this science, we shall treat: (1) Of God: (2) Of the rational creature's advance towards God: (3) Of Christ, Who as man, is our way to God.

In treating of God there will be a threefold division: —

For we shall consider (1) whatever concerns the Divine Essence. (2) Whatever concerns the distinctions of Persons. (3) Whatever concerns the procession of creatures from Him.

Concerning the Divine Essence, we must consider: —

Thomas Aquinas, *Summa Theologica,* Part I, Question 2. Reprinted by permission of Benziger Brothers, Inc.

(1) Whether God exists? (2) The manner of His existence, or, rather, what is *not* the manner of His existence. (3) Whatever concerns His operations — namely, His knowledge, will, power.

Concerning the first, there are three points of inquiry: —

(1) Whether the proposition 'God exists' is self-evident? (2) Whether it is demonstrable? (3) Whether God exists?

FIRST ARTICLE

WHETHER THE EXISTENCE OF GOD IS SELF-EVIDENT?

We proceed thus to the First Article: —

Objection 1. It seems that the existence of God is self-evident. Now those things are said to be self-evident to us the knowledge of which is naturally implanted in us, as we can see in regard to first principles. But as Damascene says (*De Fid. Orth. i.* I, 3), *the knowledge of God is naturally implanted in all.* Therefore the existence of God is self-evident.

Obj. 2. Further, those things are said to be self-evident which are known as soon as the terms are known, which the Philosopher (1 *Poster.* iii) says is true of the first principles of demonstration. Thus, when the nature of a whole and of a part is known, it is at once recognized that every whole is greater than its part. But as soon as the signification of the word 'God' is understood, it is at once seen that God exists. For by this word is signified that thing than which nothing greater can be conceived. But that which exists actually and mentally is greater than that which exists only mentally. Therefore, since as soon as the word 'God' is understood it exists mentally, it also follows that it exists

actually. Therefore the proposition 'God exists' is self-evident.

Obj. 3. Further, the existence of truth is self-evident. For whoever denies the existence of truth grants that truth does not exist: and, if truth does not exist, then the proposition 'Truth does not exist' is true: and if there is anything true, there must be truth. But God is truth itself: *I am the way, the truth, and the life* (John xiv. 6). Therefore 'God exists' is self-evident.

On the contrary, No one can mentally admit the opposite of what is self-evident; as the Philosopher (*Metaph.* iv., lect. vi) states concerning the first principles of demonstration. But the opposite of the proposition 'God is' can be mentally admitted: *The fool said in his heart, There is no God* (Ps. lii. I). Therefore, that God exists is not self-evident.

I answer that, A thing can be self-evident in either of two ways; on the one hand, self-evident in itself, though not to us; on the other, self-evident in itself, and to us. A proposition is self-evident because the predicate is included in the essence of the subject, as 'Man is an animal,' for animal is contained in the essence of man. If, therefore the essence of the predicate and subject be known to all, the proposition will be self-evident to all; as is clear with regard to the first principles of demonstration, the terms of which are common things that no one is ignorant of, such as being and non-being, whole and part, and suchlike. If, however, there are some to whom the essence of the predicate and subject is unknown, the proposition will be self-evident in itself, but not to those who do not know the meaning of the predicate and subject of the proposition. Therefore, it happens, as Boethius says (*Hebdom.*, the title of which is: '*Whether all that is, is good*), 'that there are some mental concepts self-evident only to the learned, as that incorporeal substances are not in space.' Therefore I say that this proposition, 'God exists,' of itself is self-evident, for the predicate is the same as the subject; because God is His own existence as will be hereafter shown (Q. III., A. 4). Now because we do not know the essence of God, the proposition is not self-evident to us; but needs to be demonstrated by things that are more known to us, though less known in their nature — namely, by effects. . . .

★ ★ ★

Reply Obj. 1. To know that God exists in a general and confused way is implanted in us by nature, inasmuch as God is man's beatitude. For man naturally desires happiness, and what is naturally desired by man must be naturally known to him. This, however, is not to know absolutely that God exists; just as to know that someone is approaching is not the same as to know that Peter is approaching, even though it is Peter who is approaching; for many there are who imagine that man's perfect good which is happiness, consists in riches, and others in pleasures, and others in something else.

Reply Obj. 2. Perhaps not everyone who hears this word 'God' understands it to signify something than which nothing greater can be thought, seeing that some have believed God to be a body. Yet, granted that everyone understands that by this word 'God' is signified something than which nothing greater can be thought, nevertheless, it does not therefore follow that he understands that what the word signifies exists actually, but only that it exists mentally. Nor can it be argued that it actually exists, unless it be admitted that there actually exists something than which nothing greater can be thought;

and this precisely is not admitted by those who hold that God does not exist.

Reply Obj. 3. The existence of truth in general is self-evident, but the existence of a Primal Truth is not self-evident to us.

SECOND ARTICLE

WHETHER IT CAN BE DEMONSTRATED THAT GOD EXISTS?

We proceed thus to the Second Article: — *Objection* 1. It seems that the existence of God cannot be demonstrated. For it is an article of faith that God exists. But what is of faith cannot be demonstrated, because a demonstration produces scientific knowledge; whereas faith is of the unseen (Heb. xi. I). Therefore it cannot be demonstrated that God exists.

Obj. 2. Further, the essence is the middle term of demonstration. But we cannot know in what God's essence consists, but solely in what it does not consist; as Damascene says (*De Fid. Orth.* i. 4.). Therefore we cannot demonstrate that God exists.

Obj. 3. Further, if the existence of God were demonstrated, this could only be from His effects. But His effects are not proportionate to Him, since He is infinite and His effects are finite; and between the finite and infinite there is no proportion. Therefore, since a cause cannot be demonstrated by an effect not proportionate to it, it seems that the existence of God cannot be demonstrated.

On the contrary, The Apostle says: *The invisible things of Him are clearly seen, being understood by the things that are made* (Rom. i. 20). But this would not be unless the existence of God could be demonstrated through the things that are made; for the first thing we must know of anything is, whether it exists.

I answer that, Demonstration can be made in two ways: One is through the cause, and is called *a priori,* and this is to argue from what is prior absolutely. The other is through the effect, and is called a demonstration *a posteriori;* this is to argue from what is prior relatively only to us. When an effect is better known to us than its cause, from the effect we proceed to the knowledge of the cause. And from every effect the existence of its proper cause can be demonstrated, so long as its effects are better known to us; because since every effect depends upon its cause, if the effect exists, the cause must pre-exist. Hence the existence of God, in so far as it is not self-evident to us, can be demonstrated from those of His effects which are known to us.

Reply Obj. 1. The existence of God and other like truths about God, which can be known by natural reason, are not articles of faith, but are preambles to the articles; for faith presupposes natural knowledge, even as grace presupposes nature, and perfection supposes something that can be perfected. Nevertheless, there is nothing to prevent a man, who cannot grasp a proof, accepting, as a matter of faith, something which in itself is capable of being scientifically known and demonstrated.

Reply Obj. 2. When the existence of a cause is demonstrated from an effect, this effect takes the place of the definition of the cause in proof of the cause's existence. This is especially the case in regard to God, because, in order to prove the existence of anything, it is necessary to accept as a middle term the meaning of the word, and not its essence, for the question of its essence follows on the question of its existence. Now the names given to God are derived from His effects; consequently, in demonstrating the existence of God from His effects, we may take for the middle term the meaning of the word 'God.'

Reply Obj. 3. From effects not proportionate to the cause no perfect knowledge of that cause can be obtained. Yet from every effect the existence of the causes can be clearly demonstrated, and so we can demonstrate the existence of God from His effects; though from them we cannot perfectly know God as He is in His essence.

THIRD ARTICLE

WHETHER GOD EXISTS?

We proceed thus to the Third Article: —

Objection 1. It seems that God does not exist; because if one of two contraries be infinite, the other would be altogether destroyed. But the word 'God' means that He is infinite goodness. If, therefore, God existed, there would be no evil discoverable; but there is evil in the world. Therefore God does not exist.

Obj. 2. Further, it is superfluous to suppose that what can be accounted for by a few principles has been produced by many. But it seems that everything we see in the world can be accounted for by other principles, supposing God did not exist. For all natural things can be reduced to one principle, which is nature; and all voluntary things can be reduced to one principle, which is human reason, or will. Therefore there is no need to suppose God's existence.

On the contrary, It is said in the person of God: *I am Who am* (Exod. iii. 14).

I answer that, The existence of God can be proved in five ways.

The first and more manifest way is the argument from motion. It is certain, and evident to our senses, that in the world some things are in motion. Now whatever is in motion is put in motion by another, for nothing can be in motion except it is in potentiality to that towards which it is in motion; whereas a thing moves inasmuch as it is in act. For motion is nothing else than the reduction of something from potentiality to actuality. But nothing can be reduced from potentiality to actuality, except by something in a state of actuality. Thus that which is actually hot, as fire, makes wood, which is potentially hot, to be actually hot, and thereby moves and changes it. Now it is not possible that the same thing should be at once in actuality and potentiality in the same respect, but only in different respects. For what is actually hot cannot simultaneously be potentially hot; but it is simultaneously potentially cold. It is therefore impossible that in the same respect and in the same way a thing should be both mover and moved, *i.e.,* that it should move itself. Therefore, whatever is in motion must be put in motion by another. If that by which it is put in motion be itself in motion, then this also must needs be put in motion by another, and that by another again. But this cannot go on to infinity, because then there would be no first mover, and, consequently, no other mover; seeing that subsequent movers move only inasmuch as they are put in motion by the first mover; as the staff moves only because it is put in motion by the hand. Therefore it is necessary to arrive at a first mover, put in motion by no other; and this everyone understands to be God.

The second way is from the nature of the efficient cause. In the world of sense we find there is an order of efficient causes. There is no case known (neither is it, indeed, possible) in which a thing would be prior to itself, which is impossible. Now in efficient causes it is not possible to go on to infinity, because in all efficient causes following in order, the first is the cause of the intermediate cause, and the intermediate is the cause of the ultimate cause, whether the intermediate cause be several, or one only. Now to take away the cause is to take away the effect. Therefore, if there be no first cause among efficient causes, there will be no ultimate, nor any intermediate cause. But if in efficient causes it is possible to go on to infinity, there will be no first efficient cause, neither will there be an ultimate effect, nor any intermediate efficient causes; all of which is plainly false. Therefore it is necessary to admit a first efficient cause, to which everyone gives the name of God.

The third way is taken from possibility and necessity, and runs thus. We find in nature things that are possible to be and not to be, since they are found to be generated, and to corrupt, and consequently, they are possible to be and not to be. But it is impossible for these always to exist, for that which is possible not to be at some time is not. Therefore, if everything is possible not to be, then at one time there could have been nothing in existence. Now if this were true, even now there would be nothing in existence, because that which does not exist only begins to exist by something already existing. Therefore, if at one time nothing was in existence, it would have been impossible for anything to have begun to exist; and thus even now nothing would be in existence — which is absurd. Therefore, not all beings are merely possible, but there must exist something the existence of which is necessary. But every necessary thing either has its necessity caused by another, or not. Now it is impossible to go on to infinity in necessary things which have their necessity caused by another, as has been already proved in regard to efficient causes. Therefore we cannot but postulate the existence of some being having of itself its own necessity, and not receiving it from another, but rather causing in others their necessity. This all men speak of as God.

The fourth way it taken from the gradation to be found in things. Among beings there are some more and some less good, true, noble, and the like. But 'more' and 'less' are predicated of different things, according as they resemble in their different ways something which is the maximum, as a thing is said to be hotter according as it more nearly resembles that which is hottest; so that there is something which is truest, something best, something noblest, and, consequently, something which is uttermost being; for those things that are greatest in truth are greatest in being, as it is written in *Metaph.* ii. Now the maximum in any genus is the cause of all in that genus; as fire, which is the maximum of heat, is the cause of all hot things. Therefore there must also be something which is to all beings the cause of their being, goodness, and every other perfection; and this we call God.

The fifth way is taken from the governance of the world. We see that things which lack intelligence, such as natural bodies, act for an end, and this is evident from their acting always, or nearly always, in the same way, so as to obtain the best result. Hence it is plain that not fortuitously, but designedly, do they achieve their end. Now whatever lacks intelligence cannot move towards an end, unless it be directed by some being endowed with knowledge and intelligence; as the arrow is shot to its mark by the archer. Therefore some intelligent being exists by whom all natural things are directed to their end; and this being we call God.

Reply Obj. 1. As Augustine says (*Enchir.* xi.): *Since God is the highest good, He would not allow any evil to exist in His works, unless His omnipotence and goodness were such as to bring good even out of evil.* This is part of the infinite goodness of God, that He should allow evil to exist, and out of it produce good.

Reply Obj. 2. Since nature works for a determinate end under the direction of a higher agent, whatever is done by nature must needs be traced back to God, as to its first cause. So also whatever is done voluntarily must also be traced back to some higher cause other than human reason or will, since these can change and fail; for all things that are changeable and capable of defect must be traced back to an immovable and self-necessary first principle, as was shown in the body of the *Article.*

B

The question here before us is this: Have we any evidence rendering it probable that God exists? The question is a large one, and I can do no more than summarize the arguments. And yet I think this summary, though brief, may be conclusive. The conclusion I

wish to establish is as I have said: — There is *no* probability that God exists. That is all: a purely negative conclusion. I am an infidel, and do not believe that God exists; and I think the evidence will justify my disbelief. But just as I think there is no evidence for his existence, I think there is also no evidence that he does not exist. I am not an atheist in one sense: I do not deny that God exists. My

G. E. Moore, "The Value of Religion," *The International Journal of Ethics,* Vol. 12, 1902, pp. 88–98. Reprinted by permission of the publisher, The University of Chicago Press.

arguments will only urge that there is no reason for thinking that he does; they will *not* urge that there is reason for thinking he does not. I do *not* believe that he does exist, but also I do *not* believe that he does not exist. That is the attitude I am concerned to recommend.

Is there, then, evidence that God exists? Is his existence at all probable?

We say we have evidence for a thing, when it can be inferred from another thing that we suppose established. The question of evidence for God's existence is then the question whether there are any other truths from which we can infer it. To mention evidence at all implies that other things are true beside the thing we want to prove. He who would prove by evidence that God exists must first assume that something else is true.

Now the truths from which we can start on such a proof are what we call the facts of common life — experience. We all believe that we are here, between four walls, alive and able to move; nay, more, thinking and feeling. Such are the facts of observation, from which the Natural Sciences infer their laws. In these things we all do believe; we cannot help believing them, whether we like it or not. That they are true indeed, we cannot prove. Our belief is no evidence that they are so. And so far they are just on a level with a belief that God exists: that belief also is no evidence that he exists. I believe that I exist, and some one else, I grant you, believes that God exists; and so far as these beliefs go, there is not a bit of difference between the two things that are believed. Both have an equal right to be taken for true and an equal right to be taken for false. But when we come to the question of evidence and probability, then there is all the difference in the world between them. There is evidence, in plenty, that I exist and there is none that God exists.

For my existence is an object of such a nature that it can be inferred from other objects of belief. These also are, like it and God, mere objects of belief, they cannot be proved true. But they are such that *if* any one of them be true, the others and my existence are so too. The simplest statement as that "This hand moves," involves a host of others, from which again a crowd of other simple statements, as that *I* moved it, may be deduced. And all the arguments to prove the existence of God rest upon evidence like this. The evidence is certainly as good as we can get; it is what we cannot help believing, although it may be false. To the evidence, then, I have no objection: *but* — the existence of God will not rest upon it. That I have a scar on my hand is excellent evidence of something: the scar is visible and palpable, and no doubt it had some cause. I cannot prove that these things are so; and you cannot either, except from premises equally doubtful in themselves. All of them are possibly not true. But if you grant me that the scar is there, then I maintain there is no evidence, no probability, that an angel with a burning sword came down and made it; but there is much evidence, much probability that it came about in a way that I could mention.

People take, then, the world as we think we know it, and they infer that because it is such as they and we all believe it to be, God must exist. To the facts they start from I have no objection, although we must admit they may be false: but the inference they draw from them is as absurd as the inference from my scar to that angel. There are two well-known arguments of this kind — the stock arguments of what is called Natural Theology — arguments which in one form or another are still in use. These are the arguments to a First Cause and the argument from Design. The inadequacy of both these arguments was finally pointed out a hundred years ago by Kant. With the first, as distinguished from the second, we need not deal, for, even if some First Cause were necessary, it would yet remain to prove that this Cause was intelligent and good: it must be both, you remember, to come within our meaning of personal God. That this Cause is intelligent and good as well as powerful is what the argument from Design attempts to prove. The only argument, therefore, with which we have to deal is that: From the nature of the world, as it appears on observation, we can infer that it or parts of it were or are caused by a being immensely intelligent, wise or good. The answer to this is summary but sound. We assume that useful and beautiful objects we find in the world were made by man — had for their cause a being of some intelligence and goodness. By these useful and beautiful objects I mean houses and drains, hospitals and works of art — if you like, a watch — and I call it an assumption that they were made by man, in order not to overstate my case. We have as our premise, then, that certain objects, which I am far from denying to be either useful or beautiful or sometimes both, had for their cause some tolerably good people. Then, says the Natural Theologian, we may infer that anything useful or good we find in the world, that is not a work of man's designing — man himself, above all, the most useful and beautiful of all — had also for its cause a person of intelligence and goodness. This is the argument. For what reason have we for supposing that anything at all of any kind in the world was caused by a good person? Simply the assumption that certain things of one kind were caused by man. And what reason have we for this assumption? Simply and solely the fact that we can follow the series of causes back from them to the working of man. And if we are therefore going to call man their

cause, we must also ascribe all other events to those which preceded them in the same way as man's work plainly preceded houses and drains. If houses and drains are the effect of man's work, then man himself and all other things, must be the effect of events in the world which preceded him, and so on *ad infinitum*. If, on the other hand, houses and drains were not caused by man, then we have no reason for supposing that anything useful or beautiful ever was caused by a good person. Either of these two alternatives wrecks the theologian's argument completely. If we are to infer from the nature of an effect to the nature of a cause, we can only do so on the assumption that we can find the *complete causes* of events in the course of nature. But if every natural event has a natural cause, then unless God is a natural cause, he is not a cause of anything at all. I have put this argument in a simple instance, for the sake of clearness: but it is of universal application. It has the advantage of being a question of logic, and not of fact; no new instances can overthrow it. It is as with the law of contradiction. If you have contradicted yourself, within the meaning of logic, then you must have made some mistake, however trivial. And so, if you use this argument, in whatever form you dress it, it must be worthless since your conclusion will not follow from your premises. One of your premises must be: This is the cause of that; and the other: Every event has a cause. And your conclusion is: God is the cause of these other events; his existence alone will explain them. But your first premise assigns as the cause of one natural event, another natural event. And you cannot be sure of this, unless every natural event is caused by another natural event: otherwise the effect you began with might not have had the cause which you assign — the hospital might have been made by miracle and not made by man. Either then God must be one or more among natural events, or else you have no reason to assert that he is more like one than another, more like a man than a billiard-ball. But you have asserted him to be more like a man than a billiard-ball; and you certainly cannot show that any natural event is a personal God. Either then God is a cause in some sense utterly different from that in which man is a cause: and then we cannot infer either to his existence or his nature; or else he is a cause in the sense in which man is a cause, and then we can infer his existence but not his nature: we can infer that the events in question had a cause, but not that their cause was God. This dilemma applies in general to every argument from Design — and not only to these, but to every metaphysical argument that tries to mount from Nature and Mind to any superior Reality. All such arguments infer from the nature and existence of some or all the things that are agreed to exist that something else, of a different nature, also exists. But the only known valid principle by which we can infer from the existence of one thing to the existence of something else is this same principle of causality, according to which that "something else" must be one among natural events. All these arguments must therefore involve the fallacy involved in the vulgar argument from Design. On the basis of such arguments modern philosophers are fond of offering to us, in place of a personal God, a more or less consoling Reality or Absolute. But the skeleton of any such construction is nothing more than this old fallacy. They muffle it up in garments infinitely complicated, many of which are in themselves sound stuff. But the more they muffle and the sounder the stuff, the less attractive their Absolute becomes. We have, I think, every reason to prefer the old God of Christianity. In him the artifice is

more transparent, and the product, none the less, by far more beautiful.

We cannot then make a single step towards proving God's existence from the nature of the world, such as we take it to be in common life or such as Natural Science shows it. That we are here to-night, that we were not here this morning, that we came here by means of cabs or on our feet: all facts of this sort, in which we cannot help believing, — these facts, with all the implications, which Science or Philosophy can draw from them, offer us not one jot of evidence that God exists. But there are other arguments which start like this one from experience. There is the argument from general belief. I will admit at once that most people, who have existed heretofore, have believed in a God of some sort. I have, indeed, no reason to believe that there are or have been other people and still less that they have had this belief, except on the same grounds as I believe in the facts of common life. If we are not here now, there is no evidence even that most people have believed in God. The mere fact of general belief, then, is no more certain than the facts of experience: if we reject the latter as untrue, we cannot use the former as evidence for God's existence. You cannot argue, as many people do: The facts of science are merely matters of general belief, and God's existence is the same; therefore the one is as certain as the other. For, unless the facts of science are true, you have no title to your statement that God's existence is a matter of general belief. But now, granting that it is a matter of general belief, does this fact establish any probability that God exists? I think it cannot. For many things which we now all admit to be errors, have in the past been matters of general belief: such, for instance, as that the sun went round the earth, which Galileo controverted. All the probability is, then, in favor of the supposition that many things which are still generally believed, will in time be recognized as errors. And what ground can we have for holding that the belief in God is not among their number? The probabilities seem all the other way. For I think it will be admitted that the belief in God has in the past derived much support from ignorance of Natural Science and from such arguments as those of Natural Theology. If, then, as I have tried to show, those arguments are fallacious, in proportion as this is recognized, the belief in God will become less general. You can therefore only hold that belief in God will persist undiminished, while other beliefs disappear, if you maintain the continued triumph of ignorance and fallacious reasoning. But a belief which persists from causes like these has surely no claim to be therefore considered true. In short, if you are to argue from general belief to truth, you must have independent grounds for thinking that the belief in question is true. If you can show a probability that it is true, then the fact of general belief may confirm that probability. But if, as I try to show in this case, there is no such probability, no evidence that God exists, then the fact of general belief is perfectly useless as evidence.

The argument from general belief must then break down, and I think I need hardly discuss at length any so-called historical proofs for God's existence. They are all from the nature of the case too obviously weak. If what they aim at is establishing the fact of miracles, then no historical proof can by any possibility show that an event, which happened, was in very truth a miracle — that it had no natural cause. That an event should have had no natural cause ·contradicts, as I tried to show, the very grounds of historical evidence, for this is all based on inferences from effect to cause, and if a miracle is ever

possible, we can never say that any particular thing was the cause of any other. But if you mean by miracle only a great and wonderful work, then that a man can perform astonishing feats is no proof either that he knows the truth or that he tells it. And, miracles apart, historical proofs can only show that somebody said something: whether what he said was true must be decided on quite other grounds.

The facts of common life, then, the facts with which natural science and history deal, afford no inference to God's existence. If a man still believes that God exists, he cannot support his belief by any appeal to facts admitted both by himself and the infidel. He must not attempt to *prove* that God probably exists; for that is impossible. He must be content to affirm that he sees as clearly that God exists as he sees that he himself does. Many people, I admit, may really have had this strong conviction. And many people may be content to justify belief upon this ground alone. They, I think, are right. Their position is quite unassailable. If you have this faith, this intuition of God's existence, that is enough. You may, I admit, be as certain that God exists as that you yourself exist: and no one has any right to say that you are wrong. But these are two independent facts: one is perhaps *as* certain to you as the other: but the one is *not* more likely to be true, because the other is so. The moment you use that argument, you will be wrong. You cannot argue that if you exist, God also probably exists: as you can argue that if you exist, I also probably exist. Nor can you argue that because you are so certain of God's existence, I ought to admit the slightest probability that he exists: if you do this, you are appealing to an argument similar to that from general belief. In fact, if I were the only person who could not see that God exists, and all the world agreed with you, it would yet be just as likely that I was right, as that you and all the world were right. It is equally likely we are right and equally likely we are wrong: but only equally. I have no more right to argue that probably God does not exist, because I cannot see he does, than you to argue that probably he does exist, because you see he does. This is all I have tried to show, when I maintain there is no evidence for God's existence. It is mere faith, not proof, which justifies your statement: God exists. Your belief is right, because you cannot help believing: and my unbelief is right, because I have not got that intuition. We both are justified by mere necessity.

An appeal to faith, then, — to intuition — is the sole ground for asserting the truth of religion. That truth, if it be true, is coordinate with the facts of daily life, and cannot be inferred from them, as they can be inferred from one another. And so far it would seem that religious belief stands in the same position as our moral beliefs. These moral judgments, too, it may be said, are independent of beliefs about the world: their truth also can never be inferred from that of daily facts.

That moral truth cannot be thus inferred from any facts, is, I think, quite demonstrable. But since it is denied, I must say something on this head. The argument of Mr. Balfour's book on "The Foundations of Belief" depends in part on this denial. If, he seems to say, the view of Naturalism that all things were evolved from natural causes is true, then it is inconsistent still to hold that our beliefs in the goodness of this and the beauty of that are also true. And a similar view is implied by Matthew Arnold, who seems to hold, that unless we can verify the existence of a power not ourselves that makes for righteousness, then our belief that certain conduct is righteous and other conduct wicked, must also justly perish. But is this so? Is it inconsistent

to hold that this is right and that is wrong, and at the same time to hold that we only think this right, that wrong, because in fact such beliefs have helped us to survive? Or can it be less true that right is right, even if there be no power that will reward it? The former argument refutes itself. For if it be true that beliefs were evolved, then the belief that they were so must also have been evolved. And this, according to Mr. Balfour, is a reason why we must doubt its truth. That is to say, the fact of evolution is a reason for doubting the fact of evolution. It is inconsistent to believe in the fact of evolution, if we at the same time believe in the fact of evolution. The inconsistency, we may well reply, is all the other way. It is, in fact, self-contradictory to hold that the validity of a belief depends in any way upon the manner in which it was acquired. And hence the truth of our moral beliefs *must* be independent of any scientific facts. Just so, we may answer Matthew Arnold: In order to verify the fact that righteous conduct is rewarded, we must already know what righteous conduct is: and to know that it is righteous is to know we ought to do it.

There is, therefore, no more evidence for moral than for religious beliefs; and the religious believer may be tempted to say, "I have as much right to my belief that God exists, as you have to any of your moral beliefs." But this claim, it should be pointed out, refutes itself. For his assertion that he has "as much right" to believe in God is itself a moral judgment. It can only rest upon the moral principle that necessity will justify beliefs: and this principle must have a prior validity to that of any particular instances which may be brought under it. The believer is therefore admitting that there is one moral principle to which he has more right than to his belief in God. It must be true, according to him, that necessity is a moral justification, whether his belief in God is so justified or not. In fact he cannot attempt to *defend* his belief in God except by a moral judgment; and by so doing he gives up the supposed parity between moral and religious beliefs in general, although it may still be true that such parity exists between religious belief and *most* moral judgments.

It remains true, however, that if a man really cannot help believing in God, nothing can be said against him. But I very much doubt whether this is often the case. With most believers, I think, the disparity between their moral and their religious convictions is much more striking. Their religious belief gains much of its strength from the fact that they think they ought to have it. They have a direct moral feeling that it is wicked to doubt of God's existence; and without this belief, which is a strong one, their direct religious certainty would offer but a weak resistance to scepticism. For such persons the final question arises: Are they right in thinking that infidelity is wicked?

Now they can no longer urge in defence of this opinion that belief in God is good, because it is true. On the contrary it is only because they believe it to be good that they hold it to be true. They must therefore rest their claim to its goodness solely upon its effects; and in the inquiry whether its effects are good, they must, as I pointed out above, carefully discount the vicious tendency to think the effects must be good, on the ground that the belief is true. They should bear in mind that the belief is possibly false; and that, if they shall decide that its effects are good, they will be committed to the theory that all this good is possibly a result of mere error.

Now whether they are or are not the better, the more strongly they believe that God exists is no longer a matter to dogmatize upon. The manners in which religious belief may act on different minds are infinitely various. But I think there is at least good room to doubt whether it ever does much good. That there is a power who is willing and able to help you would be, no doubt, an encouraging thought. But from this, if our argument holds, our believers are in any case excluded. God cannot interfere in the course of natural events. This belief, which has played such a large part in the religions of the past, is demonstrably untrue. At most, then, the encouragement must come from the knowledge that he sympathizes with us. And this is certainly no small comfort. But how are we to get it? We are faced by this dilemma. The encouragement will only be strong in proportion to our belief. But, on the other hand, our efforts to strengthen this belief are only too likely to fail, if we do not find we get the encouragement. That this difficulty is a real one I think most people for whom the present question has been raised, will acknowledge. That consolation, for the sake of which they desire to believe, must be already felt, before they can acquire it. They desire to "see that the Lord is good," in order that they may "taste" it; but on the other hand, unless they first do taste it, they cannot get to see it. It may well be urged that it would be better to give up this fruitless endeavor; especially when we consider that in so far they believe that God exists, is no longer a matter to dogmatize as they succeed, they are deliberately acquiring a belief, which, for all they know, is false.

And moreover, I agree with Matthew Arnold that a more important element in religion than this is the belief that the good will triumph. If we could rest in this belief, we might surely give up the belief in God, and yet get all the comfort that we needed. But for this belief also I am afraid we have no reason. That Good will triumph as that God exists is possible but only possible. Matthew Arnold's God too, is not, as he thought, verifiable. Naturalism, as Mr. Balfour argues, does fail to verify him. We have reason to believe that human life upon this planet will presently be extinguished. We certainly have no reason to believe the contrary; nor yet that our souls will persist and grow better after death.

But though our belief in this God fails us too, I think it may be doubted whether we may not still retain the very elements which have rendered religion most effective for good in the past. They are in fact elements which have no logical connection with belief in God.

(1) First, there is that valuable element in religious emotion, which proceeds from the contemplation of what we think to be most truly and perfectly good. We are indeed only entitled to think of this as what ought to be; not as what is or will be. But I doubt if this emotion need lose much of its force, because its object is not real. The effects of literature show how strongly we may be moved by the contemplation of ideal objects, of which we nevertheless do not assert the existence. It may indeed be doubted whether the most effective part in all religious belief has not always been similar to that which we have in objects of imagination — a belief quite consistent with a firm conviction that they are not facts. (2) And secondly, that some good objects should be real, is indeed necessary for our comfort. But these we have in plenty. It surely might be better to give up the search for a God whose existence is and remains undemonstrable, and to divert the feelings which the religious wish to spend on him, towards those of our own kind, who though perhaps less good than we can imagine God to be, are worthy of all the affections that we can feel; and whose help and sympathy are much more certainly real. We might perhaps with advantage worship the real creature a little more, and his hypothetical Creator a good deal less.

SUGGESTIONS FOR THOUGHT

1. "Many a modern man would be startled by the recognition of how little God means to him in his daily life and would probably be angered by a sudden Nietzschean announcement that God is dead." (A. Eustace Haydon) What are the factors that may have prompted Haydon's observation?

2. In what ways has your concept of God changed since childhood? What benefits do you derive from your conception of God?

3. When you think about the natural world do you find a place for God? Is the God-concept required when you consider the problem of values in the cosmos?

4. What sort of evidence for the existence of God do you find most conclusive? Are you disturbed by the difficulties in demonstrating that there is a God?

5. How do you account for the varying views of the nature of God found in the Old and New Testaments? Does the comparative study of the religions of various cultures indicate that God is a concept of the human imagination? Is it possible to distinguish between God and man's concept of God?

6. Some theologians have described God as an eternal creature. What would be some of the interesting aspects of a being that was not "bound" by time?

7. St. Thomas Aquinas wrote that human reason is able to establish the existence of God but it is not able to establish that God is a

Trinity. How can one distinguish between the existence of something and the qualities of that thing?

8. Compare the philosophical and the devotional approach to God. E.g., W. R. Inge once said of the ontological argument for the existence of God that one can't love a valid inference.

9. "Concerning the gods there are some who say that the Divine does not exist, others that it exists but is inactive and indifferent and takes no thought for anything, others again that God does exist and take thought but only for great things and things in the heaven but for nothing on earth; and a fourth class say that God takes thought also for earthly and human things, but only in a general way, and has no care for individuals; and there is a fifth class to whom belong Odysseus and Socrates, who say 'where'er I move Thou seest me.'" (Epictetus) Criticize this list of the possible views of the nature of God.

10. F. W. Robertson, a well-known English clergyman of the nineteenth century, is reported to have said at a period of his life when he had given up all belief in God, "If there be no God and no future state, yet even then it is better to be generous than to be selfish, better to be true than false, better to be brave than a coward." Is God necessary as a support of moral values? What are the strengths and weaknesses of a morality rooted in deity?

11. Ivan in Dostoyevsky's *The Brothers Karamozov* says: "What's strange, what would be marvellous, is not that God should really exist; the marvel is that such an idea, the idea of the necessity of God, could enter the head of such a savage, vicious beast as man. So holy it is, so touching, so wise and so great credit it

does to man." What are some of the factors which may have caused the idea to arise in the mind of man?

12. Santayana has said that "if all went well and acceptably, we should attribute divinity only to ourselves." What does this suggest about man and God?

13. Some people believe that they know the will of God; e.g., the Massachusetts Bay Colony wrote to Rhode Island asking that Rhode Island cease to allow Quakers to enter, and added that if the colony did not take favorable action, Massachusetts "would have to consider seriously what further provision God may call us to make to prevent the aforesaid mischiefe." Is the "will of God" a meaningful idea? How can people be sure that they know the will of God?

14. "The only really important question before us today is this: What do you mean by God?" (A. N. Whitehead) "At present the question whether God exists or not, seems to have ceased to be of public interest." (G. E. Moore) Which one do you think is right, or have both Whitehead and Moore made correct observations?

15. Man's tendency to picture his gods in his own image has been recognized and deplored by scholars for centuries, perhaps never more devastatingly than by Samuel Butler, who observes in his *Notebooks:* "The turnips may say 'Our turnip, which art in heaven,' etc., and 'There is not even one man falleth to the ground but by the will of our heavenly turnip.'" Can anthropomorphism be entirely avoided? What is wrong with anthropomorphism?

16. Are unbelievers bad? William P. Montague thinks "Atheism leads not to badness but only to an incurable sadness and loneliness."

SUGGESTIONS FOR FURTHER READING

BRIGHTMAN, E. S., *A Philosophy of Religion*, New York, Prentice-Hall, 1940, ch. 7.

COOK, ALBERT A., "The Ontological Argument for the Existence of God," *Proceedings of the Aristotelian Society,* Vol. 18, 1918, pp. 363–384.

EWING, A. C., *The Fundamental Questions of Philosophy,* New York, The Macmillan Company, 1951, ch. 11.

FINDLAY, J. N., "Can God's Existence Be Disproved?" *Mind,* Vol. 57, 1948, pp. 176–183.

HARKNESS, GEORGIA, *The Recovery of Ideals,* New York, Charles Scribner's Sons, 1937, chs. 9, 10.

HORTON, WALTER M., "Reasons for Believing in God," *The Journal of Religion,* Vol. 3, 1923, pp. 598–615.

HUME, DAVID, *Dialogues Concerning Natural Religion.*

KRONER, RICHARD, *How Do We Know God?,* New York, Harper and Brothers, 1943.

MATTHEWS, W. R., "The Moral Argument for Theism," *Proceedings of the Aristotelian Society,* Vol. 18, 1918, pp. 385–409.

PRINGLE-PATTISON, A. S., *The Idea of God,* London, Oxford University Press, 1920.

SMYTH, NATHAN A., *Through Science to God,* New York, The Macmillan Company, 1937, ch. 11.

SPERRY, WILLARD L., *What We Mean by Religion,* New York, Harper and Brothers, 1940, ch. 5.

STACE, W. T., *Time and Eternity,* Princeton, Princeton University Press, 1952, chs. 3, 9.

TSANOFF, RADOSLAV A., *Religious Crossroads,* New York, E. P. Dutton and Company, 1942, ch. 9.

WIEMAN, HENRY NELSON, "Can God Be Perceived?" *The Journal of Religion,* Vol. 23, 1943, pp. 23–32.

15

EVIL

EVERY HUMAN CULTURE has struggled with the problem of evil. In some respects a rationale of evil has been more urgent than a rationale of goodness. St. Augustine (354–430), whom many consider to be the father of Christian theology, has offered some of the explanations most common in Western civilization. Rabindranath Tagore (1861–1941) speaks for a segment of the East in his essay. Tagore is best known as a poet. His writings are filled with feeling for the beauty of the universe. He did much to interpret the deeper thinking of the people of Bengal to the West. In 1901 he founded a school in Bolpur near Calcutta. The school continues to this day to offer an education in keeping with the philosophy of Tagore. In 1913 he won the Nobel prize for literature, and in 1915 he was knighted by the British government.

A

By the Trinity, thus supremely and equally and unchangeably good, all things were created; and these are not supremely and equally and unchangeably good, but yet they are good, even taken separately. Taken as a whole, however, they are very good, because their *ensemble* constitutes the universe in all its wonderful order and beauty.

Augustine, "The Enchiridion," chs. 10–14, 96, translated by J. F. Shaw, "On Continence," sections 14–16, translated by C. L. Cornish, in *A Select Library of the Nicene and Post-Nicene Fathers of the Christian Church*, Vol. 3, edited by Philip Schaff, Buffalo, The Christian Literature Company, 1887.

And in the universe, even that which is called evil, when it is regulated and put in its own place, only enhances our admiration of the good; for we enjoy and value the good more when we compare it with the evil. For the Almighty God, who, as even the heathen acknowledge, has supreme power over all things, being Himself supremely good, would never permit the existence of anything evil among His works, if He were not so omnipotent and good that He can bring good even out of evil. For what is that which we call evil but the absence of good? In the bodies of animals, disease and wounds mean nothing but the absence of health; for when a cure is effected, that does not mean that the evils which were present — namely, the diseases and wounds — go away from the body and dwell elsewhere: they altogether cease to exist; for the wound or disease is not a substance, but a defect in the fleshly substance, — the flesh itself being a substance, and therefore something good, of which those evils — that is, privations of the good which we call health — are accidents. Just in the same way, what are called vices in the soul are nothing but privations of natural good. And when they are not transferred elsewhere: when they cease to exist in the healthy soul, they cannot exist anywhere else.

All things that exist, therefore, seeing that the Creator of them all is supremely good, are themselves good. But because they are not, like their Creator, supremely and unchangeably good, their good may be diminished and increased. But for good to be diminished is an evil, although, however much it may be diminished, it is necessary, if the being is to continue, that some good should remain to constitute the being. For however small or of whatever kind the being may be, the good which makes it a being cannot be destroyed without destroying the being itself. An uncorrupted nature is justly held in esteem. But if, still further, it be incorruptible it is undoubtedly considered of still higher value. When it is corrupted, however, its corruption is an evil, because it is deprived of some sort of good. For if it be deprived of no good, it receives no injury; but it does receive injury, therefore it is deprived of good. Therefore, so long as a being is in process of corruption, there is in it some good of which it is being deprived; and if a part of the being should remain which cannot be corrupted, this will certainly be an incorruptible being, and ac-

cordingly the process of corruption will result in the manifestation of this great good. But if it do not cease to be corrupted, neither can it cease to possess good of which corruption may deprive it. But if it should be thoroughly and completely consumed by corruption, there will then be no good left because there will be no being. Wherefore corruption can consume the good only by consuming the being. Every being, therefore, is a good; a great good, if it can not be corrupted; a little good, if it can: but in any case, only the foolish or ignorant will deny that it is good. And if it be wholly consumed by corruption, then the corruption itself must cease to exist, as there is no being left in which it can dwell.

Accordingly, there is nothing of what we call evil, if there be nothing good. But a good which is wholly without evil is a perfect good. A good, on the other hand, which contains evil is a faulty or imperfect good; and there can be no evil where there is no good. From all this we arrive at the curious result: that since every being, so far as it is a being, is good, when we say that a faulty being is an evil being, we just seem to say that what is good is evil, and that nothing but what is good can be evil, seeing that every being is good, and that no evil can exist except in a being. Nothing, then, can be evil except something which is good. And although this, when stated, seems to be a contradiction, yet the strictness of reasoning leaves us no escape from the conclusion. We must, however, beware of incurring the prophetic condemnation: "Woe unto them that call evil good, and good evil: that put darkness for light, and light for darkness: that put bitter for sweet, and sweet for bitter." And yet our Lord says: "An evil man out of the evil treasure of his heart bringeth forth that which is evil." Now what is an evil man but an evil being? for a man is a being. Now, if a man is a good thing because he is a being, what is an evil man but an evil good? Yet when we accurately distinguish these two things, we find that it is not because he is a man that he is an evil, or because he is wicked that he is a good; but that he is a good because he is a man, and an evil because he is wicked. Whoever, then, says, "To be a man is an evil," or, "To be wicked is a good," falls under the prophetic denunciation: "Woe unto them that call evil good, and good evil!" For he condemns the work of God, which is the man, and praises the defect of man, which is the wickedness. Therefore, every being, even if it be a defective one, in so far as it is a being is good, and in so far as it is defective is evil.

Accordingly, in the case of these contraries which we call good and evil, the rule of the logicians, that two contraries cannot be predicated at the same time of the same thing, does not hold. No weather is at the same time dark and bright: no food or drink is at the same time sweet and bitter: no body is at the same time and in the same place black and white: none is at the same time and in the same place deformed and beautiful. And this rule is found to hold in regard to many, indeed nearly all, contraries, that they cannot exist at the same time in any one thing. But although no one can doubt that good and evil are contraries, not only can they exist at the same time, but evil cannot exist without good, or in anything that is not good. Good, however, can exist without evil. For a man or an angel can exist without being wicked; but nothing can be wicked except a man or an angel: and so far as he is a man or an angel, he is good; so far as he is wicked, he is an evil. And these two contraries are so far co-existent, that if good did not exist in what is evil, neither could evil exist; because corruption could not have either a place to dwell in, or a source to

spring from, if there were nothing that could be corrupted; and nothing can be corrupted except what is good, for corruption is nothing else but the destruction of good. From what is good, then, evils arose, and except in what is good they do not exist; nor was there any other source from which any evil nature could arise. For if there were, then, in so far as this was a being, it was certainly a good: and a being which was incorruptible would be a great good; and even one which was corruptible must be to some extent a good, for only by corrupting what was good in it could corruption do it harm. . . .

Nor can we doubt that God does well even in the permission of what is evil. For He permits it only in the justice of His judgment. And surely all that is just is good. Although, therefore, evil, in so far as it is evil, is not a good; yet the fact that evil as well as good exists, is a good. For if it were not a good that evil should exist, its existence would not be permitted by the omnipotent Good, who without doubt can as easily refuse to permit what He does not wish, as bring about what He does wish. And if we do not believe this, the very first sentence of our creed is endangered, wherein we profess to believe in God the Father Almighty. For He is not truly called Almighty if He cannot do whatever He pleases, or if the power of His almighty will is hindered by the will of any creature whatsoever. . . .

And some indeed, who are used to excuse their own sins, complain that they are driven to sin by fate, as though the stars had decreed this, and heaven had first sinned by decreeing such, in order that man should after sin by committing such, and thus had rather impute their sin to fortune: who think that all things are driven to and fro by chance accidents, and yet contend that this their wisdom and assertion is not of chance rashness, but of ascertained reason. What madness then is it, to lay to reason their discussions, and to make their actions subject to accidents! Others refer to the devil the whole of what they do ill: and will not have even a share with him, whereas they may suspect whether he by hidden suggestions hath persuaded them to evil, and on the other hand cannot doubt that they have consented to those suggestions, from whatever source they have come. There are also they who extend their defense of self unto an accusation of God, wretched by the divine judgment, but blasphemers by their own madness. For against Him they bring in from a contrary principle a substance of evil rebelling, which He could not have resisted, had He not blended with that same that was rebelling a portion of His own Substance and Nature, for it to contaminate and corrupt; and they say that they then sin when the nature of evil prevails over the nature of God. This is that most unclean madness of the Manichaeans, whose devilish devices the undoubted truth most easily overthrows; which confesses that the nature of God is incapable of contamination and corruption. But what wicked contamination and corruption do they not deserve to have believed of them, by whom God, Who is good in the very highest degree, and in a way that admits not of comparison, is believed to be capable of contamination and corruption?

And there are also they who in excuse of their sins so accuse God, as to say that sins are pleasing to Him. For, if they were dis-pleasing, say they, surely by His most Almighty power He would by no means suffer them to take place. As though indeed God suffered sins to be unpunished, even in the case of those whom by remission of sins He frees from eternal punishment! No one forsooth receives pardon of more grievous punishment due, unless he hath suffered some punishment, be it what it may, although far less that what was due: and the fullness of mercy is so conveyed, as that the justice also of discipline is not abandoned. For also sin, which seems unavenged, hath its own attendant punishment, so that there is no one but by reason of what he hath done either suffers pain from bitterness, or suffers not through blindness. As therefore you say, Why doth He permit those things, if they are displeasing? so I say, Why doth He punish them, if they are pleasing? And thus, as I confess that those things would not take place at all, unless they were permitted by the Almighty, so confess thou that what are punished by the Just One ought not to be done; in order that, by not doing what He punishes, we may deserve to learn of Him, why He permits to exist what He punishes. For, as it is written, "solid food is for the perfect," wherein they who have made good progress already understand, that it pertained rather unto the Almighty power of God, to allow the existence of evils coming from the free choice of the will. So great forsooth is His Almighty goodness, as that even of evil He can make good, either by pardoning, or by healing, or by fitting and turning unto the profit of the pious, or even by most justly taking vengeance. For all these are good, and most worthy a good and Almighty God: and yet they are not made save of evils. What therefore better, what more Almighty, than He, Who, whereas He maketh no evil, even of evils maketh well? They who have done ill cry unto Him, "Forgive us our debts;" He hears, He pardons. Their own evils have hurt the sinners; He helps and heals their sicknesses. The enemies of His people rage; of their rage He makes martyrs. Lastly, also, He condemns those, whom He judges worthy of condemnation; although they suffer their own evils, yet He doeth what is good. For what is just cannot but be good, and assuredly as sin is unjust, so the punishment of sin is just.

But God wanted not power to make man such as that he should not be able to sin: but He chose rather to make him such, as that it should lie in his power to sin, if he would; not to sin, if he would not; forbidding the one, enjoining the other; that it might be to him first a good desert not to sin, and after a just reward not to be able to sin. For such also at the last will He makes His Saints, as to be without all power to sin. Such forsooth even now hath He His angels, whom in Him we so love, as to have no fear for any of them, lest by sinning he become a devil. And this we presume not of any just man in this mortal life. But we trust that all will be such in that immortal life. For Almighty God Who worketh good even of our evils, what good will He give, when He shall have set us free from all evils? Much may be said more fully and more subtilely on the good use of evil; but this is not what we have undertaken in our present discourse, and we must avoid in it excess of length.

B

The question, Why is there evil in existence? is the same as, Why is there imperfection? or, in other words, Why is there creation at all?

We must take it for granted that it could not be otherwise; that creation must be imperfect, must be gradual, and it is futile to ask the question why we are.

But the real question is, Is this imperfection the final truth? is evil absolute and ultimate? The river has its boundaries, its banks; but is the river all banks? or are the banks the final facts about the river? Do not these obstructions themselves give its water an onward motion? The towing-rope binds a boat; but is the bondage its meaning? Does it not at the same time draw it forward?

The current of the world has its bound-

Rabindranath Tagore, "The Problem of Evil," *The Hibbert Journal*, Vol. 11, 1913, pp. 705–715. Reprinted by permission of the Editor of *The Hibbert Journal*.

aries, otherwise it could have no existence; but its meaning is not in its boundaries, which are fixed, but in its movement, which is towards perfection. The wonder is not that there should be obstacles and sufferings in this world, but that there should be law and order, beauty and joy, goodness and love. The idea of God that man has in his being is the wonder of all wonders. He has felt in the depth of his life that what appears as imperfect is the manifestation of the perfect; just as a man who has the ear for music realises the perfectness of a song while in fact he is only listening to a succession of notes. Man has found out the great paradox that what is limited is not imprisoned within its limits; it is ever moving, thus shedding its finitude every moment. In fact, imperfection is not a negation of perfectness; finitude is not contradictory to infinity. It is completeness manifested in parts, infinity revealed within bounds.

Pain, which is the feeling connected with our finiteness, is not a fixture in our life. It is not an end in itself as joy is. To meet it is to know that it cannot be the principle of permanence in the creation. It is like what error is in our intellectual life. To go through the history of the development of science is, among other things, to go through the maze of mistakes it made current in different times. Yet there is one who really believes that science is the most perfect system of disseminating mistakes. The principle of ascertaining truth is the most important thing to consider in the history of science, not its innumerable mistakes. For error by its nature cannot be stationary; it cannot fit in with truth; like a tramp it must quit its lodging when it cannot pay its bill to the full.

As in intellectual error, so in evil in any other form, its essence is impermanence, for it cannot fit in with the whole. Every moment it is being corrected by the totality of things and is changing its aspects. We exaggerate its importance by imagining it as at a standstill. Could we collect the statistics of the immense amount of death and putrefaction to be found every moment in this earth they would appal us. But evil is ever moving; so with all its incalculable immensity it does not effectually clog the current of our life, and, on the whole, the earth, water, and air remain sweet and pure for living beings. All statistics consist of our deliberate attempts to represent statically what is in motion; so by this process things assume a weight in our mind which they have not in reality. This is the reason why a man, who by his profession or for other reasons, is specially concerned with any particular aspect of life, is apt to magnify its proportions, and by giving undue stress upon facts to lose hold upon truth. A detective may have the opportunities of studying crimes in details, but he loses his bearings as to their relative place in the whole society. When science collects facts to illustrate the struggle for existence that goes on in the kingdom of life, it raises a picture in our minds of "Nature red in tooth and claw." But in these mental pictures we give a fixity to the colours and forms which are really evanescent. It is like calculating the weight of the air on each square inch of our body to show that it is crushingly heavy on us. But with this weight there is the adjustment of weight, and we lightly bear our burden. With the struggle for existence in Nature there is the reciprocity, there is the love for children, for comrades; there is the sacrifice of self, which springs from love; and love is the positive element in life.

If we throw our bull's-eye light of observation upon the fact of death, the world will appear to us like a huge charnelhouse; but it is surprising to think that in the world of life the thought of death has the least hold upon our minds. Not because it is the least apparent, but because it is the negative aspect of life; just as, in spite of the fact that we shut our eyelids every second, it is the openings of the eyelids that count. Life as a whole never takes death seriously. It laughs and dances and plays, it builds and hoards and loves in its face. Only when we detach an individual fact of death we see merely the blankness and are dismayed. We lose sight of the wholeness of life whose part is death. It is like looking at a piece of cloth through a microscope — it appears like a net; we wonder at the big holes and shiver in imagination. But the truth is, death is not an ultimate reality. It looks black as the sky looks blue, but it does not blacken existence, as the sky does not leave its stain upon wings of birds.

When we watch a child trying to walk we see its countless failures; its successes are few. If we had to limit our observation within a narrow space of time the sight would be cruel.

But we find that, in spite of its repeated un-successes, there is an impetus of joy in the child which sustains it in its seemingly impossible task. We see it does not set store by its falls so much as by its ability to keep its balance even for a moment.

Like these accidents in a child's attempt to walk, we meet with sufferings in various forms in our life every day, showing our imperfection in knowledge, power, and application of will. But if it only revealed our weakness to us, we should die of utter depression. When we take for observation a limited area of our activities, our individual failures and miseries loom large in our minds; but our life instinctively takes a wider view, it has an ideal of perfection which ever carries it beyond its present limitations. Within us, he have a hope which always walks in front of our present narrow experience; it is an undying faith in the infinite in us; it will never accept any of our disabilities as a permanent fact; it sets no limit to its scope; it dares to assert that man has his oneness with God; and its wildest dreams become true every day.

We see truth when we set our mind towards the infinite. The ideal of truth is not in the narrow present, not in our immediate sensations, but in the consciousness of the whole which gives us a taste of what we should have in what we have. Consciously or unconsciously we have in our life this feeling of truth which is ever more than its appearance, for our life is facing the infinite, it is on the move. Therefore its aspiration is infinitely more than its achievements; therefore it always finds that no realisation of truth ever leaves it stranded on the desert land of finality, but carries it on to a further beyond. Therefore evil cannot stop the course of life altogether on the highway and rob it of its possessions. For the evil has to pass on, it has to grow into good; it cannot stand at a fixed point and ever remain at war with all. If the least evil could stop anywhere indefinitely it would sink deep and eat into the marrow of existence. As it is, man does not really believe in evil, just as he cannot believe that violin chords have been purposely made to create the most exquisite form of torture in discordant notes, though by the aid of statistics it can be mathematically proved that actual possibilities of discords are far greater than that of harmonious notes, for where one can play a violin there are thousands who cannot. Potentiality of perfection outweighs actual contradictions. Of course, there have been people who asserted existence to be an absolute evil, but man can never take them seriously. For our pessimism is a mere pose, either intellectual or sentimental; our life itself is optimistic, it wants to go on. Pessimism is a form of mental dipsomania, it disdains healthy nourishment, indulges in the strong drink of denunciation, creates an artificial dejection to fall back upon a stronger draught to drink. If existence were an evil, we should wait for no philosopher to prove it. It is like incriminating a man of suicide while all the time he stands before you in the flesh. Existence itself is here to prove that it cannot be an evil.

An imperfection which is not all imperfection, but which has perfection for its ideal, must go through a perpetual realisation. Thus, it is the function of our intellect to realise the truth through untruths, and knowledge is nothing but continually burning up mistakes to set free the light of truth. Our will, our character has to attain perfection by continually overcoming evils, either inside or outside us, or both. Our physical life is burning bodily materials every moment to maintain the life fire, and our moral life has its fuel to burn. This life process is going on — we know it, we have felt it, and we have a faith which no individual instances to the contrary can shake, that the direction of humanity is from evil to good. For we feel that good is the positive element in man's nature, and in every age and every clime what a man values most is his ideal of goodness. We have known the good, we have loved it, and we have paid our highest reverence to men who have shown in their lives what goodness could be.

The question will be asked, What is goodness? What does our moral nature mean? My answer to that is, that when a man begins to have an extended vision of his self, when he realises that he is much more than what he is at present, he begins to grow conscious of his moral nature. Then he knows that what he is yet to be, the state not yet experienced by him, is real, more real than what is under his direct experience. Necessarily, his perspective of life changes, and his will takes the place of his wishes. For will is the wish of the larger life, life whose greater portion is out of our present reach and most of whose objects are not before our sight. Then comes the conflict of our lesser man with our greater man, our wish with our will, the desire for things that are before our senses with our purpose which is within our mind. Then we begin to distinguish between what we desire and what is good. For good is that which is desirable for our greater self. Thus the sense of the goodness comes out of the truer view of our life, which is the connected view of the wholeness of the field of life, that takes into account not only what is present before us, but what is not, and perhaps never shall be. The man who is provident feels for that life of his which is not yet existent, feels much more for that than for the life that is with him; therefore he is ready to sacrifice his present inclination for the unrealised future. In this he becomes great, for he realises truth. Even to be efficiently selfish one has to recognise this truth, and has to curb his immediate impulses of selfishness; in other

words, he must be moral. For our moral faculty is the faculty by which we know that life is not made up of fragments purposeless and discontinuous. This moral sense of man not only gives him the power to see that his self has a contiguity in time, but it also enables him to see that he is not true when he is only restricted to his own self. He is more in truth than he is in fact. He truly belongs to individuals who are not included in his own individuality and whom he is never likely to know. As he has a feeling for his future self which is outside him, so he has a feeling for his greater self which is outside his limits of personality. There is no man who has it not to some extent, who never sacrificed his selfish desire for the sake of some other person, who never felt a pleasure in undergoing some loss or trouble because it pleased somebody else. It is a truth that man is not a detached being; he has a universal aspect, and when he recognises it, he becomes great. Even the most evil-disposed selfishness has to recognise this when it requires power to do evil; for it cannot ignore truth and yet be strong. So, in order to claim its aid from truth, selfishness has to be unselfish to some extent. A band of robbers must be moral; by this they are made into a band; they may rob the whole world, but not each other. To make immoral intention successful some of its weapons must be moral. In fact, very often it is our moral strength which gives us the power effectively to do evil, to exploit other individuals for our benefits, to rob other people of their rights. The life of an animal is unmoral, for it is aware only of an immediate present; the life of a man can be immoral, but that means that the life of a man must have a moral basis. What is immoral is imperfectly moral, just as what is false is true to a small extent, or it cannot even be false. Not to see is to be blind, but to see wrong is to see only in an imperfect manner. Man's selfishness is a beginning to see some connection, some purpose in life; and to act accordingly requires self-restraint and regulation of conduct. A selfish man voluntarily takes trouble for the sake of his self, he suffers hardship and privation without murmur, simply because he knows that what is pain and trouble, looked at from the point of view of a limited area of time, is just the opposite when seen at a larger perspective. What is a loss to the smaller man is a gain to the greater, and *vice versa.*

To the man who lives for an idea, for his country, for the good of humanity, life has an extensive meaning, and to that extent pain becomes less important to him. To live the life of goodness is to live the life of all. Pleasure is for one's own self, but goodness is happiness for all humanity and for all time. So from the point of view of the good, pleasure and pain must appear in a different meaning; so much so, that pleasure may be shunned and pain may be courted in its place, that death may be made welcome as giving a higher value to life. So there is a standpoint, which is the highest standpoint of a man's life, and from that standpoint of the good, pleasure and pain lose their absolute value. Martyrs prove it in history, and we prove it every day in our life in our little martyrdoms. When we take a pitcherful of water from the sea it has its weight, but when we take a dip into the sea itself a thousand pitcherfuls of water flow above our head and we do not feel its weight. Our self is the pitcher, we have to carry it with our strength; so on the plane of selfishness pleasure and pain have their full weight, but on the moral plane they are so much lightened that the man who has reached it appears to us almost superhuman in his patient cheerfulness under crushing trials and his forbearance in the face of malignant persecution.

To live in perfect goodness is to realise one's life in the infinite. This is the most comprehensive view of life which we can have by our inherent power of the moral vision of the wholeness of life. . . .

Man comes to grief at every step when he tries to walk in this world as if it were specially made for him. His complaint against Nature is that she takes no heed of his individual desires and needs. He seems to think that if he had a world all to himself, where he could enjoy sun when he wished and rain when he would, where there would be no law, but only his wish, he would be satisfied. But this is an illusion. For, leaving aside the question that he could have no wish if there were no obstacles to his wishes, we must keep in mind that his finite individuality is not his highest truth; there is that in him which is universal. If he were made to live in a world where his own self would be the only factor to consider, then that would be the worst prison imaginable to him. Man's deepest joy is in growing more and more by perfecting his union with the all. Which would be an impossibility if there were no law common to all. Thus, only by discovering the law and following it we become great, we realise the universal; and so long as our individual desires are in conflict with the universal law we suffer pain and are beaten.

There was a time when we prayed for special concessions, we expected that laws of Nature could be held in abeyance for our own convenience. But now we know better. We know that law could not be set aside, and in this knowledge we have become strong. For this law is not something apart from us, it is our own. The universal power which is manifested in the universal law is our own power. It will thwart us where we are small, where we are against the whole current of things; but it will help us where we are great, where we are one with the all. Thus, through the help of science, as we come to know more of the laws of Nature we gain more in power; we seem to attain a universal body; our organ of sight, our organ of locomotion, our bodily strength become world-wide; electricity and steam become our nerve and muscle. Thus we find that, just as throughout our bodily organisation there is a principle of relation by virtue of which we can call this entire body our own, and can use it, so all through the universe there is that principle of uninterrupted relation by virtue of which we can call the whole world as our extended body and use it accordingly. And in this age of science it is our endeavour fully to establish our claim to this our world-self. We know all our poverty and sufferings are owing to our inability to realise this legitimate claim of ours. Really, there is no limit to our powers, for we are not outside the universal power which is the expression of universal law. We are on our way to overcome disease and death, to conquer pain and poverty; for through scientific knowledge we are ever on our way to realise the universal in its physical aspect. And as we make progress we find that pain, disease, and poverty or power are not absolute, but that it is only the want of adjustment of our individual self to our universal self which gives rise to them.

It is the same with our moral life. When the individual man in us chafes against the lawful rule of the universal man we become morally small and we must suffer. In such a condition our successes are our greatest failures and fulfilment of our desires leaves us poorer. We hanker after special gains for ourselves, we want to enjoy privileges which none else can share with us. But everything that is absolutely special must keep up a perpetual warfare with what is general. In such a state of civil war man always lives behind barricades, and in civilisation which is selfish our homes are not real homes, but artificial barriers around us. Yet we complain that we are not happy; as if there were something inherent in the nature of things to make us miserable. The spirit universal is waiting to crown us with happiness, but our individual spirit would not accept it. It is our life of the self that causes conflicts and complications everywhere, upsets the normal balance of society, gives rise to miseries of all kinds, and brings things to such a pass that to maintain order we have to create artificial coercions and organised forms of tyranny, and tolerate infernal institutions in our midst where humanity is humiliated every moment.

We have seen that in order to be powerful we have to submit to laws of the universal forces, and thus to realise that they are our own. So, in order to be happy, we have to submit our individual will to the sovereignty of the universal will, and thus to feel that it is our own will in truth. When we reach that state, when the adjustment of the finite in us to the infinite is made perfect, then pain itself becomes a valuable asset to us. It becomes a measuring rod with which to measure our true joy.

The most important lesson that man can have from his life is not that there is pain in this world, but that it depends upon him to turn it to good account, to transmute it into joy. That lesson has not been lost altogether to us, and there is no man living who would willingly be deprived of his right to suffer pain, for that is his right to be a man. One day the wife of a poor labourer came to me and complained bitterly that her eldest boy was going to be sent away to a rich relative's house for a part of the year. It was the kind intention of trying to relieve her of her trouble that gave her the shock, for a mother's trouble is a mother's own by her inalienable right of love, and she was not going to surrender it to any dictates of expediency. Man's freedom is never to be saved troubles, but it is freedom to take trouble for his own good, to make it an element of his joy. It can be made so only when we realise that our individual self is not the highest meaning of our being, that in us we have the world-man who is immortal, who is not afraid of death or sufferings, and who looks upon pain as only the other side of joy. He knows that it is the pain which is our true wealth as imperfect beings, and this has made us great and worthy to take our seat with the perfect. He knows that we are not beggars, we have to pay with the hard coins of pain for everything valuable in this life, for our power, our wisdom, our love; that in pain is symbolised the infinite possibility of perfection, the eternal unfolding of joy; and that the man who loses all pleasure in taking pain sinks down and down to the lowest depth of penury and degradation. It is only when we invoke the aid of pain for our self-gratification that she becomes evil and takes her vengeance for the insult done to her by hurling us to misery. For she is the vestal virgin consecrated to the service of the immortal perfection, and when she takes her true place before the altar of the infinite she casts off her dark veil and bares her face to the beholder as the revelation of supreme joy.

SUGGESTIONS FOR THOUGHT

1. St. Augustine and many theologians since have explained that evil is required in order that good may exist. Lewis Mumford, on the other hand, opines that "life would still be amusing and significant were every vexatious devil banished, were every thorn plucked, were every mosquito exterminated." What do you think?

2. How might the various kinds of evils be classified? Should earthquakes and storms be counted as evils, or should evils be limited to the sins and sufferings that man brings upon himself?

3. "There must always remain something which is antagonistic to good." (Plato) Why? Wouldn't good acts be just as good without evil to serve as contrast? If evils are as essential as some of its defenders claim, why should mankind work for the elimination of evils? Is the existence of good also a problem?

4. How has the concept of a devil served to explain the existence of evil?

5. Would man be satisfied in Utopia? William James wrote after a week at Chautauqua: "This order is too tame, this culture too second-rate, this goodness too uninspiring. This human drama without a villain or a pang; this community so refined that ice-cream soda-water is the utmost offering it can make to the brute animal in man; this city simmering in the tepid lakeside sun; this atrocious harmlessness of all things — I cannot abide with them. Let me take my chances again in the big outside worldly wilderness with all its sins and sufferings." How do you explain James's dissatisfaction with a "perfect society"?

6. Kant thought that the final evidence for the basically unsatisfactory nature of human life is the fact that no one of sound understanding who had lived long enough and meditated on the worth of human existence would want to live again on any conditions. Freud believed that the "death wish" was basic to man. The Buddhist conception of nirvana also fits well in this pattern of thought. But how can one account for the hope for immortality which is so important in Christianity?

7. What are the chief "solutions" to the problem of evil? Are any of them actually *solutions* — that is, is an intellectual explanation of evil actually a solution to the practical problem of evil? What would you say to a man who claimed that the only solution to the problem of evil

is to get busy and do something about the evils in the world?

8. "Aurora forgot to ask youth for her lover, and though Tithonus is immortal, he is old. Achilles is not quite invulnerable; the sacred waters did not wash the heel by which Thetis held him. Siegfried, in the Nibelungen, is not immortal, for a leaf fell on his back whilst he was bathing in the dragon's blood, and that spot which it covered is mortal. And so it must be. There is a crack in every thing God has made." (Emerson) Why? If God is good and all-powerful, then why did He not make everything perfect?

9. "Either God is willing to remove evils, and not able; or able and not willing, or neither able nor willing, or both able and willing. If he be willing and not able he is impotent, which cannot be applied to the Deity. If he be able and not willing, he is envious, which is gen-erally inconsistent with the nature of God. If he be neither willing nor able, he is both envious and impotent, and consequently no God. If he be both willing and able, which is the only thing that answers to the notion of a God, from whence come evils? Or why does he not remove them?" (Lactatius) How do you answer Lactatius?

10. Which is more evil, man or nature? John Stuart Mill has written: "In sober truth, nearly all the things which men are hanged or imprisoned for doing to one another, are nature's everyday performances. Killing, the most criminal act recognized by human laws, Nature does once to every being that lives; and in a large proportion of cases, after protracted tortures such as only the greatest monsters whom we read of ever purposely inflicted on their living fellow-creatures." How would you answer Mill? Compare killing by man and killing by nature.

SUGGESTIONS FOR FURTHER READING

BENNETT, JOHN C., "The Problem of Evil," *The Journal of Religion,* Vol. 18, 1938, pp. 401–421.

COLLINGWOOD, R. G., *Religion and Philosophy,* New York, The Macmillan Company, 1916, Part II, ch. 4.

DUBS, HOMER H., "The Problem of Evil — A Modern Solution," *The Journal of Religion,* Vol. 11, 1931, pp. 554–569.

FERRE, NELS F. S., *Evil and the Christian Faith,* New York, Harper and Brothers, 1947.

JOAD, C. E. M., *God and Evil,* New York, Harper and Brothers, 1943, ch. 3.

KING, ROY ALBION, *The Problem of Evil,* New York, Ronald Press, 1952.

KOHN, JACOB, "God and the Reality of Evil," *The Personalist,* Vol. 33, 1952, pp. 117–130.

LEWIS, C. S., *The Problem of Pain,* New York, The Macmillan Company, 1944.

MONTAGUE, W. P., *Belief Unbound,* New Haven, Yale University Press, 1930, ch. 3.

ROYCE, JOSIAH, *Studies of Good and Evil,* New York, D. Appleton and Company, 1915, ch. 1.

TRUEBLOOD, D. ELTON, *The Logic of Belief,* New York, Harper and Brothers, 1942, ch. 17.

TSANOFF, RADOSLAV A., *The Nature of Evil,* New York, The Macmillan Company, 1931, ch. 14.

WEISS, PAUL, "Good and Evil," *The Review of Metaphysics,* Vol. 3, 1949, pp. 81–94.

WISDOM, JOHN, "God and Evil," *Mind,* Vol. 44, 1935, pp. 1–20.

16

RELIGION AND KNOWLEDGE

RELIGIOUS BELIEF springs from both evidence and desire. The following selections from Clifford and James are typical of many discussions of belief in that they cannot agree about the role desire may rightfully play in belief. Clifford demands complete intellectual objectivity, whereas James defends and justifies believing beyond that which can be fully supported by evidence. William Kingdon Clifford (1845–1879), an English mathematician and philosopher, was professor of mathematics at University College, London, at the time of his early death. The hard-hitting essays from his pen were sufficient reason for James's description of him as "that delicious *enfant terrible*." It was Clifford's essay "The Ethics of Belief" which prompted William James to write his famous essay "The Will to Believe."

A

A shipowner was about to send to sea an emigrant-ship. He knew that she was old, and not over-well built at the first; that she had seen many seas and climes, and often had needed repairs. Doubts had been suggested to him that possibly she was not seaworthy.

William Kingdon Clifford, "The Ethics of Belief," *Contemporary Review*, January, 1877 (in part). Reprinted in *Lectures and Essays by the Late William Kingdon Clifford*, edited by Leslie Stephen and Frederick Pollock, London and New York, Macmillan and Company, 1879.

These doubts preyed upon his mind and made him unhappy; he thought that perhaps he ought to have her thoroughly overhauled and refitted, even though this should put him to great expense. Before the ship sailed, however, he succeeded in overcoming these melancholy reflections. He said to himself that she had gone safely through so many voyages and weathered so many storms that it was idle to suppose she would not come safely home from this trip also. He would put his trust in Providence, which could hardly fail to protect all these unhappy families that were leaving their fatherland to seek for better times elsewhere. He would dismiss from his mind all ungenerous suspicions about the honesty of builders and contractors. In such ways he acquired a sincere and comfortable conviction that his vessel was thoroughly safe and seaworthy; he watched her departure with a light heart, and benevolent wishes for the success of the exiles in their strange new home that was to be; and he got his insurance-money when she went down in mid-ocean and told no tales.

What shall we say of him? Surely this, that he was verily guilty of the death of those men. It is admitted that he did sincerely believe in the soundness of his ship; but the sincerity of his conviction can in no wise help him, because *he had no right to believe on such evidence as was before him.* He had acquired his belief not by honestly earning it in patient investigation, but by stifling his doubts. And although in the end he may have felt so sure about it that he could not think otherwise, yet inasmuch as he had knowingly and willingly worked himself into that frame of mind, he must be held responsible for it.

Let us alter the case a little, and suppose that the ship was not unsound after all; that she made her voyage safely, and many others after it. Will that diminish the guilt of her owner? Not one jot. When an action is once done, it is right or wrong for ever; no accidental failure of its good or evil fruits can possibly alter that. The man would not have been innocent, he would only have been not found out. The question of right or wrong has to do with the origin of his belief, not the matter of it; not what it was, but how he got it; not whether it turned out to be true or false, but whether he had a right to believe on such evidence as was before him.

There was once an island in which some of the inhabitants professed a religion teaching neither the doctrine of original sin nor that of eternal punishment. A suspicion got abroad that the professors of this religion had made use of unfair means to get their doctrines taught to children. They were accused of wresting the laws of their country in such a way as to remove children from the care of their natural and legal guardians; and even of stealing them away and keeping them concealed from their friends and relations. A certain number of men formed themselves into a society for the purpose of agitating the public about this matter. They published grave accusations against individual citizens of the highest position and character, and did all in their power to injure these citizens in the exercise of their professions. So great was the noise they made, that a Commission was appointed to investigate the facts; but after the Commission had carefully inquired into all the evidence that could be got, it appeared that the accused were innocent. Not only had they been accused on insufficient evidence, but the evidence of their innocence was such as the agitators might easily have obtained, if they had attempted a fair inquiry. After these disclosures the inhabitants of that country looked upon the members of the agitating society, not only as persons whose judgment was to be distrusted, but also as no longer to be counted honourable men. For although they had sincerely and conscientiously believed in the charges they had made, *yet they had no right to believe on such evidence as was before them.* Their sincere convictions, instead of being honestly earned by patient inquiring, were stolen by listening to the voice of prejudice and passion.

Let us vary this case also, and suppose, other things remaining as before, that a still more accurate investigation proved the accused to have been really guilty. Would this make any difference in the guilt of the accusers? Clearly not; the question is not whether their belief was true or false, but whether they entertained it on wrong grounds. They would no doubt say, "Now you see that we were right after all; next time perhaps you will believe us." And they might be believed, but they would not thereby become honourable men. They would not be innocent, they would only be not found out. Every one of them, if he chose to examine himself *in foro conscientiae,* would know that he had acquired and nourished a belief, when he had no right to believe on such evidence as was before him; and therein he would know that he had done a wrong thing.

It may be said, however, that in both of these supposed cases it is not the belief which is judged to be wrong, but the action following upon it. The shipowner might say, "I am perfectly certain that my ship is sound, but still I feel it my duty to have her examined, before trusting the lives of so many people to her." And it might be said to the agitator, "However convinced you were of the justice of your cause and the truth of your convictions, you ought not to have made a public attack upon any man's character until you had examined the evidence on both sides with the utmost patience and care."

In the first place, let us admit that, so far as it goes, this view of the case is right and necessary; right, because even when a man's belief is so fixed that he cannot think otherwise, he still has a choice in regard to the action suggested by it, and so cannot escape the duty of investigating on the ground of the strength of his convictions; and necessary, because those who are not yet capable of controlling their feelings and thoughts must have a plain rule dealing with overt acts.

But this being premised as necessary, it becomes clear that it is not sufficient, and that our previous judgment is required to supplement it. For it is not possible so to sever the belief from the action it suggests as to condemn the one without condemning the other. No man holding a strong belief on one side of a question, or even wishing to hold a belief on one side, can investigate it with such fairness and completeness as if he were really in doubt and unbiased; so that the existence of a belief not founded on fair inquiry unfits a man for the performance of this necessary duty.

Nor is that truly a belief at all which has not some influence upon the actions of him who holds it. He who truly believes that which prompts him to an action has looked upon the action to lust after it, he has committed it already in his heart. If a belief is not realised immediately in open deeds, it is stored up for the guidance of the future. It goes to make a part of that aggregate of beliefs which is the link between sensation and action at every moment of all our lives, and which is so organised and compacted together that no part of it can be isolated from the rest, but every new addition modifies the structure of the whole. No real belief, however trifling and fragmentary it may seem, is ever truly insignificant; it prepares us to receive more of its like, confirms those which resembled it before, and weakens others; and so gradually it lays a stealthy train in our inmost thoughts, which may some day explode into overt action, and leave its stamp upon our character forever.

And no man's belief is in any case a private matter which concerns himself alone. Our lives are guided by that general conception of the course of things which has been created by society for social purposes. Our words, our phrases, our forms and processes and modes of thought, are common property, fashioned and perfected from age to age; an heirloom which every succeeding generation inherits as a precious deposit and a sacred trust to be handed onto the next one, not unchanged but enlarged and purified, with some clear marks of its proper handiwork. Into this, for good or ill, is woven every belief of every man who has speech of his fellows. An awful privilege, and an awful responsibility, that we should help to create the world in which posterity will live.

In the two supposed cases which have been considered, it has been judged wrong to believe on insufficient evidence, or to nourish belief by suppressing doubts and avoiding investigation. The reason of this judgment is not far to seek: it is that in both these cases the belief held by one man was of great importance to other men. But forasmuch as no belief held by one man, however seemingly trivial the belief, and however obscure the believer, is ever actually insignificant or without its effect on the fate of mankind, we have no choice but to extend our judgment to all cases of belief whatever. Belief, that sacred faculty which prompts the decisions of our will, and knits into harmonious working all the compacted energies of our being, is ours not for ourselves, but for humanity. It is rightly used on truths which have been established by long experience and waiting toil, and which have stood in the fierce light of free and fearless questioning. Then it helps to bind men together, and to strengthen and direct their common action. It is desecrated when given to unproved and unquestioned statements, for the solace and private pleasure of the believer; to add a tinsel splendour to the plain straight road of our life and display a bright mirage beyond it; or even to drown the common sorrows of our kind by a self-deception which allows them not only to cast down, but also to degrade us. Whoso would deserve well of his fellows in this matter will guard the purity of his belief with a very fanaticism of jealous care, less at any time it should rest on an unworthy object, and catch a stain which can never be wiped away.

It is not only the leader of men, statesman, philosopher, or poet, that owes this bounden duty to mankind. Every rustic who delivers in the village alehouse his slow, infrequent sentences, may help to kill or keep alive the fatal superstitions which clog his race. Every hard-worked wife of an artisan may transmit to her children beliefs which shall knit society together, or rend it in pieces. No simplicity of mind, no obscurity of station, can escape the universal duty of questioning all that we believe.

It is true that this duty is a hard one, and the doubt which comes out of it is often a very bitter thing. It leaves us bare and powerless where we thought that we were safe and strong. To know all about anything is to know how to deal with it under all circumstances. We feel much happier and more secure when we think we know precisely what to do, no matter what happens, than when we have lost our way and do not know where to turn. And if we have supposed ourselves to know all about anything, and to be capable of doing what is fit in regard to it, we naturally do not like to find that we are really ignorant and powerless, that we have to begin again at the beginning, and try to learn what the thing is and how it is to be dealt with — if indeed anything can be learnt about it. It is the sense of power attached to a sense of knowledge that makes men desirous of believing, and afraid of doubting.

This sense of power is the highest and

best of pleasures when the belief on which it is founded is a true belief, and has been fairly earned by investigation. For then we may justly feel that it is common property, and holds good for others as well as for ourselves. Then we may be glad, not that *I* have learned secrets by which I am safer and stronger, but that *we men* have got mastery over more of the world; and we shall be strong, not for ourselves, but in the name of Man and in his strength. But if the belief has been accepted on insufficient evidence, the pleasure is a stolen one. Not only does it deceive ourselves by giving us a sense of power which we do not really possess, but it is sinful, because it is stolen in defiance of our duty to mankind. That duty is to guard ourselves from such beliefs as from a pestilence, which may shortly master our own body and then spread to the rest of the town. What would be thought of one who, for the sake of a sweet fruit, should deliberately run the risk of bringing a plague upon his family and his neighbours?

And, as in other such cases, it is not the risk only which has to be considered; for a bad action is always bad at the time when it is done, no matter what happens afterwards. Every time we let ourselves believe for unworthy reasons, we weaken our powers of self-control, of doubting, of judicially and fairly weighing evidence. We all suffer severely enough from the maintenance and support of false beliefs and the fatally wrong actions which they lead to, and the evil born when one such belief is entertained is great and wide. But a greater and wider evil arises when the credulous character is maintained and supported, when a habit of believing for unworthy reasons is fostered and made permanent. If I steal money from any person, there may be no harm done by the mere transfer of possession; he may not feel the loss, or it may prevent him from using the money

badly. But I cannot help doing this great wrong towards Man, that I make myself dishonest. What hurts society is not that it should lose its property, but that it should become a den of thieves; for then it must cease to be society. This is why we ought not to do evil that good may come; for at any rate this great evil has come, that we have done evil and are made wicked thereby. In like manner, if I let myself believe anything on insufficient evidence, there may be no great harm done by the mere belief; it may be true after all, or I may never have occasion to exhibit it in outward acts. But I cannot help doing this great wrong towards Man, that I make myself credulous. The danger to society is not merely that it should believe wrong things, though that is great enough; but that it should become credulous, and lose the habit of testing things and inquiring into them; for then it must sink back into savagery.

The harm which is done by credulity in a man is not confined to the fostering of a credulous character in others, and consequent support of false beliefs. Habitual want of care about what I believe leads to habitual want of care in others about the truth of what is told to me. Men speak the truth to one another when each reveres the truth in his own mind and in the other's mind; but how shall my friend revere the truth in my mind when I myself am careless about it, when I believe things because I want to believe them, and because they are comforting and pleasant? Will he not learn to cry, "Peace," to me, when there is no peace? By such a course I shall surround myself with a thick atmosphere of falsehood and fraud, and in that I must live. It may matter little to me, in my cloud-castle of sweet illusions and darling lies; but it matters much to Man that I have made my neighbours ready to deceive. The credulous man is father to the liar and the cheat; he lives in the bosom of this his family, and it is no marvel if he should become even as they are. So closely are our duties knit together, that whoso shall keep the whole law, and yet offend in one point, he is guilty of all.

To sum up: it is wrong always, everywhere, and for any one, to believe anything upon insufficient evidence.

If a man, holding a belief which he was taught in childhood or persuaded of afterwards, keeps down and pushes away any doubts which arise about it in his mind, purposely avoids the reading of books and the company of men that call in question or discuss it, and regards as impious those questions which cannot easily be asked without disturbing it — the life of that man is one long sin against mankind.

If this judgment seems harsh when applied to those simple souls who have never known better, who have been brought up from the cradle with a horror of doubt, and taught that their eternal welfare depends on *what* they believe, then it leads to the very serious, *Who hath made Israel to sin?*

It may be permitted me to fortify this judgment with the sentence of Milton —

"A man may be a heretic in the truth; and if he believes things only because his pastor says so, or the assembly so determine, without knowing other reason, though his belief be true, yet the very truth he holds becomes his heresy."

And with this famous aphorism of Coleridge —

"He who begins by loving Christianity better than Truth, will proceed by loving his own sect or Church better than Christianity, and end in loving himself better than all."

Inquiry into the evidence of a doctrine is not to be made once for all, and then taken as finally settled. It is never lawful to stifle a doubt; for either it can be honestly answered by means of the inquiry already made, or else it proves that the inquiry was not complete.

"But," says one, "I am a busy man; I have no time for the long course of study which would be necessary to make me in any degree a competent judge of certain questions, or even able to understand the nature of the arguments." Then he should have no time to believe.

B

I have long defended to my own students the lawfulness of voluntarily adopted faith; but as soon as they have got well imbued with the logical spirit, they have as a rule refused to admit my contention to be lawful philosophically, even though in point of fact they were personally all the time chock-full of some faith or other themselves. I am all the while, however, so profoundly convinced that

William James, "The Will to Believe," *New World,* June, 1896 (in part).

my own position is correct, that your invitation has seemed to me a good occasion to make my statements more clear. Perhaps your minds will be more open than those with which I have hitherto had to deal. I will be as little technical as I can, though I must begin by setting up some technical distinctions that will help us in the end.

Let us give the name of *hypothesis* to anything that may be proposed to our belief; and just as the electricians speak of live and dead wires, let us speak of any hypothesis as either *live* or *dead.* A live hypothesis is one which appeals as a real possibility to him to whom it is proposed. If I ask you to believe in the Mahdi, the notion makes no electric connection with your nature, — it refuses to scintillate with any credibility at all. As an hypothesis it is completely dead. To an Arab, however (even if he be not one of the Mahdi's followers), the hypothesis is among the mind's possibilities: it is alive. This shows that deadness and liveness in an hypothesis are not intrinsic properties, but relations to the individual thinker. They are measured by his willingness to act. The maximum of liveness in an hypothesis means willingness to act irrevocably. Practically, that means belief; but there is some believing tendency wherever there is willingness to act at all.

Next, let us call the decision between two hypotheses an *option.* Options may be of several kinds. They may be — 1, *living* or *dead;* 2, *forced* or *avoidable;* 3, *momentous* or *trivial;* and for our purposes we may call an option a *genuine* option when it is of the forced, living, and momentous kind.

1. A living option is one in which both hypotheses are live ones. If I say to you: "Be a theosophist or be a Mohammedan," it is probably a dead option, because for you neither hypothesis is likely to be alive. But if I say: "Be an agnostic or be a Christian," it is otherwise: trained as you are, each hypothesis makes some appeal, however small, to your belief.

2. Next, if I say to you, "Choose between going out with your umbrella or without it," I do not offer you a genuine option, for it is not forced. You can easily avoid it by not going out at all. Similarly, if I say, "Either love me or hate me," "Either call my theory true or call it false," your option is avoidable. You may remain indifferent to me,

neither loving nor hating, and you may decline to offer any judgment as to my theory. But if I say, "Either accept this truth or go without it," I put on you a forced option, for there is no standing place outside of the alternative. Every dilemma based on a complete logical disjunction, with no possibility of not choosing, is an option of this forced kind.

3. Finally, if I were Dr. Nansen and proposed to you to join my North Pole expedition, your option would be momentous; for this would probably be your only similar opportunity, and your choice now would either exclude you from the North Pole sort of immortality altogether or put at least the chance of it into your hands. He who refuses to embrace a unique opportunity loses the prize as surely as if he tried and failed. *Per contra,* the option is trivial when the opportunity is not unique, when the stake is insignificant, or when the decision is reversible if it later prove unwise. Such trivial options abound in the scientific life. A chemist finds an hypothesis live long enough to spend a year in its verification: he believes in it to that extent. But if his experiments prove inconclusive either way, he is quit for his loss of time, no vital harm being done.

It will facilitate our discussion if we keep all these distinctions well in mind.

The next matter to consider is the actual psychology of human opinion. When we look at certain facts, it seems as if our passional and volitional nature lay at the root of all our convictions. When we look at others, it seems as if they could do nothing when the intellect had once said its say. Let us take the latter facts up first.

Does it not seem preposterous on the very face of it to talk of our opinions being modifiable at will? Can our will either help or hinder our intellect in its perceptions of truth? Can we, by just willing it, believe that Abraham Lincoln's existence is a myth, and that the portraits of him in McClure's Magazine are all of some one else? Can we, by any effort of our will, or by any strength of wish that it were true, believe ourselves well and about when we are roaring with rheumatism in bed, or feel certain that the sum of the two one-dollar bills in our pocket must be a hundred dollars? We can *say* any of these things, but we are absolutely impotent to believe them; and of just such things is the whole fabric of the truths that we do believe in made up, — matters of fact, immediate or remote, as Hume said, and relations between ideas, which are either there or not there for us if we see them so, and which if not there cannot be put there by any action of our own.

In Pascal's Thoughts there is a celebrated passage known in literature as Pascal's wager. In it he tries to force us into Christianity by reasoning as if our concern with truth resembled our concern with the stakes in a game of chance. Translated freely his words are these: You must either believe or not believe that God is — which will you do? Your human reasons cannot say. A game is going on between you and the nature of things which at the day of judgment will bring out either heads or tails. Weigh what your gains and your losses would be if you should stake all you have on heads, or God's existence: if you win in such case, you gain eternal beatitude; if you lose, you lose nothing at all. If there were an infinity of chances, and only one for God in this wager, still you ought to stake your all on God; for though you surely risk a finite loss by this procedure, any finite loss is reasonable, even a certain one is reasonable, if there is but the possibility of infinite gain. Go, then, and take holy water, and have masses said; belief will come and stupefy your scruples, — *Cela vous fera croire et vous*

abêtira. Why should you not? At bottom, what have you to lose?

You probably feel that when religious faith expresses itself thus, in the language of the gaming-table, it is put to its last trumps. Surely Pascal's own personal belief in masses and holy water had far other springs; and this celebrated page of his is but an argument for others, a last desperate snatch at a weapon against the hardness of the unbelieving heart. We feel that a faith in masses and holy water adopted willfully after such a mechanical calculation would lack the inner soul of faith's reality; and if we were ourselves in the place of the Deity, we should probably take particular pleasure in cutting off believers of this pattern from their infinite reward. It is evident that unless there be some pre-existing tendency to believe in masses and holy water, the option offered to the will by Pascal is not a living option. Certainly no Turk ever took to masses and holy water on its account; and even to us Protestants these means of salvation seem such foregone impossibilities that Pascal's logic, invoked for them specifically, leaves us unmoved. As well might the Mahdi write to us, saying, "I am the Expected One whom God has created in his effulgence. You shall be infinitely happy if you confess me; otherwise you shall be cut off from the light of the sun. Weigh, then, your infinite gain if I am genuine against your finite sacrifice if I am not!" His logic would be that of Pascal; but he would vainly use it on us, for the hypothesis he offers us is dead. No tendency to act on it exists in us to any degree.

The talk of believing by our volition seems, then, from one point of view, simply silly. From another point of view it is worse than silly, it is vile. When one turns to the magnificent edifice of the physical sciences, and sees how it was reared; what thousands of disinterested moral lives of men lie buried in its mere foundations; what patience and post-ponement, what choking down of preference, what submission to the icy laws of outer fact are wrought into its very stones and mortar; how absolutely impersonal it stands in its vast augustness,—then how besotted and con-temptible seems every little sentimentalist who comes blowing his voluntary smoke-wreaths, and pretending to decide things from out of his private dream! Can we wonder if those bred in the rugged and manly school of science should feel like spewing such sub-jectivism out of their mouths? The whole system of loyalties which grow up in the schools of science go dead against its tolera-tion; so that it is only natural that those who have caught the scientific fever should pass over to the opposite extreme, and write some-times as if the incorruptibly truthful intellect ought positively to prefer bitterness and un-acceptableness to the heart in its cup.

It fortifies my soul to know
That, though I perish, Truth is so—

sings Clough, while Huxley exclaims: "My only consolation lies in the reflection that, however bad our posterity may become, so far as they hold by the plain rule of not pre-tending to believe what they have no reason to believe, because it may be to their advan-tage so to pretend [the word 'pretend' is surely here redundant], they will not have reached the lowest depth of immorality." And that delicious *enfant terrible* Clifford writes: "Be-lief is desecrated when given to unproved and unquestioned statements for the solace and private pleasure of the believer. . . . Whoso would deserve well of his fellows in this mat-ter will guard the purity of his belief with a very fanaticism of jealous care, lest at any time it should rest on an unworthy object, and catch a stain which can never be wiped away. . . . If [a] belief has been accepted on insufficient evidence [even though the belief be true, as Clifford on the same page explains] the pleasure is a stolen one. . . . It is sinful because it is stolen in defiance of our duty to mankind. That duty is to guard ourselves from such beliefs as from a pestilence which may shortly master our own body and then spread to the rest of the town. . . . It is wrong always, everywhere, and for every one, to be-lieve anything upon insufficient evidence." . . .

★ ★ ★

The thesis I defend is, briefly stated, this: *Our passional nature not only lawfully may, but must, decide an option between proposi-tions, whenever it is a genuine option that cannot by its nature be decided on intellectual grounds; for to say, under such circumstances, "Do not decide, but leave the question open," is itself a passional decision,—just like de-ciding yes or no,—and is attended with the same risk of losing the truth.* . . .

★ ★ ★

I fear here that some of you, my hearers, will begin to scent danger, and lend an in-hospitable ear. Two first steps of passion you have indeed had to admit as necessary,—we must think so as to avoid dupery, and we must think so as to gain truth; but the surest path to those ideal consummations, you will prob-ably consider, is from now onwards to take no further passional step.

Well, of course, I agree as far as the facts will allow. Wherever the option between losing truth and gaining it is not momentous, we can throw the chance of *gaining truth* away, and at any rate save ourselves from any chance of *believing falsehood*, by not making up our minds at all till objective evidence has come. In scientific questions, this is almost always the case; and even in human affairs in general, the need of acting is seldom so urgent that a false belief to act on is better than no belief at all. Law courts, indeed, have to decide on the best evidence attainable for the moment, because a judge's duty is to make law as well as to ascertain it, and (as a learned judge once said to me) few cases are worth spending much time over: the great thing is to have them decided on *any* acceptable principle, and got out of the way. But in our dealings with objective nature we obviously are recorders, not makers, of the truth; and decisions for the mere sake of deciding promptly and getting on to the next business would be wholly out of place. Throughout the breadth of physical nature facts are what they are quite independently of us, and seldom is there any such hurry about them that the risks of being duped by believing a premature theory need be faced. The questions here are always trivial options, the hypotheses are hardly living (at any rate not living for us spectators), the choice between believing truth or falsehood is seldom forced. The attitude of sceptical balance is therefore the absolutely wise one if we would escape mistakes. What difference, indeed, does it make to most of us whether we have or have not a theory of the Röntgen rays, whether we believe or not in mind-stuff, or have a conviction about the causality of conscious states? It makes no difference. Such options are not forced on us. On every account it is better not to make them, but still keep weighing reasons *pro et contra* with an indifferent hand.

I speak, of course, here of the purely judging mind. For purposes of discovery such indifference is to be less highly recommended, and science would be far less advanced than

she is if the passionate desires of individuals to get their own faiths confirmed had been kept out of the game. See for example the sagacity which Spencer and Weismann now display. On the other hand, if you want an absolute duffer in an investigation, you must, after all, take the man who has no interest whatever in its results: he is the warranted incapable, the positive fool. The most useful investigator, because the most sensitive observer, is always he whose eager interest in one side of the question is balanced by an equally keen nervousness lest he become deceived. Science has organized this nervousness into a regular *technique,* her so-called method of verification; and she has fallen so deeply in love with the method that one may even say she has ceased to care for truth by itself at all. It is only truth as technically verified that interests her. The truth of truths might come in merely affirmative form, and she would decline to touch it. Such truth as that, she might repeat with Clifford, would be stolen in defiance of her duty to mankind. Human passions, however, are stronger than technical rules. "Le cœur a ses raisons" as Pascal says, "que la raison ne connaît pas;" and however indifferent to all but the bare rules of the game the umpire, the abstract intellect, may be, the concrete players who furnish him the materials to judge of are usually, each one of them, in love with some pet 'live hypothesis' of his own. Let us agree, however, that wherever there is no forced option, the dispassionately judicial intellect with no pet hypothesis, saving us, as it does, from dupery at any rate, ought to be our ideal.

The question next arises: Are there not somewhere forced options in our speculative questions, and can we (as men who may be interested at least as much in positively gaining truth as in merely escaping dupery) always wait with impunity till the coercive evidence shall have arrived? It seems *a priori* improbable that the truth should be so nicely adjusted to our needs and powers as that. In the great boarding-house of nature, the cakes and the butter and the syrup seldom come out so even and leave the plates so clean. Indeed, we should view them with scientific suspicion if they did.

Moral questions immediately present themselves as questions whose solution cannot wait for sensible proof. A moral question is a question not of what sensibly exists, but of what is good, or would be good if it did exist. Science can tell us what exists; but to compare the *worths,* both of what exists and of what does not exist, we must consult not science, but what Pascal calls our heart. Science herself consults her heart when she lays it down that the infinite ascertainment of fact and correction of false belief are the supreme goods for man. Challenge the statement, and science can only repeat it oracularly, or else prove it by showing that such ascertainment and correction bring man all sorts of other goods which man's heart in turn declares. The question of having moral beliefs at all or not having them is decided by our will. Are our moral preferences true or false, or are they only odd biological phenomena, making things good or bad for *us,* but in themselves indifferent? How can your pure intellect decide? If your heart does not *want* a world of moral reality, your head will assuredly never make you believe in one. Mephistophelian scepticism, indeed, will satisfy the head's play-instincts much better than any rigorous idealism can. Some men (even at the student age) are so naturally cool-hearted that the moralistic hypothesis never has for them any pungent life, and in their supercilious presence the hot young moralist always feels strangely ill at ease. The appearance of knowingness is on their side, of *naïveté* and

gullibility on his. Yet, in the inarticulate heart of him, he clings to it that he is not a dupe, and that there is a realm in which (as Emerson says) all their wit and intellectual superiority is no better than the cunning of a fox. Moral scepticism can no more be refuted or proved by logic than intellectual scepticism can. When we stick to it that there *is* truth (be it of either kind), we do so with our whole nature, and resolve to stand or fall by the results. The sceptic with his whole nature adopts the doubting attitude, but which of us is the wiser, Omniscience only knows.

Turn now from these wide questions of good to a certain class of questions of fact, questions concerning personal relations, states of mind between one man and another. *Do you like me or not?* — for example. Whether you do or not depends, in countless instances, on whether I meet you half-way, am willing to assume that you must like me, and show you trust and expectation. The previous faith on my part in your liking's existence is in such cases what makes your liking come. But if I stand aloof, and refuse to budge an inch until I have objective evidence, until you shall have done something apt, as the absolutists say, *ad extorquendum assensum meum,* ten to one your liking never comes. How many women's hearts are vanquished by the mere sanguine insistence of some man that they must love him! he will not consent to the hypothesis that they cannot. The desire for a certain kind of truth here brings about that special truth's existence; and so it is in innumerable cases of other sorts. Who gains promotions, boons, appointments, but the man in whose life they are seen to play the part of live hypotheses, who discounts them, sacrifices other things for their sake before they have come, and takes risks for them in advance? His faith acts on the powers above him as a claim, and creates its own verification.

A social organism of any sort whatever, large or small, is what it is because each member proceeds to his own duty with a trust that the other members will simultaneously do theirs. Wherever a desired result is achieved by the co-operation of many independent persons, its existence as a fact is a pure consequence of the precursive faith in one another of those immediately concerned. A government, an army, a commercial system, a ship, a college, an athletic team, all exist on this condition, without which not only is nothing achieved, but nothing is even attempted. A whole train of passengers (individually brave enough) will be looted by a few highwaymen, simply because the latter can count on one another, while each passenger fears that if he makes a movement of resistance, he will be shot before any one else backs him up. If we believed that the whole car-full would rise at once with us, we should each severally rise, and train-robbing would never even be attempted. There are, then, cases where a fact cannot come at all unless a preliminary faith exists in its coming. *And where faith in a fact can help create the fact,* that would be an insane logic which should say that faith running ahead of scientific evidence is the 'lowest kind of immorality' into which a thinking being can fall. Yet such is the logic by which our scientific absolutists pretend to regulate our lives!

In truths dependent on our personal action, then, faith based on desire is certainly a lawful and possibly an indispensable thing.

But now, it will be said, these are all childish human cases, and have nothing to do with great cosmical matters, like the question of religious faith. Let us then pass on to that. Religions differ so much in their accidents that in discussing the religious question we must make it very generic and broad. What then do we now mean by the religious hypothesis? Science says things are; morality says some things are better than other things; and religion says essentially two things.

First, she says that the best things are the more eternal things, the overlapping things, the things in the universe that throw the last stone, so to speak, and say the final word. "Perfection is eternal," — this phrase of Charles Secrétan seems a good way of putting this first affirmation of religion, an affirmation which obviously cannot yet be verified scientifically at all.

The second affirmation of religion is that we are better off even now if we believe her first affirmation to be true.

Now, let us consider what the logical elements of this situation are *in case the religious hypothesis in both its branches be really true.* (Of course, we must admit that possibility at the outset. If we are to discuss the question at all, it must involve a living option. If for any of you religion be a hypothesis that cannot, by any living possibility, be true, then you need go no farther. I speak to the 'saving remnant' alone.) So proceeding, we see, first, that religion offers itself as a *momentous* option. We are supposed to gain, even now, by our belief, and to lose by our non-belief, a certain vital good. Secondly, religion is a *forced* option, so far as that good goes. We cannot escape the issue by remaining sceptical and waiting for more light, because, although we do avoid error in that way *if religion be untrue,* we lose the good, *if it be true,* just as certainly as if we positively chose to disbelieve. It is as if a man should hesitate indefinitely to ask a certain woman to marry him because he was not perfectly sure that she would prove an angel after he brought her home. Would he not cut himself off from that particular angel-possibility as decisively as if he went and married some one else? Scepticism, then, is not avoidance of option; it is option of a certain particular kind of risk. *Better risk loss of truth than chance of error,* — that is your faith-vetoer's exact position. He is actively playing his stake as much as the believer is; he is backing the field against the religious hypothesis, just as the believer is backing the religious hypothesis against the field. To preach scepticism to us as a duty until 'sufficient evidence' for religion be found, is tantamount therefore to telling us, when in presence of the religious hypothesis, that to yield to our fear of its being error is wiser and better than to yield to our hope that it may be true. It is not intellect against all passions, then; it is only intellect with one passion laying down its law. And by what, forsooth, is the supreme wisdom of this passion warranted? Dupery for dupery, what proof is there that dupery through hope is so much worse than dupery through fear? I, for one, can see no proof; and I simply refuse obedience to the scientist's command to imitate his kind of option, in a case where my own stake is important enough to give me the right to choose my own form of risk. If religion be true and the evidence for it be still insufficient, I do not wish, by putting your extinguisher upon my nature (which feels to me as if it had after all some business in this matter), to forfeit my sole chance in life of getting upon the winning side, — that chance depending, of course, on my willingness to run the risk of acting as if my passional need of taking the world religiously might be prophetic and right.

All this is on the supposition that it really may be prophetic and right, and that, even to us who are discussing the matter, religion is a live hypothesis which may be true. Now, to most of us religion comes in a still further way that makes a veto on our active faith even more illogical. The more perfect and more eternal aspect of the universe is represented in our religions as having personal form. The universe is no longer a mere *It* to us, but a *Thou,* if we are religious; and any relation that may be possible from person to person might be possible *here.* For instance, although in one sense we are passive portions of the universe, in another we show a curious autonomy, as if we were small active centres on our own account. We feel, too, as if the appeal of religion to us were made to our own active good-will, as if evidence might be forever withheld from us unless we met the hypothesis half-way. To take a trivial illustration: just as a man who in a company of gentlemen made no advances, asked a warrant for every concession, and believed no one's word without proof, would cut himself off by such churlishness from all the social rewards that a more trusting spirit would earn, — so here, one who should shut himself up in snarling logicality and try to make the gods extort his recognition willy-nilly, or not get it at all, might cut himself off forever from his only opportunity of making the gods' acquaintance. This feeling, forced on us we know not whence, that by obstinately believing that there are gods (although not to do so would be so easy both for our logic and our life) we are doing the universe the deepest service we can, seems part of the living essence of the religious hypothesis. If the hypothesis *were* true in all its parts, including this one, then pure intellectualism, with its veto on our making willing advances, would be an absurdity; and some participation of our sympathetic nature would be logically required. I, therefore, for one, cannot see my way to accepting the agnostic rules for truth-seeking, or wilfully agree to keep my willing nature out of the game. I cannot do so for this plain reason, that *a rule of thinking which would absolutely prevent me from acknowledging certain kinds of truth if those kinds of truth were really there, would be an irrational rule.* That for me is the long and short of the formal logic of the situation, no matter what the kinds of truth might materially be.

I confess I do not see how this logic can be escaped. But sad experience makes me fear that some of you may still shrink from radically saying with me, *in abstracto,* that we have the right to believe at our own risk any hypothesis that is live enough to tempt our will. I suspect, however, that if this is so, it is because you have got away from the abstract logical point of view altogether, and are thinking (perhaps without realizing it) of some particular religious hypothesis which for you is dead. The freedom to 'believe what we will' you apply to the case of some patent superstition; and the faith you think of is the faith defined by the schoolboy when he said, "Faith is when you believe something that you know ain't true." I can only repeat that this is misapprehension. *In concreto,* the freedom to believe can only cover living options which the intellect of the individual cannot by itself resolve; and living options never seem absurdities to him who has them to consider. When I look at the religious question as it really puts itself to concrete men, and when I think of all the possibilities which both practically and theoretically it involves, then this command that we shall put a stopper on our heart, instincts, and courage, and *wait* — acting of course meanwhile more or less as if religion were *not* true — till doomsday, or till such time as our intellect and senses working together may have raked in evidence enough, — this command, I say, seems to me the queerest idol ever manufactured in the philosophic cave. Were we scholastic absolutists, there might be more excuse. If we had an infallible intellect with its objective certitudes, we might feel ourselves disloyal to such a perfect organ of

knowledge in not trusting to it exclusively, in not waiting for its releasing word. But if we are empiricists, if we believe that no bell in us tolls to let us know for certain when truth is in our grasp, then it seems a piece of idle fantasticality to preach so solemnly our duty of waiting for the bell. Indeed we *may* wait if we will, — I hope you do not think that I am denying that, — but if we do so, we do so at our peril as much as if we believed. In either case we *act,* taking our life in our hands. No one of us ought to issue vetoes to the other, nor should we bandy words of abuse. We ought, on the contrary, delicately and profoundly to respect one another's mental freedom: then only shall we bring about the intellectual republic; then only shall we have that spirit of inner tolerance without which all our outer tolerance is soulless, and which is empiricism's glory; then only shall we live and let live, in speculative as well as in practical things.

I began by a reference to Fitz James Stephen; let me end by a quotation from him. "What do you think of yourself? What do you think of the world? . . . These are questions with which all must deal as it seems good to them. They are riddles of the Sphinx, and in some way or other we must deal with them. . . . In all important transactions of life we have to take a leap in the dark. . . . If we decide to leave the riddles unanswered, that is a choice; if we waver in our answer, that, too, is a choice: but whatever choice we make, we make it at our peril. If a man chooses to turn his back altogether on God and the future, no one can prevent him; no one can show beyond reasonable doubt that he is mistaken. If a man thinks otherwise and acts as he thinks, I do not see that any one can prove that *he* is mistaken. Each must act as he thinks best; and if he is wrong, so much the worse for him. We stand on a mountain pass in the midst of whirling snow and blinding mist, through which we get glimpses now and then of paths which may be deceptive. If we stand still we shall be frozen to death. If we take the wrong road we shall be dashed to pieces. We do not certainly know whether there is any right one. What must we do? 'Be strong and of a good courage.' Act for the best, hope for the best, and take what comes. . . . If death ends all, we cannot meet death better."

SUGGESTIONS FOR THOUGHT

1. What reasons has one for believing in the existence of his appendix? Of Santa Claus? Of God?

2. Tertullian said of the Incarnation, "It is believable, because it is absurd; it is certain because it is impossible." Gregory wrote: "Faith that is supported by human reason has no merit." And Bacon admonished that we must "believe in the Word of God though our reason is shocked at it." What is the relation between faith and reason?

3. Is a man ever justified in *believing* something when he might be able to establish its reality or its irreality by observation? E.g., what would you think of a man who treasures a box *believing* that it contains a priceless jewel but refuses to open the box lest he lose a pleasant belief? What would be your reply to a person who says: "I believe in the existence and the goodness of God; I do not wish to seek philosophical proof nor scientific evidence for God lest I weaken my belief"?

4. The human mind, says E. S. Ames, is "unable to satisfy itself that an irrational religion can answer its needs but also doubtful whether a rational religion is possible." What religious beliefs are commonly held, not because they are reasonable, but because they are effective or desirable, or simply because men have never dared consider them intelligently?

5. Rashdall tells of a Roman Catholic priest who said to an Anglo-Catholic clergyman: "You seem to hold much the same doctrines that I do; but you hold them on the totally irrelevant ground that you believe them to be true." Is the truth or falsity of a belief irrelevant? If a proposition is true, do we "believe" it or do we just "accept it as true"?

6. Would it be an adequate evaluation of science and religion to say that science gives us things to live on, religion things to live for?

7. Does science deal only with facts, and religion only with values? Can a religious doctrine that is not in harmony with scientific facts be satisfactory? Must religious beliefs be subjected to scientific testing? Defend your answers.

8. Why has religion been critical of modern science? E.g., heliocentric view of the solar system, geology, evolution. Will science in time make the religious approach to the natural world impossible for educated people?

9. Can science itself become a religion? Pavlov said that science demands an undivided allegiance filled with passion; Kagawa has spoken of science as a "splendid religion."

10. Examine carefully the statement that science describes while religion interprets.

11. David Hume wrote, " . . . the errors in religion are dangerous; those in philosophy only ridiculous." Why the difference?

12. "The religious consciousness seeks being; the philosophical consciousness seeks knowledge . . . The religious consciousness refuses to deal with intellectual problems. It will not make life wait upon logical solutions; instead, it adopts working hypotheses." (J. H. Leuba) But why have religious leaders insisted that religious ideas are true as well as effective? Does philosophy suffer by trying to be practical? What are the basic differences between philosophy and religion? Can one through philosophical interests realize the essential religious values?

13. "Christians and Jews simply use the Bible to aid in rationalizing any practice or idea which they were carrying out and believed to be justified." (Ray H. Abrams) What is the proper use of the Bible?

14. What effect have the critical and literary approaches to the Bible had upon your evaluation of the Bible? Are sacred books revered more when understood less?

15. In what sense can the Bible be called an inspired book? What historical process is necessary to make a book a sacred book? Do we have any secular literature today that might under the proper circumstances become sacred literature? What are the advantages and disadvantages of having a work declared sacred? Did St. Paul know he was writing a book of the Bible when he wrote his letters? (See I Corinthians 1:25.)

SUGGESTIONS FOR FURTHER READING

BIXLER, JULIUS SEELYE, "The Problem of Religious Knowledge," *The Philosophical Review,* Vol. 51, 1942, pp. 574–586.

BOSLEY, HAROLD A., *The Quest for Religious Certainty,* Chicago, Willett, Clark and Company, 1939.

BURNS, C. DELISLE, "What is Religious Knowledge?" *International Journal of Ethics,* Vol. 24, 1914, pp. 253–265.

BURTT, EDWIN A., *Types of Religious Philosophy,* New York, Harper and Brothers, 1939, pp. 449–472.

KALLEN, HORACE M., "Is Belief Essential in Religion?" *International Journal of Ethics,* Vol. 21, 1910, pp. 51–67.

LYMAN, EUGENE WILLIAM, *The Meaning and Truth of Religion,* New York, Charles Scribner's Sons, 1938, Part II.

MORE, PAUL ELMER, *The Skeptical Approach to Religion,* Princeton, Princeton University Press, 1934, ch. 1.

NEWMAN, JOHN HENRY, *Fifteen Sermons Preached Before the University of Oxford,* London, Rivingtons, 1890, Sermons X, XI.

RAMSDELL, EDWARD THOMAS, "Concerning the Nature of Religious Faith," *The Journal of Religion,* Vol. 23, 1943, pp. 186–193.

SCHILLER, F. C. S., "Faith, Reason, and Religion," *The Hibbert Journal,* Vol. 4, 1905–6, pp. 329–345.

SCHNEIDER, HERBERT W., "Faith," *The Journal of Philosophy,* Vol. 21, 1924, pp. 36–40.

SCHURMAN, J. G., "Agnosticism," *The Philosophical Review,* Vol. 4, 1895, pp. 241–263.

SMITH, H. BOMPAS, "What is Religious Knowledge?" *The Hibbert Journal,* Vol. 44, 1945, pp. 54–58.

STOCKS, J. L., *Reason and Intuition,* London, Oxford University Press, 1939.

URBAN, WILBUR M., "The Will to Make-Believe," *International Journal of Ethics,* Vol. 19, 1909, pp. 212–233.

17

RELIGION AND VALUES

John Stuart Mill (1806–1873), English philosopher and economist, had the fortune (or misfortune) to be the son of a philosopher. James Mill, intending to make a philosopher out of his son, supervised the boy's education. John Stuart describes this amazing education in his *Autobiography*. Although Mill later reacted against the strict discipline of his father, he accepted most of the basic philosophical ideas of his father, e.g., empiricism, utilitarianism, and antipathy to metaphysics and religion. The following selection from his essay on "The Utility of Religion" illustrates his attitude toward religion. James Bissett Pratt (1875–1944) spent his entire professional career at Williams College. He was a leader in the American philosophy called Critical Realism. He was also a student of oriental religions, especially Buddhism. Pratt, unlike Mill, was sympathetic to religion.

A

It has sometimes been remarked how much has been written, both by friends and enemies, concerning the truth of religion, and how little, at least in the way of discussion or controversy, concerning its usefulness. This, however, might have been expected; for the truth, in matters which so deeply affect us, is our first concernment. If religion, or any partic-

John Stuart Mill, "The Utility of Religion," in *Three Essays on Religion,* New York, Longmans, Green, Reader, and Dyer, 1874 (in part).

ular form of it, is true, its usefulness follows without other proof. If to know authentically in what order of things, under what government of the universe it is our destiny to live, were not useful, it is difficult to imagine what could be considered so. Whether a person is in a pleasant or in an unpleasant place, a palace or a prison, it cannot be otherwise than useful to him to know where he is. So long, therefore, as men accepted the teachings of their religion as positive facts, no more a matter of doubt than their own existence or the existence of the objects around them, to ask the use of believing it could not possibly occur to them. The utility of religion did not need to be asserted until the arguments for its truth had in a great measure ceased to convince. People must either have ceased to believe, or have ceased to rely on the belief of others, before they could take that inferior ground of defence without a consciousness of lowering what they were endeavouring to raise. An argument for the utility of religion is an appeal to unbelievers, to induce them to practise a well meant hypocrisy, or to semi-believers to make them avert their eyes from what might possibly shake their unstable belief, or finally to persons in general to abstain from expressing any doubts they may feel, since a fabric of immense importance to mankind is so insecure at its foundations, that men must hold their breath in its neighbourhood for fear of blowing it down.

In the present period of history, however, we seem to have arrived at a time when, among the arguments for and against religion, those which relate to its usefulness assume an important place. We are in an age of weak beliefs, and in which such belief as men have is much more determined by their wish to believe than by any mental appreciation of evidence. The wish to believe does not arise only from selfish but often from the most disinterested feelings; and though it cannot produce the unwavering and perfect reliance which once existed, it fences round all that remains of the impressions of early education; it often causes direct misgivings to fade away by disuse; and above all, it induces people to continue laying out their lives according to doctrines which have lost part of their hold on the mind, and to maintain towards the world the same, or a rather more demonstrative attitude of belief, than they thought it

necessary to exhibit when their personal conviction was more complete.

If religious belief be indeed so necessary to mankind, as we are continually assured that it is, there is great reason to lament, that the intellectual grounds of it should require to be backed by moral bribery or subornation of the understanding. Such a state of things is most uncomfortable even for those who may, without actual insincerity, describe themselves as believers; and still worse as regards those who, having consciously ceased to find the evidences of religion convincing, are withheld from saying so lest they should aid in doing an irreparable injury to mankind. It is a most painful position to a conscientious and cultivated mind, to be drawn in contrary directions by the two noblest of all objects of pursuit, truth, and the general good. Such a conflict must inevitably produce a growing indifference to one or other of these objects, most probably to both. Many who could render giant's service both to truth and to mankind if they believed that they could serve the one without loss to the other, are either totally paralysed, or led to confine their exertions to matters of minor detail, by the apprehension that any real freedom of speculation, or any considerable strengthening or enlargement of the thinking faculties of mankind at large, might, by making them unbelievers, be the surest way to render them vicious and miserable. Many, again, having observed in others or experienced in themselves elevated feelings which they imagine incapable of emanating from any other source than religion, have an honest eversion to anything tending, as they think, to dry up the fountain of such feelings. They, therefore, either dislike and disparage all philosophy, or addict themselves with intolerant zeal to those forms of it in which intuition usurps the place of evidence, and internal feeling is made the test of objective truth. The whole of the prevalent metaphysics of the present century is one tissue of suborned evidence in favour of religion; often of Deism only, but in any case involving a misapplication of noble impulses and speculative capacities, among the most deplorable of those wretched wastes of human faculties which makes us wonder that enough is left to keep mankind progressive, at however slow a pace. It is time to consider, more impartially and therefore more deliberately than is usually done, whether all this straining to prop up beliefs which require so great an expense of intellectual toil and ingenuity to keep them standing, yields any sufficient return in human well being; and whether that end would not be better served by a frank recognition that certain subjects are inaccessible to our faculties, and by the application of the same mental powers to the strengthening and enlargement of those other sources of virtue and happiness which stand in no need of the support or sanction of supernatural beliefs and inducements.

Neither, on the other hand, can the difficulties of the question be so promptly disposed of, as sceptical philosophers are sometimes inclined to believe. It is not enough to aver, in general terms, that there never can be any conflict between truth and utility; that if religion be false, nothing but good can be the consequence of rejecting it. For, though the knowledge of every positive truth is an useful acquisition, this doctrine cannot without reservation be applied to negative truth. When the only truth ascertainable is that nothing can be known, we do not, by this knowledge, gain any new fact by which to guide ourselves; we are, at best, only disabused of our trust in some former guide-mark, which, though itself fallacious, may have pointed in the same direction with the best indications we have, and if it happens to be more con-spicuous and legible, may have kept us right when they might have been overlooked. It is, in short, perfectly conceivable that religion may be morally useful without being intellectually sustainable: and it would be a proof of great prejudice in any unbeliever to deny, that there have been ages, and that there are still both nations and individuals, with regard to whom this is actually the case. Whether it is the case generally, and with reference to the future, it is the object of this paper to examine. We propose to inquire whether the belief in religion, considered as a mere persuasion, apart from the question of its truth, is really indispensable to the temporal welfare of mankind; whether the usefulness of the belief is intrinsic and universal, or local, temporary, and, in some sense, accidental; and whether the benefits which it yields might not be obtained otherwise, without the very large alloy of evil, by which, even in the best form of the belief, those benefits are qualified.

With the arguments on one side of the question we all are familiar: religious writers have not neglected to celebrate to the utmost the advantages both of religion in general and of their own religious faith in particular. But those who have held the contrary opinion have generally contented themselves with insisting on the more obvious and flagrant of the positive evils which have been engendered by past and present forms of religious belief. And, in truth, mankind have been so unremittingly occupied in doing evil to one another in the name of religion, from the sacrifice of Iphigenia to the Dragonnades of Louis XIV. (not to descend lower), that for any immediate purpose there was little need to seek arguments further off. These odious consequences, however, do not belong to religion in itself, but to particular forms of it, and afford no argument against the usefulness of any religions except those by which such enormities are encouraged. Moreover, the worst of these evils are already in a great measure extirpated from the more improved forms of religion; and as mankind advance in ideas and in feelings, this process of extirpation continually goes on: the immoral, or otherwise mischievous consequences which have been drawn from religion, are, one by one, abandoned, and, after having been long fought for as of its very essence, are discovered to be easily separable from it. These mischiefs, indeed, after they are past, though no longer arguments against religion, remain valid as large abatements from its beneficial influence, by showing that some of the greatest improvements ever made in the moral sentiments of mankind have taken place without it and in spite of it, and that what we are taught to regard as the chief of all improving influences, has in practice fallen so far short of such a character, that one of the hardest burdens laid upon the other good influences of human nature has been that of improving religion itself. The improvement, however, has taken place; it is still proceeding, and for the sake of fairness it should be assumed to be complete. We ought to suppose religion to have accepted the best human morality which reason and goodness can work out, from philosophical, christian, or any other elements. When it has thus freed itself from the pernicious consequences which result from its identification with any bad moral doctrine, the ground is clear for considering whether its useful properties are exclusively inherent in it, or their benefits can be obtained without it. . . .

★   ★   ★

The inquiry divides itself into two parts, corresponding to the double aspect of the subject; its social, and its individual aspect. What does religion do for society, and what for the individual? What amount of benefit to social interests, in the ordinary sense of the phrase, arises from religious belief? And what influence has it in improving and ennobling individual human nature?

The first question is interesting to everybody; the latter only to the best; but to them it is, if there be any difference, the more important of the two. We shall begin with the former, as being that which best admits of being easily brought to a precise issue.

To speak first, then, of religious belief as an instrument of social good. We must commence by drawing a distinction most commonly overlooked. It is usual to credit religion *as such* with the whole of the power inherent in any system of moral duties inculcated by education and enforced by opinion. Undoubtedly mankind would be in a deplorable state if no principles or precepts of justice, veracity, beneficence, were taught publicly or privately, and if these virtues were not encouraged, and the opposite vices repressed, by the praise and blame, the favourable and unfavourable sentiments, of mankind. And since nearly everything of this sort which does take place, takes place in the name of religion; since almost all who are taught any morality whatever, have it taught to them *as* religion, and inculcated on them through life principally in that character; the effect which the teaching produces as teaching, it is supposed to produce as religious teaching, and religion receives the credit of all the influence in human affairs which belongs to any generally accepted system of rules for the guidance and government of human life.

Few persons have sufficiently considered how great an influence this is; what vast efficacy belongs naturally to any doctrine received with tolerable unanimity as true, and impressed on the mind from the earliest childhood as duty. A little reflection will, I think, lead us to the conclusion that it is this which is the great moral power in human affairs, and that religion only seems so powerful because this mighty power has been under its command.

Consider first, the enormous influence of authority on the human mind. I am now speaking of involuntary influence; effect on men's conviction, on their persuasion, or their involuntary sentiments. Authority is the evidence on which the mass of mankind believe everything which they are said to know, except facts of which their own senses have taken cognizance. It is the evidence on which even the wisest receive all those truths of science, or facts in history or in life, of which they have not personally examined the proofs. Over the immense majority of human beings, the general concurrence of mankind, in any matter of opinion, is all powerful. Whatever is thus certified to them, they believe with a fulness of assurance which they do not accord even to the evidence of their senses when the general opinion of mankind stands in opposition to it. When, therefore, any rule of life and duty, whether grounded or not on religion, has conspicuously received the general assent, it obtains a hold on the belief of every individual, stronger than it would have even if he had arrived at it by the inherent force of his own understanding. If Novalis could say, not without a real meaning, "My belief has gained infinitely to me from the moment when one other human being has begun to believe the same," how much more when it is not one other person, but all the human beings whom one knows of. Some may urge it as an objection, that no scheme of morality has this universal assent, and that none, therefore, can be indebted to this source for whatever power it possesses over the mind. So

far as relates to the present age, the assertion is true, and strengthens the argument which it might at first seem to controvert; for exactly in proportion as the received systems of belief have been contested, and it has become known that they have many dissentients, their hold on the general belief has been loosened, and their practical influence on conduct has declined: and since this has happened to them notwithstanding the religious sanction which attached to them, there can be no stronger evidence that they were powerful not as religion, but as beliefs generally accepted by mankind. To find people who believe their religion as a person believes that fire will burn his hand when thrust into it, we must seek them in those Oriental countries where Europeans do not yet predominate, or in the European world when it was still universally Catholic. Men often disobeyed their religion in those times, because their human passions and appetites were too strong for it, or because the religion itself afforded means of indulgence to breaches of its obligations; but though they disobeyed, they, for the most part, did not doubt. There was in those days an absolute and unquestioning completeness of belief, never since general in Europe.

Such being the empire exercised over mankind by simple authority, the mere belief and testimony of their fellow creatures; consider next how tremendous is the power of education; how unspeakable is the effect of bringing people up from infancy in a belief, and in habits founded on it. Consider also that in all countries, and from the earliest ages down to the present, not merely those who are called, in a restricted sense of the term, the educated, but all or nearly all who have been brought up by parents, or by any one interested in them, have been taught from their earliest years some kind of religious belief, and some precepts as the commands of the heavenly powers to them and to mankind. And as it cannot be imagined that the commands of God are to young children anything more than the commands of their parents, it is reasonable to think that any system of social duty which mankind might adopt, even though divorced from religion, would have the same advantage of being inculcated from childhood, and would have it hereafter much more perfectly than any doctrine has it at present, society being far more disposed than formerely to take pains for the moral tuition of those numerous classes whose education it has hitherto left very much to chance. Now it is especially characteristic of the impressions of early education, that they possess what it is so much more difficult for later convictions to obtain — command over the feelings. We see daily how powerful a hold these first impressions retain over the feelings even of those, who have given up the opinions which they were early taught. While on the other hand, it is only persons of a much higher degree of natural sensibility and intellect combined than it is at all common to meet with, whose feelings entwine themselves with anything like the same force round opinions which they have adopted from their own investigations later in life; and even when they do, we may say with truth that it is because the strong sense of moral duty, the sincerity, courage and self-devotion which enabled them to do so, were themselves the fruits of early impressions.

The power of education is almost boundless: there is not one natural inclination which it is not strong enough to coerce, and, if needful, to destroy by disuse. In the greatest recorded victory which education has ever achieved over a whole host of natural inclinations in an entire people — the maintenance through centuries of the institutions of Lycurgus, — it was very little, if even at all, indebted to religion: for the Gods of the Spartans were the same as those of other Greek states; and though, no doubt, every state of Greece believed that its particular polity had at its first establishment, some sort of divine sanction (mostly that of the Delphian oracle), there was seldom any difficulty in obtaining the same or an equally powerful sanction for a change. It was not religion which formed the strength of the Spartan institutions: the root of the system was devotion to Sparta, to the ideal of the country or State: which transformed into ideal devotion to a greater country, the world, would be equal to that and far nobler achievements. Among the Greeks generally, social morality was extremely independent of religion. The inverse relation was rather that which existed between them; the worship of the Gods was inculcated chiefly as a social duty, inasmuch as if they were neglected or insulted, it was believed that their displeasure would fall not more upon the offending individual than upon the state or community which bred and tolerated him. Such moral teaching as existed in Greece had very little to do with religion. The Gods were not supposed to concern themselves much with men's conduct to one another, except when men had contrived to make the Gods themselves an interested party, by placing an assertion or an engagement under the sanction of a solemn appeal to them, by oath or vow. I grant that the sophists and philosophers, and even popular orators, did their best to press religion into the service of their special objects, and to make it be thought that the sentiments of whatever kind, which they were engaged in inculcating, were particularly acceptable to the Gods, but this never seems the primary consideration in any case save those of direct offence to the dignity of the Gods themselves. For the enforcement of human moralities secular inducements were almost exclusively relied on. The case of

Greece is, I believe, the only one in which any teaching, other than religious, has had the unspeakable advantage of forming the basis of education: and though much may be said against the quality of some part of the teaching, very little can be said against its effectiveness. The most memorable example of the power of education over conduct, is afforded (as I have just remarked) by this exceptional case; constituting a strong presumption that in other cases, early religious teaching has owed its power over mankind rather to its being early than to its being religious.

We have now considered two powers, that of authority, and that of early education, which operate through men's involuntary beliefs, feelings and desires, and which religion has hitherto held as its almost exclusive appanage. Let us now consider a third power which operates directly on their actions, whether their involuntary sentiments are carried with it or not. This is the power of public opinion; of the praise and blame, the favour and disfavour, of their fellow creatures; and is a source of strength inherent in any system of moral belief which is generally adopted, whether connected with religion or not.

Men are so much accustomed to give to the motives that decide their actions, more flattering names than justly belong to them, that they are generally quite unconscious how much those parts of their conduct which they most pride themselves on (as well as some which they are ashamed of), are determined by the motive of public opinion. Of course public opinion for the most part enjoins the same things which are enjoined by the received social morality; that morality being, in truth, the summary of the conduct which each one of the multitude, whether he himself observes it with any strictness or not, desires that others should observe towards him. People are therefore easily able to flatter themselves that they are acting from the motive of conscience when they are doing in obedience to the inferior motive, things which their conscience approves. We continually see how great is the power of opinion in opposition to conscience; how men "follow a multitude to do evil;" how often opinion induces them to do what their conscience disapproves, and still oftener prevents them from doing what it commands. But when the motive of public opinion acts in the same direction with conscience, which, since it has usually itself made the conscience in the first instance, it for the most part naturally does; it is then, of all motives which operate on the bulk of mankind, the most overpowering.

The names of all the strongest passions (except the merely animal ones) manifested by human nature, are each of them a name for some one part only of the motive derived from what I here call public opinion. The love of glory; the love of praise; the love of admiration; the love of respect and deference; even the love of sympathy, are portions of its attractive power. Vanity is a vituperative name for its attractive influence generally, when considered excessive in degree. The fear of shame, the dread of ill repute or of being disliked or hated, are the direct and simple forms of its deterring power. But the deterring force of the unfavourable sentiments of mankind does not consist solely in the painfulness of knowing oneself to be the object of those sentiments; it includes all the penalties which they can inflict: exclusion from social intercourse and from the innumerable good offices which human beings require from one another; the forfeiture of all that is called success in life; often the great diminution or total loss of means of subsistence; positive ill offices of various kinds, sufficient to render life miserable, and reaching in some states of society as far as actual persecution to death.

And again the attractive, or impelling influence of public opinion, includes the whole range of what is commonly meant by ambition: for, except in times of lawless military violence, the objects of social ambition can only be attained by means of the good opinion and favourable disposition of our fellow-creatures; nor, in nine cases out of ten, would those objects be even desired, were it not for the power they confer over the sentiments of mankind. Even the pleasure of self-approbation, in the great majority, is mainly dependent on the opinion of others. Such is the involuntary influence of authority on ordinary minds, that persons must be of a better than ordinary mould to be capable of a full assurance that they are in the right, when the world, that is, when *their* world, thinks them wrong: nor is there, to most men, any proof so demonstrative of their own virtue or talent as that people in general seem to believe in it. Through all departments of human affairs, regard for the sentiments of our fellow-creatures is in one shape or other, in nearly all characters, the pervading motive. And we ought to note that this motive is naturally strongest in the most sensitive natures, which are the most promising material for the formation of great virtues. How far its power reaches is known by too familiar experience to require either proof or illustration here. When once the means of living have been obtained, the far greater part of the remaining labour and effort which takes place on the earth, has for its object to acquire the respect or the favourable regard of mankind; to be looked up to, or at all events, not to be looked down upon by them. The industrial and commercial activity which advance civilization, the frivolity, prodigality, and selfish thirst of aggrandizement which retard it, flow equally from that source. While as an instance of the power exercised by the terrors derived from public opinion, we know how many murders have been committed merely to remove a witness who knew and was likely to disclose some secret that would bring disgrace upon his murderer.

Any one who fairly and impartially considers the subject will see reason to believe that those great effects on human conduct, which are commonly ascribed to motives derived directly from religion, have mostly for their proximate cause the influence of human opinion. Religion has been powerful not by its intrinsic force, but because it has wielded that additional and more mighty power. The effect of religion has been immense in giving a direction to public opinion: which has, in many most important respects, been wholly determined by it. But without the sanctions superadded by public opinion, its own proper sanctions have never, save in exceptional characters, or in peculiar moods of mind, exercised a very potent influence, after the times had gone by, in which divine agency was supposed habitually to employ temporal rewards and punishments. When a man firmly believed that if he violated the sacredness of a particular sanctuary he would be struck dead on the spot, or smitten suddenly with a mortal disease, he doubtless took care not to incur the penalty: but when any one had had the courage to defy the danger, and escaped with impunity, the spell was broken. If ever any people were taught that they were under a divine government, and that unfaithfulenss to their religion and law would be visited from above with temporal chastisements, the Jews were so. Yet their history was a mere succession of lapses into Paganism. Their prophets and historians, who held fast to the ancient beliefs (though they gave them so liberal an interpretation as to think it a sufficient manifestation of God's displeasure towards a king if any evil happened to his great grandson), never ceased to complain that their countrymen turned a deaf ear to their vaticinations; and hence, with the faith they held in a divine government operating by temporal penalties, they could not fail to anticipate (as Mirabeau's father without such prompting, was able to do on the eve of the French Revolution) *la culbute générale;* an expectation which, luckily for the credit of their prophetic powers, was fulfilled; unlike that of the Apostle John, who in the only intelligible prophecy in the Revelations, foretold to the city of the seven hills a fate like that of Nineveh and Babylon; which prediction remains to this hour unaccomplished. Unquestionably the conviction which experience in time forced on all but the very ignorant, that divine punishments were not to be confidently expected in a temporal form, contributed much to the downfall of the old religions, and the general adoption of one which without absolutely excluding providential interferences in this life for the punishment of guilt or the reward of merit, removed the principal scene of divine retribution to a world after death. But rewards and punishments postponed to that distance of time, and never seen by the eye, are not calculated, even when infinite and eternal, to have, on ordinary minds, a very powerful effect in opposition to strong temptation. Their remoteness alone is a prodigious deduction from their efficacy, on such minds as those which most require the restraint of punishment. A still greater abatement is their uncertainty, which belongs to them from the very nature of the case: for rewards and punishments administered after death, must be awarded not definitely to particular actions, but on a general survey of the person's whole life, and he easily persuades himself that whatever may have been his peccadilloes, there will be a balance in his favour at the last. All positive religions aid this self-delusion. Bad religions teach that divine vengeance may be bought off, by offerings, or personal abasement; the better religions, not to drive sinners to despair, dwell so much on the divine mercy, that hardly any one is compelled to think himself irrevocably condemned. The sole quality in these punishments which might seem calculated to make them efficacious, their over-powering magnitude, is itself a reason why nobody (except a hypochondriac here and there) ever really believes that he is in any very serious danger of incurring them. Even the worst malefactor is hardly able to think that any crime he has had it in his power to commit, any evil he can have inflicted in this short space of existence, can have deserved torture extending through an eternity. Accordingly religious writers and preachers are never tired of complaining how little effect religious motives have on men's lives and conduct, notwithstanding the tremendous penalties denounced.

We may now have done with this branch of the subject, which is, after all, the vulgarest part of it. The value of religion as a supplement to human laws, a more cunning sort of police, an auxiliary to the thief-catcher and the hangman, is not that part of its claims which the more highminded of its votaries are fondest of insisting on: and they would probably be as ready as any one to admit, that if the nobler offices of religion in the soul could be dispensed with, a substitute might be found for so coarse and selfish a social instrument as the fear of hell. In their view of the matter, the best of mankind absolutely require religion for the perfection of their own character, even though the coercion of the worst might possibly be accomplished without its aid.

Even in the social point of view, however,

under its most elevated aspect, these nobler spirits generally assert the necessity of religion, as a teacher, if not as an enforcer, of social morality. They say, that religion alone can teach us what morality is; that all the high morality ever recognized by mankind, was learnt from religion; that the greatest uninspired philosophers in their sublimest flights, stopt far short of the christian morality, and whatever inferior morality they may have attained to (by the assistance, as many think, of dim traditions derived from the Hebrew books, or from a primaeval revelation) they never could induce the common mass of their fellow citizens to accept it from them. That, only when a morality is understood to come from the Gods, do men in general adopt it, rally round it, and lend their human sanctions for its enforcement. That granting the sufficiency of human motives to make the rule obeyed, were it not for the religious idea we should not have had the rule itself.

There is truth in much of this, considered as matter of history. Ancient peoples have generally, if not always, received their morals, their laws, their intellectual beliefs, and even their practical arts of life, all in short which tended either to guide or to discipline them, as revelations from the superior powers, and in any other way could not easily have been induced to accept them. This was partly the effect of their hopes and fears from those powers, which were of much greater and more universal potency in early times, when the agency of the Gods was seen in the daily events of life, experience not having yet disclosed the fixed laws according to which physical phenomena succeed one another. Independently, too, of personal hopes and fears, the involuntary deference felt by these rude minds for power superior to their own, and the tendency to suppose that beings of superhuman power must also be of superhuman

knowledge and wisdom, made them disinterestedly desire to conform their conduct to the presumed preferences of these powerful beings, and to adopt no new practice without their authorization either spontaneously given, or solicited and obtained.

But because, when men were still savages, they would not have received either moral or scientific truths unless they had supposed them to be supernaturally imparted, does it follow that they would now give up moral truths any more than scientific, because they believed them to have no higher origin than wise and noble human hearts? Are not moral truths strong enough in their own evidence, at all events to retain the belief of mankind when once they have acquired it? I grant that some of the precepts of Christ as exhibited in the Gospels — rising far above the Paulism which is the foundation of ordinary Christianity — carry some kinds of moral goodness to a greater height than had ever been attained before, though much even of what is supposed to be peculiar to them is equalled in the Meditations of Marcus Antoninus, which we have no ground for believing to have been in any way indebted to Christianity. But this benefit, whatever it amounts to, has been gained. Mankind have entered into the possession of it. It has become the property of humanity, and cannot now be lost by anything short of a return to primaeval barbarism. The "new commandment to love one another;" the recognition that the greatest are those who serve, not who are served by, others; the reverence for the weak and humble, which is the foundation of chivalry, they and not the strong being pointed out as having the first place in God's regard, and the first claim on their fellow men; the lesson of the parable of the Good Samaritan; that of "he that is without sin let him throw the first stone;" the precept of doing as we would be done by; and such other noble moralities as are to be found, mixed with some poetical exaggerations, and some maxims of which it is difficult to ascertain the precise object; in the authentic sayings of Jesus of Nazareth; these are surely in sufficient harmony with the intellect and feelings of every good man or woman, to be in no danger of being let go, after having been once acknowledged as the creed of the best and foremost portion of our species. There will be, as there have been, shortcomings enough for a long time to come in acting on them; but that they should be forgotten, or cease to be operative on the human conscience, while human beings remain cultivated or civilized, may be pronounced, once for all, impossible.

On the other hand, there is a very real evil consequent on ascribing a supernatural origin to the received maxims of morality. That origin consecrates the whole of them, and protects them from being discussed or criticized. So that if among the moral doctrines received as a part of religion, there be any which are imperfect — which were either erroneous from the first, or not properly limited and guarded in the expression, or which, unexceptionable once, are no longer suited to the changes that have taken place in human relations (and it

is my firm belief that in so-called christian morality, instances of all these kinds are to be found) these doctrines are considered equally binding on the conscience with the noblest, most permanent and most universal precepts of Christ. Wherever morality is supposed to be of supernatural origin, morality is stereotyped; as law is, for the same reason, among believers in the Koran.

Belief, then, in the supernatural, great as are the services which it rendered in the early stages of human development, cannot be considered to be any longer required, either for enabling us to know what is right and wrong in social morality, or for supplying us with motives to do right and to abstain from wrong. Such belief, therefore, is not necessary for social purposes, at least in the coarse way in which these can be considered apart from the character of the individual human being. That more elevated branch of the subject now remains to be considered. If supernatural beliefs are indeed necessary to the perfection of the individual character, they are necessary also to the highest excellence in social conduct: necessary in a far higher sense than that vulgar one, which constitutes it the great support of morality in common eyes.

B

In every discussion it is well to know what one is talking about: and we are going to talk about religion.

To say exactly what the word religion means is not an easy thing. At any rate it is not an easy thing to work out a definition of religion which will satisfy everyone. And if

James Bissett Pratt, "Why Religion Lives," *The Personalist,* Vol. 21, 1940, pp. 352–354, 364–373. Reprinted by permission of the Editor of *The Personalist.*

you talk with many people about the subject you will see that the reason for the ambiguity of the word is to be found not only in the complex and abstract matters into which a discussion of religion leads you, but also in the fact that people really do not have at the back of their minds the same thing, the same meaning, when they use the word. The many connotations of *religion* can, by analysis and classification, be reduced to two groups, but these two refuse further reduction; neither of them can be subsumed under the other. I refer to the cosmic and to the ethical meanings. Sometimes the term is used to refer to man's consciousness of, and his relation to, the ultimate Determiner of Destiny; sometimes to indicate man's sense of, and his aspirations for, the highest values.

It will be part of my contention that religion at its richest and best must include both of these meanings, that it belongs both in the field of value and in the field of ontology. But even so, one must choose upon which of the two to place one's emphasis. Neither the valuational nor the ontological can be reduced to the other, but in the last analysis one of the two must probably be the dominant factor in determining one's notion of what constitutes religion. This being the case, I owe it to you to say frankly that the cosmic or ontological appears to me the most distinguishing feature, the most characteristic character of religion. In short, if I must define religion I should say something like this: that it is an attitude of the human mind, — and by this I mean not only a belief but also an emotional and volitional attiude, — toward what is deemed the ultimate cosmic power, the final Determiner of Destiny. Religion must be distinguished from both morality and metaphysics. The emotional and volitional attitudes to which I have referred differentiate it from metaphysics, the sense of cosmic relationship distinguishes it from morality.

The cosmic reference seems to me the *sine qua non* of religion. Without it there would be no real difference between it and the moral sense. Those who would define religion purely in terms of ideals and values usually mean by the word what Matthew Arnold meant — "Morality touched with emotion." But morality, as such, morality as distinguished from mere ethical theory, is already and always touched with emotion. If that is what we want to talk about we have the good old word *morality* to use, for it means just that. But when we say *religion* most of us mean more than that. We mean more than "the consciousness of the highest social values," as Professor Ames has worded it, more than "the quest of the ages for the good life shared in a good world," as Professor Haydon has expressed it. We mean more also than Professor Dewey has in mind when he writes that "religious faith is the unification of the self in allegiance to inclusive ideal ends which imagination presents to us, and to which the human will responds as worthy of controlling our desires and choices." Unless my experience is quite misleading, the word *religion* as one finds it in "the best usage," both written and spoken, usually has a cosmic reference. And quite aside from this factual question of actual usage, it is for me decisive that we need the word religion for this attitude of man toward the ultimate Power, and do not need it to express a moral or social tendency toward ideal conduct, for which we already possess an entirely adequate term.

Now if we take religion in the cosmic sense I have suggested — man's attitude toward the Determiner of Destiny — it is easy to see why religion lives. It has lived throughout the past of the race and may be counted upon to live through all his future because man is the kind of being that cannot help taking an attitude toward the universe, or Reality as such. And by taking an attitude I mean more than assenting to a philosophy. I mean *thinking about* ultimate matters, wondering about the decisive cosmic powers, cherishing emotions and sentiments concerning them, directing one's behavior in accordance with one's belief about the kind of universe one is living in. If religion be taken in this large sense, if it be thus defined psychologically rather than creedally, it is plain that all earnest and serious men are bound to be religious.

Men believe in God because they need Him. Religion has thus far weathered every storm, repulsed every attack, survived every malady, because it satisfies as nothing else can do some of the deepest needs of human nature. Serious criticisms can be brought against each of the particular religions. Some of them have a great deal to answer for. Terrible crimes have been committed in their names, and designing men have sometimes used them as opium for the people. But there are certain great and fundamental values which religion has regularly contributed and still contributes to life; and it is the realization of this fact by the generality of mankind that largely explains their persistent and unquestioning clinging to religious faith and practice, through evil report and good report, through joy and through disaster, through lightning and tempest, through plague, pestilence and famine, through battle, murder, and sudden death, with the passionate resolution: "though He slay me, yet will I trust in Him."

It may be worth our while, therefore, to consider some of the principal values which mankind owes to religion, some of the precious things which religion brings to the individual and the race. I will suggest three of them. In the first place, religion enlarges the mind. It lifts the individual out of his little world, out of his cares and petty interests, his personal ambitions, his gossip and his business rounds, into an ampler sky, into an infinite world. This does not mean that all religious people are broad minded or have large interests; but it does mean — and I do not see how anyone can deny it — that religious people

have broader minds and have larger interests than they would have if they were not religious. To think occasionally upon themes that transcend the local and immediate, to be concerned about cosmic matters, to take an attitude toward the Determiner of Destiny, this is an exercise and an experience which can hardly fail to stretch the mind, to enlarge the man. Religion does for the common man somewhat the same work that philosophy does for the thinker. It gets him for a time away from the paltry, it gives him a momentary vision of wider horizons. It *disturbs* him: disturbs him "with the joy of elevated thoughts." And to nearly all religious men even of a very commonplace sort, a few times at least in their lives, it gives

> . . . a sense sublime
> Of something far more deeply interfused,
> Whose dwelling is the light of setting suns,
> And the round ocean and the living air,
> And the blue sky, and in the mind of man:
> A motion and a spirit that impels
> All thinking things, all objects of all thought,
> And rolls through all things.

Moments such as these, though they come but rarely, are among the high points of life, and affect all one's other moments and hours and days and years. And aside from them, the habitual living of one's life upon a conscious background of infinity and eternity, marks off the religious man from his merely moral and efficient neighbor.

The neighbor may be quite as moral as he. But while it is true that high and noble living is perfectly possible without what most of us would call religion, there can be little doubt that other things being equal, the average man is likely to live a purer and nobler life if he be religious than if he have no conscious and reverend attitude toward the Determiner of Destiny. For religion helps morality. It helps it in many ways. The thought which many a Christian and Moslem and Jew carries in the background of his mind through hours of temptation and trial, "Thou God seest me," has its enormously restraining and guiding power. In the midst of danger when opportunity presents itself for heroism, little or big, the confidence that comes from faith that the ultimate Power of the Universe is on the side of the Ideal brings to the irresolute mind and the weak flesh a courage which could ill be spared. And nowhere else, I suppose, can one find so great a source of strength for righteous decision and noble living as in devotion to the Founder of one's faith, in the image of the Living Christ, the Eternal Buddha, or of the great cloud of witnesses, never wholly beyond the horizon, whose arms are always stretched out to receive the faithful soul into the communion of saints.

In the noblest religions, moreover, this stimulus to individual morality has been supplemented by a clear call to social morality. The new application to the problems of society of the ideals long held aloft for personal conduct and aspiration is one of the characteristic developments of contemporary Christianity and Judaism, and of some forms of Buddhism, Hinduism, and Islam. Religion, I know, is often criticized for not reforming the world and putting an end to war and bringing about other consummations devoutly to be wished. And indeed I wish churches and synagogues and Buddhist sects would and could do more than they are doing. But how much are the non-religious people accomplishing? And can one picture a more deadly blow to all the causes of economic and civic and social reform and helpfulness and of international good will than the world would suffer if all the religious people lost their religion?

But in my opinion the greatest gift which religion brings to man is the gift of happiness.

I believe that religion brings more happiness to man than any other one thing does. It would be impossible to prove this; but I think that careful observation of religious people and of unreligious people will show both that the former group are notably the happier, and also that the chief source of the happiness of these happy people is, directly or indirectly, their religion. I do not say that religious people are jollier than others, or that they have more than their share of pleasure. But I am convinced that they have an equanimity amid the vicissitudes of life, that they offer a resistance to the slings and arrows of outrageous Fortune, that they possess a confidence and an inner peace, which the non-religious man notably lacks.

We can see why this should be if we will take a moment to analyze what we mean by happiness. In the first place, happiness is not pleasure, not sensuous pleasure nor temporary exhilaration. Happiness is a steadier thing than that and a more fundamental one. It has to do not with superficial ticklings but with the state of the whole man; not with the special senses nor with muscle and joint and glandular sensations, but with the fundamental urges and the long-lasting purposes of life. And I think we might say that happiness is, first, the sense of the harmonious and successful working of these purposes and instinctive drives, and then, in a larger way, the sense of our own harmony with our ultimate environment and the successful working of the larger and impersonal causes that we love.

Pivotal in this suggestion of the meaning of happiness are the words *harmony* and *sense of success*. And a little reflection will show that it is doubtful whether anything else can contribute so much to both the confident feeling of success and the realization of inner and outer harmony as can religion. Of course any powerful passion tends to unify a man's life so long as it lasts and violently asserts itself; but religion is distinguished from other sentiments or emotional interests and passions, in its steady persistence and in the width of its spread. Religion as it is found in the average religious man does not flare up suddenly and as suddenly die down: it exerts a uniquely steady influence. The religious man is not religious merely while he is in church, as the hungry man is hungry only before meals. There is seldom an hour in the day or the year of the religious man's life when the attitude toward the ultimate cosmic Power and supreme ideal and object of reverence and source of inspiration is not present in the background or the foreground of his consciousness. And it is only the subordinate and incidental purposes of life to which religion is felt to be irrelevant. Usually it is knit-up with the individual's supreme moral ideal or aspiration, and thus it presides over all the other aims of life, prevents their mutual warring, and either inspires among them, or forces upon them, a considerable degree of harmony, a kind of "King's Peace," as a monarch does among his vassals. It is not always successful. Civil wars occasionally arise. But there are few forces known to man that can rival religion in power to quell rebellion, transform a turbulent psycho-physical organism into a unified and effective man, and thus diffuse through life a sense of efficiency, wholeness, and self-realization. Largely, it does this through the inspiration of loyalty, loyalty to what is conceived at the same time as the supreme cosmic Power and as the highest object of reverence and worship. And not only inner harmony is the result of the dominance of religion when at its best, but also the sense of being in accord and at one with the ultimate environment, the everlasting arms which are always underneath. "Lord, thou hast been our dwelling-place in all generations."

Happiness, I have suggested, means both harmony and the sense of success. It is hard to be happy when the causes that we love are failing. Therefore, perfect happiness in this world is rarely found, and when found is of brief duration. Religion does not claim, nor try, to give complete and unbroken happiness. But from the very fact of its combined cosmic and ideal nature, it does shed a kind of assurance over the supreme values. Its kingdom is of this world, but not wholly of this world. And the cosmic faith that it inspires throws a new light upon passing sorrows, and builds for one an interior stronghold or keep, which, for many a man, can never be captured by any foe.

A considerable majority of religious people — even of seemingly commonplace ones — possess, I believe, a castle of this sort. A considerable majority find their unruly impulses partly controlled and their lives largely unified and harmonized by a religious ideal and a religious faith. In sunny weather and in stormy, millions of rather average "folks" find in their religion both consolation, confidence, and hope. And if we consider the more intensely religious souls, we shall find they have inner sources of joy and deep delight quite beyond the imagination of those to whom religion is largely meaningless. I have taken some pains in past years to gather information on this subject, and as a result of what I have learned from observation, from books, from questionnaires, from conversations, I feel convinced that religion contributes more than any other one influence to human calmness, confidence, and joy.

It is largely because of these fundamental and lasting values which religion contributes to human life that men have always been unwilling to give it up. Religion lives because men need it and love it. But here we are brought up square against a fact of considerable theoretical and practical importance. It is seldom religion in the abstract, religion as such, that has been the giver of these gifts to man. The first of the three values I have named — the enlargement of the mind — may, indeed be brought about by a more abstract type of religion, but the second and third values — nobility of life and joyfulness of heart — come only from a more concrete and individual faith and worship. It is usually some historical religion, some particular religious tradition, that has brought, and still brings, these great values to mankind. A few intellectual or exceptionally spiritual individuals — a Spinoza, a Goethe, an Emerson — may find their life-needs satisfied in the highly rarified air of noble religious generalities; but something more concrete, some definite teaching and belief, some sanctified form of worship, some recognized and shared sentiment, something that is specifically Christian or Hebrew or Buddhist or Hindu, is needed, is almost prerequisite, for the nourishment of the spiritual life of all communities and of nearly all individuals. For most, a religious philosophy will not suffice; a religious *tradition* is essential.

A religious tradition is something much richer and more complex than a creed. Creeds, indeed, form, or may form, parts of it. But tradition goes deeper down into the roots of a social group and of an individual than anything merely intellectual can go. It includes much of a man's emotional outlook, his volitional tendencies, his ingrained sympathies, the sense of reverence and awe, the hope and aspiration, that he has brought with him from his childhood, and which ever retain in the background of his mind, the aura of the Past. Through it he finds himself bound together with an immense society of contemporaries, and feels himself bound together with a long procession of past generations, with the great dead, with prophets and apostles, all merged in one mighty Communion of Saints. Such

tradition gets itself expressed, not in philosophies and theologies, but in sacred and glowing symbols the emotional significance of which means to the devout soul immeasurably more than any words can ever fully and definitely express.

Tradition belongs not to religion as such, but always to some particular religion. And the great life-giving values which tradition contributes, it gives only to individual religions. This fact has an obvious bearing on our question, why religion lives. It has lived in the past largely because it has been embodied in particular religious traditions. Those purists who would "liberate religion" (as they say) from the particularities of the individual, historical religions, and purify it of everything but the universal, would make it pay for its heightened purity by an almost fatal loss in strength. A religion so well filtered of all special symbols, history, and tradition would be so tenuous and transparent that the ordinary man, not a philosopher, might have difficulty in distinguishing it from just nothing at all. Religion of such a sort would live, would always live. But it might not be very important. If religion in the future is to play the great and beneficent role it has played in the past, it will still have to work through the traditions and symbols of particular religions.

There have been, there are, and there always will be individuals to whom religion of the more abstract sort, religion loosed from tradition, religion without the sanction of Society and of the Past, will minister, and for whom it will suffice. It may be that the proportion of such individuals will increase as the human race advances in intellectual and spiritual development. But up to the point we have now reached, and so far as the generality, the rank and file of mankind is concerned, one might almost say that religion of the abstract sort will never die because it has never lived. For most people it is something like the triangle:

it inhabits the realm of essence rather than that of existence. It is eternal because it is out of time: it belongs rather to the mathematical than to the biological category.

For the great mass of mankind only the specific, historical, traditional religions are alive. Bright individuals can indeed invent bright, new "religions," and these can sometimes get a temporary following among other bright people. But unless these religions can make connection with one or another of the great historical religious traditions, they have little chance of long survival. The promoters of Theosophy, to take only one example, have understood this very well; they have done their best to graft their teachings upon the ancient root of Indian thought and tradition.

Let me repeat: except for unusual individuals only specific religions are alive. And if they are to live into the future it will be because they are really alive today. If they settle down into abstractions and conventional ceremonies, into pious tabulations of past beliefs or into religious etiquette and religious millinery, they will gradually dessicate and disappear, for the good reason that they will already have lost what real life they had. "Unto him that hath shall be given, and he shall have abundantly: but from him that hath not shall be taken that little which he seemeth to have." If the religions are to live they must permanently retain their vigor and their power of adaptation and growth.

In conclusion then, I would say that religion has lived through the past because it has fitted human nature and because it has nourished the spiritual life of man: and that it has been able to do this because it has, in the past, got itself embodied in living faiths, in moving symbols, in uplifting ideals, in commanding traditions.

SUGGESTIONS FOR THOUGHT

1. When did you first begin to have doubts about some of the religious ideas and practices of your religious group?

2. How is religion able to serve as an integrating factor in human life? To what extent does it serve this function in your life?

3. What is salvation? How does religion bring about salvation?

4. Does religion take one's mind off the troubles of this world and give one a rosy otherworldliness, or does it make one work harder to make this world a decent place?

5. What are the dangers of making religious commitments too early in life? Are there any dangers in delaying the adoption of a particular religious view?

6. Is it possible to be religious in general and not identify one's self with any church or religious group?

7. Herbert Gray has said, " . . . many religious young people are rabbits. A human rabbit is a person without a healthy interest in athletics, society, politics, the other sex, and vigorous life in general." Why does religion sometimes have this effect?

8. What does a person mean when he says, "Golf is my religion"? Can devotion to scientific research, artistic creation, or social melioration contribute all essential religious values to the life of an individual?

9. "The more men are absorbed in the business of self-maintenance, or the more they are given up to intellectual, aesthetic, and ethical interests, the more the strictly religious interest falls into the background — if indeed it does not entirely disappear." (Höffding) What are these "strictly religious interests"? Is religion more significant to urban or to rural people?

10. Have you ever had emotions that might be called religious in secular surroundings? E.g.,

have you ever had a "religious experience" at the movies or at a symphony concert?

11. "A religion does not need to be true in order to be valuable; it needs only to be believed." (E. S. Brightman) Believed as what?

12. A criminologist has pointed out that most criminals belong to a church. (Cf.: Carl Murchison, *Criminal Intelligence,* 1926, p. 144.) Can we infer from this that the criminal is not religious enough, or that religion has not been as effective in fostering moral behavior as is commonly supposed?

13. "Those are not at all to be tolerated who deny the being of God. Promises, covenants, and oaths, which are the bonds of human society, can have no hold upon an atheist." (John Locke) Does it seem possible that a man keeps his promises only in so far as he believes in God? Can you name some other sanctions for promise-keeping besides fear (or love) of God?

SUGGESTIONS FOR FURTHER READING

AMES, EDWARD SCRIBNER, "Religious Values and the Practical Absolute," *International Journal of Ethics,* Vol. 32, 1922, pp. 347–365.

BRIGHTMAN, EDGAR S., "The More-than-Human Values of Religion," *The Journal of Religion,* Vol. 1, 1921, pp. 362–377.

CALIFORNIA UNIVERSITY ASSOCIATES, *Knowledge and Society,* New York, D. Appleton-Century Company, 1938, ch. 5.

EDWARDS, D. MIALL, "Religion as a Value-Experience," *The Hibbert Journal,* Vol. 28, 1929–30, pp. 493–511.

GARNETT, A. CAMPBELL, *God in Us,* Chicago, Willett, Clark and Company, 1945, ch. 1.

HARKNESS, GEORGIA, *Conflicts in Religious Thought,* New York, Henry Holt and Company, 1929, ch. 2.

HAYDON, A. EUSTACE, *Man's Search for the Good Life,* New York, Harper and Brothers, 1937, ch. 8.

HOCKING, W. E., and others, *Preface to Philosophy,* New York, The Macmillan Company, 1946, Part IV.

HOUF, HORACE T., *What Religion Is and Does,* New York, Harper and Brothers, 1945, ch. 2.

KALLEN, HORACE M., *Why Religion,* New York, Boni and Liveright, 1927, chs. 5, 11.

LUARD, T. B., "Why I do not go to Church," *The Hibbert Journal,* Vol. 35, 1936–37, pp. 327–340.

MARITAIN, JACQUES, *An Introduction to Philosophy,* New York, Sheed and Ward, 1933, ch. 7.

ROGERS, ARTHUR KENYON, "Is Religion Important?" *Religious Realism,* edited by D. C. Macintosh, New York, The Macmillan Company, 1931, pp. 3–32.

TAYLOR, HENRY OSBORN, *Human Values and Verities,* New York, The Macmillan Company, 1928, ch. 6.

18

THE NATURE OF ART

THOMAS REID (1710–1795) was the founder of the Scottish school of thought which is sometimes called the "Common Sense Philosophy." This philosophy was in the main a revulsion from the skepticism of David Hume. Reid contended that experience is immediately and directly of something external to itself. Reid taught philosophy at the universities of Aberdeen and Glasgow. The Russian novelist and moral philosopher Leo Nikolayevich Tolstoy (1828–1910) is probably best known for his novel *War and Peace.* However, many of his other books would insure his place in letters and philosophy. His *What is Art?* (1896) has been described as one of the most remarkable books ever written on the subject. Probably one of the reasons for this observation is the fact that Tolstoy defines art without appeal to the concept of beauty.

A

Beauty is found in things so various and so very different in nature, that it is difficult to say wherein it consists, or what there can be common to all the objects in which it is found.

Of the objects of sense, we find beauty in colour, in sound, in form, in motion. There are beauties of speech, and beauties of thought; beauties in the arts, and in the sciences; beauties in actions, in affections, and in characters.

In things so different and so unlike is there any quality, the same in all, which we can call by the name of beauty? What can it be that is common to the thought of a mind and the form of a piece of matter, to an abstract theorem and a stroke of wit?

I am indeed unable to conceive any quality in all the different things that are called beautiful, that is the same in them all. There seems to be no identity, not even similarity, between the beauty of a theorem and the beauty of a piece of music, though both may be beautiful. The kinds of beauty seem to be as various as the objects to which it is ascribed.

Thomas Reid, *Essays on the Intellectual Powers of Man* (in *The Works of Thomas Reid*), Edinburgh, James Thin, 1895, Essay VIII, ch. IV (in part).

But why should things so different be called by the same name? This cannot be without a reason. If there be nothing common in the things themselves, they must have some common relation to us, or to something else, which leads us to give them the same name.

All the objects we call beautiful agree in two things, which seem to concur in our sense of beauty. First, when they are perceived, or even imagined, they produce a certain agreeable emotion or feeling in the mind; and, secondly, this agreeable emotion is accompanied with an opinion or belief of their having some perfection or excellence belonging to them....

Though we may be able to conceive these two ingredients of our sense of beauty disjoined, this affords no evidence that they have no necessary connection. It has indeed been maintained, that whatever we can conceive, is possible: but I endeavoured, in treating of conception, to shew, that this opinion, though very common, is a mistake. There may be, and probably are, many necessary connections of things in nature, which we are too dim-sighted to discover.

The emotion produced by beautiful objects is gay and pleasant. It sweetens and humanises the temper, is friendly to every benevolent affection, and tends to allay sullen and angry passions. It enlivens the mind, and disposes it to other agreeable emotions, such as those of love, hope, and joy. It gives a value to the object, abstracted from its utility....

As we ascribe beauty, not only to persons, but to inanimate things, we give the name of love or liking to the emotion, which beauty, in both these kinds of objects, produces. It is evident, however, that liking to a person is a very different affection of mind from liking to an inanimate thing. The first always implies benevolence; but what is inanimate cannot be the object of benevolence. The two affections, however different, have a resemblance in some respects; and, on account of that resemblance, have the same name. And perhaps beauty, in these two different kinds of objects, though it has one name, may be as different in its nature as the emotions which it produces in us.

Besides the agreeable emotion which beautiful objects produce in the mind of the spectator, they produce also an opinion or judgment of some perfection or excellence in the object. This I take to be a second ingredient in our sense of beauty, though it seems not to be admitted by modern philosophers....

Mr. Locke's doctrine concerning the secondary qualities of body, is not so much an error in judgment as an abuse of words. He distinguished very properly between the sensations we have of heat and cold, and that quality or structure in the body which is adapted by Nature to produce those sensations in us. ... Mr. Locke made heat and cold to signify only the sensations we feel, and not the qualities which are the cause of them. And in this, I apprehend, lay his mistake. For it is evident, from the use of language, that hot and cold, sweet and bitter, are attributes of external objects, and not of the person who perceives them. Hence, it appears a monstrous paradox to say, there is no heat in the fire, no sweetness in sugar; but, when explained according to Mr. Locke's meaning, it is only, like most other paradoxes, an abuse of words.

The sense of beauty may be analysed in a

manner very similar to the sense of sweetness. It is an agreeable feeling or emotion, accompanied with an opinion or judgment of some excellence in the object, which is fitted by Nature to produce that feeling.

The feeling is, no doubt, in the mind, and so also is the judgment we form of the object: but this judgment, like all others, must be true or false. If it be a true judgment, there is some real excellence in the object. And the use of all languages shews that the name of beauty belongs to this excellence of the object, and not to the feelings of the spectator.

To say that there is, in reality, no beauty in these objects in which all men perceive beauty, is to attribute to man fallacious senses. But we have no ground to think so disrespectfully of the Author of our being; the faculties he hath given us are not fallacious; nor is that beauty which he hath so liberally diffused over all the works of his hands, a mere fancy in us, but a real excellence in his works, which express the perfection of their Divine Author.

We have reason to believe, not only that the beauties we see in nature are real, and not fanciful, but that there are thousands which our faculties are too dull to perceive. We see many beauties, both of human and divine art, which the brute animals are incapable of perceiving; and superior beings may excel us as far in their discernment of true beauty as we excel the brutes.

The man who is skilled in painting or statuary sees more of the beauty of a fine picture or statue than a common spectator. The same thing holds in all the fine arts. The most perfect works of art have a beauty that strikes even the rude and ignorant; but they see only a small part of that beauty which is seen in such works by those who understand them perfectly, and can produce them.

This may be applied, with no less justice, to the works of Nature. They have a beauty that strikes even the ignorant and inattentive.

But the more we discover of their structure, of their mutual relations, and of the laws by which they are governed, the greater beauty, and the more delightful marks of art, wisdom, and goodness, we discern.

Thus the expert anatomist sees numberless beautiful contrivances in the structure of the human body, which are unknown to the ignorant.

Although the vulgar eye sees much beauty in the face of the heavens, and in the various motions and changes of the heavenly bodies, the expert astronomer, who knows their order and distances, their periods, the orbits they describe in the vast regions of space, and the simple and beautiful laws by which their motions are governed, and all the appearances of their stations, progressions, and retrogradations, their eclipses, occultations, and transits are produced — sees a beauty, order, and harmony reign through the whole planetary system, which delights the mind. The eclipses of the sun and moon, and the blazing tails of comets, which strike terror into barbarous nations, furnish the most pleasing entertainment to his eye, and a feast to his understanding.

In every part of Nature's work, there are numberless beauties, which, on account of our ignorance, we are unable to perceive. Superior beings may see more than we; but He only who made them, and, upon a review, pronounced them all to be very good, can see all their beauty.

Our determinations with regard to the beauty of objects, may, I think, be distinguished into two kinds; the first we may call instinctive, the other rational.

Some objects strike us at once, and appear beautiful at first sight, without any reflection, without our being able to say why we call them beautiful, or being able to specify any perfection which justifies our judgment. Something of this kind there seems to be in brute animals, and in children before the use of reason; nor does it end with infancy, but continues through life.

In the plumage of birds and of butterflies, in the colours and form of flowers, of shells, and of many other objects, we perceive a beauty that delights; but cannot say what it is in the object that should produce that emotion.

The beauty of the object may in such cases be called an occult quality. We know well how it affects our senses; but what it is in itself we know not. But this, as well as other occult qualities, is a proper subject of philosophical disquisition; and, by a careful examination of the objects to which Nature hath given this amiable quality, we may perhaps discover some real excellence in the object, or, at least, some valuable purpose that is served by the effect which it produces upon us.

This instinctive sense of beauty, in different species of animals, may differ as much as the external sense of taste, and in each species be adapted to its manner of life. By this perhaps the various tribes are led to associate with their kind, to dwell among certain objects rather than others, and to construct their habitation in a particular manner. . . .

In the human kind there are varieties in the taste of beauty, of which we can no more assign a reason than of the variety of their features, though it is easy to perceive that very important ends are answered by both. These varieties are most observable in the judgments we form of the features of the other sex; and in this the intention of nature is most apparent.

As far as our determinations of the comparative beauty of objects are instinctive, they are no subject of reasoning or of criticism;

they are purely the gift of nature, and we have no standard by which they may be measured.

But there are judgments of beauty that may be called rational, being grounded on some agreeable quality of the object which is distinctly conceived, and may be specified.

This distinction between a rational judgment of beauty and that which is instinctive, may be illustrated by an instance.

In a heap of pebbles, one that is remarkable for brilliancy of colour and regularity of figure, will be picked out of the heap by a child. He perceives a beauty in it, puts a value upon it, and is fond of the property of it. For this preference, no reason can be given, but that children are, by their constitution, fond of brilliant colours, and of regular figures.

Suppose again that an expert mechanic views a well constructed machine. He see all its parts to be made of the fittest materials, and of the most proper form; nothing superfluous, nothing deficient; every part adapted to its use, and the whole fitted in the most perfect manner to the end for which it is intended. He pronounces it to be a beautiful machine. He views it with the same agreeable emotion as the child viewed the pebble; but he can give a reason for his judgment, and point out the particular perfections of the object on which it is grounded.

Although the instinctive and the rational sense of beauty may be perfectly distinguished in speculation, yet, in passing judgment upon particular objects, they are often so mixed and confounded, that it is difficult to assign to each its own province. Nay, it may often happen, that a judgment of the beauty of an object, which was at first merely instinctive, shall afterwards become rational, when we discover some latent perfection of which that beauty in the object is a sign.

As the sense of beauty may be distinguished into instinctive and rational; so I think beauty itself may be distinguished into original and derived.

As some objects shine by their own light, and many more by light that is borrowed and reflected; so I conceive the lustre of beauty in some objects is inherent and original, and in many others is borrowed and reflected. . . .

There is nothing in the exterior of a man more lovely and more attractive than perfect good breeding. But what is this good breeding? It consists of all the external signs of due respect to our superiors, condescension to our inferiors, politeness to all with whom we converse or have to do, joined in the fair sex with that delicacy of outward behaviour which becomes them. And how comes it to have such charms in the eyes of all mankind; for this reason only, as I apprehend, that it is a natural sign of that temper, and those affections and sentiments with regard to others, and with regard to ourselves, which are in themselves truly amiable and beautiful.

This is the original, of which good breeding is the picture; and it is the beauty of the original that is reflected to our sense by the picture. The beauty of good breeding, therefore, is not originally in the external behaviour in which it consists, but is derived from the qualities of mind which it expresses. And though there may be good breeding without the amiable qualities of mind, its beauty is still derived from what it naturally expresses.

Having explained these distinctions of our sense of beauty into instinctive and rational, and of beauty itself into original and derived, I would now proceed to give a general view of those qualities in objects, to which we may justly and rationally ascribe beauty, whether original or derived.

But here some embarrassment arises from the vague meaning of the word beauty, which I had occasion before to observe.

Sometimes it is extended, so as to include everything that pleases a good taste, and so comprehends grandeur and novelty, as well as what in a more restricted sense is called beauty. At other times, it is even by good writers confined to the objects of sight, when they are either seen, or remembered, or imagined. Yet it is admitted by all men, that there are beauties in music; that there is beauty as well as sublimity in composition, both in verse and in prose; that there is beauty in characters, in affections, and in actions. These are not objects of sight; and a man may be a good judge of beauty of various kinds, who has not the faculty of sight.

To give a determinate meaning to a word so variously extended and restricted, I know no better way than that is suggested by the common division of the objects of taste into novelty, grandeur, and beauty. Novelty, it is plain, is no quality of the new object, but merely a relation which it has to the knowledge of the person to whom it is new. Therefore, if this general division be just, every quality in an object that pleases a good taste, must, in one degree or another, have either grandeur or beauty. It may still be difficult to fix the precise limit betwixt grandeur and beauty; but they must together comprehend everything fitted by its nature to please a good taste — that is, every real perfection and excellence in the objects we contemplate.

In a poem, in a picture, in a piece of music, it is real excellence that pleases a good taste. In a person, every perfection of the mind, moral or intellectual, and every perfection of the body, gives pleasure to the spectator, as well as to the owner, when there is no envy nor malignity to destroy that pleasure.

It is, therefore, in the scale of perfection and real excellence that we must look for what is either grand or beautiful in objects. What is the proper object of admiration is grand, and what is the proper object of love and esteem is beautiful.

This, I think, is the only notion of beauty that corresponds with the division of the objects of taste which has been generally received by philosophers. And this connection of beauty with real perfection, was a capital doctrine of the Socratic school. It is often ascribed to Socrates, in the dialogues of Plato and Xenophon

B

What then is this conception of beauty, so stubbornly held to by people of our circle and day as furnishing a definition of art?

In the subjective aspect, we call beauty that which supplies us with a particular kind of pleasure.

In the objective aspect, we call beauty something absolutely perfect, and we acknowledge it to be so only because we receive, from the manifestation of this absolute perfection, a certain kind of pleasure; so that this objective definition is nothing but the subjective conception differently expressed. In reality both conceptions of beauty amount to one and the same thing, namely, the reception by us of a certain kind of pleasure, i.e., we call "beauty" that which pleases us without evoking in us desire.

Such being the position of affairs, it would seem only natural that the science of art should decline to content itself with a definition of art based on beauty (i.e. on that which pleases), and seek a general definition, which should apply to all artistic productions, and by reference to which we might decide whether a certain article belonged to the realm of art or not. But no such definition is supplied, as

Leo Tolstoy, *What is Art?*, translated by Aylmer Maude, New York, Thomas Y. Crowell & Company, and London, Oxford University Press, 1898, chs. 4, 5. Reprinted by permission of the publishers.

the reader may see from those summaries of the aesthetic theories which I have given, and as he may discover even more clearly from the original aesthetic works, if he will be at the pains to read them. All attempts to define absolute beauty in itself — whether as an imitation of nature, or as suitability to its object, or as a correspondence of parts, or as symmetry, or as harmony, or as unity in variety, etc. — either define nothing at all, or define only some traits of some artistic productions, and are far from including all that everybody has always held, and still holds, to be art.

There is no objective definition of beauty. The existing definitions, (both the metaphysical and the experimental), amount only to one and the same subjective definition which (strange as it seems to say so) is, that art is that which makes beauty manifest, and beauty is that which pleases (without exciting desire). Many aestheticians have felt the insufficiency and instability of such a definition, and, in order to give it a firm basis, have asked themselves why a thing pleases. And they have converted the discussion on beauty into a question concerning taste, as did Hutcheson, Voltaire, Diderot, and others. But all attempts to define what taste is must lead to nothing, as the reader may see both from the history of aesthetics and experimentally. There is and can be no explanation of why one thing pleases one man and displeases another, or *vice versa*. So that the whole existing science of aesthetics fails to do what we might expect from it, being a mental activity calling itself a science, namely, it does not define the qualities and laws of art, or of the beautiful (if that be the content of art), or of the nature of taste (if taste decides the question of art and its merit), and then, on the basis of such definitions, acknowledge as art those productions which correspond to these laws, and reject those which do not come under them. But this science of aesthetics consists in first acknowledging a certain set of productions to be art (because they please us), and then framing such a theory of art that all those productions which please a certain circle of people should fit into it. There exists an art canon, according to which certain productions favoured by our circle are acknowledged as being art, — Phidias, Sophocles, Homer, Titian, Raphael, Bach, Beethoven, Dante, Shakespeare, Goethe, and others, — and the aesthetic laws must be such as to embrace all these productions. In aesthetic literature you will incessantly meet with opinions on the merit and importance of art, founded not on any certain laws by which this or that is held to be good or bad, but merely on the consideration whether this art tallies with the art canon we have drawn up.

The other day I was reading a far from ill-written book by Folgeldt. Discussing the demand for morality in works of art, the author plainly says that we must not demand morality in art. And in proof of this he advances the fact that if we admit such a demand, Shakespeare's *Romeo and Juliet* and Goethe's *Wilhelm Meister* would not fit into the definition of good art; but since both these books are included in our canon of art, he concludes that the demand is unjust. And therefore it is necessary to find a definition of art which shall fit the works; and instead of a demand for morality, Folgeldt postulates as the basis of art a demand for the important (*Bedeutungsvolles*).

All the existing aesthetic standards are built on this plan. Instead of giving a definition of true art, and then deciding what is and what is not good art by judging whether a work conforms or does not conform to the definition, a certain class of works, which for some reason please a certain circle of people, is accepted as being art, and a definition of art is then devised to cover all these productions. I recently came upon a remarkable instance of this method in a very good German work, *The History of Art in the Nineteenth Century,* by Muther. Describing the pre-Raphaelites, the Decadents and the Symbolists (who are already included in the canon of art), he not only does not venture to blame their tendency, but earnestly endeavours to widen his standard so that it may include them all, they appearing to him to represent a legitimate reaction from the excesses of realism. No matter what insanities appear in art, when once they find acceptance among the upper classes of our society a theory is quickly invented to explain and sanction them; just as if there had never been periods in history when certain special circles of people recognised and approved false, deformed, and insensate art which subsequently left no trace and has been utterly forgotten. And to what lengths the insanity and deformity of art may go, especially when, as in our days, it knows that it is considered infallible, may be seen by what is being done in the art of our circle to-day.

So that the theory of art, founded on beauty, expounded by aesthetics, and, in dim outline, professed by the public, is nothing but the setting up as good, of that which has pleased and pleases us, i.e. pleases a certain class of people.

In order to define any human activity, it is necessary to understand its sense and importance. And, in order to do that, it is primarily necessary to examine that activity in itself, in its dependence on its causes, and in connection with its effects, and not merely in relation to the pleasure we can get from it.

If we say that the aim of any activity is merely our pleasure, and define it solely by that pleasure, our definition will evidently be a false one. But this is precisely what has occurred in the efforts to define art. Now, if we consider the food question, it will not occur to anyone to affirm that the importance of food consists in the pleasure we receive when eating it. Everyone understands that the satisfaction of our taste cannot serve as a basis for our definition of the merits of food, and that we have therefore no right to presuppose that the dinners with cayenne pepper, Limburg cheese, alcohol, etc., to which we are accustomed and which please us, form the very best human food.

And in the same way, beauty, or that which pleases us, can in no sense serve as the basis for the definition of art; nor can a series of objects which afford us pleasure serve as the model of what art should be.

To see the aim and purpose of art in the pleasure we get from it, is like assuming (as is done by people of the lowest moral development, e.g. by savages) that the purpose and aim of food is the pleasure derived when consuming it.

Just as people who conceive the aim and purpose of food to be pleasure cannot recognise the real meaning of eating, so people who consider the aim of art to be pleasure cannot realise its true meaning and purpose, because they attribute to an activity, the meaning of which lies in its connection with other phenomena of life, the false and exceptional aim of pleasure. People come to understand that the meaning of eating lies in the nourishment of the body only when they cease to consider that the object of that activity is pleasure. And it is the same with regard to art. People will come to understand the meaning of art only when they cease to consider that the aim of that activity is beauty, i.e. pleasure. The acknowledgment of beauty (i.e. of a certain kind of pleasure received from art) as being the aim of art, not only fails to assist us in finding a definition of what art is, but, on the contrary, by transferring the question into a region quite foreign to art (into metaphysical, psychological, physiological, and even historical discussions as to why such a production pleases one person, and such another displeases or pleases someone else), it renders such definition impossible. And since discussions as to why one man likes pears and another prefers meat do not help towards finding a definition of what is essential in nourishment, so the solution of questions of taste in art (to which the discussions on art involuntarily come) not only does not help to make clear what this particular human activity which we call art really consists in, but renders such elucidation quite impossible, until we rid ourselves of a conception which justifies every kind of art, at the cost of confusing the whole matter.

To the question, What is this art, to which is offered up the labour of millions, the very lives of men, and even morality itself? we have extracted replies from the existing aesthetics, which all amount to this: that the aim of art is beauty, that beauty is recognised by the enjoyment it gives, and that artistic enjoyment is a good and important thing, because it is enjoyment. In a word, that enjoyment is good because it is enjoyment. Thus, what is considered the definition of art is no definition at all, but only a shuffle to justify existing art. Therefore, however strange it may seem to say so, in spite of the mountains of books written about art, no exact definition of art has been constructed. And the reason of this is that the conception of art has been based on the conception of beauty.

What is art, if we put aside the conception of beauty, which confuses the whole matter? The latest and most comprehensible definitions of art, apart from the conception of beauty, are the following: — (1a) Art is an activity arising even in the animal kingdom, and springing from sexual desire and the propensity to play (Schiller, Darwin, Spencer), and (1b) accompanied by a pleasurable excitement of the nervous system (Grant Allen). This is the physiological-evolutionary definition. (2) Art is the external manifestation, by means of lines, colours, movements, sounds, or words, of emotions felt by man (Véron). This is the experimental definition. According to the very latest definition (Sully), (3) Art is "the production of some permanent object, or passing action, which is fitted not only to supply an active enjoyment to the producer, but to convey a pleasurable impression to a number of spectators or listeners, quite apart from any personal advantage to be derived from it."

Notwithstanding the superiority of these definitions to the metaphysical definitions which depended on the conception of beauty, they are yet far from exact. (1a) The first, the physiological-evolutionary definition, is inexact, because, instead of speaking about the the artistic activity itself, which is the real matter in hand, it treats of the derivation of art. The modification of it (1b), based on the physiological effects on the human organism, is inexact, because within the limits of such definition many other human activities can be included, as has occurred in the neo-aes-

thetic theories, which reckon as art the preparation of handsome clothes, pleasant scents, and even of victuals.

The experimental definition (2), which makes art consist in the expression of emotions, is inexact, because a man may express his emotions by means of lines, colours, sounds, or words, and yet may not act on others by such expression; and then the manifestation of his emotions is not art.

The third definition (that of Sully) is inexact, because in the production of objects or actions affording pleasure to the producer and a pleasant emotion to the spectators or hearers apart from personal advantage, may be included the showing of conjuring tricks or gymnastic exercises, and other activities which are not art. And, further, many things, the production of which does not afford pleasure to the producer, and the sensation received from which is unpleasant, such as gloomy, heart-rending scenes in a poetic description or a play, may nevertheless be undoubted works of art.

The inaccuracy of all these definitions arises from the fact that in them all (as also in the metaphysical definitions) the object considered is the pleasure art may give, and not the purpose it may serve in the life of man and of humanity.

In order correctly to define art, it is necessary, first of all, to cease to consider it as a means to pleasure, and to consider it as one of the conditions of human life. Viewing it in this way, we cannot fail to observe that art is one of the means of intercourse between man and man.

Every work of art causes the receiver to enter into a certain kind of relationship both with him who produced, or is producing, the art, and with all those who, simultaneously, previously or subsequently, receive the same artistic impression.

Speech, transmitting the thoughts and experiences of men, serves as a means of union among them, and art acts in a similar manner. The peculiarity of this latter means of intercourse, distinguishing it from intercourse by means of words, consists in this, that whereas by words a man transmits his thoughts to another, by means of art he transmits his feelings.

The activity of art is based on the fact that a man, receiving through his sense of hearing or sight another man's expression of feeling, is capable of experiencing the emotion which moved the man who expressed it. To take the simplest example: one man laughs, and another, who hears, becomes merry; or a man weeps, and another, who hears, feels sorrow. A man is excited or irritated, and another man, seeing him, comes to a similar state of mind. By his movements, or by the sounds of his voice, a man expresses courage and determination, or sadness and calmness, and this state of mind passes on to others. A man suffers, expressing his sufferings by groans and spasms, and this suffering transmits itself to other people; a man expresses his feeling of admiration, devotion, fear, respect, or love to certain objects, persons or phenomena, and others are infected by the same feelings of admiration, devotion, fear, respect, or love to the same objects, persons, and phenomena.

And it is on this capacity of man to receive another man's expression of feeling, and experience those feelings himself, that the activity of art is based.

If a man infects another or others, directly, immediately, by his appearance, or by the sounds he gives vent to at the very time he experiences the feeling; if he causes another man to yawn when he himself cannot help yawning, or to laugh or cry when he himself is obliged to laugh or cry, or to suffer when he himself is suffering — that does not amount to art.

Art begins when one person, with the object of joining another or others to himself in one and the same feeling, expresses that feeling by certain external indications. To take the simplest example: a boy, having experienced, let us say, fear on encountering a wolf, relates that encounter; and in order to evoke in others the feeling he has experienced, describes himself, his condition before the encounter, the surroundings, the wood, his own lightheartedness, and then the wolf's appearance, its movements, the distance between himself and the wolf, etc. All this, if only the boy when telling the story, again experiences the feelings he had lived through and infects the hearers and compels them to feel what the narrator had experienced, is art. If even the boy had not seen a wolf but had frequently been afraid of one, and if, wishing to evoke in others the fear he had felt, he invented an encounter with a wolf, and recounted it so as to make his hearers share the feelings he experienced when he feared the wolf, that also would be art. And just in the same way it is art if a man, having experienced either the fear of suffering or the attraction of enjoyment (whether in reality or in imagination), expresses these feelings on canvas or in marble so that others are infected by them. And it is also art if a man feels or imagines to himself feelings of delight, gladness, sorrow, despair, courage, or despondency, and the transition from one to another of these feelings, and expresses these feelings by sounds, so that the hearers are infected by them, and experience them as they were experienced by the composer.

The feelings with which the artist infects others may be most various — very strong or very weak, very important or very insignificant, very bad or very good: feelings of love for native land, self-devotion and submission to fate or to God expressed in a drama, raptures of lovers described in a novel, feelings of voluptuousness expressed in a picture, courage expressed in a triumphal march, merriment evoked by a dance, humour evoked by a funny story, the feeling of quietness transmitted by an evening landscape or by a lullaby, or the feeling of admiration evoked by a beautiful arabesque — it is all art.

If only the spectators or auditors are infected by the feelings which the author has felt, it is art.

To evoke in oneself a feeling one has once experienced, and having evoked it in oneself, then, by means of movements, lines, colours, sounds, or forms expressed in words, so to transmit that feeling that others may experience the same feeling — this is the activity of art.

Art is a human activity, consisting in this, that one man consciously, by means of certain external signs, hands on to others feelings he has lived through, and that other people are infected by these feelings, and also experience them.

Art is not, as the metaphysicians say, the manifestation of some mysterious Idea of beauty, or God; it is not, as the aesthetical physiologists say, a game in which man lets off his excess of stored-up energy; it is not the expression of man's emotions by external signs; it is not the production of pleasing objects; and, above all, it is not pleasure; but it is a means of union among men, joining them together in the same feelings, and indispensable for the life and progress towards well-being of individuals and of humanity.

As, thanks to man's capacity to express thoughts by words, every man may know all that has been done for him in the realms of thought by all humanity before his day, and can, in the present, thanks to this capacity to understand the thoughts of others, become a sharer in their activity, and can himself hand on to his contemporaries and descendants the thoughts he has assimilated from others, as well as those which have arisen within himself; so, thanks to man's capacity to be infected with the feelings of others by means of art, all that is being lived through by his contemporaries is inaccessible to him, as well as the feelings experienced by men thousands of years ago, and he has also the possibility of transmitting his own feelings to others.

If people lacked this capacity to receive the thoughts conceived by the men who preceded them, and to pass on to others their own thoughts, men would be like wild beasts, or like Kaspar Hauser.

And if men lacked this other capacity of being infected by art, people might be almost more savage still, and, above all, more separated from, and more hostile to, one another.

And therefore the activity of art is a most important one, as important as the activity of speech itself, and as generally diffused.

We are accustomed to understand art to be only what we hear and see in theatres, concerts, and exhibitions; together with buildings, statues, poems, novels. . . . But all this is but the smallest part of the art by which we communicate with each other in life. All human life is filled with works of art of every kind — from cradle-song, jest, mimicry, the ornamentation of houses, dress and utensils, up to church services, buildings, monuments, and triumphal processions. It is all artistic activity. So that by art, in the limited sense of the word, we do not mean all human activity transmitting feelings, but only that part which we for some reason select from it and to which we attach special importance.

This special importance has always been given by all men to that part of this activity which transmits feelings flowing from their religious perception, and this small part of art they have specifically called art, attaching to it the full meaning of the word.

That was how men of old — Socrates, Plato, and Aristotle — looked on art. Thus did the Hebrew prophets and the ancient Christians regard art; thus it was, and still is, understood by the Mahommedans, and thus is it still understood by religious folk among our own peasantry.

Some teachers of mankind — as Plato in his *Republic,* and people such as the primitive Christians, the strict Mahommedans, and the Buddhists — have gone so far as to repudiate all art.

People viewing art in this way (in contradiction to the prevalent view of to-day, which regards any art as good if only it affords pleasure) considered, and consider, that art (as contrasted with speech, which need not be listened to) is so highly dangerous in its power to infect people against their wills, that mankind will lose far less by banishing all art than by tolerating each and every art.

Evidently such people were wrong in repudiating all art, for they denied that which cannot be denied — one of the indispensable means of communication, without which mankind could not exist. But not less wrong are the people of civilised European society of our class and day, in favouring any art if it but serves beauty, i.e. gives people pleasure.

Formerly, people feared lest among the works of art there might chance to be some causing corruption, and they prohibited art altogether. Now, they only fear lest they should be deprived of any enjoyment art can afford, and patronise any art. And I think the last error is much grosser than the first, and that its consequences are far more harmful.

SUGGESTIONS FOR THOUGHT

1. What are the essential characteristics of a work of art? Should art portray only the beautiful, or should it reflect all aspects of life? How realistic should art be in showing us our world?

2. Why is a landscape not called art, whereas a painting of a landscape is called art?

3. "Clearness and consistency are a logician's virtues; and a poet does not present and pursue thought in the spirit of the logician. Rather does he seek it for what it is worth to him, imaginatively and emotionally, and for what he can make of it as he casts his magic spell." (L. W. Flaccus) Is the poet free from the obligation to speak truthfully? Or is there some sense in which a poet must make true statements?

4. What is the difference between the artistic temperament and the scientific temperament?

5. Is it possible for a work of art to have too much unity? What are the relative advantages of the sonnet and free verse? Does disharmony have a place in music? Is flawless art the best art, or is a work of art better because it contains some discordant elements?

6. Is art a luxury? Should a person satisfy all his physical needs before pursuing aesthetic satisfactions?

7. What is the source of the artist's inspiration? Must all good art be inspired art? Can an artist make up with hard work that which he lacks in talent? Is the creation of an art object work or play?

8. Is interest in art a means of diverting our thoughts from the serious troubles that oppress us? Why do many people like detective stories? Can art supply some thrill to humdrum lives?

9. Does the artist have the tastes of the public in mind as he works? To what extent can art arouse the public to eliminate social ills? Is didactic art good art? What do we mean when we say that an artist has lost himself in his art?

10. Why are sight and hearing the best avenues of aesthetic perception? Which has more aesthetic qualities — visually appreciating an attractively set table or eating the meal? Why cannot there be a symphony of odors or of tastes as well as a symphony of sounds?

11. Who possesses a work of art — the artist who created it, the student who understands it, or the patron who buys it?

12. How is it possible to take an aesthetic attitude toward an unaesthetic object?

13. Does an artist paint things as they are or as he sees them? Ludwig Richter relates that once he and three friends set out to paint the same landscape. They all resolved not to deviate from nature, yet the result was four totally different pictures. Why cannot an artist keep himself out of the picture? Would it be desirable if he could? In what art is there least of the artist? In what art does the artist appear most?

14. We hear much today about abstract art. Many people do not like abstract art because they say they cannot understand it. Some of the abstract artists, on the other hand, say they see no reason why they should paint only that which laymen can understand. Tolstoy once said about this: "The assertion that art may be good art and at the same time incomprehensible to a great number of people, is extremely unjust, and its consequences are ruinous to art itself." Do you agree with the abstract artists or with Tolstoy? In what ways would the creation of incomprehensible art be ruinous to art itself? What should art communicate?

SUGGESTIONS FOR FURTHER READING

BELL, CLIVE, *Art,* New York, Frederick A. Stokes Company, 1913, Part I.

DUCASSE, C. J., "What Has Beauty to Do with Art?" *The Journal of Philosophy,* Vol. 25, 1928, pp. 181–186.

FLACCUS, LOUIS M., *The Spirit and Substance of Art,* New York, F. S. Crofts and Company, 1931, Part I, II.

GOTSHALK, D. W., *Art and the Social Order,* Chicago, University of Chicago Press, 1947, ch. 1, 2.

HEGEL, G. W. F., *The Philosophy of Fine Art,* Introduction.

KANT, IMMANUEL, *The Critique of Judgment,* Part I, Section I, Book I.

LANGFELD, HERBERT SIDNEY, *The Aesthetic Attitude,* New York, Harcourt, Brace and Company, 1920, ch. 2.

MEAD, GEORGE H., "The Nature of Aesthetic Experience," *International Journal of Ethics,* Vol. 36, 1926, pp. 382–393.

PARKER, DE WITT H., *The Analysis of Art,* New Haven, Yale University Press, 1926, ch. 1.

PARKHURST, HELEN HUSS, *Beauty,* New York, Harcourt, Brace and Company, 1930, Prologue. ch. 1.

SANTAYANA, GEORGE, *The Sense of Beauty,* New York, Charles Scribner's Sons, 1896, ch. 1.

SCHOEN, MAX, *Art and Beauty,* New York, The Macmillan Company, 1932, Part I.

STACE, W. T., *The Meaning of Beauty,* London, Grant Richards and Humphrey Toulmin, 1929, ch. 8.

THURSTON, CARL, "The 'Principles' of Art," *The Journal of Aesthetics and Art Criticism,* Vol. 4, 1945, pp. 96–100.

TOROSSIAN, ARAM, *A Guide to Aesthetics,* Stanford, Calif., Stanford University Press, 1937, ch. 3, 4.

19

ART AND KNOWLEDGE

George Edward Moore (1873–   ), in his *Principia Ethica* (1903), defends his belief that knowledge makes a contribution to the aesthetic appreciation of an object. Henri Bergson (1859–1941), on the other hand, believes that aesthetic appreciation contributes a kind of knowledge which can be gained in no other way. Bergson, a French biologist and philosopher, was a defender of intuition. After teaching philosophy in various colleges in France, Bergson devoted himself to international affairs. After World War I he was president of the International Committee of Intellectual Cooperation. He won the Nobel prize for literature in 1927.

A

I propose to begin by examining what I have called aesthetic enjoyments, since the case of personal affections presents some additional complications. It is, I think, universally admitted that the proper appreciation of a beautiful object is a good thing in itself; and my question is: What are the main elements included in such an appreciation?

(1) It is plain that in those instances of aesthetic appreciation, which we think most

George Edward Moore, *Principia Ethica,* Cambridge, Cambridge University Press, 1903, pp. 189–202. Reprinted by permission of the publishers.

valuable, there is included, not merely a bare cognition of what is beautiful in the object, but also some kind of feeling or emotion. It is not sufficient that a man should merely see the beautiful qualities in a picture and know that they are beautiful, in order that we may give his state of mind the highest praise. We require that he should also *appreciate* the beauty of that which he sees and which he knows to be beautiful — that he should feel and see *its beauty.* And by these expressions we certainly mean that he should have an appropriate emotion towards the beautiful qualities which he cognises. It is perhaps the case that all aesthetic emotions have some common quality; but it is certain that differences in the emotion seem to be appropriate to differences in the kind of beauty perceived: and by saying that different emotions are *appropriate* to different kinds of beauty, we mean that the whole which is formed by the consciousness of that kind of beauty *together with* the emotion appropriate to it, is better than if any other emotion had been felt in contemplating that particular beautiful object. Accordingly we have a large variety of different emotions, each of which is a necessary constituent in some state of consciousness which we judge to be good. All of these emotions are essential elements in great positive goods; they are *parts* of organic wholes, which have great intrinsic value. But it is important to observe that these wholes are organic, and that, hence, it does not follow that the emotion, *by itself,* would have any value whatsoever, nor yet that, if it were directed to a different object, the whole thus formed might not be positively bad. And, in fact, it seems to be the case that if we distinguish the emotional element, in any aesthetic appreciation, from the cognitive element, which accompanies it and is, in fact, commonly thought of as a part of the emotion; and if we consider what value this emotional element would have, *existing by itself,* we can hardly think that it has any great value, even if it has any at all. Whereas, if the same emotion be directed to a different object, if, for instance, it is felt towards an object that is positively ugly, the whole state of consciousness is certainly often positively bad in a high degree.

(2) In the last paragraph I have pointed out the two facts, that the presence of some emotion is necessary to give any very high value to a state of aesthetic appreciation, and that, on the other hand, this same emotion, in itself, may have little or no value: it follows that these emotions give to the wholes of which they form a part a value far greater than that which they themselves possess. The same is obviously true of the cognitive element which must be combined with these emotions in order to form these highly valuable wholes; and the present paragraph will attempt to define what is meant by this cognitive element, so far as to guard against a possible misunderstanding. When we talk of seeing a beautiful object, or, more generally, of the cognition or consciousness of a beautiful object, we may mean by these expressions something which forms no part of any valuable whole. There is an ambiguity in the use of the term 'object,' which has probably been responsible for as many enormous errors in philosophy and psychology as any other single cause. This ambiguity may easily be detected by considering the proposition, which, though a contradiction in terms, is obviously true: That when a man sees a beautiful picture, he may see nothing beautiful whatever. The ambiguity consists in the fact that, by the 'object' of vision (or cognition), may be meant *either* the qualities actually seen *or* all the qualities possessed by the thing seen. Thus in our case: when it is said that the picture is beautiful, it is meant that it contains qualities which are beautiful; when it is said that the man sees the picture, it is meant that he sees a great number of the qualities contained in the picture; and when it is said that, nevertheless, he sees nothing beautiful, it is meant that he does *not* see those qualities of the picture which are beautiful. When, therefore, I speak of the cognition of a beautiful object, as an essential element in a valuable aesthetic appreciation, I must be understood to mean only the cognition of *the beautiful qualities* possessed by that object, and *not* the cognition of other qualities of the object possessing

them. And this distinction must itself be carefully distinguished from the other distinction expressed above by the distinct terms 'seeing the beauty of a thing' and 'seeing its beautiful qualities.' By 'seeing the beauty of a thing' we commonly mean the having an emotion towards its beautiful qualities; whereas in the 'seeing of its beautiful qualities' we do not include any emotion. By the cognitive element, which is equally necessary with emotion to the existence of a valuable appreciation, I mean merely the actual cognition or consciousness of any or all of an object's *beautiful qualities* — that is to say any or all of those elements in the object which possess any positive beauty. That such a cognitive element is essential to a valuable whole may be easily seen, by asking: What value should we attribute to the proper emotion excited by hearing Beethoven's Fifth Symphony, if that emotion were entirely unaccompanied by any consciousness, either of the notes, or of the melodic and harmonic relations between them? And that the mere *hearing* of the Symphony, even accompanied by the appropriate emotion, is not sufficient, may be easily seen, if we consider what would be the state of a man, who should hear all the notes, but should *not* be aware of any of those melodic and harmonic relations, which are necessary to constitute the smallest beautiful elements in the Symphony.

(3) Connected with the distinction just made between 'object' in the sense of the qualities actually before the mind, and 'object' in the sense of the whole thing which possesses the qualities actually before the mind, is another distinction of the utmost importance for a correct analysis of the constituents necessary to a valuable whole. It is commonly and rightly thought that to see beauty in a thing which has no beauty is in some way inferior to seeing beauty in that which really has it. But under this single description of 'seeing beauty in that which has no beauty,' two very different facts, and facts of very different value, may be included. We may mean *either* the attribution to an object of really beautiful qualities which it does not possess *or* the feeling towards qualities, which the object does possess but which are in reality not beautiful, an emotion which is appropriate only to qualities really beautiful. Both these facts are of very frequent occurrence; and in most instances of emotion both no doubt occur together: but they are obviously quite distinct, and the distinction is of the utmost importance for a correct estimate of values. The former may be called an error of judgment, and the latter an error of taste; but it is important to observe that the 'error of taste' commonly involves a false judgment *of value;* whereas the 'error of judgment' is merely a false judgment *of fact.*

Now the case which I have called an error of taste, namely, where the actual qualities we admire (whether possessed by the 'object' or not) are ugly, can in any case have no value, except such as may belong to the emotion *by itself;* and in most, if not in all, cases it is a considerable positive evil. In this sense, then, it is undoubtedly right to think that seeing beauty in a thing which has no beauty is inferior in value to seeing beauty where beauty really is. But the other case is much more difficult. In this case there is present all that I have hitherto mentioned as necessary to constitute a great positive good: there is a cognition of qualities really beautiful, together with an appropriate emotion towards these qualities. There can, therefore, be no doubt that we have here a great positive good. But there is present also something else; namely, a belief that these beautiful qualities exist, and that they exist in a certain relation to other things — namely, to some properties of the object to which we attribute these qualities: and further the object of this belief is false. And we may ask, with regard to the whole thus constituted, whether the presence of the belief, and the fact that what is believed is false, make any difference to its value? We thus get three different cases of which it is very important to determine the relative values. Where both the cognition of beautiful qualities and the appropriate emotion are present we may *also* have either, (1) a belief in the existence of these qualities, of which the object, i.e. that they exist, is true: or (2) a mere cognition, without belief, when it is (a) true, (b) false, that the object of the cognition, i.e. the beautiful qualities, exists: or (3) a belief in the existence of the beautiful qualities, when they do not exist. The importance of these cases arises from the fact that the second defines the pleasures of imagination, including a great part of the appreciation of those works of art which are *representative;* whereas the first contrasts with these the appreciation of what is beautiful in Nature, and the human affections. The third, on the other hand, is contrasted with both, in that it is chiefly exemplified in what is called misdirected affection; and it is possible also that the love of God, in the case of a believer, should fall under this head.

Now all these three cases, as I have said, have something in common, namely, that, in them all, we have a cognition of really beautiful qualities together with an appropriate emotion towards those qualities. I think, therefore, it cannot be doubted (nor is it commonly doubted) that all three include great positive goods; they are all things of which we feel convinced that they are worth having for their own sakes. And I think that the value of the second, in either of its two subdivisions, is precisely the same as the value of the element common to all three. In other words, in the case of purely imaginative ap-

preciations we have merely the cognition of really beautiful qualities together with the appropriate emotion; and the question, whether the object cognised exists or not, seems here, where there is no belief either in its existence or in its non-existence, to make absolutely no difference to the value of the total state. But it seems to me that the two other cases do differ in intrinsic value both from this one and from one another, even though the object cognised and the appropriate emotion should be identical in all three cases. I think that the additional presence of a belief in the reality of the object makes the total state much better, if the belief is true; and worse, if the belief is false. In short, where there is belief, in the sense in which we *do* believe in the existence of Nature and horses, and do *not* believe in the existence of an ideal landscape and unicorns, the *truth* of what is believed does make a great difference to the value of the organic whole. If this be the case, we shall have vindicated the belief that *knowledge,* in the ordinary sense, as distinguished on the one hand from belief in what is false and on the other from the mere awareness of what is true, does contribute towards intrinsic value — that, at least in some cases, its presence as a part makes a whole more valuable than it could have been without.

Now I think there can be no doubt that we do judge that there is a difference of value, such as I have indicated, between the three cases in question. We do think that the emotional contemplation of a natural scene, supposing its qualities equally beautiful, is in some way a better state of things than that of a painted landscape: we think that the world would be improved if we could substitute for the best works of representative art *real* objects equally beautiful. And similarly we regard a misdirected affection or admiration, even where the error involved is a mere error of judgment and not an error of taste, as in some way unfortunate. And further, those, at least, who have a strong respect for truth, are inclined to think that a merely poetical contemplation of the Kingdom of Heaven *would* be superior to that of the religious believer, *if* it were the case that the Kingdom of Heaven does not and will not really exist. Most persons, on a sober, reflective judgment, would feel some hesitation even in preferring the felicity of a madman, convinced that the world was ideal, to the condition either of a poet imagining an ideal world, or of themselves enjoying and appreciating the lesser goods which do and will exist. But, in order to assure ourselves that these judgments are really judgments of intrinsic value upon the question before us, and to satisfy ourselves that they are correct, it is necessary clearly to distinguish our question from two others which have a very important bearing upon our total judgment of the cases in question.

In the first place (a) it is plain that, where we believe, the question whether what we believe is true or false, will generally have a most important bearing upon the value of our belief *as a means.* Where we believe, we are apt to act upon our belief, in a way in which we do not act upon our cognition of the events in a novel. The truth of what we believe is, therefore, very important as preventing the pains of disappointment and still more serious consequences. And it might be thought that a misdirected attachment was unfortunate solely for this reason: that it leads us to count upon results, which the real nature of its object is not of a kind to ensure. So too the Love of God, where, as usual, it includes the belief that he will annex to certain actions consequences, either in this life or the next, which the course of nature gives no reason to expect, may lead the believer to perform actions of which the actual conse-

quences, supposing no such God to exist, may be much worse than he might otherwise have effected: and it might be thought that this was the sole reason (as it is a sufficient one) why we should hesitate to encourage the Love of God, in the absence of any proof that he exists. And similarly it may be thought that the only reason why beauty in Nature should be held superior to an equally beautiful landscape or imagination, is that its existence would ensure greater permanence and frequency in our emotional contemplation of that beauty. It is, indeed, certain that the chief importance of most *knowledge* — of the truth of most of the things which we believe — does, in this world, consist in its extrinsic advantages: it is immensely valuable *as a means.*

And secondly, (b) it may be the case that the existence of that which we contemplate is itself a great positive good, so that, for this reason alone, the state of things described by saying, that the object of our emotion really exists, would be intrinsically superior to that in which it did not. This reason for superiority is undoubtedly of great importance in the case of human affections, where the object of our admiration is the mental qualities of an admirable person; for that *two* such admirable persons should exist is greatly better than that there should be only one: and it would also discriminate the admiration of inanimate nature from that of its representations in art, in so far as we may allow a small intrinsic value to the existence of a beautiful object, apart from any contemplation of it. But it is to be noticed that this reason would not account for any difference in value between the cases where the truth was believed and that in which it was merely cognised, without either belief or disbelief. In other words, so far as this reason goes, the difference between the two subdivisions of our second class (that of imaginative contemplation) would be as great as between our first class and the second subdivision of our second. The superiority of the mere *cognition* of a beautiful object, when that object also happened to exist, over the same cognition when the object did not exist, would, on this count, be as great as that of the *knowledge* of a beautiful object over the mere imagination of it.

These two reasons for discriminating between the value of the three cases we are considering, must, I say, be carefully distinguished from that, of which I am now questioning the validity if we are to obtain a correct answer concerning this latter. The question I am putting is this: Whether the *whole* constituted by the fact that there is an emotional contemplation of a beautiful object, which both is believed to be and is *real,* does not derive some of its values from the fact that the object *is* real? I am asking whether the value of this whole, *as a whole,* is not greater than that of those which differ from it, *either* by the absence of belief, with or without truth, *or,* belief being present, by the mere absence of truth? I am not asking *either* whether it is not superior to them as a means (which it certainly is), *nor* whether it may not contain a more valuable *part,* namely, the existence of the object in question. My question is solely whether the existence of its object does not constitute an addition to the value of the whole, quite distinct from the addition constituted by the fact that this whole does contain a valuable part.

If, now, we put this question, I cannot avoid thinking that it should receive an affirmative answer. We can put it clearly by the method of isolation; and the sole decision must rest with our reflective judgment upon it, as thus clearly put. We can guard against the bias produced by a consideration of value *as a means* by supposing the case of an illusion as complete and permanent as illusions

in this world never can be. We can imagine the case of a single person, enjoying throughout eternity the contemplation of scenery as beautiful, and intercourse with persons as admirable, as can be imagined; while yet the whole of the objects of his cognition are absolutely unreal. I think we should definitely pronounce the existence of a universe, which consisted solely of such a person, to be *greatly* inferior in value to one in which the objects, in the existence of which he believes, did really exist just as he believes them to do; and that it would be thus inferior *not only* because it would lack the goods which consist in the existence of the objects in question, but *also* merely because his belief would be false. That it would be inferior *for this reason alone follows* if we admit, what also appears to me certain, that the case of a person, merely imagining, without believing, the beautiful objects in question, would, *although these objects really existed,* be yet inferior to that of the person who also believed in their existence. For here all the additional good, which consists in the existence of the objects, is present, and yet there still seems to be a great difference in value between this case and that in which their existence is believed. But I think that my conclusion may perhaps be exhibited in a more convincing light by the following considerations. (1) It does not seem to me that the small degree of value which we may allow to the existence of beautiful inanimate objects is nearly equal in amount to the difference which I feel that there is between the appreciation (accompanied by belief) of such objects, when they really exist, and the purely imaginative appreciation of them when they do not exist. This inequality is more difficult to verify where the object is an admirable person, since a *great* value must be allowed to his existence. But yet I think it is not paradoxical to maintain that the superiority of reciprocal affection, where both objects are worthy and both exist, over an unreciprocated affection, where both are worthy but one does not exist, does not lie solely in the fact that, in the former case, we have two good things instead of one, but also in the fact that each is such as the other believes him to be. (2) It seems to me that the important contribution to value made by true belief may be very plainly seen in the following case. Suppose that a worthy object of affection does really exist and is believed to do so, but that there enters into the case this error of fact, that the qualities loved, though exactly like, are yet not the *same* which really do exist. This state of things is easily imagined, and I think we cannot avoid pronouncing that, *although* both persons here exist, it is yet not so satisfactory as where the very person loved and believed to exist is also the one which actually does exist.

If all this be so, we have, in this third section, added to our two former results the third result that a true belief in the reality of an object greatly increases the value of many valuable wholes. Just as in sections (1) and (2) it was maintained that aesthetic and affectionate emotions had little or no value apart from the cognition of appropriate objects, and that the cognition of these objects had little or no value apart from the appropriate emotion, so that the whole, in which both were combined, had a value greatly in excess of the sum of the values of its parts; so, according to this section, if there be added to these wholes a true belief in the reality of the object, the new whole thus formed has a value greatly in excess of the sum obtained by adding the value of the true belief, considered in itself, to that of our original wholes. This new case only differs from the former in this, that, whereas the true belief, by itself, has quite as little value as either of the two other

constituents taken singly, yet they, taken together, seem to form a whole of very great value, whereas this is not the case with the two wholes which might be formed by adding the true belief to either of the others.

The importance of the result of this section seems to lie mainly in two of its consequences. (1) That it affords some justification for the immense intrinsic value, which seems to be commonly attributed to the mere *knowledge* of some truth, and which was expressly attributed to some kinds of knowledge by Plato and Aristotle. Perfect knowledge has indeed competed with perfect love for the position of Ideal. If the results of this section are correct, it appears that knowledge, though having little or no value by itself, is an absolutely essential constituent in the highest goods, and contributes immensely to their value. And it appears that this function may be performed not only by that case of knowledge, which we have chiefly considered, namely, knowledge of the reality of the beautiful object cognised, but also by knowledge of the numerical identity of this object with that which really exists, and by the knowledge that the existence of that object is truly good. Indeed all knowledge, which is directly concerned with the nature of the constituents of a beautiful object, would seem capable of adding greatly to the value of the contemplation of that object, although, by itself, such knowledge would have no value at all. — And (2) The second important consequence, which follows from this section, is that the presence of true belief may, in spite of a great inferiority in the value of the emotion and the beauty of its object, constitute with them a whole equal or superior in value to wholes, in which the emotion and beauty are superior, but in which a true belief is wanting or a false belief present. In this way we may justify the attribution of equal or superior value to an appreciation of an inferior real object, as compared with the appreciation of a greatly superior object which is a mere creature of the imagination. Thus a just appreciation of nature and of real persons may maintain its equality with an equally just appreciation of the products of artistic imagination, in spite of much greater beauty in the latter. And similarly though God may be admitted to be a more perfect object than any actual human being, the love of God may yet be inferior to human love, *if* God does not exist.

(4) In order to complete the discussion of this first class of goods — goods which have an essential reference to *beautiful* objects — it would be necessary to attempt a classification and comparative valuation of all the different forms of beauty, a task which properly belongs to the study called Aesthetics. I do not, however, propose to attempt any part of this task. It must only be understood that I intend to include among the essential constituents of the goods I have been discussing, every form and variety of beautiful object, if only it be truly beautiful; and, *if* this be understood, I think it may be seen that the consensus of opinion with regard to what is positively beautiful and what is positively ugly, and even with regard to great differences in degree of beauty, is quite sufficient to allow us a hope that we need not greatly err in our judgments of good and evil. In anything which is thought beautiful by any considerable number of persons, there is probably *some* beautiful quality; and differences of opinion seem to be far more often due to exclusive attention, on the part of different persons, to different qualities in the same object, than to the positive error of supposing a quality that is ugly to be really beautiful. When an object, which some think beautiful, is denied to be so by others, the truth is *usually* that it lacks some beautiful quality or is

deformed by some ugly one, which engage the exclusive attention of the critics.

I may, however, state two general principles, closely connected with the results of this chapter, the recognition of which would seem to be of great importance for the investigation of what things are truly beautiful. The first of these is (1) a definition of beauty, of what is meant by saying that a thing is truly beautiful. The naturalistic fallacy has been quite as commonly committed with regard to beauty as with regard to good: its use has introduced as many errors into Aesthetics as into Ethics. It has been even more commonly supposed that the beautiful may be *defined* as that which produces certain effects upon our feelings; and the conclusion which follows from this — namely, that judgments of taste are merely *subjective* — that precisely the same thing may, according to circumstances, be *both* beautiful *and* not beautiful — has very frequently been drawn. The conclusions of this chapter suggest a definition of beauty, which may partially explain and entirely remove the difficulties which have led to this error. It appears probable that the beautiful should be *defined* as that of which the admiring contemplation is good in itself. That is to say: To assert that a thing is beautiful is to assert that the cognition of it is an essential element in one of the intrinsically valuable wholes we have been discussing; so that the question, whether it is *truly* beautiful or not, depends upon the *objective* question whether the whole in question is or is not truly good, and does not depend upon the question whether it would or would not excite particular feelings in particular persons. This definition has the double recommendation that it accounts both for the apparent connection between goodness and beauty and for the no less apparent difference between these two conceptions. It appears, at first sight, to be a strange coincidence, that there should be two *different* objective predicates of value, 'good' and 'beautiful,' which are nevertheless so related to one another that whatever is beautiful is also good. But, if our definition be correct, the strangeness disappears; since it leaves only one *unanalysable* predicate of value, namely 'good,' while 'beautiful,' though not identical with, is to be defined by reference to this, being thus, at the same time, different from and necessarily connected with it. In short. on this view, to say that a thing is beautiful is to say, not indeed that it is itself good, but that it is a necessary element in something which is: to prove that a thing is truly beautiful is to prove that a whole, to which it bears a particular relation as a part, is truly good. And in this way we should explain the immense predominance, among objects commonly considered beautiful, of *material* objects — objects of the external senses; since these objects, though themselves having, as has been said, little or no intrinsic value, are yet essential constituents in the largest group of wholes which have intrinsic value. These wholes themselves may be, and are, also beautiful; but the comparative rarity, with which we regard them as themselves *objects* of contemplation, seems sufficient to explain the association of beauty with external objects.

And secondly (2) it is to be observed that beautiful objects are themselves, for the most part, organic unities, in this sense, that they are wholes of great complexity, such that the contemplation of any part, by itself, may have no value, and yet that, unless the contemplation of the whole includes the contemplation of that part, it will lose in value. From this it follows that there can be no single criterion of beauty. It will never be true to say: This object owes its beauty *solely* to the presence of this characteristic; nor yet that: Wherever this characteristic is present, the object must be beautiful. All that can be true is that certain objects are beautiful, *because* they have certain characteristics, in the sense that they would not be beautiful *unless* they had them. And it may be possible to find that certain characteristics are more or less universally present in all beautiful objects, and are, in this sense, more or less important conditions of beauty. But it is important to observe that the very qualities, which differentiate one beautiful object from all others, are, if the object be truly beautiful, as *essential* to its beauty, as those which it has in common with ever so many others. The object would no more have the beauty it has, without the specific qualities, than without those that are generic; and the generic qualities, *by themselves,* would fail, as completely, to give beauty, as those which are specific.

B

A comparison of the definitions of metaphysics and the various conceptions of the absolute leads to the discovery that philoso-

Henri Bergson, *An Introduction to Metaphysics,* translated by T. E. Hulme, New York, G. P. Putnam's Sons, 1912, pp. 1–9, 25–29, 89–92. Reprinted by permission of the publishers.

phers, in spite of their apparent divergencies, agree in distinguishing two profoundly different ways of knowing a thing. The first implies that we move round the object; the second that we enter into it. The first depends on the point of view at which we are placed

and on the symbols by which we express ourselves. The second neither depends on a point
of view nor relies on any symbol. The first
kind of knowledge may be said to stop at the
relative; the second, in those cases where it is
possible, to attain the *absolute.*

Consider, for example, the movement of
an object in space. My perception of the motion will vary with the point of view, moving or stationary, from which I observe it.
My expression of it will vary with the systems of axes, or the points of reference, to
which I relate it; that is, with the symbols
by which I translate it. For this double reason I call such motion *relative:* in the one
case, as in the other, I am placed outside the
object itself. But when I speak of an *absolute*
movement, I am attributing to the moving
object an interior and, so to speak, states of
mind; I also imply that I am in sympathy
with those states, and that I insert myself in
them by an effort of imagination. Then, according as the object is moving or stationary,
according as it adopts one movement or another, what I experience will vary. And what
I experience will depend neither on the point
of view I may take up in regard to the object, since I am inside the object itself, nor
on the symbols by which I may translate the
motion, since I have rejected all translations
in order to possess the original. In short, I
shall no longer grasp the movement from
without, remaining where I am, but from
where it is, from within, as it is in itself. I
shall possess an absolute.

Consider, again, a character whose adventures are related to me in a novel. The author
may multiply the traits of his hero's character,
may make him speak and act as much as he
pleases, but all this can never be equivalent
to the simple and indivisible feeling which I
should experience if I were able for an instant
to identify myself with the person of the hero

himself. Out of that indivisible feeling, as
from a spring, all the words, gestures, and actions of the man would appear to me to flow
naturally. They would no longer be accidents
which, added to the idea I had already formed
of the character, continually enriched that
idea, without ever completing it. The character would be given to me all at once, in its
entirety, and the thousand incidents which
manifest it, instead of adding themselves to
the idea and so enriching it, would seem to
me, on the contrary, to detach themselves
from it, without, however, exhausting it or
impoverishing its essence. All the things I am
told about the man provide me with so many
points of view from which I can observe him.
All the traits which describe him, and which
can make him known to me only by so many
comparisons with persons or things I know
already, are signs by which he is expressed
more or less symbolically. Symbols and points
of view, therefore, place me outside him; they
give me only what he has in common with
others, and not what belongs to him and to
him alone. But that which is properly himself, that which constitutes his essence, cannot be perceived from without, being internal
by definition, nor be expressed by symbols,
being incommensurable with everything else.
Description, history, and analysis leave me
here in the relative. Coincidence with the person himself would alone give me the absolute.

It is in this sense, and in this sense only,
that *absolute* is synonymous with *perfection.*
Were all the photographs of a town, taken
from all possible points of view, to go on indefinitely completing one another, they would
never be equivalent to the solid town in which
we walk about. Were all the translations of a
poem into all possible languages to add together their various shades of meaning and,
correcting each other by a kind of mutual re-

touching, to give a more and more faithful image of the poem they translate, they would yet never succeed in rendering the inner meaning of the original. A representation taken from a certain point of view, a translation made with certain symbols, will always remain imperfect in comparison with the object of which a view has been taken, or which the symbols seek to express. But the absolute, which is the object and not its representation, the original and not its translation, is perfect, by being perfectly what it is.

It is doubtless for this reason that the *absolute* has often been identified with the *infinite.* Suppose that I wished to communicate to some one who did not know Greek the extraordinarily simple impression that a passage in Homer makes upon me; I should first give a translation of the lines, I should then comment on my translation, and then develop the commentary; in this way, by piling up explanation on explanation, I might approach nearer and nearer to what I wanted to express; but I should never quite reach it. When you raise your arm, you accomplish a movement of which you have, from within, a simple perception; but for me, watching it from the outside, your arm passes through one point, then through another, and between these two there will be still other points; so that, if I began to count, the operation would go on for ever. Viewed from the inside, then, an absolute is a simple thing; but looked at from the outside, that is to say, relatively to other things, it becomes, in relation to these signs which express it, the gold coin for which we never seem able to finish giving small change. Now, that which lends itself at the same time both to an indivisible apprehension and to an inexhaustible enumeration is, by the very definition of the word, an infinite.

It follows from this that an absolute could only be given in an *intuition,* whilst every-

thing else falls within the province of *analysis.* By intuition is meant the kind of *intellectual sympathy* by which one places oneself within an object in order to coincide with what is unique in it and consequently inexpressible. Analysis, on the contrary, is the operation which reduces the object to elements already known, that is, to elements common both to it and other objects. To analyze, therefore, is to express a thing as a function of something other than itself. All analysis is thus a translation, a development into symbols, a representation taken from successive points of view from which we note as many resemblances as possible between the new object which we are studying and others which we believe we know already. In its eternally unsatisfied desire to embrace the object around which it is compelled to turn, analysis multiplies without end the number of its points of view in order to complete its always incomplete representation, and ceaselessly varies its symbols that it may perfect the always imperfect translation. It goes on, therefore, to infinity. But intuition, if intuition is possible, is a simple act.

Now it is easy to see that the ordinary function of positive science is analysis. Positive science works, then, above all, with symbols. Even the most concrete of the natural sciences, those concerned with life, confine themselves to the visible form of living beings, their organs and anatomical elements. They make comparisons between these forms, they reduce the more complex to the more simple; in short, they study the workings of life in what is, so to speak, only its visual symbol. If there exists any means of possessing a reality absolutely instead of knowing it relatively, of placing oneself within it instead of looking at it from outside points of view, of having the intuition instead of making the analysis: in short, of seizing it without any expression, translation, or symbolic representation — metaphysics is that means. *Metaphysics, then, is the science which claims to dispense with symbols. . . .*

It is incontestable that every psychical state, simply because it belongs to a person, reflects the whole of a personality. Every feeling, however simple it may be, contains virtually within it the whole past and present of the being experiencing it, and, consequently, can only be separated and constituted into a "state" by an effort of abstraction or of analysis. But it is no less incontestable that without this effort of abstraction or analysis there would be no possible development of the science of psychology. What, then, exactly, is the operation by which a psychologist detaches a mental state in order to erect it into a more or less independent entity? He begins by neglecting that special coloring of the personality which cannot be expressed in known and common terms. Then he endeavors to isolate, in the person already thus simplified, some aspect which lends itself to an interesting inquiry. If he is considering inclination, for example, he will neglect the inexpressible shade which colors it, and which makes the inclination mine and not yours; he will fix his attention on the movement by which our personality *leans towards* a certain object: he will isolate this attitude, and it is this special aspect of the personality, this snapshot of the mobility of the inner life, this "diagram" of concrete inclination, that he will erect into an independent fact. There is in this something very like what an artist passing through Paris does when he makes, for example, a sketch of a tower of Notre Dame. The tower is inseparably united to the building, which is itself no less inseparably united to the ground, to its surroundings, to the whole of Paris, and so on. It is first necessary to detach it from all these; only one aspect of the whole is noted, that formed by the tower of Notre Dame. Moreover, the special form of this tower is due to the grouping of the stones of which it is composed; but the artist does not concern himself with these stones, he notes only the silhouette of the tower. For the real and internal organization of the thing he substitutes, then, an external and schematic representation. So that, on the whole, his sketch corresponds to an observation of the object from a certain point of view and to the choice of a certain means of representation. But exactly the same thing holds true of the operation by which the psychologist extracts a single mental state from the whole personality. This isolated psychical state is hardly anything but a sketch, the commencement of an artificial reconstruction; it is the whole considered under a certain elementary aspect in which we are specially interested and which we have carefully noted. It is not a part, but an element. It has not been obtained by a natural dismemberment, but by analysis.

Now beneath all the sketches he has made at Paris the visitor will probably, by way of memento, write the word "Paris." And as he has really seen Paris, he will be able, with the help of the original intuition he had of the whole, to place his sketches therein, and so join them up together. But there is no way of performing the inverse operation; it is impossible, even with an infinite number of accurate sketches, and even with the word "Paris" which indicates that they must be combined together, to get back to an intuition that one has never had, and to give oneself an impression of what Paris is like if one has never seen it. This is because we are not dealing here with real *parts,* but with mere *notes* of the total impression. To take a still more striking example, where the notation is more completely symbolic, suppose that I am shown, mixed together at random, the letters which make up a poem I am ignorant of. If the letters were *parts* of the poem, I could attempt to reconstitute the poem with them by trying the different possible arrangements, as a child does with the pieces of a Chinese puzzle. But I should never for a moment think of attempting such a thing in this case, because the letters are not *component parts,* but only *partial expressions,* which is quite a different thing. That is why, if I know the poem, I at once put each of the letters in its proper place and join them up without difficulty by a continuous connection, whilst the inverse operation is impossible. Even when I believe I am actually attempting this inverse operation, even when I put the letters end to end, I begin by thinking of some plausible meaning. I thereby give myself an intuition, and from this intuition I attempt to redescend to the elementary symbols which would reconstitute its expression. The very idea of reconstituting a thing by operations practised on symbolic elements alone implies such an absurdity that it would never occur to any one if they recollected that they were not dealing with fragments of the thing, but only, as it were, with fragments of its symbol. . . .

In conclusion, we may remark that there is nothing mysterious in this faculty. Every one of us has had occasion to exercise it to a certain extent. Any one of us, for instance, who has attempted literary composition, knows that when the subject has been studied at length, the materials all collected, and the notes all made, something more is needed in order to set about the work of composition itself, and that is an often very painful effort to place

ourselves directly at the heart of the subject, and to seek as deeply as possible an impulse, after which we need only let ourselves go. This impulse, once received, starts the mind on a path where it rediscovers all the information it had collected, and a thousand other details besides; it develops and analyzes itself into terms which could be enumerated indefinitely. The farther we go, the more terms we discover; we shall never say all that could be said, and yet, if we turn back suddenly upon the impulse that we feel behind us, and try to seize it, it is gone; for it was not a thing, but the direction of a movement, and though indefinitely extensible, it is infinitely simple. Metaphysical intuition seems to be something of the same kind. What corresponds here to the documents and notes of literary composition is the sum of observations and experience gathered together by positive science. For we do not obtain an intuition from reality — that is, an intellectual sympathy with the most intimate part of it — unless we have won its confidence by a long fellowship with its superficial manifestations. And it is not merely a question of assimilating the most conspicuous facts; so immense a mass of facts must be accumulated and fused together, that in this fusion all the preconceived and premature ideas which observers may unwittingly have put into their observations will be certain to neutralize each other. In this way only can the bare materiality of the known facts be exposed to view. Even in the simple and privileged case which we have used as an example, even for the direct contact of the self with the self, the final effort of distinct intuition would be impossible to any one who had not combined and compared with each other a very large number of psychological analyses. The masters of modern philosophy were men who had assimilated all the scientific knowledge of their time, and the partial eclipse of metaphysics for the last half-century has evidently no other cause than the extraordinary difficulty which the philosopher finds to-day in getting into touch with positive science, which has become far too specialized. But metaphysical intuition, although it can be obtained only through material knowledge, is quite other than the mere summary or synthesis of that knowledge. It is distinct from these, we repeat, as the motor impulse is distinct from the path traversed by the moving body, as the tension of the spring is distinct from the visible movements of the pendulum. In this sense metaphysics has nothing in common with a generalization of facts, and nevertheless it might be defined as *integral experience.*

SUGGESTIONS FOR THOUGHT

1. Try to describe a spiral staircase without using your hands! What difficulties would you encounter in trying to give all the information given on a blueprint by the use of words alone?

2. "The limitations of discourse are notorious and not only the deepest truths but the simplest facts may be unutterable. How describe the taste of a pear, the color of Venetian glass, the curve of a particular forehead, and the unique emotion which it produces in me at this given moment, in this given mood and light?" (Irwin Edman) What other examples can you give of "thoughts that break the backs of words"? Why is "Say it with flowers" a good slogan?

3. Can you grasp what the artist is saying in his music without reading about the composition? Can you sense the emotional situation in a movie by closing your eyes and listening to the musical background?

4. What is the difference between reading a love story and being in love? Can this difference be correctly described as experience? What is the difference between knowing by description and knowing by experience?

5. Coleridge said, "Poetry gives most pleasure when most generally and not perfectly understood; and perfect understanding will sometimes almost extinguish pleasure." Do you agree? How can one justify the use of language in such a way that one will not be perfectly understood?

6. Would poetry be improved if all the statements made in a poem were meaningful as judged by a scientific criterion of meaning? E.g., if the poet said not that the sun arose but rather that the earth turned.

7. What are the distinctions between art and science to which Brand Blanshard points in his observation: "The artist discovers when he creates, the scientist creates when he discovers"?

8. The English astronomer A. S. Eddington, in discussing possible theories of the origin of the earth, writes: " . . . it seems to me that the most satisfactory theory would be one which made the beginning not too unaesthetically abrupt." Why should scientific theories be evaluated in part on their aesthetic properties?

9. Does knowledge help or hinder one's appreciation of beauty? Ruskin, after a lengthy study of architecture in Venice, reported: "I went through so much hard, dry mechanical toil there that I quite lost the charm of the place. Analysis is an abominable business. I am quite sure that people who work out subjects thoroughly are disagreeable wretches." What would you reply to Ruskin?

SUGGESTIONS FOR FURTHER READING

COLLINGWOOD, R. G., *The Principles of Art,* London, Oxford University Press, 1938, ch. 13.

CROCE, BENEDETTO, *Aesthetic as Science of Expression and General Linguistic,* translated by Douglas Ainslie, New York, The Macmillan Company, 1909, ch. 1.

DEMOS, RAPHAEL, "The Spectrum of Knowledge," *The Philosophical Review,* Vol. 56, 1947, pp. 237–257.

GAMERTSFELDER, W. D. and EVANS, D. L., *Fundamentals of Philosophy,* New York, Prentice-Hall, 1930, pp. 202–228.

GARVIN, LUCIUS, "An Emotionalist Critique of Artistic Truth," *The Journal of Philosophy,* Vol. 43, 1946, pp. 435–441.

GREENE, THEODORE MEYER, *The Arts and the Art of Criticism,* Princeton, Princeton University Press, 1940, ch. 23.

HOSPERS, JOHN, *Meaning and Truth in the Arts,* Chapel Hill, University of North Carolina Press, 1946.

HUGHESDON, P. J., "The Relation Between Art and Science," *Mind,* Vol. 27, 1918, pp. 55–76.

JARRETT, JAMES L., "Art as Cognitive Experience," *The Journal of Philosophy,* Vol. 50, 1953, pp. 681–688.

LAIRD, JOHN, *Knowledge, Belief and Opinion,* New York, Century Company, 1930, chs. 4–6.

LEON, P., "Aesthetic Knowledge," *Proceedings of the Aristotelian Society,* Vol. 25, 1925, pp. 199–208.

OGDEN, R. M., "Science and Knowledge," *The Philosophical Review,* Vol. 51, 1942, pp. 559–573.

PARKER, DE WITT H., "Knowledge by Acquaintance," *The Philosophical Review,* Vol. 54, 1945, pp. 1–18.

PRICE, KINGSLEY BLAKE, "Is a Work of Art a Symbol?" *The Journal of Philosophy,* Vol. 50, 1953, pp. 485–503.

RICHARDS, I. A., *The Principles of Literary Criticism,* New York, Harcourt Brace and Company, 1930, ch. 34.

RUSSELL, BERTRAND, *Mysticism and Logic, and Other Essays,* New York, Longmans Green and Company, 1925, ch. 10.

20

ART AND VALUES

AS IS WELL KNOWN, Plato banished most of the artists, poets, and musicians from his ideal state. The following selection from *The Republic* is his defense of this banishment. Lawrence Pearsall Jacks (1860–   ) would place beauty as the chief of the values — a position which Plato assigned to good·ness. Jacks is an English educator and editor. He held teaching and ad-ministrative positions at Manchester College, Oxford University, from 1903 to 1931. He was editor of *The Hibbert Journal* from its founding in 1902 to his retirement from the editorship in 1947.

A

Of the many excellencies which I perceive in the order of our State, there is none which upon reflection pleases me better than the rule about poetry.

To what do you refer?

To the rejection of imitative poetry, which certainly ought not to be received; as I see far more clearly now that the parts of the soul have been distinguished.

What do you mean?

Speaking in confidence, for I should not like to have my words repeated to the tragedians and the rest of the imitative tribe — but I do not mind saying to you, that all poetical imi-tations are ruinous to the understanding of the hearers, and that the knowledge of their true nature is the only antidote to them.

Explain the purport of your remark.

Well, I will tell you, although I have al-ways from my earliest youth had an awe and love of Homer, which even now makes the words falter on my lips, for he is the great captain and teacher of the whole of that charming tragic company; but a man is not to be reverenced more than the truth, and there·fore I will speak out.

Very good, he said.

Plato, *Republic, The Dialogues of Plato,* Vol. 3, translated by Benjamin Jowett, Oxford, The Claren-don Press, Third Edition, 1892, pp. 307–323.

Listen to me then, or rather, answer me.

Put your question.

Can you tell me what imitation is? for I really do not know.

A likely thing, then, that I should know.

Why not? for the duller eye may often see a thing sooner than the keener.

Very true, he said; but in your presence, even if I had any faint notion, I could not muster courage to utter it. Will you enquire yourself?

Well then, shall we begin the enquiry in our usual manner: Whenever a number of individuals have a common name, we assume them to have also a corresponding idea or form: — do you understand me?

I do.

Let us take any common instance; there are beds and tables in the world — plenty of them, are there not?

Yes.

But there are only two ideas or forms of them — one the idea of a bed, the other of a table.

True.

And the maker of either of them makes a bed or he makes a table for our use, in accordance with the idea — that is our way of speaking in this and similar instances — but no artificer makes the ideas themselves: how could he?

Impossible.

And there is another artist, — I should like to know what you would say of him.

Who is he?

One who is the maker of all the works of all other workmen.

What an extraordinary man!

Wait a little, and there will be more reason for your saying so. For this is he who is able to make not only vessels of every kind, but plants and animals, himself and all other things — the earth and heaven, and the things which are in heaven or under the earth; he makes the gods also.

He must be a wizard and no mistake.

Oh! you are incredulous, are you? Do you mean that there is no such maker or creator, or that in one sense there might be a maker of all these things but in another not? Do you see that there is a way in which you could make them all yourself?

What way?

An easy way enough; or rather, there are many ways in which the feat might be quickly and easily accomplished, none quicker than that of turning a mirror round and round — you would soon enough make the sun and the heavens, and the earth and yourself, and other animals and plants, and all the other things of which we were just now speaking, in the mirror.

Yes, he said; but they would be appearances only.

Very good, I said, you are coming to the point now. And the painter too is, as I conceive, just such another — a creator of appearances, is he not?

Of course.

But then I suppose you will say that what he creates is untrue. And yet there is a sense in which the painter also creates a bed?

Yes, he said, but not a real bed.

And what of the maker of the bed? were you not saying that he too makes, not the idea which, according to our view, is the essence of the bed, but only a particular bed?

Yes, I did.

Then if he does not make that which exists he cannot make true existence, but only some semblance of existence; and if any one were to say that the work of the maker of the bed, or of any other workman, has real existence, he could hardly be supposed to be speaking the truth.

At any rate, he replied, philosophers would say that he was not speaking the truth.

No wonder, then, that his work too is an indistinct expression of truth.

No wonder.

Suppose now that by the light of the examples just offered we enquire who this imitator is?

If you please.

Well then, here are three beds: one existing in nature, which is made by God, as I think that we may say — for no one else can be the maker?

No.

There is another which is the work of the carpenter?

Yes.

And the work of the painter is a third?

Yes.

Beds, then, are of three kinds, and there are three artists who superintend them: God, the maker of the bed, and the painter?

Yes, there are three of them.

God, whether from choice or from necessity, made one bed in nature and one only; two or more such ideal beds neither ever have been nor ever will be made by God.

Why is that?

Because even if He had made but two, a third would still appear behind them which both of them would have for their idea, and that would be the ideal bed and not the two others.

Very true, he said.

God knew this, and He desired to be the real maker of a real bed, not a particular maker of a particular bed, and therefore he created a bed which is essentially and by nature one only.

So we believe.

Shall we, then, speak of Him as the natural author or maker of the bed?

Yes, he replied; inasmuch as by the natural process of creation He is the author of this and of all other things.

And what shall we say of the carpenter — is not he also the maker of the bed?

Yes.

But would you call the painter a creator and maker?

Certainly not.

Yet if he is not the maker, what is he in relation to the bed?

I think, he said, that we may fairly designate him as the imitator of that which the others make.

Good, I said; then you call him who is third in the descent from nature an imitator?

Certainly, he said.

And the tragic poet is an imitator, and therefore, like all other imitators, he is thrice removed from the king and from the truth?

That appears to be so.

Then about the imitator we are agreed. And what about the painter? — I would like to know whether he may be thought to imitate that which originally exists in nature, or only the creations of artists?

The latter.

As they are or as they appear? you have still to determine this.

What do you mean?

I mean, that you may look at a bed from different points of view, obliquely or directly or from any other point of view, and the bed will appear different, but there is no difference in reality. And the same of all things.

Yes, he said, the difference is only apparent.

Now let me ask you another question: Which is the art of painting designed to be — an imitation of things as they are, or as they appear — of appearance or of reality?

Of appearance.

Then the imitator, I said, is a long way off

the truth, and can do all things because he lightly touches on a small part of them, and that part an image. For example: A painter will paint a cobbler, carpenter, or any other artist, though he knows nothing of their arts; and, if he is a good artist, he may deceive children or simple persons, when he shows them his picture of a carpenter from a distance, and they will fancy that they are looking at a real carpenter.

Certainly.

And whenever any one informs us that he has found a man who knows all the arts, and all things else that anybody knows, and every single thing with a higher degree of accuracy than any other man — whoever tells us this, I think that we can only imagine him to be a simple creature who is likely to have been deceived by some wizard or actor whom he met, and whom he thought all-knowing, because he himself was unable to analyse the nature of knowledge and ignorance and imitation.

Most true.

And so, when we hear persons saying that the tragedians, and Homer, who is at their head, know all the arts and all things human, virtue as well as vice, and divine things too, for that the good poet cannot compose well unless he knows his subject, and that he who has not this knowledge can never be a poet, we ought to consider whether here also there may not be a similar illusion. Perhaps they may have come across imitators and been deceived by them; they may not have remembered when they saw their works that these were but imitations thrice removed from the truth, and could easily be made without any knowledge of the truth, because they are appearances only and not realities? Or, after all, they may be in the right, and poets do really know the things about which they seem to the many to speak so well?

The question, he said, should by all means be considered.

Now do you suppose that if a person were able to make the original as well as the image, he would seriously devote himself to the image-making branch? Would he allow imitation to be the ruling principle of his life, as if he had nothing higher in him?

I should say not.

The real artist, who knew what he was imitating, would be interested in realities and not in imitations; and would desire to leave as memorials of himself works many and fair; and, instead of being the author of encomiums, he would prefer to be the theme of them.

Yes, he said, that would be to him a source of much greater honour and profit.

Then, I said, we must put a question to Homer; not about medicine, or any of the arts to which his poems only incidentally refer: we are not going to ask him, or any other poet, whether he has cured patients like Asclepius, or left behind him a school of medicine such as the Asclepiads were, or whether he only talks about medicine and other arts at second-hand; but we have a right to know respecting military tactics, politics, education, which are the chiefest and noblest subjects of his poems, and we may fairly ask him about them. 'Friend Homer,' then we say to him, 'if you are only in the second remove from truth in what you say of virtue, and not in the third — not an image maker or imitator — and if you are able to discern what pursuits make men better or worse in private or public life, tell us what State was ever better governed by your help? The good order of Lacedaemon is due to Lycurgus, and many other cities great and small have been similarly benefited by others; but who says that you have been a good legislator to them and have done them any good? Italy and Sicily boast of Charondas, and there is a Solon who is renowned among us; but what city has anything to say about you? Is there any city which he might name?

I think not, said Glaucon; not even the Homerids themselves pretend that he was a legislator.

Well, but is there any war on record which was carried on successfully by him, or aided by his counsels, when he was alive?

There is not.

Or is there any invention of his, applicable to the arts or to human life, such as Thales the Milesian or Anacharsis the Scythian, and other ingenious men have conceived, which is attributed to him?

There is absolutely nothing of the kind.

But, if Homer never did any public service, was he privately a guide or teacher of any? Had he in his lifetime friends who loved to associate with him, and who handed down to posterity an Homeric way of life, such as was established by Pythagoras who was so greatly beloved for his wisdom, and whose followers are to this day quite celebrated for the order which was named after him?

Nothing of the kind is recorded of him. For surely, Socrates, Creophylus, the companion of Homer, that child of flesh, whose name always makes us laugh, might be more justly ridiculed for his stupidity, if, as is said, Homer was greatly neglected by him and others in his own day when he was alive?

Yes, I replied, that is the tradition. But can you imagine, Glaucon, that if Homer had really been able to educate and improve mankind — if he had possessed knowledge and not been a mere imitator — can you imagine, I say, that he would not have had many followers, and been honoured and loved by them? Protagoras of Abdera, and Prodicus of Ceos, and a host of others, have only to whisper to their contemporaries: 'You will never be able to manage either your own house or your own

State until you appoint us to be your ministers of education' — and this ingenious device of theirs has such an effect in making men love them that their companions all but carry them about on their shoulders. And is it conceivable that the contemporaries of Homer, or again of Hesiod, would have allowed either of them to go about as rhapsodists, if they had really been able to make mankind virtuous? Would they not have been as unwilling to part with them as with gold, and have compelled them to stay at home with them? Or, if the master would not stay, then the disciples would have followed him about everywhere, until they had got education enough?

Yes, Socrates, that, I think, is quite true.

Then must we not infer that all these poetical individuals, beginning with Homer, are only imitators; they copy images of virtue and the like, but the truth they never reach? The poet is like a painter who, as we have already observed, will make a likeness of a cobbler though he understands nothing of cobbling; and his picture is good enough for those who know no more than he does, and judge only by colours and figures.

Quite so.

In like manner the poet with his words and phrases may be said to lay on the colours of the several arts, himself understanding their nature only enough to imitate them; and other people, who are as ignorant as he is, and judge only from his words, imagine that if he speaks of cobbling, or of military tactics, or of anything else, in metre and harmony and rhythm, he speaks very well — such is the sweet influence which melody and rhythm by nature have. And I think that you must have observed again and again what a poor appearance the tales of poets make when stripped of the colours which music puts upon them, and recited in simple prose.

Yes, he said.

They are like faces which were never really beautiful, but only blooming; and now the bloom of youth has passed away from them?

Exactly.

Here is another point: The imitator or maker of the image knows nothing of true existence; he knows appearances only. Am I not right?

Yes.

Then let us have a clear understanding, and not be satisfied with half an explanation.

Proceed.

Of the painter we say that he will paint reins, and he will paint a bit?

Yes.

And the worker in leather and brass will make them?

Certainly.

But does the painter know the right form of the bit and reins? Nay, hardly even the workers in brass and leather who make them; only the horseman who knows how to use them — he knows their right form.

Most true.

And may we not say the same of all things?

What?

That there are three arts which are concerned with all things: one which uses, another which makes, a third which imitates them?

Yes.

And the excellence or beauty or truth of every structure, animate or inanimate, and of every action of man, is relative to the use for which nature or the artist has intended them.

True.

Then the user of them must have the greatest experience of them, and he must indicate to the maker the good or bad qualities which develop themselves in use; for example, the flute-player will tell the flute-maker which of his flutes is satisfactory to the performer; he will tell him how he ought to make them, and the other will attend to his instructions?

Of course.

The one knows and therefore speaks with authority about the goodness and badness of flutes, while the other, confiding in him, will do what he is told by him?

True.

The instrument is the same, but about the excellence or badness of it the maker will only attain to a correct belief; and this he will gain from him who knows, by talking to him and being compelled to hear what he has to say, whereas the user will have knowledge?

True.

But will the imitator have either? Will he know from use whether or no his drawing is correct or beautiful? or will he have right opinion from being compelled to associate with another who knows and gives him instructions about what he should draw?

Neither.

Then he will no more have true opinion than he will have knowledge about the goodness or badness of his imitations?

I suppose not.

The imitative artist will be in a brilliant state of intelligence about his own creations?

Nay, very much the reverse.

And still he will go on imitating without knowing what makes a thing good or bad, and may be expected therefore to imitate only that which appears to be good to the ignorant multitude?

Just so.

Thus far then we are pretty well agreed that the imitator has no knowledge worth mentioning of what he imitates. Imitation is only a kind of play or sport, and the tragic poets, whether they write in Iambic or in Heroic verse, are imitators in the highest degree.

Very true.

And now tell me, I conjure you, has not imitation been shown by us to be concerned with that which is thrice removed from the truth?

Certainly.

And what is the faculty in man to which imitation is addressed?

What do you mean?

I will explain: The body which is large when seen near, appears small when seen at a distance?

True.

And the same objects appear straight when looked at out of the water, and crooked when in the water; and the concave becomes convex, owing to the illusion about colours to which the sight is liable. Thus every sort of confusion is revealed within us; and this is that weakness of the human mind on which the art of conjuring and of deceiving by light and shadow and other ingenious devices imposes, having an effect upon us like magic.

True.

And the arts of measuring and numbering and weighing come to the rescue of the human understanding—there is the beauty of them—and the apparent greater or less, or more or heavier, no longer have the mastery over us, but give way before calculation and measure and weight?

Most true.

And this, surely, must be the work of the calculating and rational principle in the soul?

To be sure.

And when this principle measures and certifies that some things are equal, or that some are greater or less than others, there occurs an apparent contradiction?

True.

But were we not saying that such a contradiction is impossible—the same faculty cannot have contrary opinions at the same time about the same thing?

Very true.

Then that part of the soul which has an opinion contrary to measure is not the same with that which has an opinion in accordance with measure?

True.

And the better part of the soul is likely to be that which trusts to measure and calculation?

Certainly.

And that which is opposed to them is one of the inferior principles of the soul?

No doubt.

This was the conclusion at which I was seeking to arrive when I said that painting or drawing, and imitation in general, when doing their own proper work, are far removed from truth, and the companions and friends and associates of a principle within us which is equally removed from reason, and that they have no true or healthy aim.

Exactly.

The imitative art is an inferior who marries an inferior and has inferior offspring.

Very true.

And is this confined to the sight only, or does it extend to the hearing also, relating in fact to what we term poetry?

Probably the same would be true of poetry.

Do not rely, I said, on a probability derived from the analogy of painting; but let us examine further and see whether the faculty with which poetical imitation is concerned is good or bad.

By all means.

We may state the question thus:—Imitation imitates the actions of men, whether voluntary or involuntary, on which, as they imagine, a good or bad result has ensued, and they rejoice or sorrow accordingly. Is there anything more?

No, there is nothing else.

But in all this variety of circumstances is the man at unity with himself—or rather, as in the instance of sight there was confusion and opposition in his opinions about the same things, so here also is there not strife and inconsistency in his life? Though I need hardly raise the question again, for I remember that all this has been already admitted; and the soul has been acknowledged by us to be full of these and ten thousand similar oppositions occurring at the same moment?

And we were right, he said.

Yes, I said, thus far we were right; but there was an omission which must now be supplied.

What was the omission?

Were we not saying that a good man, who has the misfortune to lose his son or anything else which is most dear to him, will bear the loss with more equanimity than another?

Yes.

But will he have no sorrow, or shall we say that although he cannot help sorrowing, he will moderate his sorrow?

The latter, he said, is the truer statement.

Tell me: will he be more likely to struggle and hold out against his sorrow when he is ,seen by his equals, or when he is alone?

It will make a great difference whether he is seen or not.

When he is by himself he will not mind saying or doing many things which he would be ashamed of any one hearing or seeing him do?

True.

There is a principle of law and reason in him which bids him resist, as well as a feeling of his misfortune which is forcing him to indulge his sorrow?

True.

But when a man is drawn in two opposite directions, to and from the same object, this, as we affirm, necessarily implies two distinct principles in him?

Certainly.

One of them is ready to follow the guidance of the law?

How do you mean?

The law would say that to be patient under suffering is best, and that we should not give way to impatience, as there is no knowing whether such things are good or evil; and nothing is gained by impatience; also, because no human thing is of serious importance, and grief stands in the way of that which at the moment is most required.

What is most required? he asked.

That we should take counsel about what has happened, and when the dice have been thrown order our affairs in the way which reason deems best; not, like children who have had a fall, keeping hold of the part struck and wasting time in setting up a howl, but always accustoming the soul forthwith to apply a remedy, raising up that which is sickly and fallen, banishing the cry of sorrow by the healing art.

Yes, he said, that is the true way of meeting the attacks of fortune.

Yes, I said; and the higher principle is ready to follow this suggestion of reason?

Clearly.

And the other principle, which inclines us to recollection of our troubles and to lamentation, and can never have enough of them, we may call irrational, useless, and cowardly?

Indeed, we may.

And does not the latter — I mean the rebellious principle — furnish a great variety of materials for imitation? Whereas the wise and calm temperament, being always nearly equable, is not easy to imitate or to appreciate when imitated, especially at a public festival when a promiscuous crowd is assembled in a theatre. For the feeling represented is one to which they are strangers.

Certainly.

Then the imitative poet who aims at being popular is not by nature made, nor is his art intended, to please or to affect the rational principle in the soul; but he will prefer the passionate and fitful temper, which is easily imitated?

Clearly.

And now we may fairly take him and place him by the side of the painter, for he is like him in two ways: first, inasmuch as his creations have an inferior degree of truth — in this, I say, he is like him; and he is also like him in being concerned with an inferior part of the soul; and therefore we shall be right in refusing to admit him into a well-ordered State, because he awakens and nourishes and strengthens the feelings and impairs the reason. As in a city when the evil are permitted to have authority and the good are put out of the way, so in the soul of man, as we maintain, the imitative poet implants an evil constitution, for he indulges the irrational nature which has no discernment of greater and less, but thinks the same thing at one time great and at another small — he is a manufacturer of images and is very far removed from the truth.

Exactly.

But we have not yet brought forward the heaviest count in our accusation: — the power which poetry has of harming even the good (and there are very few who are not harmed), is surely an awful thing?

Yes, certainly, if the effect is what you say.

Hear and judge: The best of us, as I conceive, when we listen to a passage of Homer, or one of the tragedians, in which he represents some pitiful hero who is drawling out his sorrows in a long oration, or weeping, and smiting his breast — the best of us, you know, delight in giving way to sympathy, and are in raptures at the excellence of the poet who stirs our feelings most.

Yes, of course I know.

But when any sorrow of our own happens to us, then you may observe that we pride ourselves on the opposite quality — we would fain be quiet and patient; this is the manly part, and the other which delighted us in the recitation is now deemed to be the part of a woman.

Very true, he said.

Now can we be right in praising and admiring another who is doing that which any one of us would abominate and be ashamed of in his own person?

No, he said, that is certainly not reasonable.

Nay, I said, quite reasonable from one point of view.

What point of view?

If you consider, I said, that when in misfortune we feel a natural hunger and desire to relieve our sorrow by weeping and lamentation, and that this feeling which is kept under control in our own calamities is satisfied and delighted by the poets; — the better nature in each of us, not having been sufficiently trained by reason or habit, allows the sympathetic element to break loose because the sorrow is another's; and the spectator fancies that there can be no disgrace to himself in praising and pitying any one who comes telling him what a good man he is, and making a fuss about his troubles; he thinks that the pleasure is a gain, and why should he be supercilious and lose this and the poem too? Few persons ever reflect, as I should imagine, that from the evil of other men something of evil is communicated to themselves. And so the feeling of sorrow which has gathered strength at the sight of the misfortunes of others is with difficulty repressed in our own.

How very true!

And does not the same hold also of the ridiculous? There are jests which you would be ashamed to make yourself, and yet on the comic stage, or indeed in private, when you hear them, you are greatly amused by them, and are not at all disgusted at their unseemliness; — the case of pity is repeated; — there is a principle in human nature which is disposed to raise a laugh, and this which you once restrained by reason, because you were afraid of being thought a buffoon, is now let out again; and having stimulated the risible faculty at the theatre, you are betrayed unconsciously to yourself into playing the comic poet at home.

Quite true, he said.

And the same may be said of lust and anger and all the other affections, of desire and pain and pleasure, which are held to be inseparable from every action — in all of them poetry feeds and waters the passions instead of drying them up; she lets them rule, although they ought to be controlled, if mankind are ever to increase in happiness and virtue.

I cannot deny it.

Therefore, Glaucon, I said, whenever you meet with any of the eulogists of Homer declaring that he has been the educator of Hellas, and that he is profitable for education and for the ordering of human things, and that you should take him up again and again and get to know him and regulate your whole life according to him, we may love and honour those who say these things — they are excellent people, as far as their lights extend; and we are ready to acknowledge that Homer is the greatest of poets and first of tragedy writers; but we must remain firm in our conviction that hymns to the gods and praises of famous men are the only poetry which ought to be admitted into our State. For if you go beyond this and allow the honeyed muse to enter, either in epic or lyric verse, not law and the reason of mankind, which by common consent have ever been deemed best, but pleasure and pain will be the rulers in our State.

That is most true, he said.

And now since we have reverted to the subject of poetry, let this our defence serve to show the reasonableness of our former judgment in sending away out of our State an art having the tendencies which we have described; for reason constrained us. But that she may not impute to us any harshness or want of politeness, let us tell her that there is an ancient quarrel between philosophy and poetry; of which there are many proofs, such as the saying of 'the yelping hound howling at her lord,' or of one 'mighty in the vain talk of fools,' and 'the mob of sages circumventing Zeus,' and the 'subtle thinkers who are beggars after all'; and there are innumerable other signs of ancient enmity between them. Notwithstanding this, let us assure our sweet friend and the sister arts of imitation, that if she will only prove her title to exist in a well-ordered State we shall be delighted to receive her — we are very conscious of her charms; but we may not on that account betray the truth. I dare say, Glaucon, that you are as much charmed by her as I am, especially when she appears in Homer?

Yes, indeed, I am greatly charmed.

Shall I propose, then, that she be allowed to return from exile, but upon this condition only — that she make a defence of herself in lyrical or some other metre?

Certainly.

And we may further grant to those of her defenders who are lovers of poetry and yet not poets the permission to speak in prose on her behalf: let them show not only that she is pleasant but also useful to States and to human life, and we will listen in a kindly spirit; for if this can be proved we shall surely be the gainers — I mean, if there is a use in poetry as well as a delight?

Certainly, he said, we shall be the gainers.

If her defence fails, then, my dear friend, like other persons who are enamoured of something, but put a restraint upon themselves when they think their desires are opposed to their interests, so too must we after the manner of lovers give her up, though not without a struggle. We too are inspired by that love of poetry which the education of noble States has implanted in us, and therefore we would have her appear at her best and truest; but so long as she is unable to make good her defence, this argument of ours shall be a charm to us, which we will repeat to ourselves while we listen to her strains; that we may not fall away into the childish love of her which captivates the many. At all events we are well aware that poetry being such as we have described is not to be regarded seriously as attaining to the truth; and he who listens to her, fearing for the safety of the city which is within him, should be on his guard against her seductions and make our words his law.

Yes, he said, I quite agree with you.

Yes, I said, my dear Glaucon, for great is the issues at stake, greater than appears, whether a man is to be good or bad. And what will any one be profited if under the influence of honour or money or power, aye, or under the excitement of poetry, he neglect justice and virtue?

B

There is one form of philosophy now widely adopted by eminent thinkers, and much in the ascendant, from which better results may be hoped for, though as yet, it must be confessed, they are not forthcoming. We refer to the Philosophy of Value.

This philosophy has a Trinitarian doctrine of its own. It defines the Ultimate Reality, indistinguishable from the Godhead, as a Trinity of Three Values, the Good, the True and the Beautiful. Though the statement of the Three in that order, the Good first and the Beautiful last, suggests a grading of importance, with the Good, so to say, as the senior partner and the Beautiful as the junior, it is not to be so understood, any more than the last place assigned to the Holy Ghost in the theological formula is to be understood as implying inferiority to the Father and the Son. The three Values form a Trinity in Unity, in which "none is afore and none after"

in exact analogy with their theological counterpart. Many who would hesitate or refuse to call themselves Trinitarians in the theological sense, are professed Trinitarians in the philosophical. Some would maintain that the two are variant expressions of the same fundamental truth. Whether Dean Inge is one of the latter we have no means of knowing. But he never loses a fitting opportunity in his writings to repeat the philosophical formula and present it as the climax of his philosophy. He cannot repeat it too often. Nor could his philosophy come to a more significant climax.

No philosophy can claim to be complete until it embraces the field of ethics and translates its findings, if not into terms of guidance for human conduct, at least into a moral ideal. If untranslatable into such terms it would have no relation to life and be justly condemned as no philosophy at all. So much pragmatism is latent in all philosophies, from the extreme of materialism to the extreme of mysticism, and not least in those that are definitely opposed to the school known as

L. P. Jacks, "The Cinderella of the Values," *The Hibbert Journal*, Vol. 47, 1948, pp. 3–10. Reprinted by permission of the Editor of *The Hibbert Journal*.

Pragmatic. An injunction to go and do likewise is implicit in them all. By their fruits ye shall know them. And what else can these be but the fruits of the Good Life? Is not this the acid test?

How does the Philosophy of Value react to it? This philosophy, as we have seen, is notably distinguished in the fact that it brings the Beautiful into full and equal partnership with the Good and the True in the constitution of the Godhead. How does this bear on human conduct? To what moral ideal does it give birth? What would be its translation into ethical terms? The translation would surely be that the service of the Beautiful lays obligations on the human will not less binding than those which issue from the Good and the True; is as much a matter of conscience as they, and a duty incumbent on all moral beings. If the disservice of the Good and the True is sin, so too is the disservice of the Beautiful. If the Bad and the False are offensive to the Highest, or to the Greatest Happiness of the Greatest Number, or to any other conception of the *summum bonum,* so too is the Ugly. If men are sent to hell for breaking the Ten Commandments they will not be sent to heaven for defacing the countryside with mile-long rows of hideous prefabricated houses, however conducive they may think it to the Greatest Happiness of the Greatest Number. Or, if the matter be framed in terms of *creation,* is not the creation of Beauty as high a virtue as the creation of Goodness and Truth, and the creation of Ugliness as foul an offence as the creation of the evil thing and the lie? Such would be the ethical translation of a philosophy which defines the Godhead as a Trinity of the Good, the True and the Beautiful. But where is the translation to be found in contemporary exposition? We have looked for it in vain. Since Ruskin fell silent we have heard no

voice that assigns to the Beautiful the same authority as a guiding principle of human conduct as that assigned to the Good and the True. With the definition of Beauty as integral to the Godhead, the hope naturally rises that the dull grey of moral theory will now pass into the shining green of the Tree of Life, that Goethe's voice with its *Wahrheit und Schönheit* will not be heard above Kant's with its categorical imperative, that morality is about to be touched with the emotion that will transform it into religion, the faithful bidden to imitate God by becoming like Him, creators of the Beautiful, and enter thereby into his kingdom and the embrace of his love. Alas, the hope remains unfulfilled. Truth, as defined and discussed, for example, by Dean Inge in *God and the Astronomer,* is all *Wahrheit* without a trace of *Schönheit* in its composition. At the point where we expect the transition to be made something seems to be holding our professors back. The pursuit and creation of the Beautiful which we expected to be presented as a *duty,* remains permissible only, and not always even that. It is neither matter of conscience nor source of obligation. A man may neglect or even despise it, but no sin will be involved and his conscience may be at ease. On the credit side of his moral account the creation of beauty counts for nothing, and the creation of ugliness for nothing on the debit. All that is a moral no-man's land. A few words of passing lip-service to Beauty is all that remains in our ethics to remind us of her divine eminence in our metaphysics. And when in the last chapter, due contact is made between Ethics and Politics, even lip-service fades out and the Beautiful falls into total eclipse. Who ever heard of it in connection with international relations, with party politics, with the doings of Trade Unions, the Rights of Man or the constitution of the state? All that would remain just as it is if the concept of Beauty were banished from the human mind and the Godhead defined as a Trinity of the Good, the True and the Unlovely.

Why do our philosophers thus fight shy of the Beautiful in their ethics and forget all about it when they come to politics and write their *Republic* — which certainly was not Plato's way? Why do they give it no place in the deliberations of the conscience and no part in the Greatest Happiness of the Greatest Number? Why do they begin like nightingales and end like owls? Is it that their vision of the Good and the True is still derived from the Ten Commandments, which ignore the Beautiful, and coloured with the righteousness of the Scribes and Pharisees? Is it that they are still haunted by the Puritan suspicion of Beauty as a snare of the Devil? Or is it, as someone has suggested, that our halting moralists, foreseeing that they will be able to make nothing of Beauty when they pass from ethics to politics, take the precaution of dropping it out of the discussion in good time? We think the reason lies deeper. It lies in the fact that their systems are the children of the *Zeitgeist* and their proceedings in this matter, as in so many others, a reflection of the ugly civilisation which has given them birth.

If morality be understood in a sense with which Beauty has nothing to do, as the nonconformist conscience, in common with the Scribes and Pharisees, seems to understand it, it is by no means self evident that the Order of Nature is designed for promoting such morality, either by rewarding those who practice it or punishing those who practise it not. And if the ways of Nature are taken as guides to the character of Nature's God, the same conclusion will follow as to Him as to them. That Nature rewards those who obey her laws and punishes those who disobey them, is a defensible thesis so long as a very wide meaning is given to all the terms employed, but is useless as a rule for the guidance of conduct unless we know which laws are Nature's and which are not. Are the Ten Commandments among Nature's laws, and if so are they the part where obedience is most richly rewarded and disobedience most severely punished? There is no evidence for either proposition. With the law of gravity it is different. A man who disobeys it by so arranging the water-supply to his house that it has to run uphill will certainly be punished by finding that no water flows out of his taps. But the members of his household, who are perfectly innocent of his folly, and may have warned him against committing it, will be equally involved in the punishment, and the whole family, guilty and innocent, may conceivably die of thirst. This seems to show that while Nature is inexorable in punishing disobedience to the Law of Gravity, she is quite indifferent as to the incidence of the punishment. Nor would it be out of harmony with Nature's way if all the members of the household died of thirst, except the actual perpetrator of the offence. All of which leads to the conclusion that Nature has no regard to the demands of the nonconformist conscience. The sun shines and the rain falls impartially on the just and the unjust, and the plagues and catastrophes are distributed with the same impartiality. The impartial distribution of sunshine and rain is often cited as indicating a leaning towards large-heartedness and generosity. But that agreeable impression fades out when we observe that the distribution of plagues and catastrophes is equally impartial. These miscarriages of justice, as we call them, are not infrequent in Nature's proceedings. A good many must have occurred when the bomb fell on Nagasaki. That was man's doing. But is not man a part of Nature?

Would the indictment of Nature, never more forcibly presented than in Huxley's famous lecture, be lightened if we amend our conception of morality by including the Beautiful as equal partner in its constitution with the Good and the True, as the Philosophy of Value clearly requires? Is Nature as indifferent to Beauty as she is, or seems to be, to Goodness and Truth when conceived after the manner of the Mosaic Law and the nonconformist conscience? Would the definition of God as an "Eternal Power, not ourselves, that makes for righteousness," be more in harmony with our experience if we widened our conception of righteousness so as to include the creation of Beauty as an essential attribute of the righteous man? In a word, would Job's problem, which has never been solved, become less insoluble?

That the problem would be immediately solved is certainly more than can be claimed. But the righteous man, now engaged in the creation of beauty, would go about his business with a stronger feeling that Nature and presumably Nature's God, were on his side or, as Emerson puts it, that the whole universe was backing him up. Can there be any doubt that the universe is a transcendantly beautiful creation, unquestionably a work of Art, and therefore of a supreme Artist? Never did a fortuitous concourse of atoms create a work of art or an artist, working to ends of which the flowers of the field are a hint and his own creations a witness.

"Sunsets don't look like that to me," said a patron of Turner's after inspecting one of his pictures with a marvellous sunset in the background. "By God, sir," replied Turner, using an oath appropriate to the matter in hand, "by God, sir, don't you wish they did!" Measure not the beauty of the universe by what our faint eyes can see or our dull ears hear! Think of what it would reveal to the all-seeing eye, the all-hearing ear. There is good reason to believe that Beauty is omnipresent in the cosmic structure, not only in the stupendous orchestration of the Whole, but in the minutest particles of its composition, the electrons dancing round their nucleus in the atom to the same melody which governs the rhythm of the stars in their courses, the horns of elfland tuned to the same key as the archangel's trumpet and the music of the spheres. All is of one pattern, all in the same key, but with infinite variations. Whether we study the atom in its minuteness or the nebula of Andromeda in its immensity all answer the wand of the same Conductor. The microcsope says yea to the telescope, and both say yea to the mathematician. Listening to the story of the Minute you may

"Hold eternity in the palm of your hand
 And heaven in a grain of sand:"

Listening to the Immense

"There's not the smallest orb which thou beholdest
 But in his motion like an angel sings,
 Still quiring to the young-eyed cherubirs."

In such a universe the human creator of beauty, even the humblest, may feel himself in harmony, a wanted quest, a welcome collaborator and completely at home as a fellow worker with the Living God.

To verify the omnipresence of Beauty a vision that could penetrate the inside of things would be needed. Not always nor everywhere is it spread out, in form or colour, on the surface of the world, not by any means that, though even on the surface the abundance is inexhaustible. Beauty lies, for the most part, hidden away in regions which eye hath not seen nor ear heard the music of, a mine of unsearchable riches concealed in inner structures, in silent processes of change and, above all, in movements which have no voice nor language. It is in their *motions* that the great orbs in the heavens and the little ones in the atom sing their "unheard melodies." The life-process even in the smallest insect, nay in a leaf, is a marvelous orchestration; in the higher animals and in man the infinite complexity of its integrations and correlations leaves human language completely dumb. Even where Nature's works are outwardly ugly, as many are or seem so to us, especially among the animals, even there Nature seldom fails to find a place for her hallmark somewhere on the surface; the precious jewel in the head of the toad, the opalescence of the cuttle-fish, the harmony of colour on the back of the centipede, the splash of turquoise blue on the buttocks of the baboon — laid on, we imagine, with a smile. But oftenest the touch is given in the creature's *movement* as it goes about its business, the gliding of the snake, the weaving of the spider, the stealthy approach and final spring of the carnivora, the undulating arms of the octopus seeking its prey in the waters, the majestic flight of the condor sailing round the flanks of Cotopaxi. The tale would be endless. If Beauty is not omnipresent it would certainly be hard to find a place or a thing from which it is wholly absent either outwardly where it can be seen or otherwise sensed, or inwardly, where it cannot. In any case there is enough of it to set us all thinking and to challenge the very serious consideration of the philosopher. *Quod semper, ubique et ab omnibus* — of what is that truer than of Beauty, or so true?

The conception of the universe as at once a masterpiece of creation and a supreme work of Art would have profound repercussions on the moralists. Poets would become prophets and painters priests. Under their combined ministrations Beauty would return from the exile to which utilitarianism condemns her,

assert her rights and proclaim new duties to mankind. The embargo on the making of graven images would be lifted and the order go forth to make them everywhere, but always after the patterns shown in the Mount, of the bride adorned for her husband, and the city paved with gold. Like the Good and the True, Beauty would now speak with the authority of a cosmic principle, but in a language that appealed to the heart as well as to the reason. So presented, morality would become lovable and the conclusion that God is love would not be very far off — how indeed could it be otherwise with a God eternally making for loveliness and summoning his human creatures to be fellow-workers with him in the creation of it? Duty would become less minatory, but more persuasive, and the frown on the face of the "Stern Lawgiver" whom Wordsworth addresses at the beginning of his Ode would melt into the smile which he saw at the end of it, as he watched the flowers dancing in their beds at her coming, or as when he wrote the lines:

"One impulse from a vernal wood
    May teach you more of man,
Of moral evil and of good
    Than all the sages can."

And when a Plato or a Plotinus defines the *summum bonum* as "likeness to God," or the Westminster Confession, as "to glorify God and enjoy Him for ever" they would not be understood, or misunderstood, as meaning that the God, whom the virtuous man resembles and the Christian man is to glorify and enjoy, is no other than the Jehovah who commanded Samuel to hew Agag in pieces, or the hell-committing Deity of Calvin and Jonathan Edwards. God forbid that any man should desire to be conformed to the image of that one! What wonder that "our young people," to say nothing of their elders, forsake church and chapel still haunted by the ghost of that ugly conception?

All this, we imagine, would not make disobedience to the Ten Commandments more prevalent than it is to-day. On the contrary, we should anticipate a decrease of murders, robberies, treacheries, whoredoms, juvenile delinquency, the statistics of crime in general, and man's inhumanity to man. The results achieved in these departments under the stern Lawgiver and the categorical imperative are certainly nothing to boast of. War, in which man outdoes the worst ferocities of Nature's teeth and claws, would become less frequent. All governments would necessarily be Labour Governments, but with the important difference that the base motto "the minimum work for the maximum pay" (which shows them to be haters of the labour they profess to serve) would be finally abandoned, and legislation, based on the love of labour, would now be concentrated on raising it to the highest pitch of excellence, and endowing it with the skill needed for the labourer's employment in the gardens and workshops of the Living God. On the speculative side, we do not claim, as we have said, that Job's problem would be completely solved. But it would arise in an atmosphere more favourable to a solution; the burden of it would weigh less insistently on the philosophy of religion, and be less galling to the heavy-laden backs of the philosophers. Perhaps, under the genial influence of the new atmosphere, they might all come to agree with Bergson that, in Reality, the problem is non-existent, being nothing more than an artefact of the space-thinking, self-tormenting intellect, a thing made up of words, and the inquiry into the Origin of Evil nothing more than inquiry into the meaning of its name.

A religion devoted to the love, worship and service of a God of Beauty, conceived as active throughout the universe in the creation of it, himself supremely and dynamically beautiful, and therefore good and true at the same altitude; a religion with its counterpart in a code of ethics enjoining the creation of the Beautiful as the prime and all inclusive duty of man; and this matched again by an education devoted to the liberation and training of the creative faculties — such a religion has never existed on the earth, not at least in any organised, public or cosmopolitan form. But it has had many adepts, even professors, among the artists and poets, notably Spenser, Shelley, Keats and Blake; in Wordsworth also, but in rather uneasy alliance with the conscience of the moral precisian, the two juxtaposed rather than fused. Plato and Plotinus lean strongly in that direction, but are embarrassed by too many abstractions for a complete approach. "All that is beautiful," says Augustine, "comes from the Highest Beauty, which is God." Here the Religion of Beauty is embraced without reserve, but with Augustine, too, intuition fades when the intellect gets to work and abstraction begins to make mischief. The Cambridge Platonists are in the same company. And then, of course, there is Thomas Traherne, an open professor if ever there was one. We suspect the existence of a multitude of such, including many women, deeply religious, but silent about their religion, perhaps because they feel that silence is the medium in which the beauty of holiness is best discerned; perhaps fearing their speech would be misunderstood, as the Religion of Beauty is very apt to be.

That our present civilisation would not support this religion, and that it would not tolerate our present civilisation, is evident enough. But can we, by putting imagination to the utmost stretch, picture a new civilisation, a new commonwealth or republic, in which the two would be in harmony? No easy task!

We should have to be "in the spirit on the Lord's Day" and to write a new Apocalypse. All our political notions would have to be turned inside out before we could even begin to draw the picture, let alone to colour it; political operators transfigured into artists, political speeches raised to the pitch of a chorus in Samson Agonistes, Governments prophetically inspired, Parliament turned into something resembling the angelic choir, and the last remnants of Utilitarianism dismissed from our political philosophy. With all this we must imagine the churches and chapels proclaiming the creation of the Beautiful as the supreme Law of God and all inclusive duty of man, the appointed way of access to the Kingdom of Heaven and the blessedness of the saints, proclaiming *that* as the way of salvation and denouncing the creation of ugliness as the unforgivable sin against the Holy Ghost and way to the bottomless pit; while the schools, colleges and universities backed them up with an education devoted to the release of creative faculty and the acquisition of skill, which is wisdom in action. What dream of an old man, what vision of a young man less likely to come true? "Consider the lilies of the field how they grow. And yet I say unto you that Solomon in all his glory was not arrayed like one of these." But who has believed that report?

On the whole, then, we conclude that the restoration of Beauty to her rightful place in the dynamism of the Godhead would have good effect both in religion and moral philosophy and through them on human conduct. We know of few ways, if any, in which philosophy could render a great service to the cause of human betterment. *Per contra* we reckon it a disservice to that cause when philosophy, after giving to Beauty her due eminence in the metaphysical Trinity, forgets all about her in dealing with the Good and the True, thereby lowering their status and depleting their dynamism. In our youth we were wont to hear hopes of the same kind expressed, but more extravagantly, for the Religion of Science, avatar of the True, second-named in our philosophical "Trinity," and invested by its devotees with the same predominance as Saviour that Christianity assigns to the Second Person, to the Son. These hopes have been dashed. Alas, there is no salvation in science. She has proved as potent an instrument in the hands of the wicked as of the righteous, her beneficent discoveries perverted by blackguards into cruel weapons of offence against humanity. Is a better fate in store for the Beautiful? Can Art succeed where Science has failed? We profess no certainty. But to give her a chance to show what she can do would be, we think, an experiment well worth trying. Our spirits, now somewhat depressed, would rise if we saw the experiment vigorously set on foot.

How would the experiment proceed? Unquestionably the place to begin would be the schools, colleges and universities. But heaven forbid that it take the form of making Beauty a "subject" of instruction based on an "agreed" syllabus with an examination to follow. That could only end in the failure which follows (or has followed) when religion is made into a "subject" and treated as an article for mass production. No, not that way, but rather by directing the general aim of education to the release of the creative faculties innate in man as the image of a Creator, and doing this in the sure and certain hope that, when once they are released, Beauty will spontaneously take command of those faculties, which are her own children and guide them in the paths of Excellence, even though her name be hardly mentioned and no prayers be put up for her help.

Would the churches and chapels co-operate

with the schools? It is to be hoped they would. Those of them, if there are any, which stand firm in the tradition of Calvin and John Knox, and are still weighted with the Puritan bias against Beauty as a snare of the Devil, could hardly be expected to join in the experiment, though even they might be persuaded to consider the flowers of the field more attentively and to throw off, for a time, their dismal preoccupation with the wrath of God. But others, less weighted in that direction, may reasonably be asked to give consideration to what is involved in the definition of the Godhead as a Trinity in Unity of the Good, the True and the Beautiful. If they accept it, as most of them probably do, will

it not follow that the third member of that Holy Triad imposes obligations on God's servants not less essential to their salvation than those imposed by the other Two? In treating the Beautiful as the Cinderella of the Values, or allowing it to be so treated, is there not something akin to sin against the Holy Ghost? Is there nothing offensive to the Living God, nothing to awake the consciousness of sin, nothing to trouble a good man's conscience in the defacement of the countryside by mile-long ribbons of hideous prefabricated houses? A thousand such questions might be asked. We feel sure that the churches and chapels, on thinking it over, would answer favourably to our plea.

SUGGESTIONS FOR THOUGHT

1. Would you rather eat in a café that was attractive but served mediocre food or in a drab café that served excellent food? Are you more interested in style or quality in your clothes? Which parts of a modern automobile are for aesthetic purposes only?

2. "If conversation about art were suppressed, the interest in it would hardly survive." (De Witt Parker) Why is a play more enjoyable when shared and discussed with a friend?

3. An American painter has said that much modern art is in the precise category of perpetual-motion machines in that it is "a violation of the fundamental laws of real art, and hence doomed to disappear like all other untrue things." Can works of art ever be described as "untrue things"?

4. C. E. M. Joad contends that "our experiences of beauty are more vivid and frequent than our experiences of goodness or truth, or indeed of any other form of value." Do you find yourself making the evaluation "This is beautiful" more often and with greater certainty than the evaluations "This is good" or "This is true"?

5. Is it possible to establish objective stand-

ards of artistic criticism? If it is not, then how is it possible to have art contests?

6. Confucius is supposed to have said that a man has no place in society unless he understands aesthetics. What did he mean?

7. Is the appreciation of art enough, or do you feel the need to create some form of art? Is there any one who does not in some way create art?

8. Can the sense of beauty prevent business and science from "binding us to a treadmill of futile efficiency"? (A. R. Chandler)

9. "Art heightens the sense of humanity. It gives an elation of feeling which is supernatural. A sunset is glorious, but it dwarfs humanity and belongs to the general flow of nature. A million sunsets will not spur on men towards civilization. It requires art to evoke into consciousness the finite perfections which lie ready for human achievement." (A. N. Whitehead) How does it happen that although nature and art may both be beautiful, only art has a moral influence on man? Are artists aware of their ability to exert a moral influence?

10. Can one judge a work of art without at

the same time judging the life of the artist?

11. Shostakovitch withdrew his Fourth Symphony from its first performance when it was declared to be politically heterodox in 1936. When, if ever, should art be subjected to political censorship? What are some of the best reasons for the censorship of movies?

12. An African bushman and a Chinese gentleman have very divergent conceptions of feminine pulchritude. Which evaluation is "right"? Or are both "wrong"? Or are evaluations completely relative? Does it make sense to say that although X was chosen by the group Y was *really* more beautiful?

SUGGESTIONS FOR FURTHER READING

AMES, VAN METER, *Introduction to Beauty,* New York, Harper and Brothers, 1951, Part III.

BELL, CLIVE, *Art,* New York, Frederich A. Stokes Company, 1913, Part II.

CHANDLER, ALBERT R., *Beauty and Human Nature,* New York, D. Appleton-Century Company, 1934, ch. 17.

DEWEY, JOHN, *Art as Experience,* New York, Minton, Balch and Company, 1934, ch. 14.

EDMAN, IRWIN, *Arts and the Man,* W. W. Norton and Company, 1928, ch. 2.

FLACCUS, LOUIS M., *The Spirit and Substance of Art,* New York, F. S. Crofts and Company, 1931, pp. 396–407.

JORDAN, E., *Essays in Criticism,* Chicago, University of Chicago Press, 1952, ch. 7.

PARKER, DE WITT H., *The Principles of Aes-* thetics, F. S. Crofts and Company, 1946, chs. 3, 14. 15.

SCHOEN, MAX, "The Social Message of Art," *The Journal of Aesthetics and Art Criticism,* Vol. 3, 1944, pp. 118–127.

TOROSSIAN, ARAM, *A Guide to Aesthetics,* Stanford, Calif., Stanford University Press, 1937, ch. 17.

VIVAS, ELISEO, "The Use of Art," *The Journal of Philosophy,* Vol. 35, 1938, pp. 405–411.

WHITMORE, CHARLES E., "Art, Truth, and Conduct," *The International Journal of Ethics,* Vol. 36, 1926, pp. 403–423.

WIEMAN, HENRY NELSON, *The Source of Human Good,* Chicago, University of Chicago Press, 1946, ch. 6.

ZINK, SIDNEY, "The Moral Effect of Art," *Ethics,* Vol. 60, 1950, pp. 261–274.

PART FOUR
THE SOCIAL WORLD

21

KNOWLEDGE OF THE SOCIAL WORLD

AUGUSTE COMTE (1798–1857) was a French mathematician and philosopher. At a very early age he became a freethinker. He was greatly impressed by the scientific movements of his time and believed that scientific or positive thinking required the elimination of all theological and metaphysical modes of explanation. His greatest work, *Cours de philosophie positive,* was published between 1830 and 1842. Those who reject Comtean positivism have derived satisfaction in noting that toward the end of his life Comte established a religion, a cult of humanity. Wilbur Marshall Urban (1873–1952) was an American philosopher who wrote primarily in the field of values. He taught at Ursinus, Trinity, and Dartmouth Colleges and at Yale University. Urban fully appreciates scientific knowledge, but he sees a number of difficulties in establishing such knowledge in the "social sciences."

A

From the study of the development of human intelligence, in all directions, and through all times, the discovery arises of a great fundamental law, to which it is necessarily subject, and which has a solid foundation of proof, both in the facts of our organization and in our historical experience. The

Auguste Comte, *Positive Philosophy,* translated by Harriet Martineau, London, George Bell and Sons, 1896, Introduction, ch. 1 (in part); Book VI, chs. 3, 4 (in part).

law is this: — that each of our leading conceptions, — each branch of our knowledge, — passes successively through three different theoretical conditions: the Theological, or fictitious; the Metaphysical, or abstract; and the Scientific, or positive. In other words, the human mind, by its nature, employs in its progress three methods of philosophizing, the character of which is essentially different, and even radically opposed: viz., the theological method, the metaphysical, and the positive. Hence arise three philosophies, or general systems of conceptions on the aggregate of phenomena, each of which excludes the others. The first is the necessary point of departure of the human understanding; the third is its fixed and definitive state. The second is merely a state of transition.

In the theological state, the human mind, seeking the essential nature of beings, the first and final causes (the origin and purpose) of all effects, — in short, Absolute knowledge, — supposes all phenomena to be produced by the immediate action of supernatural beings.

In the metaphysical state, which is only a modification of the first, the mind supposes, instead of supernatural beings, abstract forces, veritable entities (that is, personified abstractions) inherent in all beings, and capable of producing all phenomena. What is called the explanation of phenomena is, in this stage, a mere reference of each to its proper entity.

In the final, the positive state, the mind has given over the vain search after Absolute notions, the origin and destination of the universe, and the causes of phenomena, and applies itself to the study of their laws, — that is, their invariable relations of succession and resemblance. Reasoning and observation, duly combined, are the means of this knowledge. What is now understood when we speak of an explanation of facts is simply the establishment of a connection between single phenomena and some general facts, the number of which continually diminishes with the progress of science.

The Theological system arrived at the highest perfection of which it is capable when it substituted the providential action of a single Being for the varied operations of the numerous divinities which had been before imagined. In the same way, in the last stage of the Metaphysical system, men substitute one great entity (Nature) as the cause of all phenomena, instead of the multitude of entities at first supposed. In the same way, again, the ultimate perfection of the Positive system would be (if such perfection could be hoped for) to represent all phenomena as particular aspects of a single general fact: — such as Gravitation, for instance. . . .

There is no science which, having attained the positive stage, does not bear marks of having passed through the others. Some time since it was (whatever it might be) composed, as we can now perceive, of metaphysical abstractions; and, further back in the course of time, it took its form from theological conceptions. We shall have only too much occasion to see, as we proceed, that our most advanced sciences still bear very evident marks of the two earlier periods through which they have passed.

The progress of the individual mind is not only an illustration, but an indirect evidence of that of the general mind. The point of departure of the individual and of the race being the same, the phases of the mind of a man correspond to the epochs of the mind of the race. Now, each of us is aware, if he looks back upon his own history, that he was a theologian in his childhood, a metaphysician in his youth, and a natural philosopher in his manhood. All men who are up to their age can verify this for themselves. . . .

We must bear in mind that the different kinds of our knowledge have passed through the three stages of progress at different rates, and have not therefore arrived at the same time. The rate of advance depends on the nature of the knowledge in question, so distinctly that, as we shall see hereafter, this consideration constitutes an accessory to the fundamental law of progress. Any kind of knowledge reaches the positive stage early in proportion to its generality, simplicity, and independence of other departments. Astronomical science, which is above all made up of facts that are general, simple, and independent of other sciences, arrived first; then terrestrial Physics; then Chemistry; and, at length, Physiology. . . .

In mentioning just now the four principal categories of phenomena, — astronomical, physical, chemical, and physiological, — there was an omission which will have been noticed. Nothing was said of Social phenomena. Though involved with the physiological, Social phenomena demand a distinct classification, both on account of their importance and of their difficulty. They are the most individual, the most complicated, the most dependent on all others; and therefore they must be the latest, — even if they had no special obstacle to encounter. This branch of science has not hitherto entered into the domain of Positive philosophy. Theological and metaphysical methods, exploded in other departments, are as yet exclusively applied, both in the way of inquiry and discussion, in all treatment of Social subjects, though the best minds are heartily weary of eternal disputes about divine right and the sovereignty of the people. This is the great, while it is evidently the only gap which has to be filled, to constitute, solid and entire, the Positive Philosophy. Now that the human mind has grasped celestial and ter-

restrial physics, — mechanical and chemical; organic physics, both vegetable and animal, — there remains one science, to fill up the series of sciences of observation, — Social Physics. This is what men have now most need of: and this it is the principal aim of the present work to establish.

It would be absurd to pretend to offer this new science at once in a complete state. Others, less new, are in very unequal conditions of forwardness. But the same character of positivity which is impressed on all the others will be shown to belong to this. This once done, the philosophical system of the moderns will be in fact complete, as there will then be no phenomenon which does not naturally enter into some one of the five great categories. All our fundamental conceptions having become homogeneous, the Positive state will be fully established. It can never again change its character, though it will be for ever in course of development by additions of new knowledge. Having acquired the character of universality which has hitherto been the only advantage resting with the two preceding systems, it will supersede them by its natural superiority, and leave to them only an historical existence. . . .

As Social Physics assumes a place in the hierarchy of sciences after all the rest, and therefore dependent on them, its means of investigation must be of two kinds: those which are peculiar to itself, and which may be called direct, and those which arise from the connection of sociology with the other sciences; and these last, though indirect, are as indispensable as the first. I shall review, first, the direct resources of the science.

Here, as in all the other cases, there are

three methods of proceeding: — by Observation, Experiment and Comparison.

Very imperfect and even vicious notions prevail at present as to what Observation can be and can effect in social science. The chaotic state of doctrine of the last century has extended to Method; and amidst our intellectual disorganization, difficulties have been magnified; precautionary methods, experimental and rational, have been broken up; and even the possibility of obtaining social knowledge by observation has been dogmatically denied; but if the sophisms put forth on this subject were true, they would destroy the certainty, not only of social science, but of all the simpler and more perfect ones that have gone before. The ground of doubt assigned is the uncertainty of human testimony; but all the sciences up to the most simple, require proofs of testimony: that is, in the elaboration of the most positive theories, we have to admit observations which could not be directly made, nor even repeated, by those who use them, and the reality of which rests only on the faithful testimony of the original investigators; there being nothing in this to prevent the use of such proofs, in concurrence with immediate observations. . . .

★   ★   ★

It might be supposed beforehand that the second method of investigation, Experiment, must be wholly inapplicable in Social Science; but we shall find that the science is not entirely deprived of this resource, though it must be one of inferior value. We must remember (what was before explained) that there are two kinds of experimentation, — the direct and the indirect: and that it is not necessary to the philosophical character of this method that the circumstances of the phenomenon in

question should be, as is vulgarly supposed in the learned world, artificially instituted. Whether the case be natural or factitious, experimentation takes place whenever the regular course of the phenomenon is interfered with in any determinate manner. The spontaneous nature of the alteration has no effect on the scientific value of the case, if the elements are known. It is in this sense that experimentation is possible in Sociology. . . .

[In his discussion of the third method of investigation Comte lists three types of comparisons: comparison with inferior animals; comparison with co-existing states of society; and comparison of consecutive states. The latter he calls the historical method. T.W.O.]

The historical comparison of the consecutive states of humanity is not only the chief scientific device of the new political philosophy. Its rational development constitutes the substratum of the science, in whatever is essential to it. It is this which distinguishes it thoroughly from biological science . . . The positive principle of this separation results from the necessary influence of human generations upon the generations that follow, accumulating continuously till it constitutes the preponderating consideration in the direct study of social development. As long as this preponderance is not directly recognized, the positive study of humanity must appear a simple prolongation of the natural history of Man: but this scientific character, suitable enough to the earlier generations, disappears in the course of the social evolution, and assumes at length a wholly new aspect, proper to sociological science, in which historical considerations are of immediate importance. And this preponderant use of the historical method gives its philosophical character to sociology in a logical, as well as a scientific sense. By the creation of this new department of the comparative method, sociology confers a benefit on the whole of natural philosophy; because the positive method is thus completed and perfected, in a manner which, for scientific importance, is almost beyond our estimate. . . .

It is evident that Sociology must perfect the study of the essential relations which unite the different sciences, as this inquiry constitutes an essential part of social statics, directly intended to disclose the laws of such a connection, in the same way as in all cases of connection between any of the elements of our civilization. . . . If we remember that no science can be thoroughly comprehended till its history is understood, we shall see what special improvements this new science must introduce into each of the rest, as well as into the coordination of them all.

This leads us to consider the reaction of sociology on the other sciences in regard to Method. Without entering at present upon the great subject of a general theory of the positive method, I must just point out the established truth that each of the fundamental sciences specially manifests one of the chief attributes of the universal positive method, though all are present, in more or less force, in each science. The special resource of sociology is that it participates directly in the elementary composition of the common ground of our intellectual resources. It is plain that this logical co-operation of the new science is as important as that of any of the anterior sciences. We have seen that sociology adds to our other means of research that which I have called the historical method, and which will hereafter, when we are sufficiently habituated to it, constitute a fourth fundamental means of observation. But, though sociology has given us this resource, it is more or less applicable to all orders of scientific speculation. We have only to regard every discovery, at the moment it is effected, as a true social phenomenon, forming a part of the general series of human development, and, on that ground, subject to the laws of succession, and the methods of investigation which characterize that great evolution. . . .

Thus we see that the reaction of sociology on the other sciences is as important in a logical as in a scientific view. On the one hand, positive sociology mutually connects all the sciences, and on the other hand, it adds to all resources for investigation, a new and a higher method. While, from its nature, dependent on all that went before, Social Physics repays as much as it receives by its two kinds of service towards all other knowledge. We can already perceive that such a science must form the principal band of the scientific sheaf, from its various relations, both of subordination and of direction, to all the rest. It is in this way that the homogeneous co-ordination of real sciences proceeds from their positive development, instead of being derived from any anti-scientific conceptions of a fanciful unity of different phenomena, such as have hitherto been almost exclusively resorted to.

Social science must always remain inferior in all important speculative respects to all the other fundamental sciences. Yet we cannot but feel, after this review of its spirit, its function, and its resources, that the abundance of its means of investigation may establish it in a higher position of rationality than the present state of the human mind might seem to promise. The unity of the subject, notwithstanding its prodigious extent, the conspicuous interconnection of its various aspects, its characteristic advance from the most general to more and more special researches, and finally the more frequent and important use of *a priori* considerations through suggestions furnished by the anterior sciences, and especially by the biological theory of human nature, may authorize the highest hopes of the speculative dignity of the science, — higher hopes than can be excited by such an imperfect realization as I propose to sketch out, the purpose of which is to embody, in a direct manner, and by sensible manifestations, the more abstract view which I have now taken of the general nature of this new political philosophy, and of the scientific spirit which should regulate its ulterior construction.

B

. . . We may clear the way for the real issues by noting two points upon which all of us, scientists and philosophers alike, will surely agree.

The first of these is that in the most general sense there is only one method of knowledge, namely, the scientific — in the sense, namely, of the aim at objectivity. None of us wishes to be guilty of wishful thinking, to include our own personal prejudices and valuations in our conclusions. And yet we know that this objectivity is difficult to attain in all science. It is peculiarly so in the sciences that deal with man. Indeed, some of us have become cynical on the question, for we are accustomed to see precisely those who claim the greatest objectivity and scientific method most unaware of their own prejudices and prior evaluations.

This leads us to the second question, upon which I think we should all be agreed — namely, that these sciences or this part of science, unlike the physical sciences, contains value judgments or propositions as part of the very material of science itself. It is not merely that the practitioners of these sciences find it difficult to exclude their own valuations in the reading of the facts — that, though difficult, is conceivably possible — it is rather that the so-called "facts" themselves, *as facts,* are already value charged. We may, indeed, compare two forms of the family or of the state wholly impersonally, as we may compare two minerals or two types of vertebrates. But who is any longer naive enough to suppose that we can form the concept of the family or of the state without reference to moral and social values? Thus it is that an economic, a social, or a political theory is always a theory of value and cannot, in the nature of the case, be anything else.

On these points we should all, I think, be agreed. But now appears a serious divergence of opinion — namely, concerning the notion of science itself. Science is the most ambiguous concept of the modern world, and this ambiguity has become one of the most fatal sources of misunderstanding in our present culture.

There are those who maintain what they call the "unity of science." They insist that there is only one method of science. There are others who, recognizing the difference of material of the two types of science, insist upon the *decentralization* of the sciences —

Wilbur M. Urban, "Science and Value," *Ethics,* Vol. 51, 1941, pp. 291–294, 296–305. Reprinted by permission of the publishers, The University of Chicago Press.

that the method of the science must be determined by the material.

This second view is increasing in influence and has found outstanding representatives in all countries and all sciences. Inaugurated in a certain sense by Dilthey (in his famous saying, "Things we describe — the soul we understand"), it found its most reasoned expression, perhaps, in Rickert's famous book, *Die Grenzen der naturwissenschaftlichen Begriffsbildung.* The essential point is that, in those realms of knowledge in which value is part of the material of the sciences themselves, the methods of handling the material must be different.

It is this principle of the decentralization of science that I shall maintain. I shall insist, with Professor George Birkoff, that "each science represents a distinct level and each level is a natural one in the sense that it possesses its own type of language which is largely, if not wholly, independent of that used on the other levels," and that the reduction of one type of language to the others can lead only to confusion and fallacy.

I am well aware, of course, that even among the philosophers there is still a sect that argues vociferously for the unity of science. The logical positivists suppose that, of these languages of which Professor Birkoff speaks, there is only one that has any meaning and in which meaningful propositions can be expressed — namely, what they call "physical language." But, quite apart from the fact that this represents a serious misrepresentation of the actual practice of the sciences, it suffices for our purpose to recognize that it begs the whole question at issue. It proceeds upon a wholly arbitrary, and, as I think, untenable theory of language and meaning. Into this I cannot go. It is more to our purpose to recognize that unity of science, in this sense, is possible only by the reductionism which

Birkoff deplores and which, I think, we will all agree is fatal to understanding. Carnap, for instance, recognizes this difficulty and maintains that it does not involve reductionism, but I have found no one who is convinced by the argument. . . .

Our uncertainty regarding the methods of the value sciences really arises out of our uncertainty as to the aims of these sciences. This involves the more ultimate question of the aim or objective of science itself.

This uncertainty as to the aim of science is part of the general ambiguity of the notion. Even physics, the most fundamental of the natural sciences, is torn apart by this question. Victorian science supposed that the object of science was to observe and *explain* the phenomena of nature. This idea is, however, many physicists now inform us, quite false — that is, it "does not correspond to what science actually is, whatever we think it should be." Its sole function is to correlate phenomena and thus to control them. We no longer wish to understand, but merely to describe and control.

Whatever we may say of the physical sciences, this question of aim or objective becomes pressing when we come to the sciences of man, and its solution is imperative. Most practitioners of these sciences suppose that, as in the case of history, with which they are so closely connected, the ultimate aim is to find the lessons which eventuate from the facts, that is, to pass value judgments on forms of life and on institutions. Others deny this objective completely and maintain that the object here is also merely factual description.

The issue here presented is stated clearly in the Preface to a recent *History of Political*

Theory. Such theory, the author maintains, contains among its elements certain judgments of fact. Invariably, however, it also includes valuations and predilections, personal or collective, which distort the perception of fact. The most that criticism can do is to keep these factors as distinct as possible. Taken as a whole, a political theory can hardly be said to be true. Thus, as appears in the course of the treatment, we can describe democracies and dictatorships, but we cannot evaluate them. That is a matter of personal or national opinion. He admits that he happens to like democracy and to dislike dictatorship, but that is all that there is to it. Thus the issue of fact and value is clearly stated.

Now I take it that, while there are some of us who will accept this defeatist position, most of us, philosophers and social scientists alike, will not want to. We feel that it represents a skepticism which is death to all initiative in the social sciences and which is neither possible nor necessary. These value propositions, we should feel, are not merely expressions of emotion, individual or collective, but actual judgments which may be true or false. *They are really disguised factual judgments,* and all we have to do is to read off the meaning of the facts to get the values — to read the lessons which eventuate from the facts of history and society.

This, I should suppose, is the more common position; but, as I have already indicated, it seems to me sheer illusion. I shall now attempt to show this more fully.

The untenability of this general position has been epigrammatically stated in terms of two fallacies, the so-called "genetic fallacy" and the so-called "naturalistic fallacy," the latter being the more general notion, under which the former may be subsumed.

The genetic fallacy consists in the assumption that, by going back to the origins of a social phenomenon, we can determine its present meaning and value. This is the underlying assumption not only of the popular notion that our moral values are survivals of formerly serviceable habits but also of a large part of nineteenth-century social science and is one of the reasons that our intercourse with the phenomena was so unintelligent.

This fallacy is such a vicious one, and those who deal with history and evolution have become so wary of it, that we have become nervous and now see it lurking under every bed. We no longer need to be told that the genesis of a thing does not determine its present meaning and value, but we are not so fully aware of the more fundamental fallacy of which it is a particular expression, namely, the naturalistic fallacy, as G. E. Moore has called it.

This fallacy may be stated in several ways, but the most appropriate in our present context is the notion that values and value judgments are disguised facts and factual judgments and that values emerge *of themselves* from the "unadulterated" facts of nature. In other words, that we can get the "ought" from the "is."

Let us suppose then that "nature," as here used, is intended to describe the general order of existence, of which our most adequate knowledge is afforded by the so-called "natural sciences." If so, what have the value sciences, and pre-eminently ethics, to learn from them? Surely the answer is not doubtful. If these sciences in their own proper principle contain no mention of value, nothing concerning value can be directly extracted from them. If, on the other hand, value is assigned to inferences, or "lessons," from them, it must really be assumed within them — and the argument becomes one of values (or moral) only because values have been wrapped up in them all the time.

The issue does not, of course, seriously arise in connection with the physical sciences. It is only when we come to biological science that there is any direct reference to the human and that any inferences as to human values could conceivably be drawn. Now the only conception of value, or of biological purpose, that could conceivably be extracted from the facts of this science — whether for the individual or the species — is sustenance for as long a time as possible for as great numbers as possible. The creature by filling its skin gets a better skin to fill. But surely, unless we assume that persistence and sustenance, for as long a time and in as great numbers as possible, is itself a good or value, there is no inference to be drawn from the facts. Even more surely can no inference as to human good or value be drawn unless we make prior assumption of the identity of the human with the animal, and this is the very reductionism which all genuine science should seek to avoid.

For myself, I cannot help feeling that the entire movement in the so-called "social sciences" since Darwin and Spencer is a magnificent exploitation of the naturalistic fallacy. It was Nietzsche who made that clearest to me personally. Of the British social and moral philosophers he said that they were either knaves or fools. They tried to graft on this biological naturalism the moral values of Greek and Christian civilization, which rest on wholly different premises. Either they were really conscious that this could not be done — in which case they were knaves — or they had not intelligence enough to see that it could not be done — in which case they were fools.

I can sympathize, of course, with those who so constantly commit the naturalistic fallacy and try in some way to deduce values from facts, the "ought" from the "is." Facts are

"objective," and factual propositions verifiable. Values are subjective, it is held, and in principle unverifiable. If, they will maintain, you do not in some way deduce your values from the facts, you must fall back upon an *intuition* of values of some sort — on ethics or axiology — as the science which conditions the social sciences in general.

Now I do not suppose that we can really escape this alternative. Certainly, I shall not try to escape it. I do not hesitate to say that there is a science of ethics in the broad sense of science, and that, unless there is, there is no social science in the sense that any of its theories of social good are either true or false. In any case, that is the reason why philosophers have not, in the main, attempted to escape the alternative. That is the reason why in recent years the main body of philosophers have been led to some concept of objective values and to a doctrine of value realism. In the Ninth International Congress of Philosophy fifty papers were presented on the problems of value; and the dominant tendency in the Congress was, as I have pointed out in a recent account of this phase of the Congress' work, in this direction.

If, then, there is to be any science of the human and of human values, it must find its basis in a theory of objective values. I personally cannot see any middle ground between this and the very honest, but somewhat embarrassing, position of the positivist, who sees in value judgments merely subjective expressions of feeling and emotion, recognizes them for what they are, and then passes on to what he somewhat naively describes as mere facts.

But most of you will, I feel sure, hardly accept this alternative. The situation, you will say, is not quite so hopeless as all that. There is a middle ground, a kind of quasi-objectivity to values, and to the formulation of this position many of you have doubtless been helped by the instrumentalism connected with the honored name of John Dewey.

What the position amounts to is this: Physical science has abandoned the notion of knowledge of an antecedent world and its structure, for the control of process through experiment. Let us apply this notion analogously to the material of the social sciences and the value propositions which they contain. Values, in other words, like anything else, are to be tested by experiment, either actually or in thought. Thus, the past of any value is to be used just as in a laboratory experiment. We neither glorify it nor condemn it. It is merely to be interpreted according to the special problem created by the specific situation. When we "operate" with values in this way, we shall, just as in the physical sciences, achieve not certainty but control.

Now I shall not argue against Professor Dewey's position explicitly — that would involve the introduction of more philosophical technicalities into my paper than is either possible or desirable. I shall rather concern myself with the general position in the social sciences, which, while undoubtedly influenced by him, is yet the outgrowth of many tendencies in our present-day science and culture. On the face of it, this argument for an analogous instrumentality test of values seems quite cogent. But it is surprising how many difficulties immediately present themselves.

How do we, in the first place, test the success of a value? Values undeniably work, but they don't necessarily succeed or fail. We have monogamy, bigamy, polyandry, and a dozen other systems of marriage. They have all worked, since people seem to have lived and sung under each of them. Taboo against murder works, since societies flourish where the taboo is present; a systematic killing of aged parents also works. The latter custom is

even necessary where food is scarce and existence hard; perhaps to that extent it is even a pragmatic value. To an extent, then, despite all the dangers of the genetic fallacy, we may perhaps admit that knowledge of process and of the genesis of values can contribute significantly to our understanding of them. But the situation is wholly different when we attempt a *revaluation* of values — when, in other words, we attempt to pass to the judgment of new values (economic, social, or political) which are proposed. When judging the effectiveness, the workability of a value, we have to use some other value to appraise it. We may know the processes by which people are made fat, lean, or middling; but we shall have to decide whether we ought to make them fat, lean, or middling, for *there is no judgment* inherent in a mere process. Suppose that we decide to make them lean in order that they may run faster. Then we have founded our value of leanness upon the value of speed in running, which must, in turn, be founded on another value, and so on. Where, then, is our key value or values? By the method proposed, there could obviously be no key value in the sense of its antecedent existence, an existence which we must mutually acknowledge.

I need scarcely labor my point. Such a method is obviously powerless before the moral and political issues that face man today. And need I add, the social or humanistic sciences that employ it have nothing to say on these issues. If they suppose that they have, they are deceiving both themselves and us. Oh I know, of course, how an argument such as this is usually turned aside. In popular circles the appeal is always made to "all intelligent, right-thinking, and forward-thinking people." And in principle the argument is no different in the circles called scientific and philosophical, where, in like manner, the appeal is made to "intelligence" and to progress somehow implicit in mere *process.* The instrumentalist has a *key value,* although he, of course, denies it strenuously. That value is intelligence. It is assumed that wherever intelligence is employed good results will follow, and thus intelligence becomes the absolute value. In short, what is really done is to fall back upon certain empirically and logically unsupported judgments of value which have been implicit in all social thinking of the nineteenth century.

But suppose these assumptions are denied; suppose we are anti-intellectualists, as many of the keenest minds of the twentieth century are? Suppose that we deny that intelligence always produces the good? Is there any reply to this? Suppose we deny that process is progress. Is there any reply to this? I have already said that the social science of the nineteenth century was a gigantic exploitation of the naturalistic fallacy. Is it too much to say that the instrumentalism of the twentieth is a gigantic begging of the entire issue in question?

I said in the beginning that I should try to fulfil my function of splitting the whole problem of fact and value wide open. In doing so, I have consciously and consistently pointed my position in such a way as to invite disagreement and debate. In conclusion I shall adopt a method which is notorious for its ability to do just this thing, namely, the presentation of dilemmas.

This is an era of crises. In our present mood every tension is a crisis — and tends to become a crisis in civilization, if not in the universe. This tension, or crisis, extends itself to our knowledge and science. I know of very few sciences today in which such a crisis is not heralded — the crisis in physics, the crisis in psychology, and certainly a crisis in the social or humanistic sciences. Now, as far as this latter crisis is concerned, if there be one, it arises out of certain dilemmas which are at least felt if they are not explicitly formulated. The embarrassment in which these sciences find themselves at the moment is due to a fundamental dualism and contradiction in their very aims and methods.

The first of these dilemmas I shall formulate as follows: It is admitted that the social and political sciences contain both fact and value — factual propositions and value propositions. Either these value propositions are subjective or they are not. If they are subjective, then they are merely the expression of liking and disliking, whether individual or collective — and the notions of truth and falsity are irrelevant. If they are objective, as I believe, and judgments about them can be true or false, then this is possible only if there are objective values and an objective order of values. In that case there is a science, of ethics or axiology, with its own problems and methods. That such a science has also its own difficulties I am well aware, but there is no other alternative and that is all with which I am here concerned.

In his *Proposed Roads to Freedom* Bertrand Russell enunciates the proposition that, "while freedom may not be the highest good, it is the highest political good." When he says this, he means to make a significant assertion. To do so, however, he must assume that both the subject "freedom" and the predicate "highest good" are in some sense real or objective, otherwise, presumably, he would not make the assertion. Now, either the proposition is an expression of his own feeling and emotion, or it is objective in the sense that the predicates of truth and falsity are relevant. If it is the former, then the above noble sentiment is but his own sentiment and does not interest us further. If it is the latter then it is a statement about reality which interests us greatly and is most significant, not only for human culture and welfare but for any science of the human.

This leads to a second and most fundamental of all the dilemmas that face us at the moment. Either there is science or knowledge of the good or of value, or there is not. If there is not, if there is only knowledge of fact — of individual and collective desires and interests — then all attempts of the sciences to pronounce on values are either irrelevant or impudent. All belief that they can tell us what ought to be, in the economic, social, and political spheres, is sheer illusion; and if the practitioners of these sciences continue to let it be understood that such pronouncements are possible, they are securing the public's interest under false pretenses. The wise man will look upon history as the final judge of all social good and will accept the principle that

right, if not necessarily on the side of the heaviest battalions, is certainly on the side of the most powerful economic forces.

I have presented these dilemmas not in order to coerce your thought — I probably could not do so even if I wished to — but merely as a methodological device to make as pointed as possible the issues raised by our subject, "Fact and Value in the Social Sciences." It may be that to some of you they may seem to be significant enough to merit their disproof by showing that there is a middle ground. I do not believe it can be done, as my criticism of the instrumentalist point of view has, I think, shown. But I should certainly welcome such a solution if it were possible. It is because I am sure that it is not possible that I have tried to show what are, as it seems to me, the alternatives before us.

SUGGESTIONS FOR THOUGHT

1. "There is a popular belief that only a very clever man can be a mathematician or a physicist, while any fool can succeed in the social sciences." (A. D. Ritchie) This assumption is even expressed at college registration time, when students are sometimes heard to say, "I'm not smart enough to major in the sciences, so I'll major in something like history or sociology." What justification is there for this belief?

2. Even the most ardent social scientist will have to admit that there is a time lag between natural and social science. Is this because we do not yet know how to apply causal concepts to the subject matter of the social sciences, or is it because causal concepts cannot grasp the real essence of human group behavior?

3. Poincaré once remarked, "Sociology is the science which has most methods and fewest results." How might one argue that Poincaré

does not properly understand what is a "result" in the social sciences?

4. Some have ridiculed man's efforts to solve social problems by comparing the way a garage mechanic repairs an automobile and the way the United States Congress repairs damage in the state. Do you think the comparison is fair? What factors must the congressman take into consideration which are non-existent in the problem facing the mechanic?

5. If public-opinion polls are reliable instruments for measuring public opinion, why not substitute such polls for general elections?

6. Can one argue logically that since certain methods have been fruitful in the study of the physical world these methods will also give good results in the study of human societies? What differences are there in the subject matter of the natural sciences and the social sciences to

indicate that they require different methods?

7. Compare the concept of measurement in physics and in psychology. E.g., does an I.Q. test measure intelligence in the same sense in which a galvanometer measures electricity?

8. Carl Becker has said in regard to the scientific method: "The method is less successful in the field of social than in the field of physical phenomena for various and obvious reasons, all of which may be reduced to one: knowledge of social phenomena acquired by the sociologist modifies the behavior of social phenomena, whereas knowledge of physical phenomena acquired by the physicist has no effect on the behavior of physical phenomena." Do you agree with this?

SUGGESTIONS FOR FURTHER READING

BENOIT-SMULLYAN, EMILE, "Value Judgments and the Social Sciences," *The Journal of Philosophy,* Vol. 42, 1945, pp. 197–210.

BIERSTEDT, ROBERT, "Social Science and Social Policy," *Bulletin of the American Association of University Professors,* Vol. 34, 1948, pp. 310–319.

COLUMBIA ASSOCIATES IN PHILOSOPHY, *An Introduction to Reflective Thinking,* Boston, Houghton Mifflin Company, 1923, pp. 227–237.

GARBUNY, SIEGFRIED, "The Social Scientists of Today," *Bulletin of the American Association of University Professors,* Vol. 34, 1948, pp. 711–718.

GINSBERG, MORRIS, "Causality in the Social Sciences,"*Proceedings of the Aristotelian Society,* Vol. 35, 1935, pp. 253–270.

HEATH, A. E., "Some Notes on Methodology in the Social Sciences," *Proceedings of the Aristotelian Society,* Vol. 31, 1931, pp. 263–284.

KAUFMAN, FELIX, *Methodology of the Social Sciences,* New York, Oxford University Press, 1944.

KECSKEMETI, PAUL, *Meaning, Communication, and Value,* Chicago, University of Chicago Press, 1952, pp. 210–235.

KNIGHT, FRANK, "Fact and Value in Social Science," *Science and Man,* edited by R. N. Asher, New York, Harcourt, Brace and Company, 1942, pp. 325–345.

LARRABEE, HAROLD A., *Reliable Knowledge,* Boston, Houghton Mifflin Company, 1945, ch. 13.

MEAD, GEORGE H., "Scientific Method and the Moral Sciences," *The International Journal of Ethics,* Vol. 33, 1923, pp. 229–247.

RITCHIE, A. D., "Scientific Method in Social Sciences," *Philosophy,* Vol. 20, 1945, pp. 3–16.

SMITH, E. ELBERTON, "Value Judgments and the Social Scientist," *Bulletin of the American Association of University Professors,* Vol. 35, 1949, pp. 628–642.

22

THE NATURE OF MAN

THE PSALMIST'S QUESTION "What is man, that thou art mindful of him?" is a pertinent question for scientists and philosophers as well as for theologians. Sterling Power Lamprecht (1890–   ) answers the question from the naturalistic position. Lamprecht has taught philosophy at Amherst College since 1928. Paul Tillich (1886–   ) represents a position in theology known as Neo-supernaturalism. Tillich was educated and did his early teaching in Germany. From 1933 to 1954 he was Professor of Philosophical Theology at Union Theological Seminary in New York City. He is now at Harvard University.

A

Man's place in nature is an old, old problem which has been frequently and variously treated in the great literature of the world. In ancient Greece Plato and Aristotle analyzed the problem with brilliance and defined a precise and convincing answer. At Rome Lucretius wrote his long poem to set forth a different and startling solution. Christian art and theology, though primarily concerned with God and the life to come, have formulated a series of theories about nature and man's relation to nature. Dante and Hobbes, Spinoza and Milton, Descartes and Hume have

Sterling P. Lamprecht, "Man's Place in Nature," *The American Scholar,* Vol. 7, 1938, pp. 60–77. Reprinted by permission of the author and the publishers.

discussed the matter at length. Developments in biology and affiliated sciences in the last few generations have suggested fresh ideas bearing directly upon the problem. Yet it remains to haunt us today and to tempt us to formulate our own answer. The problem remains to haunt us because even the wiser and more illuminating of the earlier answers have not been identical. The problem remains to tempt us to formulate our own answer because almost surely, at moments of reflection on our persistent purposes and aims, we have to dispose of the problem or become listless in carrying out our purposes. A final answer, we can confidently say, has never been given. A final answer, and for good and sufficient reason, will never be given. It is, however, possible to indicate the general outlines of a satisfactory answer, emphasizing the fundamental points and leaving it to future generations to fill in the outlines with materials from their more amplified experience.

The good and sufficient reason why no final answer will ever be given is this. The place of man in nature is not one definite and settled affair. The place of civilized man in nature is by no means the same as that of savage man. In some respects the place of civilised and savage man is the same. All men are born of women; they inhabit animal bodies and are prey to ravages of disease, age, and death; they suffer from passions that are functions of their bodily constitutions. But where savage man practices crude rites in honor of a vaguely conceived spirit of vegetation, civilized man has learned to cultivate his fields. Where savage man recites charms over the sick, civilized man uses the arts of surgery and medicine. Where savage man regards the stars in order to discover the destiny in store for him, civilized man regards the stars in order to guide his own destiny towards ports of his own choice. In short, where savage man is the victim of forces he feels but knows not, civilized man is in part gaining mastery over his environment and dreams of greater mastery yet to come. Thus the place which man may come to have in nature is still in the making. Descartes 300 years ago expressed the hope that we might so follow his method as to "render ourselves lords and possessors of nature." We are not generally following his method today. Yet we still hope for the indicated outcome. And hence we cannot honestly give a final answer to the problem of man's place in nature. We can do much to describe the conditions of man's origin in nature and development through nature, but we cannot profitably undertake to prophesy the future status man may come to achieve.

In the light of the changing place of man in nature we may, however, say one thing with assurance. We may say (borrowing the eloquent phrase of Spinoza) that man's place in nature was originally one of bondage and is potentially one of freedom. In origin man is in servile status, bound by narrow limitations of time and space, bound by ignorance, crude impulse and passion. In destiny man may in part become supreme among the varying forms which nature exhibits, emancipated by disciplined imagination from superstition, brutality and blind chance. The essential point about this passage from bondage to freedom must not be overlooked — the passage itself is natural. In man nature comes to her most significant realization. In man nature manifests some of the most splendid potentialities that have lain forever within her. Man is, if we may speak boldly while humbly recognizing the extent of our own present inadequacies, the finest product of nature's art. His arts are her arts because she made him who thereby remakes her. Nature with man left out is not the whole of nature; and even nature as it was before man appeared and developed contained already the traits which made man possible and which, brought to focus in him and refashioned in specifically human form, are at once man's responsibility and nature's glory.

Man's place in nature, then, though varying from time to time, is at all stages an exploitation of nature's resources. That is, every fundamental characteristic of man's life is a peculiarly human form of a basic trait in nature. Let us see how this is so, beginning with obvious instances.

Man walks, we may say, because things in nature move. Of course other natural forms besides man walk, for the transition from inanimate nature to man is gradual. Indeed the gradual development from "mere motion," as in the fall of a meteor, to human walking is itself one of the minor verifications of the thesis that man's life must be viewed, not as distinct from nature generally but as a modification of nature's general traits. But for the purposes of this discussion we may at present neglect the intermediate forms between inanimate nature and man and may concentrate on man himself. Motion becomes walking, not because some agency has been injected into nature from without but because nature has in man acquired certain unique structural developments. We do not need to entertain any fantastic notion about a supernatural walker who mysteriously enters into human bodies and uses them to display his supernatural power and function. Given the physiological transformations of organic forms involved in the biped, man, we find that nature is quite able to account for walking without inventing strange fairy-stories to help her out. Did not things in nature move, man could not walk. Since things in nature move, man is bound, when he develops, to walk. Walking is the form, or one form, which the motion of nature assumes in man.

Similarly man digests because nature is chemical. That nature's chemistry should become digestion was always potential. It has become actual in man and in animal life generally. The conditions for the development of nature's chemistry into human digestion are altogether physiological: they consist of stomach and intestines and the like. But nature is quite competent to provide these conditions and has indeed done so with marvellous fertility. Nature needs no outside agency to effect the transition from inorganic to organic. Nature's chemistry takes on many forms of which digestion is one of the most complex and important. Nature is chemical and man digests; man's digestion is analogous to man's walking. Man's digestion is an exploitation, due to the occurrence of specialized organic conditions, of one of nature's ever-present chemical potentialities.

Now if we proceed beyond these obvious facts in which man resembles many simpler forms of life and turn our consideration to certain peculiarly human activities in which man is perhaps differentiated from all other natural things the same type of cosmological relation continues to hold. Man thinks because nature is intelligible. Thinking is not something which goes on within the head, as if some materialist would identify it with cortical processes. But neither is it something which goes on in a mind apart from nature, as if some transcendentalist would dignify the intellectual life by keeping it altogether distinct from nature. Of course there are images galore which distract our thinking; but we should not allow the psychological play of images to be confused with genuine thinking. There are errors galore which ruin our thinking but we should not allow the perversities of man to make us blind to man's genuine achievements. There is no more reason to import mind into nature from without than there is to import a walker or a digester. Thinking occurs quite naturally, as walking and digesting occur when physiological developments give rise to specialized bodily structures. There is no need to question the reality of the significant and unique processes which the term thinking means. There are mental processes, there is the *actio mentis* as the scholastics of the Middle Ages called it, and these processes have the exact character which candid examination and detailed analysis reveal. Thinking can occur, so far as we know, only when brain and nervous system have developed to a high degree of perfection. But it is not to be identified with brain any more than walking is to be identified with legs or digestion with stomach. Man thinks by means of his brain. And what he thinks are the forms which natural objects about him have. Thinking is, as Spinoza put it, a union of the mind with the rest of nature. And such a union is only possible because nature even before that union occurs is already intelligible. In thinking we enter into the very being of things just as in walking we explore nature's spatiality. What we think and what occurs in nature are then not two things but one. Again to quote Spinoza, "substance thinking and substance extended is one and the same substance, which is comprehended now under this, now under that, attribute." Spinoza will not even use a plural verb with his seemingly two subjects, sacrificing grammatical meticulousness to philosophical accuracy and emphasis. The act in thinking is man's and may well be called mental but that with which this act of thinking is concerned is nature's form and may well be called intelligible. Some good souls, animated by a praiseworthy desire to exalt the importance of the intellect, treat nature and mind as two realities, separate and distinct; but these good souls invariably reduce both nature and mind to mysteries, making nature void of intelligibility and mind incapable of knowledge. In place of such separation and its attendant mysteries we should view man's effective thinking as an exploration of nature's intelligible forms. Only then can we properly grasp man's place in nature, as in him nature's intelligibility becomes his knowledge. Thus thinking, like walking and digesting, is an exploitation of a basic trait of nature.

Man predicts, we may now go on to say, because nature is mechanical. This does not mean that nature is wholly or solely what the science of mechanics describes with accuracy. The science of mechanics achieves its high degree of accuracy just because it abstracts one special aspect of nature's complicated behavior and, neglecting all else, gives a concise statement of this selected phase. Nature is much more than even a correct and fairly completed science of mechanics would set forth for our instruction. So when we say that nature is mechanical our reference is to a trait of nature that is apparent far beyond the phase with which the science of mechanics is concerned. Our reference is to the regularities of sequence and correlation we find to hold good in all departments of nature, in human passions and in social movements as much as in the parabolic path of a projectile and the swing of a pendulum. Everywhere in nature we find uniformity of causal connection, necessity in the structure of events, constancy in the way in which antecedents of a given type lead on to their sure consequences. Mechanism is a term by which we mean to sum up all that is involved in uniformity, necessity and constancy. In saying that nature is mechanical we are denying that it is capricious or whimsical. We are affirming that it is regular and dependable. That nature is mechanical throughout is an assertion that runs beyond available evidence and contains an element of faith. It is an assertion, however, that every increase of scientific knowledge seems to substantiate and no evidence contradicts.

Man predicts because nature is mechanical. Human foresight is an exploitation of nature's regularities and constancies. Were nature not mechanical, man could not predict or profitably plan. Since nature is mechanical, man can learn in part to control and through control he may advance the course of civilization. The advance of the race is not wholly a function of man's foresight: advance is conditioned by other factors also, moral and cultural. But advance could not occur unless man could rely upon uniformity, necessity and constancy in the materials with which he works. Prediction is not due to man's will power or his determination to drive nature according to his fancy. Man can no more coerce an atom than he can fling back an avalanche or chain the winds. Nature is full of variety too and this variety, taken superficially as it first appears, may well be the natural basis of man's waywardness and of many of his curious errors. But discipline progressively discloses that even nature's variety is a manifestation of hidden order. This discipline, disclosing nature's order, raises man from petulance to maturity. Thereby the mechanism of nature becomes the technique of prediction in man.

Philosophers and theologians have sometimes tried to deny that nature is fundamentally mechanical. The reason for their denial seems often to be the sad notion that if nature is mechanical man is doomed to imprisonment in nature. And some disillusioned and disappointed men with a little taint of what they regard as scientific information add that man is in fact already imprisoned in nature and is gradually learning the tragic extremity of his unfortunate plight. Such a theory is quite pathetically contrary to the abundant facts of experience and the sure fruits of practice. The theory may be an inevitable consequence of some curious conception of mechanism which as a suppressed premise in their argument subtly controls their conclusion but it is hardly tenable in the light of the actual procedures of the laboratory and of reflection upon the course of modern history. The more we discover of the detail of nature's mechanism the more we are able to predict, guide, control. Through reliance on nature's mechanism we mold nature to our human interests. More than 300 years ago Francis Bacon saw this clearly. Picturing a great center of learning and of scientific research he spoke of the purpose of the institution in these glowing terms, "The end of our foundation is the knowledge of causes, and secret motions of things; and the enlarging of the bounds of human empire, to the effecting of all things possible." These glowing terms are also sober terms. Bacon speaks of the effecting of all things *possible*. He does not let imagination run wild and picture the effecting of all things dreamed of and feverishly desired. We control, not through arrogant insistence but through studious observance of nature's ways. We have learned to fly, not because we like to be aloft in the air but because we know much about physical forces. We can reach no other conclusion than that nature's mechanism, exploited by man, becomes prediction and control as nature's motion becomes walking and nature's chemistry becomes digestion.

Man is a moral being, we may further say, because nature is characterized by incessant flux. In speaking of man as a moral being there is no intent to refer to him as excellent or noble. He may be that or he may be quite the opposite. But in any case he is a being whose life is perennially a moral affair. And this incessant urgency of the moral quality throughout human life reflects nature's incessant flux. In a world such as ours there is no refuge where gains remain secure and strife gives place to permanent peace. Wistful men, men lacking in courage to face existence squarely, have dreamed of escape from peril: they have built up fanciful pictures of a New Jerusalem whose inhabitants reside beyond the reach of corruption. Braver men have faced the turmoil of affairs with frank recognition that passage of time and occurrence of change are the very condition of all life. "You may not enter the same rivers twice" said Heraclitus long ago "for other waters pour in upon them." Human life inevitably assumes moral character in such a world. There are final goods, there are final goods abundantly in the sense of ends intrinsically and immediately justifiable and justifying. There are no final goods in the sense of ends beyond which new adventures do not lie. We do of course solve some problems, solve them excellently; but the solution of any problem is itself but the setting for new problems to which there is no end. Life cannot be good unless it is restlessly forward-looking. And that is why the popular objectives of most men are not sufficiently rewarding. Were the goods we gained for a moment to be ours forever the search for pleasure and the lure of material profit might be more worthy of consideration. But pleasure is trivial unless it be the by-product of activities that increase human capacities for further growth, and material profit is futile unless it be effectively organized in an expanding range of human activities. Every good occurs, and so every good ought to be judged, in its context in a developing world and an onward sweep of events.

Failure to see the basis of human goods in the flux of nature is a conspicuous cause of many cases of frustration and disillusionment today (and at all times). Some men waste time wishing for conditions they regard as requisite in order to permit them, in the possession of those conditions, to begin to lead the "good life." But that attitude is equivalent to making morals a matter of rare chance. In nature all things must be seized in their passage. The good life, put into its natural context, involves the meeting of actual conditions instead of dreaming of more fortunate ones —the meeting of actual conditions with a bold love of adventure and a ripe fund of wisdom. And it is in the light of this truth that we may understand why certain moralists from Plato to our own day have dared to speak of certain goods as "ideal goods." Ideal goods are not ideal because they are ethereal and nebulous. They are ideal because they increase the range of human powers and enable man to respond

to a vastly larger environment. Knowledge is an ideal good, and so are technical skills and sensitive tastes and mutual confidence between persons — because they function in the urgency of nature's passage and make for practical effectiveness in meeting a variety of predicaments. Pleasures of sense and material possessions have no such role except they are in the hands of men who also possess the ideal goods. Thus it is the forward-driving character of nature by which choice between goods must be determined. The flux of nature becomes in man the inescapable fact of morality.

Once more, man is free because nature is contingent. Contingency is often regarded as an alternative to mechanism. In fact it is a correlative aspect of nature's ways. In our world we find that forces, once initiated, work out to their inevitable consequences. But the initiation of forces is not itself decreed. The laws of nature are statements of the mechanical phase of nature. They state the uniformities of correlation and sequence which events manifest. The laws of nature are not, however, dictates that compel procedure — they are not statutes or prescriptive enactments. The presence of contingency in nature is not evident at a glance because it is not effectively exploited by inanimate agents. Inanimate agents react to the actual stimulus of the moment; they react, it might be said, to the superficial. Intelligent agents react to more than the actual stimulus; they react to the potentialities of the actual. And these potentialities are always plural. The plural potentialities of nature are the significant basis of human choice. It is insufficient to argue that because things are as they are they will be as they will be. Rather, because things are as they are, an agent who imaginatively foresees the diverse potentialities of things may choose freely within given limits. Freedom is never total — it is not freedom *from* the world. But it is genuine — it is freedom *within* the world. There is at least no supernatural agency introduced into a mechanical nature in order to give man freedom at the expense of nature's laws. Rather there is natural development in the powers of agents within nature, and with the appearance of the physiologically developed organism of man there emerges the ability to handle materials in the light of their alternative possibilities. But the alternative possibilities were present in nature from the start even though they received no notable exploitation until intelligent creatures came to pass.

Stones, plants, even most animals are not free. They react only to the actuality which forces itself upon them with insistent pressure. Man is supreme among the products of nature just because, in imagination disciplined by stern experience, he can look through the actual to the potential, can respond to the actual in the light of the potential, can choose between the contingent factors of nature. Freedom is perhaps the latest development of a basic trait of nature; it is latest in time but supreme in importance. It is late because its appearance is consequent to the prior development of memory, imagination, knowledge. But even this latest development was latent in nature from the start, waiting for such a creature as man to enter through its possession into mastery over the rest of nature. Freedom is then the exploitation of nature's contingency.

Finally, man is religious. It is no simple feat to explain upon what basic trait of nature man's religious character rests. Yet the story of man's place is not told unless this problem is resolved. Many anthropologists have said, both recently and back through the centuries, that man is religious because nature is terrifying. "Fear made the gods" is an ancient saying whose earliest utterance in lit-

erature seems to be already a monotonous repetition of a hoary tradition. And doubtless man's fears do people the dark with threatening forces before which he then quails. Yet an unbiased student can hardly accept this anthropological opinion as an adequate comment on the entire history of religion. Like many generalizations it throws much light on human acts but fails to tell the whole story. Man has often groveled abjectly before what he has feared, but he has found joy and serenity in his religious life too, and release from fears. Perhaps it would be more just to say that man is superstitious because nature is terrifying. But even this is not quite adequate, for it might well be contended that it is not nature that is terrifying but man that is afraid. To be terrifying is not a basic trait of nature but an illusion which nature rouses in the ignorant and weak. We can say no more than that man is often superstitious because nature appears to him terrifying.

If then we reject the old attempt to explain religion, by a kind of *tour de force,* as a function of subjective fears in man what then shall we say? Man is as surely and as universally religious as he is a walking or digesting or thinking thing. Man is indeed so persistently religious that his religious life must have some profound lesson to teach us about his place in nature. Perhaps we should boldly venture to claim that religion is not so much an exploitation of a trait of nature as it is a means whereby man seeks to establish against nature a glory that is all his own. Yet even if this be true, man is religious because nature is what it is, because of what nature lacks, because he craves something for himself which nature does not automatically give. That is, religion is not so much an exploitation of a basic trait of nature as it is man's comment on nature's insufficiency. Nature is essentially pluralistic: man craves unity. The basic pluralism of nature can hardly be over-stated. Nature is a welter of diverse things and forces. In such a pluralistic world man can only live by turning the energies that singly would destroy him into a rhythmic unity that sustains him. Religion is man's experimental device for making nature humanly habitable.

Nature is raw material for all man is and does. It remains for man to transform it into the finished products of civilization and art. In itself it manifests no coordinating purpose and no sure outcome. Others besides Tennyson have fancied one far-off divine event to which the whole creation moves. Hegel saw the entire course of European history leading up to and finding fulfilment in the German nation — and since Hegel, Germany itself has tried out Bismarck, William II and Hitler, with other intervening régimes. Man cannot endure the unsystematic course of nature; he needs to establish order upon variety and unity upon diversity. He cannot abrogate nature's traits; he can, however, build for himself, out of the materials which nature profusely offers, institutions and programs and integrated arrangements. Religion is the imaginative enterprise in which this essentially human function is carried to ideal completion.

Of course religion is of many forms, some good, others bad, some wise, others stupid. There is no point at this place in weighing the merits of different religious types. Rather the point is this: that every form of religion, even the bad form, is some man's effort to bring much of nature's pluralism into the harmonious outline of an embracing plan. If his plan be vicious or silly his religion will be base or stupid. If this plan be noble and wise his religion will be of world import. Yet no religion, however excellent, can possibly be final. As Professor Whitehead has written, "The progress of religion is defined by the denunciation of gods; the keynote of idolatry is contentment with the prevalent gods." No effort of man to achieve harmony within nature is worthy of all men's loyalty. Such loyalty would quickly become subservience, as the fundamentalisms of history fully prove. Nature's pluralism may elicit man's religious integration as a response; it also forbids the taking of any such integration as a last word. To worship at others' shrines is always idolatry; we must abandon others' gods in order to be nobly religious ourselves. So man, outgrowing all religions, must yet be religious if he is to make life fine and full. Unless man come to love some enriching and embracing good, unless he create some rich harmony out of nature's pluralism, he will remain like other things in nature, a merely brutal and casual force. The embryonic goods which nature offers in almost disastrous profusion will be still-born unless brought into the embrace of an aspiration fruitful in organizing the whole of human life. Yet no aspiration can hope to organize the whole of nature and therefore other men must continually build their own alternative harmonies. But some religion is inevitable if man is to rise above the natural welter of things. Religion is the technique whereby man throughout the centuries has sought, and whereby he has in a measure found, effective integration. Religion is that aspect of life without which impulse does not become conduct, desire does not become aspiration, wonder does not become wisdom. If religion so conceived is not an exploitation of nature's pluralism it is man's rejoinder to that pluralism. Thus religion has its inception and its roots in nature, even if it has ever pointed beyond nature towards sheerly human goals.

The theme of this discussion could be indefinitely expanded. Man walks and digests, he thinks and predicts, he is moral and free and religious because nature is in motion and is chemical, is intelligible and mechanical, is incessantly changing and contingent and pluralistic. Man depends for what he is on nature and nature finds its fullest and most significant expression in man. Neither an adequate conception of nature nor an adequate conception of man can be developed in isolation from the other. The two belong together in theory as they exist together in fact. To deal with man is to deal with nature's potentialities; to deal with nature fully is, among other things, to deal with man. Nature and man are not two kinds of substance: rather they are related as raw material and finished product. Nature is essentially process: it is an endless process in which substance takes on varied forms, among which significantly is man. Man is process too; he is a process in which temporarily the course of nature is gloriously exemplified.

Other philosophies have given quite different answers to the problem of man's place in nature. Some of these answers deserve mention here, not to encourage controversy but to make more clear what the position above defended really involves. Perhaps two rather extreme and opposed answers are sufficient, if our purpose in introducing their discussion is briefly to draw sharp contrasts. The two answers that stand most opposed to each other and are also instructive in contrast to the position above outlined are materialism and transcendentalism.

Materialism arises from exclusive emphasis upon the *origin* of man in nature. Since man arises within nature, so the argument runs, he is "nothing but" another natural phenomenon, more intricate indeed than most substances but made out of the same elements and limited to the same types of mechanical action. Life, we are then told, is but the physical-chemical properties of protoplasm.

Man is a purposeless cluster of material particles whose entire mental activity is a quaint illusion, whose ideals are but compensatory imaginings by which we describe hidden bodily functions and drives, whose meaning is exhausted in the interplay of his internal bodily organs.

Transcendentalism arises from exclusive emphasis upon the *end* and *fulfilment* of human nature in its highest forms. The full integrity of man's mental life and the full validity of man's moral aspirations are asserted against the brutality of material forces, and therefore man is pictured as standing significantly outside the nexus of nature which constrains and compels all other things. Man, it seems, is more than a physical body. He must then be, so it is said, a soul, independent of nature in origin, entering strangely into the body and hence into the turmoil of nature but in his destiny preserved intact against nature. Whereas nature is blind, mechanical, void of value, man is capable of foresight, purposeful, the seat of all value. As black marks on paper, however complicated and however numerous, cannot produce significance except to a mind able to understand more than it immediately sees, so atoms, however complex and however cleverly arranged, cannot give rise to consciousness or mind or soul. Man is spirit, entering into nature from "on high," mysteriously consenting for a time to occupy a material body but capable of keeping itself free from taint from the temporary union with the body, and is released at last to return to the higher level of existence which is its true portion.

Both of these answers, the materialistic and the transcendental, have their merits. Both are exaggerations, however, of one element in a more integrated view of the relation of nature and man. The materialist sees the facts of human origins so forcefully that he treats the whole career and outcome of human life in terms of that origin. The transcendentalist recognizes so sensitively the glory of man's moral and intellectual development that he would give to man an origin imaginatively pictured in terms of his development. Both materialism and transcendentalism have a partially empirical basis. But neither is empirical enough. Man has both origin and developed capacities: he has, in a classic phrase from Santayana, both natural basis and ideal fulfilment. And both the identification of basis with fulfilment by the materialist and the separation of fulfilment from its basis by the transcendentalist are artificial solutions of a problem that ought to be treated in the light of man's continual experience of his unique transformations of nature's basic traits.

The root of the inadequacy of both materialism and transcendentalism is a false view of nature. Diametrically opposed as these two philosophies are, they rest on a common premise — a theory that views nature as a myriad of tiny material particles, changing position relatively to each other, remaining fixed in constitution, dead, void of meaning, restlessly entering into combinations and breaking up again into elements, but capable of no genuine novelty. Were nature such, man would have to be debased into a futile material entity as materialism suggests or rescued from nature by some miraculous faith such as transcendentalism demands. But it would be wiser to resolve the problem by reconsidering what nature is. There is no need to deny the reality of the material particles, whether they be atoms or electrical charges, centers of force or some other entity defined by physical science. There are only waste of effort and futility of conclusion in combating the hypotheses which experimental scientists bring forward with evidence in their favor. Not all hypotheses of scientists prove acceptable in

the end; but their correction is the task of those who can weigh the evidence and gather further evidence. It is not at all the prerogative of those who shudder at the seemingly "dangerous" implications which the hypotheses suggest for some general philosophical position. In considering the place of man in nature it is wise to begin by accepting humbly the probabilities which the physicist or other scientist tentatively sets forth as indicated by sufficient evidence; and the analysis of things into molecules, atoms and smaller particles is one of the credible conclusions of experimental science. But even if one may not deny the reality of the entities into which physical science analyzes matter one may, indeed one must, remember the reality of the things of which that analysis is given. Nature is what we have to analyze and is not exhausted by any one method. If nature is discovered to be molecular and atomic, well and good. It is much else too. The premature theories about nature that have grown out of temporary phases of scientific analysis are legion. The fault is not with the scientific analysis (at least the major fault is not here, though no analysis is infallible) but with the supposition that the analysis has disclosed the single "ultimate" truth about the nature of things. Descartes became so entranced with the geometrical aspect of nature that he defined nature in terms of extension and then he got into strange, even weird, difficulties which he could not solve. More recently people have been prone to define nature in terms of atoms or similar particles and then they either have to demote man to atomic motions or snatch him from nature entirely.

We ought to accept nature more piously for all it is and may be discovered to be without exalting a favorite aspect of nature into *the* reality of which all else is either a disguised form or a perverted fancy. If rocks and butterflies have atomic constitution and this constitution throws light upon their behavior, well and good. The atoms are not, however, the ultimate elements out of which rocks and butterflies are obtained. Rather rocks and butterflies are real in the full plenitude of their being and their atomic structure is one special aspect which a special kind of handling discloses. Examine nature in one way and you will discover its atomic structure. Examine it in other ways and you will discover its mechanical operation, its contingent occurrence, its rich potentialities, its vast resources and fertility of productive energies. There is after all only one philosophy that is not subject to Hamlet's criticism that

> There are more things in heaven and earth, Horatio,
> Than are dreamt of in your philosophy.

And that one philosophy is a philosophy which accepts nature in all its phases and aspects, open in mind to recognize new phases and aspects, neither credulous in taking fancies for facts nor arrogant in taking one system of information as setting limits to nature's infinite possibilities.

There are many truths about nature which cannot conceivably be deduced from the principles of atomic structure. These truths are no more and no less fundamental than the principles of atomic structure. He who has a petty view of nature will have either a petty or a superstitious view of man. The system of nature, if we dare refer to nature as a system, is of inexhaustible potency. It is no tight little system, definable in a few chosen postulates and then exclusive of whatever does not follow from these postulates. Nature is not a system in the sense in which we may speak of a system of mechanics or a system of cataloguing books in a library. Mechanics is a system in the sense that whatever does

not fit into the framework of its principles is not a proper concern for the men who are developing the system of mechanics. Cataloguing books is a system in the sense that it must be adequate to enable us to find our way around among the books already acquired but it need not be a prophecy of the new kinds of books that future genius may compose. Nature has justified men in formulating the system of mechanics and in inventing the system of cataloguing books. But nature is still more, and its full capacities are immeasurably vast. Perhaps it would be better not to speak of the *system* of nature at all. Perhaps it would be better to speak of nature as that to which all our systems must be referred, by which our systems may be warranted, beyond which our systems have no meaning, yet of which our systems can hardly hope to convey the whole truth.

We deepen the significance of our lives by full and frank appreciation of our roots in nature. From nature we emerged, by nature our bodies and our minds are sustained, through nature we rise to whatever of achievement we may call our own. A wholesome respect for nature and its potentialities is the beginning of civilization. It is therefore the end of philosophic wisdom. This respect is not to be confused with worship: we may worship the excellence and beauty which nature makes possible but we must respect the whole of nature, even that which brings evil and disaster in its train. Only by acknowledging the dependence of our vital human characteristics upon basic traits of nature can we take the true measure of man. Only thus can we formulate an adequate theory of man's place in nature and an adequate practice whereby to improve that place. Even in the noblest role man comes to play in nature he remains nature's child. To grasp the significance of this claim is, I believe, the best means whereby man may learn to walk with assurance, to digest with health, to think with precision, to predict with accuracy, to meet moral responsibility with courage, to turn freedom into accomplishment and to pray with piety.

B

Man is a unity and a totality. Therefore it is inadequate to develop several doctrines of man: a scientific and a philosophical one, a secular and a religious one, a psychological and a sociological one. Man is an indivisible unity. All the methods contribute to one and the same picture of man. There are, however, many elements and strata in human nature; and each of them demands a special approach — a special method. The unity of man does not imply that it is possible to examine him in one way only. Since man includes all elements of reality, every stratum of being, it is necessary to use all methods in order to deal with him adequately. He is the microcosmos, the description of which should not neglect any tool used in the description of the macrocosmos. Therefore it is wrong to make *one* method of approaching man the only one or to subordinate all other methods to one single approach, whether the theological methods in early times or the rationalistic method in modern times or the empirical method today. On the other hand, we must avoid any atomism of methods. It must be shown that in each method elements appear which drive to the others; that the empirical approach cannot be used without elements discovered by the rationalistic method; and that this in turn presupposes certain elements furnished by theology. The methods of studying human nature should be neither

Paul Tillich, "The Conception of Man in Existential Philosophy," *The Journal of Religion,* Vol. 19, 1939, pp. 201–215. Reprinted by permission of the publishers, The University of Chicago Press.

exclusive nor merely atomistic and summative, but dialectical and mutually interdependent.

There are three main groups of methods: First, the experimental-calculating method which refers to things as completely objective without any element of subjectivity in them — the method of mathematical sciences applicable as far as quantitative and calculable relations reach. In the second place there is the intuitive-descriptive method which refers to things in so far as they have subjectivity, individuality, spontaneity — the method of the so-called natural history as well as of the history of man. And in the third place there is the method of "responsible understanding" which refers to subjectivity as such, to the norms, values, creations, and meaning of personal life. In understanding personal life and its contents the distance between subject and object is overcome. There is knowledge in which we are involved ourselves; there is knowledge which concerns us infinitely. Understanding in this respect necessarily has responsible or existential character.

Man's nature must therefore be approached by these three methods since he belongs to the three realms which correspond to them. He belongs to the physical world and is subject to the laws and structures of this world, and in every moment of human life much of man's activity is calculable, such as the chemical, biological, psychological, and sociological reactions as well as his existence as a moving body in the physical space. It is not only justifiable but necessary that in order to control human body and soul the knowledge of those calculable elements should be extended as far as possible.

But there is a limit to this method. Man is a living subject, a *Gestalt,* a totality of interdependent relations in which no part can be isolated as long as the living process goes on. Therefore any normal (not artificially isolated) reaction is a reaction of the totality and has that creative character which we admire in living beings and which, in difference from mechanical dependence, appears as "spontaneity." In man this spontaneity takes on the character of freedom. Since freedom is the characteristic which distinguishes man from all other beings and since all other human characteristics follow from this, the doctrine of human nature has its center in the doctrine of human freedom (the doctrine of man's essential nature). In it the results of all the preceding approaches are united and out of it the questions arise as to the contents of human freedom and the self-realization of human freedom in personality and community. The answers to these questions lead beyond the range of the second, intuitive-descriptive method to the method of responsibile understanding. Norms and values cannot be grasped by a mere description. There is a decision implied, rooted in freedom and confirming freedom. But freedom does not mean arbitrariness and decision does not mean choice without any criterion. There is an essential relation between freedom and reason. Freedom falls down if it decides against reason; that is, against its essential content. Freedom either confirms itself or destroys itself, which is the possibility of good or evil. This ambiguous character of human freedom forces the doctrine of man to go beyond the doctrine of human freedom.

We call the doctrine of man, from the standpoint of the ambiguity of freedom, the doctrine of human servitude (the doctrine of man's existential nature). This step does not constitute a new method. The doctrine of human existence must use all the methods referred to. The theological approach to man is, so to speak, transmethodological. It is in and beyond the methods at the same time. In dealing with human existence we must show the ambiguity of this existence in the realm of calculable reactions as well as in the realm of life and spontaneity; in the realm of norms and values as well as in their realization in creative culture; and in personality as well as in community. Here we need responsible understanding as well as intuitive description and experimental calculation. But we need it from a special or, more exactly, from the all-embracing point of view. Theology asks: What do these facts, structures, values, mean for man's very existence? What do they mean for him in his standing between freedom and servitude, between finiteness and infinity, and between guilt and salvation? The theological doctrine of man deals with the problems of physical motion, of stimulus and response, of complex and repression of the sociology of the masses; it deals with the system of ethical and aesthetic norms and with the realization of them in the history of human culture. But it deals with all this not in terms of its relation to the essential structure of being but in so far as it concerns human existence. Theology has no method of its own, but it has a point of view for all methods and in all realms.

The theological doctrine of man, then, has two main sections: the doctrine of human freedom and the doctrine of human servitude; or, in other words, the doctrines of man's essential and of man's existential nature. The reason for the duality of the doctrine of man is found in the possibility that human freedom may deny itself its own essential nature. And this possibility is real.

We turn, then, to the doctrine of human

freedom — that is of man's essential nature. This is the first task of a theological anthropology; and the fact that it often has been omitted is a reason for many confusions in traditional theology. Using words like "man," "freedom," "necessity," "choice," etc., without giving an exact phenomenological description of their meaning, their presuppositions, and their implications, is a perpetual source of mistakes, wrong questions, and misleading controversies. A clear distinction, for instance, of man's essential freedom and existential servitude and an exact description of servitude as presupposing freedom and of freedom as surrendering itself into servitude would have made the debate over predestination much more fruitful. Erasmus was as right in the essential realm as Luther was in the existential realm, and the human situation cannot be described correctly if either of these realms is omitted.

This holds true of the discussion regarding determinism and indeterminism. The traditional doctrine of human freedom is restricted to the doctrine of the so-called "free will" and man is considered as a "thing with qualities." His special character is negated before the discussion starts, and consequently, in this discussion determinism is always right from the logical point of view while indeterminism represents a true experience expressed, however, in absurd terms. The mistake of the whole discussion is that the nature of man is taken for granted without freedom and that then, too late in the logical sequence, the question for freedom is raised. But it is impossible to give a description of man's essential nature without giving a description of freedom in all its implications, of which the "freedom of choice" is only one and by no means a fundamental one. Finally, theology needs a doctrine of human freedom in order to make intelligible in concrete terms such concepts as "innocence," "temptation," "sin,"

"guilt," etc. Lack of such a doctrine has deprived these concepts of their actual significance in the experience of daily life and has made them expressions of an abstract ideology.

Human freedom is identical with the fact that man has a world which is at once unitary and infinite, set over against himself, from which he is separated and to which he belongs at the same time; or, taken from the other side, that man is a definite self, centered in himself and being the center for his world. Being between himself and his world, man is free from both of them even while he is bound to both of them. This situation in all its ambiguity is the situation of human freedom. No being is free for which the world and the self are not strictly distinguished. Such a being as, for instance, an animal has a limited world to be called "environment" and an indefinite self to be called "self-awareness." A relation between the self and his world is possible only if the world is a structural unity and man is able to understand these structures and, through them, his world. And man is able to do so because the structural unity of his self and his world correspond with each other, however this correspondence may be explained (in idealistic or monistic or realistic terms). Having a world, therefore, means having the structural forms of a meaningful unity in which infinite elements are related to one another and to the whole. These structural forms are universals such as categories, concepts, laws, and principles, which make every single experience intelligible as "belonging to our world" or as "being a possible content of our self-consciousness."

Man is a definite self, set over against his world although belonging to it. In order to be a self he must be an individual, an ultimately separate part of reality, realizing itself in time and space, embodying in itself a certain power of being, a certain bodily space, and a certain duration and uniqueness that make it different from any other individual. Man is more individual than any other being. He is the complete individual because, on the other hand, he is a definite self. He alone cannot be considered as a mere exemplar of a species. As an individual self he is beyond the contrast of species and exemplar — he is "spirit." Man is spirit: this means he is the dynamic unity of reason and power, of mental universality and vital individuality. Human freedom is identical with the fact that man is spirit. Man is not only mind, statically related to the universals, but he is spirit, dynamically creating a world of his own beyond the world that he finds. And man is not only vital individuality, dynamically realizing himself in a natural process, but he is spirit, creating in unity with the eternal forms and norms of being. He has the freedom of creation, which is the first and fundamental characteristic of freedom. Human creative freedom expresses itself in four degrees: It is first the freedom of transcending any given situation and of imagining and realizing something new. Man is not bound to the actuality and to the needs of a given situation as any animal is. He can transcend any given situation infinitely. His freedom is technical freedom. He never has, and never will, cease to sketch the world of tomorrow. Man's creative freedom is, in the second place, the freedom of transcending himself in the direction of complete unity of universality and individuality. Man is able to become personality and community. His freedom is moral freedom. Moral freedom is actual only in the so-called "I-Thou relation." The ego is freed from its natural self-realization by meeting another ego which demands unconditionally to be respected as such and not to be abused as a mere thing. Here the seriousness of human freedom becomes manifest. The other self represents the inescapable

demand coming from the unity of our world and ourselves. Freedom is freedom to receive unconditional demands. The third degree of man's creative freedom is the freedom of creating with purpose. This is cultural freedom. It has elements of the two preceding degrees. It transcends the given world and it transcends the given self. But it transcends them in order to have the infinite meaning of our world and ourselves represented in temporal symbols. In language and music, poetry and art, science and philosophy, man expresses his freedom by elevating being to meaning. Man is free from being in so far as he lives in meaning. Spirit creates meaningful symbols — things which express more than they are in themselves. The freedom of cultural creativity presupposes a being which transcends its own being — it presupposes spirit. This leads to a fourth degree of freedom which, in a paradoxical phrase, could be called freedom-from-one's-own-freedom or the freedom to play with one's world and one's self. This is the counterpart of the seriousness of moral freedom. Nevertheless, it belongs to the structure of human creative freedom since it prevents man from being enslaved by his own freedom. The significance of aesthetic romanticism lies in the fact that it stresses this element against puritan moralism. Freedom which is not able to play is law and not creation.

In all these degrees of creative freedom the freedom of choice is presupposed. Creativity demands different possibilities; spirit demands the ability to decide. Freedom of choice is the fact from which the traditional discussions on freedom and necessity have started. Instead of becoming involved in that controversy which is insoluble in principle, we may describe the freedom of choice in such terms as these: Man like all beings receives stimuli and makes responses; but the line from the one to the other goes through the totality of man, of his self, and consequently of his world. Man acts freely since he acts as a definite self and not merely as a section of the world to which he belongs. The problem of the freedom of choice is answered by the description of man as having a world and being a self.

Human freedom is human peril. The ability to transcend any given situation implies the possibility of losing one's self in the infinity of transcending one's self. Technical freedom may become technical servitude if the means become ends in themselves. Moral freedom may become moral servitude if the individual self, in order to preserve itself, resists the demand coming from the other self and loses both personality and community. Cultural freedom can become *cultural servitude* if it finds expression in the will to power or the will to draw the totality of one's world into the limitations of one's individual self. Freedom to play may become the *surrender of one's own freedom,* thus wasting one's self and one's world. All this can happen because freedom implies the freedom of choice. We can decide against our essential being, thus perverting our freedom into servitude. For freedom can maintain itself only in so far as it chooses the content, the norms, and the values in which our essential nature, including our freedom, expresses itself. Freedom can act against freedom, surrendering itself into servitude. And freedom is always tempted to do so. The infinite possibility causes *Angst* — fear, horror, anxiety: the *Angst* of not actualizing all possibilities and the *Angst* of leaping from possibility into actuality. Man is afraid not to use this freedom and yet he is afraid to use it. Human possibility is human temptation. There the temptation is primarily spiritual in character. Sensual temptation is possible only after the bond between

mind and life has been torn — after the spirit has been cleft. And temptation, being spiritual, is real temptation. It is a matter of free choice. Innocence cannot be lost by a natural process but only by a spiritual decision. If this decision is made, man's existence as determined by this decision contradicts his essential nature. Man's freedom is surrendered to servitude; but servitude is not necessity. It is servitude only because it is the servitude of him who is free in his essential nature. Man does not cease to be man. It is still human existence which we must examine.

Let us consider, therefore, the doctrine of human servitude or of man's existential nature.

When freedom surrenders itself it becomes servitude. But since even in the act of surrender freedom remains active, freedom and servitude are not simply contradictions. This becomes manifest in the exact description of man's existential nature. The creativity which is the main characteristic of man in his freedom does not disappear in his servitude, but it is transformed — it becomes tragic and sinful. The doctrine of the existential nature of man must therefore deal first with human creativity under the law of tragic servitude and then with human creativity under the law of sinful servitude. The two phases are interdependent, and in both of them an element of freedom is struggling with an element of servitude. But servitude is predominant.

Man's creative freedom is the participation of man in the primary creativity on which both he and his world depend. This creativity is primary because everything depends on it and it is unconditional because it itself depends on nothing. Creating is achieving something new. But the new which is created by man is dependent on the given which he finds — on himself as well as on his world. Man does not exist by himself alone nor does his world. Both are dependent on the original creation in relation to which he and his world are "creatures." On the other hand, he, the creature, is creating; by his creative freedom he participates in the creative process. Man is a creative creature. He has finite infinity. He has the eternal Logos in temporal and individual limitations. So far as man is essentially free, his finiteness, his temporality, his creatureliness are united with his infinity, his eternity, and his creativity. So far as man existentially is in servitude the unity is lost and man is subject to the law of tragedy. We can imagine a finiteness which is continuously overcome and conserved by our infinity. We have experiences of a transitoriness which does not defy our eternity but is an element in it. We know a feeling in which the very fact that we are able to face our nothingness includes the certainty that we are beyond it. It is not our finiteness that is our tragedy but our finiteness in so far as it tries to elevate itself to infinity. This attempt is the possibility implied in freedom, and the consequence of this attempt is servitude. In order to become a free or definite self man must be an individual. His finiteness is expressed in his individuality which, at the same time, is the presupposition of his infinity, of his being able to become personality and community, technical and cultural creator. The individual thinking to make himself universal instead of subjecting himself to the universal is the tragic individual. The servitude to which he is subjected is the law of tragedy. Human creativity when it is accompanied by the determination of the individual to be the ground of himself (or in classical terms "to be like God") is the tragic servitude of man. It is servitude from a double point of view: it drives man endlessly from one finiteness to another in inexhaustible desire and in this dynamic trend it destroys the individual's

own structure in tragic conflict with other individuals. It is inescapable crime and inescapable punishment at the same time. It is important to realize that this description of human existence is similar to that given in the Bible (Gen. 3) and in the first known words of Greek philosophy in the fragment of Anaximander.

Man's tragic servitude finds many expressions in his existential nature. The *Angst* which we have described in connection with temptation as the *Angst* of innocence becomes tragic *Angst* in human contradictory existence. *Angst* is the situation of the isolated individual facing the abyss of nothingness and the threat of annihilation all around him. Man tries to escape this horrible vision by creative courage, by cultural or technical civilization, by morality, or by play. Man flees forever from his own *Angst*. In doing so he is driven from one courageous action to another, transforming *Angst* into fear and overcoming fear by courage. There is no more courageous being than man, since even in his servitude he has not lost his freedom. Nevertheless, no courage can liberate him from his *Angst* — the horrible experience of facing his own finiteness without being able to conquer it by his infinity. Animals are limited but they are neither finite nor infinite. Consequently they have neither human courage nor human *Angst*.

The *Angst*, which is the expression of human finiteness separated from human infinity, manifests itself in many forms. A theory of human existence would have to deal with all these forms. Some of them may be mentioned. There is the feeling of loneliness, which is as strong in the midst of crowds or friends or family members as it is in complete physical solitude. For it is the feeling by the individual self that he is infinitely separated from the essential unity to which he belongs. The tragedy of loneliness is that man tries to overcome it by flight to the other individual without being able to bridge the cleavage, by flight to the crowd in order to forget his loneliness as one among many, or by flight to a group in order to lose his existence as an individual in the "we-self" of the group. But since he cannot lose his individual self and since he is separated from the essential unity to which he belongs he cannot lose his loneliness. The loneliness of life becomes manifest in the loneliness of death.

The same can be said with respect to the melancholy of having to die. The fact that men call themselves mortals shows that there is something in them which rebels against mortality and tries to make life infinite by glorious memory, by perpetuating their life in their offspring, by rational argument for the immortality of the soul. In these ways human courage tries to overcome the tragedy of having to die. But it cannot, and the higher man's power and his courage the deeper the tragedy, as the great tragedians have shown.

Another evidence of human servitude is man's being anxious, to which Jesus refers in the Sermon on the Mount. The separate individual is threatened by the vicissitudes which come from the world of which he is a part. In creative freedom he struggles for security or in heroic gambling he makes a security of his insecurity. A great many of the creations of human civilization can be understood in terms of the "quest of security," and a great deal of creative — and destructive — heroism can be understood in terms of a flight from a security which is felt to be superficial and, in the end, betraying. This tragic law of insecurity has come to the foreground of consciousness in our time because of political and economic insecurity, on the one hand, and the lack of meaning in life, on the other.

Tragic servitude exists in mutual dependence with the servitude of sin. Sin is the act in which the free self turns away from its essential being and surrenders itself to servitude. The tragic servitude which is implied in our finiteness (in so far as it is separated from our infinity) is dependent on sin, for it is in the act of sin that this separation occurs in which the finite self claims for itself infinity. Sin, therefore, is the arrogance of the finite, made possible by man's having a world which stands over against him. Sin is possible through the essential good which makes man human. Therefore sin cannot extinguish human essential goodness. Sin is dependent upon it. Man can never lose his infinity and spirituality. He can never become a "stone and stump"; and therefore he can never cease to be the "image of God." To deny this in order to emphasize the gravity of sin means to destroy the very presupposition of sin.

Man retains his essential goodness; but the situation is that this goodness condemns rather than determines his existence. This is a situation which Paul and Luther have called law. The law — for instance the Ten Commandments — is not the order of some transcendental tyrant. It is our own essential goodness set over against us as a threat, as a criterion, and as a condemnation. It consequently arouses the rebellion of the individual self against the law although at the same time he must acknowledge that the law is good since it is his own goodness set over against himself. Law — not as the essential order of reality but as the command above and opposed to reality — expresses more than anything else the cleavage within man's individual and social existence.

The law creates despair. The whole description of the servitude of sin could be given in terms of despair (as Kierkegaard has done). Despair — a word which is less expressive than the German word *Verzweiflung* (split into two parts) — is freedom aware of its servitude or finiteness which is separated from its infinity. In religious terms man is separated from God. Despair is the conflict between the will to maintain one's self and the will to lose one's self; to maintain one's self by gaining the whole world, thus acknowledging through one's infinite desire the unity and totality to which one belongs, and to lose one's self by returning to the natural servitude of living below the level of freedom, thereby acknowledging that freedom is the inescapable presupposition of despair. The struggle between courage and despair expresses itself in many forms. A full description of it would have to cover large fields of human psychological and sociological behavior. It would have to deal with conscience, with the subconscious and the conscious, with the will to death and meaninglessness, and with doubt and guilt. But all this is an expression of human servitude — of the personal and social distortion of the human spirit.

The servitude of sin is universal. Only because this is the case is it servitude. Otherwise, every individual would have the chance to escape servitude in all its forms. But this is impossible. No one can escape, because the existential situation is a universal situation. The idea of original sin has no other meaning than this: the embracing universality of servitude which is at the same time an individual and a cosmic event.

Existence itself is under the law of guilt. Therefore sin has a tragic inescapability. The two sides of our description are united: Sin is rooted and tragedy is rooted in sin. The nontragic view of sin as we find it in moralism and in Pelagianism misses the connection between human finiteness and human guilt. Sin makes our finiteness tragic and finiteness makes our sin tragic. In this very human freedom is human servitude.

As the doctrine of human freedom drives us to the doctrine of human servitude, so the doctrine of human servitude forces us to consider the doctrine of human liberation. And as the transition from human servitude follows no necessity but has the character of a leap, so the transition from servitude to liberation cannot be derived from servitude. It is something new, coming from beyond human existence. A description of it would imply the whole system of theology and therefore lies beyond the scope of this article.

A full picture of human nature can be developed only if it is approached from the three points of view to which we have referred. Not only man's essential nature but also his existential and his eschatological nature must be dealt with. The doctrine of man which speaks only of the existential nature of man necessarily leads to destructive pessimism without criteria and without hope. A doctrine of man which ignores the existential nature of man leads to a shallow optimism without revelation and without grace. Only the threefold doctrine of human nature which we have here suggested can be the foundation of a Christian theology.

SUGGESTIONS FOR THOUGHT

1. Do people achieve worth because they serve institutions, or are institutions valuable because they serve human needs? John MacMurray said once, "No institution is big enough to be worth the sacrifice of the meanest person — not even the British Constitution." By what right can a nation ask its citizens to endanger their lives in war?

2. Is any person ever voluntarily bad, or are people bad only from inability to know the good?

3. Compare these three statements about human nature made by contemporary philosophers and theologians: (1) "The picture of man over against nature is a contradiction in terms. Man is one of the forms and habits of nature." (Irwin Edman) (2) "Man is not merely an animal of nature, like a skylark or a bear. He is also an animal of culture, whose race can subsist only within the development of society and civilization." (Jacques Maritain) (3) "In its purest form the Christian view of man regards man as a unity of God-likeness and creatureliness in which he remains a creature even in the highest spiritual dimensions of his existence and may reveal elements of the image of God even in the lowliest aspects of natural life." (Reinhold Niebuhr)

4. How do you interpret the words of a recent philosopher: "What is great in man is that he is a bridge and not a goal"?

5. When is a person justified in risking his life for another? Would a great scientist be expected to go into a burning building in order to save a feeble-minded child? Are all people of equal worth? Was Nietzsche right in condemning Christianity for teaching that all human life is sacred?

6. What might have led Hitler to describe humanitarianism as a "mixture of stupidity, cowardice, and superciliousness, which will melt away like snow in the March sunshine"?

7. "There are two classes of people in this world, those who sin, and those who are sinned against; if a man must belong to either, he had better belong to the first than to the second." (Samuel Butler) Do you agree?

8. "Scientists animated by the purpose of proving that they are purposeless constitute an interesting subject for study." (A. N. Whitehead) Can you name other ways in which scientists reveal more of the nature of man by their actions than they teach in their writings?

9. "We are all called men but only those of us are human who have been civilized by the studies proper to culture." (Cicero) What might those studies be?

10. What assumptions about the nature of man are made by modern democracies? By totalitarian states?

SUGGESTIONS FOR FURTHER READING

AUBREY, EDWIN EWART, "The Naturalistic Conception of Man," *The Journal of Religion,* Vol. 19, 1939, pp. 189–200.

CARR, H. W., *The Unique Status of Man,* New York, The Macmillan Company, 1928.

CARREL, ALEXIS, *Man the Unknown,* New York, Harper and Brothers, 1935.

CONKLIN, EDWIN GRANT, *Man, Real and Ideal,* New York, Charles Scribner's Sons, 1943, ch. 18.

DEWEY, JOHN, *Human Nature and Conduct,* New York, Henry Holt and Company, 1922, Introduction.

HERSCHEL, BAKER, *The Dignity of Man,* Cambridge, Harvard University Press, 1947.

HOCKING, W. E., and others, *Preface to Philos-ophy,* New York, The Macmillan Company, 1946, Part I.

KAHLER, ERICH, *Man the Measure,* New York, Pantheon Books, 1943, pp. 6–16.

KANT, IMMANUEL, *Religion Within the Limits of Reason Alone,* translated by T. M. Greene and H. H. Hudson, Chicago, Open Court Publishing Company, 1934, Books I, II.

KORZYBSKI, ALFRED, *Manhood of Humanity,* New York, E. P. Dutton and Company, 1921, ch. 4.

MORRIS, CHARLES, *The Open Self,* New York, Prentice-Hall, 1948, ch. 2.

NIEBUHR, REINHOLD, *The Nature and Destiny of Man,* Vol. 1, New York, Charles Scribner's Sons, 1941, ch. 1.

OTTO, M. C., "What is Man?" *The International Journal of Ethics,* Vol. 39, 1929, pp. 190–204.

PERRY, RALPH BARTON, "A Definition of the Humanities," in *The Meaning of the Humanities,* edited by T. M. Greene, Princeton, Princeton University Press, 1940, pp. 1–42.

PRATT, J. B., *Can We Keep the Faith?,* New Haven, Yale University Press, 1941, ch. 8.

ROBERTS, W. H., "Are We Machines? And What of It?" *The Journal of Philosophy,* Vol. 28, 1931, pp. 347–356.

WEISS, PAUL, *Nature and Man,* New York, Henry Holt and Company, 1947, ch. 7.

23

THE NATURE
OF SOCIETY

THE CONTROVERSY over whether or not society is an organism has been called the first of the moot questions of sociology. Hobbes regards society as an unfortunate necessity; Herbert Spencer (1820–1903) takes a much happier attitude toward man and society. Thomas Hobbes (1588–1679) was an English philosopher who spent most of his long life fleeing from partly-real, partly-imagined persecution of the clergy both in England and on the Continent. His greatest work, *The Leviathan,* was published in 1651.

A

Nature hath made men so equal, in the faculties of the body and mind; as that, though there be found one man sometimes manifestly stronger in body or of quicker mind than another, yet when all is reckoned together the difference between man and man is not so considerable, as that one man can thereupon claim to himself any benefit, to which another may not pretend as well as he. For as to the strength of body, the weakest has strength enough to kill the strongest, either by secret machination, or by confederacy with others that are in the same danger with himself.

And as to the faculties of the mind — setting aside the arts grounded upon words, and especially that skill of proceeding upon general and infallible rules, called science; which very few have, and but in few things; as being not a native faculty, born with us; nor attained, as prudence, while we look after somewhat else — I find yet a greater equality amongst men, than that of strength. For prudence is but experience which equal time equally bestows on all men, in those things they equally apply themselves unto. That

Thomas Hobbes, *Leviathan,* 1651, chs. 13, 17 (in part).

which may perhaps make such equality incredible, is but a vain conceit of one's own wisdom, which almost all men think they have in a greater degree than the vulgar; that is, than all men but themselves, and a few others, whom by fame, or for concurring with themselves, they approve. For such is the nature of men, that howsoever they may acknowledge many others to be more witty, or more eloquent, or more learned, yet they will hardly believe there be many so wise as themselves; for they see their own wit at hand and other men's at a distance. But this proveth rather that men are in that point equal, than unequal. For there is not ordinarily a greater sign of the equal distribution of anything, than that every man is contented with his share.

From this equality of ability, ariseth equality of hope in the attaining of our ends. And therefore if any two men desire the same thing, which nevertheless they cannot both enjoy, they become enemies; and in the way to their end, which is principally their own conservation, and sometimes their delectation, only, endeavor to destroy, or subdue one another. And from hence it comes to pass that where an invader hath no more to fear than another man's single power; if one plant, sow, build, or possess a convenient seat, others may probably be expected to come prepared with forces united, to dispossess and deprive him, not only of the fruit of his labor, but also of his life or liberty. And the invader again is in the like danger of another.

And from this diffidence of one another, there is no way for any man to secure himself so reasonable as anticipation; that is, by force or wiles to master the persons of all men he can, so long, till he sees no other power great enough to endanger him: and this is no more than his own conservation requireth, and is generally allowed. Also because there be

some, that taking pleasure in contemplating their own power in the acts of conquest, which they pursue farther than their security requires; if others, that otherwise would be glad to be at ease within modest bounds, should not by invasion increase their power, they would not be able long time, by standing only on their defense, to subsist. And by consequence, such augmentation of dominion over men being necessary to a man's conservation, it ought to be allowed him.

Again, men have no pleasure, but on the contrary a great deal of grief, in keeping company, where there is no power able to overawe them all. For every man looketh that his companion should value him at the same rate he sets upon himself; and upon all signs of contempt, or undervaluing, naturally endeavors, as far as he dares (which amongst them that have no common power to keep them in quiet, is far enough to make them destroy each other), to extort a greater value from his contemners by damage, and from others by the example.

So that in the nature of man, we find three principal causes of quarrel. First, competition; second, diffidence; thirdly, glory.

The first maketh men invade for gain; the second, for safety; and the third, for reputation. The first use violence to make themselves masters of other men's persons, wives, children, and cattle; the second, to defend them; the third, for trifles, as a word, a smile, a different opinion, and any other sign of undervalue, either direct in their persons, or by reflection in their kindred, their friends, their nation, their profession, or their name.

Hereby it is manifest that during the time men live without a common power to keep them all in awe, they are in that condition which is called war; and such a war as is of every man against every man. For war consisteth not in battle only, or the act of fighting, but in a tract of time where the will to contend by battle is sufficiently known, and therefore the notion of time is to be considered in the nature of war, as it is in the nature of weather. For as the nature of foul weather lieth not in a shower or two of rain, but in an inclination thereto of many days together; so the nature of war consisteth not in actual fighting, but in the known disposition thereto, during all the time there is no assurance to the contrary. All other time is peace.

Whatsoever therefore is consequent to a time of war, where every man is enemy to every man; the same is consequent to the time, wherein men live without other security than what their own strength and their own invention shall furnish them withal. In such condition there is no place for industry, because the fruit thereof is uncertain: and consequently no culture of the earth; no navigation, nor use of the commodities that may be imported by sea; no commodious building; no instruments of moving, and removing, such things as require much force; no knowledge of the face of the earth; no account of time; no arts; no letters; no society; and which is worst of all, continual fear, and danger of violent death; and the life of man, solitary, poor, nasty, brutish, and short.

It may seem strange to some man that has not well weighed these things, that nature should thus dissociate, and render men apt to invade and destroy one another; and he may therefore, not trusting to this inference, made from the passions, desire perhaps to have the same confirmed by experience. Let him therefore consider with himself, when taking a journey, he arms himself and seeks to go well accompanied; when going to sleep, he locks his doors; when even in his house he locks his chests; and this when he knows there be laws, and public officers, armed, to revenge all injuries shall be done him; what opinion he has of his fellow-subjects, when he rides armed; of his fellow-citizens, when he locks his doors; and of his children, and servants, when he locks his chests. Does he not there as much accuse mankind by his actions, as I do by my words? But neither of us accuse man's nature in it. The desires, and other passions of man, are in themselves no sin. No more are the actions that proceed from those passions, till they know a law that forbids them: which till laws be made they cannot know; nor can any law be made, till they have agreed upon the person that shall make it.

It may peradventure be thought, there was never such a time nor condition of war as this; and I believe it was never generally so, over all the world: but there are many places where they live so now. For the savage people in many places of America, except the government of small families, the concord whereof dependeth on natural lust, have no government at all; and live at this day in that brutish manner, as I said before. Howsoever, it may be perceived what manner of life there would be, where there were no common power to fear; by the manner of life which men have formerly lived under a peaceful government, use to degenerate into in a civil war.

But though there had never been any time wherein particular men were in a condition of war one against another; yet in all times, kings, and persons of sovereign authority, because of their independency, are in continual jealousies, and in the state and posture of gladiators; having their weapons pointing, and their eyes fixed on one another; that is, their forts, garrisons, and guns upon the frontiers of their kingdoms; and continual spies upon their neighbors; which is a posture of war. But because they uphold thereby the industry of their subjects, there does not follow from it that misery which accompanies the liberty of particular men.

To this war of every man against every man, this also is consequent: that nothing can be unjust. The notions of right and wrong, justice and injustice, have there no place. Where there is no common power, there is no law; where no law, no injustice. Force and fraud are in war the two cardinal virtues. Justice and injustice are none of the faculties neither of the body nor mind. If they were, they might be in a man that were alone in the world, as well as his senses and passions. They are qualities that relate to men in society, not in solitude. It is consequent also to the same condition, that there be no propriety, no dominion, no mine and thine distinct; but only that to be every man's, that he can get; and for so long as he can keep it. And thus much for the ill condition which man by mere nature is actually placed in; though with a possibility to come out of it, consisting partly in the passions, partly in his reason.

The passions that incline men to peace are fear of death, desire of such things as are necessary to commodious living, and a hope by their industry to obtain them. And reason suggesteth convenient articles of peace, upon which men may be drawn to agreement....

The final cause, end, or design of men who naturally love liberty and dominion over others, in the introduction of that restraint upon themselves in which we see them live in commonwealths, is the foresight of their own preservation, and of a more contented life thereby; that is to say, of getting themselves out from that miserable condition of war, which is necessarily consequent . . . to the natural passions of men, when there is no visible power to keep them in awe, and tie them by fear of punishment to the perform-

ance of their covenants and observation of those laws of nature set down in the fourteenth and fifteenth chapters.

For the laws of nature, as justice, equity, modesty, mercy, and, in sum, doing to others as we would be done to, of themselves, without the terror of some power to cause them to be observed, are contrary to our natural passions, that carry us to partiality, pride, revenge, and the like. And covenants, without the sword, are but words, and of no strength to secure a man at all. Therefore notwithstanding the laws of nature, which everyone hath then kept, when he has the will to keep them when he can do it safely; if there be no power erected, or not great enough for our security, every man will, and may, lawfully rely on his own strength and art, for caution against all other men. And in all places where men have lived by small families, to rob and spoil one another has been a trade, and so far from being reputed against the law of nature, that the greater spoils they gained, the greater was their honor; and men observed no other laws therein but the laws of honor; that is, to abstain from cruelty, leaving to men their lives, and instruments of husbandry. And as small families did then; so now do cities and kingdoms, which are but greater families, for their own security enlarge their dominions, upon all pretenses of danger and fear of invasion, or assistance that may be given to invaders, and endeavor as much as they can to subdue or weaken their neighbors, by open force and secret arts, for want of other caution, justly; and are remembered for it in after ages with honor.

Nor is it the joining together of a small number of men, that gives them this security; because in small numbers, small additions on the one side or the other make the advantage of strength so great, as is sufficient to carry the victory, and therefore gives encouragement to an invasion. The multitude sufficient to confide in for our security, is not determined by any certain number, but by comparison with the enemy we fear; and is then sufficient, when the odds of the enemy is not of so visible and conspicuous moment, to determine the event of war, as to move him to attempt.

And be there never so great a multitude, yet if their actions be directed according to their particular judgments and particular appetites, they can expect thereby no defense nor protection, neither against a common enemy nor against the injuries of one another. For being distracted in opinions concerning the best use and application of their strength, they do not help but hinder one another; and reduce their strength by mutual opposition to nothing: whereby they are easily, not only subdued by a very few that agree together; but also when there is no common enemy, they make war upon each other, for their particular interests. For if we could suppose a great multitude of men to consent in the observation of justice, and other laws of nature, without a common power to keep them all in awe, we might as well suppose all mankind to do the same; and then there neither would be, nor need to be any civil government or commonwealth at all, because there would be peace without subjection.

Nor is it enough for the security, which men desire should last all the time of their life, that they be governed and directed by one judgment for a limited time, as in one battle or one war. For though they obtain a victory by their unanimous endeavor against a foreign enemy; yet afterwards, when either they have no common enemy, or he that by one part is held for an enemy, is by another part held for a friend, they must needs by the difference of their interests dissolve, and fall again into a war amongst themselves.

It is true that certain living creatures, as bees and ants, live sociably one with another, which are therefore by Aristotle numbered amongst political creatures; and yet have no other direction than their particular judgments and appetites; nor speech, whereby one of them can signify to another what he thinks expedient for the common benefit: and therefore some man may perhaps desire to know why mankind cannot do the same. To which I answer:

First, that men are continually in competition for honor and dignity, which these creatures are not; and consequently amongst men there ariseth on that ground, envy and hatred, and finally war; but amongst these not so.

Secondly, that amongst these creatures, the common good differeth not from the private; and being by nature inclined to their private, they procure thereby the common benefit. But man, whose joy consisteth in comparing himself with other men, can relish nothing but what is eminent.

Thirdly, that these creatures, having not, as man, the use of reason, do not see, nor think they see, any fault in the administration of their common business; whereas amongst men, there are very many that think themselves wiser, and able to govern the public better, than the rest; and these strive to reform and innovate, one this way, another that way; and thereby bring it into distraction and civil war.

Fourthly, that these creatures, though they have some use of voice in making known to one another their desires and other affections; yet they want that art of words by which some men can represent to others, that which is good in the likeness of evil, and evil in the likeness of good, and augment or diminish the apparent greatness of good and evil; discontenting men and troubling their peace at their pleasure.

Fifthly, irrational creatures cannot distinguish between injury and damage; and therefore as long as they be at ease, they are not offended with their fellows: whereas man is then most troublesome when he is most at ease; for then it is that he loves to shew his wisdom, and control the actions of them that govern the commonwealth.

Lastly, the agreement of these creatures is natural; that of men is by covenant only, which is artificial: and therefore it is no wonder if there be somewhat else required, besides covenant, to make their agreement constant and lasting; which is a common power, to keep them in awe, and to direct their actions to the common benefit.

The only way to erect such a common power, as may be able to defend them from the invasion of foreigners and the injuries of one another, and thereby to secure them in such sort as that, by their own industry, and by the fruits of the earth, they may nourish themselves and live contentedly; is, to confer all their power and strength upon one man, or upon one assembly of men, that may reduce all their wills, by plurality of voices, unto one will: which is as much as to say, to appoint one man, or assembly of men, to bear their person; and everyone to own and acknowledge himself to be author of whatsoever he that so beareth their person, shall act or cause to be acted in those things which concern the common peace and safety; and therein to submit their wills, everyone to his will, and their judgments, to his judgment. This is more than consent, or concord; it is a real unity of them all, in one and the same person, made by covenant of every man with every man, in such manner as if every man should say to every man, "I authorize and give up my right of governing myself to this man,

or to this assembly of men, on this condition, that thou give up thy right to him, and authorize all his actions in like manner." This done, the multitude so united in one person, is called a commonwealth, in Latin *civitas*. This is the generation of that great LEVIATHAN, or rather, to speak more reverently, of that mortal god, to which we owe under the immortal God, our peace and defense. For by this authority, given him by every particular man in the commonwealth, he hath the use of so much power and strength conferred on him, that by terror thereof he is enabled to perform the wills of them all, to peace at home and mutual aid against their enemies abroad. And in him consisteth the essence of the commonwealth; which to define it, is one person, of whose acts a great multitude, by mutual covenants one with another, have made themselves every one the author, to the end he may use the strength and means of them all, as he shall think expedient, for their peace and common defense.

And he that carrieth this person, is called sovereign, and said to have sovereign power; and everyone besides, his subject.

The attaining to this sovereign power is by two ways. One, by natural force; as when a man maketh his children to submit themselves and their children to his government, as being able to destroy them if they refuse; or by war subdueth his enemies to his will, giving them their lives on that condition. The other, is when men agree amongst themselves to submit to some man, or assembly of men, voluntarily, on confidence to be protected by him against all others. This latter, may be called a political commonwealth, or commonwealth by institution; and the former, a commonwealth by acquisition.

B

Sir James Macintosh got great credit for the saying, that "constitutions are not made, but grow." In our day, the most significant thing about this saying is, that it was ever thought so significant. As from the surprise displayed by a man at some familiar fact, you may judge of his general culture; so from the admiration which an age accords to a new thought, its average degree of enlightenment may be inferred. That this apophthegm of Macintosh should have been quoted and re-quoted as it has, shows how profound has been the ignorance of social science. A small ray of truth has seemed brilliant, as a distant rushlight looks like a star in the surrounding darkness.

Such a conception could not, indeed, fail to be startling when let fall in the midst of a system of thought to which it was utterly alien. Universally in Macintosh's day, things were explained on the hypothesis of manufacture, rather than that of growth; as indeed they are, by the majority, in our day. It was held that the planets were severally projected round the Sun from the Creator's hand, with just the velocity required to balance the Sun's attraction. The formation of the Earth, the separation of sea from land, the production of animals, were mechanical works from which God rested as a labourer rests. Man was supposed to be moulded after a manner somewhat akin to that in which a modeller makes a clay-figure. And of course, in harmony with such ideas, societies were tacitly assumed to be arranged thus or thus by direct interposition of Providence; or by the regulations of law-makers; or by both.

Herbert Spencer, "The Social Organism," *The Westminster Review,* Vol. 74, 1860 (in part).

Yet that societies are not artificially put together, is a truth so manifest that it seems wonderful men should ever have overlooked it. Perhaps nothing more clearly shows the small value of historical studies, as they have been commonly pursued. You need but to look at the changes going on around, or observe social organization in its leading traits, to see that these are neither supernatural, nor are determined by the wills of individual men, as by implication the older historians teach; but are consequent on general natural causes. The one case of the division of labour suffices to prove this. It has not been by command of any ruler that some men have become manufacturers, while others have remained cultivators of the soil. In Lancashire, millions have devoted themselves to the making of cotton-fabrics; in Yorkshire, another million lives by producing woolens; and the pottery of Staffordshire, the cutlery of Sheffield, the hardware of Birmingham, severally occupy their hundreds of thousands. These are large facts in the structure of English society; but we can ascribe them neither to miracle, nor to legislation. It is not by "the hero as king," any more than by "collective wisdom," that men have been segregated into producers, wholesale distributors, and retail distributors. Our industrial organization, from its main outlines down to its minutest details, has become what it is, not simply without legislative guidance, but, to a considerable extent, in spite of legislative hindrances. It has arisen under the pressure of human wants and resulting activities. While each citizen has been pursuing his individual welfare, and none taking thought about division of labour, or conscious of the need of it, division of labour has yet been ever becoming more complete. It has been doing this slowly and silently: few having observed it until quite modern times. By steps so small, that year after year the industrial arrangements have seemed just what they were before — by changes as insensible as those through which a seed passes into a tree; society has become the complex body of mutually-dependent workers which we now see. And this economic organization, mark, is the all-essential organization. Through the combination thus spontaneously evolved, every citizen is supplied with daily necessaries; while he yields some product of aid to others. That we are severally alive to-day, we owe to the regular working of this combination during the past week; and could it be suddenly abolished, multitudes would be dead before another week ended. If these most conspicuous and vital arrangements of our social structure have arisen not by the devising of any one, but through the individual efforts of citizens to satisfy their own wants; we may be tolerably certain that the less important arrangements have similarly arisen.

"But surely," it will be said, "the social changes directly produced by law, cannot be classed as spontaneous growths. When parliaments or kings order this or that thing to be done, and appoint officials to do it, the process is clearly artificial; and society to this extent becomes a manufacture rather than a growth." No, not even these changes are exceptions, if they be real and permanent changes. The true sources of such changes lie deeper than the acts of legislators. To take first the simplest instance. We all know that the enactments of representative governments ultimately depend on the national will: they may for a time be out of harmony with it, but eventually they must conform to it. And to say that the national will finally determines them, is to say that they result from the aver-

age of individual desires; or, in other words — from the average of individual natures. A law so initiated, therefore, really grows out of the popular character. In the case of a Government representing a dominant class, the same thing holds, though not so manifestly. For the very existence of a class monopolizing all power, is due to certain sentiments in the commonalty. Without the feeling of loyalty on the part of retainers, a feudal system could not exist. We see in the protest of the Highlanders against the abolition of heritable jurisdictions, that they preferred that kind of local rule. And if to the popular nature must be ascribed the growth of an irresponsible ruling class; then to the popular nature must be ascribed the social arrangements which that class creates in the pursuit of its own ends. Even where the Government is despotic, the doctrine still holds. The character of the people is, as before, the original source of this political form; and, as we have abundant proof, other forms suddenly created will not act, but rapidly retrograde to the old form. Moreover, such regulations as a despot makes, if really operative, are so because of their fitness to the social state. His acts being very much swayed by general opinion — by precedent, by the feeling of his nobles, his priesthood, his army — are in part immediate results of the national character, and when they are out of harmony with the national character, they are soon practically abrogated. The failure of Cromwell permanently to establish a new social condition, and the rapid revival of suppressed institutions and practices after his death, show how powerless is a monarch to change the type of the society he governs. He may disturb, he may retard, or he may aid the natural process of organization; but the general course of this process is beyond his control. Nay, more than this is true. Those who regard the histories of societies as the histories of their great men, and think that these great men shape the fates of their societies, overlook the truth that such great men are the products of their societies. Without certain antecedents — without a certain average national character, they neither could have been generated nor could have had the culture which formed them. If their society is to some extent re-moulded by them, they were, both before and after birth, moulded by their society — were the results of all those influences which fostered the ancestral character they inherited, and gave their own early bias, their creed, morals, knowledge, aspirations. So that such social changes as are immediately traceable to individuals of unusual power, are still remotely traceable to the social causes which produced these individuals; and hence, from the highest point of view, such social changes also, are parts of the general developmental process.

Thus that which is so obviously true of the industrial structure of society, is true of its whole structure. The fact that "constitutions are not made, but grow," is simply a fragment of the much larger fact, that under all its aspects and through all its ramifications, society is a growth and not a manufacture.

A perception that there exists some analogy between the body politic and a living individual body, was early reached; and has from time to time re-appeared in literature. But this perception was necessarily vague and more or less fanciful. In the absence of physiological science, and especially of those comprehensive generalizations which it has but lately reached, it was impossible to discern the real parallelisms.

The central idea of Plato's model Republic, is the correspondence between the parts of a society and the faculties of the human mind. Classifying these faculties under the heads of Reason, Will, and Passion, he classifies the members of his ideal society under what he regards as three analogous heads: — councillors, who are to exercise government; military or executive, who are to fulfill their behests; and the commonalty, bent on gain and selfish gratification. In other words, the ruler, the warrior, and the craftsman, are, according to him, the analogues of our reflective, volitional, and emotional powers. Now even were there truth in the implied assumption of a parallelism between the structure of a society and that of a man, this classification would be indefensible. It might more truly be contended that, as the military power obeys the commands of the Government, it is the Government which answers to the will; while the military power is simply an agency set in motion by it. Or, again, it might be contended that whereas the Will is a product of predominant desires, to which the Reason serves merely as an eye, it is the craftsmen, who, according to the alleged analogy, ought to be the moving power of the warriors.

Hobbes sought to establish a still more definite parallelism: not, however, between a society and the human mind, but between a society and the human body. In the introduction to the work in which he develops this conception, he says —

"For by art is created that great LEVIATHAN called a COMMONWEALTH, or STATE, in Latin CIVITAS, which is but an artificial man; though of greater stature and strength than the natural, for whose protection and defence it was intended, and in which the *sovereignty* is an artificial *soul,* as giving life and motion to the whole body; the *magistrates* and other *officers* of judicature and execution, artificial *joints; reward* and *punishment,* by which, fastened to the seat of the sovereignty, every joint and member is moved to perform his duty, are the *nerves,* that do the same in the body natural; the *wealth* and *riches* of all the particular members are the *strength; salus populi,* the *people's safety,* its *business; counsellors,* by whom all things needful for it to know are suggested unto it, are the *memory; equity* and *laws* an artificial *reason* and *will; concord, health; sedition, sickness;* and *civil war, death."* And Hobbes carries this comparison so far as actually to give a drawing of the Leviathan — a vast human-shaped figure, whose body and limbs are made up of multitudes of men. Just noting that these different analogies asserted by Plato and Hobbes, serve to cancel each other (being, as they are, so completely at variance), we may say that on the whole those of Hobbes are the more plausible. But they are full of inconsistencies. If the sovereignty is the *soul* of the body-politic, how can it be that magistrates, who are a kind of deputy-sovereigns, should be comparable to *joints?* Or, again, how can the three mental functions, memory, reason, and will, be severally analogous, the first to counsellors, who are a class of public officers, and the other two to equity and laws, which are not classes of officers, but abstractions? Or, once more, if magistrates are the artificial joints of society, how can reward and punishment be its nerves? Its nerves must surely be some class of persons. Reward and punishment must in societies, as in individuals, be *conditions* of the nerves, and not the nerves themselves.

But the chief errors of these comparisons made by Plato and Hobbes, lie much deeper. Both thinkers assume that the organization of a society is comparable, not simply to the organization of a living body in general, but to the organization of the human body in particular. There is no warrant whatever for assuming this. It is in no way, implied by the evidence; and is simply one of those fancies which we commonly find mixed up with the truths of early speculation. Still more errone-ous are the two conceptions in this, that they construe a society as an artificial structure. Plato's model republic — his ideal of a healthful body-politic — is to be consciously put together by men, just as a watch might be; and Plato manifestly thinks of societies in general as thus originated. Quite specifically does Hobbes express a like view. "For by *art,"* he says, "is created that great LEVIATHAN called a COMMONWEALTH." And he even goes so far as to compare the supposed social contract, from which a society suddenly originates, to the creation of a man by the divine fiat. Thus they both fall into the extreme inconsistency of considering a community as similar in structure to a human being, and yet as produced in the same way as an artificial mechanism — in nature, an organism; in history, a machine.

Notwithstanding errors, however, these speculations have considerable significance. That such likenesses, crudely as they are thought out, should have been alleged by Plato and Hobbes and others, is a reason for suspecting that *some* analogy exists. The untenableness of the particular parallelisms above instanced, is no ground for denying an essential parallelism; since early ideas are usually but vague adumbrations of the truth. Lacking the great generalizations of biology, it was, as we have said, impossible to trace out the real relations of social organizations to organizations of another order. We propose here to show what are the analogies which modern science discloses.

Let us set out by succinctly stating the points of similarity and the points of difference. Societies agree with individual organisms in four conspicuous peculiarities: —

1. That commencing as small aggregations, they insensibly augment in mass: some of them eventually reaching ten thousand times what they originally were.

2. That while at first so simple in structure as to be considered structureless, they assume, in the course of their growth, a continually-increasing complexity of structure.

3. That though in their early, undeveloped states, there exists in them scarcely any mutual dependence of parts, their parts gradually acquire a mutual dependence; which becomes at least so great, that the activity and life of each part is made possible only by the activity and life of the rest.

4. That the life of a society is independent of, and far more prolonged than, the lives of any of its component units; who are severally born, grow, work, reproduce, and die, while the body-politic composed of them survives generation after generation, increasing in mass, in completeness of structure, and in functional activity.

These four parallelisms will appear the more significant the more we contemplate them. While the points specified, are points in which societies agree with individual organisms, they are also points in which individual organisms agree with one another, and disagree with all things else. In the course of its existence, every plant and animal increases in mass, in a way not paralleled by inorganic objects: even such inorganic objects as crystals, which arise by growth, show us no such definite relation between growth and existence as organisms do. The orderly progress from simplicity to complexity, displayed by bodies-politic in common with living bodies, is a characteristic which distinguishes living bodies from the inanimate bodies amid which they move. That functional dependence of parts, which is scarcely more manifest in animals than in nations, has no counterpart elsewhere. And in no aggregate except an organic or a social one, is there a perpetual removal and replacement of parts, joined with a continued integrity of the whole. Moreover, societies and

organisms are not only alike in these peculiarities, in which they are unlike all other things; but the highest societies, like the highest organisms, exhibit them in the greatest degree. We see that the lowest animals do not increase to anything like the sizes of the higher ones; and, similarly, we see that aboriginal societies are comparatively limited in their growths. In complexity, our large civilized nations as much exceed primitive savage tribes, as a mammal does a zoophyte. Simple communities, like simple creatures, have so little mutual dependence of parts, that mutilation or subdivision causes but little inconvenience; but from complex communities, as from complex creatures, you cannot remove any considerable organ without producing great disturbance or death of the rest. And in societies of low type, as in inferior animals, the life of the aggregate, often cut short by division or dissolution, exceeds in length the lives of the component units, very far less than in civilized communities and superior animals; which outlive many generations of their component units.

On the other hand, the leading differences between societies and individual organisms are these: —

1. That societies have no specific external forms. This, however, is a point of contrast which loses much of its importance, when we remember that throughout the vegetal kingdom, as well as in some lower divisions of the animal kingdom, the forms are often very indefinite — definiteness being rather the exception than the rule; and that they are manifestly in part determined by surrounding physical circumstances, as the forms of societies are. If, too, it should eventually be shown, as we believe it will, that the form of every species of organism has resulted from the average play of the external forces to which it has been subject during its evolution as a species; then, that the external forms of societies should

depend, as they do, on surrounding conditions, will be a further point of community.

2. That though the living tissue whereof an individual organism consists, forms a continuous mass, the living elements of a society do not form a continuous mass; but are more or less widely dispersed over some portion of the Earth's surface. This, which at first sight appears to be an absolute distinction, is one which yet to a great extent fades when we contemplate all the facts. For, in the lower divisions of the animal and vegetal kingdoms, there are types of organization much more nearly allied, in this respect, to the organization of a society, than might be supposed — types in which the living units essentially composing the mass, are dispersed through an inert substance, that can scarcely be called living in the full sense of the word. It is thus with some of the *Protococci* and with the *Nostoceae,* which exist as cells imbedded in a viscid matter. It is so, too, with the *Thalassicollae* — bodies made up of differentiated parts, dispersed through an undifferentiated jelly. And throughout considerable portions of their bodies, some of the *Acalephae* exhibit more or less this type of structure. Now this is very much the case with a society. For we must remember that though the men who make up a society are physically separate, and even scattered, yet the surface over which they are scattered is not one devoid of life, but is covered by life of a lower order which ministers to their life. The vegetation which clothes a country makes possible the animal life in that country; and only through its animal and vegetal products can such a country support a society. Hence the members of the body-politic are not to be regarded as separated by intervals of dead space, but as diffused through a space occupied by life of a lower order. In our conception of a social organism, we must include all that lower

organic existence on which human existence, and therefore social existence, depend. And when we do this, we see that the citizens who make up a community may be considered as highly vitalized units surrounded by substances of lower vitality, from which they draw their nutriment: much as in the cases above instanced.

3. The third difference is that while the ultimate living elements of an individual organism are mostly fixed in their relative positions, those of the social organism are capable of moving from place to place. But here, too, the disagreement is much less than would be supposed. For while citizens are locomotive in their private capacities, they are fixed in their public capacities. As farmers, manufacturers, or traders, men carry on their businesses at the same spots, often throughout their whole lives; and if they go away occasionally, they leave behind others to discharge their functions in their absence. Each great centre of production, each manufacturing town or district, continues always in the same place; and many of the firms in such town or district, are for generations carried on either by the descendants or successors of those who founded them. Just as in a living body, the cells that make up some important organ severally perform their functions for a time and then disappear, leaving others to supply their places; so, in each part of a society the organ remains, though the persons who compose it change. Thus, in social life, as in the life of an animal, the units as well as the larger agencies formed of them, are in the main stationary as respects the places where they discharge their duties and obtain their sustenance. And hence the power of individual locomotion does not practically affect the analogy.

4. The last and perhaps the most important distinction is, that while in the body of an animal only a special tissue is endowed with

feeling, in a society all the members are endowed with feeling. Even this distinction, however, is not a complete one. For in some of the lowest animals, characterized by the absence of a nervous system, such sensitiveness as exists is possessed by all parts. It is only in the more organized forms that feeling is monopolized by one class of the vital elements. And we must remember that societies, too, are not without a certain differentiation of this kind. Though the units of a community are all sensitive, they are so in unequal degrees. The classes engaged in laborious occupations are less susceptible, intellectually and emotionally, than the rest; and especially less so than the classes of highest mental culture. Still, we have here a tolerably decided contrast between bodies-politic and individual bodies; and it is one which we should keep constantly in view. For it reminds us that while, in individual bodies, the welfare of all other parts is rightly subservient to the welfare of the nervous system, whose pleasurable or painful activities make up the good or ill of life; in bodies-politic the same thing does not hold, or holds to but a very slight extent. It is well that the lives of all parts of an animal should be merged in the life of the whole, because the whole has a corporate consciousness capable of happiness or misery. But it is not so with a society; since its living units do not and cannot lose individual consciousness, and since the community as a whole has no corporate consciousness. This is an everlasting reason why the welfare of citizens cannot rightly be sacrificed to some supposed benefit of the State, and why, on the other hand, the State is to be maintained solely for the benefit of citizens. The corporate life must here be subservient to the lives of the parts, instead of the lives of the parts being subservient to the corporate life.

Such, then, are the points of analogy and the points of difference. May we not say that the points of difference serve but to bring into clearer light the points of analogy? While comparison makes definite the obvious contrasts between organisms commonly so called, and the social organism, it shows that even these contrasts are not so decided as was to be expected. The indefiniteness of form, the discontinuity of the parts, and the universal sensitiveness, are not only peculiarities of the social organism which have to be stated with considerable qualifications; but they are peculiarities to which the inferior classes of animals present approximations. Thus we find but little to conflict with the all-important analogies. Societies slowly augment in mass; they progress in complexity of structure; at the same time their parts become more mutually dependent; their living units are removed and replaced without destroying their integrity; and the extents to which they display these peculiarities are proportionate to their vital activities. These are traits that societies have in common with organic bodies. And these traits in which they agree with organic bodies and disagree with all other things, entirely subordinate the minor distinctions: such distinctions being scarcely greater than those which separate one half of the organic kingdom from the other. The *principles* of organization are the same, and the differences are simply differences of application.

SUGGESTIONS FOR THOUGHT

1. Whitehead has said that routine is dominant in any society that is not collapsing. Why do you think that he regarded routine as a sign of social life rather than social decay?

2. What are some of the forces that unite men in social groups?

3. During the French revolution Condorcet wrote: "No bounds have been fixed to the improvement of the human faculties; the perfectibility of man is absolutely indefinite." What foundation did he have for such an optimistic judgment? Is such an evaluation necessary to ensure continued efforts toward social improvement?

4. Some have claimed that the difference between insect societies and human societies is that the former are not progressive. Would a rebuttal consist in pointing out that insect societies have reached perfect adjustment through instinct and therefore progress is impossible for them?

5. Charles Perrault, a French historian, wrote in 1687: "Our age is, in some sort, arrived at the very summit of perfection. . . . it is pleasant to think that there are probably not many things for which we need envy future generations." Is such thinking ever justified?

6. "The world is probably closer to disintegration now than at any time since the fall of the Roman Empire." What aspects of contemporary society might have prompted R. M. Hutchins to make this gloomy observation?

7. D. Eldon Trueblood has characterized our civilization as a "cut-flower civilization." "Beautiful as cut flowers may be, and much as we may use our ingenuity to keep them looking fresh for a while, they will eventually die, and they die because they are severed from their sustaining roots." What are the roots of our civilization from which we are now cut off?

8. Why are most of the contemporary philosophies of history pessimistic? Is it because there

have been two world wars and a depression within twenty-five years?

9. What constitutes race prejudice? What are the problems of intermarriage between Negroes and white people? What is the purpose of the segregation of white and colored that is practiced in certain parts of the United States? Is this segregation undemocratic?

10. Why has prejudice arisen in the United States against the Negro but not to any large extent against the American Indian? What has fostered prejudice against the Jews? How can this prejudice be put down? What are the effects of race prejudice upon individuals?

11. Nations have found nothing more powerful than war as a means of prompting social solidarity. What rivals does war have in this respect?

12. William James said that we need to find a moral equivalent of war. What are the moral values of war? What are some of the possible equivalents?

13. Freud has claimed that wars are caused in part by the sadistic tendencies of people. One of America's top generals in World War II is reported to have said, "War is hell, but how I love it!" Was he sadistic? What is the attraction of war?

14. General MacArthur said at the time of the surrender of Japan: "The problem basically is theological and involves a spiritual recrudescence and improvement of human character that will synchronize with our almost matchless advances in science, art, literature, and all material and cultural developments of the past two thousand years. It must be of the spirit, if we are to save the flesh." What is the theological problem to which General MacArthur referred? How can religion aid the cause of peace?

15. Would the use of a world language necessarily imply that the nations of the world would get along more peacefully? Would the United

Nations Organization function more smoothly if one language could be used?

16. Woodrow Wilson said in an address before the United States Senate on January 22, 1917, "The equality of nations upon which peace must be founded, if it is to last must be an equality of rights." What are these rights? Do these rights refer to nations or to individuals? In international affairs is it possible for nations to count as equals?

17. How can East and West be brought together when they are so different in attitudes toward life? Is the following a fair statement of their differences: " . . . the West has a positive philosophy of action, but has little comprehension of any ultimate goal of action. . . . The East, on the other hand, has concentrated its attention on the goal but has often lost sight of the means of better living"? (Charles A. Moore)

18. Does nationalism sometimes make it difficult for us to think in terms of internationalism? What would prompt large and wealthy nations to give up national sovereignty?

19. "Nationalism is the only way thus far through which men have escaped from provincialism." (T. V. Smith) Or is nationalism the last provincialism?

SUGGESTIONS FOR FURTHER READING

BENEDICT, RUTH, *Patterns of Culture,* Boston, Houghton Mifflin Company, 1934, ch. 7.

BRADLEY, F. H., *Ethical Studies,* London, Oxford University Press, 1927, pp. 163–173.

BROTHERSTON, BRUCE W., "Society, an Original Fact," *The International Journal of Ethics,* Vol. 35, 1924, pp. 24–40.

BROWN, HAROLD CHAPMAN, "Human Nature and the State," *The International Journal of Ethics,* Vol. 26, 1916, pp. 177–192.

DOWDALL, H. C., "What is a Society?" *Proceedings of the Aristotelian Society,* Vol. 24, 1924, pp. 19–40.

EMERSON, RALPH WALDO, "Politics," *The Complete Works of Ralph Waldo Emerson,* Boston and New York, Houghton Mifflin Co., 1876, Vol. III, pp. 199–221.

FRANCKE, KUNO, "German Literature and the American Temper," *Atlantic Monthly,* November 1914.

HARLEY, J. H., "The Theory of the State," *Proceedings of the Aristotelian Society,* Vol. 25, 1925, pp. 175–198.

HARTMANN, NICOLAI, *Ethics,* Vol. II, translated by Stanton Coit, New York, The Macmillan Company, 1932, ch. 9.

LEWIS, H. D., "Is There a Social Contract?" *Philosophy,* Vol. 15, 1940, pp. 64–79, 177–189.

MACMURRAY, J., "The Concept of Society," *Proceedings of the Aristotelian Society,* Vol. 31, 1931, pp. 127–142.

PERRY, R. B., *General Theory of Value,* New York, Longmans Green and Company, 1926, chs. 14–17.

24

FREEDOM IN SOCIETY

HOW MUCH FREEDOM can and should be allowed the individual citizen in the state? Probably no problem that a democracy faces is more crucial than this one. In his essay *On Liberty* John Stuart Mill (1806–1873) offers one of the best defenses of the theory that the individual should be granted the maximum of personal liberty. A more cautious view is given by the English idealist Bernard Bosanquet (1848–1923). Bosanquet taught philosophy at University College and at St. Andrews University.

A

The object of this Essay is to assert one very simple principle, as entitled to govern absolutely the dealings of society with the individual in the way of compulsion and control, whether the means used be physical force in the form of legal penalties, or the moral coercion of public opinion. That principle is, that the sole end for which mankind are warranted, individually or collectively, in interfering with the liberty of action of any of their number, is self-protection. That the only purpose for which power can be rightfully exercised over any member of a civilized community, against his will, is to prevent harm to others. His own good, either physical or moral, is not a sufficient warrant. He cannot rightfully be compelled to do or forbear because it will be better for him to do so, because it will make him happier, because, in the opinions of others, to do so would be wise, or even right. These are good reasons for remonstrating with him, or reasoning with him, or persuading him or entreating him, but not for compelling him, or visiting him with any evil, in case he do otherwise. To justify that, the conduct from which it is desired to deter him must be calculated to produce evil to some one else. The only part of the conduct of any one, for which he is amenable to society, is that which concerns others. In the part which merely concerns himself, his inde-

John Stuart Mill, *On Liberty,* 1859 (in part).

pendence is, of right, absolute. Over himself, over his own body and mind, the individual is sovereign.

It is, perhaps, hardly necessary to say that this doctrine is meant to apply only to human beings in the maturity of their faculties. We are not speaking of children, or of young persons below the age which the law may fix as that of manhood or womanhood. Those who are still in a state to require being taken care of by others, must be protected against their own actions as well as against external injury. For the same reason, we may leave out of consideration those backward states of society in which the race itself may be considered as in its nonage. The early difficulties in the way of spontaneous progress are so great, that there is seldom any choice of means for overcoming them; and a ruler full of the spirit of improvement is warranted in the use of any expedients that will attain an end, perhaps otherwise unattainable. Despotism is a legitimate mode of government in dealing with barbarians, provided the end be their improvement, and the means justified by actually effecting that end. Liberty, as a principle, has no application to any state of things anterior to the time when mankind have become capable of being improved by free and equal discussion. Until then, there is nothing for them but implicit obedience to an Akbar or a Charlemagne, if they are so fortunate as to find one. But as soon as mankind have attained the capacity of being guided to their own improvement by conviction or persuasion (a period long since reached in all nations with whom we need here concern ourselves), compulsion, either in the direct form or in that of pains and penalties for non-compliance, is no longer admissible as a means to their own good, and justifiable only for the security of others.

It is proper to state that I forego any advantage which could be derived to my argument from the idea of abstract right, as a thing independent of utility. I regard utility as the ultimate appeal on all ethical questions; but it must be utility in the largest sense, grounded on the permanent interests of man as a progressive being. Those interests, I contend, authorize the subjection of individual spontaneity to external control, only in respect to those actions of each, which concern the interest of other people. If any one does an act hurtful to others, there is a *primâ facie* case for punishing him, by law, or, where legal penalties are not safely applicable, by general disapprobation. There are also many positive acts for the benefit of others, which he may rightfully be compelled to perform; such as, to give evidence in a court of justice; to bear his fair share in the common defence, or in any other joint work necessary to the interest of the society of which he enjoys the protection and to perform certain acts of individual beneficence, such as saving a fellow creature's life, or interposing to protect the defenceless against ill-usage, things which whenever it is obviously a man's duty to do, he may rightfully be made responsible to society for not doing. A person may cause evil to others not only by his actions but by his inaction, and in either case he is justly accountable to them for the injury. The latter case, it is true, requires a much more cautious exercise of compulsion than the former. To make any one answerable for doing evil to others, is the rule; to make him answerable for not preventing evil, is, comparatively speaking, the exception. Yet there are many cases clear enough and grave enough to justify that exception. In all things which regard the external relations of the individual, he is *de jure* amenable to those whose interests are concerned, and if need be, to society as their protector. There are often good reasons for not holding him to the responsibility; but these reasons must arise from the special expediences of the case: either be-cause it is a kind of case in which he is on the whole likely to act better, when left to his own discretion, than when controlled in any way in which society have it in their power to con-trol him; or because the attempt to exercise control would produce other evils, greater than those which it would prevent. When such reasons as these preclude the enforcement of responsibility, the conscience of the agent him-self should step into the vacant judgment-seat, and protect those interests of others which have no external protection; judging himself all the more rigidly, because the case does not admit of his being made accountable to the judgment of his fellow-creatures.

But there is a sphere of action in which society, as distinguished from the individual, has, if any, only an indirect interest; compre-hending all that portion of a person's life and conduct which affects only himself, or, if it also affects others, only with their free, vol-untary, and undeceived consent and participa-tion. When I say only himself, I mean directly, and in the first instance: for what-ever affects himself, may affect others *through* himself; and the objection which may be grounded on this contingency, will receive consideration in the sequel. This, then, is the appropriate region of human liberty. It com-prises, first, the inward domain of conscious-ness; demanding liberty of conscience, in the most comprehensive sense; liberty of thought and feeling; absolute freedom of opinion and sentiment on all subjects, practical or specu-lative, scientific, moral, or theological. The liberty of expressing and publishing opinions may seem to fall under a different principle, since it belongs to that part of the conduct of an individual which concerns other people; but, being almost of as much importance as the liberty of thought itself, and resting in great part on the same reasons, is practically

inseparable from it. Secondly, the principle requires liberty of tastes and pursuits; of fram-ing the plan of our life to suit our own char-acter; of doing as we like, subject to such con-sequences as may follow; without impediment from our fellow-creatures, so long as what we do does not harm them even though they should think our conduct foolish, perverse, or wrong. Thirdly, from this liberty of each in-dividual, follows the liberty, within the same limits, of combination among individuals; freedom to unite, for any purpose not involv-ing harm to others; the persons combining being supposed to be of full age, and not forced or deceived.

No society in which these liberties are not, on the whole, respected, is free, whatever may be its form of government; and none is com-pletely free in which they do not exist abso-lute and unqualified. The only freedom which deserves the name, is that of pursuing our own good in our own way, so long as we do not attempt to deprive others of theirs, or impede their efforts to obtain it. Each is the proper guardian of his own health, whether bodily, or mental and spiritual. Mankind are greater gainers by suffering each other to live as seems good to themselves, than by compell-ing each to live as seems good to the rest.

Though this doctrine is anything but new, and, to some persons, may have the air of a truism, there is no doctrine which stands more directly opposed to the general tendency of existing opinion and practice. Society has ex-pended fully as much effort in the attempt (according to its lights) to compel people to conform to its notions of personal, as of social excellence. The ancient commonwealths thought themselves entitled to practice, and the ancient philosophers countenanced, the regulation of every part of private conduct by public authority, on the ground that the State had a deep interest in the whole bodily and mental discipline of every one of its citizens, a mode of thinking which may have been admissible in small republics surrounded by powerful enemies, in constant peril of being subverted by foreign attack or internal commotion, and to which even a short interval of relaxed energy and self-command might so easily be fatal, that they could not afford to wait for the salutary permanent effects of freedom. In the modern world, the greater size of political communities, and above all, the separation between the spiritual and temporal authority (which placed the direction of men's consciences in other hands than those which controlled their worldly affairs), prevented so great an interference by law in the details of private life; but the engines of moral repression have been wielded more strenuously against divergence from the reigning opinion in self-regarding, than even in social matters; religion, the most powerful of the elements which have entered into the formation of moral feeling, having almost always been governed either by the ambition of a hierarchy, seeking control over every department of human conduct, or by the spirit of Puritanism. And some of those modern reformers who have placed themselves in strongest opposition to the religions of the past, have been noway behind either churches or sects in their assertion of the right of spiritual domination: M. Comte, in particular, whose social system, as unfolded in his *Traité de Politique Positive,* aims at establishing (though by moral more than by legal appliances) a despotism of society over the individual, surpassing anything contemplated in the political ideal of the most rigid disciplinarian among the ancient philosophers.

Apart from the peculiar tenets of individual thinkers, there is also in the world at large an increasing inclination to stretch unduly the powers of society over the individual, both by the force of opinion and even by that of legislation: and as the tendency of all the changes taking place in the world is to strengthen society, and diminish the power of the individual, this encroachment is not one of the evils which tend spontaneously to disappear, but, on the contrary, to grow more and more formidable. The disposition of mankind, whether as rulers or as fellow-citizens, to impose their own opinions and inclinations as a rule of conduct on others, is so energetically supported by some of the best and by some of the worst feelings incident to human nature, that it is hardly ever kept under restraint by anything but want of power; and as the power is not declining, but growing, unless a strong barrier of moral conviction can be raised against the mischief, we must expect, in the present circumstances of the world, to see it increase.

It would be convenient for the argument, if, instead of at once entering upon the general thesis, we confine ourselves in the first instance to a single branch of it, on which the principle here stated is, if not fully, yet to a certain point, recognized by the current opinions. This one branch is the Liberty of Thought: from which it is impossible to separate the cognate liberty of speaking and of writing. Although these liberties, to some considerable amount, form part of the political morality of all countries which profess religious toleration and free institutions, the grounds, both philosophical and practical, on which they rest, are perhaps not so familiar to the general mind, nor so thoroughly appreciated by many even of the leaders of opinion, as might have been expected. Those grounds, when rightly understood, are of much wider application than to only one division of the subject, and a thorough consideration of this part of the question will be found the best introduction to the remainder. Those to whom nothing which I am about to say will be new, may therefore, I hope, excuse me, if on a subject which for now three centuries has been so often discussed I venture on one discussion more.

The time, it is to be hoped, is gone by when any defence would be necessary of the "liberty of the press" as one of the securities against corrupt or tyrannical government. No argument, we may suppose, can now be needed, against permitting a legislature or any executive, not identified in interest with the people, to prescribe opinions to them, and determine what doctrines or what arguments they shall be allowed to hear. This aspect of the question, besides, has been so often and so triumphantly enforced by preceding writers, that it needs not be specially insisted on in this place. Though the law of England, on the subject of the press, is as servile to this day as it was in the time of the Tudors, there is little danger of its being actually put in force against political discussion, except during some temporary panic, when fear of insurrection drives ministers and judges from their propriety; and, speaking, generally, it is not, in constitutional countries, to be apprehended that the government, whether completely responsible to the people or not, will often attempt to control the expression of opinion, except when in doing so it makes itself the organ of the general intolerance of the public. Let us suppose, therefore, that the government is entirely at one with the people, and never thinks of exerting any power of coercion unless in agreement with what it conceives to be their voice. But I deny the right of the people to exercise such coercion, either by themselves or by their government. The power itself is illegitimate. The best government has no more title to it than the worst. It is as noxious, or more noxious, when exerted in accordance with public opinion, than when in opposition to it. If all mankind minus one, were of one opinion, and only one person were of the contrary opinion, mankind would be no more justified in silencing that one person, than he, if he had the power, would be justified in silencing mankind. Were an opinion a personal possession of no value except to the owner; if to be obstructed in the enjoyment of it were simply a private injury, it would make some difference whether the injury was inflicted only on a few persons or on many. But the peculiar evil of silencing the expression of an opinion is, that it is robbing the human race; posterity as well as the existing generation; those who dissent from the opinion, still more than those who hold it. If the opinion is right, they are deprived of the opportunity of exchanging error for truth: if wrong, they lose, what is almost as great a benefit, the clearer perception and livelier impression of truth, produced by its collision with error. . . .

★　★　★

What, then, is the rightful limit to the sovereignty of the individual over himself? Where does the authority of society begin? How much of human life should be assigned to individuality, and how much to society?

Each will receive its proper share, if each has that which more particularly concerns it. To individuality should belong the part of life in which it is chiefly the individual that is interested; to society, the part which chiefly interests society.

Though society is not founded on a contract, and though no good purpose is answered by inventing a contract, in order to deduce social obligations from it, every one who receives the protection of society owes a return for the benefit, and the fact of living in society renders it indispensable that each should be bound to observe a certain line of conduct towards the rest. This conduct consists, first, in not injuring the interests of one another; or rather certain interests, which either, by express legal provision or by tacit understanding, ought to be considered as rights; and secondly, in each person's bearing his share (to be fixed on some equitable principle) of the labors and sacrifices incurred for defending the society or its members from injury and molestation. These conditions society is justified in enforcing, at all costs to those who endeavor to withhold fulfilment. Nor is this all that society may do. The acts of an individual may be hurtful to others, or wanting in due consideration for their welfare, without going to the length of violating any of their constituted rights. The offender may then be justly punished by opinion, though not by law. As soon as any part of a person's conduct affects prejudicially the interests of others, society has jurisdiction over it, and the question whether the general welfare will or will not be promoted by interfering with it, becomes open to discussion. But there is no room for entertaining any such question when a person's conduct affects the interests of no persons besides himself, or needs not affect them unless they like (all the persons concerned being of full age, and the ordinary amount of understanding). In all such cases there should be perfect freedom, legal and social, to do the action and stand the consequences.

It would be a great misunderstanding of this doctrine, to suppose that it is one of selfish indifference, which pretends that human beings have no business with each other's conduct in life, and that they should not concern themselves about the well-doing or well-being of one another, unless their own interest is involved. Instead of any diminution, there is need of a great increase of disinterested exertion to promote the good of others. But disin-

terested benevolence can find other instruments to persuade people to their good, than whips and scourges, either of the literal or the metaphorical sort. I am the last person to undervalue the self-regarding virtues; they are only second in importance, if even second, to the social. It is equally the business of education to cultivate both. But even education works by conviction and persuasion as well as by compulsion, and it is by the former only that, when the period of education is past, the self-regarding virtues should be inculcated. Human beings owe to each other help to distinguish the better from the worse, and encouragement to choose the former and avoid the latter. They should be forever stimulating each other to increased exercise of their higher faculties, and increased direction of their feelings and aims towards wise instead of foolish, elevating instead of degrading, objects and contemplations. But neither one person, nor any number of persons, is warranted in saying to another human creature of ripe years, that he shall not do with his life for his own benefit what he chooses to do with it. He is the person most interested in his own well-being; the interest which any other person, except in cases of strong personal attachment, can have in it, is trifling, compared with that which he himself has; the interest which society has in him individually (except as to his conduct to others) is fractional, and altogether indirect: while, with respect to his own feelings and circumstances, the most ordinary man or woman has means of knowledge immeasurably surpassing those that can be possessed by any one else. The interference of society to overrule his judgment and purposes in what only regards himself, must be grounded on general presumptions; which may be altogether wrong, and even if right, are as likely as not to be misapplied to individual cases, by persons no better acquainted with the circumstances of such cases than those are who look at them merely from without. In this department, therefore, of human affairs, individuality has its proper field of action. In the conduct of human beings towards one another, it is necessary that general rules should for the most part be observed, in order that people may know what they have to expect; but in each person's own concerns, his individual spontaneity is entitled to free exercise. Considerations to aid his judgment, exhortations to strengthen his will, may be offered to him, even obtruded on him, by others; but he, himself, is the final judge. All errors which he is likely to commit against advice and warning, are far outweighed by the evil of allowing others to constrain him to what they deem his good. . . .

I have reserved for the last place a large class of questions respecting the limits of government interference, which, though closely connected with the subject of this Essay, do not, in strictness, belong to it. These are cases in which the reasons against interference do not turn upon the principle of liberty: the question is not about restraining the actions of individuals, but about helping them: it is asked whether the government should do, or cause to be done, something for their benefit, instead of leaving it to be done by themselves, individually, or in voluntary combination.

The objections to government interference, when it is not such as to involve infringement of liberty, may be of three kinds.

The first is, when the thing to be done is likely to be better done by individuals than by the government. Speaking generally, there is no one so fit to conduct any business, or to determine how or by whom it shall be conducted, as those who are personally interested

in it. This principle condemns the interferences, once so common, of the legislature, or the officers of the government, with the ordinary processes of industry. But this part of the subject has been sufficiently enlarged upon by political economists, and is not particularly related to the principles of this Essay.

The second objection is more nearly allied to our subject. In many cases, though individuals may not do the particular thing so well, on the average as the officers of government, it is nevertheless desirable that it should be done by them, rather than by the government, as a means to their own mental education — a mode of strengthening their active faculties, exercising their judgment, and giving them a familiar knowledge of the subjects with which they are thus left to deal. This is a principal, though not the sole, recommendation of jury trial (in cases not political); of free and popular local and municipal institutions; of the conduct of industrial and philanthropic enterprises by voluntary associations. . . .

The third, and most cogent reason for restricting the interference of government, is the great evil of adding unnecessarily to its power. Every function superadded to those already exercised by the government, causes its influence over hopes and fears to be more widely diffused, and converts, more and more, the active and ambitious part of the public into hangers-on of the government, or of some party which aims at becoming the government. If the roads, the railways, the banks, the insurance offices, the great joint-stock companies, the universities, and the public charities, were all of them branches of the government; if, in addition, the municipal corporations and local boards, with all that now devolves on them, became departments of the central administration; if the employees of all these different enterprises were appointed and paid by the government, and looked to the government for every rise in life; not all the freedom of the press and popular constitution of the legislature would make this or any other country free otherwise than in name. And the evil would be greater, the more efficiently and scientifically the administrative machinery was constructed — the more skillful the arrangement for obtaining the best qualified hands and heads with which to work it. . . .

★   ★   ★

To determine the point at which evils, so formidable to human freedom and advancement begin, or rather at which they begin to predominate over the benefits attending the collective application of the force of society, under its recognized chiefs, for the removal of the obstacles which stand in the way of its well-being, to secure as much of the advantages of centralized power and intelligence, as can be had without turning into governmental channels too great a proportion of the general activity, is one of the most difficult and complicated questions in the art of government. It is, in a great measure, a question of detail, in which many and various considerations

must be kept in view, and no absolute rule can be laid down. But I believe that the practical principle in which safety resides, the ideal to be kept in view, the standard by which to test all arrangements intended for overcoming the difficulty, may be conveyed in these words: the greatest dissemination of power consistent with efficiency; but the greatest possible centralization of information, and diffusion of it from the centre. . . .

★   ★   ★

The worth of a State, in the long run, is the worth of the individuals composing it; and a State which postpones the interests of their mental expansion and elevation, to a little more of administrative skill, or the semblance of it which practice gives, in the details of business; a State which dwarfs its men, in order that they may be more docile instruments in its hands even for beneficial purposes, will find that with small men no great thing can really be accomplished; and that the perfection of machinery to which it has sacrificed everything, will in the end avail it nothing, for want of the vital power which, in order that the machine might work more smoothly, it has preferred to banish.

B

Our object in the present chapter is to enforce the reality of the difficulties which attach to the idea of political self-government, so long as current assumptions as to the union of individuals in society are maintained. And

Bernard Bosanquet, *The Philosophical Theory of the State,* London, Macmillan and Company, 1899, ch. 3 (in part). Reprinted by permission of the publishers.

for this purpose we are to examine the views of some very distinguished philosophers to whom the paradox has appeared irreconcilable, and law or government has seemed essentially antagonistic to the self or true individuality of man; while the term "self," if applied to the collective group by or within which government is undoubtedly exercised, appears to them an empty and misleading expression. The curious and significant point to which we shall call attention is, in brief, that while maintaining law and government to be in their nature antagonistic to the self of man — whether as pain to pleasure or as fetters to individuality — they nevertheless admit with one voice that a certain minimum of this antagonistic element is necessary to the development of the sentient or rational self. We have here a dualism which challenges examination.

The attitude towards law and government which Bentham adopted (1748–1832) was in a great degree that of the philanthropic reformer. His principle of the greatest happiness of the greatest number is said to have been derived from Beccaria, whose work on "Crimes and Penalties" had great influence throughout Europe. And Howard, "the philanthropist," who was just twenty-two years Bentham's senior (1726–1790), represented a revolt against the abuses of the treatment of criminals at that time, by which Bentham, who eulogised him as "a martyr and apostle," was strongly affected. The movement which Bentham led was, in short, markedly hostile to the existing system of law, and to the reasonings of its advocates. And substantial as his knowledge and constructive genius proved to be, it never lost the character which the direction of his approach to the subject had marked upon it, a character of suspicion and antagonism, which is expressed in his description of law as a necessary evil, and government as a choice of evils.

Pain being the ultimate evil, it is clear why, on Bentham's principles, every law is an evil. For every law, for him, is contrary to liberty; and every infraction of liberty is followed by a natural sentiment of pain. Against those who would deny the proposition that every law is contrary to liberty he brings a charge of perversion of language, in that they restrict liberty to the right of doing what is not injurious to others. They give the term, that is to say, a partly positive implication. For him then liberty has the simplest and apparently widest meaning, which includes liberty to do evil, and is defined, we must suppose, purely as the absence of restraint. And he therefore has no doubt whatever that the citizen can acquire rights only by sacrificing part of his liberty. And in this there is an appearance of truth, if we forget that in saying that a part of one's liberty is sacrificed it is implied that one had, to begin with, a certain area of liberty, of which a portion is abandoned to save the rest. But the idea of any such antecedent liberty is just such a fiction as Bentham himself delighted to expose. It is true, however, that some degree of restraint on what we can *now* easily imagine ourselves free to do, is involved in political society. The point on which we have to fix our attention, for the purposes of social theory, is the remarkable representation of this state of things under the figure, as it were, of an amount of general liberty, which is increased by subtraction, or which can only attain its maximum by the conversion of a certain edge or border of it, so to speak, into constraint. This border of constraint is implied to be capable of a minimum, such as to condition a maximum of liberty, or possible individual initiative; a relation which, being at first sight contradictory, demands further analysis. For it would appear that if the sacrifice of some liberty is to be instrumental to the increase of the whole amount, that whole can hardly be a homogeneous given quantity, like, for instance, a piece of land; for such a one must surely be diminished by the subtraction of any part of it. It must, one would infer, be something which has a complex nature like that of a living plant, such that certain restrictions or negations which are essential to its prosperity are dictated by its individual characteristics (which must be positive), and express the same principle with them, and therefore are wholly relative to the positive type and phase of the plant to be cultivated. Only in some such sense can it be intelligible how constraint is instrumental to effective self-assertion.

But if this is so, the restrictive influences of law and government, which are the measure of the constraint imposed, cannot be alien to the human nature which they restrict, and ought not to be set down as in their own nature antagonistic to liberty or to the making the most of the human self. The root of the difficulty obviously lies in assuming that the pressure of the claims of "others" in society is a mere general curtailment of the liberty of the "one," while acknowledging, not contrary to fact, but contrary to the hypothesis of that curtailment, that the one, so far from surrendering some of his capacity for life through his fellowship with others, acquires and extends that capacity wholly in and through such fellowship. On the above assumption the terms of the paradox of self-government become irreconcilable, and government is made an evil of which it is impossible to explain how it ministers to the self which stands for the good. So long as to every individual, taken as the true self, the restraint enforced by the impact of others is alien and a diminution of the self, this result is inevitable.

It is instructive, therefore, to note Bentham's uncompromising hostility to all the theories of philosophical jurists. The common point of all their theories, from Hobbes and Grotius to Montesquieu and Rousseau, not to mention Kant and his successors, has lain in the fact that their authors divined under the forms of power and command, exercised by some over others, a substantive and general element of positive human nature, which they attempted to drag to light by one analogy after another. But neither Montesquieu's "eternal relations," nor the "Social Contract," nor "General Will," nor "Natural Rights" of other thinkers finds favour in Bentham's eyes. One and all they are to him fiction and fallacy. He can understand nothing in law but the character of a command; he can see no positive relation of it to human nature beyond the degree in which it dispenses with the pain of restraint while increasing the pleasure of liberty.

To describe the magnificent success which attended the use of this rule of thumb in the practical work of reform does not fall within our immediate subject. Our purpose was merely to illustrate the paradox implied in the conception of self-government, by pointing out how fundamentally hostile to one another Bentham took its constituent elements to be.

The same point may be further insisted on by examining the main idea of Mill's "Liberty," without by any means professing to give a full account of Mill's opinions on the relation of individuals to society. What indeed is instructive in his position, for our immediate purpose, is that, having so deep a sense, as he has, of social solidarity, he nevertheless treats the central life of the individual as something to be carefully fenced round against the impact of social forces.

Mill's idea of Individuality is plainly biassed by the Benthamite tradition that law is an evil. It is to be remembered that Anarchism of a speculative kind, the inevitable complement of a hide-bound Conservatism, was current in the beginning of this century, as in Godwin and Shelley. Thus we find concentrated in a few pages of the "Liberty" all those ideas on the nature of Individuality, Originality, and Eccentricity which are most

opposed to the teaching derived by later generations in England from the revival of philosophy and criticism. It is worth while, after
reading Mill's observations upon the relation
of individuality to the Calvinistic theory of
life, to turn to the estimate expressed by Mark
Pattison of the force of the individual character generated by the rule of Calvin at Geneva.
That the individuality, or genius, the fulness
of life and completeness of development
which Mill so justly appreciates, is not nourished and evoked by the varied play of relations and obligations in society, but lies in
a sort of inner self, to be cherished by enclos-
ing it, as it were, in an impervious globe, is
a notion which neither modern logic nor modern art criticism will admit. In the same way,
the connection of originality and eccentricity,
on which Mill insists, appears to us to-day to
be a fallacious track of thought; and in general, in all these matters, we tend to accept
the principle that, in order to go beyond a
point of progress, it is necessary to have
reached it; and in order to destroy a law, it
is necessary to have fulfilled it. Here, however, is the heart of the point on which we are
insisting. If individuality and originality mean
or depend upon the absence of law and of
obligation; if eccentricity is the type of the
fully developed self, and if the community,
penetrated by a sense of universal relations,
is therefore a prey to monotony and uniformity, then it needs no further words to show
that law is a curtailment of human nature,
the necessity of which remains inexplicable,
so that self-government is a contradiction in
terms.

How then does Mill bring the two terms
into relation? How does he represent the
phenomenon that, in the life of every society,
the factors of self and of government have
to be reconciled, or at any rate to coexist?

To find the answer to this question, the
whole of the chapter, "Of the limits of the

authority of society over the individual,"
should be carefully studied. A few characteristic sentences may be quoted here.

"What, then, is the rightful limit to the
sovereignty of the individual over himself?
Where does the authority of society begin?
How much of human life should be assigned
to individuality, and how much to society?

"Each will receive its proper share, if each
has that which more particularly concerns it.
To individuality should belong the part of
life in which it is chiefly the individual that
is interested; to society, the part which chiefly
interests society."

Every one who lives in society, he continues
in effect, is bound not to interfere with certain interests of others (explicitly or implicitly constituted as "rights"), and is bound to
take his fair share of the sacrifices incurred
for the defence of society and its members.
These conditions society may enforce, at all
costs to recalcitrants. Further, it may punish
by opinion, though not by law, acts hurtful
to others, but not going so far as to violate
their rights. But acts which affect only the
agent, or need not affect others unless they
like, may be punished, we are given to understand, neither by law nor by opinion. Mill
expects his conclusion to be disputed, and the
following is the conclusion of the passage in
which he explains and reaffirms it: ". . . when
a person disables himself, by conduct purely
self-regarding, from the performance of some
definite duty incumbent on him to the public,
he is guilty of a social offence. No person
ought to be punished simply for being drunk;
but a soldier or policeman should be punished
for being drunk on duty. Wherever, in short,
there is a definite damage, or a definite risk
of damage either to an individual or to the
public, *the case is taken out of the province
of liberty, and placed in that of morality or
law.*"

It will probably occur at once to the reader

that, considered as a practical rule, the view here maintained would by no means curtail unduly the province of social interference. We should rather anticipate that it would leave an easy opening for a transition from administrative nihilism to administrative absolutism; and some such transition seems to have taken place in Mill's later views. This tendency to a complete *bouleversement* is the characteristic of all conceptions which proceed by assigning different areas to the several factors of an inseparable whole, which then reasserts itself in its wholeness within the area of either factor to which we may happen to attend. Indeed, even in the passage before us, the defence of individuality has already wellnigh turned round into its annihilation. Every act that carries a definite damage to any other person belongs to the sphere of law, and every act that can be supposed likely to cause such a damage, to that of morality; and individuality has what is left. The extraordinary demarcation between the sphere of morality and that of liberty is to be accounted for, no doubt, by the Benthamite tradition which identified the moral and social sanctions; so that in this usage the sphere of morality means much the same as what, in the first passage referred to, was indicated as the sphere of opinion.

Now, it is obvious that the distinction which Mill is attempting to describe and explain is one practically recognised by every society. The question is whether it can be rightly described and explained by a demarcation which, if strictly pressed, excludes individuality from every act of life that has an important social bearing; while, owing to the twosided nature of all action, it becomes perfectly arbitrary in its practical working as a criterion. For every act of mine affects both myself and others; and it is a matter of mood and momentary urgency which aspect may be pronounced characteristic and essential. It

may safely be said that no demarcation between self-regarding and other-regarding action can possibly hold good. What may hold good, and what Mill's examples show to be present to his mind, is a distinction between the moral and the "external" aspects of action on the ground of their respective accessibility to the means of coercion which are at the disposal of society. The peculiar sense in which the term "external" is here employed will explain itself below.

For our present purpose, however, what we have to observe is merely that the demarcation between individuality and society, contrived in defence of the former, has pretty nearly annihilated it. And thus we see once more how overwhelming is the *prima facie* appearance that, in the idea of self-government, the factors of self and government are alien and opposed; and yet how hopeless it remains to explain the part played by these factors in actual society, so long as we aim at a demarcation between them as opposites, rather than at a relative distinction between them as manifestations of the same principle in different media.

A few words may here be said on the applications by which Mill illustrates his doctrine, in order to point out what confusion results from relying on a demarcation which cannot strictly be made.

It will be noted in the first place that he objects altogether to the attempt to prevent by punishment either immorality or irreligion as such. This objection a sound social theory must uphold. But if we look at Mill's reason for it, we find it simply to be that such an attempt infringes liberty, by interfering with action which is purely self-regarding. Without entering further upon the endless argument whether this or any action is indeed purely self-regarding, we may observe that by taking such ground, Mill causes the above objection, which is substantially sound, to appear as on all fours with others which are at any rate very much more doubtful. Such is the objection on principle to all restrictions imposed upon trade with a distinct view to protecting the consumer, not from fraud, but from opportunities of consumption injurious to himself. The regulation or prohibition of the traffic in alcoholic liquors is of course the main question here at issue; and it may be admitted that Mill's discussion, with the many distinctions which he lays down, is full of shrewdness and suggestiveness. But the ultimate ground which he takes, as above stated, is quite different from the genuine reasons which exist against attempting to enforce morality by law and penalty, and introduces confusion into the whole question of State interference by ranking the two objections together. Closely analogous are his objections to the statutes respecting unlawful games, which, whether wise or unwise, are quite a different thing from an attempt to punish personal immorality as such. And lastly, the same principle is illustrated by his whole attitude to the strong feeling and the various legal obligations which determine and support the monogamous family. In maintaining the general indissolubility of marriage, and supporting the parental power, the State is interfering, for him, with the freedom of parties to a contract, and conferring power over individuals, the children, who have a right to be separately considered. Such interference is for him *ipso facto* of a suspected nature. It is an interference hostile to liberty; and whether it is or is not an external condition of good life, which the State is able effectively to maintain, is a question which he does not discuss. Throughout all these objections to authoritative interference we trace the peculiar prejudice that the criterion of its justifiability lies in the boundary line between self and others, rather than in the nature of what coercive

authority is and is not able to do towards the promotion of good life. On many points indeed, when the simple protection of "others" is concerned, Mill's doctrine leads to sound conclusions. Such, for example, is the problem of legislation after the pattern of the Factory Acts.

But yet a strange nemesis attaches to grounds alleged with insufficient discrimination. Just as, by ranking inner morality and outer action alike under the name of freedom, Mill is led to object to interference which may be perfectly justified and effectual; so by the same confusion he is led to advocate coercive treatment in impossibly stringent forms, and in cases where it runs extreme risk of thwarting a true moral development. We are amazed when he strongly implies, in respect to the education of children and the prospect of supporting a family, that the existence of a moral obligation to an act is a sufficient ground for enforcing the act by law. The proposal of universal State-enacted examinations by way of enforcing the parental duty of educating children, to the exclusion of the task of providing education by public authority, in which Mill sees danger to individuality, opens a prospect of a Chinese type of society, from which, happily, the good sense of Englishmen has recoiled. And just the reverse of his proposal has come to pass under the influence of the logic of experience. The State has taken care that the external conditions of an elementary education are provided, and while doing this, has no doubt exercised compulsion, in order that these conditions may be a reality. But the individual inquisition by examination is tending to drop out of the system; and the practical working of the public education is more and more coming to be that the State sees to it that certain conditions are maintained, of which the parents' interest and public spirit leads them to take advantage. Sheer compulsion is not the way to enforce a moral obligation.

Still more startling is the suggestion that it might be just to interdict marriage to those unable to show the means of supporting a family, on the ground of possible evil both to the children themselves through poverty, and to others through over-population. This is a case in which authoritative interference (except on account of very definite physical or mental defects) must inevitably defeat its object. No foresight of others can gauge the latent powers to meet and deal with a future indefinite responsibility; and the result of scrupulous timidity, in view of such responsibilities, is seen in the tendency to depopulation which affects that very country from which Mill probably drew his argument. To leave the responsibility as fully as possible where it has been assumed is the best that law can do, and appeals to a spring of energy deeper than compulsion can reach.

Thus we have seen that by discriminating the spheres of non-interference and interference, according to a supposed demarcation between the sphere of "self" and of "others," a hopelessly confused classification has been introduced. Sometimes the maintenance of external conditions of good life, well within the power of the State, is forbidden on the same grounds as the direct promotion of morality, which is impossible to it. In other cases the enforcement of moral obligations is taken to lie within the functions of the State, although not only is the enforcement of moral obligations *per se* a contradiction in terms, but almost always, as in the cases in question, the attempt to effect it is sure to frustrate itself, by destroying the springs on which moral action depends.

It is worth noticing, in conclusion, that in two examples, the one trivial, the other that of slavery, both theoretically and practically very important, Mill recognises a principle wholly at variance with his own. Here he is aware that it may be right, according to the principle of liberty, to restrain a man, for reasons affecting himself alone, from doing what at the moment he proposes to do. For we are entitled to argue from the essential nature of freedom to what freedom really demands, as opposed to what the man momentarily seems to wish. "It is not freedom to be allowed to alienate his freedom," as it is not freedom to be allowed to walk over a bridge which is certain to break down and cause his death. Here we have in germ the doctrine of the "real" will, and a conception analogous to that of Rousseau when he speaks of a man "being forced to be free."

Before referring to Mill's explicit utterances on the problem of self-government, which are of the same general character as those of Mr. Herbert Spencer, it will be well to note some instructive points in the views of the latter thinker. The study of Mr. Spencer's writings, and more especially of those which appear most directly opposed to the popular conceptions of the day, cannot be too strongly urged upon the sociological student. And this for two reasons. In the first place, no other writer has exhibited with equal vividness the fatal possibilities of a collective governmental stupidity. That in practice these possibilities are continually tending to become facts, just as in theory they are represented by recurrent fallacies, is a proof of the extreme arduousness of the demands made by the task of self-government upon the people which undertakes it. And no theorist is fitted to discuss the problem of social unity who has not realised the arduousness of these demands in all its intensity. And, in the second place, the student will observe an instructive meeting of extremes between elements of Mr. Spencer's ideas and popular social theories of an opposite cast. The revival of doctrines of the natural rights of man on a biological foundation is a case in point. An uncriticised individualism is always in danger of transformation into an uncritical collectivism. The basis of the two is in fact the same.

A comparison of the conception of "right" as entertained by Bentham and by Herbert Spencer forms a striking commentary on ideas in which "government" is antagonistic to "self." Bentham, seeing clearly that the claims of the actual individual, taken as he happens to be, are casual and unregulated, fulminates against the idea of natural right as representing those claims. Right is for him a creation of the State, and there can be no right which is not constituted by law. And the truth of the contention seems obvious. How, in fact, could individual claims or wishes constitute a right, except as in some way ratified by a more general recognition?

But to Mr. Herbert Spencer the contrary proposition is absolutely convincing, and, indeed, on their common premises, with equal reason. It is ridiculous, he points out, to think of a people as creating rights, which it had not before, by the process of creating a government in order to create them. It is absurd to treat an individual as having a share of rights *qua* member of the people, while in his private capacity he has no rights at all.

We need not labour this point further. It is obvious that Mr. Herbert Spencer is simply preferring the opposite extreme, in the antithesis of "self" and "government," to that which commended itself to Bentham. If it is a plain fact that "a right" can only be recognised by a society, it is no less plain that it can only be real in an individual. If individual claims, apart from social adjustment, are arbitrary, yet social recognitions, apart from individual qualities and relations, are meaningless. As long as the self and the law are alien and hostile, it is hopeless to do more than choose at random in which of the two we are to locate the essence of right.

And how alien and hostile the self and the law may seem we see even more crudely enunciated in Herbert Spencer than in Bentham or Mill, as the fundamental principle of the tradition has worked itself more definitely to the front. "The liberty which a citizen enjoys is to be measured, not by the nature of the governmental machinery he lives under, whether representative or other, but by the relative paucity of the restraints it imposes on him." And so we are astounded to find it maintained that the positive and active element in the right to carry on self-sustaining activities is of a non-social character, depending only on the laws of life, and if the matter were pushed home, would have to be identified, one must suppose with the more strictly animal element of the mind; while only the negative element arises from social aggregation, and it is this negative element alone which gives ethical character to the right to live. Though these distinctions apply primarily to the ground of the *right to live,* yet it appears inevitable that they represent the point of view from which the active self or individuality must be regarded on the principle we are pursuing. The ground of the right to live, as here stated, is simply the recognition that life is good; and if the positive element of this good is non-social and only the negative is of social origin, and this alone is ethical, it seems clearly to follow that the making the most of life — its positive expansion and intensification — is excluded from the ethical aspects of individuality, and, indeed that individuality has no ethical aspect at all. Here is the ultimate result of accepting as irreducible the distinction between the self and government, or the negative relation of individuality and law. Liberty and self are divorced from the moral end, a tendency which we noted even in Mill. Selves in society are regarded as if they were bees building their cells, and their ethical character becomes comparable to the absence of encroachment by which the workers maintain the hexagonal outline due to their equal impact on each other as they progress evenly from equidistant centres. The self, which has ranked throughout these views as the end, to whose liberty all is to be sacrificed, turns out to be the non-ethical element of life.

Thus, when Professor Huxley speaks of "self-restraint as the essence of the ethical process," while "natural liberty" consists in "the free play of self-assertion," we see how the whole method of approaching social and ethical phenomena is turned upside down unless the paradox of self-government is conquered once for all. The idea that assertion and maximisation of the self and of the individuality first become possible and real in and through society, and that affirmation and not negation is its main characteristic; these fundamental conceptions of genuine social philosophy can only be reached through a destructive criticism of the assumptions which erect that paradox into an insoluble contradiction.

SUGGESTIONS FOR THOUGHT

1. What are the various types of freedom that seem desirable in modern societies? Which freedoms have we found necessary to curtail?

2. Thomas Jefferson, in an argument for freedom of expression, said: "It does me no injury for my neighbor to say there are twenty gods, or no god. It neither picks my pocket nor breaks my leg." Might not his polytheistic or atheistic neighbor influence Jefferson's children in ways that he would regard as injurious?

3. Must democratic America be tolerant of those who hold and propagate ideologies that conflict with democracy? How can America restrain such people and still be a democracy?

4. In the song "America the Beautiful" is the phrase "thy liberty in law." What does that phrase mean?

5. John Stuart Mill said: "He who knows only his own side of the case, knows little of that." How could one convince a dogmatic person that even to know his own position he would have to consider other positions?

6. Do you consider the following rights or obligations? Voting, paying taxes, giving to the Community Chest, using the public library, worshipping in a church of one's own choice.

7. What are the so-called natural rights of man? Why is the appeal to natural rights seldom made today?

8. John Stuart Mill said: "The only part of the conduct of any one, for which he is amenable to society, is that which concerns others. In the part which merely concerns himself, his independence is, of right, absolute." But how many instances are there in which one's conduct concerns only one's self?

9. Eric Johnston has said that we must cultivate tolerance for everything except intolerance. Can you think of some things besides intolerance which we must not tolerate? How about indifference?

10. Matthew Arnold said the older he became the less he cared about his rights and the more he cared about his duties. Is this the result of growing old? Or was Arnold fooling himself? What is the relation between rights and duties?

11. Freedom of speech has been described as the right to say what one thinks without thinking what one says. Can one separate freedom of speech from the responsibility for what one says?

12.

> In controversial moments
> My perception's rather fine.
> I always see both points of view,
> The one that's wrong and mine.

Can one be convinced one is right and also show tolerance to one who has another opinion? If one tolerates resentfully and reluctantly, he may be practising tolerance without feeling tolerant; is that tolerance?

SUGGESTIONS FOR FURTHER READING

BEACH, WALDO, "The Basis of Tolerance in a Democratic Society," *Ethics,* Vol. 57, 1947, pp. 157–169.

BECKER, CARL L., *Freedom and Responsibility in the American Way of Life,* New York, Alfred A. Knopf, 1945.

BERDYAEV, NICOLAS, *The Realm of Spirit and the Realm of Caesar,* translated by Donald A. Lowrie, London, Victor Gollancz, 1952, chs. 5, 6.

FREEMANTLE, H. E. S., "Liberty and Government," *The International Journal of Ethics,* Vol. 10, 1900, pp. 439–463.

JOAD, C. E. M., "Liberty and the Modern State," *Aristotelian Society Supplementary Volume,* Vol. 13, 1934, pp. 16–30.

LIPPMANN, WALTER, *The Method of Freedom,* New York, The Macmillan Company, 1934.

MARTIN, EVERETT DEAN, *Liberty,* New York, W. W. Norton and Company, 1930, ch. 17.

MILTON, JOHN, "Areopagitica," *Complete Poetry and Selected Prose of John Milton,* New York, Random House, 1942, pp. 677–724.

PAINE, THOMAS, *The Rights of Man,* London, J. M. Dent and Sons, 1950.

PERICLES, "Funeral Oration," *Thucydides Translated Into English,* translated by B. Jowett, Boston, D. Lathrop and Company, 1883, pp. 116–124.

PERRY, RALPH BARTON, *Shall Not Perish from the Earth,* New York, Vanguard Press, 1940, ch. 4.

RADER, MELVIN, *Ethics and Society,* New York, Henry Holt and Company, 1950, ch. 11.

RITCHIE, E., "The Toleration of Error," *The International Journal of Ethics,* Vol. 14, 1904, pp. 161–171.

STACE, W. T., *The Destiny of Modern Man,* New York, Reynal and Hitchcock, 1941, ch. 7.

VAN LOON, HENDRIK WILLEM, *Tolerance,* New York, Boni and Liveright, 1925.

25

DEMOCRACY

THE ARISTOCRATIC PLATO believed that individual freedom, the unique feature of democracy, is also the source of democracy's corruption. Plato's ideal form of government might be described as benevolent dictatorship. The following selection from *The Republic* traces the theoretical decline and fall of a democracy. Walter Terence Stace (1886–   ) accepts a typically Platonic conception of the rationality of human nature, but from man's rationality he derives social values that would be repugnant to Plato. Stace was born in London and educated in Scotland and Ireland. From 1910 to 1932 he was in the British Civil Service in Ceylon. He came to the United States in 1932 to become Professor of Philosophy at Princeton University. He has written widely in philosophy since 1920, when he published his *Critical History of Greek Philosophy.* He is probably most widely known as the author of *The Destiny of Western Man,* a volume which appeared in 1942.

A

Next comes democracy; of this the origin and nature have still to be considered by us; and then we will enquire into the ways of the democratic man, and bring him up for judgment.

That, he said, is our method.

Well, I said, and how does the change from

Plato, *Republic, The Dialogues of Plato,* Vol. 3, translated by Benjamin Jowett, Oxford, The Clarendon Press, Third Edition, 1892, pp. 261–279.

oligarchy into democracy arise? Is it not on this wise? — The good at which such a State aims is to become as rich as possible, a desire which is insatiable?

What then?

The rulers, being aware that their power rests upon their wealth, refuse to curtail by law the extravagance of the spendthrift youth because they gain by their ruin; they take interest from them and buy up their estates and thus increase their own wealth and importance?

To be sure.

There can be no doubt that the love of wealth and the spirit of moderation cannot exist together in citizens of the same state to any considerable extent; one or the other will be disregarded.

That is tolerably clear.

And in oligarchical States, from the general spread of carelessness and extravagance, men of good family have often been reduced to beggary?

Yes, often.

And still they remain in the city; there they are, ready to sting and fully armed, and some of them owe money, some have forfeited their citizenship; a third class are in both predicaments; and they hate and conspire against those who have got their property, and against everybody else, and are eager for revolution.

That is true.

On the other hand, the men of business, stooping as they walk, and pretending not even to see those whom they have already ruined, insert their sting — that is, their money — into some one else who is not on his guard against them, and recover the parent sum many times over multiplied into a family of children: and so they make drone and pauper to abound in the State.

Yes, he said, there are plenty of them — that is certain.

The evil blazes up like a fire; and they will not extinguish it, either by restricting a man's use of his own property, or by another remedy:

What other?

One which is the next best, and has the advantage of compelling the citizens to look to their characters: — Let there be a general rule that every one shall enter into voluntary contracts at his own risk, and there will be less of this scandalous moneymaking, and the evils of which we were speaking will be greatly lessened in the State.

Yes, they will be greatly lessened.

At present the governors, induced by the motives which I have named, treat their subjects badly; while they and their adherents, especially the young men of the governing class, are habituated to lead a life of luxury and idleness both of body and mind; they do nothing, and are incapable of resisting either pleasure or pain.

Very true.

They themselves care only for making money, and are as indifferent as the pauper to the cultivation of virtue.

Yes, quite as indifferent.

Such is the state of affairs which prevails among them. And often rulers and their subjects may come in one another's way, whether on a journey or on some other occasion of meeting, on a pilgrimage or a march, as fellow-soldiers or fellow-sailors; aye and they may observe the behaviour of each other in the very moment of danger — for where danger is, there is no fear that the poor will be despised by the rich — and very likely the wiry sunburnt poor man may be placed in battle at the side of the wealthy one who has never spoilt his complexion and has plenty of superfluous flesh — when he sees such a one puffing and at his wits'-end, how can he avoid drawing the conclusion that men like him are only rich because no one has the courage to despoil them? And when they meet in private will not people be saying to one another 'Our warriors are not good for much'?

Yes, he said, I am quite aware that this is their way of talking.

And, as in a body which is diseased the addition of a touch from without may bring on illness, and sometimes even when there is no external provocation a commotion may arise within — in the same way wherever there is weakness in the State there is also likely to be illness, of which the occasion may be very slight, the one party introducing from without their oligarchical, the other their democratical allies, and then the State falls sick, and is at war with herself; and may be at times distracted, even when there is no external cause.

Yes, surely.

And then democracy comes into being after the poor have conquered their opponents, slaughtering some and banishing some, while to the remainder they give an equal share of freedom and power; and this is the form of government in which the magistrates are commonly elected by lot.

Yes, he said, that is the nature of democracy, whether the revolution has been effected by arms, or whether fear has caused the opposite party to withdraw.

And now what is their manner of life, and what sort of a government have they? for as the government is, such will be the man.

Clearly, he said.

In the first place, are they not free; and is not the city full of freedom and frankness — a man may say and do what he likes?

'Tis said so, he replied.

And where freedom is, the individual is clearly able to order for himself his own life as he pleases?

Clearly.

Then in this kind of State there will be the greatest variety of human natures?

There will.

This, then, seems likely to be the fairest of States, being like an embroidered robe which is spangled with every sort of flower. And just as women and children think a variety of colours to be of all things most charming, so there are many men to whom this State, which is spangled with the manners and characters of mankind, will appear to be the fairest of States.

Yes.

Yes, my good Sir, and there will be no better in which to look for a government.

Why?

Because of the liberty which reigns there — they have a complete assortment of constitutions; and he who has a mind to establish a State, as we have been doing, must go to a democracy as he would to a bazaar at which they sell them, and pick out the one that suits him; then, when he has made his choice, he may found his State.

He will be sure to have patterns enough.

And there being no necessity, I said, for you to govern in this State, even if you have the capacity, or to be governed, unless you like, or to go to war when the rest go to war, or to be at peace when others are at peace, unless you are so disposed — there being no necessity also, because some law forbids you to hold office or be a dicast, that you should not hold office or be a dicast, if you have a fancy — is not this a way of life which for a moment is supremely delightful?

For a moment, yes.

And is not their humanity to the condemned in some cases quite charming? Have you not observed how, in a democracy, many persons, although they have been sentenced to death or exile, just stay where they are and walk about the world — the gentleman parades like a hero, and nobody sees or cares?

Yes, he replied, many and many a one.

See too, I said, the forgiving spirit of democracy, and the 'don't care' about trifles, and the disregard which she shows of all the fine principles which we solemnly laid down at the foundation of the city — as when we said that, except in the case of some rarely gifted nature, there never will be a good man who has not from his childhood been used to play amid things of beauty and make of them a joy and a study — how grandly does she trample all these fine notions of ours under her feet, never giving a thought to the pursuits which make a statesman, and promoting to honour any one who professes to be the people's friend.

Yes, she is of a noble spirit.

These and other kindred characteristics are proper to democracy, which is a charming form of government, full of variety and disorder, and dispensing a sort of equality to equals and unequals alike.

We know her well.

Consider now, I said, what manner of man the individual is, or rather consider, as in the case of the State, how he comes into being.

Very good, he said.

Is not this the way — he is the son of the miserly and oligarchical father who has trained him in his own habits?

Exactly.

And, like his father, he keeps under by force the pleasures which are of the spending and not of the getting sort, being those which are called unnecessary?

Obviously.

Would you like, for the sake of clearness, to distinguish which are the necessary and which are the unnecessary pleasures?

I should.

Are not necessary pleasures those of which we cannot get rid, and of which the satisfaction is a benefit to us? And they are rightly called so, because we are framed by nature to desire both what is beneficial and what is necessary, and cannot help it.

True.

We are not wrong therefore in calling them necessary?

We are not.

And the desires of which a man may get rid, if he takes pains from his youth upwards — of which the presence, moreover, does no good, and in some cases the reverse of good — shall we not be right in saying that all these are unnecessary?

Yes, certainly.

Suppose we select an example of either kind, in order that we may have a general notion of them?

Very good.

Will not the desire of eating, that is, of simple food and condiments, in so far as they are required for health and strength, be of the necessary class?

That is what I should suppose.

The pleasure of eating is necessary in two ways; it does us good and it is essential to the continuance of life?

Yes.

But the condiments are only necessary in so far as they are good for health?

Certainly.

And the desire which goes beyond this, of more delicate food, or other luxuries, which might generally be got rid of, if controlled and trained in youth, and is hurtful to the body, and hurtful to the soul in the pursuit of wisdom and virtue, may be rightly called unnecessary?

Very true.

May we not say that these desires spend, and that the others make money because they conduce to production?

Certainly.

And of the pleasures of love, and all other pleasures, the same holds good?

True.

And the drone of whom we spoke was he who was surfeited in pleasures and desires of this sort, and was the slave of the unnecessary desires, whereas he who was subject to the necessary only was miserly and oligarchical?

Very true.

Again, let us see how the democratical man grows out of the oligarchical: the following, as I suspect, is commonly the process.

What is the process?

When a young man who has been brought up as we were just now describing, in a vulgar and miserly way, has tasted drones' honey and has come to associate with fierce and crafty natures who are able to provide for him all sorts of refinements and varieties of pleasure — then, as you may imagine, the change will begin of the oligarchical principle within him into the democratical?

Inevitably.

And as in the city like was helping like, and the change was effected by an alliance from without assisting one division of the citizens, so too the young man is changed by a class of desires coming from without to assist the desires within him, that which is akin and alike again helping that which is akin and alike?

Certainly.

And if there be any ally which aids the oligarchical principle within him, whether the influence of a father or of kindred, advising or rebuking him, then there arises in his soul a faction and an opposite faction, and he goes to war with himself.

It must be so.

And there are times when the democratical principle gives way to the oligarchical, and some of his desires die, and others are banished; a spirit of reverence enters into the young man's soul and order is restored.

Yes, he said, that sometimes happens.

And then, again, after the old desires have been driven out, fresh ones spring up, which are akin to them, and because he their father does not know how to educate them, wax fierce and numerous.

Yes, he said, that is apt to be the way.

They draw him to his old associates, and holding secret intercourse with him, breed and multiply in him.

Very true.

At length they seize upon the citadel of the young man's soul, which they perceive to be void of all accomplishments and fair pursuits and true words, which make their abode in the minds of men who are dear to the gods, and are their best guardians and sentinels.

None better.

False and boastful conceits and phrases mount upwards and take their place.

They are certain to do so.

And so the young man returns into the country of the lotus-eaters, and takes up his dwelling there in the face of all men; and if any help be sent by his friends to the oligarchical part of him, the aforesaid vain conceits shut the gate of the king's fastness; and they will neither allow the embassy itself to enter, nor if private advisers offer the fatherly counsel of the aged will they listen to them or receive them. There is a battle and they gain the day, and then modesty, which they call silliness, is ignominiously thrust into exile by them, and temperance, which they nickname unmanliness, is trampled in the mire and cast forth; they persuade men that moderation and orderly expenditure are vulgarity and meanness, and so, by the help of a rabble of evil appetites, they drive them beyond the border.

Yes, with a will.

And when they have emptied and swept clean the soul of him who is now in their power and who is being initiated by them in great mysteries, the next thing is to bring back to their house insolence and anarchy and waste and impudence in bright array having garlands on their heads, and a great company with them, hymning their praises and calling them by sweet names; insolence they term breeding, and anarchy liberty, and waste magnificence, and impudence courage. And so the young man passes out of his original nature, which was trained in the school of necessity, into the freedom and libertinism of useless and unnecessary pleasures.

Yes, he said, the change in him is visible enough.

After this he lives on, spending his money and labour and time on unnecessary pleasures quite as much as on necessary ones; but if he be fortunate, and is not too much disordered in his wits, when years have elapsed, and the heyday of passion is over — supposing that he then re-admits into the city some part of the exiled virtues, and does not wholly give himself up to their successors — in that case he balances his pleasures and lives in a sort of equilibrium, putting the government of himself into the hands of the one which comes first and wins the turn; and when he has had enough of that, then into the hands of another; he despises none of them but encourages them all equally.

Very true, he said.

Neither does he receive or let pass into the fortress any true word of advice; if any one says to him that some pleasures are the satisfactions of good and noble desires, and others of evil desires, and that he ought to use and honour some and chastise and master the others — whenever this is repeated to him he shakes his head and says that they are all alike, and that one is as good as another.

Yes, he said; that is the way with him.

Yes, I said, he lives from day to day indulging the appetite of the hour; and sometimes he is lapped in drink and strains of the flute; then he becomes a water-drinker, and tries to get thin; then he takes a turn at gymnastics; sometimes idling and neglecting everything, then once more living the life of a philosopher; often he is busy with politics, and starts to his feet and says and does whatever comes into his head; and, if he is emulous of any one who is a warrior, off he is in that direction, or of men of business, once more in that. His life has neither law nor order; and this distracted existence he terms joy and bliss and freedom; and so he goes on.

Yes, he replied, he is all liberty and equality.

Yes, I said; his life is motley and manifold and an epitome of the lives of many; — he answers to the State which we described as fair and spangled. And many a man and many a woman will take him for their pattern, and many a constitution and many an example of manners is contained in him.

Just so.

Let him then be set over against democracy; he may truly be called the democratic man.

Let that be his place, he said.

Last of all comes the most beautiful of all, man and State alike, tyranny and the tyrant; these we have now to consider.

Quite true, he said.

Say then, my friend, In what manner does tyranny arise? — that it has a democratic origin is evident.

Clearly.

And does not tyranny spring from democracy in the same manner as democracy from oligarchy — I mean, after a sort?

How?

The good which oligarchy proposed to itself and the means by which it was maintained was excess of wealth — am I not right?

Yes.

And the insatiable desire of wealth and the neglect of all other things for the sake of money-getting was also the ruin of oligarchy?

True.

And democracy has her own good, of which the insatiable desire brings her to dissolution?

What good?

Freedom, I replied; which, as they tell you in a democracy, is the glory of the State — and that therefore in a democracy alone will the freeman of nature deign to dwell.

Yes, the saying is in every body's mouth.

I was going to observe, that the insatiable desire of this and the neglect of other things introduces the change in democracy, which occasions a demand for tyranny.

How so?

When a democracy which is thirsting for freedom has evil cup-bearers presiding over the feast, and has drunk too deeply of the strong wine of freedom, then, unless her rulers are very amenable and give a plentiful draught, she calls them to account and punishes them, and says that they are cursed oligarchs.

Yes, he replied, a very common occurrence.

Yes, I said; and loyal citizens are insultingly termed by her slaves who hug their chains and men of naught; she would have subjects who are like rulers, and rulers who are like subjects: these are men after her own heart, whom she praises and honours both in private and public. Now, in such a State, can liberty have any limit?

Certainly not.

By degrees the anarchy finds a way into private houses, and ends by getting among the animals and infecting them.

How do you mean?

I mean that the father grows accustomed to descend to the level of his sons and to fear them, and the son is on a level with his father, he having no respect or reverence for either of his parents; and this is his freedom, and the metic is equal with the citizen and the citizen with the metic, and the stranger is quite as good as either.

Yes, he said, that is the way.

And these are not the only evils, I said — there are several lesser ones: In such a state of society the master fears and flatters his scholars, and the scholars despise their masters and tutors; young and old are all alike; and the young man is on a level with the old, and is ready to compete with him in word or deed; and old men condescend to the young and are full of pleasantry and gaiety; they are loth to be thought morose and authoritative, and therefore they adopt the manners of the young.

Quite true, he said.

The last extreme of popular liberty is when the slave bought with money, whether male or female, is just as free as his or her purchaser; nor must I forget to tell of the liberty and equality of the two sexes in relation to each other.

Why not, as Aeschylus says, utter the word which rises to our lips?

That is what I am doing, I replied; and I must add that no one who does not know would believe, how much greater is the liberty which the animals who are under the dominion of man have in a democracy than in any other State: for truly, the she-dogs, as the proverb says, are as good as their she-mistresses, and the horses and asses have a way of marching along with all the rights and dignities of freemen; and they will run at any body who comes in their way if he does not leave the road clear for them: and all things are just ready to burst with liberty.

When I take a country walk, he said, I often experience what you describe. You and I have dreamed the same thing.

And above all, I said, and as the result of all, see how sensitive the citizens become; they chafe impatiently at the least touch of authority, and at length, as you know, they cease to care even for the laws, written or unwritten; they will have no one over them.

Yes, he said, I know it too well.

Such, my friend, I said, is the fair and glorious beginning out of which springs tyranny.

Glorious indeed, he said. But what is the next step?

The ruin of oligarchy is the ruin of democracy; the same disease magnified and intensified by liberty overmasters democracy — the truth being that the excessive increase of anything often causes a reaction in the opposite direction; and this is the case not only in the seasons and in vegetable and animal life, but above all in forms of government.

True.

The excess of liberty, whether in States or individuals, seems only to pass into excess of slavery.

Yes, the natural order.

And so tyranny naturally arises out of democracy, and the most aggravated form of tyranny and slavery out of the most extreme form of liberty?

As we might expect.

That, however, was not, as I believe, your question — you rather desired to know what is that disorder which is generated alike in oligarchy and democracy, and is the ruin of both?

Just so, he replied.

Well, I said, I meant to refer to the class of idle spendthrifts, of whom the more courageous are the leaders and the more timid the followers, the same whom we were comparing to drones, some stingless, and others having stings.

A very just comparison.

These two classes are the plagues of every city in which they are generated, being what phlegm and bile are to the body. And the good physician and lawgiver of the State ought, like the wise bee-master, to keep them at a distance and prevent, if possible, their ever coming in; and if they have anyhow found a way in, then he should have them and their cells cut out as speedily as possible.

Yes, by all means, he said.

Then, in order that we may see clearly what we are doing, let us imagine democracy to be divided, as indeed it is, into three classes; for in the first place freedom creates rather more drones in the democratic than there were in the oligarchical State.

That is true.

And in the democracy they are certainly more intensified.

How so?

Because in the oligarthical State they are disqualified and driven from office, and therefore they cannot train or gather strength; whereas in a democracy they are almost the entire ruling power, and while the keener sort speak and act, the rest keep buzzing about the bema and do not suffer a word to be said on the other side; hence in democracies almost everything is managed by the drones.

Very true, he said.

Then there is another class which is always being severed from the mass.

What is that?

They are the orderly class, which in a nation of traders is sure to be the richest.

Naturally so.

They are the most squeezable persons and yield the largest amount of honey to the drones.

Why, he said, there is little to be squeezed out of people who have little.

And this is called the wealthy class, and the drones feed upon them.

That is pretty much the case, he said.

The people are a third class, consisting of those who work with their own hands; they are not politicians, and have not much to live upon. This, when assembled, is the largest and most powerful class in a democracy.

True, he said; but then the multitude is seldom willing to congregate unless they get a little honey.

And do they not share? I said. Do not their leaders deprive the rich of their estates and distribute them among the people; at the same time taking care to reserve the larger part for themselves?

Why, yes, he said, to that extent the people do share.

And the persons whose property is taken from them are compelled to defend themselves before the people as they best can?

What else can they do?

And then, although they may have no desire of change, the others charge them with plotting against the people and being friends of oligarchy?

True.

And the end is that when they see the people, not of their own accord, but through ignorance, and because they are deceived by informers, seeking to do them wrong, then at last they are forced to become oligarchs in reality; they do not wish to be, but the sting of the drones torments them and breeds revolution in them.

That is exactly the truth.

Then come impeachments and judgments and trials of one another.

True.

The people have always some champion whom they set over them and nurse into greatness.

Yes, that is their way.

This and no other is the root from which a tyrant springs; when he first appears above ground he is a protector.

Yes, that is quite clear.

How then does a protector begin to change into a tyrant? Clearly when he does what the man is said to do in the tale of the Arcadian temple of Lycaean Zeus.

What tale?

The tale is that he who has tasted the entrails of a single human victim minced up with the entrails of other victims is destined to become a wolf. Did you ever hear it?

O yes.

And the protector of the people is like him; having a mob entirely at his disposal, he is not restrained from shedding the blood of kinsmen; by the favourite method of false accusation he brings them into court and murders them, making the life of man to disappear, and with unholy tongue and lips tasting the blood of his fellow citizens; some he kills and others he banishes, at the same time hinting at the abolition of debts and partition of lands: and after this, what will be his destiny? Must he not either perish at the hands of his enemies, or from being a man become a wolf — that is, a tyrant?

Inevitably.

This, I said, is he who begins to make a party against the rich?

The same.

After a while he is driven out, but comes back, in spite of his enemies, a tyrant full grown.

That is clear.

And if they are unable to expel him, or to get him condemned to death by a public accusation, they conspire to assassinate him.

Yes, he said, that is their usual way.

Then comes the famous request for a bodyguard, which is the device of all those who have got thus far in their tyrannical career — 'Let not the people's friend,' as they say, 'be lost to them.'

Exactly.

The people readily assent; all their fears are for him — they have none for themselves.

Very true.

And when a man who is wealthy and is also accused of being an enemy of the people sees this, then, my friend, as the oracle said to Croesus,

'By pebbly Hermus' shore he flees and rests not, and is not ashamed to be a coward.'

And quite right too, said he, for if he were, he would never be ashamed again.

But if he is caught he dies.

Of course.

And he, the protector of whom we spoke, is to be seen, not 'larding the plain' with his bulk, but himself the overthrower of many, standing up in the chariot of State with the reins in his hand, no longer protector, but tyrant absolute.

No doubt, he said.

And now let us consider the happiness of the man, and also of the State in which a creature like him is generated.

Yes, he said, let us consider that.

At first, in the early days of his power, he is full of smiles, and he salutes every one whom he meets; — he to be called a tyrant, who is making promises in public and also in private! liberating debtors, and distributing land to the people and his followers, and wanting to be so kind and good to every one!

Of course, he said.

But when he has disposed of foreign enemies by conquest or treaty, and there is nothing to fear from them, then he is always stirring up some war or other, in order that the people may require a leader.

To be sure.

Has he not also another object, which is that they may be impoverished by payment of taxes, and thus compelled to devote themselves to their daily wants and therefore less likely to conspire against him?

Clearly.

And if any of them are suspected by him of having notions of freedom, and of resistance to his authority, he will have a good pretext for destroying them by placing them at the mercy of the enemy; and for all these reasons the tyrant must be always getting up a war.

He must.

Now he begins to grow unpopular.

A necessary result.

Then some of those who joined in setting him up, and who are in power, speak their minds to him and to one another, and the more courageous of them cast in his teeth what is being done.

Yes, that may be expected.

And the tyrant, if he means to rule, must get rid of them; he cannot stop while he has a friend or an enemy who is good for anything.

He cannot.

And therefore he must look about him and see who is valiant, who is high-minded, who is wise, who is wealthy; happy man, he is the enemy of them all and must seek occasion against them whether he will or no, until he has made a purgation of the State.

Yes, he said, and a rare purgation.

Yes, I said, not the sort of purgation which the physicians make of the body; for they take away the worse and leave the better part, but he does the reverse.

If he is to rule, I suppose that he cannot help himself.

What a blessed alternative, I said: — to be compelled to dwell only with the many bad, and to be by them hated, or not to live at all!

Yes, that is the alternative.

And the more detestable his actions are to the citizens the more satellites and the greater devotion in them will he require?

Certainly.

And who are the devoted band, and where will he procure them?

They will flock to him, he said, of their own accord, if he pays them.

By the dog! I said, here are more drones, of every sort and from every land.

Yes, he said, there are.

But will he not desire to get them on the spot?

How do you mean?

He will rob the citizens of their slaves; he

will then set them free and enrol them in his body-guard.

To be sure, he said; and he will be able to trust them best of all.

What a blessed creature, I said, must this tyrant be; he has put to death the others and has these for his trusted friends.

Yes, he said; they are quite of his sort.

Yes, I said, and these are the new citizens whom he has called into existence, who admire him and are his companions, while the good hate and avoid him.

Of course.

Verily, then, tragedy is a wise thing and Euripides a great tragedian.

Why so?

Why, because he is the author of the pregnant saying,

'Tyrants are wise by living with the wise;' and he clearly meant to say that they are the wise whom the tyrant makes his companions.

Yes, he said, and he also praises tyranny as godlike; and many other things of the same kind are said by him and by the other poets.

And therefore, I said, the tragic poets being wise men will forgive us and any others who live after our manner if we do not receive them into our State, because they are the eulogists of tyranny.

Yes, he said, those who have the wit will doubtless forgive us.

But they will continue to go to other cities and attract mobs, and hire voices fair and loud and persuasive, and draw the cities over to tyrannies and democracies.

Very true.

Moreover, they are paid for this and receive honour — the greatest honour, as might be expected, from tyrants, and the next greatest from democracies; but the higher they ascend our constitution hill, the more their reputation fails, and seems unable from shortness of breath to proceed further.

True.

But we are wandering from the subject: Let us therefore return and enquire how the tyrant will maintain that fair and numerous and various and ever-changing army of his.

If, he said, there are sacred treasures in the city, he will confiscate and spend them; and in so far as the fortunes of attainted persons may suffice, he will be able to diminish the taxes which he would otherwise have to impose upon the people.

And when these fail?

Why, clearly, he said, then he and his boon companions, whether male or female, will be maintained out of his father's estate.

You mean to say that the people, from whom he has derived his being, will maintain him and his companions?

Yes, he said; they cannot help themselves.

But what if the people fly into a passion, and aver that a grown-up son ought not to be supported by his father, but that the father should be supported by the son? The father did not bring him into being, or settle him in life, in order that when his son became a man he should himself be the servant of his own servants and should support him and his rabble of slaves and companions; but that his son should protect him, and that by his help he might be emancipated from the government of the rich and aristocratic, as they are termed. And so he bids him and his companions depart, just as any other father might drive out of the house a riotous son and his undesirable associates.

By heaven, he said, then the parent will discover what a monster he has been fostering in his bosom; and, when he wants to drive him out, he will find that he is weak and his son strong.

Why, you do not mean to say that the tyrant will use violence? What! beat his father if he opposes him?

Yes, he will, having first disarmed him.

Then he is a parricide, and a cruel guardian of an aged parent; and this is real tyranny, about which there can be no longer a mistake: as the saying is, the people who would escape the smoke which is the slavery of freemen, has fallen into the fire which is the tyranny of slaves. Thus liberty, getting out of all order and reason, passes into the harshest and bitterest form of slavery.

True, he said.

Very well; and may we not rightly say that we have sufficiently discussed the nature of tyranny, and the manner of the transition from democracy to tyranny?

Yes, quite enough, he said.

B

First of all, I shall state what I understand democracy to be. I think that in essence it means that our lives should be governed by *reason* and not by *force*. The Greeks, who were the inventors of democracy — however much their democracies differed from ours — asked themselves the question, "What is the difference between men and brutes?" And they answered, "The difference lies in the fact that men possess reason, which the brutes do not." It is from the Greeks that we get the common, but now often decried, definition: Man is a rational animal. The Greek idea was this: men share with the animals most of their faculties; for example, sense perception, the appetites of hunger, thirst and sex, the basic emotions such as anger and fear. That wherein man rises above the brute is that he is a rational being. Other differences of course there are. Man alone has speech, lights fires, invents tools, wears clothes, possesses moral ideas, creates works of art. Man also is the only animal which laughs. But all these differences, even the gift of laughter, will be found ultimately to depend upon the fact that man alone, among all animals, possesses what we call reason. Reason, the Greeks

thought, is the divine element in man. "Live in the light of reason" was the Greek message to the world, just as "Live in the light of Love" was the Christian message. And those two messages are not incompatible, but complementary. We can follow them both.

Before I go any further, I had better try to protect myself against the volley of objections and protests which I see, even at this stage, are certain to rain down upon me. My philosopher friends will object that the word "reason" is utterly vague and ambiguous. It has been used, and misused, in all sorts of ways. I know some philosophers who are so sensitive about this that they are allergic to any mention of reason at all and will show signs of extreme anguish if you so much as use the word at all in their presence. I am painfully aware of the ambiguities of the word and the mischief that has been done by it in philosophy. But I think that a sensible account of it can be given. I must not go too deeply into this, because to do so would lead us into philosophical technicalities, but I think the essence of the matter can be put quite simply.

I think the essence of reason is the power of abstract thought. If you think about *this* man, or *this* circular wheel, you are thinking about concrete or individual things. But if you think about men in general or circles in

W. T. Stace, *What Are Our Values?*, Lincoln, Nebraska, The University of Nebraska, 1950, pp. 30–44. Reprinted by permission of the publisher.

general, you are thinking abstractly. That is why geometry is an abstract subject. It never discusses this circle or this triangle, but always the circle or the triangle in general, or, as we say, in the abstract.

Now it is certain that animals do not possess this power of abstract thought, but that men do. This is why animals cannot speak, because words, apart from proper names, always stand for abstract ideas. This is also why, although you can, I expect, condition a dog to distinguish between a particular circle and a particular triangle — to wag his tail, shall we say, when he sees a circle, and to bark when he sees a triangle; for there is no end to the wonderful things which modern experimental psychologists can do — although you can teach the dog to do this, yet the fact remains that you can never teach him geometry. The reason is that to distinguish between this circle here before your eyes and this triangle here before your eyes, all you require is the gift of physical vision. You require eyes, nothing more. But to learn geometry, you must be capable of abstract thought, and of this the dog is incapable. I do not deny of course that the doctrine of evolution requires us to suppose that abstract thinking has somehow or other developed out of potentialities in the animal mind. But it also requires us to believe that animals with eyes have somehow developed from animals which had no eyes. And just as we have eyes now and those other organisms do not, so too we have reason now and the animals from which we developed it do not.

I have very little doubt that all the other capacities which men possess and animals lack, such as speaking, lighting fires, inventing tools, wearing clothes, possessing moral ideas, and the like, can be shown to be the result of his capacity for abstract thought. But to show this in any detail would require us to become very technical. I will say only that "reasoning," in the sense of arguing, proving, passing from a set of premises to a conclusion, depends entirely on the use of abstract thought. And if these things are true, I think they justify my statement that abstract thought is the essence of reason or intelligence. They also justify the Greek belief that it is essentially reason which distinguishes us from the brutes. For all the other important differences flow from this.

Another set of objections to all I am saying will come from those who keep on telling us nowadays that man is *not* a rational animal. Emphasis on irrationalism is a characteristic mark of our age. We have Freud, and the psychoanalysts, and the pragmatists and other voluntarists, all dinning into our ears what a very irrational creature man is. What governs man, they tell us, is passion, desire, the will, unconscious sex, the Oedipus complex and all that. Reason is nothing but a cork tossed helplessly about on the top of the dark ocean of desire. We deceive ourselves if we imagine that we are governed by reason.

Well, I will make an offer to these people who keep telling us these things. Abraham said to the Lord, "If there be fifty righteous people in Sodom, will you hold your hand and not destroy the city?" And Jehovah agreed. Then Abraham, who was a business man, beat Jehovah down from fifty to forty, to thirty, to twenty, and ultimately to only ten people. If there were even ten righteous people in Sodom, God would not destroy it. I should like to strike a similar bargain with the irrationalists. If I admit that man is 95% governed by these dark unconscious forces: the Oedipus complex, the Electra complex, the superiority complex, the inferiority complex, and the whole complex of complexes; if I admit that man is the whole frightful psychological mess that you say he is, will you admit on your side that he is 5% rational? No? Well, will you give me 3%? No? Well, will you give me even 1%? You surely cannot refuse that. Well, if you give me that, I will accept that bargain, and I will go on. I will rephrase my previous remarks as follows. When I define man as a rational animal, I mean that he is 1% rational, and that the brutes are zero per cent. When I say that the Greeks thought men ought to try to live more rationally, and that the life of reason is the good life, and that I agree with this, then I will claim that what I and the Greeks mean is that we ought to try to be 2% rational. And when I say man's reason is the cause of his speech, his tool-making, his morals, his art, and his civilization, I mean that this 1% is the cause of these things. Have I said enough about this kind of objection? And can I now go on?

Well, the next point is this. If reason is what distinguishes us from the brutes, if it is what is divine in man, then what is the proper life for man? Plato answered this question in the *Republic*. The proper life for man is the life governed by the highest part of man, his reason. Because the brute lacks reason you can rule him only by force. But because man is a rational being, the only government which is consistent with his nature is that he be ruled by *reason*. This great insight of Plato's has been, along with the Christian ideal of the rule of love, the guiding light of Western civilization; and I say that it is the essence of democratic philosophy, although it is true that Plato himself did not at all understand democracy in this way.

Before I explain this further, let me add one more thought. If it is true that reason is what raises man above the brute, and if it is also true, as I affirm, that government by reason is the essence of democracy, then we have here a proof of what I alleged earlier — that

the values of democracy are universal human values, not merely particular values. For if man is a rational animal, if reason is of his essence, this means that reason is a common element of all men. It means that all men are rational. It is true that there are insane people — freaks and exceptions from the human rule — just as there are freaks and exceptions born with three legs or none at all, instead of two. But the existence of insane or otherwise totally irrational people will not prevent me from saying that all men, that is all normal men, are rational, and that rationality is of the essence of man, any more than the existence of freaks with three legs will prevent me from saying that two-leggedness is an essential character of the human animal. Now if reason is a universal human character and democracy is justified because it is government by man's highest part, his reason, it will follow that democracy is the ideal government for all men and not merely for Americans, or Britishers, or Frenchmen. This is the proof that the values of democracy are universal values. But of course, it depends upon the assertion that democracy is, as I have said, government by reason. And this is what we now have to show. We have to ask, *"Is government by reason the essence of democracy?"*

We have two opposite possibilities of government: government by force, which is the way to deal with animals, and government by reason, which is the way to deal with men. The former I am asserting is the way of totalitarianism or any autocratic government. The latter is the way of democracy. In order to see this let us ask ourselves what, in any state, is the relation between the rulers and the ruled. In a totalitarian state the rulers impose their will by force upon the ruled. In a democracy the rulers, whether they be a President and Congress, or a Parliament and Prime Minister, have to *persuade the people by rational argument* that the measures they propose are the best. And if they cannot do this they have to get out and make way for others who can. They have to use the instrument of *persuasion,* not the instrument of force. That, in bold outline, is what I mean by saying that democracy simply means government by reason. Stalin or Hitler simply compel their subjects to do as they will. Force is the principle of their government. President and Congress do not compel us against our will. They have to *persuade* us that the measures they propose are right. Persuasion is the principle of democratic governments. They have to use rational means to persuade us as rational men.

I foresee an obvious criticism of this. It is true, you will say, that a democratic government has to persuade its citizens, but it is quite untrue that they persuade them by reason, by rational arguments. It is notorious that our politicians almost never appeal to reason. They appeal to the ignorance, the prejudice, the self-interest of the electorate. Sometimes they appeal to the basest passions. Sometimes they use unworthy tricks and even deceit and lies and false promises to persuade the people. And where is reason to be found in all this?

The charge, of course, is perfectly true. The facts are as stated. But these facts do not show that I am wrong in saying that the essence of the democratic ideal is government by reason. What they show is that actual democracies fall far short of the essential ideal of democracy, that they are not what they ought to be, that they are not truly democratic. They point to the abuses of democracy, not to the ideal of democracy in which alone, of course, democratic values would perfectly flower. And it is about democratic values that we are talking, not about human failures to reach them. An ideal democracy would be a government in which the people and the rulers "reasoned together," in which the rulers would have to persuade the people by rational means that their policy was good, and in which the people would refuse to be misled by prejudice, passion, and ignorance. That is the real ideal of democracy, not the mass of selfish grabbing, vote-catching, and corruption which actual democracies unfortunately are. We are accustomed to saying that there are some peoples who are not yet fit for democracy. And we self-righteously plume ourselves that we are not among them. The truth is that there is no nation in the world yet fit for democracy, and perhaps there never will be.

Democracy is an ideal, not a fact. But it is an ideal we can strive for. The facts we are discussing — the corruption, the greed, the base deceit and lying and false promises which are found in existing democracies — these are the very facts which are seized upon by our enemies in criticism of democracy. Look, they say, how the self-styled democratic countries are actually governed — by falsehood, ignorance, and shameless greed. Is it not better to be ruled by a man, or by a few men, who are above the necessity of sinking to these levels, who can do what they know to be best without having to count the votes of the base and foolish mob? It is a clever argument. But it means the utter abandonment of the ideals of reason. And the answer to it is that it is better to struggle upwards towards the light of reason, badly as we do it, than to lower our standards and to admit once and for all that we are only animals for whom the proper government is by force.

We do not usually think of rationality as the main value of democracy. We think of freedom, equality, and individualism. We shall find, however, that these really depend on the central notion of rationality. They flow from it and are its corollaries. Freedom, equality, and individualism are only values because they are required by the rationality of man. Let us take them in order and examine them. Then we shall find that this is true.

First, freedom. What does it mean? The word, of course, is very ambiguous, and the thing itself has been variously conceived. I cannot hope to distinguish all possible meanings or to offer an accurate definition. But to get rid of at least one ambiguity, I will say that I do not think that what we call political freedom has anything at all to do with the controversy about free will. I think that a determinist, who denies the existence of what philosophers call free will, can perfectly well believe in political freedom. For the determinist's point is merely that all human actions are determined by causes, that there is no such thing as an uncaused action. The believer in democratic freedom need not deny this because his creed is, as I shall try to show, merely that reason, not force, should govern men's actions. In other words what a man does should be caused by the rational motives which proceed from within himself, not by forces applied to him externally. It is true that there is supposed to be a difficulty as to how reason can cause a man to act, since it is said that only desires cause action. I will not go into the technicalities of that matter. But there is no real difficulty. It is obvious that if a man is acting wildly and we ask him to be "controlled by reason," what we mean is simply that he ought to consider all the evidence, all the facts relevant to his action, its consequences both to himself and to other people, and not be led by some single blind passion or desire which is in him. And it is obvious that in this sense there cannot be any psychological difficulty in being "controlled by reason," since sensible people commonly are so controlled in greater or less degree. Thus liberty as a political ideal has nothing

at all to do with free will in the metaphysical sense.

Next we have of course to follow the common practice in distinguishing liberty from license. License means lawlessness, doing whatever you please and being controlled by no law at all. Liberty means being controlled by a law, but a law which you impose on yourself, or which the people in a democracy impose on themselves, and which is not merely imposed on them by an alien or external force.

The essence of the matter seems to be that that man is free who is able to decide for himself, by the use of his own reason, what he should do. We may, if we like, define freedom simply as acting from one's own internal motives, uncompelled by any external force. We need not mention reason at all. In that case an animal too is free in so far as he roams about unconstrained. But if we do this, we leave out the notions of freedom as a right and freedom as a value. You can, if you like, allow very young children and insane people to do exactly as they please without any external control. And they are then no doubt in a sense "free." But they have not the right to their freedom, nor is it a value. For the *right* of freedom flows from rationality, and those who have not yet gained, or have lost, rationality, do not have the right of freedom and have to be controlled externally. It is only because, and if, I am a rational being that I have a right to decide, by the use of my own reason, what I shall do. And it is only if I do act rationally that my freedom has any value. Thus the value we call freedom is an offshoot of man's rational nature.

We see the same thing in the ideals of freedom of speech, press, assembly, religion, and the like. The freedoms of speech, press and assembly mean only the rights of people to use their own reasoning powers to decide what they will think and say. It is the same with freedom of religion. Why was it wrong to imprison Galileo for believing that the earth revolves around the sun? Why would it be wrong to burn someone alive for denying the doctrine of the Trinity? Of course I know that merely pragmatic and utilitarian reasons are commonly given. We are more likely to reach truth, it is said, if everyone is free to give his own version of it. Error is best refuted, not by force, but by giving it free reign so that it will ultimately refute itself. All this is perfectly true. But we may take higher ground. The ultimate basis for denying to the state or the church the power to coerce me in my religious beliefs is that I, as a rational being, have the right to use my reason to decide for myself.

If the right and value of democratic freedom flows from the right and value of rationality, the same is true of democratic equality. What does such equality mean? It obviously does not mean that all men are equally clever, good, or wise. Equality of opportunity comes nearer the target but does not quite hit it. Democratic equality means, I think, that every rational being has, just because he is rational, a right, equally with all others, to develop his capacities and potentialities from within himself as he thinks best without external coercion. External coercion need not take the form of actual violence. It may be exercised by the pressure of public opinion, by taboos, or simply by unreasonable customs. For instance, if a man of great potential powers is prevented by social barriers of caste or birth from realizing them, from becoming what he is capable of becoming, he is being coerced. And this is the same thing as denying his equality with other men. And this again is the same thing as denying his freedom. For freedom and equality are ultimately the same thing, or two aspects of the same thing.

Freedom means the right to act from my own internal resources, and not from compulsion, so long as I do this rationally. And equality means that all men equally have the right, and that they must not be deprived of it by class and other social barriers.

Lastly we come to the democratic value of individualism. This again is no more than another expression of the same ideal of rationality. It means the right to be myself, and not to have other people's personalities forced upon me. It means the right to develop my own individuality in whatever way seems reasonable to me. This depends on my *being* reasonable. An irrational being, for instance an insane person, has no right to develop his insane individuality as he pleases. He has to be coerced. Likewise children cannot be granted an unlimited right of individualism. The tendency of modern educational theory has been to grant them more and more the right of individualism. And this may be a good thing. A child is a potentially rational being, and rationality develops in him as he grows older. Therefore he ought to be given the right of expressing his own individuality in exact proportion to the rationality he has developed, no more and no less. It is a matter of degree. Whether former educational theory granted too little individualism to the child, and whether we are now granting him the right amount or too much, I will not try to determine. It may be added that when women were formerly kept in control, it must have been on the theory that they are less rational than men. And their present equality with men must be based on the view that they are just as rational as men. As to whether this is true or not, I shall leave you to decide.

It follows that there is a true and a false individualism. That kind of individualism, sometimes called "rugged," which consists in selfishly grabbing everything you can, trampling on other people's rights, and destroying their happiness, is the false kind, and is no part of democratic theory. For although it asserts my own rights of individuality, it destroys those of others. Individualism should rather be thought of as a duty than as a right. It means the duty to recognize that all men, and not merely I, are, as rational beings, entitled to realize their personalities to the utmost. It means that the emphasis is on the other man's right, not on mine. The democratic ideal of individualism is that every man and woman in the community should develop his inner resources to their most perfect flowering so as to contribute most to the richness of the life of the whole community. And this is precisely what is denied by that false individualism which is merely a euphemism for selfishness and anti-social behaviour.

Thus these three concepts — freedom, equality and individualism — are all based upon, or flow from, the central concept of the rationality of man. It was not an accident that the people whose philosophers defined man as the rational animal and who insisted above all upon the value of reason, thought, knowledge, learning, science, contemplation, and who in fact coined and circulated these values for the western world down to our own times, were also the peoples whose statesmen — corrupt demagogues though many of them were — invented democracy. It is not an accident that those vast portions of the globe which, however highly cultured in some respects they may be, have not inherited the Greek tradition of the supremacy of reason, have also never developed a democracy of their own, never had any — except perhaps in village institutions — until it was brought to them from the West. That democracy is an expression of the rational nature of man is the basic philosophical justification of democracy. Its justification is that it arises out of the very nature

of man. Some people think that the issue of totalitarianism or democracy is a mere matter of taste, of whether a particular people or culture happens to like the one or the other. I do not agree. I say that democracy is founded in the rational nature of man and therefore is the only government fit for men. Government by force, totalitarian or merely autocratic, is a government proper only to animals.

I will now briefly summarize the rather long and intricate argument of this lecture. My main contention has been that the democratic values — freedom, equality, and individualism — are universal human values, not particular values valid only for our West European and American culture. On this question depends the issue whether we have any right to try to democratize other peoples, and also whether there is any chance of our succeeding. In order to support this view we had to discover what this proposition that "the democratic way of life is universally a good for man, that is, for all men" *means*. We saw that it does not mean that all actually agree with it. For if it did it would be refuted by the mere existence of cultures which do not accept it. What it does mean is that we believe all peoples *would* accept democracy as a good for them on two conditions: (1) that they are sufficiently matured in their civilization, and (2) that they would give it a proper trial.

In this respect democratic values are like any other universal human values. If we say that love and charity are universally goods for all men and that hate and enmity are universally evils, we do not mean that all men accept this code of morals. We mean that if they were mature enough, and if they would give the Christian virtues of love and charity a fair trial in their lives, they would find universally that they would be happier people for doing so, far happier than those who base their lives on hate and enmity. We admitted that propositions of this sort are very difficult to prove. But in the case of democratic values we tried to show that we have good reason for believing them to be universal in this sense by the following argument. Democracy, we argued, is based on the rational nature of man, which is universal. It is not based upon, it is not an expression of, the cultural peculiarities of certain peoples, such as Americans, British, or Frenchmen. It expresses the essential nature of human kind, their rational nature, which distinguishes them from the lower animals. Animals can be governed only by force, which is the principle of total-itarianism. But democracy is government by reason and is therefore the only good government for all rational beings. Also the characteristic values of the democratic way of life — freedom, equality, and individualism — are likewise only expressions of man's rational nature. The democratic way of life is the good life for man because it grows out of the nature of man. And this is not a mere particular, local, or regional truth, but a universal truth about man as man. Ultimately, to be human is to be rational, and to be rational is to be democratic.

SUGGESTIONS FOR THOUGHT

1. Nations as different as the United States and Russia claim they are striving toward a democracy. What does "democracy" mean to the United States? To Russia?

2. Harold Laski said: "There is in America a wider disillusionment with democracy, a greater scepticism about popular institutions, than at any period in its history." What reasons can you give for the contemporary loss of faith in democracy?

3. What is the relation between the Judeo-Christian tradition and democracy? F. D. Roosevelt, in an address on the state of the nation in January, 1939, said: "Storms from abroad directly challenge three institutions indispensable to Americans, now as always. The first is religion. It is the source of the other two — democracy and international good faith. Religion by teaching man his relationship to God gives the individual a sense of his own dignity and teaches him to respect by respecting his neighbors."

4. Does allegiance to the idea of freedom in a democracy imply that those in a democracy cannot even try to spread its ideals and institutions to other peoples and nations?

5. How is it possible to strike a balance between freedom and equality? If unequal beings are given freedom, what is to prevent the stronger from destroying the weaker? Should we be more concerned with justice and less with freedom?

6. Everett Dean Martin said: "The American way of doing things is to organize them. Our genius for organization is probably our most generally recognized national characteristic." How can this be explained in a democracy that stresses individualism? Is this an indication of our sociability, our respect for the common welfare, our unwillingness to be original, or what? Walt Whitman once said, "I will accept nothing which all cannot have their counterparts of on the same terms." Is this a good definition of equality?

7. What moral qualities and intellectual abilities are essential to good citizenship in a democracy? What can formal education do to help people live together peacefully?

8. Lincoln Steffens reached the conclusion that "Educated people were the slowest to move toward any change. . . . It [education] did not aim, apparently, to make us keen with educated, intelligent curiosity about the unknown, not eager to do the undone; it taught most of us

only what was known." Is this in accord with your observations? Are the educated or the uneducated elements in America more open to change?

9. The Educational Policies Commission stated in 1938: "Popular government without universal education is a prologue to tragedy." Why did they make this statement? To what extent should the government supply free education to its citizens? If higher education is made free to all who might profit from it, is there danger of discouraging individual initiative?

10. The Master of Balliol College said after an interview of young German prisoners during World War II: "They are wonderfully skilled and technically trained. But they had no educa-

tion: they were robots. It was frightening." What did they lack that constitutes an education? What did William James mean when he said that the opposite of a liberal education is a literal education? How would a "literal education" endanger a democracy?

12. R. M. Hutchins believes it is significant that as France turned toward Fascism its educational system turned toward vocational training. What is the possible relation between Fascism and vocational training? Between democracy and non-vocational education?

13. Bertrand Russell says that a fanatical belief in democracy makes democratic institutions impossible. Why? What is wrong in ardently believing in democracy?

SUGGESTIONS FOR FURTHER READING

BECKER, CARL L., *Modern Democracy,* New Haven, Yale University Press, 1941.

BROWN, W. JETHRO, "The True Democratic Ideal," *The International Journal of Ethics,* Vol. 14, 1904, pp. 137–150.

FITE, WARNER, "The Theory of Democracy," *The International Journal of Ethics,* Vol. 18, 1907, pp. 1–18.

GABRIEL, RALPH HENRY, *The Course of American Democratic Thought,* New York, The Ronald Press Company, 1940, ch. 31.

HOOK, SIDNEY, "The Philosophical Presuppositions of Democracy," *Ethics,* Vol. 52, 1942, pp. 275–296.

MERRIAM, CHARLES E., *What is Democracy?,* Chicago, University of Chicago Press, 1941.

MILLER, JOSEPH DANA, "The Difficulties of Democracy," *The International Journal of Ethics,* Vol. 25, 1915, pp. 213–225.

PERRY, RALPH BARTON, *Puritanism and Democracy,* New York, The Vanguard Press, 1944, Part III.

REVES, EMERY, *A Democratic Manifesto,* New York, Random House, 1942.

SABINE, GEORGE H., "The Two Democratic Traditions," *The Philosophical Review,* Vol. 61, 1952, pp. 451–474.

SHELDON, W. H., "The Defect of Current Democracy," *The Journal of Philosophy, Psychology, and Scientific Methods,* Vol. 16, 1919, pp. 365–379.

SMITH, T. V., "Contemporary Perplexities in Democratic Theory," *The International Journal of Ethics,* Vol. 39, 1928, pp. 1–14.

TEAD, ORDWAY, *The Case for Democracy,* New York, Association Press, 1938.

VLASTOS, GREGORY, "Religious Foundations of Democracy," *The Journal of Religion,* Vol. 22, 1942, pp. 1–19, 137–155.

WILSON, WOODROW, *Democracy Today,* edited by Christian Gauss, New York, William R. Scott, 1917, pp. 126–140.

Index